W9-ABY-864

Courtesy of Bettmann Archive

Landing of Commodore Perry at Kanagawa, March 8, 1854

JAPAN'S MODERN CENTURY

By

HUGH BORTON

PROFESSOR OF JAPANESE AND DIRECTOR
EAST ASIAN INSTITUTE
COLUMBIA UNIVERSITY

THE RONALD PRESS COMPANY • NEW YORK

Library of Congress Catalog Card Number: 55-10667
PRINTED IN THE UNITED STATES OF AMERICA

To

Sir George B. Sansom

whose inspiration and
kindly guidance made
this book possible

History is that by means of which one records events. On the basis of events the true history shows itself that good should be rewarded and evil punished. . . . Writings should be authenticated and events be made clear. If one deviates in any direction from this, how can one call this a true history?

TOKUGAWA TSUNESADA, Preface, *Dai Nihon Shi* (The History of Japan), 1715.

Writing history is hardly private enterprise; it is public business of the republic of learning and letters, whose citizens desire that any job undertaken shall be done well.

BERNARD DEVOTO, Preface, *The Course of Empire*, 1953.

PREFACE

Events of the past years have revealed with dramatic suddenness and effect Japan's importance in world history. When the attack on Pearl Harbor occurred in December, 1941, the average American could not believe that such a small nation would have dared to challenge the greatest industrialized country in the world. It was equally sobering for him to discover that shrewd Japanese planning, a severe austerity program, and fanatical patriotism had produced a powerful military empire which capitulated only after four years of total war. Since their defeat, the Japanese people have shown an amazing degree of resilience and industry. Through a combination of foreign aid and of their own prodigious effort, they have put their country back on its feet, and it is rapidly becoming, both literally and figuratively, a strong island bastion against the communist tide in East Asia.

These developments are all the more significant in view of the fact that a century ago Japan was a secluded, semi-feudal, agrarian country of only thirty million persons. Now it is a modern industrial state with a population of more than eighty-seven million. This book endeavors to explain, therefore, Japan's phenomenal transformation, seeking answers to the twofold question: How did Japan get that way? Where is it likely to go? The necessary material is drawn from sources in Japanese and in Western languages as well as from the author's close contacts with Japan during the last three decades and his participation in the formulation of United States postwar policies for Japan.

In general this book presents Japan's modern transformation as a narrative, interpreting and analyzing the forces which brought about this change. Since the formative influences, whether political, economic, social, or international, varied in their intensity throughout the different periods, these forces are emphasized in proportion to their shifting importance. For example, in the first decade after the restoration to power of the Emperor Meiji in 1868, economic considerations were paramount. In the period beginning with the war against China in 1894, international considerations increasingly dominated the scene. The emphasis on each of the periods throughout the entire century is kept in rough balance. The selection of facts to be included, however, was a difficult problem. Anyone who writes a history of a civilization which is not rooted in the Western tradition must perforce include much background material that is new to many readers. Also, the more recent the events, the more material there is from which to choose. It was decided that detailed facts would be included where they were necessary for a clear understanding of the narrative, where the significance of events has been lost or misinterpreted by previous writers, or where information has hitherto been scanty.

Through a provocative approach to certain fundamental questions, it is hoped that this book will stimulate both the general reader and the specialist on Far Eastern affairs to re-evaluate past events and to arrive at a more accurate assessment of current developments. For example, on the basis of the record, it is questionable to what extent democratic, representative institutions existed or functioned prior to World War II. With this heritage will these new institutions prosper or decline? The record also shows clearly that a drive to dominate China was one of the basic determinants of Japanese foreign policy throughout the past century. The current prevalence in Japan of a desire for closer commercial contacts with Communist China is a natural outcome of this historical background. It cannot be dismissed as mere propaganda of the Reds. In the past, the necessity for economic survival was used as justification for strong state controls and for overseas expansion. The search for economic viability in the future may well produce the same results if alternative solutions are not found.

As for some of the technical problems—biographical material, supplementary remarks, and references to sources are relegated to notes at the end of each chapter to avoid interrupting the narrative. The bibliographical notes, referring to both Japanese and Western language sources, are suggestive rather than exhaustive but should be of assistance to the reader who wishes to pursue a particular subject further. Japanese personal names are given with the family name first. In a few cases, such as "Konoye" or "Tokyo," I have used the more popular romanization.

In conclusion, it is difficult to acknowledge adequately, and impossible to list, all those who assisted me. My initial thanks are due those closest to me who have endured my absorption in this book. My wife and children have been long-suffering and patient and have given unstintingly of their understanding, encouragement, and help. My students have made fruitful criticisms of material that was first presented in the classroom. My colleagues in the East Asian Institute of Columbia University have been generous in their interest. Through their cooperation and with the assistance of Institute's funds, I was able to devote a profitable and rewarding sabbatical year of research and study at Tokyo University.

Among my colleagues, I am eternally grateful to Sir George B. Sansom, the outstanding Occidental authority on Japanese history, who introduced me to the study of Japanese history at a private seminar which he conducted in Tokyo in the winter of 1928-29. If this book has any special merit, I am particularly in his debt. We have spent many hours discussing both its contents and its method of presentation, and he has unselfishly read the entire manuscript and made many helpful suggestions. Professor Edwin O. Reischauer of Harvard University also kindly read all but the last part of the manuscript and offered valuable criticisms. I am also grateful to Mr. Ikuo Fukuda who assisted me in Tokyo, to Mr. John Creelman, Miss Frances Weinberg, and especially to Mr. John Lane, for help in collecting material and checking many of the details; to Mrs. Creelman and Mrs. Lane for their services in typing the manuscript. To Mr. Howard Linton, Miss Miwa Kai, and Mr. Philip Yampolsky of the East Asiatic Library of Columbia University, my hearty thanks for their constant aid. Miss Kai kindly wrote the Chinese characters used in the footnotes. My colleague Dr. Osamu Shimizu graciously consented to write the Japanese title on the wrapper. The illustrations of Ii Naosuke, of his poem, and of the early cannon are gifts from his great grandson, Ii Naoyoshi. Finally, I am grateful to Miss Gwendolyn Fillman, Secretary of the East Asian Institute, who has done so much for me in the office, thereby giving me time to devote to writing.

HUGH BORTON

New York, N.Y.
August 1, 1955

CONTENTS

PART I

The Opening of Japan, 1850-1868

PART II

Formation of a Centralized Monarchy, 1868-1890

PART III

Establishment of the Japanese Empire, 1889-1915

PART IV

Leadership in Greater East Asia, 1915-1941

PART V

Japan Survives War and Defeat, 1941-1955

APPENDIX

MAPS

TABLES

ILLUSTRATIONS

PART I

THE OPENING OF JAPAN
1850-1868

> He shall have the use of two oceans—the mighty
> Pacific and the turbulent Atlantic shall be his.
>
> Speech at New Jersey
> Democratic State Convention, 1844.

Chronology

1853-1868

1846	Commodore Biddle fails to open Japan
1853, July	Perry arrives in Japan
August	Shogun seeks opinion of barons on foreign trade
	Industrialization in western clans
1854	Treaty of Kanagawa with the United States
1855	Treaty of Shimoda with Russia
1856	Arrival of U.S. Consul-General Townsend Harris
1858	United States–Japanese Commercial Treaty
1860	First Japanese Mission to the United States
1863	Western clans demand expulsion of foreigners
	Foreign bombardment of Satsuma
1864	Foreign squadron opens Straits of Shimonoseki
1865-66	Civil war in Chōshū; Shogun's army defeated
1867, November	The Shogun resigns
1868, January 3	Emperor Meiji announces restoration of power
April	Shogun surrenders at Edo (Tokyo)

1

INTRODUCTION

Flung across the great circle route from North America to the Asiatic continent lies the Empire of Japan. Its boundaries, as verified by the Treaty of Peace signed at San Francisco on September 8, 1951, were essentially the same as those of a century earlier when President Millard Fillmore and Secretary of State Daniel Webster were making plans to send a naval mission to open Japan to the West. In the mid-nineteenth century Japan was the only large Asiatic country to remain closed to the Western world. The British and the Dutch, who had already developed strong colonial empires, were anxious to expand their Far Eastern trade. Following the defeat of China by Great Britain in the Opium War, in 1842, China had been forced to relinquish important attributes of its sovereignty to the Western powers.

On the North American continent, Americans had been pressing toward the West—the sunset—until their territory had reached the Pacific. This basic urge emanated partly from fancy, partly from fact. Cabeza de Vaca, one of the first European explorers of the New World, wrote as early as 1535 that he was certain that he would find what he desired by going toward the sunset. This lure in America to follow the sun was intensified by tales of the fabulous wealth of the seven cities, of the riches of Quivira, of the "Island of California," and of the Western Sea. Even Coronado's failure to find little more than the Pueblo Indians failed to diminish men's hopes of finding their fortune in the Orient. The myth was kept alive by the Jesuit missionaries in the Mississippi Valley, who claimed that Hudson Bay was separated from Japan by 3500 miles of open water. At the beginning of the nineteenth century, as the continental ridge was conquered and its contours and sources examined at first hand by explorers such as Lewis and Clark, fancy turned into fact. There was no easy route across the continent to the shore of the Pacific Ocean. Nevertheless, America's concept of Manifest Destiny, the exuberance and energy of the young Republic, led to only one eventuality: the extension of the borders of the United States from the Atlantic to the Pacific.

But the adventurous American of the 1850's was not willing to stop at the eastern shores of the Pacific Ocean. The expansionist movement, stimulated by the growth of industrialization in both western Europe and the United States, focused the eyes of ambitious traders, merchants, and sailors on the mysterious and fabulous Orient. China was made all the more alluring by the special privileges for foreigners written into the "unequal treaties." Owners of sleek clipper ships had already profited from this trade. American whalers had found the Pacific their most lucrative region. The developments in steam navigation made shipowners keenly aware of the need for coaling stations at convenient intervals along the main sea routes. But Japan, which was the logical place for ports of refuge and for coaling stations, was closed to all foreign ships except a limited number of Dutch and Chinese boats. American seamen who had been shipwrecked on Japan's rugged and treacherous shores had been maltreated. Although Japan and the United States were separated by nearly five thousand miles of the Pacific Ocean, these factors and many others made it inevitable that it was only a matter of time before the United States would force Japan to renounce its self-imposed seclusion.

Japan's history during the past century, therefore, is the account of how it reacted to the world after its seclusion was shattered. It is the study of the response of an Oriental civilization to the challenge which faced it. It is an analysis of the effect of the stimulus from without and the struggle from within on the only Oriental country in the nineteenth century to accept the challenge of the West by westernization and to become one of the leading world powers. But Japan's sudden rise, its even more precipitous decline, and rapid postwar recuperation raise many important questions. Why did Japan react as it did to the stimulus of westernization? Why was its response in sharp contrast to the ineffectual reaction of India and China? Why was Japan able to resist colonization and carry through its own political, economic, and social metamorphosis? Why was it bold enough to challenge the United States in a life and death struggle in our own time? What is its future?

Some historians, especially the young Japanese Marxists such as Tōyama Shigeki, would interpret Japan's modernization in terms of economic determinism and Marxist phraseology. He maintains, for example, that the uprisings of the Japanese peasants, which were not antiforeign as had been the case in China, were the first sprouts of the struggle against feudalism which made the development of absolutism inevitable. Having formed itself into an absolutist state, Japan was thus able to escape the same fate as China. Other historians naïvely attribute the difference between China and Japan to geographical and social factors and especially to what they call "the superior character of the Japanese people." But the history of Japan's modernization is too complicated to be interpreted or explained by any single factor or theory. As Sir George Sansom has aptly noted, Japan's modern political development presents so many peculiar features that they cannot be reconciled with any theory, deterministic or otherwise.[1]

It will be found, for example, that Japan's ability to resist colonization and to carry through its own political, economic, and social metamorphosis was the result of a complex of factors. They included a combination of the casual coincidence of historical events, and geographical, social, and economic forces. It was comparatively easy, as Britain had also found, for Japan to industrialize a small island kingdom with protected harbors and landlocked lines of communications such as those afforded by the Inland Sea. Furthermore, the country was ruled by warriors or *samurai* who were eager to import western weapons and to build up a militarily strong, industrialized nation. Finally, the Japanese had long been blessed with a unique ability to adapt those aspects of foreign civilizations useful to them and to reject the rest. All these forces combined, therefore, to produce Japan's modernization: its rise to become the most powerful country in Asia; its final collapse and complete defeat; its re-emergence as a potentially democratic and law-abiding member of the family of nations.

In addition to attempting to answer the question of how Japan's modernization occurred and what brought it about, this book will analyze certain startling similarities between conditions confronting Japan at the middle of the nineteenth century, when this study begins, and at the middle of the twentieth century. At both times, the Western powers had a superior technical knowledge, a higher standard of living, and far greater military prowess than Japan. Most of the Western countries were larger in area and their national borders enclosed more varied and valuable resources.

On the other hand, the dissimilarities between the present time and a century ago are of even greater importance than the similarities. In the mid-nineteenth century, the West, and particularly the United States, took the initiative in forcing Japan out of seclusion. The latter had ignored and defied the Western powers. In fact, it had taken an attitude of indifference and aloofness toward them. In the mid-twentieth century, it had forced the issue and, due to ultranationalism and expansionism, had clashed directly with the national interests of the Soviet Union, China, the United States, the United Kingdom, and other Allies. Furthermore, a century ago the Tokugawa dictatorship was overthrown, the Emperor was restored to power, and feudalism was formally abolished without involving Japan in war or widespread internal revolution. Japan's capitulation in 1945 came only after an intensive, destructive, and costly war. In 1850, such nationalism as existed was directed toward the restoration of Imperial power and toward retention of territory which had been traditionally Japanese. In the decade prior to World War II, nationalism was aggressive and militant and was the inspiration for the acquisition of overseas territories and the establishment of Japanese hegemony throughout the entire Far East.

But one of the most important differences between conditions at the beginning and the end of this past century is the fact that when the Emperor regained control of state power in 1868, he and his ministers could decide their own destiny. The small group of autocrats who actually ran the country were comparatively free to choose the course they wished to follow in the realm of politics, economics, finance, and international relations. For example, the treaties with the Western powers made no mention of Japan's future form of government, nor were the Occidental diplomats particularly concerned over the question of whether Japan should have a monarchy, a republic, or a military dictatorship. The main concern of the foreigners was whether or not the Japanese government was able to maintain law and order and to protect their rights established by the treaties.

There was no outside direction as to the structure of the new economy; there was no insistence that there be strict state control or free enterprise, or that land be owned privately or granted to warriors under a feudal contract. In the realm of finance, Japan was free to choose its own type of currency system, to select either the gold or silver standard for that currency, and to decide whether or not it would seek foreign loans. In the field of international relations, however, the foreign nations had forced Japan to make concessions. The new treaties opened certain ports to foreign trade, placed limitations on import and export tariffs, and granted foreigners extraterritorial rights. In other respects, the leaders of the new Japan made their own decisions.

In contrast to this earlier freedom, in the summer of 1945 the Allied Powers dictated the terms of surrender. General Douglas MacArthur, as Supreme Commander for the Allied Powers, had absolute authority and power, and all matters of policy were decided by the Allies independently of Japan's wishes. For all practical purposes, the Japanese had no choice as to the retention of the Imperial system, the deconcentration of economic power, and dissolution of the *zaibatsu* (financial magnates), agrarian reform, the purge, the capital levy, and, above all, the type of constitution they must sponsor.

But what of the future? Is the fear of Communism and Soviet aggression the main issue of common interest between Japan and the West? Will Japan remain on the side of the democracies or will economic adversity, a smoldering nationalism, and a propensity for centralized control force it to the extreme right or into the Communist camp? An analysis of Japan's first century of modernization should go far toward making the answers to these questions obvious.

Notes

1. One of the most representative works by a leftist historian is that by Tōyama Shigeki, entitled *Ishin Shi* (A History of the Restoration; Tokyo: Iwanami, 1951). A general discussion of some of the other active members of the virile *Rekishi Gakkai* and of their historical studies, which have a strong flavor of economic determinism, will be found in John W. Hall's review of "Nihon Shakai no Shiteki Kyūmei," *Far Eastern Quarterly,* November, 1951, pp. 97-104; and in a note on the above by Sir George B. Sansom in *Far Eastern Quarterly,* August, 1952, p. 506.

2

THE UNITED STATES CHALLENGES JAPAN'S SECLUSION

Manifest Destiny and Japan

By the mid-nineteenth century, Japan had been governed for over six and a half centuries by a series of military dictatorships which had exalted the warrior class and degraded all others. One of the most successful and enduring of these dictatorships was that of the Tokugawa family which was created in 1603. For 250 years the Tokugawa generalissimos or *Shoguns* had ruled unchallenged throughout the entire country, but the evils inherent in their ruthless system of government were threatening the entire fabric of society. A dearth of capable leaders, an increase of financial indebtedness, the beginnings of nationalism, and an anti-Shogun alliance of some of the more progressive feudal barons, all contributed to the deterioration of the established order. International pressure was also increasing. In fine, the feudal government was in a precarious position and a marked increase in pressure from any of these forces could serve as the catalyst to precipitate the overthrow of the regime.

In another sense, Japan was a vacuum toward which the United States, Russia, and Great Britain were all being drawn. The rapid westward expansion of the United States, its belief in Manifest Destiny, and its desire to profit from a potentially lucrative Far Eastern trade, however, indicated that America was likely to play the decisive role in this drama. Even before their Constitution was ratified by the thirteen states, leading Americans had shown keen interest in trade with the Orient. John Jay, in the *Federalist Paper,* No. 4, warned that France, Great Britain, and other European nations would begrudge American advances in foreign trade. He reflected the deep interest of Robert Morris and other Federalists when he turned his attention on the Far East. He noted: "In the trade to China and India, we interfere with more than one nation, in as much as it enables us to partake in advantages which they had in a manner monopolized."

In the spring of 1792, three years after George Washington's inauguration as first President of the United States, a Boston captain, Robert Gray, was exploring the northwest coast of the American continent. He entered the Columbia River, gave it the name of his 212-ton ship, and claimed the river's watershed or the Oregon Territory for his country. Though England made a similar claim, which was not relinquished until 1846, Gray's voyage was the harbinger of momentous developments for an expansion-minded America.

By 1803 the threat of encirclement of the United States by Spain, England, or France, or by a combination of them, had vanished. In its stead, partly through the wisdom of Thomas Jefferson, and partly through a combination of circumstances, the position had changed completely. Jefferson had long realized that whoever controlled New Orleans controlled the Mississippi watershed. He also recognized the significance of the British explorer MacKenzie having been the first to cross the American continent. Whoever was first to consolidate an empire from the Atlantic to the Pacific Oceans would control the continent in the future. Shortly after Jefferson became President, therefore, he moved to purchase New Orleans and to possess Louisiana. Napoleon Bonaparte, as part of his plan to weaken England after the defeat in his Haitian campaign, decided to give up his American colony of Louisiana. He confidently expected that if Louisiana were turned over to the United States, the increased strength of the latter, which would result from the transfer, would weaken Britain's position vis-à-vis France.

Thus the machinations of the French Emperor played into Jefferson's hands and accelerated events which led to the opening of Japan. On April 30, 1803, Louisiana—that vast territory from the mouth of the Mississippi to the sources of the Missouri River in the far northwest—became American territory. Henry Adams wrote that this event was "so portentous as to defy measurement." For Japan, as well as for America, Adam's statement proved to be correct. This expansion of American territory westward was one more event which made it inevitable that Manifest Destiny would force the United States to shatter Japan's seclusion.

Even before Napoleon had decided to sell the Louisiana Territory, Jefferson had planned an expedition to explore the northwest, to challenge British trade in that part of the American continent, and to reach the Pacific by an overland route. When Meriwether Lewis and William Clark started out on their famous expedition in 1804, their orders were to explore particularly the portage between the Missouri and the Columbia Rivers and the relationship of these rivers with the Rio Grande and Colorado Rivers. The success of their explorations substituted knowledge for fancy. It made possible the next phase of America's Manifest Destiny, namely, the undisputed and inevitable acquisition of territory from the eastern to the western shores of the continent and the expansion of contacts with the Orient.[1]

Shortly thereafter, John Jacob Astor's dream of a profitable free trade between Astoria and the Orient was abruptly interrupted by British naval action in 1812. But the course of the American continental empire was not to be deflected. Senator Thomas Hart Benton of Missouri was the most ardent advocate of his time of the need for trade with the Orient and the profits to be derived therefrom. Always arguing that American western expansion was the highroad to the riches of Asia and the Indies, Benton claimed that Jefferson believed that the Lewis and Clark expedition would result in overland commercial relations with Asia. He fought constantly for the development of the Oregon Territory and for wresting Oriental trade from the British. To him, the Arkansas, Platte, and Yellowstone Rivers, with sources interlocking with those of rivers draining into the Pacific, would become "the lines of communication for peoples of the United States with Eastern Asia." He saw one of his dreams realized when Great Britain relinquished to the United States its rights to the Oregon Territory in 1846 and the new American domain stretched from the Atlantic to the Pacific Oceans.

When his son-in-law, John C. Fremont, declared the independence of the Republic of California the same year, his joy was unbounded. He boasted that the arrival of the Caucasian race on the shores of the Pacific Ocean was one of the most significant moments of world history. He believed that the possibilities of spiritual and economic gain from the fabulous and pagan Orient were limitless. It was easier than ever before for the advocates of Manifest Destiny to prove by historical events that America was destined to play a decisive role in the Pacific area basin.[2]

Simultaneously with the extension of the American border to the Pacific Ocean, attempts were made to force Japan out of seclusion. For several years, a formidable fleet of American whalers, averaging over 200 annually, had roamed the Pacific Ocean in search of their prey. Clipper ships, bound for the lucrative Canton trade, skirted Japan's eastern coast. Some of them never reached their destination because they were wrecked on the rocky, typhoon-swept shore. The rough and inhumane treatment which these seamen received in Japan was well known to both the American government and people. It was questionable how long the United States would tolerate this situation. Furthermore, potential trade with the Orient had always fired America's imagination. The rapid growth of steam navigation, coupled with the fact that the shortest route to the Asian mainland passed close to Japan's shores, made both the navy and merchant marine anxious to have coaling stations there. It was not surprising, therefore, that suggestions came from various quarters for an expedition to open Japan to trade, to ensure humane treatment of foreign seamen, and to secure a port where coal and provisions could be obtained.

One of the persons to demand such an expedition was Charles W. King, a member of a firm in Canton which sponsored the unsuccessful trip of an American ship, the "Morrison." Hopeful of starting private trade, he had organized the voyage ostensibly to return seven Japanese castaways. In 1837, when the ship appeared a few miles south of modern Yokohama, Japan was in a helpless position. It had absolutely no navy, and coastal defenses were pitiably weak. The authorities relied, therefore, on a strict enforcement of an old decree which declared that any foreign ship which came close to shore should be destroyed and any persons who landed should be arrested or killed. The "Morrison" fell into this category. When it dropped anchor it was immediately surrounded with a flotilla of small boats. After the boarding party had ascertained that the ship was unarmed, it was fired upon by a coastal mortar which forced its withdrawal. As a passenger on that vessel, King was piqued by the firing on his ship and by a subsequent refusal of the representatives of one of the strongest fiefs in the southwest to negotiate with him. After his return to China, he recommended that a United States naval expedition be organized immediately, that it anchor off Japan's coast and issue an ultimatum demanding trade relations and proper treatment for castaways.

Another American merchant, Aaron Haight Palmer, after an examination in Holland of official reports on Dutch-Japanese trade, returned to the United States convinced that an expedition should be dispatched to Japan as soon as possible.[3] The immediate result of this interest and enthusiasm was authorization in June, 1845, to Commodore James Biddle, chief of the East India Squadron, to carry the American Commissioner to China and thence to Japan to negotiate a trade treaty. The instructions added that if the Commissioner did not get to Japan, Biddle was free to go himself if he thought it advisable. As the Commissioner never reached the Orient, Biddle decided to attempt to break down Japan's seclusion. Thus in July, 1846, two American warships under his command anchored off the coast south of Edo (present-day Tokyo).

Unfortunately, Biddle was hampered from the start by restricting instructions. He was ordered to use utmost caution in his dealing with the Japanese, to act so as not to excite a hostile feeling toward, or a distrust of, the government of the United States. Consequently, when a low-grade Japanese seaman pushed him around when he entered a landing boat, he took no retaliatory action. Having allowed himself to be humiliated in this fashion, Biddle lost the respect of those with whom he had come to negotiate. The Japanese officials decided that he had little authority and that the United States was not capable of forcing its will on Japan. He was forced to leave empty handed.

Events within America were contributing, however, to a wider acceptance of the concept of Manifest Destiny and of a desire to play a vital role in the Far East. In the short period between 1846 and 1851, the United States established the Oregon Territory, Mexico was defeated, gold was discovered in California, the great migration to the western seaboard had begun, and the State of California was admitted to the Union. These developments convinced many Americans that their country was destined to become not only great, but also the commercial leader in the Orient. Mr. George Wilkes of New York proposed the construction of a transcontinental railway to capitalize on the potential profits from trade with what he described as "the opulent empire of Japan." The founders of the Pacific Mail Steamship Company were advised by Commodore Glynn, who had just returned from repatriating several American seamen, that they should ask the government to take steps to permit them to make use of Japanese ports. Consequently, Secretary of State Daniel Webster was easily convinced in 1851 that the United States manifestly was destined to dispatch a special expedition to force Japan out of seclusion.

Commodore Perry: Sailor of Destiny

When Commodore Matthew Calbraith Perry (1794-1858) was first informed of his assignment to lead an expedition to force open the door of Japan, he was not enthusiastic about his appointment. He believed that his outstanding career and seniority entitled him to a more important task. As he became immersed in his new undertaking, however, he became challenged by its possibilities.

Actually, he was admirably suited to succeed where others, British, Dutch, French, Russian, and American, had failed. His training, experience, and personality all contributed to his success. He approached this assignment, the success or failure of which was to effect the whole course of history in the western Pacific, from the viewpoint of one of America's leading and most experienced naval officers. He devoted all his energies to planning the entire expedition, from the selection of personnel to the adoption of basic policies that should govern his action in Japan. He was a stern disciplinarian and expected complete obedience from his men. His birth and upbringing had instilled him with a strong belief in himself. Such arrogance and pomposity which he possessed, though it might have been resented by some of his subordinates, made a deep and favorable impression on the Japanese.

He perused all available material in Washington on contemporary Japan. On the basis of this information, he insisted that he be given a flotilla strong enough to impress that nation with the prowess of America. As he had long advocated the adoption of the latest developments in steam navigation for naval craft, it was no mere coincidence that his squadron included two of the navy's best steamships. His flagship was the "Susquehanna," one of the new steam frigates. She was accompanied by the "Mississippi," which had already been under his command in 1847 and had performed creditably for him at Vera Cruz.

Long experience had also taught Perry that restrictive orders and directives were of questionable value in a situation in which former precedents could not be applied. He had complete confidence in his own ability to force a treaty on Japan providing he were given enough latitude of action and freedom to use his own discretion. Consequently, he persuaded Secretary of State Daniel Webster to allow him to decide the basic policies under which the expedition would operate. Webster supported this point of view and obtained consent of the other members of the Cabinet. As a result of this decision, Perry proceeded to write his own instructions with complete freedom. They took the form of a letter dated November 5, 1852, from the Acting Secretary of State to the Secretary of the Navy. According to these orders, the objectives of the United States in Japan were threefold:

1. To arrange for the protection of American seamen and property.
2. To obtain permission for American ships to enter one or more ports for provisions and to establish a coal depot.
3. To carry on trade by sale or barter.

The instructions then emphasized the necessity of explaining to the Japanese, because of their distrust of the British and other European powers, that the United States had no connections with any European country. Rather, it was a country with large cities extending from the Atlantic to the Pacific Ocean and from which, with the aid of steam, Japan could be reached in twenty days. Furthermore, if during the negotiations the Japanese showed no signs of willingness either to relax the system of exclusion or to guarantee humane treatment of American shipwrecked seamen, Perry was empowered to take a firm position. He was instructed to inform the Japanese "in the most unequivocal terms that it is the determination of the United States government to insist that all United States citizens be treated with humanity." Finally, Perry covered every possible contingency and protected himself against failure. His instructions concluded, "It is proper that the commodore should be invested with large discretionary powers, and should feel assured that any departure from usage, or any error of judgment he may commit will be viewed with indulgence."[4]

He was less successful, however, in his plans to assemble an imposing squadron. The new screw ship, "Princeton," which he had hoped would be completed in time, had failed in its preliminary tests. Despite the fact that only four ships were available, Perry decided sometime in November, 1852, that further delay might jeopardize the success of the whole expedition. He was afraid that the new Democratic President-elect, Franklin Pierce, might change the instructions or cancel the whole project. There was also the real possibility that other powers, notably Holland or Russia, might force Japan open before the United States could negotiate a treaty and hence put America at a disadvantage and humiliate him. Consequently, he left Norfolk, Virginia, on November 24, 1852, on the "Mississippi" en route to Hong Kong where his small fleet was to rendezvous. When he reached Hong Kong four and a half months later he was chagrined and disgruntled to find that the "Susquehanna," which he would use as flagship, had gone to Shanghai with refugees from the Taiping Rebellion. He stopped long enough, however, to add his son, Oliver, to his staff as secretary, and Dr. S. Wells Williams, an American Board Missionary in China, as chief interpreter. Williams had accompanied the "Morrison" sixteen years earlier on its abortive voyage to the Japanese coast, had acquired a reputation as a thorough scholar through the publication of his *Chinese Repository,* and had a knowledge of both Chinese and Japanese.

The two steam frigates "Susquehanna" and "Mississippi" left Shanghai in May, 1853, for Naha, the capital city of the Ryūkyū (Liuchiu) Islands. Perry hoped to serve a double purpose by his visit to the islands. In the first place, he needed a base of operations free from the suspicious and jealous eyes of Europeans. For this purpose, Naha was far superior to either Shanghai or Hong Kong. In the second place, he knew that the Ryūkyū Islands were considered to be directly under Japanese suzerainty. Hence, any activity of foreigners in that region would immediately be reported to the Japanese government. Consequently, Perry acted in a manner which he was sure would impress the Japanese on the islands. He insisted that the Regent entertain him at the palace rather than in the Regent's residence in Naha. He came and went as he pleased and demanded a house for use of the seamen. Finally, he carried out landing-party maneuvers to prepare his forces for possible similar operations in Japan.

In June, 1853, nearly seven months after he left Norfolk, Perry's squadron of four ships was ready for the last lap of their voyage. The two steam frigates sailed for Japan, towing the sailing sloops "Saratoga" and

"Plymouth." They steamed straight for the heart of the empire, Edo Bay, at whose head was located the seat of the Tokugawa dictatorship. On July 8, 1853, they were sighted off the coast at Uraga, at the foot of the bay. Japanese guard boats were immediately launched to head off the flotilla. Since the oarsmen could not keep up with the speed of the steamships, Perry ignored their shoutings and gesticulations; the flotilla continued up the bay to an anchorage of Perry's choice.

Frantic attempts were made by the Japanese to determine the plans of the Americans but Perry had issued strict orders to prevent any boarding of the vessels except by duly authorized officials. The time for either negotiations or hostilities had arrived. Perry would soon know whether or not he had received the correct intelligence concerning his enemy and whether he had made a wise estimate of the situation. If his planning had been based on sound reasoning, his arrival would mark a turning point in Japanese and world history.

Japan in the Mid-Nineteenth Century

Before the reaction to the arrival of the American naval force can be understood, it is necessary to describe briefly conditions within Japan when Perry pierced the curtain of isolation. At the beginning of the seventeenth century, the entire country had been united through the shrewdness and military power of Tokugawa Ieyasu (1542-1616). He had established his seat of government at Edo (modern Tokyo), was appointed Barbarian Subduing Generalissimo or Shogun in 1603, and ruled with an iron hand from his impregnable castle within the city.[5] For two and a half centuries his family held undisputed sway over the land by means of a military dictatorship usually called the Tokugawa Shogunate. Main branches of the family were enfeoffed at strategic centers and protected their holdings by formidable castles. Approximately 250 feudal barons (*daimyō*) held their fiefs at the pleasure of the Shogun.

These feudal barons were divided into two classes, those loyal to Ieyasu prior to a decisive battle in 1600 when he established his supremacy, and those who were his enemies at that time. The former, called "hereditary vassals," were rewarded for their services. The latter, termed "outside vassals," were isolated from the strategic positions of the realm and their fiefs were reduced in strength. Toward the end of the period, however, their isolation helped them. Some of them were able to form the core of the opposition which caused the downfall of the Tokugawa Shogun in the nineteenth century. But in the seventeenth century, any indication of infidelity by a feudal baron resulted in confiscation or reduction in size of his domain, or his transfer to an isolated region. All the barons, whether "hereditary" or "outside," swore allegiance to each new

Ploughing and Planting the Seed Bed

Transplanting

RICE—THE BASIS OF

These prints from a late seventeenth century treatise on agriculture, the *Nōgyō Zensho* by Miyazaki Yasusada, illustrate the various processes in growing rice, from preparing the

Harvesting and Threshing

Hulling and Storing

JAPANESE AGRICULTURE

ground in early spring to storing the harvest in the fall. Though they depict farming methods that are centuries old, they show scenes still common on many Japanese farms.

scion of the Tokugawa family and were required to spend half of their time in attendance at the Shogun's court.

Just as the Tokugawa family had its own retainers and vassals, each feudal baron had his own warriors who kept order within the boundaries of each fief and were subject to call for duty from the central government in time of national crisis. As further precaution against revolt, the barons were forbidden to form military or political alliances among themselves or with the Imperial court or to build or repair their castles without permission. Even the Emperor, with his small court in Kyōto, who had only ceremonial power, was dependent upon the will of the Shogun for the extent of his income.

Under this dictatorship, the country had been at peace since 1615 except for one Christian rebellion in the early seventeenth century and numerous peasant uprisings. This enforced peace had been acquired by methods which have been identified in the twentieth century with totalitarianism. Japanese society was rigidly stratified and harsh penalties restrained persons from shifting from one class to another. The warriors were the ruling class and all other classes in society were subservient to and dependent on them. Wealth was measured in terms of rice income and fiefs were assigned and incomes estimated on the basis of the productive capacity of the land. Consequently, the well-being and fortune of the warriors were dependent on the rice-producing class, the peasant or farmer.

The farmers, or second highest class in society, comprised about five-sixths of the total population of approximately thirty million. They were the economic base of feudalism and hence were recognized as an essential element in society. Nonetheless, most of them lived a primitive existence and were barely able to eke out enough to generate sufficient energy for themselves and their families to continue to cultivate the fields. They were taxed at least 50 per cent of their crop and were forbidden to sell their lands, divide their property, or leave their occupation. Since they frequently resorted to infanticide or abortion, their numbers remained static. The increasing frequency of their uprisings, despite the death penalty for every person so implicated, gave eloquent evidence that their economic plight was deteriorating.

The other two important groups in society were the artisans and the merchants. The former supplied the populace with daily necessities as well as luxuries, such as building supplies, clothing, household utensils, farming tools and simple machines, porcelain ware, lacquer, straw products, paper, silks and brocades, cotton cloth, footgear, and weapons. Until the importation in the 1850's of contemporary Western techniques of manufacturing guns and a few consumers' goods, practically all industry was in the handicraft stage. The merchants or townsmen, who were despised by the warrior, rose to power with the infiltration of money as the medium of exchange. They were the shippers, wholesalers, and storekeepers, and later business managers of the fiefs. As the bankers for the central government, for the feudal barons, and for individual warriors, the townsmen soon became creditors to the military class. Consequently, their actual power increased in proportion to their fortunes.

The dictatorship issued laws binding on all classes of society. It provided the death penalty for most crimes and for any act which could be construed as subversive, such as escaping to another fief, plotting an uprising, forgery, or counterfeiting. The laws were enforced by an elaborate system of secret police or spies who immediately reported any suspicious or irregular activity. The military power of the dictatorship was bolstered by financial and economic power. The Tokugawa family owned fiefs whose income totaled one-fourth of Japan's average annual rice crop of nearly 150 million bushels. It monopolized the mining of precious metals, taxed the merchants and guilds in the large cities, and held the feudal barons responsible for the construction and repair of its castles.

Finally, in the early seventeenth century, when the founders of the Tokugawa Shogunate believed that foreign trade could not be carried on without endangering the peace and security of the realm, Japan was sealed from the outside world. Except for limited, carefully regulated, and controlled trade with a few Chinese and Dutch merchants at Nagasaki, no foreigners were allowed within the country. No Japanese were permitted to go abroad nor to return from abroad on pain of death. Christianity was interdicted and practically exterminated through ruthless persecutions. In its stead, orthodox Confucianism, which justified absolutism, became the official philosophy of the state. Education based on this philosophy was restricted to a few select members of the warrior class. Everything possible was done to keep life static and to preserve the traditions of the founders of the dictatorship. As the German physician Von Siebold observed after his residence in Japan in 1823, that country had "condemned itself to complete immobility in the midst of universal movement."

Forces Which Challenged the Immutable Shogunate

By 1850, the Shogunate still maintained undisputed and complete control throughout the country. In fact, there was no concerted effort on the part of any class or group to usurp its power or to bring about its overthrow. Nonetheless, even the most complacent official could not fail to see indications which presaged momentous changes. In the first place, the Shoguns had long since ceased to be leaders and men of outstanding ability. For example, the eleventh Shogun, Ienari, who reigned from 1786 to 1837, longer than any member of his family, took a personal interest in the affairs of state. Certain of his characteristics, however, were not those which one usually associates with dictators. As described by one historian, "Intellectually he was a mediocrity; physically, while not exactly an invalid, he was far from robust. He was subject to epileptic fits."[6] His son and successor, Ieyoshi, who ruled from 1837 to 1853, was little better than a nonentity and rarely attempted to exert his own will or influence his ministers. A band of selfish opportunistic subordinates surrounded the ruler and vied among themselves for his favor. The situation was further complicated by the large group of ladies in waiting and concubines at the court and by the comings and goings of the priests from temples which had found favor in the eyes of the Shogun. Everyone schemed for the supremacy of his own faction. Jealousy, corruption, and weakness had led to degeneration and intrigue.

Despite the harsh edicts which forbade a shift from one class in society to another or a change in one's profession, social and economic forces produced change. For example, money had come to replace rice as the accepted medium of exchange, and the warrior, who usually lived in the castle towns or cities, was in constant need of it. His unquenchable thirst for luxury soon put him in debt to the merchant. The latter, to improve his social status, would often cancel the debt in exchange for the privilege of becoming a warrior. The warriors, who were the mainstay of the military power of the country, had become soft and degenerate. Only in rare cases were they expected to participate in exercises which improved their skill as soldiers or which kept them fit.

The peasants, who were expected to remain docile and till the land regardless of hardships, occasionally revolted. In some instances, the central government was forced to accept their demands. Others were condemned for moving to the city to live or for adopting such luxurious habits as the use of perfumed hair oil, paper raincoats, and umbrellas. They were admonished to return to the simple ways and to make their own raincoats and broad brimmed hats from home-grown straw. In fine, economic and social forces were creating changes among all groups which, in turn, stimulated the growth of new leadership. But change and new leaders are anathema to a dictatorship and were particularly intolerable to the Shogunate. While these changes could be kept to a minimum, they could not be controlled indefinitely.

The economic and financial distress of the central government and of most of the ruling class was the most striking evidence, however, that the end of the dictatorship was near. In 1605 when Ieyasu had retired as first Shogun and turned the government over to his son, he had two mil-

Ii Naosuke as Chief Councilor in Formal Court Dress

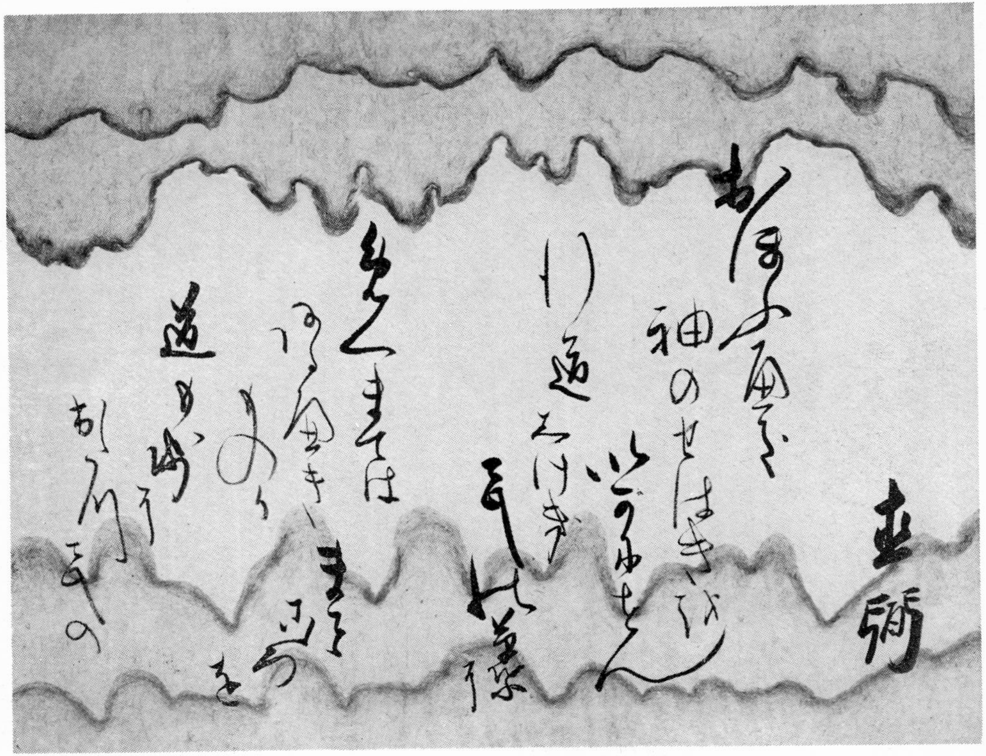

An Example of Ii's Calligraphy

Famous as the statesman who signed the Treaty of Edo with the United States in 1858, Ii was also noted for his considerable artistic talents.

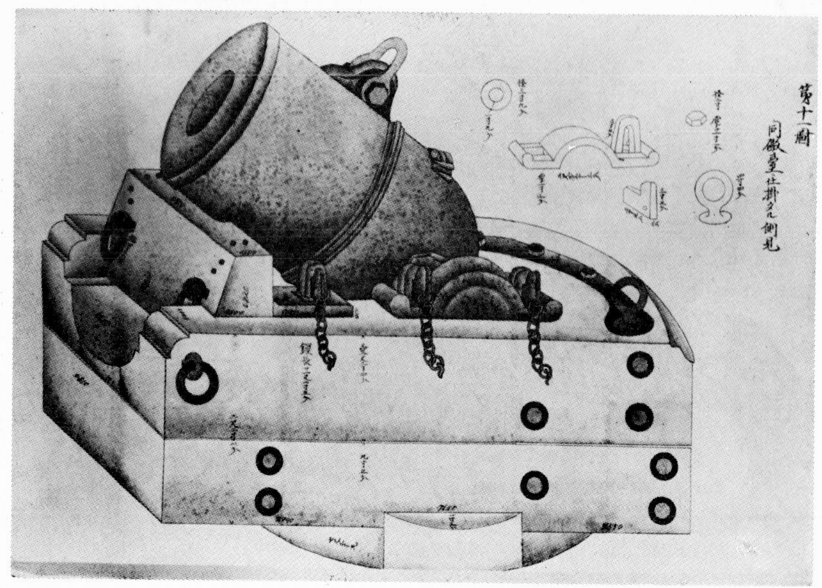

Early Type Cannon for Coastal Defense

Courtesy of Bettmann Archive

The Change From Samurai to a Conscript Army

lion gold pieces (*ryō*) stored in his warehouse. A little more than a century later, there was an estimated average yearly excess of about 200,000 bushels of rice and 250,000 gold pieces.

In the early eighteenth century, expenses increased at such an alarming rate that the annual deficit had to be met by frequent debasement of the currency, borrowing from the rich merchants, special transportation taxes, or withdrawal from the cash reserves of the government. According to a memorial prepared in 1858 by the Minister of Finance, the years 1834-36 saw an average annual deficit of 587,000 gold pieces which was offset by an excess of only 55,000 bushels of rice. Immediately thereafter, expenses suddenly jumped as a result of poor harvests, natural calamities, and the destruction by fire of one of the main castles. By 1854, the annual deficit was reported as 738,000 gold pieces.[7]

It is clear that the government was facing a financial crisis. Specific reforms had been inaugurated to decrease expenses and restrict luxuries. The monopolistic trade organizations had been temporarily abolished. Forced loans or requisitions from the rich merchants in the western cities had been increased. Half of the indebtedness of the feudal barons and the direct retainers of the Shogun had been canceled and the remainder was to be paid back without interest charges. But the basic financial weakness of the government was too fundamental to be cured by mere palliative measures. The whole feudal structure was rotten and was bound to collapse. As a leading scholar had predicted a half century earlier:

> The feudal barons have become impoverished and are unable to support those retainers who serve them. The Shogun's private retainers are luxurious in their habits and are unable to carry on their duties. If by chance there is a crisis, those in charge will be unable to cope with it.

The reactionary and conservative officials of the Shogunate were also confronted, in the philosophical and intellectual realm, with a new nationalism which was to challenge the right of the Tokugawa dictators to continue to usurp the power and authority of the Imperial throne. A small group of fearless scholars re-examined the oldest histories and discovered that Japan presumably had been produced by the Sun Goddess and that the Emperor was her direct descendant. Some scholars who hinted that the Shoguns were usurpers of the Imperial prerogatives were summarily banished from Edo. At the same time, work was progressing on a new history of Japan, the *Dai Nihon Shi* (History of Japan), which challenged even more directly the legitimacy of the Tokugawa Shogunate. This monumental compilation was begun in the middle of the seventeenth century and the sections on the "Chronicles of the Emperors" and the "Biographies" were presented to the Emperor Kōkaku in 1810.

Although for many centuries the Imperial court in Kyōto had been shorn of its political and economic power, it still possessed a limited amount of prestige. No Shogun or warlord had ever dared to rule Japan without Imperial sanction. The throne always remained as a potential political power. After the accession to the throne of Kōmei (reigned 1846-66), great grandfather of the present Emperor, Hirohito, the rivalry between the Emperor and the Shogun increased. The former was slowly becoming conscious of his importance as a new political force. The Emperor's court began to show interest and initiative in improving its status. New regulations for court behavior were issued by the youthful sovereign. They read in part as follows:

> The guards, both day and night, will cease their laziness and work together diligently.
>
> All of the officials, high and low, will be on duty and there shall not be any ignorance of the rules for ceremonies.
>
> There shall be no unauthorized goings and comings nor any arguments in a loud voice. If there is wrangling without cause, those responsible will receive heavy punishment.
>
> Drinking shall be limited to three cups full [of rice wine].
>
> Those who do not follow simplicity will be punished.

The court persisted in making requests to the Shogun for permission to expand its activities to include the reading of the Buddhist scriptures, the performance of classical plays, and the establishment of a school for the courtiers. Permission was finally granted in 1845 for a school which opened two years later under the name of Gakushūin. All courtiers under fifty years of age were required to attend the classes in reading the Chinese classics and were expected to apply Confucian ethics to their own personal conduct. By 1848, classes in the earliest Japanese laws and histories were added to the curriculum. It was a modest beginning but a first step toward preparing the Emperor's young advisers for their future leadership.

It was no mere accident that most of the fiefs which rallied around the throne and led the movement against the Tokugawa dictatorship were those which were the most advanced economically and politically. When these fiefs were able to ally themselves with the Imperial throne, their success was assured. (See Chapter 4.) This success would have been impossible, however, if the clan chieftains and their advisers had not sponsored modern technological advances and built some small Western industries. In other words, by the time Commodore Perry arrived in 1853 to open Japan's closed curtain, more effective progress toward modernization had been made in many of the outlying clans than within the Tokugawa domains. It was natural, therefore, that these clan leaders should be more enlightened and progressive than the ostentatious officials of the central government.

One of the most capable and powerful feudal barons of this period was Shimazu Nariakira (d. 1858) of Satsuma, in the southwest tip of the country. When he succeeded to his domain in 1851, many practical reforms had already been instigated. Animal husbandry had been fostered in each village where foreign-type cattle and horses were nurtured. A tremendous debt of five million gold pieces, accumulated partly as a result of supporting three mansions in Edo and a daughter at the Shogun's court, had been largely repaid by the profits from a sugar monopoly in the northern Ryūkyū Islands. Sales of sugar from the decade 1830-40 had equaled two and a half million gold pieces. When Admiral Cecille, commander of the French fleet in the Far East, sought a treaty of friendship in 1846 with the King of the Ryūkyū Islands, Nariakira obtained full responsibility over the islands, "to rule them as he saw fit." The profits which he made from continued trade were invested in industries which surpassed those of any other area. For example, a special institute, known as the Shūseikan, was established. Under its stimulus, medicine, sugar, glass, and glazed porcelain were manufactured. Smelting works were built in 1850 and two years later three small reverberatory furnaces and two blast furnaces for the production of cannon for coastal defense were completed. Translations were ordered to be made of Dutch books on naval construction and the central government had been requested to permit the fief to build a ship larger than the legal maximum tonnage, for use in foreign trade.

The fief of Hizen, which along with Satsuma, was to become one of the four leaders of the Restoration movement, was also one of the most highly advanced industrially. Hizen surrounded the city of Nagasaki, the port of call for the Dutch and Chinese traders and for ships of other countries seeking foreign trade. Consequently the domain was given responsibility for the protection of that port. The feudal lord of the domain, Nabeshima Kansō (1814-71) had realized that industrialization of his domain was essential to permit manufacture of the military installations necessary to protect the harbor. As the central government provided no funds for these coastal defenses, the fief was compelled to manufacture other goods which could be sold to help pay for the production of the military installations. Finally, contact of the clansmen with the Hollanders, who had been trading at Nagasaki for two centuries, had stimulated interest in European science and technological developments. Western techniques, including iron smelting, shipbuilding, and electricity, were officially sponsored and by 1842 cannon had been manufactured with Dutch help.

After six years of procrastination, the Tokugawa authorities reluctantly agreed to give the fief a small loan and to permit 53 cannon to be placed around Nagasaki harbor. The first successful reverberatory furnace in Japan was completed in 1850 and cannon were produced as rapidly as possible. As a contemporary described them, "Although they were not yet equal to Occidental guns, still the difference is not appreciable." Even before the country was opened to Western intercourse, the clan had secretly asked the Dutch to bring with them on their next trip a model of a steamship. By 1853, although the Hizen clan was not openly hostile to the Tokugawa dictatorship, conditions within the clan were such that it could become a strong potential rival.

Another center of both potential and real subversive activity, from the point of view of the Shogunate, was the fief of Mito. It derived its name from the castle town about seventy miles north of Edo on the edge of the fertile eastern plain. Ironically, it had been established in the early seventeenth century as one of the three main branches of the Tokugawa family to help assure the continuance of the family's military dictatorship. It produced only one Shogun, the last, but at the same time was a hotbed of antigovernment activity and intrigue. The nationalistic *Dai Nihon Shi* (History of Japan) had been compiled under its auspices. As in the case of the western clans, such as Satsuma and Hizen, the Mito clan had championed military preparedness and industrialization.

When Tokugawa Nariaki succeeded to the fief at the age of thirty in 1829, he immediately ordered the various officials of the domain to give up their luxurious habits and to emphasize learning and the military arts. He set up village schools throughout the domain for the education of the people and appointed efficient officials who soon reduced the expenditures of the fief. He also established public granaries for famine relief and instituted public work's projects such as dredging the rivers. The warriors were ordered to return to the villages and all their debts were canceled. Finally, Nariaki led his warriors on a hunting expedition in 1840 which was equivalent to military maneuvers and which became an annual affair. As he had disregarded the central government's prohibition against local fiefs building up their armament, he was forced into retirement for four years, and his program of industrialization lagged temporarily. Nevertheless, the coastal defenses were finally strengthened, Dutch books were borrowed from Satsuma, and Mito clansmen were sent to that fief to inspect the newly constructed furnaces. Subsequently, the Mito clan built its own model furnace with the help of engineers from Satsuma and elsewhere.

There were two other clans which also played a prominent role in the Imperial Restoration. One of these was Chōshū, on the western tip of the main island of Honshu, which commanded the western entrance to the Inland Sea. The other was Tosa on the south side of the island of Shikoku. Like the three examples already cited, both Chōshū and Tosa were advanced intellectually and economically and produced some of the outstanding leaders of new Japan.

In addition to the comparatively advanced economic development of several of the feudal domains which traditionally were the enemies of the military dictatorship of the Tokugawa family, there was a small but important group of intellectual leaders who advocated policies counter to those in force. As most of these persons had contacts with Western learning, they took a keen interest in the basic question of Japan's best defense against possible attack from abroad. Many of them devoted their lives to increasing their knowledge of Western military science. Others went a step further and argued that it was folly for Japan to remain secluded and that wealth and strength could be best attained by foreign trade. Their advocacy of a policy counter to that of the past was sufficient to make the government consider them subversive influences.

Two of the outstanding intellectuals in this group, who suffered severely because of their beliefs, were Watanabe Kazan (1793-1841) and Takano Chōei (1804-50). Both men were ardent students of Occidental learning and especially military science; both were convinced that Japan should take a more lenient attitude toward the foreign demands that Japan be opened to the outside world. They were members of a group of scholars and government officials who opposed the forceful expulsion of the American ship "Morrison" in 1837 and were falsely accused by a jealous, conservative official. Takano, who had written a book critical of the government, was condemned to life imprisonment. After escaping from prison when it burnt and wandering "underground" for six years, he was finally betrayed. He killed one of the police who came to arrest him and then committed suicide. Watanabe had fared badly, too. Condemned to perpetual confinement in his own clan, he committed suicide.

Takashima Shūhan (1798-1866), an employee in the city magistrate's office in the city of Nagasaki, is another example of this group of "subversives." He had studied Dutch military drill and artillery methods, ordered guns and mortars from the Dutch, and instructed about 300 of his pupils in European type drill formations. When he heard of China's defeat in the Opium War in 1840, he was convinced that Japan should reform its military system and use the newest weapons. Finally called to Edo in 1841 to give a demonstration of Dutch drill tactics and artillery practice, he made such a favorable impression that the government purchased his cannon and ordered him to start a new school for the instruction of military officers. He then became a victim of the reactionary and jealous attitude of conservative members of the government who feared any type of innovation. Imprisoned in 1842 by the same person who accused Watanabe and Takano, he was forced to remain in seclusion until after the arrival of Commodore Perry.

The fate of these men, who devoted their efforts to strengthening the military and economic position of their country, was eloquent evidence of the fact that there were men who were courageous enough to oppose the government despite the consequences. It also showed that the military dictatorship was rapidly forcing its own capitulation by refusing to recognize the tremendous external and internal changes that were taking place. The end of the universal state of the Tokugawa Shogunate was in sight.[8]

Notes

1. As will be immediately apparent to anyone familiar with his work, I have relied heavily on DeVoto for the interpretation of the events from Gray's discovery of the Columbia to the exploration of the Missouri. Although somewhat of a digression from our main theme, the events cannot be ignored since they led directly to Perry's expedition and Japan's opening. See Bernard DeVoto, *The Course of Empire* (Boston: Houghton Mifflin Co., 1953), pp. 315 ff.

2. For an interesting account of the role of Britain and others in connection with our western expansion and its relation to the road to the Indies see Henry Nash Smith, *Virgin Land* (Boston: Harvard University Press, 1949), pp. 19 ff.

3. Henry Graff, *Bluejackets with Perry in Japan* (New York: New York Public Library, 1952), pp. 35 ff.

4. Arthur Walworth, *Black Ships off Japan* (New York: Alfred A. Knopf, Inc., 1946), pp. 40 ff.

5. The present palace of the Emperor in Tokyo is on the site of the old Edo castle. The watchtowers on the east moat, the huge stone walls and ramparts surrounding the palace grounds are relics from the original castle built for Ieyasu at the expense of the feudal barons.

6. James Murdoch, *A History of Japan* (3 vols.; London: Kegan Paul, Trench, Trubner & Co., Ltd., 1926), III, p. 429.

7. Unfortunately, it is extremely difficult to obtain accurate figures on the annual budget, and it is questionable whether complete figures were kept. In any case, only fragmentary information is available. The memorial referred to gives figures for only the years 1791-93, 1811-13, 1820-22, 1834-36, and 1854-56. According to Takekoshi, who gives no sources for his data, the annual average deficit amounted to 545,000 gold pieces and the excess of rice was only 17,593 bushels for the years 1834-36. He gives no figures for 1854. See Toki Tomomasa, "Tairō Ii Naosuke bakufu zaisei kyūbō no ken," (Memorial of eleventh month, 1858) in Nakamura Katsumaro (ed.), *Shigaku Kenkyū Roku,* pp. 317-29, and Takekoshi Yosaburō, *Nihon Keizai Shi* (Tokyo: Heibonsha, 1929), III, pp. 733-43.

8. For a vivid description of these "forerunners of the revolution," see George B. Sansom, *The Western World and Japan* (New York: Alfred A. Knopf, Inc., 1950), pp. 248-75; and Ishin Shiryō Hensan Kakari (ed.), *Ishin Shi* (6 vols.; Tokyo: Meiji-shoin, 1939-41), I.

3

JAPAN IS OPENED TO THE WEST 1853-1857

Fear and Dismay Within Japan in 1853

The arrival in July, 1853, of Perry's "black ships," as they were called, created an immediate furor both among the people and the officials. Many of the fishermen and coastal villagers were astonished at the sight of the paddle-wheelers which ejected black clouds of smoke. Rumors that the barbarians had harnessed volcanoes soon swept the countryside. In Edo, thirty-five miles to the north of Perry's anchorage, the populace was thrown into near panic and feared the worst. The reports from Chinese sea captains of China's defeat in the so-called Opium War by England in 1840 were still fresh in the minds of the intellectual leaders. Some of these reports, which had been published in Japan, were surprisingly accurate.[1] They stated that China had been forced to cede territory to Great Britain, to pay an indemnity, and to open its ports to trade.

People wondered, therefore, whether the arrival of this fleet of American warships signaled a fate for Japan similar to that of China. Unlike the ordinary citizens of Edo, the leading officials of the Tokugawa government knew full well the significance of the arrival of this flotilla of warships. They knew that they were American and that Perry had come to ask for a treaty. They also knew that several of the European countries, notably Russia, England, and France were determined to break the Dutch monopoly of trade with Japan. Russian official requests for trade and attacks on Japanese outposts on the Kurile Islands had underlined the emergency. British warships had also appeared in Japanese waters in defiance of Japan's exclusion policy. Now that the Americans had arrived, even greater international pressure was added to the other forces working toward the overthrow of the dictatorship.

The central government, fearful lest its traditional policy of forceful expulsion of foreign ships lead to war, had modified its exclusion policy in the hope that the impending crisis might be postponed. As early as 1842, a new edict had been issued to all feudal barons responsible for coastal defenses. This decree ordered that foreign ships should be supplied with provisions and then advised to leave. Ships reconnoitering along the coast were not to be molested.

An unequivocal policy of exclusion gave way to a new policy of vacillation. The Tokugawa officials hoped that they could avoid a showdown with foreigners through threats, vacillation, and procrastination. They recognized that these objectives might be accomplished if the "red-headed barbarians" could be persuaded to carry on all their negotiations at Nagasaki. That city had special magistrates to deal with foreigners and the fortifications in the harbor were the best in the country. Furthermore, the movements of foreigners in Nagasaki could be kept from most of the country. As Perry was well aware, however, the American squadron's arrival at the entrance to Edo Bay meant that the problem must be faced immediately by the Japanese officials. There was always the possibility that the ships would proceed on toward Edo and there were no fortifications strong enough to stop them. A failure on the part of the local feudal barons or even of the forces of the Shogun, "the Barbarian Subduing Generalissimo," to resist and overcome an attack would spell disaster for the Tokugawa dictatorship.

The Ministers of State had long struggled with the all-important security problem of how to protect Japan's shores. Some of the officials, such as Tsutsui Masanori, who later negotiated with the Russian Admiral Putiatin, argued in 1846 that the coastal defenses should be greatly strengthened, naval ships should be built, and provisions supplied to foreign ships to minimize the possibility of later attack. Those persons responsible for the country's defense realized, however, that protection from foreign invasion could come only if the various clans combined their efforts. On the other hand, if these clans were to give effective protection, they would have to be permitted to rearm. There was no assurance that a newly acquired strength would not be directed against the dictatorship itself. It was finally decided, nonetheless, to take a chance on the continued loyalty of the feudal barons and to encourage increased armaments in the different fiefs.

To assist in the implementation of this new policy, the Shogunate began to acquaint the feudal lords with the actual state of affairs. In a report of December, 1849, they were informed of the most recent encroachments of foreign ships into Japanese waters in both the north and the southwest. More specifically, a British ship had entered lower Tokyo Bay and its sailors had landed on the offshore island of Ōshima. In other cases, the "barbarians" had boarded the Japanese patrol boats. The report continued that if nothing were done to alleviate the situation, Japan's dangers would increase. Consequently, it recommended: "We have often ordered that you carry out the responsibilities of protecting the country. You should, despite the opinions you may hold, be prepared to supply soldiers and obey the instructions in reference to the expulsion of foreign ships." The smaller fiefs were ordered to be ready to join a general plan of defense. The report concluded:

> The only salvation from an attack by the foreign rebels is an alliance to defend the country and the exertion of the entire national strength. The barons (*daimyō*) are the bulwarks of defense. Their direct retainers are next who are followed by the merchants and farmers who should carry out their specific duties to the best of their ability.[2]

As one of the prerequisites for their privilege of continuing to trade, the Dutch had been required to make annual pilgrimages to the court at Edo and to present written reports on conditions abroad. Hence, they were on the alert for any foreign news which would be of special interest to the Shogun's court. Through reports from their embassy in Washington they were fully aware of the plans for an American expedition. Secretary of State Daniel Webster asked the Dutch Ambassador whether Japan intended to continue its policy of exclusion. The Netherlands government seized upon the American request as an opportunity to strengthen its position. In 1852, it appointed a new chief, Donkier Curtius, to the Dutch trading outpost in Japan. He was instructed to promote, by every means in his power, the success of the American expedition and simultaneously to persuade the Japanese government to change its policy of exclusion not only toward Holland but toward America and other countries.

This plea, as well as a Dutch request for a commercial treaty, was categorically rejected. In the summer of 1852, the Dutch formally reported on the proposed American expedition and emphasized the fact that preparations were completed for landing a military force. The lethargic bureaucrats in Edo refused to give credence to the reports, but the Dutch insisted on their authenticity. When news reached the Edo government from the Ryūkyū Islands, through the *daimyō* of Satsuma, that Perry had arrived at Naha and would proceed to Japan, feverish efforts to bolster the coastal defenses were started.

The Japanese Stall for Time

When Perry finally appeared on July 8, 1853, he had already made important basic decisions on procedures which contributed greatly to the success of his expedition. In the first place, he would keep himself inaccessible except to the highest officials. Secondly, all Japanese would be treated with courtesy but firmness, and communications with nonofficials would not be tolerated. If they showed any signs of procrastination, he would take advantage of his instructions to survey Japanese waters to send ships up the bay closer to the capital city. Finally, he would brook no delay over minor matters but would deliver the letter from the President requesting a treaty, retrace his course to the Ryūkyūs and the China coast, strengthen his fleet, and return the next spring for an answer.

Consequently, when the Japanese began to bicker over where the American communication should be received, Perry was specific. He informed them that they had three days to agree to receive the letter on the shore opposite the anchorage of the squadron. From Perry's point of view, it was important to impress upon the Japanese at the start that he would not be intimidated but would carry out his own plans.

To underscore the seriousness of his demands he insisted that, "If the friendly letter of the President to the Emperor is not received and duly replied to, he will consider his country insulted and will not hold himself accountable for the consequences." Special parties from the expedition began surveying the bay for an anchorage nearer to Edo. This action had a magic effect on the Council of Elders, the chief governing body. Although the Americans were not aware of the fact, the largest Japanese shore batteries were one-fourth the size of the guns of the "Mississippi" and are reported to have had only ten rounds of ammunition. The government had little choice but to accede to Perry's wish.

Consequently, in less than a week after his arrival, he landed on shore in full dress with a strong guard and under the protective cover of the four naval ships. President Fillmore's letter was delivered. It was received by the specially appointed officials in silence. They handed the Americans a note which stated that the letter was received in opposition to Japanese law. It added tersely, "As the Uraga beach was not a place where negotiations or entertainment were authorized," and "as the letter has been received, you can depart."[3]

Perry realized that this final barb left him on the defensive and could be interpreted to mean that he had been forced to leave. Consequently, when the ceremonies were completed, the entire squadron was ordered underway, not down the bay but northeasterly toward Edo. A new anchorage was made ten miles nearer the city and later the "Mississippi" steamed close enough so that Perry could see the southern suburb of Shinagawa. That no guns were fired from the land fortifications, even though Perry approached within sight of the nerve center of the Tokugawa dictatorship, was clear proof that the Council of Elders had recognized the American squadron's superior strength and had decided that at all cost hostilities should be avoided at this time.

After the exchange of some presents, Perry headed his fleet for the open sea on July 17, having promised that he would return for an official reply to his government's request. He intimated that his squadron would be considerably augmented. He had accomplished exactly what he had intended to do. He had landed on shore at the place he, rather than the Japanese, had selected. He had officially communicated with the Japanese government and requested a formal reply. There was no question in his mind but that Japan's seclusion was near an end. He had hopes that it would come about without open hostilities. From his point of view, this would depend entirely on Japan's reply.

The Great Debate on Seclusion

Although there were many of the Councilors and lesser officials who gave a sigh of relief when the American ships disappeared over the horizon of lower Edo Bay, they knew that the basic question of whether to abolish the national policy of seclusion was still to be settled. President Fillmore's letter had stated that Perry was sent so that "the United States and Japan should live in friendship and have commercial intercourse with each other." It pointed out that the American Territory of Oregon and the State of California lay directly opposite to the Shogun's dominions and that American steamships could cover the distance in eighteen days. It requested, just as Perry's instructions had stated, that (1) the two countries should trade for mutual benefit; (2) shipwrecked sailors should be treated kindly; (3) American steamers should be allowed to stop in Japan for supplies of coal and provisions and a convenient port be designated for this purpose.

Since all these requests were diametrically opposed to the traditional and accepted policy of seclusion, a real dilemma faced the Council of Elders. If the Councilors accepted the American demands, it would be a reversal of policy. Such action would be taken as a sign of weakness by the Dutch, British, Russian, and French. They would press for even greater concessions which would require even more humiliating capitulation. The government would be left open to direct or indirect attack by its enemies at home. On the other hand, if the demands were rejected, the Americans might open hostilities and force Japan to submit to demands such as those made on China by Great Britain. To make matters worse, though he had been little interested in state affairs, the Shogun had died only a few days after Perry withdrew. Much time had to be spent on ceremonials connected with his funeral.

The immediate danger from without, however, was too real to be ignored. The crumbling dictatorship had recourse to the only alternative left to it; it made such preparations as it could against an American invasion and simultaneously sought commitments from the feudal barons to support a common program. All coastal defenses, regardless of who governed the fief in which they were to be built, were ordered to be strengthened. Individual feudal barons were permitted to make purchases of cannon and ships directly from the Dutch or to build them in their own fiefs. The Imperial Court, for whose safety the Shogun was responsible, was notified of Perry's arrival and the purpose of his trip.

Finally, Chief Councilor Abe Masahiro (1819-57), who hoped to be able to present a united front to the Americans when they returned, took an unprecedented and momentous step. In fact, it was such a significant move that it might be considered as the dawn of the first day of Japan's modern century. On August 5, 1853, he had a translation of President Fillmore's letter sent to all the feudal barons, the leading government officials, the chief Confucian scholars, independent warriors, and merchants. The official communication read as follows:

> At this time, a great crisis faces the country. In fact, it is a time of danger. It is requested that you will all give serious consideration to the purport of the American President's letter and will express your opinions freely on the matter even though they may be contrary to established policy.[4]

Perry's arrival, his refusal to move to Nagasaki or to be intimidated, and his delivery of an official letter came as a shock to all classes of society living in the Edo area. The circulation of this communication from the United States came as an even greater shock. Few had realized that the Tokugawa government was so weak and frightened that it had to ask persons outside the inner circle of Councilors what policy should be adopted. As might be expected from such an unprecedented move, many of the replies were confused and some straddled the issue. Others, largely depending on the personal experiences of the feudal barons, took a strong position either pro or contra the rejection of the American demands and the continuation of seclusion.

When the opinions of fifty-nine of the most important *daimyō* are analyzed, it is found that they fall fairly evenly into three categories. The first group of replies supported some form of trade with the United States. The second group advocated avoiding hostilities to give the country time to increase its defenses. Finally, many persons categorically refused to consider any change in policy and demanded that America's requests be rejected. Twenty-two of the barons supported trade, eighteen wanted to avoid war, and nineteen were confident that the Americans could be driven away without the necessity of giving them any concessions.

Quite naturally Kuroda Narihiro, who had joint responsibility for the protection of Nagasaki, was one of those in the first group. He argued that any victory which might be achieved would be only temporary. Hence it would be better to accede graciously to the American demands. The Lord of Hikone, Ii Naosuke, was also among those who favored a conciliatory reply. In fact, he soon came to be the leading Councilor who supported greater contacts with foreigners. Some of the persons in this first group argued that the profit from trade should be used to buy necessary guns and ships for the country's defense. This position was eloquently presented by Takashima Shūhan, who had come out of disgrace after Perry's arrival (see page 25) and whose technical and military knowledge was avidly sought by the government. He noted that Japan's plight, in terms of its supply of modern firearms, was the same as that of China. He bemoaned the fact that while every Western soldier had a gun, there were only thirty guns for each 1000 soldiers in Japan. The navy was completely undeveloped and hence the Japanese could not compete successfully with the Westerners who were equipped with warships. He concluded that trade would produce the necessary funds to pay for armaments and that it would be useless to begin a war until Japan was properly armed.[5]

Shimazu Nariakira, feudal baron of Satsuma in the extreme southwest, was one of the most powerful warriors. Because of his contacts and trade with the Ryūkyū Islands and of his personal interest in the problem, he was particularly well informed on foreign affairs. Nearly a decade earlier he had pleaded for trade on his own behalf. His vassals in the Ryūkyūs had warned him of Perry's intentions. One of his advisers, who later acted as official interpreter at the conferences with Perry, had been to America and knew of its power and strength.

Nariakira's position on what to do with the American request carried special weight. It was, in fact, far more practical than the replies of most of the barons but falls between the first and second groups. He communicated privately with two other barons seeking their support for his proposal that the entire problem of coastal defense should be placed in the hands of a single individual, namely, Tokugawa Nariaki of Mito. He argued that it was impractical to refuse flatly the requests of the United States, England, and Russia; so Japan should play for time. Funds of the Tokugawa government, rather than those of the local feudal barons, should be used for building coastal defenses. Finally, he advocated limited trade, but not with America, to strengthen Japan. Specifically, he requested that he be permitted to build twelve large ships and a steamboat and that each feudal lord possess a ship for trading with India and China. Finally, all of the feudal barons should receive copies of the Dutch reports on conditions abroad so that they would be kept abreast of international developments.

Tokugawa Nariaki of Mito, who was nominated by Shimazu Nariakira for a position comparable to that of a minister of defense, wanted to avoid hostilities, improve the nation's defenses and reject the demand for trade. It has already been observed how he had bent every effort to strengthen the defenses of his own fief. He was keenly aware, therefore, of the significance of Perry's visit. In his memorial he argued that the Shogun should decide the basic issue of war or peace. He believed that before this question was decided, all the feudal barons, the farmers, and the merchants should be ordered to live simply; all the people should strive for enlightenment; and the entire country of the gods should work together. He urged immediate use of the Dutch to augment Japan's defenses. They should be asked to import and to present to the government as a gift small and large guns and send steam warships from Europe. Shipbuilders, pilots, and mechanics should be collected and brought to Japan on the next Dutch ship. He pressed for military activities on a national scale similar to those which he had introduced into his own fief. The feudal barons should be ordered to build cannon and perfect the defenses in their respective fiefs and the warriors should be forced to take military exercises. Furthermore, all of them should study artillery. He even advocated the construction of fortresses along the seacoast with both private and public funds.

In direct opposition to customs and laws which placed the warrior class above all others and gave them special privileges, he recommended making fishermen into a coastal defense force. As he described it, "fishermen should be intermingled with soldiers to protect the coast." Finally, he called upon the national and local divinities for help. He prayed that the spiritual power of the Sun Goddess enshrined at Ise would unify all the people of the land of the gods. In another memorial, Nariaki listed numerous reasons why Perry's request for a treaty should be turned down. He feared that acquiesence would result in the other powers making similar demands. He predicted that the foreigners would first ask for trade and then would proselytize the country. The result would be strife and contention. He concluded, "Seclusion has enervated the spirit of the people. The present moment is the most auspicious one to quicken their sinews of war."

Finally, there were also many other important and influential barons who favored rejection of the American request and continuance of a tight seclusion. Significantly, these included three (Hizen, Chōshū, and Tosa) of the four powerful western clans, which were to rally around the Emperor and force the abdication of the Tokugawa Shogun. (See Chapter 4 below.) They were supported by most of the Confucian scholars, the royalists, and many of the leading political figures. As one of them tersely remarked, "There has been no attack by foreigners on the sacred soil of Japan since the Mongol invasion in the thirteenth century. If trade were granted, Japan's dignity would be lost and its unique national polity would be gone." The most ironical statement from this group was that made by the man who was to become the last Shogun and who had to capitulate in 1867 to the Imperial forces. He boasted that, "No matter how many vessels come from overseas, none of them will return—such is the strength and virtue of Japan."

The consensus seemed to support the view of this last group, namely, that Perry should be sent away without a treaty. The fact that this view was also strongly held by the Imperial Court made the situation even more difficult for the Tokugawa officials. Obviously, an ambiguous answer would receive the most support. Those officials who had already been in contact with Perry and his subordinates realized, however, that it would take more than prayers offered at seventeen-day intervals at the seven leading shrines to protect the country in its greatest crisis in history.

Perry Returns and the Treaty of Kanagawa of 1854

While Perry was wintering near Macao, replenishing his supplies, resting his crews, and awaiting re-enforcements for his flotilla, he received two important reports. The first of these was an official request from the Japanese government through the Dutch that he postpone his return because of the death of the Shogun. He immediately recognized this request as a delaying tactic so that it had no effect on his plans. The second report was that a Russian naval expedition, under the command of Admiral Putiatin, had borrowed from the precious store of coal which Perry had reserved for himself in Shanghai; had proceeded to Nagasaki in August, 1853; had returned to China for more coal; and had requested that the Americans join forces with the Russians in opening Japan. Distrustful of Russian designs and fearful lest they receive concessions prior to his obtaining a treaty, Perry advanced by several months the date of departure for his squadron.

Although Perry believed that the presence of the Russian fleet in Far Eastern waters endangered his chances of success, the timing of Putiatin's movements were actually a real advantage to him. The Russians had hoped to strengthen their East Asiatic empire by creating good relations with Japan. Admiral Putiatin had left Russia in August, 1852. His flagship sailed in October to join him in England a month before Perry departed from the United States. Both expeditions had been launched independently, but when Putiatin stopped at the Cape Verde Islands in February, 1853, he learned that Perry was ahead of him. The Russians reached Canton in the summer of 1853 only to hear that the American squadron was nearing the Japanese coast.

Four Russian warships entered Nagasaki two weeks after the feudal barons had been requested to submit their opinions regarding a treaty with the foreigners. Admiral Putiatin, the Russian Commander, demanded the settlement of boundaries in the Kuriles and Sakhalien and the opening of a port for trade. By the time Perry reached the Japanese coast a second time, Putiatin had made two visits to Japan. In fact, one of the chief negotiators with Putiatin was returning from Nagasaki along the Eastern Seaboard Route just in time to see Perry's second flotilla cast anchor in lower Edo Bay. The Russian's request for a trade treaty had been denied but his visits made the Japanese officials keenly aware of the fact that they faced a threat from both Russia and the United States. The relentless pressure from overseas was becoming unbearable.

In the meantime, Commodore Perry had taken certain steps to protect his rear in the event that his final negotiations were unsuccessful. He proposed to his government that the United States should seize both the Ryūkyū and Bonin Islands and use them as a base of operations against Japan. He recommended that if his mission failed, the Island of Okinawa, the largest in the Ryūkyūs, should come under American control in repayment for insults and injuries to American citizens.

On his second trip, he stopped again at Okinawa but set up a small American outpost on the island before starting on the last lap of his voyage. This time, he was in command of an imposing squadron. Eight ships approached the familiar Japanese anchorage on February 12, 1854. They were later joined by two others. Their total complement of 1600 men was equal to about one-fourth of the personnel in the American navy. The writings of the leading Japanese negotiators clearly indicate that they were overawed by this display of force. In fact, they grossly exaggerated the reserves which they believed were at Perry's disposal. Hayashi, the chief delegate, wrote:

> Perry said that he would enter into negotiations but if his proposals were rejected he was prepared to make war at once; that he would have 50 ships in nearby waters and 50 more in California.[6]

Believing that they were faced with an attack if they did not show a conciliatory attitude toward the American demands, the Japanese agreed to hold the negotiations at Kanagawa, a point nearer Edo than the old anchorage. The Shogun's answer to President Fillmore's letter was delivered on March 8, 1854. It agreed, subject to certain limitations, to comply with the American requests concerning coal and provisions and the proper treatment of ships and crews in distress. Coal and other supplies would be available only at Nagasaki after a year and no other form of trade would be permitted. Perry then countered unsuccessfully with a proposal that Japan sign a treaty permitting trade similar to that between the United States and China.

The remainder of the negotiations involved largely the question of suitable ports of call for American ships. Perry had rejected Nagasaki and substituted Kanagawa. Hayashi and his colleagues were without instructions. They hastened to Edo for consultations with the chief councilors including Nariaki of Mito. Obviously, from the Japanese point of view, Kanagawa was far too near the seat of government. Consequently, isolated cities were substituted and finally accepted by both sides. These cities were Hakodate on the northern island of Hokkaidō, and Shimoda on the tip of Izu peninsula, some three days' journey from the capital. One point, which remained vague, concerned the right to appoint a consul in one of these ports. So long as the Japanese had refused to agree to carry on trade, Perry considered it imperative that the treaty provide for the appointment of an American consul who could negotiate a commercial treaty. Consequently, it was agreed that after eighteen months a consul could reside at Shimoda whenever either party decided such an arrangement necessary. All these points were incorporated into the Treaty of Kanagawa, signed March 31, 1854.[7] Japan's protracted seclusion had finally come to an end. (See Frontispiece.)

As already intimated, the successful conclusion of these negotiations was enhanced by various factors. Perry had made thorough preparations and followed a policy which favorably impressed the Japanese negotiators. The requests of Russia for trade, which were made between Perry's two visits, only underlined the danger to Japan from abroad. The answers from the feudal barons concerning the advisability of abandoning the seclusion policy had shown that though a majority of persons agreed that Japan should remain closed many had concluded that war would mean defeat. The government wished to avoid war at all costs.

Finally, the presents which the Americans gave to the Shogun and the lavish entertainment showered on the negotiators had a decidedly salutary influence. The model steam train, which circled the tracks at twenty miles an hour, and the telegraph sets, which sent instantaneous messages mysteriously through wires, were tangible evidence of the technological advancement of the United States. Many who saw them began to realize that there might be many advantages to be gained by trade with the Occident. For the sake of expediency, the Council of Elders had formally informed the barons that the Americans would be sent away without granting them concessions. Actually, the treaty had made numerous concessions. Furthermore, other Western powers were to make even greater demands. But for the moment, the Tokugawa government was preoccupied with meeting the criticism that arose when it became known that the new treaty had been signed.

Other Treaties and Conventions

As was to be expected, when the European powers interested in the Orient learned that the United States had ended Japan's seclusion, there was a rush by the other powers to seek privileges for themselves. Admiral

Sir James Sterling visited Nagasaki half a year after Perry had left. His purpose was twofold, to search for Russian ships as prizes in the Crimean War and to sign a treaty. He was unsuccessful in his search for the Russian Admiral Putiatin but obtained a treaty (October, 1854) which allowed British ships to call at Nagasaki or Hakodate for supplies.

Shortly after the British squadron had left Nagasaki, the Russians arrived in the north. This time, however, Admiral Putiatin had only one ship, the "Diana." His determination to obtain a favorable answer to his requests was clear from his decision to head for Ōsaka, the port nearest the Imperial capital of Kyōto. The Tokugawa officials were thrown into a frenzy. It seeemed that their worst fears had been realized. The foreigners were even threatening to attack the Emperor's capital, which the Shogun was impotent to defend. The Japanese adamantly refused to negotiate with Putiatin at Ōsaka and ordered him to proceed elsewhere.

Although Putiatin was forced to move before he could renew negotiations, he had proved to his own satisfaction that another Japanese seaport was easily accessible to European style ships and that the Ōsaka roadstead was not as shallow as had been rumored. Since he had realized the dangers of continued procrastination by the negotiators if he returned to Nagasaki, he headed eastward toward Shimoda, one of the two ports included in the Treaty of Kanagawa. At Shimoda, while negotiations were still proceeding, the "Diana" was severely damaged in the tidal wave and whirlpool created in the landlocked harbor by the devastating earthquake of December 23, 1854. The hapless ship was completely in the clutches of the elements. It rotated around its mooring forty-two times in a period of half an hour and was thrown about mercilessly by the tides. It was only by chance that it was not dashed upon the rocks. While being towed to safety to a nearby harbor a few days later, it finally sank.

Putiatin continued his negotiations while Japanese carpenters were building a new ship for his return voyage. The final results of his negotiations were incorporated into the Treaty of Shimoda of February, 1855. This treaty opened Nagasaki to Russian trade. In other respects, it went beyond either of the two other foreign treaties. In the first place, it contained territorial clauses which conceded all of the Kurile Islands south of Urup to Japan and that island and those north of it to Russia. Sakhalien was to remain unpartitioned as heretofore. Secondly, Russian subjects were not to be under the jurisdiction of Japanese law but were to be tried in Russian consular courts. In view of the most-favored-nation clause in the other treaties, this provision for extraterritorial rights in the Russian treaty meant that extraterritoriality would soon become a universal practice for all of the Western countries.

The Netherlands and France were the next powers to obtain treaties with Japan and their demands included a request to start regular commercial activities. As pressure increased from the outside for the complete raising of the curtain of seclusion, a counter movement developed within Japan. The leaders of this movement capitalized on the potential strength and prestige of the Imperial Court in Kyōto and demanded that the barbarians be expelled from the sacred soil of Japan.

Internal Political Strife

In order to understand the intricate, and in many respects, unpredictable and apparently irrational reactions of the political leaders of Japan to the arrival of the foreigners, it is essential to realize that those statesmen were motivated by a strong sense of personal loyalty. This loyalty transcends all other beliefs of the leaders and makes Japan's history that much more fascinating yet difficult to understand. Some of the leaders, especially the responsible officials in the Tokugawa government, were primarily loyal to the Shogun. Others, particularly the feudal barons whose families had been traditional enemies of the Tokugawa dictators, were becoming conscious that their primary loyalty should be toward the Emperor. Still others paid their allegiance to one of the leaders of the numerous factions within the Shogun's government. In the decade and a half between the arrival of the foreigners in 1853, and the restoration of the Emperor to a position of supremacy in the state in 1868, there were two basic conflicts which interacted on each other. The first conflict was between the royalists and the foreigners; the second conflict was between the royalists and the Tokugawa supporters.

In the months immediately following the signing of the treaties with the foreigners, however, these two conflicts are difficult to isolate because of the struggle between two strong factions over the selection of the successor to the Shogun. As already noted, the twelfth Tokugawa Shogun had died in July, 1853, only a few days after Perry had sailed for the China coast with a promise to return. As the actual operation of the government was largely in the hands of the Council of Elders, the *Rōjū,* it made little practical difference in terms of basic policy as to who was Shogun. The office only became important when there was no direct heir to the generalissimo. Such an eventuality always presented a fertile ground for the growth of intrigues and feuds resulting from strong loyalties to the various contenders to the position of heir-apparent.

In 1853, when the thirteenth Shogun took office, he had no son nor was it considered likely that he would ever have one. Consequently, many of the feudal barons and chief Councilors of Elders aligned themselves on the side of one of two possible candidates. One contender was Tokugawa Iemochi, the first cousin of the incumbent and the closest in line of succession. The other was Tokugawa Keiki, the seventh son of the Lord of Mito, Tokugawa Nariaki. Since a final decision was not made on this question until 1858, many of the political events of this period can be understood only if it is remembered that this struggle continued in the background. Naturally, this conflict only complicated the problem of dealing with the foreigners.

More specifically, the history of the next few years is centered around the struggle for control of the Council of Elders and then shifts to the larger struggle between the Imperial Court, backed largely by the barons from the west, and the old dictatorship. The struggle to dominate the Council was between Ii Naosuke, Lord of Hikone, and Tokugawa Nariaki, Lord of Mito. Ii had recommended that a conciliatory attitude be taken toward America's request. He was unquestionably loyal to the Tokugawa government and so was selected by it to protect the Emperor from foreign contamination. On the other hand, Tokugawa Nariaki, Lord of Mito, was a royalist and antiforeign. He was already under suspicion by the authorities because of the independent military preparations he had made. He had a hard fight on his hands before he would be able to get his son chosen as successor to the Shogun.

Although neither Ii Naosuke nor Tokugawa Nariaki was a regular member of the Council of Elders, their views carried more weight than most of the Councilors. Even the President of the Council, Abe Masahiro, discovered that his tenure of office depended on the acquiescence of Nariaki. When Abe became fully aware of the crisis which faced the country, he prepared a reform program. It emphasized the need for the selection of able men to office, the reduction of expenditures, increased military preparations, and the formation of a single office for defense. He went still further and consulted Nariaki, together with several other officials, on the advisability of establishing some form of consultative body which would assist the authorities. It was to be composed of the leading Confucian scholars and students of Dutch learning, soldiers and artillerymen well versed in foreign affairs, and outstanding clan officials. He proposed that the group meet twelve times a month with officials from the office of defense to discuss problems of national preparedness.

Before this plan could be carried any further, however, Abe was involved in political intrigues. Nariaki, who had recommended the rejection of Abe's resignation in 1854, wrote to him in 1855 demanding the resignation of four of the Councilors who were jealous of Nariaki's power. A brief account of the ramification of these resignations will illustrate how closely loyalties and political events were related. Resignations of two of the Councilors were accepted. The officials in charge of the Castle guard were changed. In the far north, Hakodate, the largest city in Hokkaidō, was to be opened to foreigners. On the pretext of protecting the country from attack, the central government confiscated the fief in which Hakodate was located and placed it under the direct control of the Tokugawa family. Actually the confiscation was motivated by political reasons. Matsumae Takahiro, Lord of the fief, was a blood relative of one of the Councilors who had been jealous of Nariaki and who had been forced out of office.[8]

Just when one clique appeared to have gained the ascendency in the Council, the opposition began to take over. Ii Naosuke was displeased with the apparent control that his rival Nariaki had over the President of the Council. In the early part of 1856, when Naosuke believed he had rallied enough support to force Abe out of office, the latter resigned and picked his own successor, Hotta Masayoshi. Although Ii's designs were temporarily stalled by these tactics, he was soon able to win Hotta over to the side of the proforeign forces. Hotta is described by Townsend Harris, the first American consul in Japan, as about thirty-five years old, short in stature, of a pleasant and intelligent countenance and with a low, rather musical voice. He was to remain President of the Council for three years and to become the willing tool of Ii, especially during the latter's Regency which began on June, 4, 1858.

During this period, Ii had two strong convictions. In the first place, he favored trade with the foreigners and hoped to strengthen the country through the profits from trade. In the second place, he believed that the constant crisis which faced Japan could be met successfully by an amalgamation of the Imperial Court and the warriors, an alliance of the crown with the Tokugawa and its most loyal feudal barons. This concept, known as *Kōbu gattai,* was given added impetus when the Emperor's approval was obtained for the earliest treaties—the Emperor even thanked the Shogun for his efforts.

With Hotta as President of the Council, and Ii as the most important figure behind the scenes, both in favor of closer relations with the foreigner, the central government encouraged the official translation of Western scientific and military books. A new school was established where lectures on foreign books were given to the most talented clan warriors and where English, French, and German were taught. But the proforeign officials soon discovered that the foreigners forced them to take a position far stronger than they would have taken voluntarily. This situation only stimulated criticism against the Tokugawa dictatorship. As the foreign pressure increased, resentment and hatred against the military and against Ii Naosuke increased.

Foreign Treaties Become a Political Issue

These political maneuvers and struggles between rival groups over the appointment of an heir to the Shogun, over control of the Council of

Elders, and over foreign policy created an explosive political atmosphere. Consequently, when the American Consul, Townsend Harris, arrived at Shimoda on August 21, 1856, he found himself in an almost untenable position. Hotta had been President of the Council of State only a few months and Nariaki of Mito and other members of the pro-Imperial, antiforeign group still held considerable sway over the government's policies.

On the other hand, Harris was well prepared for these inconveniences and irritations which tried his patience. A wealthy New York banker and trader and former president of New York City's Board of Education, he had acquired early in life much firsthand experience and knowledge of the Orient through shipping as supercargo on his own boats and residing for several years in many of the cities east of Suez. He was well known by most of the leading foreigners in those ports. These facts, together with his patience and unshakable resolve to succeed, made him an admirable choice for the position. Harris' main task was to complete the work begun by Perry, namely, to place Japanese-American relations on a firm and lasting basis by the conclusion of a commercial treaty.

As is eloquently related in his *Journal,*[9] Harris was exposed to both major and minor inconveniences. The first foreign consul in Japan, he had to break down many barriers. He never relinquished his efforts, however, to be recognized and treated in a manner befitting a duly accredited representative of a foreign power and to obtain a new treaty. From his *Journal* it is clear that he fully expected his task to be a difficult one. For example, when he wrote President Pierce accepting his appointment as United States Consul General to Japan, he declared that he was prepared to endure the social banishment and mental isolation which such a mission entailed.

He was not prepared, however, for the fact that he was neither expected nor wanted by the Japanese government. This situation was the result of internal conditions and of a major difference between Japan and the United States in their interpretation of the Treaty of Kanagawa of 1854. Commodore Perry and his government had assumed that Article XI of the Treaty gave the United States the right to send a representative to Japan eighteen months after the Treaty went into effect. Hence, Townsend Harris had been dispatched as Consul General. On the other hand, the Japanese government had interpreted the Treaty to mean that a consul would be sent only if both countries considered it necessary.[10] It is also clear from the discussion which Perry had during the negotiations on the treaty that each of these interpretations reflected the desire of the respective countries. The United States wanted to obtain permission as soon as possible for Americans to reside in Japan and to begin to trade. For its part, Japan hoped to keep the foreigners out as long as possible and to postpone actual trade relations.

In such an atmosphere, Harris found it difficult during the first half of his residence to make any headway on even such minor matters as a fair rate of exchange for dollars into Japanese currency and on the right of his servants to make purchases in the public market. By February, 1857, however, he had made some progress. He had obtained permission to move about unmolested. The special guards posted around the old temple which served as a consulate were finally removed.

He then began negotiations for a new convention to expand the concessions obtained by Perry. Harris proposed four points: (1) Nagasaki should be included as a port of call for American ships; (2) American residents in Japan should be subject to American consular jurisdiction (extraterritoriality); (3) Americans should have the right to reside, lease property and construct buildings; and (4) an equitable discount rate should be set for changing money. Although the first three points asked for no more than had already been granted to the Russians and the Dutch, the Japanese were adamant about granting Americans the right to reside permanently or to lease property. They also refused to budge on the currency issue, insisting that a 25 per cent discount, instead of 6 per cent asked by Harris, was necessary to cover coinage expenses. By persistence and patience, and with the passage of sufficient time to strengthen the position of the proforeign element headed by Hotta and Ii, Harris finally obtained a convention which contained all the points which he had demanded. It was signed in June, 1857.

He had been less successful, however, on another basic issue. He insisted from the start that he be permitted, as was the accepted international custom, to present in person his credentials and a letter from the President of the United States to the Shogun, the *de facto* head of the Japanese state. As all Harris' requests set a precedent, he discovered that the Shogun's government was most deliberate in reaching decisions on such a delicate problem. Ten months after he had first raised the issue, he had still received no definitive answer. In the meantime, the officials in charge of foreign affairs had told the feudal barons in attendance on the Generalissimo that Harris' demands were in accord with usual foreign procedure. They also reminded the Councilors and others that China was paying dearly for refusal to comply with the Treaty of Nanking. In fact, a British naval squadron had bombarded Canton in October, 1856, because of Chinese recalcitrance. It was intimated that refusal to grant Harris' request might result in a similar fate for Japan. Despite these warnings, "all of the barons attending the Shogun, with one accord, said that Harris should not be permitted to enter the capital."

Nevertheless, the government, through the Council of Elders, notified Harris in September, 1857, that he was to proceed to Edo where he would be officially received at court. His vivid description of the treatment he received during his week's trip along the main roadway is clear proof of the changed, official attitude toward him. He was given treatment accorded only the leading princes. The road was swept clean, bridges were repaired, traffic was halted, and arrangements were made to lodge him at the best inns. The final act in opening Japan's closed door occurred on December 7, 1857, when Harris stepped into the audience room of the Edo castle and personally presented his letter of credence to the Shogun. The precedent having been established, he stated that he intended to work "to unite the two countries more closely in the ties of everlasting friendship." To this the Shogun Iesada is reported to have replied:

> Pleased with the letter sent with the Ambassador from a far distant country and likewise pleased with his discourse. Intercourse shall be continuous forever.[11]

The full impact of the shattering of the curtain of isolation was yet to come. From the point of view of the Tokugawa dictatorship, the policy of vacillation and procrastination had been most successful. While it had been necessary to sign treaties with the Western powers, such action had not seriously threatened the power or prestige of the government. Furthermore, by 1857, when Townsend Harris had his audience with the Shogun, there seemed no immediate danger of an attack from abroad. In view of the real weakness, militarily, economically, and politically, of the central regime, it was something of a victory to have been able to prevent a showdown with the foreigners. So long as the foreigners could be kept isolated and out of sight of the people, there was a possibility that the autocratic authority of the Shogun would not be challenged. But the arrival of Commodore Perry with President Fillmore's letter had forced the feudal barons to take sides on the vital issue of isolation or opening the country. It also aggravated the smoldering rivalry between the Imperial Court in Kyōto and the Shogunate in Edo. Those who opposed the foreigners were also those who questioned the authenticity of the Shogun's right to rule. As time passed, the increased demands of the foreigners created even greater antiforeign feeling. The Shogun's officials were accused of disloyalty to the Emperor, their orders and decrees were disregarded, and the royalists became strong enough to force the capitulation of the dictatorship.

Notes

1. For some of the books based on the war see Oka Yoshitake, *Kindai Nihon no Keisei* (Tokyo: Kōbun-dō, 1952), p. 30 *et seq.* As Sir George Sansom notes, some of

the accounts were fantastically exaggerated. One rumor which persisted stated the English flotilla was composed of 25,860 vessels and a million men. See G. Sansom, *The Western World and Japan* (New York: Alfred A. Knopf, Inc., 1950), p. 250.

2. Ishin Shiryō Hensan Kakari (ed.), *Ishin Shi* (6 vols.; Tokyo: Meijishoin, 1939-41), II, p. 44 ff.

3. See Francis L. Hawks (ed.), *Narrative of the Expedition of an American Squadron . . . Under Commodore M. C. Perry* (Washington: Nicholson, 1856), I, pp. 244 and 261, for the texts of these communications.

4. *Ishin Shi,* II, p. 69.

5. See Tsuji Zennosuke, *Kaigai Kōtsu Shiwa* (Tokyo: Naigai Shoseki Kabushiki Kaisha), p. 790 ff.

6. "Diary," *Transactions of Asiatic Society of Japan,* 2d series, VII (1930), p. 101.

7. For the text of the Treaty of Kanagawa see Hawks, *Narrative,* II, final pages. It should be noted that this first treaty with a Western power did not contain a provision for extraterritoriality. On the insistence of Dr. Williams, this sign of Occidental superiority was omitted. As Article IX provided most-favored-nation treatment, however, the United States automatically received extraterritorial privileges after the other powers had received them in their treaties.

8. *Ishin Shi,* II, p. 111.

9. See Mario Emilio Cosenza, *The Complete Journal of Townsend Harris* (New York: Doubleday & Co., Inc., 1930). Although Harris did not leave Japan until May 8, 1862, the *Journal* stops on February 27, 1858, and no manuscript is extant for the later years.

10. To a certain extent both interpretations were possible. The English text read: "There shall be appointed by the government of the United States, consuls or from the date of the signing of this treaty, provided that *either of the two govern-* agents to reside in Shimoda at any time after the expiration of eighteen months *ments deem such arrangement necessary.*" In the Japanese text, the subject of the clause, 無據儀有之候模樣ニヨリ "If conditions make it necessary" is not given and could be assumed to be either Japan, or the United States or both.

11. Cosenza, *Harris Journal,* p. 475.

4

THE DICTATORSHIP COLLAPSES 1857-1868

Embarrassment from the Foreigners

It was almost exactly a decade between December, 1857, when Harris had his audience with the Shogun, and November, 1867, when the last Tokugawa Generalissimo announced that he would resign. During that short period, each demand of the foreigners precipitated intrigues to control the Shogun's Council of Elders, rivalry between the proforeign and antiforeign factions, awakening of the Imperial Court and the powerful western clans to rally their forces to overthrow the Tokugawa usurpers, and the deterioration of the economic and financial position of the Shogunate. The final result was a complete collapse of the old dictatorship; the restoration to power of the Emperor Meiji on January 3, 1868; and the emergence of a new group of leaders. No state can undergo such a transformation overnight, especially if the change is relatively peaceful. Vestiges of the old regime will still remain despite the formation of new institutions. The Meiji Restoration of 1868 can be understood, therefore, only if it is considered as a continuing process.

The reactionary and tradition-bound bureaucrats in the Edo government had done their best to postpone the interview of American Consul Townsend Harris with the Shogun Iesada lest the foreigner make even more embarrassing demands of them. These fears were well grounded, for Harris lost no time after his audience in 1857 in making the abolition of seclusion a reality. He pressed for the commercial treaty requested in the letter from the President of the United States. He asked for (1) permission for the American Minister to reside at Edo, the seat of government; (2) freedom of trade for Americans without interference from the Japanese government officials; and (3) the opening of additional harbors to foreigners.

Both Foreign Minister Hotta and the Governor of Shimoda informed Harris that as individuals they believed his requests to be reasonable and favored their acceptance. Since they were thoroughly cognizant of the influence exerted by antiforeign barons such as Tokugawa Nariaki of Mito and by the Emperor and his advisers, however, they were not certain that their views would prevail. They warned Harris that the Shogun and many of his Councilors were still opposed to foreign intercourse. On the other hand, fear of foreign retaliation for inaction caused Foreign Minister Hotta to set about the impossible task of trying to save the dictatorship from destruction from without by obtaining approval for a commercial treaty with the United States.

He attempted to explain to the barons at the Shogun's court the reasons for the inevitability of opening the country. His arguments failed to convince the opposition. Nariaki of Mito arrogantly declared that Harris' request should be refused and yet urged, quite illogically, that his fief be allowed to carry on trade. Even the most forward-looking intellectuals attached to the western clans also argued against a commercial treaty.

Having failed in his tactics in Edo and without informing Harris, Hotta then proceeded to Kyōto to consult the Emperor and his courtiers and to obtain Imperial sanction for the proposed treaty. If Imperial approval could be secured, all other objections could be ignored. Opposition in Kyōto was even stronger than in the east. The Emperor retorted:

> The Imperial mind is deeply concerned. Things having come to the present pass, public sentiment being what it is, and in view of the importance of matters of state, We desire that the opinions of the three families [Owari, Kii, and Mito] and of the *daimyō* be sought.[1]

In other words, the Emperor had sided with Nariaki of Mito and the other antiforeign elements. The Imperial Court was fearful of the effect of having foreigners near Kyōto and the sacred shrine of Ise.

Furthermore, a smoldering hatred was beginning to take concrete form against the usurper in the east, the Tokugawa dictator. The courtiers who advised the Emperor intended to make the best possible use of any circumstances that would unbalance the opposition. They realized that the treaty issue could be a real cause of embarrassment to the government and hence opposed accepting the American commercial treaty. When Hotta returned to Edo in June, 1858, he was defeated. Several months earlier he had written Harris that the treaty would be signed and that the approval of the Imperial Court could be obtained. Now he realized this promise could not be fulfilled.

At this stage, Ii Naosuke saw an opportunity to enhance his own power and prestige. He became the central figure and took matters in his own hands. He was appointed President of the Councilors. He then signed the United State's Treaty of Commerce on July 29, 1858, and planned to secure Imperial approval later. The new treaty opened four new ports to Americans, including Kanagawa south of Edo and Hyōgo on Ōsaka Bay. Both Edo and Ōsaka were open to foreign residents. Import and export duties were established. Extraterritoriality was permitted and freedom of worship was assured. Harris had achieved his objective. Ii Naosuke was more powerful than the antiforeign forces. In particular, Ii had gained the upper hand over his rival, Tokugawa Nariaki of Mito.

The political position of Ii Naosuke was also strengthened by his manipulations which resulted in his favorite candidate being selected as heir to the Shogun. No successor had been chosen for the incumbent and Ii Naosuke and Tokugawa Nariaki had supported rival candidates. Since Ii was the most powerful Councilor in 1858, it was comparatively simple to have a proclamation issued naming the Shogun's first cousin as the new heir rather than Keiki, the son of Nariaki. Consequently Nariaki of Mito had received another severe defeat.

Since the succession issue had been settled against his wishes, Nariaki concentrated on attacking Ii's foreign policy. Both the Imperial Court and Nariaki made no secret of their anger at Ii for having signed a treaty without Imperial consent. They even intimated that the Generalissimo's leading minister was disloyal to the throne. Ii struck back ruthlessly and quickly. Nariaki and two other leading barons were ordered placed under "home arrest." Members of those clans unfriendly toward the Tokugawa family were forbidden to enter Kyōto or to confer with the Imperial Court.

Despite this ban, the Emperor became even more active in politics than previously. He ordered Ii to appear in Kyōto and explain his action. The latter refused to budge and sent one of the new Councilors, Manabe Akikatsu, in his place. The latter argued that the continual appearance of American, Russian, British, and French warships meant that these countries would all ask for treaties. In fact, he pointed out that envoys had been sent to negotiate with Harris, the American representative, because the danger of war with the Western powers was so great that there was no other alternative possible. The Imperial Court finally gave its consent reluctantly to the new treaty.

But the basic split over foreign policy continued. In fact, the leaders of the large clans in western Japan began a new movement "to exalt the throne and to expel the barbarians" (*Sonnō Jōi*). Their first move was to persuade the Emperor to issue a decree ordering the Shogunate to perfect its military preparedness and to expel the barbarians from Japan's sacred soil. Despite this basic disagreement between the Emperor and the Shogun on foreign policy, an open break had not yet occurred. There was some hope that the alliance of the courtiers and warriors might still prevent civil war. The Lord of Satsuma, after elaborate negotiations, despite his leanings to support the Emperor, had successfully concluded arrangements for his daughter to marry the Shogun. Furthermore, Ii Naosuke had arranged for the marriage of an Imperial princess to the Shogun. Strong leaders from both the royalists and proforeign groups were still working for an alliance of the Imperial Court and the Shogunate.

Assassinations of Foreigners and of Ii Naosuke

On the other hand, there was clear evidence that some of the clans were willing to support the Emperor openly. The representative in Kyōto of the powerful Chōshū clan informed one of the chief courtiers that his clan would send troops to defend the Imperial palace if hostilities developed as a result of the arbitrary action of Councilor Ii. Five days after Nariaki of Mito was arrested, one of the Imperial courtiers, Sanjō Sanenari, received a memorandum which indirectly extolled the position taken by the anti-Shogun leaders. It argued that it was a real sign of loyalty to protect the Emperor as a figure distinct from the Shogun. It suggested that if the Chōshū troops were in Ōsaka and an incident against the foreigners developed, these troops would then be available to protect the throne.[2] In other words, if an incident could be manufactured, the excuse would be at hand for a coup d'état in which the Chōshū troops would automatically become an Imperial guard ready to fight the Tokugawa forces. Little wonder, therefore, that after the arrival of Manabe (the Shogun's envoy) at the Imperial capital, forty persons were expelled from office because of their antigovernment sentiments. Further turmoil and possible open civil war was temporarily overshadowed by a smallpox epidemic in Ōsaka and Kyōto.

As time passed, the pressure against the old government gained momentum and the western clan leaders continued their intrigues and consultations with the Imperial courtiers. The Tokugawa authorities were unable to enforce their decrees prohibiting such meetings. In fact, the Emperor was persuaded to reissue the edict which required the Shogun to carry out his duty as military guardian and protector of the country to expel the barbarians from Japan's soil and to force out of office those who favored intercourse with foreigners.

The arrival of the earliest foreign residents and consuls from the various European countries, in accordance with the foreign treaties, only aggravated the situation. Many more persons, from their contacts with the foreigners, realized that there was a real possibility that the latter had come to stay. In fact, the presence of the official missions of several governments in the city of Edo and Harris' insistence that he had both a right to remain and to expect protection, despite attacks on Europeans, kept the issue at fever pitch. Murders and attacks followed one another. A Russian officer and two sailors were some of the first to be killed. Other casualties included a Chinese servant in the French consulate, a Japanese linguist in the British legation, two Hollanders, and Mr. Heusken, secretary to Mr. Harris.

By far the most significant assassination resulting from the antiforeign movement was that of Ii Naosuke. On the morning of March 24, 1860, while going to the castle in the middle of a snowstorm to consult with the Shogun, he was mortally wounded by a band of Mito warriors. Obviously they had considered him responsible for the temporary political demise of their feudal lord, Nariaki, and were violently opposed to Ii's foreign policy. His death was a serious blow to the government. In fact, it was kept a secret for nearly a month. He was not officially removed from office until April 20 and his death was not announced until the next day. Furthermore, so long as the Lord of Mito, Nariaki, remained alive, the Shogun did not feel strong enough to arrest the culprits or take any action against them. When Nariaki died in September, 1860, the Mito clan was ordered to arrest those who had murdered Ii, the Shogun's chief Minister of State. A dictatorship which dared not take action for six months against political murders obviously had become a dictatorship in name only.

Direct action on the part of the various clansmen opposed to the foreigners continued. Mito and Chōshū men attacked the British legation on separate occasions. They declared that they were carrying out "a great deed to the honor of the sovereign." They had taken upon themselves the task of the expulsion of the foreigners since they considered it intolerable to stand by and see the sacred empire violated by the presence of the barbarians.

Sponsorship of Western Techniques

While the hot-headed clansmen who opposed the government's foreign policy were taking matters into their own hands and were doing their best to expel forcefully the hated barbarians, the more enlightened leaders sponsored the use of European technical knowledge. Even before Perry had left Japan after his first visit in 1853, orders had gone out from the central government to perfect the coastal defenses. While reliance was largely placed on the individual fiefs the Tokugawa government slowly began to support policies and practices which strengthened its own military power.

The western clans were permitted to build or purchase larger ships and the Dutch were asked to import a warship for the government. In the summer of 1855, the Dutch presented the Shogunate with its first steamship, the "Kankō Maru" (formerly the "Sunbeam"). The Dutch engineers, firemen, and seamen who brought the ship to Japan, totaling twenty-two persons, were used as instructors for the twenty ambitious warriors who were the first persons assigned to the study of naval science. Others followed, mostly from the strong western clans.[3] Shortly thereafter, the first iron foundry was built under the government's auspices and the direction of a Hollander, M. H. Hardes. Other Dutch engineers remained in Japan after 1861 to provide technical guidance.

Another Hollander who was influential in spreading technical information was Pompe van Meerdervoort. Appointed to the Dutch navy to teach natural and military sciences, he conducted classes at Nagasaki in 1857 in anatomy, physiology, physics, chemistry, and geology. Lack of laboratory equipment and other necessary supplies and facilities hampered his efforts. For example, custom and law both forbade the use of cadavers in the study of anatomy, and van Meerdervoort had to wait a year for a papier mâché model of the human body to be sent from Paris before he could demonstrate his lectures. Because of the language barrier, his first lectures were little understood by his fourteen pupils, some of whom were from the Shogun's court, others from the feudal domains in Kyūshū. Although his physics classes were attended by ardent students, he regretted the fact that "their want of elementary instruction in arithmetic, algebra and mathematics" made it impossible for them to understand his explanations.[4] His most successful course appears to have been in bandaging where the pupils jumped with alacrity at the chance to strap up their classmates. Inadequate though this school may have been, it was a beginning in the instruction of Western science. Other schools, directly under the support of the Tokugawa government, were started in Edo where the young warriors concentrated on foreign languages.

One of the most important and dramatic events which impressed the Tokugawa authorities with the backwardness of Japan was the first official mission of the Shogunate to go to America. This mission was dispatched in 1860 to the United States to exchange ratification of the Treaty of Commerce. Although it was sent on an American ship, it was escorted across the Pacific by the Japanese steamship "Kanin Maru," which the Dutch had recently presented. This ship was the first steamship manned by a Japanese crew to make the trans-Pacific passage.

When the embassy arrived in San Francisco, its members were naturally surprised at many of America's customs. The square lanterns on the carriages, the clocks in evidence in hotel rooms and lobbys, the long mirrors, fireplaces, and frame pictures on the walls all struck them as strange appurtenances of Western culture. Ballroom dancing was the most difficult custom for them to understand. For example, at a reception on May 18, 1860, given by Secretary of State Cass, members of the embassy found that they were expected to shake hands with everybody around them.

After dinner, when ushered into the ballroom, they were even more astonished. Vice Ambassador Muragaki gave his impressions of the formal dance as follows:

> Immediately after we were seated, the music commenced and an officer in uniform with one arm around a lady's waist and the other hand holding one of hers, started moving round the room on his toes, many others following his example. . . . As for us, we had never seen or imagined anything like it before. It was, of course, with no small wonder that we witnessed this extraordinary sight of men and bareshouldered women hopping round the floor, arm in arm, and our wonder at the strange performance became so great that we began to doubt whether we were not on another planet.[5]

At a later party, they learned to enjoy themselves. They were amazed to learn, however, that the women danced for pleasure and were not paid entertainers but respectable members of society.

Their visit captivated the enthusiasm of the American people and left a lasting impression on them. In New York, the populace turned out in throngs to greet their triumphal procession up Broadway. Walt Whitman wrote of them:

> Over the Western sea hither from Niphon come,
> Courteous, the swart-cheek'd two-sworded envoys,
> Leaning back in their open barouches, bare-headed, impassive,
> Ride to-day through Manhattan.[6]

This adulation abruptly ended, however, when New Yorkers were distracted by the arrival from England of the gigantic steamship, "The Great Eastern" on its maiden voyage. Its appearance in New York was dramatic evidence to the Japanese of the material progress of America and Europe. They had already been intrigued with the railroads, the telegraph, the modern newspapers, and other examples of industrialization. They returned to convince many of the government officials at home that Japan was more backward militarily and economically than even the most sophisticated persons realized. They substantiated the belief of Hotta, Ii, and others that the presence in Japan of the foreigners must not only be tolerated and endured, but expected.

Outbreak of Civil War

As more foreigners appeared, the tension between the Imperial Court in Kyōto and the Shogunate increased; the antiforeign movement became intensified and central control broke down. For example, in 1862, the Emperor had summarily ordered the Shogun to appear before him in Kyōto. When the Shogun arrived, he was told that June 24, 1863, had been set as the date for the expulsion of the foreigners and that the Shogun should enforce such a policy. An Imperial decree was issued to that effect.

The Shogun's Minister was forced to report to the representatives of the foreign powers that the ports were to be closed and that the foreigners were to be driven out because the people did not desire intercourse with foreign countries.

The diplomatic and foreign community was in no mood to be intimidated. As the number of attacks on the foreigners increased, they had taken a stronger stand against the Shogun and insisted that he control the lawless elements in the country. One of the most notorious cases, which led directly to foreign military retaliation, was the murder of C. L. Richardson in September, 1862. A retinue of men from Satsuma, a center of strong royalist and antiforeign feeling, was returning from Edo after having delivered the Imperial order which had summoned the Shogun to Kyōto to explain why the foreigners had not been expelled. Near the present city of Yokohama, they met a riding party of three British subjects who refused to give the warriors the right of way. The fact that the British did not dismount was taken as an insult by the warriors and Richardson was cut down. When the British government later demanded an indemnity of $500,000 from the Tokugawa government and $125,000 from the Satsuma fief, antiforeign resistance increased.

With their patience tried by this incident as well as by attacks on the consulate, the British took retaliatory measures. In August, 1863, a British naval expedition bombarded the capital of Satsuma. The shore guns, arsenal, and steamers in the harbor of Kagoshima, which had all been locally produced, were quickly destroyed. The effect was immediate. The Satsuma clan capitulated and its warriors became entranced with the effective and technically advanced armament of the British. They swarmed over the ships in their eagerness to learn as much as possible. It was the beginning of a close friendship between many of the future leaders of the Japanese navy and British naval officers. The matter was finally closed when the Shogunate paid the indemnity and asked the British to assist it in shipbuilding.

Despite the Imperial decree directed at the foreigners, the Shogun knew it would be impossible to drive them out. When he returned from Kyōto to the safety of his own castle in Edo in the spring of 1863, he announced his inability to carry out the Emperor's command. At the same time, the position of the foreigners became even more dangerous. The Shogun was no longer able to control the activities of the most powerful barons or their retainers, such as those from Satsuma, who had killed Richardson. The old system of alternate attendance, which required that all the barons spend half of their time in Edo and, hence remain away from their fiefs, was drastically relaxed. Hostages were no longer held and attendance at the Shogun's court was required only every few years. There was an immediate exodus from Edo and the proroyalist barons flocked to Kyōto to form alliances with the Emperor.

In the fief of Chōshū, the second strongest of the proroyalist, antiforeign western clans, the persons advocating direct action also were in power. These leaders decided that they would take upon themselves the responsibility for the enforcement of the decree to expel the foreigners. As the American ship "Pembroke" neared the Shimonoseki Straits on June 24, 1863, proclaimed as the expiration date for the expulsion of the foreigners, she was fired on from the shore batteries in Chōshū province. During July, French and Dutch ships were also fired upon. Again the foreigners took matters into their own hands. American and French warships silenced the gun emplacements, but the Chōshū clansmen remained arrogant and insolent.

The advice of a young clansman named Itō Hirobumi, who had just returned from a clandestine trip to Europe, was unheeded. He pleaded that resistance was useless under the present parlous state of Japan's defenses. Twenty-five years later, however, he had completed drafting Japan's new Constitution and was so powerful that no one dared challenge his opinion (see Chapter 8). An envoy sent by the Shogun to remonstrate with the clansmen was assassinated. Their defiance was finally challenged in September, 1864, by a combined fleet of British, Dutch, French, and American warships. This allied force removed the shore batteries and exacted a promise from its local commander that the Shimonoseki Straits would be opened and that an indemnity would be paid.

In the meantime, the Imperial Court came to disagree with the wisdom of the policy of expelling the foreigners forcibly. Consequently, it ordered out of Kyōto those courtiers and the Chōshū warriors who had recommended this policy. The Shogun was again called to the capital; this time he was treated with even less respect and was shorn of power. He lost his right to invest the new feudal barons with their fiefs. He was forced to accept as his advisers those feudal barons who had the confidence of the Emperor, including the barons of Satsuma and Tosa.

This action of the Emperor against the Chōshū clansmen only exasperated them and forced them to take matters into their own hands. Convinced that the time had arrived for a showdown with the Tokugawa dictatorship, they returned to their province in the west and revolted against the Shogun. Despite an earlier decision to agree to a truce, the Shogun resolved in 1865 to crush the rebellious Chōshū clan. No decision could have been more disastrous, however, for the tottering dictatorship. The Chōshū army was an entirely new type of army. It was not composed exclusively of the hereditary warrior class but had been recruited from all classes of society. It had been trained by a dynamic leader, Takasugi Shinsaku (1839-67); it was well disciplined, and was supplied with the newest type rifles purchased from abroad. It was more than a match for the soft, indolent, ill-equipped, and undrilled warriors who composed the government's forces. After a year's delay, the Shogun's forces entered the field only to be defeated.

In the meantime, the situation in other areas continued to deteriorate for the Shogun. The leaders of the Satsuma clan, many of whom were close to the Emperor and his advisers in Kyōto, had persuaded Shimazu Hisamitsu (1817-87), the *de facto* head of the clan, to abandon the old policy of an alliance between the Imperial Court and the Shogun's court. Instead, they proposed that Satsuma form an alliance with Chōshū and other like-minded clans to work for the restoration of power of the Emperor and the overthrow of the Tokugawa dictatorship. The excellent showing of the Chōshū troops in their revolt made this argument seem more than logical. Furthermore, the British Minister, Sir Harry Parkes, let both Chōshū and Satsuma know that his government favored an Imperial restoration and gave them moral support in their efforts.

By the end of the summer of 1866, therefore, there was little left of the Tokugawa dictatorship. The Emperor had selected the advisers for the Shogun and deprived him of the right to allocate new domains. The powerful clans of Satsuma and Chōshū had openly defied the Shogun's policies. Civil war had broken out and the rebellious Chōshū forces were openly supporting the Emperor against the Shogun. There was increasing likelihood that the newly aroused loyalty for the Emperor would become the rallying force for a combined attack against the tottering dictatorship.

Economic and Financial Impotence of the Shogun

In the face of these overwhelming odds, the Shogunate had made a last-minute effort to salvage as much of its power as possible. It attempted to follow the difficult path of reliance on foreign help, both technical and financial, and of political independence from the country giving that assistance. Politically, France had shown the most interest in supporting the Shogun. Napoleon III had sent Leon Roches as his Minister to Japan in 1864 and had instructed him to give the Japanese as much assistance as possible. Ironworks, two docks, and three shipyards were planned to be built at Yokosuka over a period of four years with French assistance at a cost of $2,400,000. With the help of a $500,000 loan from France, work was begun in 1865. Japanese agents were sent to France to place the necessary orders for the machinery and to hire foreign experts. By 1866, forty-six such persons had begun to work on the project.

The French, again through their Minister Roches, offered military aid when the Shogun was engaged in the civil war in Chōshū. A treaty had been negotiated earlier with Napoleon III which included provision for military assistance. Since it was never ratified, the assistance was largely confined to French instructors in the Shogun's military school. When the government continued to be embarrassed by continued civil war in Chōshū, the brother of the Shogun was appointed head of the delegation to the Paris Exposition. Actually, he was instructed to obtain, if possible, a loan of $6,000,000, to defray the costs of the campaign in the west.

Although he failed in his mission, the French continued to be friendly to the Tokugawa cause. Leon Roches suggested certain administrative reforms. He proposed that the sincerity and loyalty of the western clans be challenged by throwing open three western ports to foreigners; namely, Hyōgo near Ōsaka, Shimonoseki in Chōshū, and Kagoshima in Satsuma. His administrative reforms included a new system of taxation by which the merchants would be subject to a regular levy and all tax-free lands would be deprived of their exemptions. The restoration of power to the Emperor came too rapidly, however, to permit the implementation of any of these suggestions.

Foreign Trade

The Tokugawa government had also hoped to strengthen its financial position through profits from foreign trade. Heretofore, no new system of taxation had been adopted, no annual budget was prepared; revenues were derived largely from the income of government-owned land and "forced loans" imposed on the merchants. These sources were far from sufficient to meet the annual deficit of approximately 700,000 gold pieces (*ryō*). The opening of the ports and necessary preparations for the arrival of the foreigners had added noticeably to the annual expenses. For example, it was estimated that 300,000 *ryō* were needed for these purposes in Hokkaidō alone.

Consequently, it is not surprising that some government officers advocated official sponsorship of trade. Thus in April, 1859, the government-leased ship, the "Kamida Maru," sailed for Siberia with a Russian interpreter aboard. The silk, rice, soybeans, and sweet potatoes which it carried were not popular with the Siberian natives and the venture was a miserable failure.

In view of the reports which reached Edo through the foreign merchants in Yokohama and elsewhere of the fabulous profits to be obtained from trade with China, a second officially sponsored ship headed for Shanghai. Named the "Senzai Maru," it sailed with Dutch traders and a Japanese crew of fifty-one aboard. The cargo of coal, dried seafoods, lacquer, camphor, and textiles was treated as Dutch merchandise but the voyage likewise made no profit. A final attempt to trade in Shanghai, this time with the use of an American ship, resulted in the modest profit of 1,300 *ryō*. Obviously, therefore, the financial plight of the Tokugawa government was not to be alleviated through officially sponsored trade.

Turning to the general trade tendencies from 1859-67, available statistics, even though they contain some contradictions, reflect certain unhealthy trends. (See Table I.) In the first place, the total volume of trade indicated

TABLE I

JAPANESE FOREIGN TRADE 1859-67[7]

		Yokohama	Nagasaki	Hakodate	Total
1859	Export	$ 400,000	$ 800,000		$ 1,200,000
	Import	150,000	600,000		750,000
1860	Export	3,904,000	600,000		4,504,000
	Import	945,700	700,000		1,645,700
1861	Export	2,682,900	789,600		3,472,500
	Import	1,478,000	604,000		2,082,000
1862	Export	6,305,126	3,000,000	$173,399	9,478,525
	Import	2,576,000	2,500,000	11,537	5,087,537
1863	Export	5,134,000	925,000		6,059,000
	Import	1,595,000	602,000		2,197,000
1864	Export	8,997,484	1,159,900	414,847	10,572,231
	Import	5,443,594	1,316,897	90,798	6,851,289
1865	Export	17,467,728	560,787	461,815	18,490,330
	Import	12,913,024	1,147,771	133,976	14,194,771
1866	Export	14,100,000	1,954,000		16,054,000
	Import	11,430,000	1,080,000		12,510,000
1867	Export	8,708,907	1,770,907	638,861	11,118,675
	Import	13,008,785	5,248,987	218,558	18,476,330

the political instability of the period. For example, there was in general a slow but steady rise in both the import and export trade from 1859 to 1862. The drop in both export and import trade in 1863 revealed the strong antiforeign movement and the effect of direct attacks by ardent nationalists on various official and nonofficial members of the foreign community. It is also likely that the chastisement that summer by the European powers of the recalcitrant fiefs of Satsuma and Chōshū had a salutary effect on the antiforeign outrages and may be partly responsible for the rapid increase in trade during the next year. Conversely, the equally rapid decrease in total trade, particularly in exports after 1865, and the shift from a favorable to an unfavorable balance of trade, were a natural consequence of the civil war in the western part of Japan and of the complete breakdown of the authority of the Shogun. (See Table II.)

Furthermore, an analysis of the composition of this trade indicates the primitive state of Japan's economy. For example, exports were mainly in the form of agricultural products. Raw silk was the dominant item, accounting for five-eighths of the exports from Yokohama in 1860 and over one-half of the total seven years later. The large export of silkworm eggs (one-fourth of the total exports from Yokohama in 1867) was the result of the precarious situation of Europe's silk industry. These shipments saved the European industry from extinction because of a disease in the Italian and French silkworms and also prevented Japan's unfavorable trade balance from becoming much worse for that particular year. At the same time, tea and camphor became important export items, the former accounting for one-fifth of the total.

TABLE II

Foreign Trade in Japan, 1859-67
(In Million Dollars)

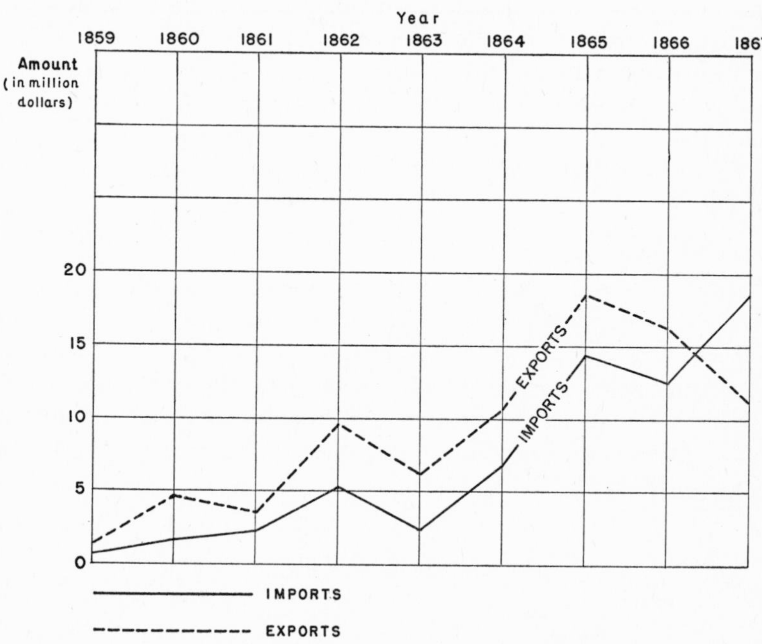

In the early years, the heavy import demands for consumers' goods, such as cotton cloth, woolen cloth, and other fabrics, were further evidence of the low state of industrialization throughout the country. For example, in 1860 cotton cloth accounted for one-half, and wool and other fabrics for one-third, of all imports into Yokohama. By 1867, infant industries had begun to fill some of the demands of the domestic market so that imports of these products had dropped to one-fourth of all imports. They were replaced by new items which gave some indication of trends to come. For example, the purchase of foreign style ships accounted for 20 per cent of Nagasaki's imports and guns and ammunition for 10 per cent of those of Yokohama. Rice and sugar, which were to be so important later when Japan began to feel the pressure of an accelerated increase in population, equaled 20 per cent of total imports. Finally, the small expenditure for military supplies indicates the precarious position of the Shogun. Although he had been faced with a civil war in 1865, military supplies were only a minor part of the total imports.

Despite a continuous favorable trade balance from 1859 to 1866, it should be remembered, however, that the benefits from this situation did not necessarily accrue to the Japanese government. Trade was not a government enterprise nor was it carried on by Japanese subjects. Foreign entrepreneurs and shippers handled practically all the trade and profited therefrom. Since most of these traders were British, over three-fourths of the total foreign trade at this time was with England.[8] Furthermore, the treaties had originally permitted an import duty of 20 per cent. In 1865 the Western powers had forced the Shogun to reduce the duty to 5 per cent. Consequently, the revenue from 5 per cent of total imports and exports could hardly be expected to meet the new demands for national expenditures.

Inflation and Loss of Bullion

Two other factors, both direct results of the opening of the ports, had a deleterious effect on Japan's economy. In the first place, the new demand for articles to be exported created a scarcity of goods and brought about an inflation in prices. As will be seen from Table III, this tendency was particularly true in 1865 when civil war broke out. Despite the government's ban on the export of rice, the country's main staple, wholesale prices rapidly rose.

TABLE III

Rice Prices, 1859-67[9]
(Unit is in *momme* or 3.75 gramme of *seiji* silver coin for 5.11 bushels of rice)

Year	Momme
1859	203.0
1860	142.0
1862	100.0
1863	325.0
1864	530.0
1865	1300.0
1866	590.0

Prices of other commodities are reported to have shown similar increases; those of tea doubled, silk tripled, and cotton quadrupled.

Another manifestation of the discontent resulting from these conditions was a steady increase in the number of peasant uprisings in the last years of the Tokugawa period. For the decade 1853 to 1862, there was an average of 5.6 uprisings per year; from 1862 to 1863 this had risen to an average of 6.2. In the year 1866, just after the sudden jump in the price of rice, there were thirty-two rebellions by the farmers.

The financial uncertainty was further aggravated by the debasement of the currency and the outflow of gold. Debasement had long been resorted to as a method of meeting increased financial needs until the standard coins equaled less than one-eighth their original value. This depreciation was also accompanied by a decrease in the metallic value of the silver and gold coins. In fact, after an analysis by the Philadelphia mint of the silver content of the *ichibu* silver coin, which Perry had stipulated should be equal to the Mexican dollar, it was discovered that it had a metallic value of about 33 cents. On the basis of the Japanese-American Commercial Treaty of 1858, which provided that metals should be exchanged weight for weight, the Mexican dollar came to be exchanged for three *ichibu* silver coins.

As soon as this exchange rate was settled and trade actually began, there was a sudden drain on Japanese gold coins which disturbed the financial market still further. For many centuries, silver had always been given a high value in Japan and was exchanged roughly in a ratio of one to six. As fifteen to twenty pieces of silver exchanged for one piece of gold on the Asiatic continent, the traders and sailors soon began to make a smart profit at the expense of Japan's supply of gold coins.[10] During the last six months of 1859, a million gold pieces were exported from Japan and the Shogunate was forced to adjust the value of silver to that comparable to the rest of the world.

Increased Strength of Western Clans

In contrast to this disorganization and deterioration of the national economy which adversely affected the Tokugawa government, the clans which were most active in the royalist movement were profiting from their progressive industrial policies. Many of the most powerful of the rival clans of the Shogunate, Mito in the north, Satsuma, Chōshū, Tosa, and Hizen in the west, were far more advanced economically than the rest of the clans or than the fiefs of the central government. (See Chapter 2.) From the significant roles played in the turbulent 1860's by Tokugawa Nariaki of Mito, by the Satsuma leaders in Kyōto, and by the Chōshū army, it is clear that the economic power of these clans had created actual and potential military and political power. Before describing the final overthrow of the Shogun by a coalition of the four western clans, therefore, it is important to stop briefly to survey the most recent economic developments in a few of these fiefs.

For example, Satsuma in the extreme southwest, through its trade with the Ryūkyū Islands, had accumulated a limited amount of mercantilist capital which had been invested locally. After the completion of the blast and reverberatory furnaces in 1853, industrialization continued apace. Dutch patterns were followed to manufacture porcelain, glass, sulfuric acid, lacquers, farm implements, shipbuilding machinery, and oil extractors. A machine to produce static electricity had been built in Edo and both a telegraph line and gas lights were installed within the garden of the feudal mansion in the domain.

Pompe van Meerderwoort, when he visited the principality's capital city of Kagoshima in 1858, reported that he saw formidable coastal batteries with guns capable of firing cannon balls of 150-pound weight built by local foundries. But these cannon were no match for the fire power of the British flotilla which attacked the city in 1863. He also stated that 1200 men were working in the fief's industrial development institute, the Shūseikan, and that one hundred more were melting, blowing, grinding, and using the latest coloring methods in the porcelain and glass factory. The clansmen were also working on a paddle-wheel steamer which they presented later to the Shogun. By 1867, a start had been made in spinning. Clansmen had been dispatched to Europe to purchase spinning machinery. It had been installed under British supervision and was operated by 200 Japanese employees under a British manager with six British assistants.

In the northwest corner of Kyūshū, surrounding the harbor of Nagasaki and center of foreign activity for nearly 300 years, the domain of Hizen had devoted much of its time and effort to the development of military industries. The iron foundry, which the Hollander Hardes had constructed, was busy on orders for the newly constructed forts at the head of Edo Bay at Shinagawa. By 1866 it was casting nearly forty cannon a month. At the same time, young technicians and engineers from neighboring clans, were receiving technical training and instruction at the foundry.

Tosa, the third of the western clans which was to take a lead in the Restoration movement, had made marked strides industrially and militarily. While the feudal baron Yamanouchi Toyonobu (d. 1872) had originally advocated continuance of Japan's seclusion policy, he was a strong advocate of Western methods of gunnery and naval construction. He used Manjiro, a waif returned from America, to assist in the modern industrialization of the clan and sent his best scientists to other fiefs to learn the latest methods. Trade associations, sponsored by the clan, were formed which gave important experience to young men such as Iwasaki Yatarō (1834-85) who was to become one of the nation's leading financiers and industrialists. A people's army, similar to that in Chōshū, composed of unattached warriors, farmers, and village officials, was organized and continued in existence until after the overthrow of the Shogun.

These industrial developments and the new types of armies which were recruited in Chōshū and Tosa were evidence that social mobility was an accepted fact. The townsmen, warriors, and farmers who had been stratified into separate classes by the Tokugawa dictatorship, now worked together, making each feudal domain self-sufficient, strong, and independent of the Shogun's power. The townsmen were active in the management of the business affairs of the fief at home and at Ōsaka, including supervision of the various clan monopolies. The farmers were being recruited into the new local people's armies and thus attained the status of warriors. The most active and intellectually alert young warriors were busy advising their feudal lords on how to participate actively in the restoration of the Emperor to power and on ways to enhance the prestige of the fief. These men, especially those from the *Satchō Dohi* group (the abbreviated name given to Satsuma, Chōshū, Tosa, and Hizen) were obtaining invaluable practical experience which was to enable them to accomplish the herculean task of modernizing the entire country within a generation.

The growing need of the individual warrior to borrow cash to meet the bare essentials of living was an added incentive to shifts in social classes. Some of the warriors were so impoverished that they could not afford to sleep on a mattress in winter or under a mosquito net in summer. Many willingly sold their preferential social status and their annual stipend of 500 bushels of rice to merchants who were willing to lend them fifty gold pieces.

The clans also were in need of money to assure the successful conclusion of their political plans. Consequently, the local merchants and bankers found themselves inextricably entwined in the political movement to overthrow the Shogun. If they were to retrieve or salvage any of the heavy indebtedness owed them by the warriors and feudal barons, they could not afford to antagonize these warriors who planned to restore the Emperor as the actual ruler of Japan. Thus they acquiesced in the political changes that took place. In view of this debtor-creditor relationship, it was unlikely that the merchants would revolt against the class from which they hoped to continue to receive interest or capital payments on loans.[11]

As the young warriors began to sponsor industries on a national scale, the merchants and bankers began to play a key role in the nation's industrialization. For example, the Mitsui family, which had been the bankers for the Shogunate, found it financially expedient and profitable to shift their allegiance from the Shogun to the Emperor after the former capitulated. Consequently, the stage was set for a small body of political, military, and business leaders to form a closely knit, elite group of autocrats. They concentrated first on restoring the Emperor to power and then they shifted to tackle those practical problems which would make Japan strong and unified under the rule of the youthful Emperor Meiji.

The Shogun Capitulates

In the summer of 1866, the Tokugawa dictatorship, which had survived for over two and a half centuries, was harassed on all sides. International, political, economic, financial, social, and military forces were aimed against it. In a little over a year, the Shogunate as an institution was to cease to exist and a new group of young, virile, imaginative leaders was to replace it. Much of the authority and power of the Shogun had been taken over by the Emperor and the most powerful rival clans. Such residual authority as remained with the Shogun was quietly transferred in 1867-68 to the Emperor so that the dictatorship expired with only a minimum of struggle and upheaval.

The most significant events leading to its demise can be simply told. In the summer of 1866, the Shogun had gone to Ōsaka to give moral support to his army which was vainly endeavoring to suppress the revolt of the royalist forces in Chōshū. When the Shogun died in August, the campaign was temporarily halted while his successor was installed. The coalition of the western clans and the Emperor, however, had not yet advanced to the point where they were strong enough to forestall the installation of a new Shogun. They contented themselves with supporting Keiki, the son of Tokugawa Nariaki of Mito, who had been the unsuccessful candidate nearly ten years earlier, as the favorite choice. Pressure was then put on Keiki who agreed to withdraw his troops from Chōshū and to give up the campaign. Shortly thereafter, on February 3, 1867, the Emperor Kōmei died to be succeeded by his fifteen-year-old son, known to the world as Meiji.

The movement to restore the young Emperor to the position of *de facto* ruler of the country rapidly gained momentum. The leaders of the intelligent group of young warriors in the western clans began to work on specific plans for an alliance. Ōkubo Toshimichi from Satsuma and Kido Kōin from Chōshū, both of whom immediately became key figures in the post-Restoration reforms, persuaded their domainial lords to give their complete support to the Emperor. Saigō Takamori, a fearless warrior from Satsuma and intensely loyal to the Emperor, led that clan's troops into Kyōto and placed them at the disposal of the youthful sovereign.[12] They were soon joined by warriors from Tosa and other royalist forces.

The Shogun, Keiki, who was virtually a prisoner in his own Nijo

Palace in Kyōto, accepted additional reforms which sheared him still further of power. Until November 8, 1867, he had hoped that he could retrieve some of the power and influence which he had lost since he took office. The staunch supporters of the Emperor had selected that day, however, for a direct attack against Keiki. Realizing that his cause was lost, he announced his intention of resigning as Shogun.[13]

The Chōshū troops and courtiers who had been banished in 1863 because of their strong antiforeign attitude were forgiven by the Emperor and permitted to return to Kyōto. The Emperor Meiji thus had at his disposal the strongest feudal barons and armies in Japan. The first step had been taken in the Meiji Restoration and in the establishment of the skeletal form of the new Imperial government from which the Shogun and his close vassals were excluded. On January 3, 1868, the Emperor announced that all power was restored to him and that the office of Shogun was abolished.

Fortunately for the new Emperor and the new volunteer army placed at his disposal by the western feudal barons, the resistance of the Tokugawa forces was at a minimum. When Keiki decided a fortnight later to fight rather than to retire gracefully, he moved to Ōsaka. His forces were quickly defeated by the Imperial army and he escaped to the protection of his castle in Edo. Again the military leader of Satsuma, Saigō Takamori, came to the fore. His fellow clansmen had already reinforced the garrison of the Edo mansion of their feudal baron. They were more than ready for a fight to the finish but this eventuality was avoided in April, 1868, when Saigō obtained the Shogun's acceptance of the Emperor's terms of surrender. The Edo castle and all military and naval supplies were to be turned over to the Emperor. All the Shogun's vassals were to leave Edo and those who had conspired against the Emperor were to be punished. Keiki, the Shogun, who at one time had expected that at the very least he would be given an important post in the new government, was incarcerated in the family castle at Mito. Aside from a small group of his followers who escaped to the north by ship, the Tokugawa Shogunate had lost its support and the dictatorship had collapsed in the two hundred and sixty-fifth year of its existence.

Notes

1. The three families were the chief branches of the Tokugawa family. The Emperor's reply was designed to embarrass Hotta, as the majority of the barons and Nariaki, head of the Mito family, were strongly opposed to any further concessions. Ishin Shiryō Hensan Kakari (ed.), *Ishin Shi* (6 vols.; Tokyo: Meijishoin, 1939-41), II, p. 330.
2. *Ishin Shi,* II, p. 535.

3. See *Ishin Shi,* II, p. 142 *et seq.* The largest number of persons assigned to training on the ship, a total of forty-seven, came from Hizen, the fief responsible for the protection of Nagasaki.

4. Thr. J. C. L. Pompe van Meerdervoort, "The Study of Natural Science in Japan," *Journal North China Branch Royal Asiatic Society,* II (1859), p. 213 *et seq.*

5. *The First Japanese Embassy to the United States of America* (Tokyo: The America-Japan Society, 1920), pp. 42-43.

6. "A Broadway Pageant," *The Poetry and Prose of Walt Whitman,* Louis Untermeyer, editor (New York: Simon & Schuster, Inc., 1949), p. 258.

7. Figures are based on Montague Paske-Smith, *Western Barbarians in Japan and Formosa in Tokugawa Days 1603-1868* (Kobe: J. L. Thompson, 1930); Kawai Toshiyasu, "Bakumatsu no bōeki gaku," *Tōkei Gaku Zasshi,* No. 109, April, 1895; and *Yokohama Kaikō Gojunenshi* as cited by Ishii Takashi: *Bakumatsu Bōeki Shi no Kenkyū,* pp. 35-38. After 1862, the *Yokohama Kaikō Gojunenshi* figures appear to be far less reliable than the others.

8. In 1863 England imported 73 per cent and exported 80 per cent of the total foreign trade. In 1865 the proportions were 81 per cent and 87 per cent respectively. Ishii, *op. cit.,* p. 80.

9. Hugh Borton, "Peasant Uprisings in the Tokugawa Period," *T.A.S.J.,* 2d series, XIV (1938), p. 209.

10. For example, if a trader arrived at Yokohama with sixty Mexican dollars, he could trade them for 180 *ichibu* silver coins. These silver coins could then be exchanged for forty-five *koban* gold pieces which could be sold in China for ninety to 150 Mexican dollars. In other words, if the trader were fortunate in the exchange he could get in Japan, he would make in currency exchange an average of 150 per cent profit on a single round trip.

11. It has been suggested by Norman that this so-called merchant-warrior coalition was inevitable as a result of the large investment of the merchants in land rented to the peasantry. The debtor-creditor relationship appears, however, to be an even stronger cementing factor. The suppression of the peasant by the warriors was merely incidental to their effort to maintain their position of supremacy rather than a conscious effort to suppress the chief productive class. See E. Herbert Norman, *Japan's Emergence as a Modern State* (New York: American Institute of Pacific Relations, 1940), p. 54.

12. Saigō Takamori (1828-77) was born in Kagoshima the capital of the Satsuma fief, of a low-rank warrior family. He was a boyhood friend and relation of Ōkubo. In February, 1854, he first came to the attention of his feudal lord, Shimazu Nariakira, on whom he made a favorable impression. Several months later, he was appointed chief gardener of Nariakira's mansion, a position which brought him into close contact with his chief. During the next few years, Saigō's royalist and antiforeign feelings were stimulated by his contacts with Nariakira and other men of like mind and by visits on clan business to Kyōto and Edo. In the fall of 1858, while Saigō was at Kyōto, Nariakira died and Saigō became involved in the struggle for power of two cliques within the clan. At the same time, Saigō became known to the Shogun as an anti-Tokugawa warrior. Consequently, when he was exiled, he tried to kill himself, but was saved from drowning by the boatmen. Except for a few months when he served as a political observer in Kyōto, Saigō remained in exile from 1859 to 1864.

In April, 1864, he was again in Kyōto and was recognized as the effective leader of the Satsuma warriors. During the next three years, he was influential in keeping Satsuma from involvement in the civil war in Chōshū and in organizing the *rap-*

prochement of those two clans. He worked closely with his own clansman, Ōkubo, and with the young royalist Kido Kōin of Chōshū. In February, 1866, Saigō and Kido hammered out the formal alliance between Satsuma and Chōshū; in early 1867 he began to negotiate with other clans concerning the formation of an anti-Shogun coalition. When the Imperial Restoration was proclaimed in January, 1868, Saigō was in charge of the Satsuma troops which formed the nucleus of the new Emperor's army.

Ōkubo Toshimichi (1830-78) was born at Kagoshima in the Satsuma clan. As the son of a warrior, he entered the clan schools where he studied Chinese literature, classics, and poetry. At the age of sixteen, he was appointed a clan official.

In August, 1858, saddened by the death of Nariakira and the near escape from death of his friend Saigō, Ōkubo went to the Satsuma mansion and formed a "league of loyal men" who vowed not to rest until their nation was unified. During the next nine years, he played a key role within his clan as well as in the formation of a strong anti-Tokugawa alliance. On his various trips to Kyōto, he met the leaders of both the Imperial Court and the Shogun's government. In 1863, following the bombardment of Kagoshima by the British, he was entrusted with the working out of the three-cornered agreement between Great Britain, Satsuma, and the Shogun. In 1864 he advised Shimazu Hisamitsu, of Satsuma, to recall Saigō from exile for the good of the royalist movement. Two years later, in a meeting at Kyōto with Saigō, Kido Kōin, and others, he helped to formalize the Satsuma-Chōshū alliance. After the Shogun surrendered, he became one of the strongest members of the new government.

The importance of the Satsuma clan in the Restoration movement is also exemplified by the activities of Shimazu Hisamitsu. Born in 1817, Hisamitsu never inherited the domain but ran it after 1859 and soon became active in the coalition movement of warriors and the Imperial Court. He continuously cautioned his warriors against too rash or precipitate action and had the most recalcitrant of them killed when they persisted in their opposition to him. In 1864 he brought about a temporary reconciliation between the Imperial Court and the Shogun. By the beginning of 1867, however, he realized that such a reconciliation was impossible and readily agreed to an alliance with the Chōshū fief to attack the Shogunate. He was appointed Minister of the Right in the new Imperial government but soon became disappointed in its policies and accomplishments. He frequently left Tokyo in disgust only to return for a short while. In 1876 he returned to his old fief to live in retirement until his death in 1887.

Kido Kōin (1835-77) was born in the Chōshū fief. A sickly youth, he studied Chinese classics, history, and fencing, and later took up Western military science. A few years later he was head of the clan's school in Edo for training its warriors.

When the cry, "Exalt the Emperor and Expel the Barbarians," arose, Kido advised his clan chieftain, Mōri Takachika, to prepare for war. In 1864, however, he advised against civil war but was overruled, and found himself later as leader of the army. After personal conferences with Saigō Takamori, leader of the rival Satsuma clan, Kido worked actively for their alliance against the Tokugawa. When the Shogun, Keiki, resigned, Kido recommended the complete destruction of his forces. He soon became one of the strongest and most active leaders in the new Imperial government.

13. For a detailed account of the events during the last days of the Shogun see Oka Yoshitake, *Kindai Nihon no Keisei* (Tokyo: Kōbun-dō, 1952), p. 101.

PART II

FORMATION OF A CENTRALIZED MONARCHY 1868-1890

We, sitting on the Throne which has been occupied by Our dynasty for over 2500 years, and now exercising in Our name and right all authority and power transmitted to us by Our ancestors, have long had in view gradually to establish a constitutional form of government, to the end that Our successors on the Throne may be provided with a rule for their guidance.

Imperial decree promising the
establishment of Parliament,
October 12, 1881.

Chronology

1868-1890

1868, January 3	Imperial restoration of Emperor Meiji
April 6	Imperial (Charter) Oath
1869, March	Four western clans (*Satchō Dohi*) petition Emperor to accept title to domain
1871, August	Imperial Decree formally abolishes clans
1872	Railroad opened between Tokyo and Yokohama
	Iwakura Mission tours United States and Europe
1873	Edict against Christianity removed
	Universal land tax in money instituted
	Creation of modern army based on conscription
October	Split over question of Korean War
1874	Formosan Expedition
1875	Territorial settlement of Kuriles with Russia
	Ōsaka Conference
1876	Treaty of Kanghwa opens Korea
	Forced commutation of feudal pensions
1877	Saigō's Rebellion
	Memorial requesting representative assembly and constitutional government
1878	Expansion of Imperial Army
1879	Ryūkyū Islands incorporated into the Empire
1880	Law for sale of factories to private industry
1881, March	Ōkuma's Memorial demanding a Parliament
July	Ōkuma exposes Hokkaidō scandal
	Iwakura establishes principles for Constitution
October 11	Ōkuma ousted
	Parliament promised by 1890
1885	Li-Itō Convention on Korea
	First Cabinet formed
1889, February 11	Meiji Constitution proclaimed

5

FIRST PRACTICAL STEPS OF THE MEIJI GOVERNMENT 1868-1873

In a study of the factors and motive forces which molded and formed Japan during the past century, one is impressed with the fact that this development was the result, as is true of any historical event, of the interaction of various forces, national or international, economic, social, or political. At the same time, a more detailed analysis of the main events of any given period in history often reveals the preponderance of one set of forces over the others. This situation appears to be particularly true of the events of the first few years of the Meiji Restoration, and yet is often neglected by the historians of the period.

As will become apparent from the following analysis, economic problems were among the most important ones during the first few years of the Meiji Period, particularly from 1868 to 1873. In these early years of the Restoration the new leaders devoted their main strength and effort toward the solution of the economic dilemma in which Japan found itself and toward the development of a sound economic base for the new state. If the political and economic structure of modern Japan is to be understood clearly, therefore, it is important to recognize that the real problems which absorbed the actual rulers of the country during the early rule of the Emperor Meiji were practical problems. They were absorbed in questions such as lighthouses, stable currency, taxes, industrial production, a new army, a merchant marine, and the development of foreign markets. Political problems began to demand the dominant attention of these leaders only after many of the basic economic issues had been settled.

This point is made patently clear by Itō Hirobumi, who became the chief architect of the Constitution. In an article which he wrote some fifteen years after the Constitution was promulgated, he makes no mention of political developments from 1868, when the Emperor Meiji was restored to power, to 1880 when the law was issued which inaugurated the system of cities and prefectures.[1] Apparently, in Itō's view, nothing important happened politically for the first twelve years of the Restoration. It is in order, therefore, to concentrate this survey of the first five years of the new government on practical issues rather than on theoretical political problems.

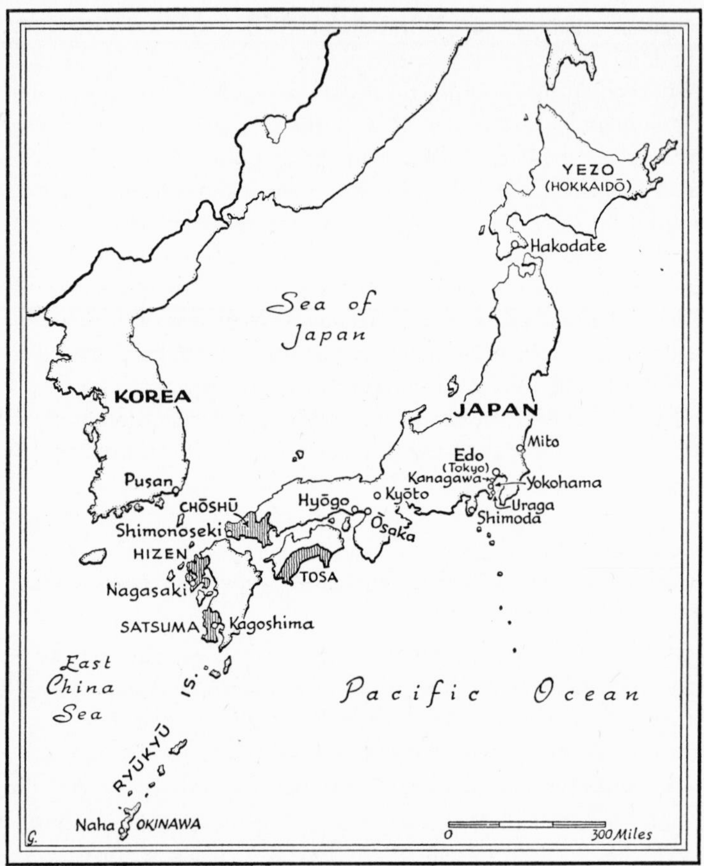

JAPAN IN 1868

Temporary Form of Imperial Government

When the youthful Emperor Meiji issued the proclamation on January 3, 1868, of the "Restoration of Imperial Government," only very limited power had actually been restored to the throne.[2] The military campaigns against the Tokugawa forces, even though they were of a limited nature, had yet to be successfully concluded. There had been no revolution, no overthrow of one class by another. The warriors were still the most powerful element in society. The feudal barons of most of the strongest fiefs had shifted their allegiance from the Tokugawa generalissimo, the Shogun, to the Emperor. Though the sovereign had an army at his disposal far stronger than the combined forces of his potential enemies, this army was available to him only so long as the feudal barons willed it.

Furthermore, the new Imperial government had not yet acquired many of the basic attributes of a government. It did not have the power to tax the land. Its treasury was completely empty. Title to the land was still both theoretically and practically in the hands of 276 separate and partially autonomous feudal barons and the peasants who tilled the soil. There was no standard currency in circulation. There was no agreed pattern for the structure of the new government and no clear concept of the relationship between the Imperial Court and the feudal barons and other classes in society. There were few experienced administrators available to take over the operation of the affairs of state. No foreign power had yet recognized the new government. Militarily, Meiji was defenseless against foreign attack as he had no navy, nor did any of the barons loyal to him have ships of sufficient size or strength to form the core of a new navy.

As Kido Kōin, the sensitive young warrior from Chōshū, described the situation ten months after the Emperor issued his Restoration Proclamation:

> If we wish the restoration of a new government to be realized and the prestige of our Emperor to be elevated abroad, we must establish the basis of government by allotting three-fifths of the expenses for military purposes, one-fifth for the government, and one-fifth for relief and for the people.

Just as the Meiji Restoration was the natural outcome of the events leading up to January 3, 1868, so the new government did not suddenly appear as a fixed pattern. The whole Restoration movement was a continuing process which extended over several years. In fact, the pattern of the new constitutional monarchy was not irrevocably set for roughly twenty years. Under these circumstances, the first few years of the Restoration were full of constant shifts in the form of government. A small group of capable and imaginative men, who had been the leading courtiers and the young warriors in the progressive clans in western Japan, became the key figures in the most important new posts in the government. They constantly shifted from one ministry to another or created new ones as the exigencies of the times demanded. They were completely engrossed with the problem of improving Japan's position through rapid modernization, industrialization, and increased military strength. They were far too occupied with practical matters in the first dozen years of Meiji's reign to have time to work out a master plan for the development of an imperialistic monarchy.

Although there was interest in human rights and liberalism, this interest was in no sense comparable to that which existed in the American or French Revolutions. The Meiji Restoration had not been sparked by Christian idealism, by the principles of equality, brotherhood, and liberty, or even by a class struggle, as the Marxists would wish one to believe. On the contrary, it had been a struggle between rival groups within the warrior class, with one group loyal to the concept of Imperial restoration. Consequently, the first forms of the new government followed a pattern familiar in Japanese history. Two councils of state were formed to be composed of courtiers and the feudal barons from those clans that had supported the Emperor against the Tokugawa Shogun. Seven departments of government were established, one of the most important of which was that of Shintō, the indigenous religion.

In addition to the military action taken against the Tokugawa forces in the early months of 1868, the new leaders made an important decision on the basic policy which should control the new government. This basic policy was formulated by the courtier Iwakura Tomomi (1825-83), assistant chief of the new State Council, and two of the young clansmen from the west, Fukuoka Kōtei (1835-1919) from Tosa and Kido Kōin from Chōshū. It was proclaimed on April 6, 1868, in the form of an Imperial oath, usually referred to as the Charter Oath. Its famous five articles stated, in familiar terms, the general principles and antifeudal aspirations under which the new monarchy would operate. It read:

1. An assembly widely convoked shall be established, and thus great stress shall be laid upon public discussion.
2. The welfare of the whole nation shall be promoted by the everlasting efforts of both the governing and the governed classes.
3. All subjects, civil and military officers, as well as other people, shall do their best and never grow weary in accomplishing their legitimate purposes.
4. All absurd usages shall be abandoned; justice and righteousness shall regulate all actions.
5. Knowledge shall be sought for all over the world and thus shall be strengthened the foundation of the Imperial polity.[3]

With these broad principles settled, it was possible for Fukuoka and his colleagues to draw up more specific plans for a national government. After they studied Chinese, European, and earlier Japanese systems of government, they presented a plan which recognized the three powers of government, namely, the legislative, executive, and judicial, and delegated them in a rather loose fashion to the Council of State (*Dajōkan*). These powers were to be exercised by a bicameral assembly, the President of the Council, and the various executive departments. This plan, often referred to as the first "Constitution" and called the *Seitaisho,* was formally adopted in June, 1868. Shortly thereafter, the name of the city of Edo was changed to Tokyo (Eastern Capital). The name of Meiji (Enlightened Government) was given to the period. The young sovereign moved his court to the new capital of Tokyo, and the old Edo castle became the Imperial Palace.

As new problems developed, it soon became apparent that the real power in the government rested in the hands of the Councilors (*sanyo*). The Imperial princes, who were the titular heads of the executive departments, became figureheads. The proposed assembly proved to be little more than an advisory body and soon disappeared. On the other hand, with the Emperor's sanction, the Councilors acted either individually or collectively as both the executive and legislative branches of government. They were men largely from the middle class warriors of the western clans who had had practical experience in local government and had participated in the Restoration.[4] They were comparatively young men when their sovereign ascended the throne; many of them had hardly reached the age of thirty. These were the men of action who were content to wait for a more propitious time before they set up a complicated national administrative structure. These were the people who were to grow as the new state grew and whose power increased with it. Once having tasted the heady effect of power, they could not give it up.

Financial Confusion and Lack of Technical Knowledge

Fortunately for the Imperial Army, there had been a minimum of military resistance by the supporters of the Tokugawa cause. Nonetheless, such battles as were fought in 1868 and 1869 placed a heavy drain on the meager resources of the new government. Of an estimated expenditure of 51.5 million yen for the first two years nearly 9 million yen was spent on the various military campaigns. Furthermore, it was too early for the new government to profit from the confiscation of the vast realm owned by the Tokugawa family. As the chief of the newly established Treasury Office described it, "The expenditures or budget of this office is a fiction. We have only resorted to borrowing and our daily expenses are barely met."

The situation was complicated by the fact that no action had been taken to abolish the outward forms of feudalism, and the central authorities still lacked the power to collect a uniform national tax. Furthermore, the currency was in a state of utter confusion. There were different varieties of gold, silver, iron, and copper coins and nearly 1700 types of gold, silver, and rice certificates with a total value of approximately 146,790,000 yen.

As had been the case a decade earlier, the foreign merchants were quick to profit from this confusion and from the favorable exchange rates between gold and silver in Japan. By exchanging foreign silver for Japanese gold they were able to make a profit of 100 per cent. Consequently, one-half million gold pieces (*ryō*) were exported in the first month of 1869 alone. The new Finance Office resorted to the only means at its disposal. It immediately requested a "loan" of 3 million yen from the rich merchants to meet the emergency and issued 48 million yen in paper currency known as "Council of State Bills" (*Dajōkan Satsu*). Of this amount, approximately half was used to meet the expenses of the new government and the remainder was loaned to the leading feudal barons to relieve their financial difficulties. This policy served the double purpose of circulating the new currency and of stimulating industrial production.

Another basic and practical problem which simultaneously confronted the new leaders and demanded adroit handling was the relation of the Imperial government to the Western powers. During the final days of the old Tokugawa government, agreement had been reached to open an additional port for foreign traders, namely Hyōgo (modern Kōbe). In fact, several foreign representatives had come to Ōsaka to observe the opening of the port. In view of the danger of hostilities between the Imperial and Tokugawa armies at the end of 1867, however, the foreigners returned to the new port under the protection of a flotilla of foreign warships anchored in the harbor. At this critical point, every effort was made by the new Imperial government to prevent a deterioration in relations with the Western countries. Their representatives were informed in February, 1868, that the Emperor and his government intended to respect the treaties already signed with the Europeans. Imperial audiences were planned with leading foreign diplomats.

During this first year, at least half of the most influential leaders in the Restoration, especially those who had already been abroad, were appointed as officials in the Office of Foreign Affairs or were in charge of relations with the foreigners in Ōsaka, Yokohama, or Nagasaki, the three places where there were the largest number of Western traders. For example, Inouye Kaoru and Itō Hirobumi, both of whom had already been to England, were successively in Nagasaki, Ōsaka, and the Foreign Office. Kido was an assistant, Ōkuma Shigenobu an Under Secretary, and Gotō Shōjirō an Assistant Secretary of that same office.[5]

A specific example of one of these obligations under the old treaties, which was carried on by the new government, is that in connection with lighthouses. In 1866, Sir Harry S. Parkes, the British Minister, had negotiated on behalf of England, Holland, France, and the United States, a convention "for various requirements necessary to the safety and well-being of Europeans and Americans." Japan was required thereby to "provide all the ports open to foreign trade with such lights, buoys or beacons as necessary to render secure the navigation of the approaches to said ports."

Through the good offices of Sir Harry Parkes, Richard Henry Brunton (1841-1901) was chosen to supervise the work to be undertaken by the Japanese government. A manuscript which he wrote of his experience in Japan throws pertinent sidelights on conditions in the early years of the Restoration.[6] Brunton arrived in June, 1868, with two assistants and equipment necessary to build lighthouses at eight key points. Surveying of the locations was begun immediately. By the beginning of the next year the light at Kannonzaki, halfway up the bay to Yokohama, was finished, and a temporary light was installed on the tip of Awa at Nojimagasaki, the point first sighted by steamers headed for Yokohama. Furthermore, the British ship "Sunrise" of about 500 tons was purchased as a lightship and anchored off Yokohama to mark the harbor entrance. Construction was also begun on a lightship with the aid of British shipwrights. The ship was finally launched in 1869 for use at Hakodate. By 1876, when Brunton resigned and returned to England, lights had been established at thirty places along the Japanese coast. The official record of the bureau reads laconically, "He had worked zealously since 1868 so he was given a reward of 2,000 yen." This sum was, of course, in addition to the monthly salary of 600 yen which he had been receiving.

The lack of technical knowledge throughout Japan is poignantly expressed by Brunton at several places in his manuscript. For example, at one point he showed considerable irritation over the refusal of the Governor of Yokohama, Terashima Munenori, to accept his proposal that the city water be conveyed in iron pipes from a reservoir rather than in hollow bamboo and that a filtration plant be built. He also refers with unrestrained disdain to the craze for steamers in Japan. He writes:

> High officers of the government, feudal barons and all who could command sufficient means purchased steamboats. . . . Unfortunately for these first purchasers, steamboats are exceedingly intricate, and, in the hands of the ignorant, dangerous instruments both as regards their guidance across the sea and their internally propelling machinery. Heedless of the fact that their own people were without experience in controlling or working them, the Japanese owners placed unskilled persons in charge of the vessels usually with frequent results of a most disastrous character.

The most common mistake was to fire the boilers without sufficient water in them. He concludes, "Soon learning to estimate justly their own utter incapacity, foreign officers and engineers were appointed to all steamships."

His efforts were not restricted, however, to lighthouses and ships. In 1870 he was asked to construct a bridge without foreign artisans to show the Japanese how bridges were built in Western countries. He designed the bridge, borrowed a punching and shearing machine from an engineering shop, cut the iron plates and made the holes for the rivets. "The whole girders were thus fitted and riveted together by Japanese mechanics who had never in their lives handled similar tools and who were completely ignorant of the exact character of the work in which they were having a part." He concludes with the cryptic remark, "Thus the first iron bridge was erected in Japan without mishap and appeared to be perfectly satisfactory."

Brunton was succeeded by another Britisher, but the Japanese who had been sent abroad to study were soon to replace the foreigners. The role of the Westerners in introducing many of the foreign skills, however, is well illustrated by the large number of foreigners hired in the lighthouse service. For example, forty-seven persons were employed during these early years as engineers, supervisors, metal workers, instructors, lighthouse keepers, and teachers. One of the lightships, the "Meiji Maru," which had been built in England, was manned by British officers until as late as 1884.

Strengthening the Emperor's Base of Power

If it was obvious to Brunton that Japan had made little preparation for the adoption of Western techniques and industrial improvements, the group of reformers were equally convinced that the future prosperity of their country lay in the rapid development of internal economic and military strength. They were painfully aware of the fact that the treaties with the West restricted their autonomy. Foreigners were allowed extraterritorial rights and severe limitations were placed on the import and export duties which Japan could charge. Most of these new leaders had had personal contact with the limited industrial developments in their own clans prior to the Restoration. Hence, they were conscious of the lack of technical knowledge throughout the country. But above all, they realized that the power of the Emperor rested on a flimsy foundation.

When the form of the new Imperial government was announced in June, 1868, the feudal barons were told to govern their fiefs temporarily as in the past and to consider themselves as provincial governors. The promise of the new government that it would assume responsibility for the income and debts of the barons was a substantial incentive to them to remain loyal to the sovereign. The most astute of the young clan leaders realized, however, that if the Emperor was to have any real power both the political and economic autonomy of the feudal barons must be destroyed. In other words, any authority or power which the barons and their retainers derived from the territory inherited by them or assigned to them from the Tokugawa Shoguns must be transferred to the Emperor. Any residual privileges which the warriors retained after the Shogun resigned must first be returned to the throne and then reassigned by the Emperor. Consequently, two of the key reformers, Kido of Chōshū and Ōkubo of Satsuma, persuaded their feudal lords to surrender voluntarily to the crown their feudal rights of suzerainty over their domains.

By March, 1869, the four powerful western clans, Satsuma, Chōshū, Tosa, and Hizen (the *Satchō Dohi* clans), petitioned together that the sovereign accept the title to their domains. Their request to "return their registers" (*hanseki hōkan*) was based on the argument that one central body of government and one universal authority was essential for the effective operation of the new Imperial government. Their plea continued, "It is now sought to establish an entirely new form of government. The land in which your servants live is the land of the Emperor and the people whom they govern are his subjects." These clan chieftains then surrendered their "registers" of the persons within their domains and entreated the Emperor to issue decrees as he deemed necessary and to deal as he saw fit with the lands and peoples of the four clans. Other clans vied with each other to follow this example. By 1870, the feudal lords of these fiefs had moved permanently to the new capital of Tokyo and had placed their troops directly under the command of the sovereign.

In August, 1871, an Imperial Decree was issued which formally abolished the clans and converted them into prefectures (*ken*). At that time, all but seventeen of the 276 feudatories had already transferred their fiefs and there was a general feeling of satisfaction over the accomplishments thus far. On that day, Kido Kōin was elated. He was confident of the feasibility of eradicating feudalism and the arbitrary power of the feudal barons. He noted in his diary: "Today my ideal has been realized and Japan's stature has become as lofty as that of the other countries of the world."[7] The outer forms of feudalism were disappearing but the new Imperial government still did not have the power to levy a universal tax in money based on the value, not the crop, of the land.

Much still needed to be accomplished, therefore, before Japan would begin to become a "prosperous country through military and industrial strength," as envisaged by its ambitious young leaders. A free labor supply, technical knowledge, an abundance of capital, an integrated plan for industrialization, and a uniform system of taxation were necessary. The first of these prerequisites came about as the result of the social changes which accompanied the Restoration. The barriers between the provinces were abolished, people were permitted to travel at will and obtain employment wherever they desired. The social classes were abolished. Even the warriors lost their identity. The jinrikisha had been invented and transportation was rapidly developing. As had already been intimated, technical knowledge was obtained by hiring foreigners and by sending groups of young men abroad to learn new skills.

On the other hand, it was more difficult to solve the problem of lack of capital. Japan's extended seclusion had reduced the possibilities of growth of a strong mercantile class. The owners of such capital as had been accumulated from internal commerce and trade were reluctant to risk investment in enterprises sponsored by a government in which they had little confidence. If capital was to be obtained, it would come about by the untiring efforts of the government leaders. It was not enough to collect a special levy on the wealthy families or to increase the paper money in circulation. Government-sponsored commercial companies (*Tsūshō Kaisha*) were established in the open ports but these failed to compete successfully with the foreign trading companies or to increase confidence in the new government's currency.

Two bold steps were taken in the field of national finance. In the first place, two of the key figures in the Restoration movement were assigned to improve the currency. Ōkuma Shigenobu, a Councilor from Hizen, and Itō Hirobumi, a Councilor from Chōshū, were assigned to the Finance Office. They proposed that the yen should be the unit coin, that the decimal system should be used, and that only one metal would be the standard. Shortly thereafter, Ōkuma was promoted to be Vice-Minister of Finance and Itō became his assistant. Itō was sent to America early in 1870 to study foreign currency systems. Since the gold standard was the most prevalent one abroad, he urged its adoption. Contrary to his recommendation, the government first settled on the silver standard. As a result of the continued objections of the European traders who practically monopolized Japan's foreign trade, the gold standard was finally adopted in 1871.

Before Itō went abroad, he and Ōkuma made a second important financial decision. They recognized the absolute necessity for a railway and yet had no funds for constructing one. They decided to try to raise the capital abroad. In November, 1869, they were appointed, together with the titular head of the Finance Office, to negotiate a loan with Great Britain for the construction of a railway between Tokyo and Hyōgo (Kōbe). After consultation with Horatio N. Lay, Customs Commissioner in China, a loan was floated in London for £930,000 at 9 per cent interest, redeemable in 1881. Work was begun on the first leg of the line, Tokyo to Yokohama, in early 1870 under the supervision of the British engineer Morrel. The line was officially opened two years later. Simultaneously a branch office was established in Ōsaka to supervise construction work of the main line in western Japan. But progress in the mountainous terrain was discouragingly slow. In 1872 only eighteen miles of track were completed and there were only ten locomotives in the country. Nine years later, 128 miles of track were finished so that many of the cities on the

Pacific coast of the main island were connected by this latest method of transportation.

This step in Japan's industrialization was also significant for two other reasons. In the first place, the loan floated in London was the first of only two foreign loans sought by Japan during the formative years and was of such a limited amount that Japan was able to remain independent of financial dominance by Great Britain. In the second place, this transaction indicated the predominant position, financially and economically, which Great Britain had over the other Western powers engaged in Far Eastern trade. For example, both the United States and France had hoped that they would be selected to finance a railroad, but they lost out to their commercial rival. As for the United States, it was also vitally interested in railroads at this time. It hoped that it would be able to recover some of the trade lost during the years of the Civil War and of the Reconstruction Period. The same year that the British loan to Japan had been floated in London, the Union Pacific Railroad had completed the final link in the first transcontinental system. It was the dream of its builders that this new route would draw some of the European-Oriental trade through the United States. Such was not to be the case. Neither the recently reunited American Republic nor Imperial Japan had yet learned how to compete successfully in Oriental trade with the more experienced British financiers and traders.

Government Sponsored Industrialization

In addition to railway construction, the Japanese government also took an early interest in strategic industries. These included communications, the old Tokugawa munitions plants, and mining. In the communications field, energies were concentrated on building a telegraph line. Technicians and experts were hired from England and the first line was opened between Tokyo and Yokohama the first year after the Restoration. Due to the lack of technical knowledge of the Japanese and the fear and objections of the peasants to this new invention, there were only sixty-five miles of line by 1871. Some believed the rumors that the wires were to be used for transmitting their blood to quench the thirst of the foreigners. Others objected to the line crossing their property and cut the wires or tore down the poles. Despite these obstacles, the Council of State persisted in its opinion that the telegraph should be extended and that it should be owned by the government for security reasons. When faced with civil war a few years later, public ownership of the telegraph assured effective communication between the capital and the troops in the field and was one of the factors which contributed materially to victory. The Council was vindicated in its decision.

After the Tokugawa dictatorship had capitulated, the new Imperial government immediately confiscated such military industries as had already been started. This move had a twofold effect. In the first place, the government had direct control over the most important strategic industries, a situation that assisted the rapid rise of a strong and effective military machine. In the second place, the normal order of industrial development from light to heavy industries was reversed in Japan. Consequently, consumers' goods industries were to develop far more slowly than heavy industries.

One of the first examples of confiscation undertaken by the Meiji authorities was that of the Nagasaki shipyard and foundry. It had been built by the Hizen clan in 1861 and was placed under the supervision of the Nagasaki city office in 1868. The Yokosuka foundry and shipyards, planned by the feudal government with the assistance of French technicians and the promise of a loan, were formally seized in 1868 and operated as a government naval yard until 1945. The two chief arsenals at Tokyo and Ōsaka were likewise appropriated, foreigners were employed to operate them and instruction was given in the manufacturing of small weapons. The difficulty in putting these plants in operation is clearly illustrated by the history of the Ōsaka arsenal. Its confiscation was not formally consummated until two full years after the Restoration; it was not ready to operate until after machinery had been shipped from the Nagasaki foundry and was installed and adapted for arsenal use.

Mining also was important both for the growth of strategic industries and for the growth of industry as a whole. The Meiji government took over the mines owned directly by the Tokugawa government and profited from earlier geological surveys made in northern Japan. It proceeded on the theory that while it theoretically owned the natural resources below the surface of the ground, private persons could open new mines with the government's permission and could sell their products to the government. In many cases the government operated the mines directly and invited European miners, geologists, and engineers to Japan to assist in their operation and to train Japanese who would eventually run them completely. In other cases, the government was glad to have the mines developed by private enterprise.

One of the most important mining projects in the latter category was the coal mine at Takashima, an island ten miles offshore from Nagasaki. Before the Meiji Restoration, the exploitation of this mine was planned as a joint enterprise of the local feudal baron and the British firm of Thomas B. Glover & Co. They installed steam-driven hoisting machinery for raising the coal from the pits, a railway for hauling the coal through the mines and a ventilating system. This equipment enabled the mine to produce 200 tons of bituminous coal daily. It continued to be operated after the Restoration by Glover until 1873 when it was purchased by, and put under the direct operation of, the government for ten months. At this point, Gotō Shōjirō, one of the more liberal of the reformers, purchased the mine. Several years later it was bought by the Iwasaki interests.

Confusion and ineptness in the early industrialization was inevitable when so many problems pressed on all sides for immediate solution. Progress was made, however, on the important problem of an organized plan of industrialization by the formation of the Ministry of Industry (*Kōbushō*) in November, 1870. This new department had the double purpose of encouraging industry among the people and enabling the state to profit financially and militarily from this industrialization. It was the center of Japanese mercantilism and the nursery of Japanese capitalism. Specifically, the Ministry was charged with the supervision over all matters relating to the opening of industrial schools, encouragement of industry of all kinds, and the supervision of all mining activities. Furthermore, it was to construct, repair, and maintain railroads, telegraphs, lighthouses and navigation buoys; construct and repair ships and warships; carry out the forging and casting of metals, such as copper, iron and lead; manufacture various types of machines; and survey land and sea areas.[8]

Some of these responsibilities were new ones and required extended planning and development, others had been transferred from the all-powerful Finance Ministry or from the experimental Ministry of People's Affairs (*Mimbushō,* 1869-71). It is extremely significant that the Ministry of Industry was directed almost exclusively in its earlier years by Itō Hirobumi. He was appointed Vice-Minister in December, 1871. As there was no Minister at that time, he had final and complete charge of its activities. This situation was formalized by his appointment to be Minister in 1873, a post he held for five years. A man like Itō, who was to play such an important role in the formation of the constitutional government, seemed to have had no time in those early years to argue about the form of government most suitable for Japan. He and his colleagues were too absorbed with other more practical matters. They postponed the formation of a constitutional monarchy until Japan was strong enough economically to withstand the various forces at work, at home and abroad, that might have destroyed the new Imperial state.

At this point, two questions present themselves. Was it possible that Itō and his colleagues had decided at an early date that the best government for Japan immediately following the Restoration was a minimum of government? Was it more likely that they had not had time to consider the matter seriously and were fortunate in the choice that was made by default? Perhaps no definitive answer can ever be made to either of these queries. On the basis of what actually happened, however, one can venture a guess. In view of the innumerable problems which confronted the small group of active members of the government and which demanded immediate attention, it is probable that the latter explanation is the more likely.

In any event, the net result for Japan's future development was the same. The concentration on practical problems accelerated industrialization and strengthened Japan militarily. This reduced interference from groups outside the clan oligarchy to a minimum during the first few years because the oligarchs alone had the technical knowledge to be leaders in the industrialization movement. Having secured important posts within the government during this transition period, they could easily shift their efforts to constitutional problems when the country was ready for them. (See Chapter 8.) In so doing, they selected and trained their own group of assistants, the lower ranking bureaucrats; there was no room for members of the opposition. In other words, this concentration on practical problems made possible a simultaneous political unification and the formation of a strong, centralized state.

Feudal Forms Abolished

But another important reform still called for completion, namely, the formation of a universal and uniform system of taxation. A few months after the fiefs were formally dissolved by edict, in October, 1871, Finance Minister Ōkubo and his assistant Inouye Kaoru permitted the sale of land in perpetuity and recommended the establishment of certificates of land ownership. When these certificates were issued the next month in Tokyo, a value was placed on the land for taxation purposes and money from taxes began to flow into the national treasury. But the difficult problem was to set a fair value on the farm land. Heretofore its worth had always been measured in terms of the amount of rice it produced. If land was to be sold or to be assessed for purposes of a tax in money, some formula must be found to determine its cash value.

Ōkubo devised such a formula by use of the facts at hand. He started with the annual crop for any given field, its income. He knew that 6 per cent interest was considered to be a fair return on an investment. Hence he argued that 6 per cent would be a fair return to the landholder for his investment. Previously, the landholder's income had been the annual crop or yield from his land. By equating these two factors, the crop and the 6 per cent interest, Ōkubo fixed the value of the land.

The average annual crop for each parcel of land was considered to be equal to 6 per cent of its value. Since each plot represented the capital investment of the landlord, and since the interest on that investment was 6 per cent, the total value of the land was 16 2/3 times the value of the crop. As the value of the crop was known, the value of any field was determined by multiplying its yield by 16 2/3. Furthermore, Ōkubo decided that the farmers should continue to pay the equivalent of half the crop in the form of rent or taxes. Under the new system, the new tax was not to be paid in rice but in money. Consequently, the cash tax would be half of the value of the average crop. As it had been decided to count the crop as equal to 6 per cent of the land value, half of it would be 3 per cent.

Hence, in 1873, the old methods of collecting taxes were abolished and a gradual examination of all the land and land certificates was begun. Thereafter, a tax of 3 per cent on the new value of the land was to be collected. The immediate effect of this move was obvious. The government was able to formulate a procedure whereby a money tax could be universally levied on the owner of the land on the basis of the value of his property, not on the annual crop of the land. Furthermore, since the tax was valued at half the value of the crop, it would be no more severe in its actual operation on the farmer than the old tax collected in rice. If the owner did not cultivate the land, it was left to him to collect the rent, but he was responsible to the government for the tax.

But the establishment of a land tax in money was not the only unsettled problem connected with the abolition of feudal rights. The new government had assumed the burden of paying the annual rice stipends of the feudal barons and of the warriors. While this arrangement assured the loyalty of many of them to the new regime, it placed a heavy charge on the impoverished treasury. Naturally, the government was anxious to be relieved of this obligation as rapidly as possible in view of the fact that the warriors comprised a nonproductive class and most of them were useless to the Emperor even as soldiers. By 1871, when the movement to transfer the fiefs to the throne gained momentum, the government offered to commute those privileges into government bonds. Such a procedure enabled it to transform immediate cash requirements into long-term obligations. In other words, it no longer would have to make heavy annual payments in rice or the cash equivalent, but would only be required to pay interest on the bonds issued.

Even though this scheme, originally devised by Ōkubo and later developed by Ōkuma, relieved the strain on the national treasury, cash was needed immediately to pay 8 per cent interest on the bonds. Furthermore, warriors with less than 500 bushels of rice income could commute half of their pensions into cash and half into bonds. Consequently, funds were sought from every possible source. The Ministry of Finance issued a new series of convertible treasury notes. The name and credit of the Mitsui family, the strongest bankers in Japan, was called upon to bolster the value of these new notes. Credit was again sought and obtained in London for £2,400,000, at an interest rate of 7 per cent, for a period of twenty-four years.

By 1876, the financial position of the government was sufficiently strong to make possible the forced commutation of all of the feudal pensions. In that year, an edict made it compulsory upon all of the former members of the warrior class to transform their incomes, if they had not already done so voluntarily, into government bonds. The interest rate of these bonds and their date of maturity varied according to the former rice income of the warrior.

From the point of view of the warriors, especially those with small income, this transfer of their perpetual feudal claims into cash or government bonds had several disadvantages. By Imperial Decree, their assets had already been reduced to less than half of their original value. Furthermore, traditionally the warriors considered money matters as degrading so that few of them had had any practical business experience. When payments were made to them in negotiable securities, many of them soon lost their assets through poor investment policies; others dissipated their limited resources in extravagant spending. Within a few years, all but 20 per cent of them had lost control of their original holdings.

On the other hand, the old feudal barons with large incomes suffered far less than the average warrior. For example, a baron with an old income of 500,000 bushels of rice ended up in 1876 with an annual income from interest on his government bonds equal to 80,000 yen.[9] In comparison to the landholder during the French or Russian Revolutions whose lands were confiscated, however, the old warrior class had come out handsomely.

Simultaneous with the abolition of the old feudal contracts of the warriors, they lost many of their special social privileges. (See Chapter 10.) For example, after 1871, they could voluntarily give up wearing their swords if they desired. In other words, the sword no longer symbolized social prestige and power. The feudal barons and the courtiers formed the new nobility; the warriors (*samurai*) comprised a new class in society called *shizoku* (gentry); all other persons became commoners. Thus the warriors lost their special exemptions and became a class in name only.

They lost even their distinction as a separate class when a modern army, based on universal conscription, was substituted for the old armies composed of hereditary warriors. The movement for a strong army coincided with Japan's industrialization and social reorganization and was made possible by it. Yamagata Aritomo, one of the young warriors from the

Courtesy of Bettmann Archive

IWAKURA PRESENTS HIS CREDENTIALS TO PRESIDENT GRANT, 1872

Over the Western sea hither from Niphon come
Courteous, the swart-cheek'd two-sworded envoys,

—"A Broadway Pageant" by Walt Whitman (Commemorating the first Japanese embassy to the United States in 1860.)

Courtesy of Bettmann Archive

Itō Hirobumi, 1841-1909

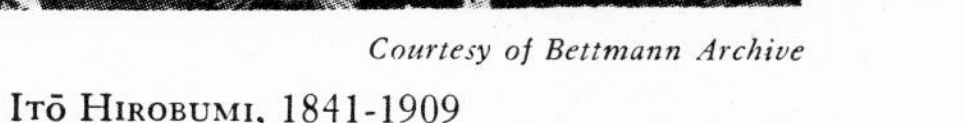

Courtesy of Bettmann Archive

Yamagata Aritomo, 1838-1922

western clan of Chōshū, was largely responsible for this policy.[10] After assisting in the subjugation of the Tokugawa forces during the early months of the Restoration, he went to Europe to study the French and Prussian armies. After his return in 1870, he was appointed Second Vice-Minister of War. Since his superior was an Imperial prince with little practical knowledge and as there was no Vice-Minister, Yamagata was the actual head of the ministry. In 1873 he became full Minister.

During this short interval, the main groundwork was laid for the Imperial Japanese Army. The first conscription law was enacted in 1870. It provided for three years of active service and two years in the reserve. It also permitted exemption from service through payment for a substitute. Many of the farmers objected to this provision and refused to serve. Consequently, national quotas could not be filled until 1873, when a new conscription law was promulgated. Although exemptions still existed which placed the heaviest burden on the lower classes, the new conscripts were chosen by lot. For the next few years, not more than 10,000 men were called to the colors annually. In fact, it was not until after the Satsuma Rebellion of 1877 that Yamagata was able to organize a strong and effective army.

Signs of Unrest and Discontent

The military campaigns between the Imperial and Tokugawa forces in the first two years of the Restoration were not extensive operations and affected only a small portion of the people. The great social and economic changes of the Restoration movement were not brought about, however, without creating more extensive disorder than these military campaigns. As more drastic changes were pushed by the authorities, more disturbances developed. These took the form of peasant uprisings similar to those of the Tokugawa days. Universal conscription, the liquidation of the fiefs, and the introduction of a tax in money were the most common causes for the uprisings. Others resulted from the abolition by decree of the four classes, the designation of a single currency as the medium of exchange, the introduction of innovations such as the telegraph, and the forceful separation of Buddhism from Shintoism. The greatest number occurred in 1873, the year in which both the land reforms and effective conscription were started. In most cases, they were local affairs arising from local conditions. In a few cases, as in Kyūshū in 1873, over one-quarter of a million persons were involved. Except for some of the political riots connected with the people's rights movement, they were not of national significance. (See Chapter 6.) Practically none of them were directly connected with the struggle between the Emperor and the Tokugawa forces. They were a symptom of the times, however, which showed that the oligarchs were not yet completely in control.

But an even more significant sign of discontent was the split which was rapidly growing within the ranks of the Emperor's chief ministers and advisers. The split came about over the policy toward Korea. In effect it was the result of a basic rift between those who advocated the further strengthening of Japan internally before venturing overseas, and those who supported expansion before the home base was secure. In 1871, the former group decided that a special mission should be sent abroad to secure as much knowledge as possible concerning Western technological progress. As the treaties with the powers provided that revisions could be considered that year, the mission was organized ostensibly to seek such revisions. If revision were possible, the tariffs could be raised, the government income increased, and the warriors given a larger compensation for their old feudal rights. If the powers refused to take seriously the matter of revision, the mission could at least increase its scientific knowledge.

Iwakura Tomomi, Vice-President of the Council and Minister of Foreign Affairs, was selected to head this special mission. He was accompanied by several of the most powerful officials in the government and especially those who were primarily concerned with first strengthening Japan internally. For example, Ōkubo Toshimichi, Minister of Finance, was an important member of the group. He had been largely responsible for the plan just inaugurated which deprived the warriors of their feudal privileges. Itō Hirobumi, newly appointed Vice-Chief of the Ministry of Industry, was another member of the mission. He was young and inexperienced but eager to make his new department the dynamic center of Japan's modernization. His fellow clansman Kido Kōin, who had drafted many of the edicts which actually brought about the Restoration, was also included. There were fifty subordinates and assistants as well as the first Japanese women to be sent abroad to study.

After the arrival of the Iwakura Mission in Washington, they were disappointed by the cold reception President Grant gave their request to revise the treaties so that their country would stand on a footing similar to that of the most enlightened nations. Their chagrin was partially placated by action of the United States Congress which appropriated a special fund of $50,000 for their entertainment. When they reached London they were greeted by Sir Harry Parkes, British Minister to Japan, and by Brunton, home on leave from the lighthouse service. The true nature of the Japanese Mission is evident from Brunton's description of their four months' stay. He wrote that Itō and his young assistants showed special interest in twenty-eight London business establishments in September alone. These included factories for candles, skivers, glue, gelatine, bricks, cement, and iron foundries and shipyards. They spent far more time in the factories than in diplomatic talks in the Foreign Office.

The group then crossed over to the continent where they were favorably impressed with Prussia and Bismarck. Iwakura's conversation in Berlin in March, 1873, with Germany's Under Secretary of Foreign Affairs, made him and his Mission realize how many reforms at home were necessary before the Western powers would consider Japan an equal. At that interview, Iwakura was asked how soon foreigners would be allowed to travel freely in the interior of Japan. He had to admit that permission for this could not be granted until legal and administrative reforms were perfected and the national police were trained. The Under Secretary replied that the Japanese government should make a request for opening negotiations to revise the treaties only after such reforms had been perfected.

Iwakura and his colleagues were in a receptive mood, therefore, when they dined with Bismarck. They listened attentively to his advice that if Japan was to become strong like Germany it must rely on its own strength. He told them that nations could not be trusted and that international law was followed only so long as it was in the self-interest of a state to do so. Iwakura and his entourage never forgot this lesson. In less than a decade, he was advocating a Prussian-type Constitution for Japan. Itō was sent back to Berlin to study Prussian political philosophy in preparation for drafting Japan's Constitution.

But this quest for practical knowledge by those most directly responsible for the program of industrialization was abruptly terminated by the ascendancy at home of a group advocating expansion. This latter group was composed of talented Councilors who had been excluded from many important conferences at which basic policies had been determined. They were disgruntled because the real power was wielded by others. They were also jealous of having been left out of Iwakura's Mission.

The most dynamic among them was Saigō Takamori, a fellow clansman of Ōkubo's from Satsuma. He had carried much of the brunt of the fighting for the Emperor against the Tokugawa Shogun at the time of the Restoration and had negotiated the settlement in early 1868 for an armistice. (See page 64.) He was, therefore, one of the key figures in the Restoration. Always an idealist and a man of action, he deplored the gradual degradation of the warriors as a class and more particularly the concentration of governmental power in the hands of such men as Ōkubo, Kido, and Itō. In other words, he realized that he was less and less influential in the government. This discontent was shared by other Councilors such as Itagaki and Gotō from Tosa and Etō from Hizen.

To assure continuance of their policies during their absence, Iwakura and the key members of his Mission had obtained assurances from Saigō and their other political rivals who remained at home. The latter had promised that no important appointments or policy changes would be made during the absence of the Iwakura Mission. In view of the struggle for power which was developing within the government and of the problems which demanded immediate settlement, it was impossible to expect that such a pledge would be kept. In fact, it was to be respected more in its breach than in its observance.

The problem of Japanese-Korean relations was the central issue which caused an open break between the two opposing factions. In the early months of 1872, Japan had sent official envoys to Korea to negotiate a treaty and to open that country from its seclusion. The envoys had been rebuffed and insulted. Subsequently, several Japanese subjects in Korea were attacked and the Korean problem was placed before the Council of State. Saigō, who had great confidence in the newly established conscript army, recommended an aggressive policy for two reasons. In the first place, Japan's national honor and pride demanded that Korea pay for its insulting conduct. In the second place, a successful military campaign would solve the distress of the dispossessed warrior class by making new territory available to them for exploitation.

Saigō, who apparently never doubted the successful outcome of this venture, was fully aware of the possibility that such a military move might result in hostilities with Russia. Nevertheless, he argued that such an eventuality would give Japan a welcome chance to extend its frontiers. "Should Japan's borders be restricted to Hokkaidō?" he queried. Rather, they should be expanded to include the territory south of a line from Possiet Bay to Nikolaevsk. By these arguments and his forceful personality, he was able to win support in the Council for a positive policy against Korea. Other Councilors, such as Etō of Hizen, and Gotō and Itagaki of Tosa, had also been piqued by the monopoly of important government positions held by Satsuma and Chōshū clansmen. They were glad to sponsor a project which would challenge this monopoly. The plan, as adopted by the Council, included Saigō's appointment as envoy to force Korea's capitulation. Confident that his efforts would lead to hostilities and a successful campaign, he was delighted at a chance to die, if necessary, for the glory of his country.

On the other hand, the members of the Iwakura Mission had been sobered by what they had observed abroad and were more convinced than ever that Japan's first task was to strengthen her internal economy and her military power. When reports from home reached them of the danger of the outbreak of war against Korea, they feared not only for their own political power but also for the future of their country. They returned home immediately and finally won support for the reversal of the decision of the Council to send Saigō to Korea and to fight if necessary. In October, 1873, the Emperor ordered the government to concentrate on internal improvements and to forget about a military expedition to Korea. The rancor created over the Korean issue caused serious repercussions for the next few years. Saigō was enraged; he immediately resigned from the government and returned to his home province of Satsuma. Other members of the opposition such as Gotō and Itagaki of Tosa and Etō of Hizen also resigned.

From external appearances, the Imperial government had successfully weathered the storm generated by the rejuvenation of the Emperor's power. The basic principle had been universally accepted that the government should be controlled and operated by a coterie of Imperial advisers and councilors. A uniform currency had been adopted. Studies had been made in important fields of industrialization with the assistance of foreign experts. Railway lines were rapidly expanding. Several industries were sponsored by the government. Feudalism was formally abolished by the liquidation of the fiefs and the commutation of the pensions of the warriors. Only two foreign loans of limited extent, and free from any political commitments, had been necessary to put the government on a comparatively sound financial basis. An official mission to America and Europe had been rebuffed in its attempt to revise the treaties but the members of that mission had obtained much practical knowledge from their trip. The first major crisis within the government had been solved to the satisfaction of the rulers. There had been few important revolts at home since the Tokugawa forces capitulated. This apparent tranquillity was, however, only the lull before the storm.

Notes

1. See Itō Hirobumi, "Some Reminiscences of the Grant of the New Constitution," in Ōkuma Shigenobu (compiler), *Fifty Years of New Japan,* English version edited by Marcus B. Huish (2 vols.; London: Smith Elders, 1910), I, p. 121 *et seq.*

2. Meiji Tennō (1850-1912). It is practically impossible to obtain detailed and objective biographical information about Emperor Meiji. His early training and outlook were strongly influenced by the court nobles such as Iwakura Tomomi and Sanjō Sanetomi. From the fact that one of his chief teachers, Motoda Eifu, was a conservative and old-style Confucian scholar, one can surmise that much of the Emperor's training was in the conservative Chinese tradition. Some of his biographers describe his chief pastimes as writing poetry, horsemanship, and reviewing troops on maneuvers.

Although he is described as a hard worker in the details of administration, as an individual he was less important in the Restoration than some of his trusted advisers.

As a symbol, he was extremely important. His public appearances added much to the budding spirit of nationalism but he was always kept away from normal contacts with the people. In times of crisis, however, his opinion was sought and followed. But the key to obtaining Imperial sanction to any policy was to obtain previous approval from his closest advisers. Hence, as will become apparent below, the importance of Emperor Meiji in history was the manner in which his chief ministers were able to use his name and his position to obtain acceptance of their policies.

3. W. W. McLaren, "Japanese Government Documents," *Transactions of the Asiatic Society of Japan,* vol. 42, p. 8.

4. These key councilors included Ōkubo Toshimichi and Saigō Takamori from Satsuma; Kido Kōin, Itō Hirobumi (1841-1909) and Yamagata Aritomo (1838-1922) from Chōshū; Gotō Shōjirō (1838-97) and Itagaki Taisuke (1837-1919) from Tosa; and Soejima Taneomi (1828-1905) and Ōkuma Shigenobu (1838-1922) from Hizen. For Japanese sources on the background of the government changes see Ishin Shiryō Hensan Kakari, *Ishin Shi* (6 vols.; Tokyo: Meijishoin, 1939-41), I. The names of the officials appointed to the various posts are given chronologically in *Meiji Shiyō* (2 vols.; Tokyo: Kinkō-dō shoseki k.k., 1933). For special studies on the period see Nobutake Ike, *The Beginnings of Political Democracy in Japan* (Baltimore: Johns Hopkins University Press, 1930); and R. A. Wilson, "Seitaisho," *Far Eastern Quarterly,* May, 1952, pp. 297-304.

5. Inouye Kaoru (1836-1915). Inouye was born of a family which had served the feudal barons of Chōshū for generations. In his youth he studied "English and Dutch Learning," concentrating on Western artillery methods. After 1854 he served as a sort of aide-de-camp for his feudal lord and soon joined other convinced partisans in the clan who worked for an Imperial restoration. He also was in the forefront of the antiforeign movement and was among the group which set fire to the British legation in Edo in 1861.

In the spring of 1863 he and Itō Hirobumi went abroad for study. While in England, he realized that the idea of "expelling the barbarians" was nonsense and henceforth concentrated his attack on the Tokugawa dictatorship. His views were not appreciated by some of his fellow clansmen, one of whom attempted to assassinate him one night while returning home. He hovered between life and death for several days but finally recovered. During the turbulent civil war days, he traveled about in disguise on various missions. After 1868 his most important posts were in the Ministries of Foreign Affairs and Finance.

Itō Hirobumi (1841-1909). Itō was born of an extremely poor warrior family in the Chōshū fief. From this lowly beginning he was to become his country's most powerful figure. When about twelve, he was adopted by the Itō family which hired him out as a page to another warrior who was quick to observe his talents. In 1855 Itō studied for five months with the loyalist Yoshida Shōin. He then studied Dutch military science at Nagasaki and was in Edo at the height of the antiforeign movement. In 1861, he participated with Inouye and other fellow clansmen in the attack on the British legation.

In 1863 he and Inouye smuggled themselves out of Japan, serving as forecastle hands on a small trading ship to London. In London Itō studied science for several months, but returned home immediately upon learning of the imminence of hostilities between Great Britain and Chōshū. When he reached home, he tried unsuccessfully to persuade his fellow clansmen to abandon their proposed attack on the foreigners. After Chōshū had been defeated, he worked out the treaty between Chōshū and the Dutch, American, and British commanders. In March, 1868, Itō received his first appointment in the new Bureau of Foreign Affairs. He shifted from there to Finance, Public Works, and finally to the head of the Cabinet.

Ōkuma Shigenobu (1838-1922). Ōkuma was one of the few outstanding leaders of the Restoration who came from the province of Hizen. Born in a warrior's family, he was sent to the various clan schools in Nagasaki where he became proficient in both Dutch and English studies. During this period he came in contact with other future leaders of the Restoration such as Saigō Takamori and Gotō Shōjirō.

In the spring of 1866 he vainly sought permission to obtain an audience with the Shogun to try to persuade him to give up his powers to the Emperor. When the Imperial Restoration was announced in 1868, Ōkuma was Governor of Nagasaki. Since he had been appointed to this position by the Shogun, he left office precipitately, only to be appointed to the same post by his feudal baron. In view of the number of foreigners at that trading center, Ōkuma's chief responsibilities were toward the foreign merchants and representatives. One of the most serious problems which faced him was the appearance of about 5000 Japanese Christians, who had been in hiding near the city. As the anti-Christian edicts were still in force, Ōkuma began rounding them up. The representatives of the Western powers protested vehemently but before Ōkuma could offer any solution, he was called to Tokyo to serve in the Foreign Office. After holding various posts, he became Under-Secretary of Foreign Affairs in 1869. Since at this period the heads of the departments of the government were either courtiers or feudal barons appointed for prestige purposes, Ōkuma in reality controlled the country's foreign affairs. Like many of his colleagues he shifted from one government department to another. He even became Prime Minister but much of his public life was devoted to various problems of foreign relations.

Gotō Shōjirō (1838-97). Born in Tosa, Gotō was a lifelong friend of Itagaki Taisuke, leader of the "liberals." After serving several months as a supervisor in the clan government, he went to Edo, entered the language school of the Tokugawa government and studied navigation and "English studies." Always an advocate of the restoration of power to the Emperor, he was often used by his feudal baron as an emissary to important anti-Tokugawa fiefs such as Satsuma and Hizen. He was among those who urged the Shogun to resign in 1867, and in early 1868 he became Assistant Secretary of Foreign Affairs. While in that office, his quick action saved the life of the British Minister, Sir Harry Parkes, when the latter was attacked in an antiforeign riot. Gotō, who had jumped from his horse and cut down Sir Harry's assailant, was later knighted by Queen Victoria for his bravery. He continued to be one of the chief leaders until his death.

6. Richard Henry Brunton, "Pioneer Engineering in Japan, A Record of Work in Helping to Relay the Foundations of the Japanese Empire 1868-78," MS in Rutgers University Library, New Brunswick, N.J. I am greatly indebted to Rutgers University Library, Rutgers University, New Brunswick, N.J., for permission to use Brunton's manuscript. It is part of their valuable manuscript collection of the "Griffiths Papers." The transfer of the Lighthouse Bureau, to which Brunton was appointed, from the jurisdiction of one Ministry to another during the early years of the Restoration was indicative of the unsettled conditions within the government and of its general policy of improvisation. The Lighthouse Office, *Tōdaikyoku,* was first established in 1868 as part of the Yokohama City Office. In the next year it was transferred to the Finance Ministry (*Ōkurashō*), then to the Foreign Office, after which it became a branch of the Internal Affairs Ministry (*Mimbushō*). Following the formation of the Ministry of Industry (*Kōbushō*) in 1870, it was one of its important branches until the general reorganization in 1885.

7. Oka Yoshitake, "Shinseifu," *Gendai Nihon Shōshi,* ed. Yanibara Tadaō (Tokyo: Misuzu-shobō, 1952), I, p. 68.

8. The official history of the Department of Industry is entitled "Kōbushō Enkaku Hokoku," *Meiji Zenki Zaisei Keizai Shiryō,* eds. Ōuchi Hyōe and Tsuchiya Takaō, (21 vols.; Tokyo: Kaizo-sha, 1931-36), XVII.

9. This figure was derived as follows: The income of 500,000 bushels had automatically been reduced by Imperial Decree in 1876 to 50,000. This was estimated to have a cash value of 320,000 yen. In 1876, when commutations were made compulsory, an income of this size had an estimated capital value of 1,600,000 yen. Bonds worth this amount bearing 5 per cent interest would produce an income of 80,000 yen.

10. Yamagata Aritomo (1838-1922). Yamagata, the power behind the throne from 1909, when Itō died, until his own death in 1922, was also the person most responsible for Japan's modern army. Born in Chōshū on June 14, 1838, his father was able to provide him with a good education. At the age of nineteen he was sent to Kyōto to serve as a clan spy and there met some of the earliest loyalists. Like his fellow clansman, Itō, he was inspired by the loyalist teacher Yoshida Shōin to work for the restoration of the power and prestige of the Emperor. He received his first military experience as an officer in the "people's army" of Chōshū, which was to prove that spirit and training were superior to tradition and prestige. Yamagata was wounded during the bombardment of the coastal defenses of Chōshū in 1863 by the Western powers. Subsequently, his clique within the clan came to power and its policies resulted in the outbreak of civil war against the Shogun. In February, 1867, Yamagata and Saigō of Satsuma began to work together to form an Imperial force strong enough to defeat the Tokugawa. In the campaign of 1868-69, he was in command of the loyalist forces which defeated the Aizu clan troops in northern Japan. For account of the early years of the Japanese army see Yamagata Aritomo, "The Japanese Army," in Ōkuma Shigenobu (compiler), *Fifty Years of New Japan,* I, pp. 194-217; and Hyman Kublin, "The Modern Army of Early Meiji Japan," *Far Eastern Quarterly,* IX (1949), pp. 20-42.

6

THE OLIGARCHS ESTABLISH THEIR POWER 1873-1880

In the previous chapter, the early practical steps taken by the young Imperial advisers and government leaders of the Meiji Restoration and their pragmatic approach to the intricacies of government have been emphasized. Munitions factories made possible a conscript army. A conscript army deprived the warrior class of their monopoly of martial virtue. The abolition of the fiefs and application of a universal tax based on the value of the land, not the crop, enabled the national treasury to be assured of a fixed income and to operate on a budget. Modern railroads and the telegraph, built by the government, helped to tie the country into a single geographic unit which could be readily protected from internal revolts or external attacks. The implementation over several years of these various reforms increased, both directly and indirectly, the strength of the Emperor and the power of the state.

When the Emperor agreed in October, 1873, with Iwakura and his group that the country should give up the expedition against Korea and should concentrate on internal improvements, the responsibility for running the government became restricted to an even smaller handful of oligarchs. Led by Iwakura, Ōkubo, Kido, Ōkuma, Yamagata, and Itō, they entrenched themselves in the key positions in the government. At times, they vied among themselves as individuals for favor and power. On the other hand, when they were challenged by the advocates of "people's rights" and by the champions of a representative, elective assembly, they gave way on unimportant issues only and presented a united front. Whenever they agreed to structural changes which ostensibly gave the people more power, they implemented such agreements as they saw fit and promulgated, in the name of the Emperor, legislation which gave them extensive powers.

The period immediately following the decision on the Korean issue, therefore, is characterized by two distinct, yet interrelated, features. There was an intensification of opposition to the oligarchs by various antigovernment groups in the form of a public demand for new, representative institutions. On the other hand, the government leaders husbanded the power they had acquired. As Sir George Sansom has aptly expressed it:

> Almost all the national energy seemed to be devoted to political questions, and the country was divided into two main camps—progressives . . . against conservatives.[1]

During this period of acute political consciousness the political philosophy of those who were to complete the Meiji Restoration was formed.

The political struggle precipitated by the resignation of the disgruntled Councilors in 1873 must not be thought of simply as a struggle between advocates of progressive and conservative political philosophy. As Sir George is careful to note, the course of events was not governed by adherence to accepted political theories. Even though ideas were given European labels such as "liberal," "progressive," or "conservative," these words cannot be interpreted in their usual Occidental meaning. They have always had their peculiar Japanese connotations.

Thus, if the term "progressive" is defined broadly to mean greater freedom and more rights for the people, it is not fully applicable to the political philosophy of all of the antigovernment leaders. For example, Saigō, who led a formidable revolt in 1877, was far from "progressive" politically. Furthermore, even the most outstanding progressives were unbelievably conservative on some subjects.

Conversely, the conservative oligarchs might be defined as those who believed in the superiority of absolute rule and in the inferiority of democratic institutions. But they, like their opponents, were often motivated by a personal thirst for power. By 1873, their initial loyalty and enthusiasm for the Emperor had begun to wear thin. Each of the young clan bureaucrats had experienced the giddying and exhilarating effects of power in his own hands. They would not and could not give it up easily. The Ministers of State came to consider themselves individually, rather than collectively, responsible to the Emperor. A new political atmosphere developed in which personal jealousies, antagonisms, and ambition often became stronger than clan ties or even a common loyalty to the throne.

Itagaki Taisuke, who was the personification of the "progressive" movement, befriended some strange fellow-travelers in his crusade to obtain a representative assembly. Saigō, the ultraloyalist, became jealous of his fellow clansman Ōkubo and willingly gave his life in open rebellion. Ōkuma, at once a "progressive" and an oligarch, was summarily ejected from power when he challenged his colleagues, the clan bureaucrats. At a later stage, though they were fellow clansmen and had been imbued with the same conservative beliefs, Yamagata and Itō became political enemies.

Effect of Opposition to the Oligarchs

The resignation of Saigō on October 24, 1873, and that of the four other Councilors on the next day, created an immediate crisis in the government. Iwakura and his group acted quickly to retain control over the reins of government. On October 25, Itō of Chōshū was designated to fill one of the vacancies on the Council. Though only thirty-three years old, he had impressed Iwakura favorably during the trip abroad and thus became one of the inner circle. He was soon preoccupied with the problems of the Ministry of Public Works. By the beginning of 1874, though no decision had yet been made on the final form for the new government, this group of bureaucrats from the western clans formed a tightly knit body. They were confident that they were in undisputed control and that their position could not be successfully challenged.[2]

It came as a shock to them, therefore, to discover that those who had resigned over the Korean issue had closed their ranks and were actively engaged in antigovernment activities. In January, 1874, all those who had resigned from the Council, except Saigō, presented a caustic memorial to the throne demanding the formation of an elected assembly. These memorialists were motivated both by a fervent desire to enhance their own political power as well as by an urge to increase the rights of the people. Furthermore, they were from the two clans of Tosa and Hizen and were keenly aware of the inferior position which their clansmen had held in the central government.

Among the chief Ministers and Councilors, Ōkuma was the only representative from these two clans who was left in the government. Itagaki Taisuke and the other memorialists saw in the people's rights movement a possibility of support to overthrow the bureaucrats from the rival Satsuma and Chōshū clans.[3] They also hoped that they might become the new leaders. Their memorial was, therefore, outspoken in its denunciation of the leaders of the government. It accused them of usurping the governing power and of depriving the crown of its prestige. It claimed that the Councilors prevented the people from expressing their grievances. If reforms were not effected, the state would be ruined. It continued:

> We have sought to devise a means to rescue the state from this danger and we find it to consist in developing public discussion in the Empire. The means of developing public discussion is the establishment of a Council Chamber chosen by the people. Then a limit will be placed to the power of the officials and both governors and governed will obtain peace and prosperity.

This indictment was too severe to be ignored. A direct reply to the memorial was made a week later by Katō Hiroyuki (1836-1916), as spokesman for the government. Katō had studied both the Dutch and German languages as a youth. He was in charge of the government school which later became Tokyo Imperial University. He was the author of various books on political science. He began as an advocate of liberal equalitarianism but became conservative as his age and administrative responsibilities increased.[4] His arguments in 1874 against Itagaki's memorial for a deliberative assembly, however, reflected his basically conservative point of view. He noted that even in the civilized and enlightened states of Europe, public opinion is not invariably just and enlightened. As neither Prussia nor Russia had deliberative assemblies, he saw no reason why Japan should have one. In fact, he concluded that only wise leaders were capable of determining what was suitable for the country under the present circumstances.

The antigovernment forces were not to be silenced. In fact, the action of some of them reflected the discontent and unsettled conditions of the times. As already noted, Saigō had returned to Satsuma and rallied a hard core of fanatical loyalists around him. Etō Shimpei lost patience and returned directly to his province of Hizen. He immediately led an open rebellion under the slogan of "War with Korea, the restoration of the feudal barons to their rightful place in the government, and the expulsion of the foreigners." When he was unable to receive active support from Saigō or from other antigovernment groups, he capitulated after fifty-two days of rebellion.

On the other hand, Itagaki and his immediate supporters did not resort to direct action but continued their attack on the government through public written statements. In February, 1874, they elaborated further on their demands for a deliberative assembly in a written rebuttal to Katō's views. This document is important not only because the authors quoted from John Stuart Mill to defend their position, but also because it reveals their own conservative, rather than radical, political philosophy. At the time their reply was written, Itagaki was the most important and most vociferous member of the movement for people's rights. If his reply is a true indication of his basic beliefs, there is little to distinguish him as a champion of equalitarian individualism, liberty, and the basic human rights as these concepts have been understood in France, England, or the United States. He and his colleagues were liberals or progressives, therefore, only in a relative sense.

As was true of most Japanese intellectuals of his day, Itagaki had accepted those concepts which impressed him favorably. He then modified or superimposed them on a basically conservative native belief. For example, he condemns the government as oligarchic and hence in need of rectification. He quotes Mill to prove that men of high caliber do not require despotic power to enable them to exert great influence. Furthermore, he deplores the extreme submissiveness of the people. He argues, with

Mill, that the government should take responsibility for the people's advance to the next stage of political development, namely, a deliberative assembly.

At this point, Itagaki injects his own concepts. He recommends that the assembly, or Council Chamber, as he calls it, be given only restricted and limited powers. As he defined it:

> If the Council Chamber is established, we do not propose that the franchise should at once be made universal. We would only give it in the first instance to the samurai and the rich farmers and merchants.

In other words, the Council would be selected by an elite minority. Furthermore, there is no demand that the Council be the most powerful executive organ of the government. In fact, it is doubtful whether even Itagaki conceived of an Assembly to which the Cabinet or Imperial Councilors would be responsible. As Dr. Yanaibara Tadaō points out, a movement of pure liberalism had not yet arisen from the people. Rather, Itagaki was motivated by what has been termed "national liberalism."[5] He was convinced of the superiority of his own class; he saw little reason to give the majority of the citizenry, the masses in the city, and the tenant farmers a vote.

Home Minister Ōkubo, who had been personally responsible for suppressing Etō's rebellion in Hizen, considered views such as those expressed by Itagaki and his followers as especially dangerous when discontent and unrest were so prevalent. In fact, he had been so fearful of the effects on the discontented warriors of the cancellation of the Korean campaign that he engineered a diversionary expedition against two of the aboriginal tribes in Formosa. His official excuse for the punitive campaign was that China had refused to chastise some Formosan natives for having killed some Ryūkyūans.

Although it required 3600 soldiers, 289 sailors and cost 3,600,000 yen, the expedition was eminently successful from the Japanese point of view. Not only did a large band of hotheaded warriors have a chance to practice their newly acquired skills, but business interests also profited from it. The merchant-banker Iwasaki of Tosa made a handsome profit on the expedition. (See page 115.) The government purchased thirteen ships which it leased to him to operate after the expedition was over; it later gave them to him with a subsidy sufficient to develop his own shipping line. By October, 1874, the Chinese government had agreed with Ōkubo, who had been sent to Peking as plenipotentiary, that the expedition was "just and rightful" as Japan was protecting its own subjects. Furthermore, this agreement gave Japan a strong legal claim later for the Ryūkyū Islands which were incorporated into the Japanese Empire in 1879. (See Chapter 9.)

But the clan oligarchs from Satsuma and Chōshū were conscious that their tenacious hold of practically all important posts in the government placed them in a vulnerable position. Consequently, they resorted to an oft repeated device. They called a conference of as many of the dissident factions as possible and reached a compromise with the opposition. This general agreement was then incorporated into an Imperial Proclamation which gave additional prestige to the agreement and placed an obligation on all parties to observe it.

Thus, early in 1875 Itagaki was called to a conference in Ōsaka where a valiant attempt was made to patch up the differences between him and the chief Councilors. As a result of Itagaki's insistence that some form of deliberative and representative assembly be formed, the conference agreed that:

1. A Senate or *Genrō-In* be called to discuss legislative matters.
2. A Supreme Court be organized.
3. A conference of Prefectural Governors be called to consider, along with the Senate, the future form of the national government.
4. The functions of the Councilors and Ministers of State be separated.

The implementation of the agreement reached at Ōsaka is illustrative of another technique which the clan oligarchs used to great effect. The Imperial Proclamation, which they had prepared, granted in general terms these privileges to the people. While it appeared to be sanctioning democratic institutions, in reality such was not the case. The detailed interpretation and implementation of the new policy was left to conservatively minded Ministers of State and their bureaucratic assistants. War Minister Yamagata, for example, was convinced that persons in the antigovernment movement planned to overthrow the government. He remonstrated, "Every day we wait, the evil poison will spread more and more over the provinces."

Thus the oligarchs, in order to be assured of control over the opposition, enacted strict laws. For example, in 1875 new press and publication laws provided for severe penalties for those who openly wrote against established policy. More than sixty persons were arrested within a year for violating these new laws. (See page 185.)

As new "freedoms" were given the people, new power to guide and to suppress them was acquired by the Emperor's responsible Ministers. This same procedure was followed in general in 1887 when strong objections were raised to the lack of progress on the revision of the treaties, in 1889 when the Constitution was promulgated, and in 1924 when universal manhood suffrage was approved. Even in 1931, when elements of the Japanese Army engineered a coup d'état in Manchuria, the same pattern was followed in modified form. In any of these or other crises in Japan's modern history, the Emperor's ministers were convinced of the justice of their cause. They firmly believed, or made themselves believe, that they knew better than anyone else what was best for the country and for the people. Consequently, they sponsored legislation or Imperial decrees which gave them sufficient authority to carry out their beliefs.

Obviously, Itagaki's efforts had resulted in some progress toward the formation of representative institutions; but the new pattern of government continued to be conservative and slow in forming. Administratively, the powers and functions of the Home Ministry were broadened. The Home Minister was responsible directly to the Emperor and had full charge of matters related to public safety, local government, taxes, and public works. With the national police force under his direct supervision, he became one of the most powerful men in the government.

Although the edict in 1875 which created the Senate seemed to augur well for greater rights for the people, its constitution and rules which were announced later, made it a conservative body. Its membership was restricted to nobles and persons of the two highest court grades who had rendered meritorious service to the throne. It functioned for only a short period and served as little more than a sounding board for new government policies. Similarly, the prefectural assemblies, promised at the Ōsaka conference, did not meet until 1878; they were composed of the upper class, and were only advisory in nature. Once more, the clan bureaucrats had made changes in the governmental structure, but of such a nature that they retained the real power.

Saigō Takamori Defies and Challenges the Clan Bureaucrats

No one was more aware of the concentration of power in the hands of a few favored Imperial Councilors than Saigō Takamori. After his resignation in 1873 from the Council and as Commander-in-chief of the Imperial guard, he had returned immediately to his home province of Satsuma. He was accompanied by his former feudal baron, the Imperial Advisor Shimazu Hisamitsu. Both men were strong supporters of the right of the Emperor to rule and they believed firmly that he was being ill-advised. They refused to participate in any of the government's activities. They had not been included in the compromise meeting in Ōsaka in early 1875. Consequently, Saigō was both shocked by and apprehensive of the news that a Senate was to be established. The conferences of prefectural governors held shortly thereafter filled him with even greater forebodings. Reportedly, they were discussing an appropriate form of a Constitution for Japan which would mean further limitation of the Imperial prerogatives.

In the meantime, Saigō had established his own private school in the prefectural capital of Kagoshima. Since many of his faculty had formerly served under him in the Imperial guards, infantry and artillery squads were formed. Chinese classics were an important part of the course of study. Saigō's purpose was to train young men adequately for government service. Eventually he hoped to have a hard core of well-disciplined persons who would take over the central government under his leadership. Furthermore, his small group of fanatic followers insisted that the warriors as a class should be supreme above all others and should rule the empire. Among the warriors, they believed none were better equipped to bear that responsibility than themselves.

Satsuma was one of the most isolated provinces in Japan, and its inhabitants had long cherished a feeling of independence from central control. Many of the graduates of Saigō's school were given positions in the Satsuma prefectural government and the governor was in agreement with Saigō's objectives.

Personal rivalries and antagonisms also contributed to the bellicose attitude of Saigō's band of warriors. They were attached to his cause by a strong personal loyalty and had an intense antipathy toward any who opposed him. The Satsuma men were particularly resentful of the power wielded within the central government by their fellow clansman, Ōkubo. Their feelings were intensified by the fact that as Home Minister he was responsible for public safety throughout the country, including Satsuma. When he requested Ōyama, the prefectural governor, to come to Tokyo to explain his insubordination and partisanship toward Saigō, the governor refused to appear. When special police agents were sent from Tokyo in retaliation to spy on the activities of the Saigō clique, its members considered it an insult to their leader. Finally, the Satsuma warriors were dissatisfied with the central government's plan for the forceful commutation of their feudal pensions. The special interest rate of 10 per cent for bonds held by Satsuma warriors, as compared to a rate of 5 to 7 per cent for all other warriors, was not a sufficient incentive to force them to change their minds. They did not desire to be tied, either financially or politically, to the fate of the new government.

The final, unbearable insult, from the point of view of Saigō's henchmen, was an order from Tokyo in January, 1877, to transfer the Army and Navy ammunition stored in the city of Kagoshima to a safer district. The Satsuma men ignored the order and took the initiative by seizing the depots. Saigō then led a force of 15,000 men northward ostensibly to carry on negotiations with the national government in Tokyo. Actually, he had revolted against the Imperial government and his campaign was supported and sanctioned by Governor Ōyama. Although the governor's jurisdiction was limited to Kagoshima Prefecture, in the extreme south of Kyūshū, he ordered all the garrisons in the entire island to give the rebels safe conduct. They were not challenged until they had marched six days and 115 miles to reach Kumamoto.

The Commander of the Imperial Army garrison of that city, who was responsible to the Chief of Staff in Tokyo, refused to permit the rebels to pass without a pitched battle. Saigō's forces, fired by his zeal and leadership, began a siege of the Imperial troops in the castle at Kumamoto. Reinforcements arrived just in time to save the castle. The entire peacetime army of 32,000 men was committed against Saigō. They were supplemented by a reserve of 10,000 men and many of the national police. It took the government nine months and cost 42 million yen to suppress the revolt. In September, 1877, Saigō, his officers, and the last of his men died in their den near Kagoshima.

As a result of the rebel's defeat, the Imperial Government had successfully met its greatest challenge. The new Imperial Army, recruited from all classes of society, proved that it could successfully meet an army composed exclusively of the old warrior class. As none of the other dissident groups, such as that led by Itagaki in Tosa, had joined Saigō's rebellion, it was clear to the central government that a widespread, effective opposition did not exist. Rather, the rebellion was a personal affair of Saigō and was motivated by his frustrations and misplaced loyalties.[6] Consequently, after the suppression of the uprising, the clan bureaucrats were in a position to push forward with the business of the formation of a permanent governmental structure and of economic development and expansion which would contribute directly to Japan's national strength.

Increased Demands for People's Rights

But the oligarchs were not as free to pursue their policies as appeared on the surface. They still had to deal with increasing political opposition. The continuing problem which faced them was how to retain the power and dignity of the throne and their own favored position and at the same time to give the people enough rights and privileges to keep them satisfied. No one had yet developed a satisfactory solution to this problem. In fact, a solution might have been ignored if it had not been forced on the clan bureaucrats by the challenges thrown at them by the advocates of "people's rights." The struggle between the oligarchs and those who demanded a representative, elected national assembly did not stop with the outbreak of Saigō's Rebellion in 1877.

On the contrary, Itagaki and his followers had no responsibility for suppressing the rebellion and thus were free to devote their entire energies to political problems. They brought the issue to a head by formation of a political society and the issuance of a scathing memorial while the rebellion was in progress. (See page 103.) In view of the danger of arrest under the new press and libel laws for the sponsorship of such views, it took considerable courage and personal conviction in the righteousness of their cause to take this action.

Many of the leaders of this movement had received inspiration from British political philosophy and from their past experiences. One of the most important of these was Fukuzawa Yukichi.[7] The first important product of his pen, *Seiyō Jijō* (Conditions in the Western World), was published in 1869. It was a description of life in Western Europe and America, especially Great Britain and the United States. It depicted their political institutions and defined the differences between monarchy, aristocracy, and republic. But Fukuzawa made it clear to the reader that he considered the British parliamentary system to be the best and that man's natural rights should be safeguarded. He introduced the Japanese reader to practical aspects of American and British life by a description of their systems of taxation, railways, steamship lines, post offices, banks, schools, libraries, museums, and joint stock companies. A first edition of 150,000 copies of the book was soon sold out and it continued to be widely read.

Simultaneously, he championed the study of the English language and advocated practical learning rather than the traditional curriculum of Chinese classics and language. A list of his more important writings reflects his increased interest and concern for political problems. In 1876, just prior to Saigō's rebellion, he wrote a treatise, entitled *Bunken Ron*, on the division of judicial, legislative, and executive powers of government. Two years later he added his weight to those demanding greater rights for the people by writing *Tsūzoku Minken Ron* (A Popular Discourse on People's Rights). Although he was more interested in general reform than in the formation of a political party to bring about these reforms, he was one of the most effective antagonists of the oligarchs and their autocratic tendencies and had a significant influence on Itagaki and his followers.

Another important foreign influence on political thinking came from France. Although French thought was not as influential as British political philosophy, it served as the basis for the most radical reformers. By the time of the Satsuma Rebellion in 1877, the works of both Montesquieu and Rousseau had been translated; Rousseau's theory of man's natural rights, as set forth in his *Contrat Social*, had been enthusiastically accepted by a small group of Japanese radicals. The concepts of "liberty and equality" became the basis for their demands that the social and political privileges inherited from feudalism should be abolished.

One of the most prominent of this group was Nakae Chōmin (1847-1901), a Tosa native who studied Dutch and French at Nagasaki before the Restoration, and then became interpreter for the French Minister Leon

Roches. At Itagaki's suggestion he was sent to France as a student on a government scholarship. After his return in 1874 he became secretary of the Senate and later devoted his time to journalism. He was always in the forefront of the fight against the oligarchs. Although his views were more radical than those of Itagaki and his immediate followers, he never advocated overt action against the government or revolution.

As already noted, steps taken thus far by the Imperial government to increase the rights and privileges of the people were not dictated by a great revolutionary movement. Furthermore, except for the Etō and Saigō Rebellions, the popular revolts or uprisings which had exploded were restricted to the peasantry, were often isolated cases, and rarely had any political motivation. In fact, they were unimportant enough to be ignored by the government in the sense that they did not demand or dictate the agrarian changes that were inaugurated. On the other hand, the movement for people's rights could not be ignored. Unrest and disturbance after 1877, although never comparable to that of Saigō's Rebellion, increased and included influential groups in society such as the landowners and manufacturers of consumers' goods. (See Chapter 7.) Even the farmers and city workers were beginning to become politically conscious and to be influenced by political leaders such as Itagaki.

Although the writings of persons such as Fukuzawa and the memorials of Itagaki and his group had been partly responsible for this increased political consciousness among the people, the formation of political societies was also important. Itagaki, who had become disappointed with results of the "reforms" in the government sponsored by the oligarchs, was convinced that progress in the people's rights movement would be possible only when public interest in governmental affairs was sufficiently aroused. He concentrated, therefore, on the formation of a political organization, on writing, and on speaking in public meetings. With his fellow Tosa clansman, Kataoka Kenkichi (1843-1903), and others he formed the Society of Independence (*Risshisha*). Its avowed purposes were to fight for the rights of the individual, to perfect the people's welfare, and to advance the concept of an elected popular assembly. Nevertheless, its membership was restricted to the gentry class.

Perhaps the most important single act of the *Risshisha* was its sponsorship of a memorial drafted in the name of Kataoka, its President. The Satsuma Rebellion was in progress when the memorial was presented in June, 1877. It claimed that the current unrest was the direct result of the despotic power excercised by the Emperor's ministers and of their refusal to take heed of the opinion of the nation.

> Laws have been enforced, taxes imposed, the collection of the land-tax reformed, wars declared against foreign countries, portions of the empire exchanged; solely at the

caprice of several officials, without allowing public opinion to have a voice in the matter. The sacred oath taken by the Emperor on his accession to the throne has been altogether set aside.[8]

The memorial then lists eight evils which prevailed. The first was the arbitrary action of the Cabinet which imposed its own oppressive measures on the people in disregard of the Emperor's will expressed in his decrees of 1868 and of 1875. The memorial decried the fact that the provincial governors had not met again and that the press and libel laws stifled all expression of public opinion. Other evils noted were the random and confused way in which the government was conducted and the concentration of authority and power in Tokyo. Furthermore, it complained that the common people were given no political rights and had no control over their welfare. While the memorial did not oppose the concept of military conscription, it disapproved of such a system so long as it was operated by a despotic government.

On financial matters, the memorial accused the authorities of favoritism in the exploitation of Hokkaidō and other regions and complained that the system of collecting taxes in cash was unfair. The eighth evil cited by the *Risshisha* was referred to as the mismanagement of foreign affairs, a point on which the government was particularly vulnerable because no progress had been made in revising the unequal treaties with the European powers. The memorial was a formidable document both in its caustic attack on prevalent evils as well as in its length. It concluded with a plea to the Emperor to "put an end to all despotic and oppressive measures, and to consult public opinion in the conduct of the government. To this end a representative assembly should be established so that the government may become constitutional in form."

The memorial was ignored officially on the grounds that it contained impolite language. Its demand for an elected assembly and charges against the oligarchs for obvious mistakes could not, however, be so easily dismissed. It was public knowledge that the Satsuma and Chōshū clansmen were acting arbitrarily and that their foreign policy belied their claim that Japan was a nation comparable to any in the Western world. Many of the other evils described in the memorial were easily recognizable by the increasing number of persons influenced by occidental political philosophy. By the issuance of this statement, the *Risshisha* had greatly intensified the struggle for people's rights.

The Conservative Oligarchs State Their Views

It is difficult to assay the influence exerted by the *Risshisha* or any of the advocates of greater people's rights at any given time. A prominent constitutional historian, Professor Ōtsu Jun'ichirō, goes so far as to claim that the demands of Kataoka and others expressed the real desire of the people and changed the political complexion of the country. As he expressed it, "The government officials, who had been oppressing public opinion, found that they had lost face and realized for the first time that they could not suppress the will of the people."[9] The facts do not seem to justify giving such importance to the "progressives."

It is clear, however, that this group did modify the action of the oligarchs on several occasions, even though the latter always retained control. For example, as early as 1876 the Emperor had requested the Senate to begin a study of various constitutional systems in preparation for drafting a constitution appropriate for Japan. It formed a special committee to conduct such investigations and made progress on a draft constitution. Furthermore, in 1877 there was a general reorganization of the governmental structure which attempted to separate the executive, legislative, and judicial powers of the government. The next year, Ōkubo, the key figure in the government, was assassinated. His assailant explained that he was motivated by a desire to revenge the death of Saigō, for which Ōkubo, as Home Minister, had been responsible. Consequently, the remaining leaders became apprehensive for the safety of their own positions and of their persons.

Under the circumstances, the government took additional steps to placate the opposition. The Ōsaka Conference and the subsequent proclamation in 1875 had promised the formation of an assembly of prefectural governors to consider the question of a constitutional system. Such a meeting had been held for a few days under the chairmanship of Kido. Many of the governors regretted that the time for discussion had been limited and no further meetings had been called.

Just prior to his death, Ōkubo called the governors together to approve a plan for local assemblies. Consequently, in July, 1878, it was announced that prefectural assemblies would be established and their members would be elected by a restricted male electorate. The assemblies were to be used to discuss prefectural budgets and other local matters. On the other hand, their power was limited by the fact that the Governor initiated all bills and could veto them. He also had power to dissolve the assembly if it became too cantankerous. Although these assemblies were a far cry from an elective national parliament, the government claimed that it was taking appropriate steps to determine the will of the people.

Far more important than any of these reforms, however, was the awakened consciousness of the oligarchs to the fact that they must crystallize their own views on the question of the permanent governmental structure. To this end, advice was sought from a distinguished foreign visiter, former President of the United States, Ulysses S. Grant. While in Tokyo in 1879 on his trip around the world, the same persons who had asked him six years earlier in Washington to approve treaty revisions now sought his opinion on the knotty problem of how much power to give to the people. General Grant was well aware of the fact that the Japanese people as a whole had had little education or experience in politics. Universal education had theoretically been in operation for a few years (see page 175) but in reality, illiteracy was more prevalent than literacy. Furthermore, the average Japanese subject had had little firsthand experience with problems which required political decisions and had not been given responsibility in government. People were content to leave such matters up to the authorities.

In view of these facts, when Grant had a conference with the Emperor Meiji, he advocated adoption of representative institutions but urged the Japanese to consider the matter with great care. He warned them that if rights of suffrage and representative institutions were once given to the people they could not be withdrawn. Hence, they should be given gradually. Under the circumstances, he urged delay in establishing an elected national legislature with full powers.

After Ōkubo's assassination Itō had succeeded to the post of Home Minister. Young Itō had already shifted his interests from practical problems of reconstruction, which he encountered as Minister of Industry, to those of a political nature and came to play an increasingly important role in the government. When he learned that the draft Constitution proposed by the Senate contained liberal provisions which he believed to be dangerous to the future of the state, he turned to his old mentor, Prince Iwakura, for help. As President of the Council of State, Iwakura was a key figure in any move to get Imperial sanction for a new policy. Consequently, on December 21, 1879, Itō wrote Iwakura requesting that the Senate be asked to abandon its work on a constitution. Shortly thereafter, obviously on Iwakura's advice, the Emperor issued such an order. At the same time, each of the members of the Council of State was requested to present his views to the throne on the question of a constitution.

By this move, Itō had outmaneuvered both the Senate and those outside the government who clamored for a parliament. In the first place, he knew that the Councilors, with the possible exception of Ōkuma, would support his own general position that extreme caution was necessary in granting additional powers to the people. Any public demands for action could now be silenced by the reply that the Emperor had requested his most esteemed advisers to give him their views. It could logically be argued that until these views were in hand, the government could take no action. Even more important, the people could be kept in ignorance of the contents of the opinions of the Councilors in the event that the views were not acceptable to Iwakura and Itō. As President of the Councilors, Iwakura would forward the memorials to the throne, and could screen them at will. At one blow Itō had thus assured himself of support for a conservative governmental system and deprived the opposition of a means of criticizing his maneuver.[10]

As was expected, the views of all the Councilors except Ōkuma were conservative and reflected the heritage of Confucianism and the German doctrine of the supremacy of the state expounded by political philosophers such as Blüntschli and Biederman. Yamagata Aritomo, who had been Minister of War until 1878, was the first Councilor to send in his reply. He was also one of the most representative of the advocates of Prussian political philosophy. Although his memorial is rambling in parts and is a combination of generalities and references to modern concepts of government, the type of government he supported is clear.

He pointed to three evils which he believed retarded Japan's governmental progress. The first evil was the rapid development of events which resulted in hasty decisions and a deviation from "the right way." The second evil was a change on the surface of society brought about by new innovations. In reality, he argued, only limited groups had benefited from changes which had already occurred. Finally, Yamagata concluded that the Restoration had caused some of the warriors and other groups to revolt. These examples were proof to Yamagata that the majority of the people had not shown proper respect for the government and refused to obey its orders. To meet these evils, Yamagata proposed that the people cease their search for novelty and follow the example of the Councilors and Ministers. The action of the latter should be based on a constitution established on sound principles. For Yamagata, such sound principles included continuance of the special prerogatives of the Emperor and of the privileges of his court.

Yamagata's views were equally conservative on the question of division of powers. He wrote:

> As for the division and establishment of the three powers of executive, legislative and judicial, though there are models in existence, these should be completely modified [to suit Japan's unique needs]. The extent of power of these branches of government should be settled. If the legislative and judicial power are not restrained by the executive power and if provision is not specifically made in the constitution for such restraints, it will be impossible to avoid contradictions.[11]

In other words, he disregarded the concept that the three estates should balance each other. Rather, he championed the position that the executive branch of the government should have power to check the legislative and judicial branches.

In view of the controversy over the question of the people's rights which Itagaki and others had aroused, Yamagata's memorial also contained his views on this issue. Like practically all key persons in the government, he opposed the idea of an elective parliament. He advocated, on the other hand, a modification of existing governmental institutions such as the appointive prefectural assemblies. The capable persons from these assemblies should be "pulled out," regardless of the prefecture from which they came, and should be used to form a single assembly. This hand-picked assembly should then discuss the principles for a new constitution. After this type of assembly had functioned for a few years, it could be changed into an elective body. As he argued:

> Put an assembly in practice secretly, learn from experience and at a time when there is no fear of contradiction and trouble, change its name, speak about it openly, and it will not be too late. Make a mixture of direct and indirect election as through an electoral college. Slowly a people's assembly could thus be organized.

In conclusion, he recognized that persons might object to his proposals on the grounds that such an assembly would be merely advisory and would automatically approve governmental policies. He was not impressed, however, by the fact that citizens of European countries participated directly in their governments. Japan could not be compared with the West. As he expressed it:

> As Japan is just beginning a new type of government, you cannot expect the Japanese to have one ten-thousandth of the rights of Europeans.

Yamagata's memorial has been quoted extensively both because of the key position he held in the Restoration government and because most of the other Councilors agreed with his conservative position. For example, Itō Hirobumi, who was to be primarily responsible for drafting Japan's new constitution, held views essentially the same as those of Yamagata. In his earliest proposals for an elective assembly, which he presented in 1879, Itō recommended that the Senate (*Genrō-In*) should be expanded and that its members should be elected from among the nobility. He believed that the chief function of a Parliament (*kokkai*) should be to protect the Imperial Household and to preserve ancient customs. Its opening should, however, be postponed. Such a plan, he maintained, would have the dual advantage of controlling changes and broadening the base of public discussions. As for an election for members of Parliament, a specific office should be formed to investigate the question before any decision should be made on it.

Continued Antigovernment Pressure, 1880-81

As if to underline his proposal that a decision be postponed on the question of an elective parliament, Home Minister Itō sponsored a new law which restricted political activity. This new edict of 1880, entitled "A Law of Public Meetings," made the usual forms of political activity illegal. Henceforth, all political meetings must be approved by the police, including the speakers, their topics, and the membership and governing rules of the body sponsoring such a meeting. The police had additional authority to disband a meeting if the speaker wandered from the approved subject or if the meeting were deemed prejudicial to public tranquillity.

Another move of the oligarchs was aimed directly at reducing participation in politics by those persons who had been the most active supporters of the movement for people's rights. An Imperial decree forbade members of the armed services, and teachers and students in both government and private schools and universities, from attending political meetings. Finally, political associations were prohibited from advertising their meetings, soliciting membership, or combining or communicating with similar societies. In other words, persons who wished to lecture on subjects such as democratic political institutions, or the right of the people to be represented in the government, and any group which wished to discuss these questions were carrying on activities branded as subversive by the government.

Despite these stringent public safety and public assembly laws, political activity advocating people's rights not only survived but increased. As will be discussed in the next chapter, one of the reasons for this growth was the close alliance of some of the organizers of the first political party and the landowner-entrepreneur group. (See Chapter 7.) Another reason was the decision of Itagaki and his followers to formalize their group into a political party. In December, 1880, they published their projected covenant for the *Jiyūtō* or Liberal party. It promised to work for the extension of civil rights, the advancement and prosperity of the nation, and for constitutional government. It also called for the publication of newspapers to expand the beliefs in liberty and to cultivate public opinion on political issues. Despite the new laws of 1880 which made such activity illegal, it advocated public lectures and a membership drive. After the platform was published, however, no immediate steps were taken to organize the party formally. This move awaited the crisis within the government created by Ōkuma's challenges of the oligarchs in 1881.

From a political point of view, therefore, the oligarchs were still faced in 1880, as they had been faced in 1873, with an irritating and embarrassing, if not formidable, opposition. They had been forced to make some concessions to the advocates of greater rights for the people, but had not capitulated on any of the vital issues. If the conservative recommendations, which the Councilors had already forwarded to the throne, could be incorporated eventually into a new, national, governmental structure, they would have no objections to such a move. On the other hand, they were in no hurry for such a change and were content with conditions as they existed.

There was one flaw in this situation. Ōkuma Shigenobu had not yet expressed his views on the question of a parliament and had shown a tendency to favor the opinion of the progressives such as Itagaki, Kataoka, and Fukuzawa. Ōkuma was an outsider; he was from Hizen rather than from Satsuma and Chōshū. Finally, he was becoming one of the strongest men of the government. A showdown between Ōkuma and the other Councilors seemed inevitable but no one was aware of the acuteness of this major political crisis. The final act in the Meiji Restoration had yet to be enacted.

Notes

1. G. B. Sansom, *The Western World and Japan* (New York: Alfred A. Knopf, Inc., 1950), p. 343.

2. Ōkubo, who also was one of the new Councilors, was transferred in 1874 to be head of the powerful, recently created Ministry of Home Affairs. In this post, he was in charge of the internal security of the country. Ōkuma became the new Minister of Finance in 1873. Yamagata, as Councilor and Minister of War, was inextricably involved in trying to make universal conscription operative.

3. Itagaki Taisuke (1837-1919) of Tosa was one of the chief signers of this memorial. He had served creditably in the campaign against the Shogun's forces at the time of the Restoration of Emperor Meiji. He was appointed Councilor in 1869. He supported the general concept of the separation of powers. In 1874 he returned to his native province of Tosa where he established the *Risshisha,* a political club. For the text of the memorial see W. W. McLaren, "Japanese Government Documents," *Transactions of the Asiatic Society of Japan,* vol. 42, p. 426 ff.

4. For example, Katō's *Shinsei Taii* (A General Outline of True Government) which appeared in 1870, was a precursor of later works by authors who demanded democratic reforms in the government. In 1875, his *Kokutai Shinron* (A Basic Treatise on National Polity) was critical of the traditional ideas of the Japanese state. He accused the leaders of believing that the Emperor is sublime and that the people are base. He argued that the nationalist scholars did violence to the truth and were despicable because they advocated complete obedience to Imperial commands without question. Shortly thereafter he recanted and withdrew the book from circulation. His later writings were conservative.

5. For Yanaibara's views see Yanaibara Tadaō (ed.), *Gendai Nihon Shōshi* (Tokyo: Misuzu-shobo, 1952), I, p. 14 *et seq.* The text of Itagaki's and his colleague's reply to Katō is in *Japanese Government Documents, op. cit.,* p. 440 *et seq.*

6. Although I have referred to Saigō as a rebel and to his campaign as a rebellion, the reader should not infer that he has been treated in Japanese history as a traitor. On the contrary, because he revolted in the name of the Emperor to protect him from evil influences, he was admired by many of his contemporaries and he has become a great national hero and a favorite subject for novels, plays, and stories of knightly valor. Even a post-World War II theater audience will weep over a classical play in which he is the hero.

7. Fukuzawa Yukichi (1835-1901) was born into a modest samurai family and

learned from an early age a high sense of duty and loyalty, self-control and contempt for worldly goods. His father was in charge of the clan's treasury in Ōsaka but performed his duties out of a sense of loyalty rather than of fondness for business matters. In 1854 when Perry forced the American Treaty on the Shogun, Yukichi was sent to Nagasaki to learn Dutch and Western style gunnery. This experience, together with his assignment to teach Dutch to his clansmen, planted seeds of disbelief in his own mind in the old traditions and myths of Japan. As he was of a rebellious nature, he resented a society which required that an ambitious youth like himself conform to certain specified patterns. In 1861, he accompanied an official mission of the Shogun to England. He returned home at a time when antiforeign feeling was at its height. In fact, it had caused all of the foreign representatives, except Townsend Harris, to leave Tokyo. Despite these circumstances, he gave glowing accounts of British wealth and prosperity. He argued that Japan, an island country, might have much to learn from England. He never filled a post in the government, but devoted his energies to teaching and writing on society and politics. In this way he became one of the most effective interpreters of foreign institutions to his fellow countrymen. He founded his own school in Edo in 1865 which developed into Keio University, one of Japan's outstanding private universities. The emblem of the school of two crossed pens, which is still worn by its students, was chosen because of his firm belief that the pen was mightier than the sword. His autobiography has been translated by his grandson, Kiyooka Eichi. Miss Carman Blacker, a Scarborough Fellow, has been in Japan recently making an exhaustive study of Fukuzawa and his writings. When completed, it should be a valuable contribution to our knowledge of the Restoration Period. For an excellent survey of Fukuzawa and his writings, see Sansom, *The Western World and Japan,* pp. 426-51.

8. For a complete translation of this memorial see *Japanese Government Documents, op. cit.,* pp. 452-79. It is purported to have been written by Ueki Enori (1854-92), one of the more radical members of the Tosa group. Called Itagaki's "brain trust" by some, Ueki took a strong position in defense of freedom of speech and thought and insisted that the people be informed of the actions of officials in regard to public affairs. On the other hand, like his contemporaries, his "liberalism" was tempered with conservatism. He favored a constitutional monarchy with the state organized on a feudal basis. Members of his own class, the warriors, should be the backbone of the electorate and should constitute the political elite. Kataoka had been selected in 1871 as one of two representatives from Tosa to study abroad. When he returned from Europe, he became an official in the Navy Department. He resigned with Itagaki over the Korean issue in 1873. He was arrested later for his political indiscretions but finally was elected to Parliament.

9. Ōtsu Jun'ichirō, *Dai Nihon Kensei Shi* (10 vols.; Tokyo: Hobun-kan, 1927-28), II, p. 366.

10. Contrast this procedure with that of John Jay, James Madison and Alexander Hamilton who in 1787-88 pleaded through their papers in the *Federalist* with the people of New York to adopt the American Constitution. The policy in Japan was to keep the people from thinking on basic issues, rather than giving them the facts and then letting them decide.

11. For the complete text of Yamagata's views see Yamagata Aritomo, *Koshaku Yamagata Den* (Tokyo: Yamagata Aritomo Kō Kinen Jigyō-kai, 1933), II, p. 842 *et seq*. For the opinions of Itō, Yamada, Inouye, and other Councilors, see Ōtsu, *op. cit.,* II, p. 370 *et seq.*

7

THE ECONOMIC AND POLITICAL BASIS FOR THE VICTORY OF CONSERVATISM IN 1881

In the years immediately following the crisis over Korea in 1873, events such as the Saigō Rebellion of 1877 and the demands of the people's rights movement compelled the oligarchs to concentrate on the solution of political problems. Nevertheless, many of the practical difficulties which had absorbed the time and energy of the chief government officials in the period prior to 1873 (see Chapter 5), had not been resolved. In fact, continued industrialization and increased economic and military power were prerequisites for the creation of conditions under which a constitutional monarchy could be established. In other words, the political power and the economic strength of the Imperial government were interdependent and the oligarchs could not have acted in one field without support from the other. Hence they devoted much time and energy to the final solution of many of these practical problems.

What, then, were the most significant developments, from the formal abolition of feudalism in 1873 to the challenge of Ōkuma in 1881, which gave the leaders in the government additional strength to combat this serious threat to their authority from within their own ranks? What was the position of the government in relation to the nation's industrialization? What role did private capital play in Japan's modernization? What specific measures did the oligarchs take to assure victory for their political and economic policies?

Government Sponsorship of Industry

The economic program during the first few years of the Meiji Restoration might be characterized as one of improvisation. It was an apprenticeship for acquiring technical skills and for creating what the young oligarchs believed to be the minimum economic essentials for a modern state: an infant Navy, a conscript Army, the beginnings of a system of transportation and communication, a universal tax in money, and a single currency. After 1873, the national government continued to encourage and control industry so that the country could guarantee its military and economic, as well as its political, independence. There developed a new tendency, however, to concentrate on stimulating new industrial and commercial activity, especially in the field of consumers' goods. After his return from Europe in 1873, Minister of Home Affairs Ōkubo Toshimichi expressed the government's position as follows:

> The wealth of the country is dependent on the quantity of goods produced. . . . The people's industries have not had sufficient encouragement from the government as they have just begun to develop. Skill and knowledge must be given to the people and complete regulations established. The government and officials all must exert every effort to encourage industry and to increase production.[1]

To give substance to his words, he proceeded to establish a special division of industrial and agricultural development within his Ministry. One of its first tasks was to try to force foreign trade into the hands of Japanese traders. Ever since Japan was opened to the Occident, foreign traders and foreign commercial houses had monopolized foreign trade in the open ports. As late as 1877, foreigners handled 94 per cent of the export and 97 per cent of the import trade. Japanese merchants had been weak in two respects: they had only limited capital funds available for foreign trade and were ignorant of international trading practices. To circumvent these obstacles, Ōkubo and his colleagues concentrated on developing native skills, raising the quality of goods, and educating foreigners about Japanese products. To achieve these objectives great importance was given to competitive industrial exhibits at home and to international expositions abroad.

Elaborate preparations were made for representation at the Vienna Exposition of 1873. Since it was Japan's first participation in that type of activity, two years were spent on the plans. A special office was established with Ōkuma as director for which 600,000 yen was appropriated. The general purpose of the program was to advertise Japanese goods abroad and to transplant to Japan as many European production methods as possible. Seventy government officials were sent to the Exposition to assist in exhibiting Japanese products which might compete in the world markets. They had an additional assignment following the close of the Exposition. Under the general direction of a European adviser, they traveled throughout Europe to study modern methods of manufacturing and marketing.

In order to capitalize on any foreign interest in Japanese products that might have been stimulated, consulates were formed wherever possible with capable persons in charge. For example, the Finance and Home Ministries each sent a representative to England and to America to "distribute samples of Japanese products, investigate conditions of industry in those countries, and to make secret investigations of the advantages and disadvantages of Japanese products in the markets of those countries."[2] Special reports were soon sent home by the new consular officers and trade agents on subjects such as the market for silk-egg sheets in Italy, porcelain in San Francisco, flannel in Shanghai, and black tea in India. The practical results of some of these reports were soon apparent. In 1875 Ōkubo announced that the policy henceforth would be to encourage exports through Japanese hands. A Tea Examination Bureau was established and the first tea was exported to the United States in October, 1875, and tea soon grew to be a large trade item. Matches were sent on consignment to special offices in China.

In fact, attempts were made to enter a field in which foreigners had practically a monopoly, namely, the sale of raw silk. The Occidental traders had been isolated in special compounds in each of the treaty ports where they lived a life apart from the country around them. Because of the extraterritoriality provisions in the treaties, they were beyond the reach of the Japanese law. For many years they had their own police, post offices, and currency, which gave them a feeling of superiority over the "natives." Naturally, their arrogant and superior attitude was carried over into any business dealings which they had with the Japanese. On many occasions the foreign merchants arbitrarily disregarded price agreements previously reached between themselves and Japanese sellers. They often refused to countenance legitimate Japanese demands for a higher price of raw silk and paid a lower price of their own choice.

Every effort was made by government officials, such as Ōkubo, to develop direct Japanese shipments of silk abroad to circumvent the necessity of dealing with the unprincipled Westerners. These silk shipments began in 1876 and slowly increased in volume. Four years later, the Yokohama silk merchants formed their own association and the government lent one million yen without interest to the Japanese wholesalers to protect their profits and to give them an advantage over the foreigners. At the same time (1880), the Yokohama Specie Bank was organized to have charge of foreign bills of exchange and to assist the Japanese with their foreign trade transactions.

Faced with these drastic developments, the foreign merchants became more tractable and amenable. They began to abide by their agreements lest they be forced out of business prematurely. As a result of the government's conscious effort to increase foreign trade, total trade rose 50 per cent from approximately 40 million yen in 1871 to 62 million yen in 1881. On the other hand, despite these efforts and except for 1868 and 1876 when silkworms were destroyed by disease in Europe which resulted in heavy exports of silkworm eggs, Japan had a continued unfavorable trade balance so that Ōkubo and his colleagues were not able to reduce the foreign debt by the profits in foreign trade. (See page 275.)

Shipping is another branch of Japan's economic program which clearly illustrates the struggle to break down a foreign monopoly through active support by the government. Special commercial offices and exchange companies had been established immediately after the Restoration to stimulate trade. They were soon found to be ineffectual against competition from such well-established companies as the American Pacific Steamship Company and the British P. & O. Company. Consequently, the government ordered the wealthy Mitsui family to form a new company. Despite public loans to the amount of 850,000 yen granted at favorable terms this company was eventually dissolved. The eighteen ships which it had operated, together with thirteen ships which the government had purchased in 1874 for the Formosan expedition, were all transferred to the Iwasaki-owned Mitsubishi Steamship Company. Home Minister Ōkubo extended his policy of protectionism still further by promising the new company an annual subsidy of 310,000 yen.

Obviously private foreign lines could not compete with this type of direct subsidy. Consequently, the American Pacific Steamship Company gave up. It sold to the new Japanese company three of its ships, which it used in the Yokohama-Kōbe-Nagasaki-Shanghai trade, and its warehouses in Kōbe and Shanghai. An additional government grant was given the Mitsubishi Company to enable it to compete successfully with the British P. & O. Company for the trade between Shanghai and Yokohama.

The Japanese government further augmented the resources of the Mitsubishi Steamship Company during the Satsuma Rebellion of 1877. Funds totaling 700,000 yen and nine ships were given to it to meet the needs for army transports to suppress the uprising. After the rebels were pacified, the Mitsubishi interests kept the ships. When two rival Japanese companies developed, the government offered a new subsidy in 1885 to an amalgamated company which was to be known as the Nippon Yūsen Kaisha (Japan Mail Line). Thanks to the close interrelationship of government and private enterprise and the active support of men like Ōkubo, within sixteen years Japan had absorbed a large part of its ever expanding trade into its own hands. In fact, it had forced its foreign rivals out of business and finally obtained another sovereign right, namely, a monopoly of its intercoastal trade.

Another general feature of Japan's rapid industrialization was the formation of model factories or other enterprises, which, it was hoped, would serve as examples and incentives to private industrialists to form their own companies. One of the most significant of these was the Sapporo Machine Shop in Hokkaidō which was developed as part of the general colonization program for that region. Steam-powered machines were imported from the United States. Forges and steam-driven sawmills and machines for manufacturing water wheels were all part of the project. In fact, Hokkaidō became the center for the manufacture of machinery, implements, sawmills, and wheat mills.[3]

In 1874, the second year Itō was chief, the Ministry of Industry constructed at government expense an equally important factory at Akabane, then a suburb of Tokyo. It was originally built on British models to encourage the production of machines and other iron products. It was particularly proud of its smelting plant and the forty-horsepower steam-driven machinery. Like many of the other machine shops and heavy industries, it was later absorbed by the military, being transferred to the jurisdiction of the Navy Department in 1883.

Along with this emphasis of the government on heavy industry and on those features of Japan's economy which would strengthen the country militarily, there was also a conscious attempt made to encourage the manufacture of consumers' goods. In some areas, such as Kagoshima in Satsuma, where limited industrialization had taken place before the Restoration, progress had already been made in cotton spinning. The first modern type factory in Japan had been established there in 1867, and four years later when Brunton visited the city, he noted a huge cotton factory which was seemingly in perfect order and operating at full capacity. The machinery had been imported from Oldham, England, through Glover & Company.

The successful operation of large spinning mills depended, however, both on the development of a uniform thread and on the training of skilled operators. Consequently, a large thread factory, under foreign direction, was established at Tomioka in 1870 by Shibusawa Eiichi, one of the outstanding private industrialists of the period.[4] Its design, materials, machines, and tools all came from France. It was completed two years later at a cost of over a quarter of a million yen and soon became the center both for the production of uniform thread and also for the training of girls in spinning skills. Because of the contribution it made to the spinning industry, Shibusawa and the other founders of the company, were reimbursed for 55 per cent of the cost of building the plant. Most of the other spinning plants, however, followed the customary pattern of direct government sponsorship and construction with machines imported from England, France, or Italy; operation for a limited period by the government; and final sale to private purchasers at a ridiculously low price. Such a procedure was followed for the spinning plants at Nagoya and Hiroshima and numerous other western cities and for the waste-silk plant in Shimmachi.

Financial reforms were also introduced to keep pace with the industrial advance. Ōkuma had been appointed Finance Minister in 1873 and re-

Courtesy of Chūō Suraido Co.

Tokyo's Ginza in an Early Stage of Westernization

Courtesy of East-West

THE NEW EDUCATION AND OLD METHODS OF CALCULATION

mained in that post until 1880. New convertible notes had been issued in 1873 to help meet the expense of commuting the rice incomes of the warriors. National banks had been organized to meet the needs of the country for currency, but the limitations placed upon them made them of questionable value. Furthermore, an unusually heavy drain on the gold reserve had reduced the value of the new government notes, which shortly had to be turned into the banks for conversion. During the period of 1875-76, therefore, the circulation of money practically stopped. New gold and silver coins were stamped and inconvertible notes were issued. In fact, the government was forced to meet the extra expenses arising from the Satsuma Rebellion by borrowing 15 million yen from the National Bank and by issuing 27 million yen in paper currency. This act brought the total paper money in circulation up to a total of 107 million yen. As a contemporary popular saying had it, "The Meiji Government ruled the Empire by cutting paper."

The steady increase in paper money continued until Matsukata Masayoshi (1835-1924) became Finance Minister in 1881 and a policy of currency reduction was inaugurated.[5] (See page 153.) Despite the popular condemnation of public finances and a rapid rise in the price of rice from 4.60 yen in 1877 to 8.79 yen in 1879 and to 12.11 yen in 1880, the financial situation was kept sufficiently under control to avoid the need for further foreign loans. Notwithstanding the multifarious programs undertaken by the government, national expenditures were kept within the limits of receipts and foreign indebtedness was at a minimum. By 1881 a policy of retrenchment began simultaneously with a search for an appropriate constitution.

Another aspect of this period which had an adverse effect both on the people in general and on the government officials was the heavy reliance on foreign experts. This fact is substantiated by the official history of the Ministry of Industry which frankly admitted that foreigners, mostly British, had in reality brought about a revolution in Japanese industry and were largely responsible for increased scientific knowledge. On the other hand, the lighthouse adviser, Brunton, noted on the basis of his own experience, that after the failure of the Iwakura Mission to obtain revisions of the treaties in 1873, his Japanese superiors were less cooperative and his colleagues less willing to take his advice. He observed an increasing desire to be rid of the foreigners as quickly as possible.

On November 15, 1879, the Council of State made an important policy decision on this problem. It specifically requested the Ministry of Public Works to reduce its expenses by asking the foreigners to resign as soon as possible. At that date, it employed 130 foreigners whose salaries totaled 342,000 yen, nearly three-fifths of the fixed expenses of the whole Ministry.

Whenever possible, the foreign experts were to be replaced by Japanese graduates of the newly formed technical schools.[6] The period of apprenticeship was fast drawing to a close.

Effect of Industrialization on Political Rivalries

The industrial capital structure, built under state auspices, had a direct bearing on the political structure of the country. In the first place, this program of government sponsorship of trade and industry had caused a close alliance between the government and the financial and industrial leaders. With the exception of a few families, such as the Mitsui family, which had acquired its wealth in the seventeenth century, the new capitalists had not been wealthy before the Restoration. They were not, as one might expect, the direct descendants of the largest feudal barons. Rather, they came largely from the same group which produced the leaders in government, namely, the middle-class warriors. They profited from a close political and economic alliance with those in power. In fact, many of the richest industrialists of the Meiji period became officials within the government or were appointed to the peerage.

Furthermore, there had not been a wealthy, effective group of merchants, financiers, or industrialists who could afford to be exponents of a European style liberal state. Such wealth as existed was dependent on the continuance of both the new economic and political structure. The new capitalists and the new government found themselves in a mutually beneficial alliance; neither desired to challenge the other and both profited from this alliance.

At the same time, this government sponsorship of industrialization resulted in two other developments which determined the social composition of the groups that opposed the government and that simultaneously supported greater rights for the people. If this alliance of oligarchs and *nouveaux riches* was to continue to their mutual profit, new industries must be protected. Such protection would normally come about through high tariffs. Because of Japan's treaties with the foreign powers, however, Japan did not have tariff autonomy. Hence, the only remaining way to protect industry was by a discriminatory tax policy.

It was to be expected that the oligarchs would not tax the infant industries which they had created. Land had traditionally been the chief source of revenue for the government and logic dictated that it should continue to be so. Consequently, land taxes continued to comprise the greatest source of income. For example, from 1875 to 1879, taxes from land equaled 80.5 per cent of the total, and from 1880 to 1884 amounted to 65.5 per cent. Furthermore, industrialization led to urbanization, which created greater interest in the cities with a proportionate neglect of rural areas. As spinning mills developed and sugar refineries were built, the farmers found that their home industries in spinning and refining could not compete with the machines. No attempt was made to recompense them nor was any program conceived to rehabilitate them.

On the contrary, in 1881 just prior to the time that Ōkuma presented his first memorial, the new Finance Minister, Matsukata, inaugurated a retrenchment policy. Rice prices fell so that the landowner, the owner-cultivator, the part-tenant, and tenant all suffered. Many of the small landowners were also entrepreneurs who manufactured products such as rice wine, bean paste, and soy sauce. Hence their businesses were likewise adversely affected by the new financial measures. This large group of discontented people naturally blamed the government for their plight. Consequently, they readily supported persons such as Itagaki and his colleagues, and later Ōkuma, who were fighting the oligarchs.

At the same time, the leaders of the "liberal movement" actively sought the support of the discontented landlord-entrepreneurs and occasionally organized them against the government. For example, in 1880 when the government proposed a special yeast tax to defray the cost of a projected naval expansion program, a Council of Rice Wine Brewers was formed to oppose the tax. Ueki Enori, who allegedly had drafted the famous memorial of 1877, was one of the founders and most active members of this council. He was one of two representatives who presented a formal protest to the government against its interference in private enterprise and against the tax. When he was arrested, he called a meeting of the Brewer's Council in Ōsaka only to have it banned by the authorities.

Thus by the beginning of 1881, political and economic policies of the oligarchs had produced three groups with a single common interest. Two of these groups, the advocates of greater rights for the people and the entrepreneurs-landowners were beginning to work together. The third group was composed of past and present members of the government who were not members of the Satchō clique but who came from other clans. All three groups were united through their hatred of the clique of former Satchō warriors who held the key posts in the government.

Ōkuma Shigenobu was the outstanding member of this last group. At this time, even though he had come from the province of Hizen, he was the senior member of the Council of State and one of the strongest figures in the government. Furthermore, he was known to be opposed to the views of all the other Councilors on the question of the early formation of a representative and elected national assembly. There was also a possibility, therefore, that Ōkuma could rally around him all these anti-government forces and thus become undisputed leader of Japan.

Ōkuma Defies the Conservatives, 1881

Without doubt, in the early months of 1881, this possibility of a united front was in Ōkuma's mind as he planned his strategy against his colleagues on the Council. Since he was the only Councilor to oppose the conservative views of the oligarchs, he was reluctant to state his position in an official memorial. On the other hand, Itō and the other conservatives were confident that they could isolate Ōkuma sufficiently to prevent him from causing too much trouble. Since all of the other Councilors had expressed their opinions, they insisted that Ōkuma could no longer remain silent. He finally stated his position in March, 1881, in a statement which was drafted by one of his young disciples and which had far greater repercussions than the government had anticipated.

This document, which was submitted directly to the Emperor, was a challenge to Ōkuma's colleagues on the Council. He prefaced his memorial with an explanation of the operation of a parliamentary form of government. Next he outlined six steps which he believed to be prerequisites for the creation of such a government. He proposed that, after the question of membership for Parliament was settled, a definite date should be set for its opening and that this date should be publicly announced. To assure conformity of the government's policy with the will of the people, the leader of the majority party in Parliament should become Premier and should resign when he lost the confidence of the legislature. As in the British system, provisions should also be made for separate parliamentary secretaries and civil servants who would not be affected by the rise and fall of cabinets and who would afford a continuity of personnel.

Yet this was the extent of his liberalism. He could not bring himself to the point of trusting the majority. A product of his times, his views were almost as conservative as his colleagues on the question of how to draft the constitution. He believed that it should be framed by Imperial command and should not be forged from heated debate in a constituent assembly or a constitutional convention.

But the point in his memorial which was most embarrassing to the oligarchs concerned the date for the opening of Parliament. Itō and the others had urged postponement of such a move to avoid any threat to their power or to the prerogatives of the Emperor. On the other hand, the public was increasing its demands for the early formation of an elective body. (See page 109.) Ōkuma capitalized on this movement and argued that the calling of a national assembly was an urgent matter. In fact, he insisted that the form of the new national government should be decided within the year (1881), that the plan of such a government should be announced the next year, that an election should be held in 1883, and that Parliament should be called immediately thereafter.[7]

The impact of Ōkuma's demands on the nation was tremendous, but in itself was not enough to force a showdown between the conservative oligarchs and the progressives. It set off a chain reaction, however, which led to Ōkuma's challenge of the economic policy of the government in the fall of 1881. These two moves together forced a crystallization of thought among the conservatives and acted as a catalyst for the precipitate steps taken by them against Ōkuma. In the end, this struggle resulted in the concentration of autocratic control in the hands of the Emperor's advisers and spelled a significant defeat for the supporters of a representative government. This defeat had both an immediate and lasting effect. The immediate result was that the oligarchs allowed the formation of a constitutional monarchy with only limited powers granted to the people. Control was concentrated in the hands of the chief ministers. The lasting effect, as will be evident from subsequent accounts of the futile efforts of the liberal forces to direct Japan's policies prior to World War II, was to stifle the growth of democracy.

Obviously, Ōkuma's views, as expressed in his memorial in March, 1881, were not acceptable to such conservative Councilors as Iwakura and Itō. In fact, Iwakura had told Ōkuma personally that his request for an election the next year was ridiculous since it would be impossible to make the necessary preparations in time. When Itō saw the memorial—whether he was officially given a copy or took one surreptitiously from the files is an open question—he was enraged that Ōkuma should make such sweeping demands.

There had been disagreements before among the chief advisers of the Emperor, but never of such a deep-seated nature. Perhaps Itō foresaw that this rift over policy would evolve rapidly into a struggle for power between the conservatives and the "liberals." The Satchō oligarchs were fighting for a form of constitutional government which would protect the interests of their sovereign and themselves. Ōkuma was fighting for continued favor with the Emperor and for a constitutional monarchy which would give the people at least a minimum of rights.

In July, 1881, Ōkuma challenged the government's economic policy. He charged that his colleagues were aiding, abetting, and profiting from the proposed sale of the Hokkaidō Colonization Office. By his cry of scandal, he made the question of the disposition of government-owned industries a vital issue in the national debate on people's rights and constitutional government. In reality, by this act he forced a showdown on the question of who was the strongest man in the government. His appeal to the people for support made the split between himself and the Itō-Iwakura-Yamagata clique irreparable.

The Hokkaidō Scandal

To understand the significance of Ōkuma's move, it is necessary to revert temporarily to the importance of Hokkaidō to the nation as a whole and to the program of liquidation of government-sponsored industries. At the beginning of the Meiji Restoration in 1868, the northern island of Hokkaidō was the one area in Japan which was not heavily populated nor developed. Colonization had been retarded because of its inaccessibility, its high mountains and heavy forests, and its cold climate. Geological surveys had revealed that it was one of the richest regions of natural resources throughout Japan and that it had great potential industrial possibilities. To capitalize on these potentialities, the government formed the Hokkaidō Colonization Office in 1869 and sponsored an energetic colonization and development program. Model factories and mines, breweries, machine shops, and sawmills were built with government funds. In fact, during the first eleven years of its existence, over 14 million yen had been invested by the Colonization Office.

The exploitation of this northern frontier had largely been the result of the energy and vision of Kuroda Kiyotaka, a clansman from Satsuma.[8] After his appointment in 1869 as Vice-Commissioner of Colonization, he visited the United States and solicited the technical assistance of leading American scientists and educators. Some of the most prominent of these included General Horace Capron, United States Commissioner of Agriculture, and Dr. William Clark, President of Massachusetts Agricultural College. These men, together with approximately seventy other foreign advisers and experts, developed the pattern which enabled Hokkaidō to become an important asset to the empire, as well as a laboratory for experiments in methods of colonization to be used later in Korea and Formosa.

Kuroda was also keenly aware of Hokkaidō's strategic importance. In this connection, he gave priority to the expansion of strategic industries. Simultaneously, colonists were transported at government expense and were formed into militia. This militia, which was organized as a defensive force against Russia, offered some protection but was not sufficient to prevent an attack from the north. To lessen the increasing tension between Japan and Russia, Kuroda urged abandonment of claims to Sakhalien and concentration on strengthening Hokkaidō. This policy led to the settlement with Russia in 1875 of Japan's northern boundary. The latter gave up all claims to Sakhalien in exchange for full control over all the Kurile Islands. (See Chapter 9.)

As in other parts of the nation, the successful operation and expansion of many of the industries started by the Colonization Office corresponded with the general shift in government policy from direct to indirect control and operation of nonstrategic industries, most of which no longer needed direct government subsidies for technical development, although many were operating at a loss. If the nonstrategic industries could be sold to private industrialists, they would no longer be a burden on the financial and technical resources of the state. Furthermore, the state then became free to devote its efforts toward enlarging the Army and Navy and developing the strategic industries necessary to support them.

Heretofore, no clear-cut policy had been developed for disposing of a particular industrial plant or enterprise. In some cases, particularly among the strategic industries, the government retained control and ownership. In others, the factory or plant was sold to the original promoter at a nominal price. In still others, the industrialist who had built the factory himself was given a subsidy to encourage expansion. In all cases, there was a close relationship between key figures in the government and the new industrialists.

In view of the criticism which was growing against this apparent collusion between industry and government and the losses which the latter was sustaining, a new policy was formulated. In November, 1880, a Law on the Sale of Factories (*Kōjō Haraisage Gaisoku*) was promulgated. The government claimed that since the factories which were established for encouraging industrial development had become prosperous, they would be turned over to private ownership. It looked forward, however, to selling unprofitable enterprises at a low price.

The law further specified the steps to be taken by anyone who wished to purchase such industries. In all cases, it was expected that the sale would be at a low price to encourage the growth of private enterprise. Such a general program released the government of responsibilities that it no longer wished to carry. It also gave undeniable advantages to private enterprise and permitted questionable deals between businessmen and key officials in the Ministry of Industry, the Home Ministry, or other branches of the government responsible for the program.

Since the ten-year, government-sponsored program for Hokkaidō expired in 1881, the future of the Colonization Office had to be settled. A group of Ōsaka merchants and some of the members of the Hokkaidō Colonization Office saw a rare chance to profit from the application of this law to the government projects under that office. In July, 1881, they set up a company in Ōsaka to purchase the real estate, distilleries, factories, mines, ships, shipyards, and other tangible assets of the Colonization Office. Their plan provided for the payment of a total of 300,000 yen for property whose actual value was probably seventy times that amount or 21,000,000 yen. It was also proposed that the new company purchase the property in thirty yearly installments and that no interest be charged on the unpaid balance. Thus the entire investment could be purchased for a down payment of 10,000 yen or 1/2000 of its estimated cost. This scheme was presented to Kuroda who approved it and forwarded it to the Council of State with a recommendation that it be accepted.

The question of whether to sell the Hokkaidō property immediately became a major political issue both within the Council of State and among the people at large. In June the Emperor had rejected outright Ōkuma's proposals for a constitution and for the formation of an elected assembly within a year. Itō and other members of the Council, who had been enraged at Ōkuma for daring to present views which differed from theirs, had supported this rejection. They saw in the move an attempt to oust them from leadership in the government. By midsummer, both sides were looking for an opportunity to challenge and embarrass the other.

Ōkuma seized upon the Hokkaidō scheme, therefore, as an opportunity to increase his strength. He denounced it for what it obviously was—a colossal and brazen attempt to make enormous profits at the expense of the taxpayer. Before the Council had acted on the proposal, the *Tokyo-Yokohama Mainichi* (newspaper) learned of the impending sale and denounced it vehemently in an editorial. Many other papers echoed this opinion. Mass meetings sprang up at which the clan bureaucrats were severely criticized and Ōkuma's position was eulogized.

In the meantime, Kuroda was anxious to have the plan for the liquidation of the government's interests in Hokkaidō approved before popular opposition became too strong. It is reported that he threatened Sanjō, President of the Council, and demanded that the Emperor's approval of the project be obtained. In any case, Imperial assent to the sale at the ridiculously low price was obtained on August 1, 1881. At this juncture, Ōkuma found himself supported by such important figures in the government as the Minister of Finance Sano and Vice-President of the Council Sasaki. Many of the followers of Itagaki and persons who were shortly to organize the Liberal party (*Jiyūtō*) were eager to join the chorus of criticism against Kuroda, his plan, and his fellow clansmen and supporters from Chōshū.

The Conservatives Triumph in 1881

In view of the power which the conservatives had already wielded in the government, it was unlikely that they would let this threat to their power and authority pass unchallenged. In fact, they were biding their time and knew that time was on their side. For several weeks, the Emperor had planned a tour of inspection to the north and northwest. It was the fifth of such carefully planned trips throughout the Empire and the first to the interior of Hokkaidō. The Imperial party, which included Ōkuma, departed from Tokyo on July 30 and did not return until October 11, 1881. In this interval, the oligarchs who remained behind in Tokyo, planned their strategy carefully and well on three vital, interconnected problems. These were (1) the basic principles for the Constitution, (2) the future of the Hokkaidō Colonization Office, and (3) the disposition to be made of Ōkuma. In reference to the all-important question of the Constitution, Ōkuma's challenge for an immediate election had been rejected but no substitute proposal had been offered.

Specific ideas were taking shape, however, in the minds of several of the key officials. Minister of the Right Iwakura, who had always been close to the Emperor, was taken ill early in the summer. Before his departure for a rest cure on July 6, 1881, he wrote a memorial to Prince Arisugawa on constitutional government and the methods which should be followed in drafting a constitution. Since his views on the procedures and on the principles which should be adopted were largely followed in the next few years, the importance of his memorial is obvious. He advocated:

1. Public announcement of the formation of a constitution-investigation commission.
2. Establishment of a drafting office within the palace under the direction of a Minister, secret preparation of the draft, and its presentation to the Council for discussion.
3. The secret preparation by three or four ministers of the draft constitution and the accompanying Imperial proclamation.[9]

In this same memorandum, Iwakura was equally explicit on the basic principles for a constitution. He argued that the Emperor should be the source and authority for all steps connected with drafting a constitution. Furthermore, procedures should be followed which permitted the gradual adoption of constitutional government. Some matters, such as the rules for succession of the Emperor, did not properly belong in the constitution. Any such basic document should permit the Emperor to retain the following powers: supreme command of the Army and Navy; the right to declare war, make peace, and conclude treaties with foreign powers; supervision of the coinage; conferring of honors; granting of an armistice; and authority to close, prorogue, dissolve, or open the Diet. He should also be given the right personally to appoint or dismiss the highest officials in the government.

Iwakura also recommended certain features for the Cabinet and Parliament which were designed to increase the power of the former and reduce the strength of the people's elected representatives in the latter. For example, he suggested that Cabinet members did not necessarily have to be members of Parliament. The various Ministers of State should be individually responsible for their action to the Emperor in contrast to the accepted concept in most constitutional monarchies of collective responsibility of the Cabinet. The Imperial Diet should be bicameral; the Senate, or upper house, to be composed of Imperial appointees or persons elected by the peerage.

According to Iwakura, the People's Elected Assembly (*Minsen In*) should have only restricted power. In the first place its members should be selected by an electorate restricted to those who were property owners. Furthermore, Parliament should not have the right to interfere with the formation of a Cabinet. His memorial contained three other suggestions, all of which appeared later in the Constitution and which strengthened the position of the Emperor and of his chosen ministers. One of these points concerned the budget and resembled a similar provision in the Prussian Constitution. He recommended that if the Cabinet and the Parliament could not agree on a budget, the budget of the previous year should automatically go into effect. Since this provision deprived Parliament of the all-important control over finances, its adoption made a nonconfidence vote meaningless. Second, Iwakura recommended that limitations should be placed on the other powers of Parliament. Third, similar restraint should control the judiciary.

He concluded his memorial by pointing to what he considered to be the weaknesses in the British parliamentary system. He noted that in England the King's wishes were subject to the majority will of Parliament and that "the Cabinet was at the mercy of the dominant party" in the House of Commons. Iwakura argued that if the British pattern were followed, the Japanese tradition of supreme power of the Imperial throne would be broken. Consequently, he urged adoption of the Prussian pattern in which Parliament was consulted, but in which the sovereign had the real authority and power.[10] Having presented his opinion, Iwakura left for the west and remained away from the capital for two months.

In the meantime, opposition among some of the other Councilors was mounting against Ōkuma. In fact, if Itō and some of his colleagues had had their wish, Ōkuma would already have been forced to resign. But such a move had been vetoed by the Emperor, and Ōkuma was permitted to go with the Imperial party on the northern tour. Shortly after he left Tokyo rumors circulated that he was in close political alliance with the educator Fukuzawa Yukichi and the financier Iwasaki Yatarō. In fact, some claimed that these two men were Ōkuma's political strategists and financial supporters and that the three of them had formed an alliance to overthrow the Satchō oligarchs, to set up their own Cabinet, and to propose a constitution acceptable to them.

These rumors were not as fantastic as they appeared. If Ōkuma had retained Imperial favor and formed a Cabinet, he would, in all probability, have supported a constitution based on a political philosophy similar to that which Fukuzawa advocated. Iwasaki, who came from Tosa, doubtless would have been delighted to see the clansmen from Chōshū and Satsuma ousted. If a new regime were established under the direction of his friends and with his financial support, he would be sure to profit from it. Moreover, there were indications of close financial ties between Ōkuma, Fukuzawa, and Iwasaki. While Ōkuma had been Minister of Finance, he had received a memorandum from Fukuzawa on the advisability of establishing a new bank. Shortly thereafter, Iwasaki helped to finance the government's new bank for foreign transactions, the Yokohama Specie Bank. Furthermore, Fukuzawa had acted as intermediary for Iwasaki when the latter purchased the Takashima Coal Mine. Finally, all three men were openly opposed to the proposed plan to sell the Hokkaidō properties for a mere pittance.

Even though Iwakura, Itō, and the other oligarchs had not yet developed a plan to oust Ōkuma, the Hokkaidō scandal continued to be increasingly embarrassing to the government leaders. In early September, 1881, Sanjō Sanetomi, acting President of the Council, became concerned over the turn of events. He wrote Iwakura, who was still away from the capital on a rest cure, that since Ōkuma had labeled the Hokkaidō sale plan as graft, the Council of State was becoming pressed to the limit. Furthermore, the ideas of Fukuzawa were being widely accepted. He pleaded that Iwakura return to the capital. This letter was followed by an urgent telegram three weeks later which brought Iwakura to the capital less than one week before the return of the Emperor and Ōkuma. The stage was rapidly set for the final scene of the drama.

Immediately upon Iwakura's return, he agreed with Sanjō that the government had made a mistake in approving the Hokkaidō deal. He realized that postponement of the sale would automatically deprive the opposition of one of its main points of grievance. Hence, he urged that Imperial sanction should be sought for a cancellation of the plan to sell the properties. Second, he recommended that a formal announcement should be made that the Emperor favored the formation of a constitutional government and that Parliament was to be opened by a specific date.

During the next few days, five of the Councilors (Sanjō, Itō, Saigō Tsugumichi, Yamada, and Iwakura) met to clarify these decisions and to put them in writing for the Emperor's approval. They also decided on procedures to be followed to oust Ōkuma. They agreed that the chief Ministers should confer with the Emperor immediately upon his return. At that time they would seek his consent to the resignation of Ōkuma and the postponement of the Hokkaidō sales. They would also present him with a draft edict for his signature, which would announce a date for the opening of Parliament and would order changes in the Council of State and the Senate.

On October 11, 1881, the Emperor and his party returned to Tokyo. That night the Councilors, except Ōkuma, who purposely was not invited, met with the Emperor. They obtained his consent to Ōkuma's resignation; they also received his approval of an innocuous announcement about the opening of Parliament. This edict, which was issued the next day, stated that a Parliament would be established, not the next year as urged by Ōkuma, but by 1890. It continued with the request that necessary preparations should be made in the meantime for formation of a constitutional government. It added that a subsequent proclamation would deal with matters such as "the limitations upon the Imperial prerogative and the constitution of parliament." Lest the opposition misinterpret what the Emperor had in mind, the edict concluded:

> We perceive the tendency of Our people is to advance too rapidly, and without that thought and consideration which alone can make progress enduring, and We warn Our subjects, high and low, to be mindful of Our will, and those who may advocate sudden and violent changes, thus disturbing the peace of Our realm, will fall under Our displeasure.[11]

Thus the die was cast on the fateful night of October 11, 1881. The counsels of the conservatives had prevailed and the Japanese were to be granted by 1890 a constitution drafted secretly by the men who had successfully ousted Ōkuma, the main threat to their position. It is quite true that this announcement of a parliamentary government stimulated the activities of the so-called political parties. It is also true that Itō, who was to be in charge of drafting the Constitution, went abroad to study foreign forms of government.

But it is equally true that Iwakura and Itō had finally realized that their concepts of a limited constitutional monarchy were threatened if Ōkuma gained control. Perhaps his criticism of the Hokkaidō proposal presaged a movement to challenge the economic policies and program of the government. It was too great a risk for the oligarchs to run. During his absence with the Emperor on his two and a half month's journey, Itō and Iwakura had worked effectively and well among their colleagues to win support for Ōkuma's ouster. They had also drafted and obtained approval of an edict on the new Constitution which permitted the acceptance of Iwakura's political philosophy. Nine years was more than enough time to win support for a form of constitutional monarchy which gave the sovereign and his ministers wide powers and limited the rights of his subjects. The conservatives had met successfully the first real challenge to the continuance of their favored position.

In conclusion, it is important to remember that many of the accounts of Japan's political history have put greater emphasis on the years *subsequent to,* rather than *prior to,* Ōkuma's ouster. Some stress the Prussian influence on Itō after 1882, others the importance of the suppressive laws of 1885 and 1888 in throttling the opposition when the Constitution was being drafted. Still others emphasize the rise of the political parties and certain "democratic features" of the Constitution.

But none of these interpretations seem to stand up against the facts. Let it be re-emphasized that Ōkuma's challenge had two phases. His first memorial in March, 1881, challenged accepted political concepts; his criticism of the Hokkaidō deal in July, 1881, was directed against basic economic policies. In reality, by his two memorials, he had raised the basic and fundamental issue of whether he or Itō was to be the leader under the new Constitution. Furthermore, the ideas expressed in Iwakura's memo of July 6, 1881; the political maneuvers during the summer and fall of that year; and the reversal of the policy on Hokkaidō all point conclusively to the fact that the key figures in the government had agreed, prior to October 11, 1881, when Ōkuma was ousted, on the type of constitution Japan should have. The important decisions were made and the stage was set for an autocratic type of government *before* rather than *after* Itō received his appointment in 1882 as Minister of Constitutional Matters. The details of content and of the drafting of the Constitution remained to be settled, but nine years was ample time for that.

Notes

1. Tsuchiya Takeo, *Zoku Nihon Keisai Shi Gaiyō* (Tokyo: Iwanami, 1941), p. 66.
2. *Ibid.,* p. 87 ff.
3. See *infra,* p. 122 ff.
4. Shibusawa Eiichi (1840-1931). Throughout his life, he vacillated between politics and positions in the government and business, but his chief interest and main energy were directed toward the formation of factories, banks, and related activities. Although theoretically opposed to the Tokugawa dictatorship, Shibusawa's personal loyalty to Tokugawa Keiki, feudal lord of Mito, compelled him to accept a position with the central government when Keiki became Shogun. As part of the retinue of the Shogun's brother to the Paris Exposition, Shibusawa was struck with the importance of businessmen in European countries. After the Emperor Meiji came to power, Shibusawa held several posts in the Imperial government, such as Chief of the Taxation Bureau and later Vice-Minister of the Treasury. He opposed large military appropriations, the expedition to Formosa, and other expansionist tendencies of the new regime. In addition to the spinning and weaving factories which he built, Shibusawa was a pioneer in banking. He organized the "First Bank" (Daiichi Ginkō) in November, 1872, under provisions of the new banking laws which he had drafted. Eight years later, his Tokyo Bankers Association developed into the Tokyo Bank. Before his retirement in 1909 he had been influential in establishing nearly 250 companies.
5. Total paper currency in circulation in 1881, when Matsukata's policy of re-

trenchment and conversion was inaugurated, equaled 170 million yen. See Asahi Shimbun, *Meiji Taishō Shi* (6 vols.; Tokyo: Asahi Shimbun, 1930-32), vol. 3, p. 38 *et seq.*

6. "Kōbushō Enkaku Hokoku," Ōuchi Hyōe and Tsuchiya Takeo, ed., *Meiji Zenki Zaisei Keizai Shiryō* (21 vols.; Tokyo: Kaiso-sha, 1931-36), XVII, p. 265 ff.

7. Ōtsu Jun'ichirō, *Dai Nihon Kensei Shi* (10 vols.; Tokyo: Hobun-kan, 1927-28), II, p. 420 ff.

8. Kuroda Kiyotaka (1840-1900) was born in Kagoshima and had fought against the British when they attacked the city in 1863. He was influential in cementing the alliance of his clan with that of Chōshū before the Restoration. He later became Prime Minister, Councilor, and finally Elder Statesman.

9. Ōtsu, *op. cit.,* II, p. 44.

10. *Ibid.,* II, pp. 411-19 for the text of Iwakura's memorial.

11. W. W. McLaren, "Japanese Government Documents," *Transactions of the Asiatic Society of Japan,* vol. 42, pp. 86-87.

8

THE ADOPTION OF THE MEIJI CONSTITUTION, 1881-1889

Although Itō and his conservative colleagues had won their battle with Ōkuma, their preferential position was not unassailable until their views and their authority had been incorporated into a new constitution. The Emperor had cautioned against precipitate action and had set nine years hence as the target date for the calling of Parliament. If the oligarchs were to capitalize on their victories thus far, they would have to be on constant guard against any significant threat to their position during the period in which the forms of a constitutional monarchy were being worked out.

By their decision to reverse themselves on the Hokkaidō deal as a result of widespread, articulate, and indignant opposition, the oligarchs had lost considerable prestige and popularity. Furthermore, there was always the possibility that an extremist might rally enough support among the general populace to resort to direct action either against the chief ministers individually or against the government as a whole. Ōkubo had been killed only a few years earlier for suppressing the Saigō Rebellion. Another fanatical nationalist might attack those who had ousted Ōkuma or any other Councilor for an alleged act of disloyalty.

Thus the history of the seven and a half years, from Ōkuma's dismissal on October 11, 1881, to the promulgation of the Constitution on February 11, 1889, is one in which the government took such action as it considered necessary to maintain control while it prepared a constitution.

New rules and regulations kept the Liberal and Progressive parties within bounds and caused their demise only a few years after they were formed. A short depression and the government failure to obtain the cancellation of "unequal clauses" in the peace treaties were prevented from creating a strong and effective antigovernment movement by strict police surveillance. The secrecy which surrounded the drafting and approval of the new Constitution by a handful of selected Ministers assured the acceptance of a document which preserved the special prerogatives of the throne and granted only a minimum of rights and privileges to the people.

No sooner had Ōkuma been eliminated than a complete reshuffle took place in the government. The first move was to order the creation of a new, semiexecutive, semilegislative body called the "*Sanji-In.*" Its functions were to assist in drafting laws and regulations forwarded from the Council of State. At the same time, it could present drafts of new laws on its own initiative for the Councils approval. The heads of the six sections of the *Sanji-In,* namely, Foreign Affairs, Home Affairs, Military Affairs, Finance, Justice, and Legislative, were to be appointed by the President from among its members. These executive departments continued to operate until the formation of a Cabinet in 1885.

As had been true of all the organs of the central government, however, the most important point was not what the avowed functions of the organs might be, but who were the key figures in these organs. Hence, it was of special significance that Itō Hirobumi was Chairman of the new *Sanji-In* which he had created. Furthermore, Terashima Munenori (1833-93) from Satsuma was the new President of the Senate, having replaced a Hizen clansman. In other words, the Satchō oligarchy had consolidated its hold over the key positions of a reorganized government.

Formation of the Liberal and Progressive Parties

These acts of the oligarchs, especially their dismissal of Ōkuma, only stimulated the leaders of the people's rights movement into action. Despite the fact that they were fighting against heavy odds, the antigovernment forces refused to be silenced. Before the end of 1881, the Liberal party (*Jiyūtō*) completed its formal inauguration and Itagaki Taisuke was elected its first president. As intimated above, it supported a form of government which would give the people a voice in public affairs. It opposed government interference in the private affairs of the individual and advocated general education so that there would be an enlightened public opinion. As Ueki Enori, one of the most articulate leaders stated, "To criticize freely the merit of legislation is necessary for the well-being of the state."

The more the leaders of the Meiji government made secret decisions, the more irate the Liberal party leaders became over the fact that they and the people were in ignorance of what transpired. Despite strenuous efforts to increase the party's numerical strength, however, it never had an important national membership. Even its advocacy of lower taxes and other policies favorable to the peasants did not materially increase its size. It was primarily a local group in Tosa and its membership was ridiculously small. Only 101 members are recorded for the early months of its existence; just prior to its dissolution in 1884 there were about 2100 members. But the influence of its leaders was far greater than that of its actual membership.

The other important antigovernment party, the Progressive party (*Kaishintō*) was founded by Ōkuma. In the previous discussion of him and his role in the struggle for a liberal constitution and for greater people's rights, he has been treated as one of the regular members of the oligarchy. Although he was the chief spokesman within the government who opposed ultraconservatism, it is not correct to classify him as a "liberal" in the same category with Itagaki, a practice followed by many of the writers on the democratic movement. It is true that in October, 1881, Ōkuma was so vitally interested in a constitution which would guarantee the rights of the people that he was willing to be broken politically for these views.

It is equally true, however, that he, like any realistic politician, hoped that his moves, plus the people's exacerbation over the Hokkaidō scandal, would increase his power and enable him to challenge Itō successfully. In other words, whereas he was interested in the movement for popular rights and constitutional government, he was a conservative-liberal on the one hand, and a politician on the other. Moreover, there are certain other factors which make Ōkuma seem of only secondary importance as a liberal. For example, he did not begin actively to organize a political party until after he was outside the government. Furthermore, his willingness in 1888 to come back into the government during the premiership of Kuroda Kiyotaka, whom he had fought on the Hokkaidō issue, indicates a vacillation and opportunism not evidenced by Itagaki.

As a politician, Ōkuma rallied around himself the urban intelligentsia, industrialists, and some conservatives outside the government. He formed his Progressive party in March, 1882, which adopted the motto of "Slow and Steady." It favored preservation of the dignity of the Imperial Household, extension of internal reforms, strengthening of local government, and the extension of the franchise. Like the Liberal party, it was small numerically but symbolized and represented the views of a much larger group. But these two parties were to go out of existence long before the Constitution was promulgated or a national election was held, so that they should not be thought of as political parties in the strict sense. They were more like political clubs whose members were loyal to the leaders and supported the loosely defined "people's rights movement."

The tragedy of the early liberal movement, from the point of view of the political parties becoming an effective leavening influence in Japan's constitutional development, was that the parties and political leaders fought among each other. Rather than closing ranks when governmental pressure increased and directing their attack at the evils of the oligarchy, the Liberal and Progressive parties allowed the government to drive a wedge between them and to increase their animosity for each other. If they had swallowed their pride and stood together against any move to suppress the people's rights, they would have been far more effective.

The outstanding example of this rift within the party movement was the treatment accorded Itagaki and the reaction it created among the followers of Ōkuma and the Progressives. In the first place, an attempt was made on Itagaki's life in April, 1882, after one of his political speeches. He was wounded but not mortally so and soon recovered. His convalescence was speeded by receipt of an Imperial gift of money, a gesture which indicated the high esteem in which he was held. At the same time, the government feared his political potentialities. Consequently, several of the chief ministers conceived of a plan whereby his influence could be temporarily diminished and he could be weaned away from his party.

They sought financial assistance from the Mitsui interests for an extended trip abroad for him and his colleague Gotō. He accepted the offer and announced his plans for the trip. Several important party leaders, including the popular writer and novelist, Suehiro Tetchō, violently opposed the project. They claimed that a trip at this critical juncture of Japan's political development was equivalent to abandoning the movement for representative government. Others, particularly members of the rival Progressive party, claimed that the funds for the trip came from a questionable deal made by the government and the Mitsui interests. They maintained that the Japanese Army had renewed its contracts with Mitsui after the latter had promised to finance Itagaki's trip. The Progressive party's newspapers insisted that he had no right to go unless he divulged the source of his support.

No one was quite sure whether Itagaki was aware, when he left, that he was traveling on Mitsui's funds. His supporters ignored the issue and launched a frontal attack on his critics. They called for the destruction of the "Sea Monster," the Mitsubishi interests, which financed the Progressive party. In doing so, they referred to the steamship monopoly which Iwasaki Yatarō, founder of the Mitsubishi, had developed largely through close association with Ōkuma and the government. Their criticism was an appropriate one as the Mitsui interests had been able to form a rival steamship company only after Ōkuma had left the Finance Ministry and been forced out of the government.

It was a public secret that the two largest financial houses, the Mitsui and Mitsubishi, had each found it to their self-interest to be closely associated with a political party. Hence, the incriminations were well-founded and a close Liberal party–Mitsui and Progressive party–Mitsubishi liaison developed. Not only was this close relationship to continue as the old parties evolved into modern parties but business rivalries came to be added to political antagonisms. In the 1880's, this ill-feeling created an irreconcilable schism between the parties. The recriminations and equally vehement denials diverted the energies and the venom of the antigovernment forces from the central issue of oligarchical control. When Itagaki returned from his trip, his colleagues were fighting the rival party, not the clan bureaucrats. Furthermore, the scandals and strife between the parties antagonized the public toward the democratic movement.

In the meantime, the conservatives took advantage of this conflict and made it even more difficult for the parties to function. The laws regulating the press and public meetings and associations were strengthened. Proprietors, managers, and editors of newspapers and magazines were made personally responsible for statements critical of established policy. The law restricting political meetings and prohibiting attendance at them by members of the armed forces, by public servants, and by teachers and students was strictly enforced. Political arrests increased, and it became almost impossible for the parties to survive.

Economic conditions also weakened the popular movement. Matsukata became the new Finance Minister in 1881 and immediately began a deflationary program. He froze government expenditures for four years, retired the notes in circulation, purchased specie abroad, and brought business expansion to a halt. Prices tumbled and land taxes increased. Whereas previously the landowner had had funds to support the party movement, after 1881 he was struggling to keep from being dispossessed from his land. At the same time, the radical elements in the two parties, particularly those in the *Jiyūtō,* found support among the hard-pressed and discontented tenants and small farmers. Revolts of farmers faced with heavier taxes or foreclosures increased in number and size. The party leaders were justifiably accused of instigating them.

Many of the revolts occurred in the silk-growing area northwest of Tokyo as a result of the fall in silk prices. A noteworthy episode was the uprising in May, 1884, in Takazaki in Gumma Prefecture. One of the ringleaders was a member of the prefectural assembly and another was a leader of the Liberal party in the adjoining prefecture. Members of the Tokyo branch of the party came to Takazaki and attended meetings with the local officials and inhabitants. They advocated direct action against the government and began to train their own special military units. Their plot to assassinate several high officials was uncovered in time to frustrate an open attack on the city's army garrison. The central government became alarmed lest the general economic depression lead to a general uprising under the leadership of the parties. Consequently, it passed new laws which made it impossible for the parties to function effectively. With a loss of their main financial support, the parties disappeared in 1884. The *Jiyūtō* dissolved and the *Kaishintō* lost its leadership.

The Clan Bureaucrats Plan a Constitution, 1882-87

With the movement for representative government under control, the Emperor's chief ministers and advisers were free to proceed with the preparation of a constitution which reflected their political philosophy. In fact, they had already started to formulate their plans. In March, 1882, only five months after the Emperor stated that a constitution would be promulgated by 1890, Itō Hirobumi received an Imperial command to proceed abroad to study foreign constitutions. As President of the newly formed *Sanji-In,* he was the key person in the government concerned with the drafting of the basic laws of the land. The Imperial Councilors had already approved a constitutional monarchy, which preserved the position, authority and dignity of the throne.

They also clearly realized that Prussia under Bismarck offered one of the most fruitful places for comparative study. This belief had been thoroughly instilled in the minds of the ruling oligarchs by their contacts with Herman Roessler, an erstwhile professor from Erlangen University, who had been an adviser to the Japanese Foreign Office since 1878.[1] Consequently, it is not surprising that Itō, when he was selected chief of the mission to study foreign constitutions, should have headed for Germany. He later wrote that he had been sent on his mission:

> . . . to make as thorough a study as possible of the actual workings of different systems of constitutional government, of their various provisions, as well as of theories and opinions actually entertained by influential persons.[2]

He went directly to Berlin, where the Japanese Minister had arranged for a special series of lectures by the famous political scientist, Rudolf von Gneist. In these lectures, which Gneist held thrice weekly for nearly three months, he argued against adopting characteristics of the American or French Constitution. In his opinion, problems of diplomacy, the organization of the military establishments, and property owned by the Imperial family should not be subject to decisions of the legislative body. In fact, the power of parliament should be limited and that of the ministers of state strengthened. Specifically, there should be a limit on the former's budgetary power and on those eligible to vote.

From Gneist, and later from Lorenz von Stein in Vienna, Itō found ample evidence to use on his return to refute the arguments of those who opposed his political philosophy. In another sense, he found verification of the basic ideas which he and Iwakura had already formulated. He could well afford, without jeopardizing his objectives, to stop in England on his return trip to listen to a single lecture on representative government by Herbert Spencer.

Itō and his party returned to Tokyo in 1883. The government, obviously guided by Itō's experience, set about making the necessary administrative changes to assure the formation of a limited constitutional monarchy consistent with his political philosophy. Gneist had argued that it would be unwise to establish a constitutional convention. Itō had been impressed with his reasoning on this point and forthwith recommended a special office for the study of constitutional and administrative reforms. A bureau, known as the Commission to Investigate the Constitution (*Seido Tori Shirabe Kyoku*), was announced in March, 1884. It was made a branch of the Imperial Household Ministry and Itō was appointed its Chairman. Consequently, work could be carried on in strictest secrecy and in collaboration with the personal wishes of the Emperor. Under these conditions, the public would neither be permitted nor dare to intervene directly.

At the same time, the system of nobility was remodeled so as to strengthen the hands of the conservatives. Finally, at the end of the next year (1885) the old system of Councilors was reorganized and a Cabinet system was set up. Itō became the first Prime Minister while several of the key posts within the Cabinet were assigned to his fellow clansmen.[3]

At the age of forty-four, he had achieved a position in the new government with powers comparable to that of his European idol, Bismarck, the German Chancellor. He was concurrently Prime Minister, Minister of the Imperial Household, and Chairman of the Commission to Investigate the Constitution. Furthermore, the new power given his fellow clansman Yamagata as Home Minister had already caused the dissolution of the political parties and broken the back of the agrarian movement. The office of Lord Keeper of the Privy Seal was created and a national civil service organized. Finally, the government talked in general terms about representative institutions which would be created by the new Constitution, but no document had yet been drafted and no official recommendations as to its contents had been made public. Consequently, the opposition had nothing tangible to criticize and simply had to wait and hope for the best. Itō and his colleagues must have been well satisfied with the way opposition to their plans had been kept to a minimum.

In the face of these developments, public interest in politics began to decline. People as a whole resigned themselves to what had always been considered as inevitable in the operation of the government; namely, that "the authorities" who were in positions of responsibility would take matters into their own hands and inform the public of their decisions after they had been made. As Fukuzawa expressed it:

> The general mass of the people is indifferent to political power and ignorant of its value. They are satisfied if the government issues an order.

Hence, there was a general apathy toward the whole question of drafting of the Constitution. This attitude was somewhat offset by a general curiosity as to how much power would be granted Parliament and what rights would be assured the Emperor's subjects.[4]

The actual drafting of the Constitution by Itō and his colleagues was not begun until 1886. In passing, it should be noted that after it had been announced in 1881 that a constitution would be prepared, the bureaucrats had taken five years to reach the point of beginning to draft the basic document. By postponing their work, much of the ardor of those who urged greater rights for the people had been cooled by the passage of time. Furthermore, Itō had been preoccupied with other duties. He had been holding conferences with Li Hung-chang on the thorny question of Japanese and Chinese rights in Korea. (See Chapter 9.) Itō also realized that the longer he postponed the completion of the final draft of the new Constitution, the less time his opponents would have to organize and solidify the opposition prior to the deadline of 1890. With important administrative changes well behind him, therefore, Itō assigned specific tasks to his associates. Inouye Ki (1844-95), a classical scholar, was made chairman of the group and was largely responsible for the draft of the Constitution and of the Imperial House Laws. Itō Miyoji, who had gone to Europe in 1882-83, worked on the laws for Parliament; and Kaneko Kentarō, a former student of Harvard University, compiled the election laws.

All of them operated under certain general principles which had formed in Itō's mind after his return from Europe. In the first place, he believed that since the Imperial system had been the essence of the country, the new Constitution and its supporting laws must preserve the Emperor's dignity and power. He insisted that, in granting rights and limited freedom to the people, special care should be taken not to limit the prestige of the Emperor. He later explained that in European countries religion was made the axis of the state, but that in Japan neither Confucianism nor Shintōism had sufficient power to control the people. Hence, neither of these religions could appropriately become such an axis. He concluded, therefore, that the Emperor alone should be the axis of the Japanese state and that the Constitution should verify and emphasize that principle. Another general principle that Itō had learned from von Stein was that the text of any constitution should be as simple as possible to permit broad latitude in its interpretation. Finally, he insisted that heavy reliance be placed on Prussian political theory.

As Inouye began the actual compilation of the text of the first draft of the Constitution he followed the suggestions of Itō on the powers to be given Parliament and the Cabinet. He also kept in close touch with Roessler, who by this time had become a Professor of Law at Tokyo Imperial University. By the spring of 1887 three drafts were completed; two were compiled by Inouye on the basis of Itō's suggestions and the third had been written by Roessler. In the summer of that year Inouye, Itō Miyoji, and Kaneko visited Itō Hirobumi at his summer villa. There all four of them, with the three drafts at hand, worked without interruption until they had produced a fourth draft to which only a few changes were made prior to its formal presentation to the Emperor and Privy Council. Except for the fact that a copy of one of the drafts had been stolen, their work was kept secret from the public. In fact, they had not even given any indication to the public of the contents of the proposed draft; nor did the public know how far the drafting had proceeded.

Complications Over Revisions of the Treaties

Just at this juncture, international developments shifted general interest away from the problems of the proposed Constitution. By their position in the Cabinet and by the methods used to prepare an official draft text, Itō and his colleagues had protected themselves from effective criticism. On the problem of the revision of the treaties with Western powers, however, they found themselves in a vulnerable position. They had constantly insisted that all their actions were motivated by a desire to exalt and strengthen their country and their Emperor. On the other hand, the lack of progress on treaty revision seemed to belie this purpose. Several clauses in the treaties with the Western powers clearly infringed on Japan's sovereignty and national dignity. For example, the clauses which permitted extraterritoriality for Europeans and limited Japan's freedom to determine its own import and export duties still remained unchanged. A rising patriotism and national pride had produced violent objections to the extraterritoriality clauses.

Practical considerations created demands for revisions of the tariffs. When Ōkuma became Minister of Finance in 1873 he realized that tariff autonomy was essential if he was to place the country's budget on a firm basis. Whereas in 1888 a country such as the United States derived half of its revenue from tariffs, Japan collected only 5 per cent of its income from import and export duties. It was imperative, therefore, for Japan to obtain tariff autonomy as soon as possible.

But early attempts at revision had failed miserably. After the Iwakura Mission had been rebuffed by the Western powers in 1873, the government leaders had realized that many domestic reforms were necessary before successful negotiations for revisions could be completed. For example, none of the Western powers would approve of revisions until modern Western-style civil and criminal codes and law courts were in operation. No European nation would be willing to have its citizens tried under a feudal code of ethics. So long as the old codes continued, the Western powers insisted on the continuation of extraterritoriality.

Futile negotiations dragged on intermittently for several years while the people clamored for their successful conclusion. After the British Minister reminded the Japanese government in 1884 that revision of the treaties was contingent upon the adoption by Japan of Western legal standards, the work of drafting new codes by foreign legal experts such as Roessler was accelerated. Their efforts had impressed the United States favorably enough for it to be willing to revise the unequal clauses but other governments still claimed that insufficient progress had been made.

The next step was a joint British-German proposal of 1886 which recommended only partial abolition of extraterritoriality. It provided that the countryside should be opened to foreigners for unrestricted travel. In the meantime, the new civil, criminal, and commercial codes and the law courts should be put in operation. Import duties would be raised, in some instances by as much as 25 per cent, but the export tariff rate would remain at 5 per cent. In spite of these concessions, however, the foreigners insisted that certain aspects of extraterritoriality should remain. For example, consular jurisdiction should be retained for a limited period in the large cities. Finally, foreign judges and procurators would be appointed in cases in which foreigners were involved. When these proposals became known, the public was indignant. They objected both to the provisions for foreign judges and that foreigners would be permitted unrestricted residence throughout the nation. Opposition to the foreigners' proposals was so strong that in September, 1887, Foreign Minister Inouye Kaoru was forced to resign.[5] (See also p. 180 ff. below.)

It was precisely at this point that Itō and his colleagues had completed their fourth draft of the Constitution. The success of their efforts in this regard was threatened by the impasse over the revision of the treaties. There was a real possibility that a leader of the opposition might be able to capitalize on this failure of the government to revise the treaties. If anyone could unify the various political elements opposed to Itō and his colleagues, the whole future of the oligarchs was at stake. In fact, all the carefully laid plans to produce a constitution which preserved the special prerogatives of the Emperor and the position of his Ministers might be for nought.

Consequently, the Cabinet took strong measures to prevent further embarrassment both on the treaty negotiations and on the type of constitution to be adopted. In the first place, Itō temporarily assumed the post of Foreign Minister. In late December, 1887, his Home Minister, Yamagata, promulgated strict regulations to preserve law and order. Under the new regulations, persons suspected of causing disturbances or "judged to be scheming something detrimental to public tranquility" could be banished from Tokyo. Both those who were the Cabinet's political opponents and those who objected to the proposed treaties with the foreigners were either intimidated or banished from the city. Under virtual martial law, nearly 600 persons active in the people's rights movement were forced to leave the political heart of the Empire.

Such was the domestic atmosphere in the spring of 1888 when Itō and his three assistants met again to put the finishing touches on the Constitution and on the texts of the Imperial House Laws. The time had also arrived to settle the question of how the basic laws should be adopted. While there had been some clamor for a constitutional convention, Itō had never favored such a procedure, and the disturbances caused by the treaty-revision fiasco made him even less enthusiastic for it. Some persons claimed that only the Emperor's approval was necessary. A partial compromise of these two extremes was adopted. In April, 1888, a Privy Council was created by Imperial Ordinance. The Emperor gave the following reasons for this move:

> Whereas We deem it expedient to consult personages who have rendered signal service to the State, and to avail Ourselves of their valuable advice on matters of state, We hereby establish Our Privy Council which shall henceforth be an institution of Our Supreme counsel.

In other words, the Emperor and a select group of his most trusted servants would discuss the draft of the Constitution in the new Council and would approve it. It would then be proclaimed as the immutable law of the Empire.

From the shifts which followed in the highest posts in the government, it is obvious that the oligarchs, under Itō's guidance, had engineered this whole scheme. He immediately resigned as Premier and became President of the Privy Council. His three assistants were made secretaries of the Council. Kuroda Kiyotaka of Satsuma, a loyal protégé of Yamagata, was the new Premier. In the second place, the two strongest adversaries of the clan oligarchs, Ōkuma and Itagaki, were asked to join the Council to make it impossible for them to lead the opposition. Ōkuma accepted a position in the Cabinet as Foreign Minister with an assignment to solve the explosive problem of the unequal treaties. It will be noted later how dangerous this undertaking became for him. (See below p. 180.) On the other hand, Itagaki remained outside the government and refused to join the Council. Nevertheless, Yamagata's strong-arm rule made it impossible for anyone opposed to the government to cause any significant trouble.

The Meiji Constitution of 1889

In May, 1888, with Yamagata having squelched or eliminated the subversives, the Privy Council began its deliberation on Itō's draft of the

Constitution in the presence of the Emperor. During forty-three subsequent sessions throughout the next nine months, the Emperor and his most trusted advisers debated the text of this basic document. Ōkuma, who was busy with negotiations with the foreigners, was the only important official to keep away from the meetings. Since he had long disagreed with Itō on many points, he was glad to have this excuse for not attending.

As in the case when the first drafts were made by Itō and his colleagues, no records are available as to what exactly transpired in the Council meetings. It seems probable that such changes as were made did not materially affect any of the important provisions of the document. In any event, the draft was approved by the Privy Council. February 11, or Empire Day, the day when the first mythological Emperor presumably ascended the throne, was selected for the promulgation of the new Constitution.

The ceremony held on February 11, 1889, was a simple one. According to Dr. Erwin Baelz, a German professor at Tokyo Imperial University, who observed the ceremony, the entire procedure lasted about ten minutes. He writes:

> On either side of the throne a high dignitary now stepped forward, one of them Duke Sanjo . . . , each of them with a roll of parchment. The one Sanjo held was the Constitution. The Emperor took the other document, opened it, and read it in a loud voice.[6]

Emperor Meiji, who by that time was thirty-seven years old, proclaimed that he promulgated the present, immutable fundamental law for the sake of his subjects and their descendants. He attributed Japan's successes in the past to the virtues of his ancestors and to the loyalty of his subjects. He concluded that since his subjects descended from his ancestors, he had no doubt that they would be guided by his views, sympathize with his endeavors, and make manifest the glory of his country, both at home and abroad.

After his speech (containing slightly more than two hundred words in the official English translation), he handed the parchment on which the Constitution was written to the Prime Minister and left the room. Thus Japan's first Constitution was given to the people more than twenty years after the Restoration was started. For fifty-eight years, from that day until May 3, 1947, when the post-World War II Constitution came into force, not a single change was made in the document which implemented Itō's desire that the Emperor be the center, the axis of the constitutional monarchy.

Although the importance of the Constitution will become apparent from the interpretation of events subsequent to its adoption, some of its features must be emphasized at this point if those events are to be understood.

The late Professor Robert K. Reischauer, an outstanding authority on Japan's government, has succinctly described the fundamentals of Japanese political theory which must be grasped if the history of Japan's constitutional government is to be understood. To him, these concepts are that society is more important than the individual, that all men are by nature unequal, that politics and ethics are synonymous, that government by men is superior to that by law, and that the patriarchal family is the ideal state.[7] To explain the document another way: it is a compromise between the concepts of statism and liberalism, with a strong preference toward statism.

But the Constitution can best be undertood by an analysis of its most salient features. (See Appendix IV.) While it delineated the three basic powers of government, it strengthened the Emperor's power on all sides. The preamble stressed the immutability of the document and the necessity of eternal allegiance to it in its present form. The power, dignity, and central position of the Emperor were guaranteed. He was sacred and inviolable. As Itō expostulated in his *Commentaries,* not only should no irreverence be shown the sovereign but he should not be made the subject of discussion nor the topic of derogatory comment. The Constitution further provided that the Emperor exercise the rights of sovereignty and of legislative power with the consent of the Diet. It also gave him wide powers to issue ordinances. It recognized his Supreme Command of the Army and Navy and his authority to determine the organization of the armed services. He had the power to make war and peace and to conclude treaties. Finally, as the initiator of amendments to the Constitution, he could control any future attempts to limit his power.

His position was further secured by the Imperial House Law. Its purpose was to assure the continuance of the Imperial line without outside interference. If amendments were necessary, they would be decided by the Emperor with the advice of the Imperial Family Council and of the Privy Council. The Imperial Household Ministry had charge of the personal affairs of the Emperor and his family, as well as restrictive control over the right of his subjects to approach him. As a result, this group of bureaucrats, who originally were conservative but in the 1930's stood up against the ultranationalists, became influential personal advisers to the sovereign and wielded much power behind the scenes.

Despite the new outward form, the Constitution perpetuated the strength of the executive branch of the government. In reality, it gave legal sanction to the wide powers already exercised in the name of the Emperor by a small group of ministers. While it established legislative and judicial branches of the government, it was careful not to give them sufficient power to infringe on the executive. Consequently, the Privy Council, which was the body composed exclusively of Imperial appointees, was continued with authority to deliberate upon important matters of state referred to it by the Emperor.

The concept of individual responsibility of Ministers of State toward the Emperor, which had existed heretofore, was strengthened. Article 55 read:

> The respective Ministers of State shall give their advice to the Emperor and be responsible for it.
>
> All Laws, Imperial Ordinances and Imperial Rescripts of whatever kind, that relate to the affairs of state, require the countersignature of a Minister of State.

The Constitution did not mention a Cabinet as such nor refer to the concept of collective responsibility. Rather, the compilers consciously omitted this important feature of parliamentary government whereby the legislative has a check on the executive. This lack of provision for collective Cabinet responsibility on the one hand, and the assignment to the Emperor of supreme command over the Army and Navy on the other, led to a policy of dual diplomacy and gave free rein to the military.[8] Since the ministers were appointed by the Emperor, and acted for him, they were nearly as far above reproach as their sovereign. In time of crisis, if they were able to retain the Emperor's personal approval for their action, they could weather the storm of criticism.

Confucian teachings and feudal concepts of loyalty had combined to create a deep reverence for one's elders in Japanese society. Japan's history is replete with examples of those who ruled indirectly from retirement. As the old leaders developed a loyal cadre of trained followers there was a tendency to promote new leaders to positions of authority. For example, Kuroda, the Premier, was from the younger group. At the same time, even with the fundamental pattern of government settled, the old leaders were neither willing nor able to relinquish control. Consequently, the informal conferences of two or more of the older statesmen came to be formalized into a body known as the *Genrō* or Elder Statesmen. The members of this extraconstitutional body were selected by the Emperor from among his most venerable contemporaries. It was used to advise him on the most important decisions and for several years was the strongest body in the governmental structure. In many respects it exercised his executive functions for him.

This tendency in Japan's political development to rely on the experience and wisdom of the conservative elite elements in society was further increased by the constitutional provisions for Parliament. The Imperial Diet was divided into a House of Peers and a House of Representatives. Membership in the former came from the nobility and a few Imperial appointees. Only the members of the lower chamber were elected. To guarantee, as Itō desired, that the appointive House of Peers serve as a stabilizing or equilibrating force within the legislative branch, it was given powers practically equal to the House of Representatives. The only exception was the right of the latter House to initiate financial bills, but in practice even this difference did not exist. Hence, the Peers had a virtual veto over legislation forwarded to it by the lower body. The basically conservative Peers could and did control any move by the Representatives to circumscribe the power of the executive and rarely took sides with the Representatives in their battle to strengthen the legislative branch of the government. Furthermore, the Constitution was worded carefully to avoid any indication that the Diet shared any sovereign power with the Emperor.

The powers of the House of Representatives, the only elective body in the national administration, were limited to such an extent that it was difficult for the political parties to operate effectively. Together with the House of Peers, it was subject to prolongation or dissolution at the will of the Prime Minister. As dissolution made an election for members of the lower house compulsory, this device was frequently used effectively by the oligarchs in their fight with the party representatives. Furthermore, when the Diet was actually in session, it met infrequently and for only a few hours each day. There was no real opportunity to discuss adequately important national and international issues. As a Minister was not responsible collectively to the Cabinet, even a vote of nonconfidence did not, as in the case of Premier Tanaka in 1928, cause his resignation.

But the numerous Premiers who ignored the wishes of the Diet were able to act independently also because of the limited budgetary powers given to the people's elected representatives. Iwakura had been impressed with the provision in the Prussian constitution whereby the budget of the previous year would automatically become operative if Parliament failed to act on a new budget prior to adjournment. He had discovered an essential device whereby a Cabinet could stay in power regardless of the wishes of the legislators. In the American and British governments, the executive is completely dependent on the legislative branch for finances to operate the government. Since Itō and his colleagues wished to avoid such an eventuality, Article 71 of the Constitution specifically stated that:

> When the Imperial Diet has not voted on the Budget or when the Budget shall not be brought into actual existence, the Government shall carry out the Budget of the preceding year.

Because of this provision the political parties and members of the opposition in the lower chamber knew full well that if they disagreed with the Cabinet, their views would have only a limited effect. Even though a vote of nonconfidence were pushed through Parliament, which was unlikely because of the right of dissolution, the government would automatically have funds to continue operations. This provision, perhaps as much as any other, permitted a degeneracy in politics in the earliest sessions of the Diet.

The treatment accorded two other groups by the Constitution must be noted. The first of these groups, the militarists, were given special privileges and advantages which enabled them to become the strongest single force in Japan's history. As indicated in the discussion of the role of the Emperor, his power of Supreme Command and authority to determine the organization of the services enhanced the special position of the military through what was termed "direct access to the throne." In other words, if the military wanted Imperial sanction for an exploit such as the invasion of Manchuria in 1931, they claimed that these provisions in the Constitution gave them the right to go directly to the throne for the Emperor's approval for their plans. The Premier and other members of the Cabinet might not even be aware that such a decision had been made. Faced with a *fait accompli,* the Cabinet would be forced to capitulate.[9]

This predominant position of the military in Japanese politics was also the result of another unique feature of the operation of the Japanese government. Under most parliamentary governments, if a new cabinet is being formed, the Prime Minister has a comparatively free hand in selecting his ministers for the various portfolios, including those of the War and Navy Departments. In Japan, however, those available to serve as Minister of War and Minister of Navy were closely circumscribed by an Imperial Ordinance. The first of these ordinances was issued in May, 1900, while General Yamagata was Premier. It provided that only Generals and Lieutenant Generals on the active list could be appointed to the post of Minister of War. Only Admirals and Vice-Admirals on active duty could be appointed as Minister of Navy.

This ordinance, more than any other single piece of legislation, gave the militarists a life-and-death hold over all subsequent Cabinets. Its operation was very simple. If the military leaders, or any strong clique in either the Imperial Army or the Imperial Navy, opposed the policies of a Prime Minister or his Cabinet, the Minister of War or Navy threatened to resign. If the government failed to heed the warning, the Minister would resign and cause the downfall of the whole Cabinet. The small group of high-ranking officers eligible for these Cabinet posts were then ordered not to serve on any future Cabinet until a Premier acceptable to the military was selected. Consequently, if a Premier wanted to stay in power, he had no choice but to bend to the wishes of the military. In 1913 this ordinance was modified to make reserve officers eligible for appointment. In 1936 it was changed back to its original form.

Finally, there remains to be considered the position of the people under the Constitution. To the extent that persons such as Itagaki and Ōkuma spoke for the people, they had forced the issue of a constitution. However, they had no part in drafting it. The central issue of the movement for a constitution and for people's rights had not been whether all men were created equal and hence should have equal rights. Furthermore, no one had seriously advocated the thesis that sovereignty resided in the people rather than in the Emperor. On the contrary, the question was the extent of the rights to be granted to the people. Itō magnanimously described the subjects of the Empire as "public treasures." He conceived of them as treasures, however, which should be protected and controlled. This acceptance of the principle of inequality within Japanese society had an obvious result.

In the first place, the Constitution referred to the people as subjects and placed more emphasis on their duties than on their rights. Even the basic right to vote was limited to property owners. At the time of the promulgation of the Constitution, those eligible to vote for members of the House of Representatives equaled less than half a million persons. This meant that only about 1¼ per cent of the population had the right of franchise.

As for basic human rights, they were restricted. Freedom of conscience, of religion, of thought, and of speech were all recognized but were made subject to the limits of the law. Hence, a Parliament composed of representatives from the elite classes passed stringent laws, such as the Peace Preservation Law, which limited the people's freedom. If a subject were arrested, custom, the Constitution, and the Civil and Criminal Codes provided for a far different "due process of law" than the traditional Western European practice. A trial by a jury composed of one's peers, the right to be confronted with the charges against the accused, the right of counsel and a speedy trial for the defendant were all principles and practices foreign to Japanese judicial practice. In fact, a man was considered guilty until he could prove his innocence. In a stratified society, privileges and judicial protection were allotted in proportion to the importance of one's social status. As for the duties of the subjects, the Constitution specified that they were "amenable" to service in the armed forces and to the duty of paying taxes.

Such was the general heritage of the Japanese people under the Meiji Constitution. It was not a heritage which was conducive to the growth of individual freedom or representative institutions. It had not been designed for that purpose. In fact, it was clearly designed to establish the supremacy of the throne and to enable the state to control the people. It had been conceived and nurtured in an atmosphere in which freedom was considered to be less of a virtue than obedience; equality less important than inequality; brotherhood less appealing than suspicion.

The process of modernization from a form of modified feudalism to a limited constitutional monarchy was similar in many respects to that of Germany, from which so much had been borrowed. As Veblen has pointed out, in Japan, as well as in Germany, the concept of the state as an overruling personal—or quasi-personal—entity had prevailed from former times. In both countries, the government rested on the suzerainty of the crown, not on the discretion of a parliamentary body, and was a government of "constitutionally mitigated absolutism" with little or no libertarian tradition to temper this absolutism. In the economic sphere, both of these nations decided to modernize their economies to meet the strategic needs of the state. The technology necessary for industrialization was taken over ready-made from other countries which had previously developed it. Such things as parliamentary tradition, democratic government, or even the needs of the people could be ignored if the state's preparation for war made it necessary.[10]

In 1890 Japan was in a particularly advantageous position. Both German absolutism and technological development were at an advanced stage when the key figures of the Meiji Restoration visited Europe in 1873 and again in 1882. These leaders were perceptive enough to recognize that they could avoid innumerable mistakes and perhaps even disaster if they relied heavily on Germany's experience. The process of modernization in Japan, therefore, so long as its national objectives were the same as those of Germany, could be speeded up by an emphasis on adaptation of those features applicable to Japan. The process of modernization described thus far, therefore, is really that of adaptation. Its success was enhanced by the economic and territorial accruals which had occurred by the time the Constitution was promulgated. Its success was assured by society's acceptance of the philosophy that the highest calling of the subject was to serve the State and to follow its dictates for the glory of the Empire.

Notes

1. Itō, Iwakura, and others, as noted in Chapter 5, had been favorably impressed with Bismarck and his concepts of government. Furthermore, the Japanese Minister in Berlin, Aoki Shūzō (1844-1914), was a staunch supporter of Prussian political philosophy. The first Japanese to study in Germany, he had absorbed much of the political atmosphere around him during his student days, and especially that of Bismarck after the latter became Minister in 1875. Without doubt, Aoki had had a hand in the selection of Roessler as an adviser to his home government.

2. Itō Hirobumi was accompanied by three younger men, Itō Miyoji (1857-1934), Hirata Tōsuke (1849-1929) and Saionji Kimmochi (1849-1940). Itō Miyoji, who was no relation to the other Itō as they had different family names, was assigned with the other two to study the Constitution of the Third Republic in France. He was the only one of the assistants to aid in the preparation of the final draft of the Constitution a few years later. For reference to Itō Hirobumi's concept of his mission

see Itō Hirobumi, "The Japanese Constitution" in Ōkuma Shigenobu, *Fifty Years of New Japan* (2 vols.; London: Smith Elders, 1910), I, p. 127.

3. Inouye Kaoru was the new Foreign Minister; Yamagata Aritomo was Home Minister; the important portfolios of Finance, Army, and Navy were held respectively by three Satsuma clansmen, Matsukata Masayoshi, Ōyama Iwaō and Saigō Tsugumichi.

4. A similar disinterest of the public toward modern political crises was evidenced in February, 1936, and in March, 1946. On February 26, 1936, a radical group in the army staged an abortive coup d'état but held parts of the heart of Tokyo under their grip for several days. The public felt no personal responsibility for what was happening or for the future course of events. If a complete military dictatorship had resulted, they would have been as complacent as they were under Hirota's Cabinet. (See *infra* page 340.) In the case of March, 1946, when the Japanese were expected to accept SCAP's proposals for a new constitution, their capitulation was rapid and complete, and there was little outside reaction to the decision. (See *infra* page 403.)

5. Since the issue of the unequal treaties was the only problem of international relations which had aroused the people during this period, it has been discussed at this point. For the other international problems see below, page 158 ff.

6. Tobu Baelz, ed., *Awakening Japan: The Diary of a German Doctor: Erwin Baelz,* translated by Eden and Cedan Paul (New York: Viking Press, Inc., 1932), p. 81.

7. See R. K. Reischauer, *Japan, Government and Politics* (New York: Thomas Nelson & Sons, 1939), pp. 22-35.

8. Itō argued that the Prime Minister had no control over his Cabinet members and that they were not responsible to him. See Itō Hirobumi, *Commentaries on the Constitution of the Empire of Japan,* tr. by Itō Miyoji (Tokyo: Chu-o Daigaku, 1931).

9. For an example of the operation of this practice see page 330.

10. See Thorstein Veblen, *Imperial Germany and the Industrial Revolution* (New York: The Macmillan Co., 1915), pp. 80 ff.; and Thorstein Veblen, "The Opportunity of Japan," Leon Ardzrooni, ed., *Essays in our Changing Order* (New York: Viking Press, Inc., 1934), pp. 248-66.

9

NATIONAL STRENGTH IN 1890

The power at the disposal of the Emperor and his Ministers at the time of the promulgation of the Constitution was dependent on much more than the provisions of that document. It depended on certain specific factors such as the condition of agriculture, potentialities for self-sufficiency, financial stability, the extent or success of the industrialization program, and the growth of the armed services. At the same time, national strength could be dissipated if dreams of territorial expansion went far beyond ability to absorb territory overseas. Conversely, if expansionism was commensurate with an integrated national growth, it could cause a net increase in national strength.

All these power potentials, as well as the sovereign rights and authority of the Emperor which were confirmed by the Constitution, were also affected by numerous variable factors and national characteristics. For example, the loyalty of the people toward the Emperor and the throne, their patriotism, their willingness and ability to work, their aptitudes and ambitions, and their subservience to authority were crucial elements in the state's program of amalgamation of the entire national effort to strengthen the Empire. On all these counts, as well as on many more which would augment the national strength, the people were not found wanting. A complete analysis of Japan's national strength in 1890 will necessitate, therefore, a brief account of Japan's general economic status, of the territorial limits of the Empire, and of the contemporary cultural and social scene.[1]

The Conditions of Agriculture

Particularly after World War I, Japan has been referred to as a "have-not" country. A paucity of natural resources, a small area, extremely limited arable land, and an ever increasing population have added to its economic plight. Good or bad standards of living and conditions within a country are relative, however, and the ordinary Japanese subject compared his plight with that of a few years earlier, not with a comparable person in one of the advanced Occidental countries. In the years immediately following the Meiji Restoration of 1868, the country was far from modernized and standards of living were low in comparison with the Occident. Nevertheless, conditions gradually improved and the main home islands were able to produce enough rice to feed the population without imports of cereals. The population had not yet begun to take a sudden spurt upward and the people's tastes were still relatively simple. Despite isolated uprisings by peasant groups, there was general acceptance of conditions as they existed.

One of the most significant features of the agrarian economy is the fact that though only one-seventh of Japan's land area is arable, the country's population is predominantly agrarian. For example, in 1872, approximately 77 per cent of the gainfully employed were agricultural workers and four years later the proportion was slightly higher; as late as 1920, half of the total workers were engaged in agriculture. From these figures it is obvious that agricultural conditions affected more people than did the conditions of any other industry; if there were weaknesses in the agrarian economy, they would eventually weaken the national economy.

During the first two decades of the Meiji Restoration, both strong and weak characteristics of agriculture appeared. As for the former, the traditional small-scale farms, many of them less than two acres, permitted the continuance of farm operations with a minimum of capital when capital funds were needed for industrialization. Moreover, the competition for good farm land had forced an intensive use of all available space. Improved methods of cultivation and better seeds increased production sufficiently to meet the demands made by a growing population. The farmer's income was also supplemented by the sale of raw silk and the products of home industries. As silk exports doubled, the growing of silkworms became an important phase of farming. So long as the market was firm, silk remained the most profitable cash crop. The agrarian economy was also bolstered by the fact that the farm population was hard working, expected little from life except enough to eat, and was inherently conservative.

On the other hand, many of the weak characteristics of agriculture were evident even before 1890. Little additional land was available for reclamation and cereal production could be increased only gradually. By 1889 it had reached 183.0 million bushels, an increase of about 16 2/3 per cent in a decade. Any additional gains would result only from prodigious efforts of time and money.

In contrast to these limited food resources, there were indications that the population of the nation would increase at a rapid rate. During the Tokugawa dictatorship, natural calamities, social practices such as infanticide and abortion, and disease had resulted in a stagnant population. Modernization, including the introduction of sanitation and hygiene and improved living standards, was bound to force a rapid rise in the net increase. Although the population had risen only 10 per cent in the decade from 1880-90, any increase, no matter how small, put a strain on the food supply. Furthermore, as the standard of living for all classes of society improved, per capita consumption of rice increased. (See Tables IV and V.)

This relentlessly increasing pressure of population on food supply is graphically demonstrated by reference to the statistics on rice exports and imports. In the decade from 1885 to 1894, there was an abrupt change from a surplus to a deficiency in the national crop. In the first half of that decade, over 3,750,000 bushels of rice were exported; in the second half, over 1 2/3 million bushels of rice were imported. Thereafter, production at home could not keep up with the demand so that rice imports steadily increased.[2]

The long-range prospects of agriculture were not good. Domestic production of foodstuffs was not going to be sufficient to meet the demands of a rapidly growing population. Hence, Japanese industry would have to manufacture goods for export to provide the foreign exchange to purchase vital food imports. If this balance could not be maintained, the national economy would be in jeopardy. For the period under discussion, however, this issue had not yet become acute but the trends indicated that it soon would be.

Another feature of the agrarian economy during this early period, which came to be permanent, was a marked increase in tenancy. This movement was greatly increased by the effects of the Restoration. After the feudal holdings were transferred into private property, the new Imperial government was obliged to establish a universal land tax. In addition, in order to meet the requirements of a centralized state, the tax was to be paid in money and paid regularly. These common features of a modern national economy became insurmountable obstacles for many of the farmers. The abolition of the fiefs had made the landlord-peasant relationship an impersonal one.

In feudal times, if the peasant were in arrears in the payment of his taxes in rice, the feudal baron knew that dispossession would only reduce the amount of rice produced within his domain. Since the feudatory was interested in as much rice income as possible, he often permitted postponement of tax payments until the farmer had a good harvest. After the certificates of ownership of land were issued, the owner must either pay his tax in cash or borrow money to do so. Moreover, he must pay the same amount each year, regardless of whether or not there was a good harvest, and could no longer count on the beneficence of a paternalistic, feudal lord. Instead, he was confronted by an impersonal tax collector who insisted on adherence to an impersonal law.

Under these circumstances, the position of the small landowner was extremely vulnerable and many of them were forced to give up their holdings. The figures on tenancy and increased dispossessions attest to this fact. For example, in 1873 the proportion of tenants to proprietors was 1:5, but in 1887 it had doubled to 2:5. For the seven years from 1883 to 1890, 367,744 agricultural producers, or about 7 per cent of the total farm households, were forced to sell their land. The most tragic aspect of this development was the fact that three-fourths of the dispossessions resulted from nonpayment of taxes while the value of the land confiscated by the government and auctioned for sale was twenty-seven times the value of the total taxes in arrears.

This tendency toward concentration of landownership in the hands of fewer landlords and the decrease in the number of cultivator-owners had additional weaknesses and permitted widespread abuses. The owner, by exaction of a heavy rent from the tenant, could pass on to the cultivator any new taxes which the government might require. On the other hand, the tenant was in a weak bargaining position because he had little freedom of action. There was only a limited demand for unskilled farm labor and a heavy demand for dwellings. Hence, the tenant held on to the job and the house which he had and accepted a heavier burden of rent. On balance, when the Constitution was promulgated in 1889, the agrarian economy showed more signs of weakness than of strength, but these weaknesses were not yet significant enough to cause any serious embarrassment to the government.[3]

Financial Strength

These weaknesses in the agrarian economy were partially mitigated by the increased stability in the nation's finances. When Matsukata Masayoshi became Minister of Finance in 1881, the nation's finances were in a chaotic condition. The experiment in national banking had been unsuccessful. The bank notes varied in value with the silver yen coins. In 1880, 1.50 yen exchanged for 1.00 yen of silver; by the next year 1.79 yen of paper money was needed to buy 1.00 yen of silver. Prices of commodities also rose. Rice cost 5.15 yen in 1877 but rose to 10.48 yen in 1881. Despite the temporary suffering which sweeping reforms might inflict on some of the population such as the farmers, Matsukata adopted radical steps to place the country on a solid financial base.

His first steps were to freeze the national expenditures and create a sinking fund to redeem the public debt. He had inherited the inconvertible notes issued to pay for the Satsuma Rebellion in 1877 and for other national expenses. When an accumulation of specie permitted it, he recalled these notes. In five years, the value of paper money rose from one-fifth its face value to a level equal to that of silver. Furthermore, during the decade 1880-90 the public debt rose only 2 per cent while the service charges paid by the government on its indebtedness were reduced. Interest charges, which had been as high as 19 per cent, were lowered to 5 per cent; a foreign loan for a new section of the railroad across the central mountains was secured at only 6 per cent.

An analysis of the annual receipts and expenditures for the nation shows the improved condition of the exchequer. In 1869, the first full year after the Restoration, both receipts and expenditures approximated 21 million yen. In 1875-76, when the new land tax was collected over a large portion of the country, receipts rose to 86 million yen and expenses were only 60 million yen. In 1882, after Matsukata had taken office, receipts and expenditures were equal again to 63 million yen. As a result of his having frozen expenditures at that amount for the next few years, the situation improved so noticeably that in 1890-91 receipts stood at 106 million yen, 24 million yen above expenditures.[4]

This improvement in national finances was also the result of institutional reforms inaugurated by Matsukata. He abolished the old National Banks because of their inability to meet the financial demands made upon them. In their stead, with the National Bank of Belgium as a model, he organized the Bank of Japan as the central banking institution. He also created special banks to perform specialized functions such as the Yokohama Specie Bank and the Hypothec Bank. As for the Yokohama Specie Bank, it acted as the chief foreign exchange bank. The state provided one-third of its capital and the Minister of Finance appointed its president and vice-president. Reserves in the treasury could be called upon for use in foreign bills of exchange. Thus by 1887, when the Specie Bank began to function effectively in foreign exchange, a Japanese financial institution was at hand to deal with foreign trade. Local producers of silk, rice, tea, and other items of export no longer dealt through foreigners in the port cities. Similarly, necessary raw materials or finished products for the growing armament program could be imported directly through Japanese firms. Finally, the Hypothec Bank accepted immovable property as security for long-term loans. Within less than a decade, the country's finances were on a firm basis, economic activity was stimulated, the foreign trade balance shifted from excess imports to excess exports, and a firm basis was established for armament expansion.

Industrial Growth

Although the limited agricultural resources and increased population pressure boded ill for Japan's economic future, the general policy of government sponsorship of industries brought encouraging results. Some of them, such as those in Hokkaidō, became extremely profitable. (See Chapter 7.) In 1882 Ōkuma reported that the following were owned by the Imperial Japanese Government:

3 shipbuilding yards
51 merchant ships
5 munitions works
52 factories
10 mines
75 miles of railway
1 telegraph system

Since some of these factories, mills, plants, and mines were offered for sale by the government at bargain prices, private capitalists were eager to absorb them. This policy of bargain sales was advantageous for both the government and for the new owners. It permitted the former to devote its energies to new fields or to concentrate on key strategic industries. It eliminated nepotism, the possibility of discriminatory and unfair subsidies, and the competition between government and private enterprise in several important industries.

As for the private industrialist, it permitted him to start out with a small amount of capital. Other things being equal, he would make a handsome profit from his new adventure. To give a few random examples, the Mitsui interests were delighted to purchase the Shimmachi Spinning Mills. Mr. Asano Sōichirō (1848-1930), who became the wealthy cement tycoon, purchased the Fukugawa Cement Company in 1884. All the large combines strengthened their position of monopolistic control of many industries through shrewd purchases.[5] This sale of government-owned industries contributed materially, therefore, to Japan's industrial strength prior to 1890.

Progress and expansion also continued in the textile industry. The success of the Tomioka Spinning Mill and the assistance Shibusawa Eiichi received from the government has already been noted. (See page 116.) In 1880 he expanded into the Ōsaka region where he founded the Ōsaka Spinning Mill with 10,000 spindles. In seven years the spindles in his factories had increased sevenfold. The demands of this plant and those of many other new ones had boosted raw cotton imports from a mere 12,000 bales in 1868 to a peak of 158,000 in 1888.

As for heavy industries (many of them under government ownership) progress was equally notable. In coal mining, for instance, the average annual output increased rapidly. During the period 1877-84 less than a million tons were mined annually, but in the next decade a yearly average of 2,600,000 tons were produced. As Japan was deficient in iron ore and coking coal, metal production was never sufficient to meet domestic needs and developed more slowly. Even after the Sino-Japanese War of 1894-95, home output of pig iron was sufficient to meet only 40 per cent of domestic needs.

Shipbuilding, which was to be so important after World War I, was still in its infancy. In fact, only one steamer over 1000 tons had been built in Japan before 1895. The importance of a merchant marine, however, had already been recognized by the authorities. The Mitsubishi interests had been encouraged, by periodic gifts of ships, to develop the powerful Japan Mail Steamship Company (N.Y.K.). In 1885 it owned 58 ships aggregating 65,000 tons, practically all of them having been built in foreign yards. Moreover, it received a subsidy which guaranteed for fifteen years a return of 8 per cent interest on the capital investment.

This rapid industrial progress was naturally reflected in the sudden shift in foreign trade from an unfavorable balance prior to 1881 to an excess of exports over imports for several years in the next decade. By 1881 the adverse balance had totaled 79 million yen with invisible foreign services having cost Japan 70 million yen in gold exports. From 1881 to 1893, however, some of the years showed a favorable trade balance. The character of foreign trade also reflected the changing economic pattern. Imports of finished manufactured goods increased and the export of foodstuffs and raw materials declined. In other words, Japan's population was absorbing all of the domestic food supply and there was a demand for finished foreign goods. Furthermore, its industries were far enough advanced to use the total production of raw materials, but it relied on foreign factories for complicated machinery. (See Table XII.)

Military Strength

If the assumption is correct that the Meiji leaders modernized their country to meet its strategic needs—and the facts thus far strongly substantiate this assumption—it was to be expected that the expansion of the Army and Navy would be commensurate with industrial growth. A review of military expenditures shows this to be true. During the period between the Satsuma Rebellion and the Sino-Japanese War (1877-94), the Imperial Army spent approximately 200 million yen and the Imperial Navy an additional 130 million yen. Following the difficulties which the government had encountered in suppressing the Satsuma Rebellion of 1877, War Minister Yamagata was able to convince his colleagues that the Army needed to be expanded and reorganized. In 1878 he organized the Army on the German pattern, established a General Staff, and laid down a ten-year expansion program. The plan included building the ground forces into an Imperial Body Guard Division and six other divisions. A Staff College was formed in 1883 which eliminated the necessity to send officers abroad to study. The old garrisons, located at several cities throughout the

Empire, were changed into Division Headquarters. The Army was organized into divisions with specialization as infantry, supply, artillery, and engineers. A peacetime army of 73,000 men, with a wartime strength of 274,000, had been hammered out so that "at last the military foundation for fighting on the continent was laid."[6]

In view of the insular character of Japan's geography, a navy was as essential as an army for security reasons. Consequently, during the same period an ambitious naval construction and development program was pursued. Naval expenditures were used largely to meet the costs of the naval building program. In 1881 a program was started which included the construction of six warships, twenty-four middle- and small-sized auxiliary craft, and twelve torpedo boats. It called for annual payments of 3.3 million yen. After 1883 the additional expenses of the program were financed largely by special bond issues which totaled 17 million yen. The program was further expanded to permit the construction of 23 ships between 1883 and 1889. But even though the Navy built its own hulks and rig, much of the machinery and armament for the vessels had to be imported. In fact, the war against China in 1894 was fought largely in ships purchased from abroad or built overseas on special order.

A strong military machine was already in the making. Although expenses were far greater toward the end of the period, during 1877-94 Japan spent an average of 20 million yen yearly on armaments. In terms of the national expenditure, which Matsukata froze at 63 million yen in 1882, these Army and Navy expenses equaled one-third of the total.[7] These expanded military establishments immediately became two of the chief pillars which supported Japan's natural strength.

At the same time, as was true of the agrarian problem, there were circumstances which made this strength more apparent than real. This program of modernization enabled Japan to win the Sino-Japanese War in 1895, the Russo-Japanese War in 1905, and to profit materially from World War I. On the other hand, military expenditures placed a heavy burden on the taxpayer and kept living standards down. The scarcity of raw materials, such as coking coal and iron ore, tempted the militarists to undertake the conquest of Manchuria and China to obtain these resources. Since they were not stopped by their own government or people, the Empire had to endure the consequences of eventual expansionism. This in turn led to a clash with the United States and its Allies in World War II and eventual defeat and humiliation. One is tempted to ask, therefore, whether this newly created strength in 1890 was real or illusory. In any event, the modernization movement of the first two decades of the Meiji Period had contributed directly to a limited expansion of the territorial boundaries of the Empire.

The Beginnings of Empire: The Kurile and Bonin Islands

Thus, by 1890 various aspects of Japanese economic life had shown marked virility and potentialities for growth. Some of these aspects, such as the rapidly expanding program of military preparedness, gave indication of bursting their bonds. But the time had not yet arrived for a correlation of political, economic, and military forces which would result in a successful, full-scale war, and the acquisition of important colonial territories. Nothing like a master plan for imperialistic expansion had been developed or accepted.

On the contrary, it was a period of trial and error in questions concerning territorial expansion. Many years earlier, individuals such as Saigō Takamori had dreamt of the conquest of territory on the mainland of Asia, but a basic policy on this question had not been decided. For example, Ōkuma's decision in 1874 to substitute a Formosan expedition for the more dangerous Korean campaign was made on an *ad hoc* basis. Improvisation, which was such an outstanding characteristic of the economic and political growth of the nation in these formative years, was the only consistent element in Japan's early foreign relations. Nevertheless, two of the territorial questions which arose prior to 1890, the issue of the Ryūkyū Islands and the question of Korean independence, had a direct bearing on the formation of the subsequent policy in relation to the continent. Furthermore, the problems which these issues raised came to be basic causes of both the Sino-Japanese War of 1894 and the Russo-Japanese War of 1904.

Even the less significant question of the final disposition of the Kurile Islands, the chain which extends from Hokkaidō northeasterly in an arc to Kamchatka, was a crucial element in Russian-Japanese relations. In the earliest treaties with Russia, the Kuriles had been divided between the two countries and the status of the Island of Sakhalien (Karafuto) had been left unsettled. In the years after the Restoration, there were divergent views within the Japanese government on the disposition which should be made of these territories. One group, stimulated by the visit to Tokyo in 1870 of the former United States Secretary of State, William H. Seward, favored a policy of expansion. This school of thought urged that negotiations be started with Russia for the purchase by Japan of the northern half of Sakhalien. In addition, Russia should be forced to accept Japan's demand for the southern half of the island and all of the Kuriles.[8]

The other group, led by Kuroda Kiyotaka, the chief of the Hokkaidō Colonization Office, supported a policy of conciliation toward Russia. He realized better than anyone else how slim a hold Japan had over Hokkaidō and how a war with Russia at that time would have meant the loss of Hokkaidō for Japan. (See Chapter 7.) Since Kuroda wanted to avoid an open break at all cost, he even advocated Japan's abandonment of any claim for Sakhalien to relieve Russian-Japanese tension.

His views prevailed so that Admiral Enomoto Takeaki was sent to St. Petersburg in 1874 with instructions to settle the Russo-Japanese boundary questions as amicably as possible. After lengthy discussions, a treaty was concluded the next year in which both countries made concessions. Japan gave up all claims to Sakhalien; Russia gave up claim to the northern half of the Kuriles and agreed to cede the entire chain of islands to Japan. This settlement remained in force until after the Russo-Japanese War when Japan acquired, by the Treaty of Portsmouth of 1905, the southern half of Sakhalien. Because of their geographic position, the Kuriles were important to Japan strategically and were incorporated into Hokkaidō and administered as an integral part of that prefecture. Because of the abundant fish in their waters, they were valuable economically. After World War II, they were occupied by Soviet forces and henceforth the Japanese have been denied access to them.

Another group of offshore islands, the sovereignty of which was disputed in the early Meiji Period, is the Bonin Islands (Ogasawara). Historically they had been considered an integral part of the Empire but their chief fame had been as a place of exile for political criminals. Claimed by the British in 1827 and by Perry for the United States in 1853, neither country had pressed its claim, but Japan had undertaken their active colonization. In 1873 United States Secretary of State Hamilton Fish had ruled that they had never been officially recognized as an American possession; two years later the United States persuaded the Western powers to agree to recognize the Bonins as Japanese territory. Despite the fact that they lie 560 miles to the southeast from Tokyo, they were incorporated in 1880 into Greater Tokyo (Tokyo Fu). They remained as part of the capital district until occupied by United States naval forces during World War II. Their poor water and mountainous terrain have made them of little value other than as a protective outpost for Japan as a whole and especially for the metropolitan areas of Yokohama and Tokyo.

The Ryūkyū (Liuchiu) Islands

One of the most important territorial issues in the early Meiji Period concerned the Ryūkyū (Liuchiu) Islands.[9] They extend for 570 miles in a southerly direction below Kyūshū and were the most important territory in dispute during this period. In 1875 they sustained an estimated population of 167,572 that had distinctive cultural and linguistic characteristics of its own. In language and customs the Ryūkyūans show similarities to both the Chinese and Japanese, but seem to be more closely related to the latter. From the fourteenth to the seventeenth centuries they were predominantly under Chinese influence. After the seventeenth century, they were conquered by the Japanese feudal baron of Satsuma. He continued to exact tribute rice from them until modern times. This relationship of suzerainty did not prevent the islands from paying tribute simultaneously to China, however, and from carrying on an active trade with both China and Japan. Furthermore, the "King of the Liuchius" considered himself independent enough of both Japan and China to sign treaties on his own behalf with the Western powers. In 1854 Perry signed one of the first of such treaties for the United States.

With the formal abolition in 1872 of the feudal domains in Japan, the disposition of the Ryūkyūs became important. The Japanese gave little credence to any Chinese claims to the territory and took steps to eradicate such claims. The King was forcibly transported to Tokyo and forbidden to leave. The United States Minister to Japan, DeLong, was informed in October, 1872, that the Ryūkyū Islands had been formally incorporated into Japan but was assured that the terms of the American treaty with "the Kingdom of the Liuchius" would be observed.

In 1873 the Japanese Foreign Minister was despatched to China to obtain redress for the killing of some Ryūkyūan waifs by an aboriginal tribe of Formosans. Japan wanted to get China to punish the Formosans for these unlawful acts or at least to accept responsibility for them. Such action would automatically establish the fact that the Ryūkyūans were Japanese subjects. It would be equivalent to China's renunciation of its claims to the islands. Shortly after the negotiations were begun, the Japanese achieved their objective. Li Hung-chang, the Chinese Viceroy, accepted China's responsibility to punish the Formosan aborigines, and made no counterclaim for Chinese sovereignty over the islands. This acquiescence to Japan's demands was interpreted by Japan, as well as by American Minister DeLong, as meaning that China had waived all claims to the islands.

In the earlier discussion on the Korean issue (see Chapter 6), it has been recorded how political developments in Tokyo led to direct action against Formosa. The Formosan Expedition had been conceived as a diversionary action to placate the expansionists who had wanted to fight Korea. It was not challenged militarily by China and enabled Japan to obtain a written agreement for indemnification of losses sustained by the Ryūkyūans. In October, 1874, the Japanese plenipotentiary and the Chinese Minister of Foreign Affairs signed a convention at Peking which recognized the Ryūkyūans as Japanese subjects. The Convention stated specifically that "certain Japanese subjects" were "wantonly murdered by the unreclaimed savages of Formosa." Japan agreed to withdraw its expeditionary forces from Formosa; China promised not to blame Japan for its action and to drop all further discussion on the matter. Furthermore, China promised to pay 100,000 taels to the families of the shipwrecked Japanese who were killed.[10]

Two points are of special significance. In the first place, the agreement makes no mention of Ryūkyūans but always refers to them in the text as "people from Japan." Secondly, China signed the agreement and paid the indemnity without any reservations. It never realized that both of these acts constituted recognition on its part of Japanese sovereignty over the Ryūkyū Islands.

Consequently, when China protested in 1879 against the incorporation of the islands into Okinawa Prefecture, it was in an extremely weak position from the point of view of international law. Nevertheless, when ex-President Ulysses S. Grant stopped at Peking on his world tour, China placed the matter before him and asked for his intercession. He proposed the appointment of a High Commissioner to settle the question. After his arrival in Tokyo, he informed China that he believed Japan would be willing to make sacrifices if China would approach the negotiations in the same spirit. This move of General Grant resulted in the renewal of direct negotiations between the Chinese and Japanese. As Grant had predicted, the Japanese proposed a compromise solution, namely, that the southernmost group of the Ryūkyūs, the Sakishima Group, be ceded to China in return for a revision of the Sino-Japanese Treaty of 1871 to include a most-favored-nation clause which would give Japan the same privileges in China granted the other powers.

Negotiations over this thorny issue continued throughout 1880. At one point, Viceroy Li Hung-chang agreed to limit China's claim to the southern group but refused to consent to revision of the old Sino-Japanese treaty. In October, 1880, the Chinese negotiator promised the Japanese Minister at Peking that he would sign an agreement which included both of Japan's demands. Two months later, the Chinese had not signed and reversed themselves. The Japanese Minister at Peking was informed that an Imperial Decree had ordered that the whole matter be taken out of the hands of the Chinese Foreign Ministry and that it was to be considered by the Northern and Southern Superintendents of Trade. By mid-January, 1881, the Japanese government was fed up with Chinese vacillations. It considered that the failure to keep the promise to sign the treaty was in reality equivalent to forfeiture of Chinese claims to the islands. It notified the Chinese government that it considered the matter closed and that its Minister had been recalled.

Apparently the Chinese government had followed these tactics to prevent signing an agreement which recognized Japanese sovereignty over the Ryūkyū Islands. In March, 1881, Li Hung-chang told the United States

Minister to China that his government would never agree to the division of "the Liuchiu Islands" between China and Japan. At the very most, it would sign a treaty whereby both powers guaranteed their absolute independence. But Li was not willing to make their disposition a cause for war and was content to leave the matter in abeyance.

He and his colleagues had underestimated the importance of actual possession of territory in such a dispute. Time was on the side of the Japanese. They continued to administer the islands as an integral part of their Empire and refused to reopen negotiations. Whether from indifference or from misjudgment, the entire archipelago, including the two southernmost islands nearest Formosa, had been lost to China indefinitely.

The issue was revived again during World War II by Generalissimo Chiang Kai-shek. In the revised Chinese edition of *China's Destiny,* he described the Liuchius, along with other border regions, as a strategic area necessary for the protection of China's existence. He assumed that the islands were Chinese territory. He concluded that "their severance from the rest of China takes away the national defenses of the country."[11]

This Chinese claim was never taken seriously, however, by the other Allies in discussions on the postwar disposition of the Ryūkyūs. They remained part of Japan until 1945 when Okinawa, the largest of the group, was seized by American forces. Since that time, the main islands of the chain have been under United States military occupation.

Although the dispute over the Ryūkyūs did not lead to open hostilities between China and Japan, it laid the groundwork for distrust and animosity which were to increase during the next decade. Each country interpreted the results of the negotiations differently. Japan believed that China's oral commitments could not be trusted and that action was preferable to endless negotiations. On the other hand, China was resentful of the arrogance of the Japanese officials and of their insistence on following Western procedures in international law. It was fearful of the military machine which Japan had developed, and was apprehensive that there would be a repetition of the Formosan affair with negotiations backed by military or naval pressure. It considered that all of the outlying territories, such as the Ryūkyūs and Korea, were under Chinese suzerainty and that Japan had no right to claim them. It was not sure, however, that Japan could be stopped.

Korean Independence and Suzerainty of China and Japan

As in the dispute over the disposition of the Ryūkyū Islands, the issues arising from the question of Korean independence went beyond the limits of that country. In fact, the problem of Korean autonomy has always, whether in the late sixteenth century, the late nineteenth century, or mid-twentieth century, involved two or more other countries. Partly because of its geographic location as the land bridge between Japan and the Asiatic mainland, partly because of its endemic weakness in comparison with its neighbors, Korea has often been one of the most baffling of international problems. In the third quarter of the nineteenth century, Korea was an independent country with its own King and separate government, yet paid tribute to both China and Japan. Each of these countries considered that it had a special interest in Korea to the exclusion of the other. Each regarded with suspicion any moves by the other within the Korean peninsula. In fact, each considered such moves as a direct threat to its national interests. For many centuries, however, Korea had had a closer relation to China than to Japan.

Under these circumstances, when Japan attempted to negotiate a treaty with Korea which would have abolished the latter's seclusion and put Japan's relations with that country on a par with those of China, complications immediately developed. In 1872-73, when its envoys received rebuffs from the arrogant Koreans, there was violent reaction in Japan. (See Chapter 5.) Japan then sought to clarify the situation by asking China to explain its position on Korea. The answer was the same as that for the Ryūkyūs. China maintained that it possessed the right of suzerainty over the Korean kingdom and that the King was a Minister of the Chinese Emperor.

Not satisfied with this answer, Japan attempted to force the issue by following a policy which Perry had used so successfully in Japan some twenty years earlier. In 1875 Japan sought a treaty with Korea through a show of naval force along the Korean coast and through diplomatic negotiations. The mission failed; so the next year Japanese naval boats surveyed the Korean coast despite gunfire from shore batteries. The Koreans were warned that the survey was in preparation for a military force which would support the next Japanese diplomatic move.

It was a bluff but it worked. In China Li Hung-chang, who had only recently agreed to concessions in the Ryūkyūs as a result of the Japanese military expedition against Formosa, was afraid of future Japanese moves. Hence he told the Koreans to receive the proposed Japanese diplomatic mission. Direct negotiations between the Japanese and the Koreans resulted in the Treaty of Kanghwa of 1876. By this first modern treaty, Korea opened two ports to Japan and granted partial extraterritorial rights to Japanese subjects. In return, Japan recognized Korea as an independent state enjoying the same sovereign rights as Japan.

But Korean and Chinese reactions to this treaty were as important for the future as were its contents. One of the objectives of the Japanese negotia-

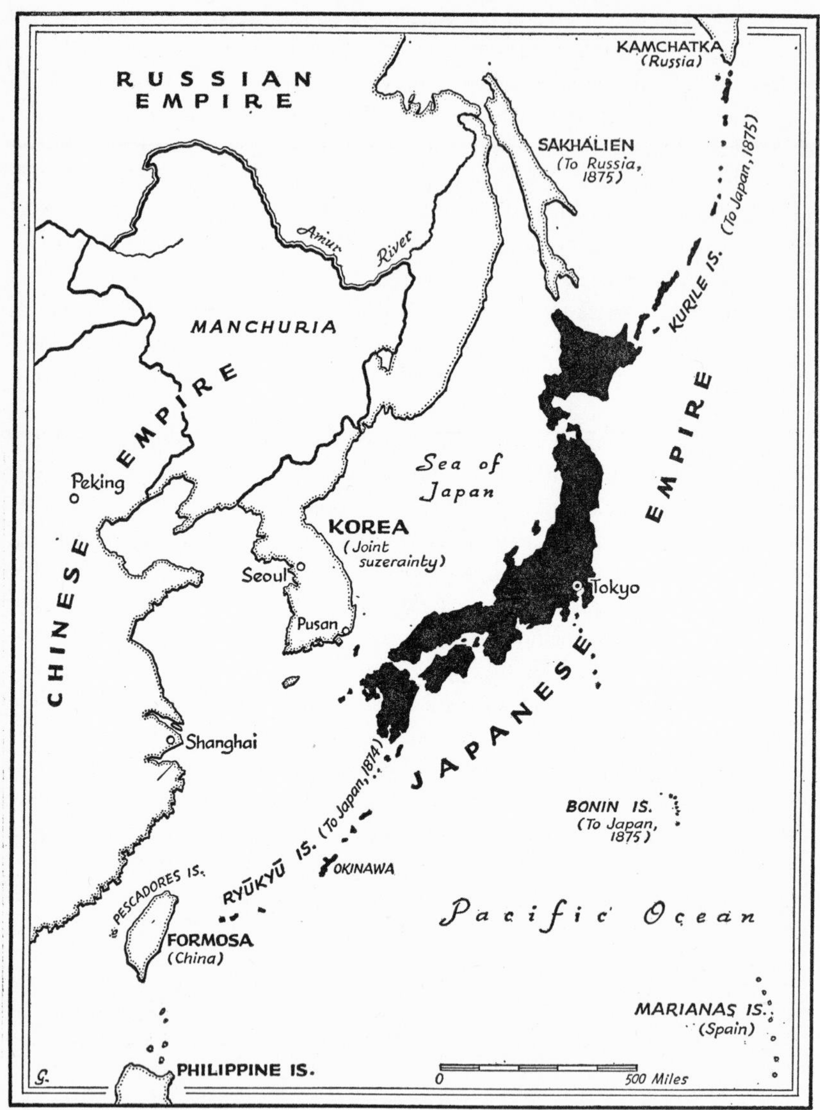

THE JAPANESE EMPIRE, 1890

tors had been to obtain an agreement which clearly established Korea as a country independent of Chinese or any other foreign influence. If this fact could be established, there was some chance of Japan being able to compete successfully for the control of Korea on an equal footing with China. Either on their own initiative or on the advice of Li Hung-chang, however, the Korean negotiators had questioned the powers of the Japanese envoy and so raised questions on the validity of the Kanghwa Treaty. Furthermore, they had kept the Chinese informed of all stages of the negotiations and had not acted as free agents. As for China, it refused to take seriously the clause in the treaty about Korean independence. In fact, the whole affair made no difference in China's attitude. Regardless of the Kanghwa Treaty, China continued to assume that it had a right to expect Korea to follow its lead on foreign affairs and to be partially subject to it.

This policy is illustrated by subsequent negotiations of the United States with Korea. The American envoy, Admiral Robert W. Shufeldt, first approached the Japanese in the hope of getting them to mediate for the United States. This move aroused Li Hung-chang into action. Since he was anxious to keep Japan from obtaining a favored position, he offered to act as mediator himself. Shufeldt assumed that this offer meant that China was agreeable to recognize Korean independence. He soon discovered, however, that such was not the case. In fact, he was asked to include a statement in the treaty which recognized Korea as a dependent state of China. Such a clause would have been a diplomatic victory for China over Japan in its relations with Korea. When Shufeldt refused to comply with this wish, the Koreans indicated that they might not be willing to sign any treaty with the United States.

The question was finally settled in a manner which protected the desires of both the United States and China. The Shufeldt Treaty, the first Korean treaty with a Western power, was signed in 1882. It provided for perpetual peace and friendship between Korea and the United States. At the same time, a letter from the Korean King accompanied the Treaty which described his country's status as inferior to China's. This letter stated specifically that Korea was a dependency of China but that the intercourse between Korea and the United States should be carried on in every respect on terms of equality. It concluded:

> In the matter of Corea being a dependency of China in any question that may arise between them in consequence of such dependency, the United States shall in no way interfere.[12]

Hence both Japan and the United States had presumably negotiated treaties with Korea as a free and equal nation. China had permitted such negotiations, however, on the assumption that there were no inconsistencies between these treaties and the concept that Korea continued in reality to be a Chinese dependency. In other words, the issue of Korea's status relative to China and Japan was as unsettled as ever.

At the same time, the effects of implementing the Kanghwa Treaty and domestic intrigues within Korea complicated Japanese-Korean-Chinese relations. During preceding decades, the autocratic and corrupt court of the Korean King at Seoul had broken into several factions, each of which supported a contender for the throne. The lines of loyalty were further confused by the support which China and Japan gave to the contending factions. One of the two most important groups was led by the father and Regent of the young King, the Taewŏnkun. In general, the Taewŏnkun and his adherents were conservative, reactionary, and antiforeign, and were supported by China.

The other group was controlled by the Min, or family of the Queen, which acted through the King. The Queen's faction was relatively progressive, proforeign and pro-Japanese. It increased in strength in direct proportion to the growth of Japanese national strength and Japanese influence in Korea. After the Treaty of Kanghwa was signed with Japan in 1875, the Taewŏnkun was ousted as Regent and the King welcomed Japanese assistance. The Taewŏnkun then retaliated by instigating an attack against the Japanese Legation which forced the Minister to seek the safety of a British warship anchored in Pusan harbor. The Japanese immediately sent reinforcements to guard their legation and China countered with a similar move. At the same time, the latter captured the Taewŏnkun and whisked him away to Tientsin on the grounds that he had revolted against the Chinese Emperor. In reality, he was in safe keeping until such time as China might want to use him for political purposes. In the end, the King retained temporary control. He apologized to Japan for the revolt started by the Taewŏnkun, granted an indemnity to Japan for the losses sustained, and permitted an increase in the Japanese Legation Guard.

During the next few years, the history of Korea's foreign relations is that of intrigue and coercion by both China and Japan in their endeavor to obtain control over Korea's politics. In 1883, China sent Yüan Shih-kai to Korea as its chief resident, who openly aided and abetted those opposed to the Japanese. As foreign pressure increased, the King was in an untenable position. He first requested protection from the Japanese Minister but finally sought refuge under Yüan's protection. The situation had deteriorated to such an extent that the differences between China and Japan had to be settled either by negotiations or by war. Neither side was yet ready for war.

Hence, in 1885, the new Japanese Premier, Itō Hirobumi, went to Tientsin to meet Viceroy Li to work out a solution. After brief negotiations, they signed the Li-Itō Convention whereby both countries agreed to withdraw their troops from the Korean peninsula within four months. Furthermore, if disturbances within Korea required either of the signatories to dispatch troops, written notice of such intention would be sent to the other. Finally, they agreed that neither Chinese nor Japanese were to be employed in the organization or training of a Korean army. This agreement settled the crisis temporarily. Japan was not yet strong enough to force the Korean issue and China was confident that propinquity and historical precedent gave it an advantage. As the American Minister in Japan described it:

> Japan's policy was to allow Korea to be recognized as belonging to China in order to forestall the designs of any other country. . . . When Japan should fight China, Korea could be taken without fear of protest from European powers.[13]

The European power most concerned over Korea's future was, of course, Russia. So long as China and Japan had vied for exclusive control over Korean affairs, Russia was content to await a more propitious moment to exert its influence. Even before the Li-Itō Convention forbade the use of Chinese or Japanese advisers in the Korean Army, Russia was in an enviable position. When Von Mollendorf, a German in the employ of the Chinese Maritime Custom, went to Korea as a foreign adviser, he advocated the use of Russian officers to modernize the Korean Army. In return, Russia was to receive exclusive permission to use Port Lazaroff, the warm-water port of Wonsan. Both China and Japan protested against this move, so that Russian influence was temporarily kept out of the crucial area. For the moment the Li-Itō Convention had prevented the crisis over Korea from deteriorating but had not settled the question of whether China or Japan would dominate the peninsula. Peace in the Far East was contingent on the willingness of both of these countries to postpone a final showdown.

When the Japanese Constitution was promulgated in 1889, therefore, the various components of the nation's strength indicated growth and expansion, both economically and territorially. Agriculture, the country's basic industry, had produced enough staple food to meet domestic needs with a surplus for export. The difficulties of increased production, a limited acreage of untilled arable land, greater per capita consumption, and a steady rise in the birth rate were to combine, in the near future, to create a deficit in the rice supply. The deficiencies were met, however, by imports paid out of exports of raw silk and a limited amount of finished goods. Moreover, a more serious agrarian crisis was to be averted by the outbreak of war.

Financially, the nation was stronger in 1890 than at any other time in its recent history. The policy of retrenchment and fixed annual expenditures sponsored by Finance Minister Matsukata had effectively reduced the public debt, regained confidence in the currency, and increased annual revenues by more than half so that they were well in excess of expenditures. Industrial growth continued in both consumers' goods and heavy industries. Foreign trade showed an excess of exports over imports. With these auspicious developments, Japan absorbed an annual military budget of 20 million yen, about one-third of the total expenses, without showing any outward signs of strain. Could it be that fate had destined Japan to become the new leader of Asia?

A survey of Japan's territorial problems prior to 1890 tends to substantiate a positive answer to this question. There were few signs which indicated that Japan could easily be held in check if it decided to expand. Thus far it seemed to have succeeded in obtaining most of what it sought. The Russian boundary question had been settled; Hokkaidō was rapidly becoming more and more secure. The Ryūkyū Islands had been incorporated into the Empire. China's demands concerning them had been ignored. Only a war could wrest them from Japan.

As for Korea, Japan had not yet recognized it officially as a key to the control of the continent. So far, efforts had been partially successful in neutralizing Chinese influence in Korea. The best that could be hoped for at the moment was recognition by China, in word and in deed, that Korea was an independent country. As the realization grew that China intended to persist in its overlordship of Korea, Japan became obsessed with the desire to control the peninsula. It was an easy step in reasoning, therefore, to conclude that this control was necessary for national survival.

Japan had gone a long way in less than forty years. When Perry arrived it feared for its very existence. Now it dared to consider the use of force to obtain acceptance of its desires in territories such as Korea, which had not traditionally been considered a real or potential part of Imperial Japan. The thirst for empire was just beginning, as the thirst for power had already held the oligarchs in its grip.

Only one basic international question still remained unsettled. This was the revision of the unequal treaties with the Western powers. But even in the face of these difficulties, the oligarchs had retained complete control over the opposition. In the immediate future, however, this question of treaty revision and the problem of Japan's relations toward Korea were to absorb much of their thought and energy. For the next three decades, they were to be primarily concerned with carving out and consolidating an Empire which made Japan the dominant force in East Asia.

Notes

1. Since economic features for the earlier years of the Restoration have already been noted in Chapters 5 and 7, the economic sections of this chapter will concentrate on economic conditions covering the decade 1880-90. Some of the territorial questions, such as the settlement with Russia over the Kurile Islands and Sakhalien and the Formosan Expedition of 1874, have already been mentioned. Nevertheless, since it is important to have a comprehensive picture of Japan's territorial strength in 1890, these events have been repeated and elaborated for emphasis in the second half

of the present chapter. A description of the social and cultural scene in 1890 is postponed to Chapter 10.

2. See Ishii Ryoichi, *Population Pressure and Economic Life in Japan* (London: P. S. King & Staples, Ltd., 1937), p. 165. Also Table V, page 265.

3. It will be recalled that even the distress among the landowners, entrepreneurs, and farmers, which the *Jiyūtō* attempted to capitalize on, had largely subsided by 1889. (See *supra* page 135.)

4. Matsukata Masayoshi, "Japan's Finance," in Ōkuma Shigenobu, *Fifty Years of New Japan* (2 vols.; London: Smith Elders, 1910), I, pp. 364-65.

5. The following table indicates the large differential between the cost of the industries to the government and the sale price:

	Sale Price	Government Cost
Furukawa Cement	250,000 yen	468,000 yen
Innai Mine	75,000 "	195,000 "
Kosaka Mine	200,000 "	547,000 "
Shinagawa Glass Co.	80,000 "	189,000 "

See E. Herbert Norman, *Japan's Emergence as a Modern State* (New York: American Institute of Pacific Relations, 1940), p. 31.

6. Ono Guichi, *War and Armament Expenditures in Japan* (New York: Oxford University Press, 1922), p. 40. That the Army had grown up is clearly illustrated by Yamagata's willingness to shift from Minister of War in 1878 to other posts and to become Home Minister in 1885.

7. Edwin A. Falk, *Togo and the Rise of Japanese Sea Power* (New York: Longmans, Green & Co., Inc., 1936), p. 125; and Gombey Yamamoto, "The Japanese Navy," in Ōkuma Shigenobu, *Fifty Years of New Japan,* I, pp. 218-30.

8. Seward made these suggestions on the basis of his own experiences with Russia. He had purchased Alaska for the United States in 1867.

9. Political events pose a real problem as to what name should be used for the archipelago. The Chinese reading of the characters used for the islands is Liu-ch'iu; the Japanese reading of the same characters is Ryūkyū. Though perhaps confusing to the reader, I have decided to refer to them as the Ryūkyū Islands.

10. As the clauses in this treaty have an important bearing on the Chinese claim, the last clause reads as follows in the original:

日本國從前被害難民之家

See United States Government, *Chinese Treaties 1908,* II. For details of the Sino-Japanese negotiations which follow see *United States Department of State Archives 56,* "China," James B. Angell, November 16, 1880–February, 1881, Despatch No. 103, January 25, 1881. See also T. F. Tsiang, "Sino-Japanese Diplomatic Relations 1870-94," *Chinese Social and Political Science Review,* 1933, p. 45 *et seq.*

11. For the Chinese edition of Chiang's work see Chiang Kai-shek, *Chung Kuo Chih Ming Yun* (Chunking, December 15, 1945), pp. 6-7.

12. United States Department of State, *United States Foreign Relations 1888,* Part II, pp. 255-56.

13. Frederick Nelson, *Korea and the Old Order in Eastern Asia* (Baton Rouge: University of Louisiana Press, 1946), p. 206.

10

THE SOCIAL AND CULTURAL SCENE

Something of the conglomerate character of Japanese society in 1890 can be imagined from the preceding material, but the contributions of this society to the aggregate strength of the growing Empire have yet to be analyzed. The problem at hand is more than an elaboration of national characteristics and habits and a description of the social scene in the chief urban centers and in the remote villages. Rather, it is essential to determine the extent and effectiveness of the efforts of the Imperial government to mold the masses of society to become obedient, loyal, and industrious subjects of the Emperor. It is also important, if the true nature of the Japanese people in modern times is to be understood, to indicate the influences and acceptability of other forces on both those who led and those who followed. The subsequent description of the social scene will enumerate, therefore, some of the specific reforms deemed necessary to complete the process of national modernization. It will give illustrations of the effects, in many cases incongruous and unpredictable, of the conflict between an innate conservatism and nascent nationalism on the one hand, and an insatiable appetite for Western knowledge on the other. It will note the growth of a state-controlled educational system and a new legal system both of which attempted to preserve old concepts and to make all subjects amenable to the duties imposed upon them by virtue of the fact that they were Japanese.

As has been pointed out previously on numerous occasions, a highly developed ability to *adapt* foreign cultural attributes, an extensive eclecticism, has been a significant national characteristic of Japan. At no time in its history was this more clearly illustrated than in the first twenty years of the Meiji Period; in no aspect of life was this more apparent than in the effort toward modernization. In fact, thanks to this ability to select rather than to a blind desire to imitate, much of the friction which would normally be expected from the clash of Occidentalism with traditional Oriental customs and thought was avoided. In its place, the new government and many of the most brilliant young men of the country were able to combine a strong belief in the national heritage with technical knowledge of Western civilization.

The Two Currents of Nationalism and Occidentalism

In 1884, when Itō had returned from Germany and began to think specifically about drafting a constitution, a young man, twenty years his junior, had just been sent to the United States as a student. This young man, Nitobe Inazō, was to personify in his life this eclecticism in a unique manner. In the year that his country promulgated the Constitution, he was expounding on the two currents of Western civilization and of Japanese culture. Later he wrote eloquently of the conflict between the former, with its scientific, practical, and democratic approach, and the latter, with its literary, artistic, and aristocratic base. Learning in Japan meant a knowledge of religion, belles lettres, and Chinese ethics; education in the West covered all branches of knowledge. He concluded:

> Japan is experimenting with Western arts and sciences to see how far she can make them her own. . . . She will not repeat the folly . . . of introducing an exotic civilization wholesale; she could not do it now as she has too much at stake.[1]

To Nitobe, as well as to his contemporaries, the new Japan was not an accretion produced by foreign cultures, but the result of the application of an innate eclecticism to new circumstances and new stimuli.

In the first years of the Meiji Period, this sophistication was not as apparent as was the blind eagerness to learn the English language, a naïve belief that all foreigners had a superior knowledge of any subject, whether the foreigner was a drunken sailor, a profligate, a merchant, or a pious missionary of the Gospel. But by 1890 modernization had come to mean to people of all ranks, whether urban resident or lowly peasant, the prohibition of many of the customs and practices which had been accepted for centuries. The famous Charter Oath of 1868 set forth some of the basic objectives for the new society. All classes were to have a chance to fulfill their proper functions, absurd usages were to be abandoned, and knowledge was to be sought throughout the world. (See page 72 above.)

All general policies of this nature required time and effort to implement. Since an agrarian society such as that of Japan is inherently averse to change, and since the government's leaders had more important issues to solve than social changes, many of the old customs disappeared slowly. Social mobility was sanctioned and encouraged and people were free to travel and seek employment at will. Nevertheless, nearly everyone remained conscious of rank and class; few ventured away from familiar haunts in exchange for insecurity of a strange place or the uncertainty of a new position.

Fukuzawa Yukichi, who zealously awaited all decrees which abolished many of the outward signs of feudalism, relates a personal experience which illustrates this aversion to social change. Feudal custom and the common law had required that if a farmer or merchant were on horseback and met a warrior, he must immediately dismount and prostrate himself at the side of the road while the warrior passed by. Beginning in 1871, many new privileges had been given to the "commoners" to elevate their status. They could use a family name, ride horseback, marry into a warrior family, and even refuse to dismount when passing a warrior.

Sometime after the issuance of the edict cancelling the custom of dismounting before warriors, Fukuzawa, who by his attire gave away the fact that he was a member of the warrior class, met a farmer on horseback. The latter immediately jumped from his horse. Fukuzawa then ordered him to remount or he would beat him. Both the farmer and Fukuzawa showed that they were victims of the society in which they had been raised. The peasant, fearful lest he be beaten for observing the new custom, observed the old. On the other hand, though Fukuzawa intellectually accepted the new custom, he reacted in the old tradition as a warrior toward a peasant by threatening to force him to accept the new custom by a flogging.

Certain attributes of a modern state, however, dictated certain changes in custom. For example, the topknot, a kimono with long flowing sleeves, and a full skirt might have been little hindrance to a knight in battle who relied on old weapons and who duelled with a sword. For a modern army, however, requiring concerted action, mobility, and the use of modern firearms, all of these customs were a hindrance. The modern soldier wore a hat and had no time after reveille to fix an elaborate "hair-do." He must be ready to move easily and freely and march as a group. He could not be encumbered by broad kimono sleeves which were drafty in winter and easily snared at all times. Hence the Army was the moving spirit behind the abolition of many old social customs. To cut one's hair in the Western style, or to wear Western style hats, coats, shirts, and trousers on official government duty first became voluntary and then compulsory. To give incentive to the reform movement, the adverse reactions of the foreigners to old customs were often emphasized.

But the process of acculturation often produced a hodgepodge. A young blade might consider himself well-dressed with a derby, waistcoat, kimono, and wooden clogs. A Tokyo barber, with a beautifully styled headdress, and flowing kimono sleeves kept out of the way by a Western style apron, would see little incongruity in the fact that he was giving his client a Western style haircut. The government official, on the other hand, was not considered aptly dressed unless he wore a morning coat, striped pants, and a high silk hat to his office. When he returned home, he would change into his native dress.

The new national telegraph bureau was more disturbed than pleased over the farmer's misunderstanding of this new device. To the simple peasant, if men's thoughts could be transmitted over wires, it seemed logical that men's possessions likewise could be sent by the new invisible force. Consequently, they would constantly hang packages on the wires in the naïve belief that they would be mysteriously spirited away to their destination. Such practices, plus the farmer's fear of the purpose of the telegraph, became so prevalent that riders had to patrol the line constantly to keep it clear.[2] The peasant also had little use for the new law which forbade him to appear naked in public. His habit of not wearing clothes was dictated by utility. It was cooler in summer without them and it was far simpler to clean himself than his clothes after a day in the muck of the rice fields.

Many of these new restrictions on old customs, however, were full of political overtones. The peasant who was on the lookout for a way to ameliorate his economic plight used the enforcement of such decrees as conscription into the army as the immediate cause for local uprisings. The warrior who had been taught from childhood that it was more honorable to part with his life than with his sword, and who still considered himself superior to all other groups, received a blow to his pride and social status when forbidden after March 22, 1876, to wear his swords in public. He had been well prepared for this eventuality, however, by a decree issued as early as 1871 which made sword-wearing optional. Consequently, there was no public demonstration when the edict went into force. As observed above, by this time almost everyone (except Saigō and his men in Kyūshū) had accepted the inevitable changes which accompanied the elimination of the outward forms of feudalism.

Since these specific "reforms" were believed to be requisites on the road toward "modernization," they covered a wide range. For example, the government encouraged eating of beef for health reasons. When much publicity was given to the fact that the Emperor had eaten a dinner with roast beef, meat eating became a fad. Men believed that they understood modern civilization if they wore watches and jewelry, lit their houses with gas lamps, and rode in trains.

On some occasions, the nation was shocked by the official sponsorship of exhibitions of some of the less commendable manifestations of "Western civilization." One of the most notorious examples of this type of activity was the construction in 1883 by the government of a Western style pavilion, the *Rokumeikan*, for social engagements. Here meetings were held on foreign cooking and dressmaking, Western music, the renovation of art, novel writing, and the theater. Regular dances and social gatherings with the foreign community were officially sponsored by Foreign Minister Inouye. A fancy dress ball, held on April 20, 1887, brought severe criticism on Prime Minister Itō and his Cabinet, most of whom had attended the affair.[3] The public was shocked at the spectacle of a leading statesman cavorting in public over a dance floor in the arms of a foreign woman and dressed in a ridiculous costume. Their excuse for these activities was that they would bring a *rapprochement* between the Japanese and the foreigners and the revision of the unequal treaties that much closer. The argument soon lost weight, however, since negotiations for treaty revision were broken off only a few weeks later.

But all of this private and public interest in westernization made little difference to some of the basic, ingrained, social practices and concepts. Far more progress was made in changing superficial practices than in creating new social concepts. A feminist movement, including sponsorship of foreign education for a select group of young women, the first of whom were chaperoned as far as the United States by the Iwakura Mission in 1871, had little effect on the inferior position of women in Japanese society. The Constitution and the new codes verified this unequal status. The attempted liberation in 1871 of the professional entertainers (*geisha*) and of the prostitutes, who were indentured to their masters, was a useless gesture and had no effect on the universal acceptance of a double standard of morality for men and women.

The abolition of the pariah class (*eta*), who had performed the "unclean" tasks of scavengers, executioners, slaughterers, and tanners, was ordered in 1871, but their absorption into the general ranks of the common people was more theoretical than real. This group of three-quarters of a million persons continued to live in separate villages, married out of their group with difficulty, and were limited in the occupations open to them. In fact, their disparity was officially recognized by the approbrium of "new commoner" which was given to them.

Former social classes were abolished but a strong consciousness of class distinction continued. A new class, the nobles (*kazoku*), took the place of the former ruling warrior class in the minds of the common people. The Confucian concept of superior and inferior continued and was underscored by the constitutional provision for a House of Peers to "be composed of members of the Imperial Family, of Nobles, and of Deputies who have been appointed by the Emperor." Likewise, the family pattern continued largely unchanged on the basis of a vertical relationship. Marriages were arranged through a "go-between"; the daughter-in-law, who lived with her husband's parents, was subservient to their wishes; the head of the household was supreme and considered that the family existed for him and was subservient to his demands.

Education to Serve the State

Despite the tenacious hold which tradition had on society, old concepts and institutions gave way to new ones. As in the case of economic and political institutions already described, there were tremendous renovations in education but they came about slowly and their general purposes and patterns did not take final shape until shortly after the Constitution was promulgated. Traditionally, education had theoretically been limited to the warrior class, had been based on Confucian learning, and had been the responsibility of the feudal clans. The word of the teacher was not open to question and the greatest of deference was due him. Did not the pupil walk seven feet behind his instructor to avoid indiscreetly treading on his shadow? Many of the townsmen had been sufficiently educated to read popular literature. Time and patience were required before the concept was accepted that teaching was a science and that education was something to be organized into a system.

The leaders of the new government under Emperor Meiji had early recognized, however, the importance of education and the need for technical information on the subject. This need had been expressed in the Charter Oath of 1868 by the provision which specified that knowledge should be sought for "all over the world." (See page 72.) In the first years of the Restoration, foreign knowledge on education was largely limited, however, to that of the French system. Hence the Education Law of 1872, which established compulsory elementary education, was based on a French model. Education was described as being essential for success in all lines of pursuit, whether farming, manual arts, or business.

The system, as it was laid down on paper, was magnificent. It provided that boys and girls of all classes should receive primary education and that the more gifted should be given advanced training. The country was divided into university, middle school, and primary school districts with interlocking supervision. Many of the old urban schools and their teaching staffs were brought within the system, thereby giving it continuity with the old educational concepts and methods. But in reality, much had to be done to implement this new code. It could not be put into practice overnight or even within a few years. Buildings had to be constructed, teachers trained, curricula established, textbooks written and published, and the people educated to accept and cooperate with this new concept of compulsory education. Actually, as late as 1890 only half of those eligible for a primary education were taken care of.

Some of these obstacles were partly overcome by a first-hand survey of conditions abroad, by the employ of foreign advisers in key spots, and by improvisation. For example, the Iwakura Mission had a special educational section which spent several weeks in the United States surveying the

American educational system. It was greatly assisted by the Japanese Minister in Washington, Mōri Arinori[4] and by the United States Commissioner of Education. During this visit, members of the Mission made other important personal contacts with leading American educators and decided to employ some of them as advisers to their government.

For example, Professor David Murray (1830-1905) of Rutgers University was appointed adviser to the Ministry of Education in 1873. After his arrival in Japan, he spent nearly a year traveling and observing the newly created educational system at work and investigating the nation's needs before he wrote his first report in which he made several significant recommendations. In the first place, he urged instruction in Japanese rather than in foreign languages. The dearth of teachers and the immediate need for adequately trained instructors had necessitated the employment of a large proportion of foreigners. In the seven most important government schools, for example, there were fifty-one Japanese teachers and forty-six foreigners. He concluded:

> No system of universal education can be successfully carried out which shall not employ as its vehicle the common language of the people. . . . It must, therefore, be fully understood that the efforts to carry forward the national education in the languages of Europe are only temporary expedients.[5]

In the second place, Murray outlined the general lines to be followed in training future teachers. A select group of persons should first be trained in the principles of the projected primary school system. They should then become the staff of a normal school to introduce to others the new methods of teaching. Simultaneously, textbooks should be prepared and the requisite number of normal schools should be established to supply the needs of the country. For the next few years, his general recommendations were followed.

Another American, Marion M. Scott, trained the first teachers; American primary school textbooks were translated *in toto* for use in the Japanese schools. Foreign experts, estimated at 5000 persons at its peak, were used to instruct Japanese students especially in the sciences and technology. For example, British instructors in the various naval schools were largely responsible for the growth of the modern Imperial Navy. As soon as a core of Japanese were trained in the new techniques, the foreigners were replaced by their Japanese understudies.

But this initial emphasis of education on the needs of the individual, rather than those of the state, was gradually but effectively replaced by an educational system whose purpose was to train the individual to serve the state. This shift in policy followed the general political trend toward oligarchical control. By about 1880 the government leaders had developed a philosophy based largely on Prussian concepts. This new Prussian influence was soon reflected in the general reorganization of the national government and in the functions and authority delegated to the Ministry of Education. The new regulations of December, 1880, were directed against an attempt made the year before by Vice-Minister Tanaka Fujimarō to decentralize the system by the formation of local school boards.[6]

The new law bluntly decreed that the educational affairs of the whole country would be administered by the Department of Education. Furthermore, any important act of the Minister of Education had to be approved by the Privy Council. A new educational proclamation, or law, the selection of members of an educational mission or of students to go abroad, the framing of rules for government sponsored schools, or any deviation from existing rules, all had to receive the sanction of the Councilors. Since these same Councilors also determined the political policies of the government, it was obvious that the final shape of the educational system was going to be such as to strengthen the state.

During the decade from 1880, when the concept of a strongly centralized school system was accepted, to the issuance of a conservative, reactionary Edict on Education in 1890, most vestiges of liberalism in education disappeared. The mania for Western knowledge was replaced by a conscious effort to teach the old concepts of morality based on Confucian doctrines and national patriotism. After 1882, university courses in which the instructor lectured in a foreign language were dropped. Three years later, Mōri Arinori, who had become converted to Bismarck's political philosophy, was appointed Minister of Education. He was convinced that the primary purpose of education was to serve the state. The primary object of the schools (whose curricula now emphasized Oriental morality, the Chinese classics, and Japanese language and history) was to train the pupil in complete obedience to the wishes of the state.[7] Privately established schools, such as Keio University in Tokyo, founded by Fukuzawa, or the special school of Ōkuma, which developed into Waseda University, were not allowed to issue the same type of degree as that of the leading Imperial Universities, so that their graduates were unable to obtain government employment. The private institutions did serve a useful purpose, however, in training the core of leaders in the fields of industry, finance, and private education.

The central government strengthened its means of controlling national thought still further by the issuance in 1890 of the Imperial Rescript on Education. This edict, which had far more to say about patriotism, loyalty, and moral principles than about education, was the ultimate expression of the philosophy which had motivated the whole movement toward autocratic control. It was the basis of the nation's morals and ethics for the next half century and hence deserves to be quoted in its entirety. Its official translation follows:

Know Ye, Our Subjects:

Our Imperial Ancestors have founded Our Empire on a basis broad and everlasting and have deeply and firmly implanted virtue; Our subjects ever united in loyalty and filial piety have from generation to generation illustrated the beauty thereof. This is the glory of the fundamental character of Our Empire and herein also lies the source of Our Education. Ye, Our Subjects, be filial to your parents, affectionate to your brothers and sisters; as husbands and wives be harmonious; as friends be true; bear yourselves in modesty and moderation; extend your benevolence to all; pursue learning and cultivate arts, and thereby develop intellectual faculties and perfect moral powers; furthermore, advance public good and promote common interests; always respect the Constitution and observe the laws; should emergency arise, offer yourselves courageously to the State; and thus guard and maintain the prosperity of Our Imperial Throne coeval with heaven and earth. So shall ye not only be Our good and faithful subjects, but render illustrious the best traditions of your forefathers.

The Way here set forth is indeed the teaching bequeathed by Our Imperial Ancestors to be observed alike by the Descendants and the subjects, infallible for all ages and true in all places. It is Our wish to lay it to heart in all reverence in common with you, Our subjects, that we may all attain to the same virtue.[8]

This pronouncement and elaboration of the moral precepts which should guide all loyal Japanese subjects was in a sense a reversal of the fifth paragraph of the Charter Oath of 1868 which advocated seeking universal knowledge throughout the world. It was a triumph for Emperor Meiji's Confucian teacher, Motoda Eifu, who was convinced that Western ethical teachings were not suitable for Japan. It was a boon to Itō Hirobumi's philosophy that the Emperor, and loyalty to him, should be the axis around which the state and its subjects should revolve. In terms of modern methods of propaganda, it was a powerful weapon of thought control. In fine, it was a conscious and effective way of steering the people away from the exotic Western stream of civilization toward an amplified, intensified, national stream of culture which was to sweep all before it for the next half century.

A New Legal System

The problem of the creation of a legal system which would serve the needs of the new constitutional monarchy was extremely complicated. It involved both the conflict between Western and traditional concepts, a difficulty which was common to most of the reforms, and a diplomatic struggle between the Western powers and Japan over the question of revision of the treaties. It was necessary to reconcile such diametrically opposed ideas as the old feudal belief of complete subservience to authority and the modern concept of individual rights. Right of ownership of property was more essential than the right to receive an annual rice stipend. The state's power to collect a tax on personal holdings and recognition of individual indebtedness were a far cry from the old practices whereby the feudal baron possessed economic and financial autonomy within his own fief and the head of the household was held responsible for the debts of any of its members.

As for the conflict over the revision of the unequal treaties, various aspects of this problem have already been discussed (see Chapter 8), but its relation to the formulation of a new legal system has only been implied. In 1858, when the Western powers insisted that their nationals be tried in their own consular courts rather than in the local courts, the Japanese legal system left much to be desired. Such laws as existed discriminated in favor of the warrior. The townsman, craftsman, or peasant was intimidated by the overbearing warriors, lived in constant fear for his life, and was kept in ignorance of the law. Whenever anyone was arrested, he was expected to confess the crime of which he was accused. If no confession was forthcoming, it was exacted from him by ingenious and effective torture. Since the foreigners refused to be placed under the jurisdiction of this type of legal system, they had insisted on their own consular courts and other special privileges.

On the other hand, the nationalist-minded reformers were eager to eliminate these inequalities as rapidly as possible while the political opponents of the oligarchs kept relentless pressure on the government to revise the treaties. Many of the responsible ministers realized, however, that drastic reforms in the legal system would have to be inaugurated before any real progress could be made in treaty revision. Like many of the other features of the Restoration, it was not until after the Iwakura Mission returned in 1873 that the Council of State realized how formidable the problem was. Iwakura, who had been sent abroad specifically to revise the treaties had met with rebuffs in Washington, London, Paris, and Berlin. When he and his colleagues saw the differences of Western legal practices with those of Japan, they were forced to admit that their laws were inadequate.

The first written penal code, which was largely a codification of seventeenth-century Chinese legal concepts, had not been promulgated until 1870. Japanese jurists began to study Western legal institutions, particularly those of France, and a special law section of the Department of Justice translated French codes and gave instruction in French law. Foreign legal specialists were appointed to assist in the modernization program; Gustave Boissonade de Fontarabie from France began drafting a new criminal code. With the *Code Napoleon* as a model, it was completed in

1882 and remained in force until a decade after the Constitution was promulgated.

Since there had been even less progress in the codification of the civil law than of the criminal law, the government emphasized the importance of local usage in civil cases. In 1875, in an attempt to regularize civil procedure, orders were issued which provided that civil cases, in the event that there was no written statute, were to be decided according to custom. In default of common procedure, they were to be settled by reason and justice. In reality, the judge decided cases on the basis of whatever legal system he might have studied. Simultaneously, work continued on various drafts of a civil code which was finally placed under Boissonade's supervision.

By 1885, when Itō became Premier and was prepared to begin the serious preparation of the new Constitution, the legal system was in complete confusion. A Criminal Code, similar to that of the *Code Napoleon* was in force; the draft of the new Civil Code was unsatisfactory; a Commercial Code had yet to be accepted. The Western powers were in no mood, therefore, to concede that the Japanese legal system had been revised sufficiently to permit them to abandon extraterritoriality.

In 1886 the negotiations were again begun with the foreign powers to conclude a new series of treaties. (See page 140.) At the same time, a Bureau to Study the Legal Codes was formed. It produced a revised Civil Code as well as new drafts for the treaties. When it was published in 1888 the public became indignant at its recommendations, which permitted use of foreign judges in cases that involved foreigners, and which opened the hinterland to them. The Japanese people objected strenuously to having the foreigners roam over their country at will. They also saw no further need for any form of extraterritorial rights. Despite this widespread opposition, a series of Imperial Conferences were held in 1889 to consider these recommended revisions for the treaties. At this point, public indignation produced dramatic consequences. Ōkuma had been appointed Foreign Minister to solve the knotty treaty problem. (See page 141.) He was considered responsible, therefore, for these unpopular proposals and criticism was aimed at him. As he returned home from one of the Conferences a bomb was thrown at him which resulted in the loss of his leg. It also postponed the settlement of the issue of unequal clauses in the treaties for another few years.

By 1890, however, when Parliament first met, a strict Criminal Code was in effect, a new Civil Code had been drafted, and the German jurist, Herman Roessler, had codified the Commercial Code on the basis of the German model. As the new parliamentary government began to function and as the foreigners insisted on further legal reforms before they would agree to revision of the treaties, innumerable changes were made in the Codes before they were acceptable.[9] At the same time, these changes in the legal system strengthened the state's control over the individual. France's influence in the Civil Code had been replaced by that of Germany.

Some of the unique features of Japanese society were preserved under the new laws. For example, they recognized that all persons in a household were under the control of the head of the house. Nevertheless, new rights were given individual members of the house, such as the right to own property. Furthermore, since property was inherited by members of the house rather than by the group as a whole, the head of the household was no longer liable for the debts of all its members. Society's assumption that women had an inferior status was recognized in the marriage, divorce, and inheritance laws. From the point of view of the government, the legal system was an effective partner of the educational system in making the subject a servant of the state to be used by the state to make it strong.

Religion and Thought

In the early years of the Meiji Restoration, the national government had taken a direct interest in the control of religion. This interest was reflected in the first reorganization of the government, which placed the Bureau of Shintō Religion above all of the other departments of the Council of State. This temporary elevation of Shintōism, an indigenous polytheistic animism and ancestor worship, to become the state religion created a violent anti-Buddhist movement (*Shimbutsu bunri*). For a few months immediately following the abolition of the Shogunate in 1868, all Shintō shrines were forced to rid themselves of Buddhist influence or risk destruction at the hands of fanatical exponents of the new national faith. But the movement petered out as rapidly as it had arisen and Shintoism was temporarily forgotten.

The active interest of the government in religious problems was next aroused by the activities of the Christians. The traditional anti-Christian attitude of the country and its people has already been emphasized. (See Chapter 2.) Despite bans proscribing it as a religion and the imposition of the death penalty for all believers, a number of households in southwestern Japan had secretly maintained their faith in Catholicism. Even before the Restoration, both Catholic and Protestant missionaries appeared in Japan but were restricted in their evangelical activities because of the continuance of the anti-Christian edicts and of the laws forbidding foreigners to leave the port cities. As late as 1870, the government received complaints from the Buddhist priests that the ban on Christianity was being flaunted. Consequently notices were again posted which proclaimed that "the evil religion of Christianity was strictly prohibited as heretofore," and nearly 4000 Catholic communicants were removed from the Nagasaki area.

This move had a calamitous effect on both Protestants and Catholics as many of the native Christians gave up working for the missionaries. But the picture abruptly changed in 1873 when the edict against Christianity was removed. As Dr. Daniel Crosby Greene, a missionary of the Congregational Church in Kōbe recorded:

> Soon there followed the dawn of a better day. The edicts against Christianity were taken down from the notice broad; Roman Catholic Christians were restored to their homes and it was a privilege to minister to some of them as they passed through the streets of Kobe. Gradually the consciousness of freedom spread among the people and our little chapel was thronged with curious believers.[10]

Evangelical activities were now openly undertaken by the small band of Protestant missionaries, and a committee began to translate the Bible into Japanese. New converts were made but progress was slow. The Japanese had difficulty in comprehending some of the basic Christian concepts, and other aspects of Western civilization seemed more appealing and more utilitarian than the new religion. English Bible classes were often attended more for the practice which they afforded in the language than for the theology which was taught. By 1881, there were roughly 4500 Protestants and 25,000 Roman Catholic converts; by 1889 the numbers had risen to 32,000 and 26,000 respectively, together with 16,000 Greek Orthodox adherents.

But the strength of this new movement can better be measured in terms of official and unofficial reaction to it rather than by citing the number of converts. Aside from the relaxation of the restrictions on Christians, the government took little interest in the movement until it decided in 1890 to issue a general statement on the moral principles which should guide the Empire. By that time, thanks to the tireless efforts of a small band of ardent believers, Christianity had begun to make an impression on the Japanese intellectual world. One of the most significant projects was Dōshisha University in Kyōto. Its founder, Niishima Jo (Reverend Joseph Hardy Neeshima), had graduated from Amherst College, had been ordained as a Congregational minister and had returned home to establish a Japanese center of Christian training. In 1884 he toured the United States for funds to build Dōshisha into a first-class university. His return coincided with the increasingly intense conflict between Christianity and the new nationalism as later expressed in the Edict on Education. Although Dōshisha was not disbanded, its expansion and rise were retarded, while national education, including the Imperial Universities, expanded. It also suffered from what Niishima described as too much emphasis on the Bible to the neglect of scientific teaching.

Both the influence of the missionaries and the national significance of the growing conflict between Christianity and nationalism are clearly illustrated by the activities of Uchimura Kanzō (1861-1930). After studying English in Tokyo, Uchimura decided in 1877 to enter the Sapporo Agricultural School which was training leaders for the economic exploitation of Hokkaidō. Although the school was a government school, it had a strong Christian influence. For example, when Uchimura arrived he learned that the entire first class had been baptized by the Methodist missionary, M. C. Harris. Dr. William S. Clark, who had been brought from Massachusetts, had refused to teach ethics unless he were permitted to teach the Bible. Deeply religious, he left a permanent influence on the lives of men such as Uchimura and Nitobe. (See page 171.)

After graduation, Uchimura worked in the Ministry of Agriculture but interrupted his bureaucratic career to go to the United States to see a Christian country in action. He hoped that such a trip would teach him how to serve his own country better. He was at first disillusioned by what he found but was later inspired by those who befriended him. He, like Niishima, graduated from Amherst College, studied theology, and returned home in May, 1888. Unlike Niishima, however, he refused to cooperate with the foreign missionaries and declined to teach at Dōshisha because of the foreign support it received.

This emphasis on a native Christian Church, independent of foreign support, which later grew into the strong *Mukyōkai,* brought Uchimura into personal conflict with the new nationalism and with the authorities. After his return to Japan, he became an English teacher and spiritual adviser to 600 dormitory students in the First Higher School, one of the chief preparatory schools for Tokyo Imperial University. Subsequent to the promulgation of the Rescript on Education, the Principal of the First Higher School announced a meeting of the faculty and students of the school to acknowledge formally the receipt of this document. Each member of the faculty was ordered to go singly to the platform and to bow to the Imperial signature affixed to the Rescript.

Uchimura considered this performance similar to the obeisance required at Buddhist and Shintoist ceremonies. He concluded:

> I took a safer course for my Christian conscience and in the august presence of sixty professors . . . and over one thousand students, I took my stand and did not bow.[11]

The effect of his adamant stand was electrifying. The national press and public opinion branded him as a traitor. Despite a subsequent compromise with his conscience and promise to bow before the Rescript, pressure was so strong and opinion was so united in the view that he had committed lese majesty that he was forced to resign from the school.

This incident, while it did not prevent Uchimura from becoming one of the most effective advocates of Christianity, sharpened the schism between those who believed their greatest loyalty was to God and those who considered their paramount patriotism and loyalty was to the throne. It was used by Christianity's arch enemies as an illustration of the incompatibility of Christianity with the ideals set forth in the Rescript. The most eloquent advocate of this position was the outstanding philosopher, Professor Inouye Tetsujirō. In a famous article published in 1893, which expressed the views of most of the Imperial University scholars, Inouye argued that Christianity was contrary to the concept of national polity (*kokutai*), that monotheism and undivided loyalty to God were subversive to the principles of obedience, loyalty, and nationalism as expounded in the Rescript. Inouye's blast was only the first round of an extended polemic whose results were inconclusive.

The Constitution provided that ". . . subjects shall within limits not prejudicial to peace and order, and not antagonistic to their duties as subjects, enjoy freedom of religious beliefs." (Article 28.) The matter boiled down, therefore, to the question of whether the beliefs of the Japanese Christians or missionaries forced them, as had been true of Uchimura, to run counter to existing laws and whether these laws were strictly enforced. In reality, Christianity and a strong nationalism coexisted and tolerated each other. The government was confident, however, that the universal dissemination of morals and ethics based on traditional nationalism would more than counteract any subversive effect of Christianity.

The Press and Literature

Even before the Restoration, no aspect of life was free from the influences of the Western stream of culture which had been trickling past the curtain of isolation. Since this stream brought with it new knowledge, new concepts, and new techniques, the curtain became perforated and ever more numerous aspects of Occidental culture appealed to the imagination of the Japanese. But the mysteries of this new culture could not be solved unless its languages could be understood. Prior to Perry's arrival no one had considered it important to learn any foreign language other than Chinese or Dutch.

After the country was formally opened to the West and foreign consulates were established, however, there was a shift away from the study of Dutch toward English and French. Increased contacts with the foreigners required a much larger body of competent interpreters than heretofore. Official communications between the representatives of the foreign powers and the central government, business transactions between foreigners and Japanese merchants, trips abroad of individuals and official missions, all required a minimum language competence at least by a corps of interpreters. Consequently, by 1868, the first year of the Meiji Restoration, more than a decade had elapsed to permit comparatively widespread competence in European languages by many of the leaders of the country. Under the new Imperial regime, this movement gained momentum.

At the same time, not only these persons but any Japanese who had direct or indirect contact with the foreigners, became exposed to new media for the dissemination of ideas and new forms of writing. One of the most significant of these innovations of the foreigners was the newspapers. As early as 1862, the Tokugawa government had ordered its Foreign Language Investigation Office to translate news sheets published by the Dutch in Batavia. These included the *Batavia Nieuws* and shortly thereafter the *Javaische Courant.* The next efforts in newspaper publishing were undertaken by the foreigners and included the Yokohama publications of the *Japan Commercial News* and the *Japan Times,* which were also translated by the government officials.

During the next few years, stimulated by the innovations inaugurated by the new Imperial government, a host of papers, many of them small and published irregularly, appeared in the Japanese language. Toward the end of 1870, the *Yokohama Mainichi,* a single sheet published daily on foreign paper by movable lead type, became the first regular Japanese daily. It was followed shortly by papers published by foreigners or sponsored by individuals who used them to gain support for their point of view. But their influence was restricted because their distribution was limited to the metropolitan areas, particularly Yokohama, Ōsaka, and Tokyo, and only a small number of copies were printed. For example, the largest paper, the *Nishin Shijishi,* printed by J. R. Black, had a daily circulation of only 1500 copies.[12]

In 1874, when the leaders of the movement for people's rights, such as Itagaki Taisuke, used their own papers to criticize the policies of the oligarchs, the central government moved in. It could not afford to let such issues as the national financial crisis, the Korean expedition, or the form and content of a constitution be discussed indiscriminately by the budding journalists. It might be disastrous to the privileged position of the oligarchs, particularly in view of the adoption of universal education and the rapid increase in literacy, if these papers were allowed freedom of expression and if this concept were accepted by their readers as a fundamental right of the people. Consequently, restricting legislation was adopted in this field just as it had been imposed in others.

In 1875, while the debate raged between the "liberals" and the government on the question of liberty and rights for the people (see Chapter 6), the Meiji government issued a Press Law which gave it extensive powers of control. There followed a struggle, which was to continue until the 1930's with varying degrees of intensity, between the government which tried to enforce the laws and the papers which sought ways and means of evading them. The latter, as they received public support, became bolder and more open in their criticism which stimulated the issuance of even more restricting laws. Specifically, the Press Law of 1875 provided for a fine and imprisonment of editors whose papers criticized government policy. The papers evaded the laws by hiring dummy editors, who were popularly known as "prison editors," who paid the fine and served the jail sentence for the paper while it continued to appear. The government remedied this weakness in the law the next year by an amendment which called for suspension of publication as well as the penalties of fines and imprisonment.

Humorous as this contest may seem in retrospect, the authorities zealously kept control over public opinion and never allowed it to get out of hand. When the issues of the Constitution and the revision of the treaties with the foreigners were still unsettled, the laws were again strengthened in 1883 and 1885. Under the new laws, each paper had to deposit 1000 yen which was forfeited any time the Home Ministry decided an article was inimical to the public welfare.

As a result of these limitations, as well as the need of extensive capital dictated by modern plant facilities, the number of newspapers was radically reduced and there was a shift away from polemics to the reporting of facts. The outstanding leader in this new trend was the *Asahi* papers published by Maruyama Ryūhei in Ōsaka and Tokyo. Maruyama founded the papers in 1879 and immediately introduced innovations. He developed his own wire and news services to enable his papers to base their stories on facts rather than on hearsay reports. These innovations had a leavening effect on the standards of the entire newspaper world. Rival papers, such as the *Jiji Shimpō*, founded in 1882 by Fukuzawa Yukichi,[13] adopted similar methods of operation. With the opening of Parliament in 1890, the best papers had their permanent correspondents in Tokyo and other important cities, subscribed to foreign telegraph services through Reuters, speeded publication through the use of the revolving press, and relegated police stories to the third page.

A unique contribution which the newspapers made to the nation's cultural development was through the publication in serial form of many of the early novels and translations of Western books. While it is true that some published separate books, many of the literati supported themselves by writing novels in serials for the newspapers. Although the novel had long been a popular type of literature in Japan,[14] it had differed in form from the Western style novel, had lacked the concept of a sustaining plot, and, in later years, had fallen under the influence of Chinese literary tradition. With the influx of the numerous practical aspects of Western civilization and a popular desire to learn about Europe, the newspapers sponsored the translations of Occidental novels. These translations, which at one time comprised nearly 90 per cent of the books published, were accepted with great enthusiasm by their readers.

During the period from 1877 to 1890, these translations of foreign novels awakened the Japanese writers and the public to new possibilities of literature. Such works as Bulwer Lytton's *Ernest Maltravers,* which was translated in 1878, or Disraeli's *Coningsby,* which received the translated title of "Spring Warblings" in 1884, caused a sensation. They appeared just when political problems absorbed men's minds and motivated their actions. Some of the most popular Japanese authors, both out of political conviction and because of the profits involved, began to turn to political problems. The result was the emergence of a new, virile novel which recorded the disappointments, the hopes, and aspirations of its author. It centered about the history of Japan and hinted at dissatisfaction with existing political conditions.

One of the most representative and popular authors of the political novel was Suehiro Tetchō (1848-96). He was educated in his fief's school, became one of its teachers, and went to Tokyo in 1870 to continue his studies. He was an active member of Itagaki's "liberal movement" and first expressed his views in the newspapers for which he worked. When he criticized the Press Law of 1875, he was fined and restricted to his home for three months. His first important political novel, *Setchū Bai* (1886), dealt with contemporary politics and indirectly advocated, by its descriptions of governments in other countries, the adoption of a popular representative government in Japan. This was followed the next year by another novel (*Kakan-ō*) which ends with the Liberal party (*Jiyūtō*) triumphant in the national political struggle. After the new Constitution was promulgated in 1889, however, his political writings, as well as those of his contemporary political novelists, lost their popularity.

Two other important influences on the development of the modern novel must be noted. In the first place, Tsubouchi Shōyō (1859-1935) had a profound influence on the form and substance of the novel. At the age of fourteen, he began the study of English at the Foreign Language School in Nagoya. Shortly thereafter, he was sent to Tokyo where he continued his studies of English and began translations of Shakespeare and Scott. By 1885, after he had been greatly influenced by the English literature which he had read, translated, and taught, he wrote *The Essence of Fiction* (*Shōsetsu Shinsui*). This work was the first to explain the meaning and purpose of a European style novel. He emphasized the necessity to free the novel from the deadening effects of traditions of the Tokugawa Period, to emphasize realism, and to depict life accurately. He also advocated a psychological penetration which was new to Japanese authors and readers.

This work was so important that some literary historians consider its appearance as the beginning of the modern novel in Japan.

The final stage in the development of modern Japanese literature was reached with the publication of Futabatei Shimei's (1864-1909) famous novel *Drifting Cloud* (*Ukigumo*) in a semicolloquial style. Its first installment appeared in 1888. Futabatei, unlike both Suehiro and Tsubouchi, who had largely been influenced by British thought, was a follower of Russian writers such as Tolstoy and Gorky, whose works he also translated. The characters in his books were taken from the crowds and, like those around him, were tormented and uncertain. His style was simple and his works were the inspiration for future young writers of the naturalist school and made the novel understandable to the average graduate of the new educational system.

By the opening of the first session of Parliament in 1890, when the new Constitution began to operate, the cultural and social phases of society reflected the same tendencies as those in the political and economic spheres. While certain practical manifestations of Western civilization had been incorporated into new social customs, into the national educational system, in the law courts and legal codes, in journalism and modern literature, there was not blind acceptance of both the form and substance of these foreign practices. Rather, a highly developed eclecticism permitted the adaptation of elements compatible with traditional customs and beliefs and amenable to regulation and control by the state. In the first few years of the Meiji Period, both the government and people were confused by the complexity and number of the problems which must be solved. The impact of Christianity and of British and American advisers in various branches of the Imperial government, notably in education, bode well for the universal acceptance of democratic principles and concepts of government by and for the people. The widespread influence of France in the early organization of the Army and in the legal codes gave added strength to the movement.

But as the power of the central government increased, a small group of oligarchs defeated the supporters of a modified form of the political philosophy of Mill and of Rousseau and kept these advocates under close surveillance. The clan bureaucrats sought, by every means at their disposal, to make their country strong and to perpetuate and to enhance the privileges and prerogatives of the Emperor and of themselves. Consequently, the oligarchs turned to the supervision of the cultural traits of society to make them consistent with accepted political philosophy. By the time that Itō and his colleagues had agreed that a modified form of Prussian style constitutional monarchy was applicable to Japan, that the state was supreme, and that the subject existed to serve the state, changes were ordered in the educational and legal systems.

By 1890, when the new Constitution was in operation, the earlier democratic influences of England, the United States, or France had been eradicated from the national system of education, from the law codes, and from the press. As an extra precaution against the re-emergence of these influences or against an untoward increase in the effectiveness of Christianity, the conservatively minded statesmen obtained Imperial sanction for the issuance of a new set of moral principles to which all loyal subjects must prescribe on pain of social ostracism, economic purge, or even death. Hence men's thoughts, as well as the form of government and the economic system under which they lived, were to be cast into an increasingly rigid, nationalistic mold. The first half century of Japan's modern history had seen a phenomenal modernization, but it had also witnessed a centralization of control, a subordination of the individual to serve the purposes of the state, and a pronouncement of acceptable and prescribed beliefs and practice. Those who conformed to the will of the state, whether neighboring nations or Japanese subjects, would receive the benevolent blessings of the Emperor. Those who dared to challenge that will would have to be forced to accept it or perish.

Notes

1. Nitobe Inazō (1862-1933) was born into a warrior family of Morioka fief. While a student at Sapporo Agricultural College, he came under the influence of Dr. C. T. Clark and was a close personal friend of the outstanding Christian, Uchimura Kanzō. Nitobe received his Ph.D. degree at Johns Hopkins University, married a Philadelphia Quaker girl, and returned the year the Constitution was promulgated to be President of his alma mater. After holding various teaching posts, he was Under-Secretary General of the League of Nations (1920-26). Long an advocate of internationalism, he was an archopponent of the Army's policies toward Manchuria and North China in the 1930's but died on a visit to America when it appeared as though he had given up his opposition to them. The quotation is from his *Western Influences in Modern Japan* (Chicago: University of Chicago Press, 1931), p. 22.

2. For illustrations of the strange mixture of the exotic strains of the East and the West see *Gaihō Kindai Hyakunenshi,* Nos. 3-6, 1951 (Tokyo: Kokusai Bunka Johosha, 1951). One picture is of special interest, a photograph of the Iwakura Mission taken at San Francisco in January, 1872, shows Ōkubo, Kido, Itō, and Yamaguchi in formal western attire, and Iwakura in a Japanese costume and topknot. *Ibid.,* No. 3, p. 203.

3. *Ibid.,* No. 5, pp. 394-95 for description, cartoons, and pictures of what it refers to as the Rokumeikan Period.

4. Mōri Arinori (1847-89) was from Satsuma. He realized at an early age the need for information on foreign affairs and hence devoted himself to "Western

studies." After his clan's bombardment by the British in 1863, promising young men were sent to England to study. Mōri was one of them and arrived in London in June, 1865. There he studied mathematics, chemistry, physics, and Russian naval techniques. He returned home in 1868, to be sent to Washington as Japanese Minister in 1870, where he immediately started a survey of the American educational system. Fifteen years later, when he was to become Minister of Education, he had abandoned American concepts of education for those of Germany. He was murdered in 1889, purportedly for not having shown proper respect to the Emperor.

5. United States, Bureau of Education, *Circular of Information,* No. 2, 1875, p. 20.

6. Tanaka Fujimarō (1846-1909) was, like several of the members of the Iwakura Mission, a student of the American missionary, Guido F. Verbeck. The latter had been in Japan since 1859. Despite his connection with Christianity, Verbeck was president of a school which was the forerunner of Tokyo Imperial University. Tanaka became Vice-Minister of Education in 1876. With the preference for German pedagogical methods after 1880, his influence rapidly declined. Dr. David Murray, who supported Tanaka's views, had left Japan in 1879.

7. This Herbartian pedagogical philosophy was expounded after 1887 at Tokyo Imperial University by the German philosopher and educator, Emil Hausknecht. His conservative philosophy became prevalent not only because it appeared to be applicable to Japan but because it was consistent with the whole philosophy of the state developed by the oligarchs. Obviously, if they had not approved of his point of view, they would not have approved his appointment. For an interesting discussion of Hausknecht's influence, see Nitobe, *Western Influences,* p. 43 ff.

8. Japan, Department of Education, *A General Survey of Education in Japan* (Tokyo: 1937), p. ii. It should be said in the government's defense that emphasis on old concepts of morality was perhaps the safest antedote to the prevalence of amorality and aversion to the past.

9. The chronology of the drafting and promulgation of the Civil Code indicates the confusion which existed. The part of the Code dealing with property was published in 1890. In 1893 the effective date of the entire code was postponed to permit further changes. Three books, those on General Provisions, Real Rights, and Obligations were promulgated in 1896. The entire code was revised and published just prior to the effective date of the new treaties in 1898.

10. Evarts B. Greene, *A New Englander in Japan* (Boston: Houghton Mifflin Co., 1927), p. 113. The timing of this edict can be traced to the return of the Iwakura Mission. The Mission had been partly inspired by Verbeck, and its members could not but have been impressed by the fact that it was the Christian Occident that was strong and the anti-Christian Japan that was weak.

Figures on total converts vary widely and are increased by the inclusion of children. The figures quoted are those accepted by Anesaki Masaharu, *History of Japanese Religion* (London: Kegan Paul, Trench, Trubner & Co., Ltd., 1930); and Otis Cary, *A History of Christianity in Japan* (2 vols.; New York: Fleming H. Revell Co., 1902).

11. It was the universal practice for all schools to have copies of the Rescript on Education. The Rescript and the portrait of the Emperor were considered to be the most valuable possessions of the school. Yearly ceremonies were held at which the Rescript was read to the entire school, during which everyone bowed reverentially. The quotation from Uchimura is from a letter, dated March 6, 1891, to David C. Bell, a Minneapolis banker, ardent Christian and lifelong inspiration to Uchimura. It is contained in Uchimura's *Collected Works* (Tokyo: Iwanami Shoten,

1932-33). The most thorough study of Uchimura in English to date is that of John Howes, *Uchimura Kanzo (1861-1930)*, Master of Arts Thesis, Columbia University, New York, 1953.

12. Black was most disdainful of the veracity and caliber of his competitors. In his *Young Japan. Yokohama and Yedo* (2 vols.; London: Trubner & Co., 1880-81), he has given some pertinent information on the period.

13. Fukuzawa, who had close ties with Itagaki's "Liberal Movement," described the purpose of his paper as follows:

> To describe modern civilization, to discuss the ways and methods of attaining this civilization, and to furnish information to the public that it will not fall behind.

Both the *Jiji Shimpō* and the *Asahi* continue to be published today, but the latter remains the more powerful paper.

14. The reader is doubtless familiar with *The Tales of Genji* (London: George Allen & Unwin, Ltd., 1935) through the admirable translation by Arthur Waley of the eleventh-century novel *Genji Monogatari* by Murasaki Shikibu. This novel has always been popular with Japanese readers. In the eighteenth century there was a rash of "realistic" novels, many of them centering around life in the licensed quarters in the cities.

PART III

ESTABLISHMENT OF THE JAPANESE EMPIRE 1889-1915

There is a Law of Nations, it is true,
But when the moment comes, remember,
The Strong eat up the Weak.

From a *Song of Diplomacy* by
Komuro, translated by G. B. Sansom,
in *The Western World and Japan*

Chronology

1890-1915

1890, November	First Diet opened
1892, February	Violence in elections
	Itō becomes Premier
1894	Treaty with Great Britain abolishing extraterritoriality
July 25	Outbreak of Sino-Japanese War
1895, April 17	Treaty of Shimonoseki
	The Triple Intervention, forcing the return of Liaotung
1898	Acquisition of Liaotung by Russia
	Rosen-Nishi Agreement
1899	The Open Door Policy
1900	Boxer Uprising
	Yamagata-Itō rivalry; Itō forms Seiyūkai party
1902	Anglo-Japanese Alliance
1904, February 8	Outbreak of Russo-Japanese War
1905, July	Taft-Katsura Agreement
	Anglo-Japanese Alliance renewed and strengthened
September 5	Treaty of Portsmouth
November	Itō becomes Resident General of Korea
1907, July 25	Protectorate over Korea
1908	Katsura Cabinet
1909, October	Itō assassinated at Harbin
1910, August 22	Korea annexed by Japan
1912, July 30	Death of Emperor Meiji
1914, April	Ōkuma becomes Premier
August 23	Japan declares war on Germany
November	Japan completes capture of German-leased territory in Shantung
1915, January 15	Twenty-One Demands presented to China
May 25	China reluctantly agrees to demands

11

THE OLIGARCHS IN POWER UNDER THE CONSTITUTION, 1889-1895

In a little more than a generation, from Perry's arrival in Japan in 1853 to the promulgation of the Constitution on February 11, 1889, Japan had undergone dramatic changes. Some of this transformation was, however, more superficial than real. Most of it had been inspired and directed by a small group of oligarchs. Many of the reforms which they had inaugurated, such as the promulgation of a new Constitution, had yet to be tried by experience. Nevertheless, the basic prerequisites for a modern state were at hand: an effective central government, a conscript army, a system of universal education, an abundant labor supply, a potentially important industrial and commercial society, and an agrarian production sufficient to meet immedate demands. Obviously Japan had met the challenge of Western civilization by *adapting* the basic elements of Westernization.

The significant question to be answered in 1890 was not whether Japan was to become a modern state. It was rather, "What type of state and how important a country was it to become?" Would the oligarchs continue to retain control through the manipulation of the constitutional government which they had created? Would the civil or military group among the oligarchs finally gain the ascendancy? What influence would modernization have upon the country? Could the economic and political aspirations of a virile people be met within the territorial confines of the empire as of 1890? If not, what effect would international forces have on the course of the Japanese Empire? How significant would that empire become? Could it possibly become strong enough to play a leading part in world politics? What would be the net effect of the interaction of these forces on Japan and on the world during the next generation?

In view of the fact that the next quarter century covered by this study saw the creation of a strong Japanese Empire with formidable colonies, international problems dominate the scene. As the empire grew, Japan became increasingly involved in world politics. By May, 1915, this involvement had reached its climax. Japan took advantage of the preoccupation of the Allies in the war in Europe to consolidate its position in China. It demanded and received preferential treatment and special privileges on the Asiatic continent and became the undisputed leader of East Asia.

While achieving this prominent position as a world power, the oligarchs had successfully met every challenge to their supremacy from the people and from the political parties. Such struggles as took place between Parliament and the Cabinet, or between the party members in the House of Representatives and the oligarchs were over domestic issues and for control of the reins of government. On the all-important issue of establishment of a strong empire, all groups supported an aggressive foreign policy. Such differences as existed on questions of diplomacy were on matters of method rather than on questions of policy.

The Oligarchs Retain Control, 1890-94

Before describing Japan's successes in the war against China in 1894, it is necessary to turn to the bitter domestic struggle between the political parties and the oligarchs after the new Constitution went into effect. The conclusion of the short ceremonies on February 11, 1889, which promulgated the Meiji Constitution, was the signal for the renewal of the political battle silenced two years earlier by the harsh measures enforced by Home Minister Yamagata. With elections for members of the lower branch of Parliament in the offing, the political parties (*mintō*) had a new *raison d'être*.[1] At last, they had a legitimate opportunity to prove both their strength and their worth by sponsoring candidates in the election.

Although they were resentful of the conservative nature of the Constitution, the party leaders placed great hopes in the power they would be able to exert through Parliament. Despite the constitutional limitations on the powers of the House of Representatives, they fully expected that the new national government would be operated on the principle that the Premier would be selected from the largest party in the House. They anticipated that if a majority of the members of the House of Representatives belonged to the parties, the political parties and those who supported "popular rights" would be in a strong position to counteract the influence of their opponents, the clan oligarchs. In fact, the parties might even be able to control the executive as well as the legislative branch of the government. As the strength of the parties lay in the general unpopularity of the oligarchs among the people, every effort was made to capitalize on this situation. For example, the party candidates criticized the slow progress of the negotiations for the revision of the unequal treaties with the Western powers. They also challenged the right of the oligarchs to continue to monopolize the key positions in the government and to refuse to inaugurate democratic practices.

On the other hand, the clan bureaucrats had no intention of allowing the Constitution to deprive them of their authority. They had moved adroitly and cautiously toward a constitutional monarchy. Whenever they made concessions toward popular representation in government, they contrived safeguards to protect the prerogatives of the throne and to assure the predominance of the executive over the legislative. They had conceived and drafted the Constitution in such a way as to provide a bare minimum of representative institutions and a maximum of Imperial absolutism.

Certain ingrained social concepts and patterns of action gave the oligarchs a distinct advantage over the political parties in the fight to retain control. In the first place, the Constitution had been granted by the Emperor to the people. This act was a natural consequence of the feudal concept of subordination of the inferior to the authority of the superior. Furthermore, the basic social concept of group responsibility greatly assisted the leaders of the government. Anyone familiar with contemporary Japan is aware of the importance of group consideration (*sōdan*) of a problem before a decision is made. This traditional procedure of passing judgment on any issue—whether a family or national problem—had not been affected by the Meiji Restoration. On the contrary, examples already cited clearly indicate that group decisions determined basic policies throughout the Restoration Period. Such a procedure exonerated any single individual from blame if the policy proved unsuccessful. In society in general, individual opinions and private initiative had to give way to compromise and group harmony. Diversity of views and individual responsibility were sacrificed for the good of the whole. Hence these traditional practices tended to strengthen support for the oligarchs and to handicap the popular movement.

But perhaps the greatest advantage for the oligarchs in their struggle with the parties was the fact that the former had held the reins of government for the past twenty-three years. When the Constitution was promulgated, all of the key posts in the government were filled by oligarchs.[2] There was no indication that they would abdicate their favored position just because a Parliament was to be formed. On the contrary, it was clear from what they had already done and said that they intended to continue to rule and to fight the concept of popular government. It was inevitable, therefore, that the first period of parliamentary government should be one of conflict between the party representatives on the one hand and the oligarchs on the other.

During the first five years of constitutional government, the constant changes in Cabinets, the frequent dissolution of the Lower House, and the violence during the general elections all indicate the extent and intensity of the struggle for control of Parliament. In this half decade there were four separate Cabinets and three general elections. The demise of the first Cabinet, even before the elections were held, illustrates the instability of the political scene.

Foreign Minister Ōkuma had been having great difficulty with the Western powers, with his political opponents, and with the public on the question of revision of the unequal clauses in the treaties. Because of his willingness to compromise, an attempt had been made on his life on October 18, 1889. (See above, page 180.) The shock of this terroristic act had been too great for Prime Minister Kuroda to withstand. His Cabinet resigned *en bloc* within ten days. The oligarchs had been challenged in this first instance not by those who clamored for greater people's rights but by ultranationalists. As was to be the case so often in the future, the terrorists were to achieve their aims by illegal direct action to the detriment of the plans and policies of the moderates.

The selection of the new Prime Minister was of the utmost importance to the oligarchs. They realized that the elections scheduled for July 1, 1890, and the opening of the first session of the Diet would put a great strain on their position. To assure continuance of their control, they needed a strong, steady hand to guide the Cabinet. Consequently, General Yamagata was chosen as the new Prime Minister. Aoki, the Minister in Berlin when Itō was studying the Prussian Constitution and who looked and behaved more like a German than a Japanese, was selected as Foreign Minister. Yamagata and Aoki were known for their opposition to representative institutions. All of the important Cabinet positions were filled by men from Satsuma and Chōshū. Thus the oligarchs hoped to keep Parliament from interfering with the operation of national affairs. They talked about the "transcendental" character of the Cabinet. Leaders such as Itō argued that since the administrative rights of the government were part of the Emperor's prerogatives, Cabinet ministers were responsible for their actions to the Emperor and to no one else. They were above the political parties and beyond the reach or the reproach of Parliament.

As a result of this attitude, considerable opposition to the Cabinet developed prior to the election. The party leaders made full use of this discontent and of the popular demand for immediate revision of the treaties. Consequently, at the first national election, the Liberal party (*Jiyūtō*) and the Progressive party (*Kaishintō*) together were able to obtain 171 seats out of the total of 300 in the Lower House.[3] A large number of the remaining members of Parliament were independents and Prime Minister Yamagata controlled only 89 votes. When Yamagata met the First Diet in November, 1890, the lines were clearly drawn between the oligarchs and the party members of the House of Representatives. In his opening speech, which was arrogant and contemptuous, he represented the extreme attitude of the bureaucrats. He assumed that his colleagues, with their twenty-five years' experience in statecraft, knew what was best for the country. His omission of any reference to his legislative program indicated his intention to ignore Parliament.

On the other hand, the people's parties had a clear majority of votes in the House of Representatives. Although they were not united behind a single leader, they were united on several issues. They were enraged that no progress had been made on revising the treaties. They were anxious to challenge the Satchō (Satsuma Chōshū) clans' monopoly in government and to exercise fully the powers given them under the Constitution. When the national budget was presented to the Diet, the Lower House immediately slashed 10 per cent off the appropriations. These reductions were primarily concentrated on the salaries of the civil and military officials who had actually been operating the government for the past two decades. The newly elected members of Parliament knew that the civil service was replete with conservative bureaucrats who were as uncompromisingly opposed to the political parties as were the oligarchs.

In the face of this possible reduction in available funds, Yamagata adopted two separate tactics; one was parliamentary but the other was of questionable propriety. He contended that the Lower House was exceeding its power in demanding reductions in the budget and prorogued the Lower House for a week. He justified this action on the basis of Article 67 of the Constitution, which prohibited the reduction of fixed expenditures without the concurrence of the Cabinet. The questionable tactics which he espoused included hiring thugs to intimidate the members of Parliament who were opposed to the government and to prevent them from entering the Diet Building. At the same time, bribes and special favors were used to induce other members to abandon their party allegiance. In the end, the budget was passed but Yamagata had weakened his position.

He was criticized by his colleagues for the tactics which he used. Itō, the leader of the civil group among the oligarchs, questioned the applicability of Article 67 to the Diet's decision to reduce the budget.[4] These were the first signs that cracks were appearing in the armor of the oligarchs. Divisive tendencies, created by jealousies and the rivalry between civil and military leaders were increasing. This criticism of the Prime Minister led to his resignation in May, 1891. Nevertheless, during his tenure of office, the Diet had been unable to exert its influence effectively in the operation of state affairs. In fact, the independence of the executive from the legislative branch of the government had only increased.

Two important precedents, which had been established in selecting the last two Prime Ministers, were again followed in 1891. In the first place, the oligarchs decided among themselves by informal conferences who should be selected from among their group to head the Cabinet. Their choice was in complete disregard for the strength of the parties in Parliament. Thus, the hope and dream of the advocates of people's rights that the leader of the largest party in Parliament would be the Prime Minister remained only a dream. There was apparently no effective way that the parties could break up the oligarchs' monopoly.

The second precedent which the oligarchs followed was to choose the new Premier alternately from Satsuma and Chōshū. Thus, Matsukata Masayoshi from Satsuma, who had been such a successful Finance Minister a decade earlier, was selected to head the government. Like his predecessors, he had little patience with the political parties or respect for their representatives in the Diet. He soon antagonized the legislators, who retaliated by obstructing any new legislation by a filibuster. Faced with these tactics, Matsukata answered in kind. He received Imperial consent to dissolve the Diet in December, 1891, making a new election compulsory.

The election of February 15, 1892, was a sordid example of the ruthless attitude of the oligarchs toward the people and their parties. The politicians maintained that Matsukata's dissolution of Parliament was a retaliatory act and was contrary to the public will. Consequently, the parties' candidates were bitterly opposed to the oligarchs and all they stood for. On the other hand, the government took an equally uncompromising attitude. It hoped to smash the direct connection of the popular parties with the people and to strengthen its own representation in Parliament at the expense of the parties. Men like Itō, who now recognized that the Diet could not be ignored completely, were beginning to advocate a government party. They realized that they must have a legislative program and win the support of the legislators for such a program.

As the first move in a campaign of the Cabinet to win greater support in Parliament, Shinagawa Yajirō, a ruthless and ultraconservative bureaucrat from Chōshū and henchman of Yamagata, was appointed Home Minister. He ordered all of the prefectual governors and the police, who were directly responsible to him, to support the government's candidates in each district. The result of these instructions was the bloodiest election in Japan's history. Twenty-five persons were killed and nearly 400 wounded. The election, despite the strong-arm police methods, gave the Cabinet only ninety-five seats as opposed to a total of 163 seats for the "people's parties."

After such violence and in view of the comparatively poor showing of the government's candidates in the election, the struggle between the oligarchs and the parties increased in intensity. A resolution to impeach the Cabinet lost in the Lower House by only three votes. The Third Diet, which met in May, 1892, refused to pass the annual budget. But in effect, like so much of Parliament's obstructionism, it made little difference. The Constitution provided that if a budget was not approved, the one for the previous year automatically went into effect.

Despite this rebuff, therefore, Matsukata continued as Premier until challenged by the military. The furor created by the election scandal had been partially placated by the removal of Shinagawa as Home Minister. His successor tried to restore public confidence by the transfer or dismissal of the prefectual governors who had been responsible for the outrages. Since Shinagawa was a representative of the military faction of the oligarchs, such action was a direct affront to the military. Consequently, both the Minister of War and of the Navy showed their disapproval of the policies of the bureaucrats in the Cabinet by resigning. This action, like many other precedents set in these early years, was to become a common practice in later years and assured control of the cabinets by the military.

When Matsukata was forced to resign in midsummer of 1892, the party leaders were elated. They believed that their uncompromising attitude and the refusal of their representatives in the Diet to cooperate with the oligarchs had shown conclusively that the concept of a transcendental Cabinet was both impractical and inoperative. They assumed that the constant turnover in Cabinets and the resignation of three Premiers since October, 1889, was attributable to their maneuvers. They saw the resignation of Yamagata as Premier as the first sign of a breach among the oligarchs. The parties anticipated that the oligarchs would soon offer concessions in the hope of obtaining cooperation from the Diet. If such an eventuality came about, the importance of the House of Representatives would be established and the parties would become the dominant power in Japanese politics.

It is impossible to determine how much of this reasoning, accepted largely both by Itagaki and Ōkuma, was wishful thinking and how much of it reflected the actual position of power of the parties. In historical retrospect, however, one fact does become patently clear. The party leaders had underestimated the solidarity of the oligarchs whenever the latter's power was challenged. Furthermore, the proponents of people's rights had not yet realized that the Constitution had created a political paradox—a parliamentary form of government, yet one in which the Emperor and his advisers retained autocratic power.

Political developments during the next Cabinet demonstrated both of these facts. The elder statesmen immediately closed ranks and selected the most venerable civil oligarch as Prime Minister, namely, Itō Hirobumi. He proceeded to use the politicians to discredit themselves. For example, in November, 1892, when the antioligarch members of the Lower House presented a memorial to the throne censuring the Cabinet, Itō refused to show any signs of weakness. He arranged for the Emperor to call together the Cabinet ministers and leaders of both houses of Parliament, to admonish them and to order them to compose their differences. After the Emperor offered to contribute one-tenth of his income for defense expenditures, he asked the members of Parliament and other officials to allocate a similar proportion of their own salaries for the same purpose. It would have been impossible for them to have refused and still retained their jobs. This use of the prestige of the throne to placate the opposition had the desired effect. The party members became dispirited and even agreed to approve the national budget with only minor changes. Itō had clearly won his first round.

During the next year and a half prior to the outbreak of the Sino-Japanese War in August, 1894, Itō and the oligarchs were at loggerheads with the House of Representatives. Parliament was dissolved twice and Itō carried out his policies despite a hostile legislature. When the parties began to fight each other, the Prime Minister encouraged their disunity. In December, 1893, they united again over the issue of revision of the unequal clauses in the treaties and sent a resolution to the Emperor which requested the dismissal of the Premier.

At this point, the prestige of the Privy Council was brought to bear on the obstreperousness of the Representatives. Answering for the Emperor the Privy Council made the terse statement, "As for the resignation of my Chief Minister, I will not permit outside interference."

In a crisis, the oligarchs, not only in the Cabinet but also in the Privy Council, had stood firm against the people's representatives in Parliament. Finally, Parliament was dissolved and the use of strong tactics against the opposition was renewed. These took the familiar form of suppression of the opposition's newspapers, prohibition of political meetings, and the liquidation of the most "radical" organizations.

In the elections in March, 1894, voting at most of the polls was without incident but resulted in a House of Representatives hostile to Itō. As previously, it passed a nonconfidence resolution, but this time by an overwhelming majority of 253 to 17. Both Itō and the Emperor refused to accept the resolution and did not even give the Representatives the satisfaction of a written reply. In effect, the parties had again brought the legislative branch of the government to a standstill. They seemed determined that if they could not control the government, they would obstruct its operation whenever possible. In retaliation for their lack of support, Itō dissolved the Diet again on June 2, 1894. He did so on the pretext that it had refused to cooperate on the issue of treaty revision. Actually, his action had been precipitated by the crisis in Korea. Before Parliament met again, Japan was at war with China and domestic political differences were forgotten.

Political Differences Dissolved by War With China, 1894

Nothing more effectively quieted the futile efforts of the political parties to control the reins of government than the international crisis. In fact, international problems dominated Japan's development during the years to come and were of far greater import than domestic political struggles. Heretofore, the two most crucial international questions following the Restoration had been the revision of the unequal treaties and the struggle for the dominance over Korea. (See Chapters 8 and 9.) Both of these questions became acute, however, during the premiership of Itō.

The question of treaty revision was always a politically explosive issue. Many a Foreign Minister had been forced to resign and several Cabinets had faced a crisis over their inability to persuade the foreigners to relinquish their extraterritorial rights. Even when war clouds thickened over Korea, Parliament was more critical of Itō's inability to solve the question of treaty revision than of his policy toward China. Treaty revision was the central issue of the debates on foreign affairs in 1893 and 1894. Prime Minister Itō had used Parliament's attitude on the treaties as the excuse for dissolution.

Just prior to the outbreak of the Sino-Japanese War in 1894, however, the thorny issue was largely resolved. Aoki Shūzō, who had been Foreign Minister under Yamagata, was sent to London on special assignment to negotiate with Great Britain for the abolition of consular courts (extraterritoriality) and for tariff autonomy for Japan. As a result of Aoki's successful mission, the first treaty with Japan abolishing the unequal clauses was signed in London on July 16, 1894, to be effective in 1899. Similar treaties with other powers soon followed. The end of the fight for equality with the West was in sight.

The controversy with China over Korea was incomparably more significant for Japan than the revision of the treaties with the Western powers. If China gained undisputed control of Korea, Japan's chances for expansion on the Asiatic continent were lost. In 1885 the possibility of a Sino-Japanese war had been averted by the successful conclusion of the Li-Itō Convention. (See above, page 166.) At that time, both China and Japan had temporarily forsaken their claim for exclusive control of Korea. They also promised to notify each other if either power intended to send troops into the Korean peninsula. Nevertheless, China continued to contend that it had jurisdiction over Korean foreign affairs. For example, it had asked the United States Chargé d'Affaires Foulke be recalled from Seoul because of his activities on behalf of Korean independence. Furthermore, Yüan Shih-kai had continued as the Chinese Resident to assure Korean compliance with China's wishes.

On the other hand, Japan tenaciously refused to accept China's special position. The conservative clique in Tokyo had restrained the ultra-nationalists from going to war over Korea in 1873 because their country was not politically and economically solidified. Twenty years later such arguments were no longer convincing or pertinent. Furthermore, Itō and his Cabinet colleagues had not forgotten what they considered to be China's procrastination and pusillanimous attitude over the question of the disposition of the Ryūkyū Islands. (See page 161.) They had not given Korea up but were waiting for a more propitious moment to settle permanently the question of whether Japan or China was to control Korean affairs.

When a band of anti-Japanese nationalists known as the Tonghaks revolted in south Korea in June, 1894, Prime Minister Itō was convinced that the time for decision was at hand. The Tonghaks were a reactionary group of Korean patriots inspired by a desire to preserve "Eastern Learning" and to expel all vestiges of Western civilization from their country. They considered the Japanese as Oriental renegades and as degenerate as Occidentals. Politically the Tonghaks were the enemies of the Min or Queen's family and were supported by the former Regent, Taewŏnkun. After the Tonghaks revolted, the Japanese Minister in Seoul telegraphed his government that they probably were not strong enough to overthrow the King but that their revolt might endanger the lives of Japanese nationals.

Since the Korean King's troops were defeated in their first skirmish with the rebels, he asked Li Hung-chang for military aid. On June 6, 1894, in accordance with the provisions of the Li-Itō Convention, Li informed the Japanese government that Chinese troops were being dispatched to Korea to suppress the rebellion. He added that they would be withdrawn as soon as the disturbance was quelled.

The Japanese government considered this announcement of Chinese intentions as a threat to Japan's position in Korea and as a challenge to the Imperial Army and Navy. The Cabinet, General Yamagata, and the Chiefs of Staff agreed that China's action could not go unchallenged. As a countermeasure, it was decided that Japanese troops should also be sent immediately to Korea. Li and the Chinese government were so informed.

From this point, events developed rapidly. By June 10, 1894, Chinese troops were south of the Korean capital of Seoul. Despite the fact that the rebel Tonghaks were put under control during the next two weeks, both Japan and China refused to withdraw their troops. When Great Britain and other powers inquired of the intentions of the two countries, Japan gave evasive answers. At home, it completed preparations for the mobilization of both its land and naval forces. Hostilities seemed inevitable.

Itō's offer to send a joint Sino-Japanese Commission to Korea was rejected by China. Henceforth, Japan disregarded the Li-Itō Convention. On June 26, it demanded that the King carry out certain administrative reforms to be recommended by it and informed him that Japanese troops would remain in Korea until the reforms were completed. Two days later the Japanese Cabinet, the Elder Statesmen (*Genro*), and the Privy Council agreed that Japan would go to war if that were necessary to force China out of Korea. By mid-July, Japan warned China that the despatch of more troops to Korea would be considered as a hostile act. On July 23, 1894, the King's palace was entered by Japanese troops. As a captive, the King signed an agreement for the expulsion of the Chinese. Two days later a Chinese troopship of British registry, the "Kowshing" was sunk by the Imperial Japanese Navy.[5]

In Japan, opposition to Itō and his Cabinet vanished instantaneously with the outbreak of war. The entire nation realized that the stakes in Korea were too high to be lost by internal bickering. Moreover, the party members in the House of Representatives had opposed the oligarchs not because of the latter's aggressive China policy. On the contrary, the various factions, regardless of their differences on matters of internal politics, had never disagreed on the advisability of greater Japanese control on the Asiatic mainland. Such differences as had appeared had been more over the method and the timing of such control rather than over the wisdom of control. In 1891, for example, the *Jiyūtō* had demanded a more, rather than a less, aggressive policy. Since Itō had taken the nation into a war which might give Japan control over Korea, everyone willingly bent to the task of winning that war as rapidly as possible.

Because of this sudden disappearance, with the outbreak of war, of the struggle between the oligarchs and the politicians, it has been claimed that Itō started hostilities to extricate himself from a difficult position politically. Such an argument is, however, an oversimplification of a very complex problem. In fact, many factors indicate its fallaciousness. Naturally, it made his political life much simpler to have Parliament's support for his war effort. But he was far more fearful of the extension of Chinese hegemony over Korea than of the continuous bickerings of the politicians. He had drafted a Constitution which assured the pre-eminence of the executive and the Emperor's advisers. During the past five years, the parties had not seriously threatened that pre-eminence, so that Itō could continue, if necessary, to ignore Parliament. If Japan's international status was not to be impaired, however, he could not ignore Chinese troop movements in Korea. Whether war meant the political solidification of the home front was of only secondary importance. Of supreme importance was whether China could be forced to give up its suzerainty over Korea.

First Fruits of Victory

The Declaration of War by Japan on August 1, 1894, six days after the Chinese troopship had been sunk, was an anticlimax. From the beginning of hostilities, there was no question as to the outcome of the struggle. China was weak and disorganized. The Imperial court was still living in a blissful isolation. Its army was practically as outmoded as that of Japan thirty years earlier. Although two of the Chinese battleships outclassed those from Japan, the training and equipment of the Chinese Navy was inferior. By mid-September, Japan controlled the Gulf of Chihli which meant that it could effectively prevent the shipment of Chinese reinforcements to Manchuria and Korea. Port Arthur fell on November 21. Three months later, Japan was in possession of all of Korea and of the rich Liaotung Peninsula, the entrance to South Manchuria.

Having completed these valuable conquests within little more than six months, Japan was willing to negotiate for peace. Its demands as a price for an armistice indicated, however, that it hoped to profit directly from its military victories. The armistice conditions specified that Viceroy Li Hung-chang be sent as the chief Chinese envoy and that three important northern Chinese cities be ceded to Japan. These cities were Shanhaikwan, gateway through the Great Wall to the north; the industrial city of Tientsin; and its port of entry, Tangku. As possession of these three centers by Japan would be a constant threat to the capital city of Peking, Li refused to accept the demands. Nevertheless, he came to Shimonoseki to see if he could negotiate a settlement.

The deadlock in the preliminary negotiations was broken and Japan's attitude toward China was abruptly changed by an unexpected attack on Li's life. Although he was not even seriously wounded, this terroristic act caused immediate repercussions in Japan and abroad. Throughout the war, Japan had gone to considerable pains to demonstrate to the world that it was "modern" enough to be able to follow the practices prescribed by international law. Its failure to declare war after hostilities had started had not been considered too serious an infraction. The unwarranted shooting of an official peace envoy, however, was an entirely different matter.

The Japanese government suddenly realized that unless amends were made speedily and magnanimously, this one irresponsible act might jeopardize all of the prizes of the war. Consequently, Itō, the Japanese Premier and chief peace delegate, visited Li and apologized to him officially. The Emperor sent his personal physician to care for the wounded envoy and issued a decree deploring the incivility of the act. The conditions for an armistice were withdrawn and Japan made concessions in its peace demands. The proposed war indemnity was reduced by one-third and the demands that Japanese subjects be given exceptional privileges in the interior of China were dropped. The right to occupy Mukden in South Manchuria as a guarantee that the terms of the treaty would be carried out was also waived.[6]

As a result of this attack on Li, the final settlement was far more moderate than originally intended by Japan. By the Treaty of Shimonoseki, which Li and Itō signed on April 17, 1895, China "recognized definitely the full and complete independence and autonomy of Korea." It also agreed to cede to Japan in perpetuity and full sovereignty the island of Formosa and the adjacent Pescadores Islands and the Liaotung Peninsula in South Manchuria. It promised to pay an indemnity of 200 million taels of silver (360 million yen) to defray the cost of the war. Four additional Chinese cities were opened for commercial and industrial purposes. Finally, the treaty specified that the port of Weihaiwei, on the northern shore of the Shantung Peninsula, would continue to be occupied by Japanese forces until the indemnity was paid and a treaty of commerce was negotiated between the two nations.

The Sino-Japanese War had been eminently successful for the victor. Japan had conclusively defeated one of the strongest nations in the Orient. The indemnity was more than sufficient to repay Japan for its war effort. New, rich colonial territories had been acquired both in the south and on the continent of Asia. Formosa, which was contiguous to the Ryūkyū Islands, formed a natural bridge to further expansion southward. In Japanese hands, the Liaotung Peninsula was a protection from future encroachments by China or by Russia on Korea. Finally, Chinese hegemony over, and special privileges in, Korea had been eliminated and the political vacuum created thereby was rapidly filled by Japan.

The American Minister in Seoul claimed that there was evidence everywhere that Japan was running Korea. The Korean Army was drilled and officered by Japanese. The post office, the telegraph system, and the railway from Seoul to Pusan were taken over and operated by them. Taxes were assessed according to Japanese laws. China had more than given up suzerainty over Korea. The peninsula kingdom was at the mercy of a rapidly expanding Japanese Empire which had become the predominant force in East Asia.

The Bitter Price of Victory—The Triple Intervention

Such appeared on the surface to be the rewards of victory. One of the leading dailies, the *Kokumin Shimbun,* had boasted:

> As a result of the war, Japan's position in the world has been changed by the revelation of three basic Japanese characteristics. First, the Japanese people excel throughout the world in their patriotic love of country. Secondly, they have a unique ability to digest, utilize, and apply modern civilization. Thirdly, they have a solid and strong-nature or temper.[7]

But no historical event is isolated or detached from other contemporary developments and the peace negotiations at Shimonoseki were no exception to this rule. The Western powers had begun to look upon Japan's activities with considerable misgivings. They were particularly apprehensive lest Japan win special privileges in China. Some of them were determined to prevent such an eventuality from coming to pass. When the Japanese Minister in London had asked in 1893 about Britain's attitude in the event of a war between Japan and China, he had been told that while Great Britain would welcome an amelioration of the internal chaos in Korea it would not tolerate the transfer of Korea to Japan.

The Russian Minister in Tokyo had likewise stated that his government would not countenance the violation of Korean independence. The newspaper *Novoye Vremya* had warned Japan not to go too far lest a joint Chinese-Russian protectorate be necessary for Korea. Vice-Foreign Minister Hayashi had been told by some of the European diplomats that a demand for territory on the Chinese mainland might result in intervention by the powers. Despite these warnings, the Japanese Chiefs of Staff had insisted that they receive territorial concessions and an indemnity as the reward for military victory. Consequently, the clauses which ceded Liaotung to Japan had been included in the Treaty of Shimonoseki.

Prime Minister Itō was fully aware, however, that it was unlikely that the Western powers would allow Japan to retain this territory. He also knew that the powers had been kept informed of the progress of the negotiations. Viceroy Li, who was conscious of the value of international support for his position, had kept the foreign diplomats abreast of the developments. For example, on April 1, 1895, nearly three weeks before the Treaty was signed, they learned of Japan's request for the Liaotung Peninsula.

Itō and his colleagues did not know until later, however, the extent of the impact which this news had had on the Western powers. It was particularly startling to Russia. That country had long desired a warm-water port either in Korea or in the Liaotung Peninsula. Such a port would be a natural eastern terminus for the Trans-Siberian Railway which had been under construction for three years. The Sino-Japanese War had decreased the chances of Russia obtaining a port in Korea. From the Russian point of view, therefore, the Liaotung Peninsula remained as an alternate potential Russian sphere of influence so long as it did not fall into Japanese hands.

After learning of Japan's request for Liaotung, the Russian Minister of Finance, Count Serge Witte, who was one of the chief architects of Russian Far Eastern policy, acted quickly to forestall Japan. He proposed to Great Britain, France, and Germany that intervention was in order to discourage Japan from asking for Liaotung. Great Britain, fearful of Russian advances on the Asiatic continent and contemptuous of China, preferred to see Japan rather than Russia in a favorable position in Korea and South Manchuria. Hence it showed little interest in Witte's proposal. On the other hand, France and Germany were quick to agree that if Port Arthur and the Liaotung Peninsula were in Japanese hands, they would be a menace to the peace of the Far East.

As soon as the contents of the Treaty of Shimonoseki were announced on April 17, 1895, Russia formally approached the powers concerning intervention. Thus Japan's destiny became entwined in the intricacies of European diplomacy. It had asked for something which conflicted with the self-interests of one of the European powers. From the point of view of this self-interest, such interference could not be tolerated, especially by an upstart nation which might be impertinent enough to defy the "advice" of a single power. A week later, the first formal step of the tripartite intervention took place. Vice-Foreign Minister Hayashi was jointly "advised" by the French, German, and Russian Ministers in Tokyo that Japan should renounce its claims to the Liaotung Peninsula.

Two days later, a formal note from Russia stated:

> The Government of His Majesty the Emperor of all the Russians, in examining the conditions of peace which Japan has imposed on China, finds that the possession of the Peninsula of Liaotung, claimed by Japan, would be a menace to the Capital of China, would at the same time render illusory the independence of Korea and would henceforth be a perpetual obstacle to the peace of the Far East.

It concluded, in diplomatic language, by "advising" Japan to renounce its claim.

Despite the fact that Itō and some of his Cabinet had expected this *démarche,* they found it difficult to accept the inevitable. It was clear that Russia had taken the initiative and had challenged Japan to a showdown. The Japanese Minister at St. Petersburg reported that Russia was adamant and was making military preparations for any eventuality. It was common knowledge that the Russian Pacific fleet was concentrated at Vladivostok ready for action at a moment's notice. Faced with these unpleasant facts, an Imperial Conference was hastily called at which it was tentatively decided that the "advice" would have to be accepted. Of the key persons at the conference, Foreign Minister Mutsu appears to have been the only one who insisted that the "advice" be rejected.

As for the public at large, they had been kept in ignorance of the latest developments. News of the Russian demands had leaked out and caused an immediate wave of antigovernment criticism. The government immediately closed all of those newspapers which had referred to the matter in an unfavorable light. The only news available on this vital issue came from the foreign press, *The Japan Times and Mail.* The Foreign Minister was unable, therefore, to capitalize on public support for his position.

In the end, it was decided to present a compromise proposal to the Russians. Japan promised to renounce, after the treaty was ratified, all of Liaotung except the southern tip of the peninsula. In return it would ask for additional indemnity and would occupy Chinese territory until the terms had been carried out. Russia rejected this suggestion unequivocally.[8]

The original Russian demand that Liaotung be given up was finally accepted by Japan. The final draft of the Treaty of Shimonoseki was revised accordingly. A few days later, the Emperor tried to soften the blow for his subjects and to minimize the humiliation by stating in an Imperial rescript that Japan had accomplished its aims in the war. He concluded that the retrocession in no way reflected on Japan's honor and hence the people should accept the decision passively.

The Triple Intervention Stimulates Nationalism

But even the prestige of the Emperor was not sufficient to make the Japanese public willing to accept this forceful intervention in their affairs by Russia and its allies. In fact, the official and formal acquiescence to the demands of the European *triplice* had both immediate and far-reaching results. The immediate effect was seen in the outburst of violent public indignation directed against the contents of the treaty and the Itō Ministry. All shades of political opinion criticized the government's action. For example, Gotō Shōjirō, one of the leaders of the *Jiyūtō* and Agriculture Minister in the Itō Cabinet, advocated an expansionist program in a memorial which he forwarded to the Cabinet. He proposed the acquisition of the Three Eastern Provinces in Manchuria and of Korea. He recommended that these territories be linked by the construction of a Japanese-owned railway. He also urged necessary political alliances to protect China from European encroachments.[9]

This international capitulation also acted as a stimulant to ultranationalists who found a receptive public ear for their proposals for an aggressive foreign policy. Heretofore, leaders of nationalist thought had taken a negative attitude. They had hoped to preserve certain basic national characteristics and to protect them from the deleterious effects of European civilization. Henceforth, a new national self-consciousness concentrated on how to improve Japan's international position in the world at large. As one of the new intellectual leaders, Takayama Chogyū expressed it:

> The Constitution, which was promulgated in 1889, clarified Japan's unique national polity, destroyed the empty principles of democracy and thereby unified national political thought. Likewise, the Imperial Edict on Education of 1890 is a model for national morality and in its turn unified national moral thought. Thus for the first time the spirit of Nipponism was able to control the public spirit of society. . . . It became the principle which was to represent the clearly awakened consciousness of Japanese nationalism.

A new type of patriotism, to be known as Nipponism (*Nihon Shūgi*) had arisen during the war. It was a virulent nationalism which throve on self-sacrifice and adversity. The war period had raised the people's loyalty to a high pitch. As a contemporary writer expressed it, "the special features and most glorious points of Japan's constitutional government were made manifest at home and abroad."

The far-reaching results of the aftermath of the Sino-Japanese War of 1894-95 are difficult to assay in view of the congeries of forces which molded Japan's modern development. But one development is clear. Slowly but steadily the Japanese people and nation came to be convinced that their chance for an important place in the sun was in direct proportion to their material and spiritual strength. The growth and tenacity of this spiritual force was increased by the intervention of the powers. The bitterness of this humiliating experience was intensified in 1898 when Russia acquired for itself the same territory it had forced Japan to renounce.

One can make a strong case, therefore, for the contention that the tripartite intervention was the most important single event in recent times which diverted Japan toward a policy of nationalistic aggression. The nation had been struggling peacefully for over twenty years to revise the unequal clauses in the treaties with the Western powers. At last, real progress had been made toward that end. The recent victory against China had been won at the cost of a concerted, national effort. Furthermore, in asking for territory from its former enemy, Japan was following what it believed to be accepted international procedure. Spain, Portugal, the Netherlands, and Great Britain had long since carved out empires in Asia as a result of military conquest. Germany, Russia, and France showed clear signs of following a policy whereby "might makes right."

In the face of victory, more and more Japanese, both statesmen and humble subjects, were convinced that these three powers had taken advantage of Japan's weakness to prevent it from acquiring territory they wanted for themselves. Henceforth, anyone within Japan who opposed a strong, aggressive policy toward China, toward Russia, or toward the West found scanty historical evidence to support the position that cooperation and concessions would win more respect than aggression and an adamant position. It was argued with cogent consistency that the only true steps to national survival and salvation were through military strength and aggressive nationalism. Consequently, it will constantly be noted that the emphasis for the next half century was on military preparedness, expansion, and making the most out of the weaknesses of China or of the Western powers. Russia, Germany, and France had sown the wind; a half century later, the United Nations were to reap the whirlwind.

Notes

1. A word of caution is in order concerning terms such as "political parties" (*mintō*) and "popular rights" (*minken*). These terms are used loosely by Japanese political scientists to refer to the various groups who favored greater rather than fewer rights for the people and who supported candidates not sponsored by the government for the House of Representatives. A more exact meaning of these terms will become clear as the controversy between the oligarchs and the parties is explained.

2. From among the original instigators of the Imperial Restoration, Itō, Yamagata, Ōkuma, and Inouye Kaoru were the most important persons still living. On February 11, 1889, Itō was President of the Privy Council. Matsukata was Home Minister. Ōkuma, who had opposed Itō and his colleagues so bitterly seven years earlier, was Minister of Foreign Affairs in a Cabinet headed by his former political enemy, Kuroda. Inouye Kaoru was a Minister of Agriculture. Other members of the Kuroda Cabinet were Matsukata Masayoshi as Finance Minister, Ōyama Iwaō as Minister of War, Saigō Tsugumichi as Minister of Navy, Yamada Kengi, Justice, and Mōri Arinori as Minister of Education.

3. After their demise in 1884, the parties had been revived to meet the election challenge. Itagaki's Liberal party was by far the strongest with 130 seats. It had carried on a campaign based on the following points: revision of the treaties on the basis of equality, extension of Japanese control over Korea, abrogation of the stringent press and peace preservation laws, and adoption of the concept of a Cabinet responsible to the Diet. Ōkuma's opportunism confused the picture. When a Cabinet member, he usually acted as an oligarch. When outside the Cabinet, he considered himself the leader of a "liberal party." His Progressive party secured 41 seats. Of the 450,865 persons eligible to vote for the members of the Lower House, all but 6 per cent had voted. For reference to the expediency of Yamagata's action see George B. Sansom, *Japan in World History* (New York: American Institute of Pacific Relations, 1951), p. 87.

4. When Article 67 was drafted, Itō apparently had in mind such expenditures as the ordinary expenses of the Army and the Navy, of diplomatic missions, of the Diet, and of the obligations on the national debt. See Itō Hirobumi, *Commentaries*

on the Constitution of the Empire of Japan, tr. by Itō Miyoji (Tokyo: Chu-ō Daigaku, 1931), pp. 128-31.

5. F. Nelson, *Korea and the Old Order in Eastern Asia* (Baton Rouge: University of Louisiana, 1946), p. 206.

6. H. B. Morse and Harley F. McNair, *Far Eastern International Relations* (Boston: Houghton Mifflin Co., 1931), p. 402.

7. Ōtsu Jun'ichirō, *Dai Nihon Kensei Shi* (10 vols.; Tokyo: Hobun-kan, 1927-28), IV, p. 218 *et seq.*

8. *Ibid.,* p. 282.

9. *Ibid.,* p. 451.

12

INTERNATIONAL PRESSURES AND THE GROWTH OF EMPIRE, 1895-1904

The Predominance of International Forces

It has just been shown how the rivalry between Japan and China for the control of Korea was the central issue leading directly to the Sino-Japanese War. This issue was presumably settled by the Treaty of Shimonoseki of 1895 by which both countries recognized Korea's complete independence. The intervention of the three Western powers in 1895 had forced Japan to give up its hopes of acquiring the Liaotung Peninsula. But during the next decade, the same struggle for control over Korea persisted, with Russia replacing China as one of the challengers. Furthermore, this was the period in which the leading European countries carved out concessions and spheres of influence for themselves in China. This movement was an outcome of their drive to maintain a balance of power in Europe and led to Japan's involvement in an alliance with Great Britain against Russia.

Even the United States, which had been largely absorbed with its own internal problems, suddenly became a colonial power with important possessions in the central and western Pacific Ocean. Likewise it became implicated in the future of China through the advocacy of the Open Door Policy and the outbreak of the Boxer Uprising in North China. The decade closed with the conclusive defeat of Russia by Japan in the Russo-Japanese War of 1904-5. Obviously it was a period in which international forces were predominant among those which directed Japan's course of history. The question to be answered, therefore, is: What was the effect of these international events on the growth of the Japanese Empire?

Conditions within Japan also added to the relative importance of international problems. With the conclusion of the war against China in 1895, political instability became even more pronounced than before the war. The House of Representatives constantly opposed the domestic program of the Cabinet and the oligarchs. In retaliation, the latter dissolved

Parliament whenever the government's program was stymied by the obstructionism of the legislators. The Prime Minister continued to be selected alternately from the leaders from Chōshū and Satsuma. Specifically, from 1895 to 1901 there were seven different Cabinets and four dissolutions of Parliament. One new feature of this period was the realization by the oligarchs that it was to their advantage to obtain party support rather than party antagonism. Hence a pattern developed whereby the premier-designate obtained support of one of the main parties in return for political promises and the appointment of a party representative to a Cabinet post.

Despite the unpopularity of the final settlement of the War with China in 1895, Itō had been able to stay in power until 1896 with the support of the Liberal party. When the Liberals objected to Ōkuma, their long-time political rival, serving on the Cabinet, Itō lost their support. The premiership shifted to Matsukata of Satsuma who was able to last until January, 1898, largely because of the backing he received from the Progressive party.

Itō again was selected as Prime Minister but failed to win the support of either of the party groups. In fact, the political events which followed made him realize, though reluctantly, that the new constitutional form of government could not operate effectively without a closer working arrangement between the Cabinet and the party members of the House of Representatives. In the summer of 1898, Itagaki and Ōkuma, the leaders of the two rival parties, settled their differences and formed a single party, the Constitutional party (*Kenseitō*) to challenge the oligarchs and to press for party cabinets and the principle of a cabinet responsible to Parliament.[1]

Heretofore, there had been no significant disunity among the oligarchs, especially when they were confronted with a challenge from the political parties. By 1898, however, Itō and Yamagata had become political rivals if not enemies. Although they were fellow clansmen from Chōshū, personal jealousies and the antagonism between the civil group, led by Itō, and the military group, under Yamagata's tutelage, caused an open break.[2] Hence, as Premier in 1898, Itō knew that he would have weak support at home for any move he made abroad. Likewise, when Ōkuma and Itagaki jointly formed a Cabinet in the summer of that same year, they were in an even more precarious political position. Faced with these internal weaknesses, Japan adopted a generally conciliatory and cooperative policy throughout the decade between the Sino-Japanese and the Russo-Japanese Wars (1895-1904). It concentrated on negotiations, treaties, and alliances to bolster its international position. After a false start in Korea in 1895, it bided its time until powerful enough to force its will on both Korea and Russia.

Russian Influence in Korea Temporarily Paramount, 1895-97

To revert to developments after peace was concluded with China in 1895, Korea remained the central issue. The war had eliminated the menace of China to Japan, but the Russian Empire represented an even greater menace. From Japan's point of view, an "independent Korea" meant a country both independent of foreign control and amenable to Japan. Though this policy may not yet have been officially expressed, Japan's representatives in Korea acted on the basis of such a policy.

As a first step toward Japanese control of Korean affairs, the King was placed under "protective custody" and other members of the court, including the Queen, were prevented from interfering in the operation of Korean affairs. Naturally the Queen became anti-Japanese but soon found herself opposed by her old political rival, the Taewŏnkun. Always a political opportunist, he had conceived of a plot to murder the Queen to win Japanese favor and to increase his political power. He then proposed to run Korean affairs in accordance with Japan's wishes and thus be in an unassailable position. The new Japanese Minister in Seoul, General Miura Gorō (1846-1926) became privy to this plot through a colleague who was adviser in the Korean War Department. The Taewŏnkun was encouraged to carry out his plan; the Queen was murdered on October 8, 1895. When the news broke, the foreign diplomats in Seoul were shocked, and the Korean people were enraged. Since Miura's implication in the plot was publicly known, the Koreans held Japan accountable for what had happened and that country immediately lost influence and prestige both in Korea and among the Western powers.

The incident is also significant as an early example of two recurring and dangerous themes in Japan's recent history: dual diplomacy and the refusal of the Japanese courts to convict political assassins. As for the first of these themes, when the American Minister in Tokyo inquired about the incident, he was assured by the Foreign Minister in the most positive fashion "that the recent revolution at Seoul was a complete surprise to the Japanese Government and that the Japanese Government had nothing whatever to do with it."[3] Prime Minister Itō insisted that the usurpation of power by the Taewŏnkun must be immediately repudiated by Japan.

After the Foreign Office received a report a few days later on what had transpired, the American Minister was told that Miura and his staff were being recalled. The Japanese Government now knew that their Minister had been in direct communication with the Taewŏnkun concerning the plot. It also knew that Miura had acted independently of instructions from the Foreign Office and that it could repudiate his acts only with difficulty. The harm had been done and Japan had to face the consequences.

As for the reluctance of the courts to act against political assassins or their accomplices, Miura's treatment was surprisingly lenient. He, members of his staff, and several military officers stationed at Seoul were arrested upon their return to Japan. They were tried at a court martial held early in 1896. The tribunal found that prior to the murder of the Queen, Miura did "enter into conspiracy with the Taewŏnkun to overthrow the existing government and murder the Queen." The court concluded, however, that despite their findings there was not sufficient evidence to prove that any of the accused actually committed the crimes which they had originally planned. Consequently, six military officers, General Miura, and forty-seven civilian members of his staff were all acquitted. On January 29, 1896, the *Official Gazette* announced that Miura's ranks and honors, of which he had temporarily been deprived, had been restored. As far as both he and his government were concerned, the matter was closed.

Miura and his henchmen had hoped to improve both their own position and that of their country in Korea by their participation in the plot to murder the Queen. On the contrary, however, they had aroused widespread resentment. It became increasingly difficult for Japan to gain support within Korea for its policies. On the other hand, Russia was quick to take advantage of this situation and to fill the breach caused by China's withdrawal and by Japan's self-incrimination.

When the Queen's palace was attacked in early October, 1895, the Russian Minister in Seoul offered his quarters as an asylum for the Korean King and the Crown Prince. Their escape and liberation from the Japanese automatically destroyed any *de facto* or *de jure* basis for Miura's projected puppet regime. Under this new protection and in view of the sudden appearance of a strong anti-Japanese feeling, the Korean King was quick to brand the pro-Japanese members of his Cabinet as traitors. A new Cabinet was created which annulled the "reform laws" which had been imposed on Korea by Japan. For the next year, during which time the King continued to reside in the Russian Legation, Russia's influence in Korea was predominant. At the same time, the King had considerable freedom and by May, 1896, willingly sent his brother-in-law to Moscow to ask for Russian protection over Korea.

After Japan's victory over China in 1895, Russia also strengthened its general position in East Asia. Together with France, it loaned China funds to pay for the indemnity provided for in the Treaty of Shimonoseki.

As security against default in payment on the loans, Russia obtained a prior claim on Chinese revenue. But of even greater importance to Russia's power status in Asia was the successful conclusion of diplomatic negotiations at Peking which resulted in the Li-Lobanov Treaty of June 3, 1896. This agreement between China and Russia provided for mutual military assistance in the event that Japan attacked either of them or took military action against Korea. It also approved the construction of a railway through North Manchuria to Vladivostok. By these moves, Russia had temporarily replaced Japan as the most influential foreign power in Korea and had allied itself with China against their mutual rival, Japan.

Yet both Russia and Japan found themselves in vulnerable positions. Neither of them was strong enough to force the other to capitulate. It was impossible for Russia to compete with Japan in the Far East so long as the last lap of the Trans-Siberian Railway through North Manchuria to Vladivostok was not completed. Japan's position was equally weak. It had suffered a severe setback in Korea by Miura's indiscretions. Most of its proposed expansion of the Army and Navy was still in the planning stage. It would take several years to build them up to the projected strength.

Though Japanese-Russian rivalries for Korea's control were intense, both sides were forced to make concessions for the next few years. For example, when General Yamagata was sent to Russia in 1896 to represent Japan at the coronation of the Russian Emperor, he suggested that Korea might be divided into two spheres of interest with the thirty-eighth degree parallel as the dividing line. By this arrangement Russian encroachments could be kept within bounds and Japan would have time to build up south Korea and to solidify its position.[4]

His offer was rejected by Russia on the grounds that Japan had already recognized Korean independence and that the demarcation of two spheres of influence would be counter to this pledge. Actually, Russia hoped to get much more than a sphere just in the northern half of Korea. In the meantime it had to be content with a joint declaration with Japan whereby both countries agreed to help the Korean King build a police force and an army, to guarantee foreign loans when necessary, and to consult each other prior to dispatching troops to Korea. Obviously, both sides were consciously making concessions to avoid antagonizing the other.

Such an unstable balance could not be maintained for long. Although the Korean King was given personal freedom, he governed with Russia behind the throne. Even after he moved into his new palace in the early months of 1897, he discovered that he was a victim of Russian machinations. The new Russian chargé d'affaires in Seoul, De Speyer, both advocated and implemented an aggressive policy. He increased pressure on the Korean government to bend to his will and to that of the Czar. He threatened to force out of office those Korean officials who opposed him. He obtained an acknowledgment that Kir Alexeviev was to be chief Financial Adviser and Superintendent of Customs with power to control and supervise all matters relating to Korea's finances. Further concessions concerned Russia's long-standing request for a coaling station in southern Korea. Deer Island in Pusan Harbor was agreed upon as the site. By mid-February, 1898, the Russo-Korean Bank opened for business with authority to handle all of the government's revenue. Russia's predominant position appeared assured and De Speyer's policies seemed to have been accepted.[5]

But two completely separate forces contributed to the sudden withdrawal of Russian influence. A new nationalist consciousness was rapidly developing in Korea under the leadership of Dr. Philip Jaisohn (Shu Chai Pil). His Independence Club, which included many influential leaders, had been carrying on an effective educational program to train Koreans for independence. It had also castigated the venality of Korean officials and the disloyalty of those who cooperated with the Russians. As Russian pressure increased, the Independence Club became political in nature and advocated resistance to foreign subservience. This plea of the club strengthened the King's determination to oppose any further Russian demands.

Simultaneously with the growth of an independence movement, a new Russian policy had been adopted for Korea. The Czar had been persuaded that if he wished to retain possession of the Liaotung Peninsula, which he had acquired from China in 1898, and if he expected to avoid antagonizing Great Britain and Japan, his advisers to the Korean government would have to be withdrawn. Alexeviev and the Russian military advisers were ordered home, the Russo-Korean Bank was closed and Russian influence dwindled.

But these moves, as well as Japan's future action which filled the vacuum created by Russia's withdrawal, must be placed against the larger background of events in East Asia as a whole. Many of these events emerged from the whole complex of European rivalries and balance of power. They involved the struggle for foreign concessions in China and the emergence of the United States as a world power with a colonial empire in the Pacific.

Spheres of Influence of the European Powers in China

The participation of Germany and France, on Russia's initiative, in the demand on Japan in 1895 that the Liaotung Peninsula be returned to China was representative of their growing interest in Asia. Although both Great Britain and the United States had maintained a strict neutrality on this issue, these countries also were by no means disinterested observers in the fate of China or in the growth of the Japanese Empire. In fact, all of these Western powers were on the point of consolidating their spheres of influence in Asia either on the continent or in the Pacific.

These acts of imperialism had a dual result. They not only dismembered China but also had a controlling effect on Japan's foreign relations and hence are an essential element in this narrative. For example, Germany's constant search for an effective means to reduce the strength of France turned the attention of William II to China. He recognized that if he could obtain Russia's support for his plans in the Far East, he might reduce the effectiveness of the Franco-Russian Alliance. Hence he had been glad to join Russia in 1895 in a common move to check Japan.

Furthermore, he was in immediate need of a commercial and naval base in Pacific waters to protect his farflung empire. Specifically, he sought a coaling station for German naval and commercial vessels as a counterbalance against British-held Hong Kong. Surveys were made in the Philippines, the Pacific Islands, and along the China coast to discover a suitable location for such a base. Kiaochow Bay, on the south-central coast of Shantung Peninsula, was finally agreed upon as the most desirable site. The only question which remained was how to secure this territory.

In view of Germany's desire to use Russia rather than antagonize it, Russian opinion was sought on this proposal. Since the Czar contemplated similar action in reference to the port of Py'onyang on the northwestern coast of Korea, he replied that he had no objections to Germany's plan to acquire Kiaochow. After this clarification of aims, Germany informed the Chinese government in September, 1897, of its desire to acquire Kiaochow Bay. China temporized and evaded the issue.

In November, 1897, two German missionaries in Shantung were killed by Chinese robbers. This incident gave Emperor William the excuse for which he had been waiting. Despite effective Chinese action against the robbers, Germany acted. Tsingtao, the important port at the mouth of Kiaochow Bay, was successfully occupied by a small German military contingent. Germany then demanded complete compensation for the murder of its subjects, the granting of railway and mining concessions on the Shantung Peninsula, and a naval base at Kiaochow Bay.

When China balked at some of these demands, William II jumped at the chance to become the self-appointed protector of the Holy Church. He claimed that it was his duty to defend Christendom from the peril of the infidels and the barbaric hordes of the "Yellow Race." He organized a squadron to be sent to China to enforce his demands and to save Europe from the "yellow peril." By the time his brother, who headed the naval force, arrived, China was ready to capitulate.

This decision of William II to take direct action against China also stimulated Russia to make a similar move into the Liaotung Peninsula. The Czar had decided to acquire by naval action the key harbors of Dairen (Dalny) and Port Arthur on the southern tip of Liaotung. Germany was informed in December, 1897, that a Russian squadron would shortly anchor at Port Arthur. When the fleet arrived, it had the desired effect. China granted Russia liberal concessions in the form of leased territories and other privileges.[6]

One can well imagine the Japanese reaction to these latest moves by the Western powers. It was easily discernible that William II considered the Japanese in the same category as the Chinese. Furthermore, as indemnification for the murder of two of its missionaries, Germany had obtained a lease for one of the most important strategic ports in northeast China and important economic privileges in Shantung. As for Russia, by a show of force it had secured the exact territory which Japan had demanded at the peace conference at Shimonoseki in 1895. Japan, which had defeated China in a full-scale war, had received nothing on the Asiatic mainland. To the Japanese people and government, it was obvious why Germany had a leased territory in Shantung and why Russia, rather than Japan, was in possession of Liaotung. Germany and Russia were each stronger than Japan and also had the support of one another. Confronted with the stark reality of the times that in international politics "might makes right," and in view of the political disunity within Japan, its status on the Asiatic Continent was at the mercy of the other powers.

Fortunately for Japan, Russia had abruptly changed its Korean policy and had decided to withdraw from Korea. (See page 219.) It acquiesced in a new settlement with Japan, which was a windfall for the latter. Instead of having to watch Russian influence and power increase in Korea, Japan obtained assurances of its own preferential position in the peninsula. These were incorporated in the Rosen-Nishi agreement of April, 1898, which outlined the procedures which Japan and Russia would follow in the immediate future in Korea. The signatories promised to refrain from direct interference in the internal affairs of Korea. They would nominate at Korea's request only those military instructors and financial advisers approved by both Russia and Japan. But most important of all, Russia recognized Japan's preferential economic and commercial position in Korea and promised not to interfere with Japanese-Korean commercial and industrial developments.

Although Japan hoped that this agreement meant that the day of Russian dominance in Korea was over, there was no guarantee that this would be true. These gains seemed scant recompense in comparison with what other powers were obtaining throughout Asia. In fact, this disparity of position in Asia between Japan and the leading European powers made a deep and lasting impression on the Japanese. A little over a generation later, when Japan followed similar tactics in Manchuria, European action in 1895 was taken as a precedent. The argument ran as follows: Japan happened to modernize in 1930 not in 1895. If it had been strong at the earlier date, it could have kept Liaotung. If it had insisted upon doing so, it might have obtained a lease in China when the powers carved out their spheres. It might even have acquired possession of Korea at the same time. Why should it be condemned for similar action a few years later when it had much greater provocation for its action?

The United States Becomes a Pacific Power

Simultaneously with these manifestations of imperialism by the European powers, the United States likewise became a victim of the expansionist fever. The disunity and weaknesses caused by the struggle over slavery, the stultifying effect of the tragedies of the Reconstruction in the South, and the challenge of vast undeveloped areas had kept the United States occupied primarily with national issues. Since 1856-62, when Townsend Harris was the first American Consul, it had played only a limited role in Japan's historical development. Most of the technical foreign assistants, with the exception of those selected by Kuroda for Hokkaidō, had come from Europe. The preference for American ideas and materials for the educational system was of short duration. American political institutions, which were based on a philosophy incongruous with the basic concepts of the oligarchs, had never been accepted. Japan's trade with America was only a fraction of that with other foreign countries.

By 1895, therefore, there were only a limited number of basic interests which the United States and Japan had in common. On the other hand, a rapid industrialization, the growth of transcontinental transportation, and the desire for overseas markets were underlying forces which contributed to a new American nationalism. This expansionism, which was advocated by the Republicans, collided with Japan's ambitions in the Pacific and with Europe's designs in China.

The collision with Japan was the result of both American and Japanese desires to possess the Hawaiian Islands. By a treaty with Hawaii in 1887, the United States had obtained a naval base and the use of port facilities in the Islands. In the previous year, Hawaii had made an agreement with Japan concerning the immigration of Japanese laborers. Japan, on the basis of an earlier commercial treaty, insisted that its subjects receive treatment equal to that of native Hawaiians. On the other hand, it had disregarded the quota for immigrants as set by the treaty. To stop this limitless flow of foreign laborers, the Hawaiian government permitted only those with valid permits to land. Japan countered this move by the dispatch of a warship to Honolulu and by demanding unrestricted entry privileges for Japanese subjects.

American reaction to these Japanese maneuvers varied with the party in power in Washington. The Democrats, who headed the government when the treaty was concluded in 1887, were against formal annexation of the Islands. The Republicans, who came to power when President Benjamin Harrison was elected in 1888, favored expansion. In 1893, he presented a treaty for the annexation of Hawaii. Before action was taken, the Democrats again took office and President Cleveland withdrew the treaty. In 1896, William McKinley, a Republican, won the election by a considerable majority and the annexation movement was revived. The *Honolulu Star,* in commenting on Japan's request for unlimited immigration, wrote, "It is the white race against the yellow. . . . Nothing but annexation can save the islands."

This plea fell on sympathetic ears. By the middle of 1897, McKinley had resubmitted the treaty for the annexation of Hawaii. This action brought a fiery protest from the Japanese Minister in Washington, Hoshi Toru. In an official communciation to the American government, he claimed that the maintenance of the status quo in the Hawaiian Islands was "essential to a good understanding of the powers which have interests in the Pacific." He feared that annexation would postpone the settlement of Japanese claims in the islands. Finally, he argued that the residential, commercial, and industrial rights of Japanese subjects would be endangered by annexation.

Despite these protests, the United States pushed ahead with its plans for annexation. The Republican administration of President McKinley did not intend to let anything stand in its way. The American Minister at Honolulu was prepared for any eventuality. His instructions read that if the Japanese resorted to forceful occupation, he was to consult with the local authorities and the American naval commanders, "land a suitable force and announce provisional assumption of a protectorate by the United States over Hawaii pending consummation of the annexation treaty."[7]

In the Congressional debates on the treaty, the chief argument for annexation was the danger to the United States of Japanese infiltration of the Islands. Other senators noted the need for a coaling station for American ships in the mid-Pacific. Finally, it was claimed that annexation was the only way to assume protection of American property which amounted to over three-fourths of the area of the Islands. The Senate Foreign Relations Committee reported in a prophetic vein:

> The present Hawaiian-Japanese controversy is the preliminary skirmish in the great coming struggle between the civilization and the awakening forces of the East and civilization of the West.[8]

After the United States entered the war against Spain in 1898, which John Hay had characterized as both necessary and righteous, the fate of Hawaii was sealed. The defeat of the Spanish fleet in Manila Bay stimulated Congress to pass a Joint Resolution for annexation. The Hawaiian Islands were formally annexed on August 12, 1898, and the United States immediately became a power with colonial territory in the Pacific. Two days later, the Japanese Minister was assured that the Japanese on the Hawaiian Islands would receive just and equitable treatment. Faced with a *fait accompli,* as in the case of Russia in Liaotung, the Japanese government was powerless to push its objections further, and remained skeptical as to future developments.

The American acquisition of the Philippine Islands, though a much richer and larger prize than Hawaii, had only an indirect bearing at this juncture on Japanese-American relations. In the debate on their annexation, American commercial advantages, the political prestige which a sizable territorial possession in the western Pacific would give to the United States, and the desire to protect the Filipinos from potential oppressors, such as Germany, were some of the most recurrent arguments. No mention was made of the need to place the islands under American sovereignty to keep Japan from acquiring them. On the contrary, after Manila's occupation by American forces, Japan formally expressed its acquiescence to the extension of United States sovereignty over the Islands. It added that such a solution of the question would be entirely satisfactory to Japan.[9]

This solution was likewise satisfactory and satisfying to the American people. They were proud of their colonial empire and gloried in it. They were too naïve to realize that empire building carried heavy responsibilities. They had little suspicion that the protection of these possessions forty years later would involve them in a war against Japan. In 1898, the American sphere of influence, though not on the Asiatic mainland, was even more real, more comprehensive, and more exclusive than that of the European powers in China, or of Russia or Japan in Korea.

The Open Door Policy

At the same time, the United States was apprehensive lest the European powers would exclude it from trade in their respective spheres of influence

Japanese Empire and European Concessions in China, 1900

in China. If the expansion of these spheres continued, American commercial interests would suffer. When John Hay circulated his famous Open Door Note in 1899, European imperialism had reached its peak in Eastern Asia. The United States had taken possession of the Philippines and of the Hawaiian Islands. Germany had acquired concessions in

Shantung and the Micronesia Islands north of the equator. Russia was ensconced in southern Manchuria and was threatening Korea. France was negotiating for territory in South China.

Although Great Britain was a free-trade country and would have welcomed imports from America in its sphere in China, its actions appeared to follow the same pattern as the other European countries. It had nearly doubled the territory of the Crown Colony of Hong Kong and held a leasehold at Weihaiwei. It also sought recognition of its special sphere of influence in central China in the rich Yangtze River Valley. Its ships hauled two-thirds of the tonnage of the goods in the China trade and it was determined to retain this commercial advantage.

Conversely, Japan was woefully unstable after the victory over China. The political parties and the oligarchs were at loggerheads. It needed to buy time to be able to perfect its military machine, to exploit its newly acquired colony of Formosa, and to hold its own against Russia in Korea. Obviously, it would be intrigued by any move toward China which would increase its status on the Asiatic mainland.

The Open Door Policy, which was designed to preserve and enhance American commercial interests in China, became one of the basic elements in American foreign policy. Like many such policy pronouncements, however, it underwent elaboration and expanded interpretations. By the time of the abortive negotiations with Japan in November, 1941, the United States referred to the Open Door Policy in terms such as the inviolability of territorial integrity, the noninterference in the internal affairs of other countries, and the equality of commercial opportunity. At its inception at the end of the nineteenth century, however, the Open Door Policy not only had a very limited connotation but it also was originally a British concept.

If Great Britain was to maintain its trade advantages in China, it was necessary to check Russian and German economic and political penetration in East Asia. British Foreign Secretary Balfour had declared that he did not regard China as a place for conquest but rather as a profitable place for British and world trade. Shortly thereafter, the British government acted to implement this policy. In early 1898 it sent a note to China demanding that no territory in the British sphere of influence, the Yangtze Valley, be alienated to another power.

At the same time, both Japan and England became conscious of their joint interests in checking Russia. Accordingly, the British Colonial Secretary Chamberlain began conversations with the Japanese Minister to London, Katō, looking toward closer Anglo-Japanese cooperation. Katō saw many advantages to an alliance with Britain. It would afford both partners undisputed naval control of the Far East and would be especially beneficial for Japan, which would become the leading partner in Asia. But Katō received little support from his government because Prime Minister Itō had a distinct preference for an alliance with Russia rather than with Great Britain. Consequently, further diplomatic talks were held in abeyance.

At this point, Britain sought the help of the United States as a counter force against both Germany and Russia. Immediately following the German seizure of Tsingtao in 1897, the British proposed to the United States that the two countries work together to insure equal economic opportunity in China. The United States was, however, completely absorbed with the question of war with Spain and turned down Britain's suggestion. By September, 1898, the fighting with Spain was over and America was suddenly conscious of the Far East as a new area in which to exert its influence. John Hay was appointed Secretary of State and selected as one of his advisers, W. W. Rockhill, an old China hand.

Secretary Hay recognized that the recent formation by the European powers of separate spheres of influence in China called for a new formulation of American policy. He asked Rockhill to prepare a memorandum on American policy for China. Rockhill, in turn, consulted a life-long friend and fellow-resident in China, Alfred E. Hippisley, a British subject who had been Commissioner of the Chinese Maritime Customs. His experience in that position had made him keenly conscious of the dangers to China of the predatory commercial and territorial policy advocated by the foreign powers. From a practical viewpoint, he believed that monopolistic trends could best be checked by a new policy which gave equal opportunity to everyone.

The recommendations which he sent to Rockhill, therefore, concentrated on the question of how equal economic opportunity could be achieved within the framework of conditions as they actually obtained in China in 1899. He advocated acceptance of the existence of the various spheres of influence, arguing that it would be impossible for citizens of any country to obtain treatment within a sphere equal to that of the nationals of the state controlling that sphere. Specifically, United States citizens could not expect preferential treatment. Nevertheless, the United States could and should insist that its citizens be given treatment in these spheres equal to that afforded other nations.

This memorandum of Hippisley's to Rockhill became the basis for Hay's Open Door Note of September 6, 1899. The Note was concerned primarily with customs problems and nondiscriminatory commercial treatment within the spheres of influence. It asked the powers with concessions in China to agree that they would not interfere with any foreign investments within the spheres or leased territory which they had in China, and requested that Chinese tariffs be applied to goods shipped to these ports. Finally, it proposed that equal harbor dues and railroad fares be levied on the goods of all countries.

Secretary Hay's note was circulated to England, France, Germany, Japan, Italy, and Russia. As was to be expected, Great Britain readily accepted this move which would protect its commercial interests in the spheres of other powers. Germany also sent a favorable answer. Japan's reply was evasive and equivocal, but it agreed to accede to Hay's proposal if the other powers did likewise. Secretary Hay seized upon this indecisive attitude of Japan to make the first expansion of the Open Door Policy. He informed the Japanese Foreign Minister that the other governments intended, so long as the other powers acted in the same manner,

> . . . to maintain liberty of trade and equality of treatment for all the world within the territory in China over which they can exercize control or influence.

There was one important flaw in the American proposal. It came from a country which had no leasehold and no sphere of influence in China. When Hay claimed that the principle of commercial equality had been accepted by states with interests in China, he assumed that these powers would deny special privileges for their own subjects within their spheres. At the same time, the United States adopted a closed door policy in its own Asiatic possessions. It is not surprising, therefore, that the various powers to whom the Open Door Note had been sent saw little reason to take their commitments seriously. To Japan, the whole proceedings seemed naïve and useless.

The Boxer Uprising

The internal events in China were to endanger its territorial integrity even more than the avarice of the Western powers. Ever since China's defeat in 1895, political and economic conditions had deteriorated and an antiforeign feeling had increased. A few enlightened Chinese leaders, such as the reformers K'ang Yu-wei and Liang Ch'i-ch'ao, had persuaded the young Emperor to adopt innovations similar to those inaugurated in Japan. The conservative elements in China had prevailed upon the reactionary Empress Dowager, however, to seize the Emperor and to rescind the Imperial decrees inaugurating reforms. K'ang and Liang, with the assistance of Itō Hirobumi, fled to Japan. China soon settled back into its reactionary ways.

The complacency of the Celestial Kingdom was soon shattered, however, by a national, anti-Christian, antiforeign revolutionary movement known as the Boxer Uprising. The central government was too impotent to be able to check the uprisings. In 1899 the movement gained momentum under the Boxers in Shantung Province and spread to the chief cities with foreign settlements in North China. In June, 1900, the Boxers captured the capital city of Peking and cut off the foreign legations from outside contact. For the next three months, China was in reality at war with the foreign powers. Faced with this common danger to their diplomatic missions, the powers temporarily forgot their political and economic rivalries. An Allied military force was organized to relieve the beleaguered Peking legations. Japan, because of its proximity to the scene, supplied about half of the forces, Russia and Britain a little less than one-fourth each, while the remainder came largely from the United States and France.

The United States, which was aware of the tepid reaction of the powers to the Open Door Policy, was fearful that the Boxer Uprising would be used by them as an excuse to demand even greater concessions from China. To forestall such a move, Secretary Hay issued a new policy statement on China a month before the Allied forces were ready to advance from Tientsin to relieve the Peking legations. This statement of July, 1900, required no reply from the other powers. It left no question in their minds, however, as to America's attitude. It stated:

> The policy of the United States is to seek a solution which may bring about permanent safety and peace to China, preserve Chinese territorial integrity and administrative entity, protect all rights guaranteed to friendly powers by treaty and international law and safeguard trade with all parts of china.

In less than a year after the Open Door Note had been circulated, therefore, the United States had added another important element to its China policy. Henceforth, it was committed to the principle of preserving what was left of Chinese territorial integrity.

The final settlement of the Boxer Uprising required the payment by China of an indemnity to the powers of 450 million taels ($334,000,000). The special privileges, which the powers required as guarantees for the safety of their diplomatic representatives and their nationals, were far more important than the cash settlement. They were made at the expense of Chinese sovereignty and to the military advantage of the powers. Special guards were permitted to be quartered in each legation in Peking. Certain key points between Peking and the sea were occupied and the Paiho River to Tientsin was to be deepened. China's obvious disintegration and inability to maintain law and order within its borders left it at the mercy of the foreign powers. On the other hand, each of the powers watched the moves of the others like a hawk. In fact, these mutual suspicions and national jealousies were far more effective than the Open Door Notes in saving China from further dismemberment.[10]

The Anglo-Japanese Alliance of 1902

Contrary to fears of the European nations which participated in the defeat of the Boxers, Japan took the most conciliatory attitude toward China of all the powers. Its troops acted in an exemplary fashion. Half of its forces were withdrawn immediately upon the relief of the legations. It was not yet ready to insist on its own sphere within China proper. For the moment, it would be content to concentrate on consolidating its position in Korea.

From the point of view of its internal political condition Japan was in no position to enforce its will abroad. Throughout the Boxer Uprising, General Yamagata had been Prime Minister for the second time and the rivalry between him and Itō had come to the surface. The latter had finally decided that political parties were necessary for the operation of the government. To achieve this end and to strengthen his own position in his fight for supremacy with Yamagata, Itō and his followers formed their own party, the Seiyūkai party. As President of the party, Itō expected all its members to follow his commands, to approve any appointments he might make to Cabinet posts, and to consent to any selection of Prime Minister made by the Elder Statesmen. The party was formed, therefore, for the sake of political expediency rather than as any large concession to a popular demand for party cabinets.

Shortly after the Seiyūkai party was formed, Yamagata resigned as Prime Minister and the Elder Statesmen selected Itō as his successor. The new Cabinet, except for the War, Navy, and Foreign Ministers, was composed of Seiyūkai members. It remained in power until the next year when General Katsura, a protégé of Yamagata, became Premier and retained that post until 1906, the year after victory over Russia. Although Itō failed to gain appreciable strength by launching his new party, the Seiyūkai party was henceforth an important force in Japan's political history.

To return to international events and their effect on Japan, it became obvious to the participants in the joint expedition against the Boxers that Russia was the one power most desirous of taking advantage of China's weakness. With its leasehold in the Liaotung Peninsula, Russia was in the strongest position to wrest concessions from the Chinese Imperial Court in nearby Peking. Russia had suggested that the powers withdraw their troops from Peking to Tientsin. Since this move would have enhanced Russian control over Manchuria, the other powers objected. Russia then acted unilaterally and increased its pressure on China. This caused Peking to ask the powers to mediate on its behalf.

This request of March, 1901, was particularly embarrassing for Prime Minister Itō. He had personally advocated a Japanese-Russian *rapprochement.* On the other hand, he could not agree to Russian dominance over

China. He was forced to concur with Yamagata and the Privy Council that military preparations should be speeded up because of the danger of war with Russia. He also sent a stiff note to Russia intimating that its intended demands on China for special concessions in Manchuria should be withdrawn. As a result, Russia temporarily capitulated by acceding to Japan's request.

With the downfall of the Itō Cabinet in 1901 and the selection of Katsura as Prime Minister, Japan's policy toward Russia and Great Britain changed markedly. General Katsura was a protégé of Yamagata. He was also strongly anti-Russian. He and his colleagues in the Cabinet were determined to keep Russia out of Korea and were willing to go to war, if necessary, to prevent it. Furthermore, they estimated that victory would be assured if the war was fought before Russia completed the Trans-Siberian Railway and if France was kept out of the struggle.

With a view to attaining these goals, it was decided to explore further the possibility of an Anglo-Japanese alliance. Ambassador Hayashi Tadasu was recalled from St. Petersburg and assigned to London with instructions to renew negotiations which had been broken off by Katō three years earlier. The successful conclusion of this proposed alliance was hindered by several factors. In the first place, there was Germany's desire to check Russia and the suggestion that it join the alliance. Hayashi endorsed this proposal but it was received coolly by the British. Secondly, the differences of opinion among the leaders in Japan confused the issue.

Itō, although he was outside the Cabinet, was one of the most influential of the Elder Statesmen. He was opposed to policies advocated by Yamagata and Premier Katsura. Itō believed that Japan's interests in Korea could best be preserved by an alliance with Russia rather than with England. In addition, he doubted seriously whether England would emerge from its "splendid isolation" sufficiently to join an alliance with Japan. Nevertheless, he agreed with the Cabinet that negotiations should proceed in London. In October, 1901, Hayashi received formal authorization to proceed. By November the first British draft of an agreement was presented to him.

At this point, the negotiations were complicated by Itō's maneuvers. He had been invited to Yale University to receive an honorary degree at its bicentennial celebration in October, 1901. Itō had accepted the invitation and was determined to extend his trip to Europe and especially to Russia. Apparently he hoped to negotiate, as a private citizen, an agreement with Russia which would assure Japan's hegemony over Korea, prevent a war with Russia, and forestall the necessity of an alliance with England. He was too powerful a figure to be ignored and so was allowed to take his trip. Hayashi was ordered to Paris to confer with him and to report on the

London negotiations. Itō was amazed to learn how far the discussions had progressed and that the British were pressing for an early conclusion of the alliance. Consequently, he agreed that the conversations must continue.

Hayashi returned to London with instructions to temporize while Itō proceeded to St. Petersburg, where he claimed he expected to carry on "harmless gossiping." In the Russian capital, he received a warm reception. Although he had left home without official instructions to negotiate, he was convinced that he could conclude an alliance. On his own initiative he proposed a mutual guarantee of Korean independence and a mutual promise not to use the peninsula for strategic purposes. He also was willing to recognize Russia's paramount interest in Manchuria in return for a similar acknowledgment of Japan's special political, industrial, and commercial interests in Korea.

Since the British Foreign Office was fearful of a Russo-Japanese alliance, it looked askance at Itō's movements. Hayashi, who personally was strongly opposed to Itō's plans, was also anxious to conclude the alliance with Britain. Time and distance were on the side of the pro-British group in the Japanese government. By the time Itō cabled Katsura the gist of his proposals, Hayashi had reached agreement with the British government on most of the points to be included in the alliance. In December, 1901, the Privy Council and the Emperor decided to accept the proposed Anglo-Japanese Alliance and to reject Itō's proposal for an alliance with Russia.[11]

The Anglo-Japanese Alliance was signed on January 30, 1902. It recognized the special interests of Great Britain in China and of Japan in Korea. It provided that either of them could take necessary measures to safeguard those interests if threatened by the aggressive action of another power or by disturbances within China or Korea. Both countries promised to remain neutral if either of them should become involved in a war to protect those interests. They also pledged themselves to come to the assistance of the other if a third power should join in any such hostilities. The agreement was to remain in force for five years.

The effect of this Alliance was immediate. While the victory over China in 1895 had increased Japan's prestige abroad, the Alliance with Great Britain was far more significant. Japan was elated over the fact that it was an ally with one of the most powerful European states. Moreover, it had achieved by diplomacy one of its objectives, namely, the prevention of another power entering a war with Russia as the latter's ally. In view of Britain's pledge, it was certain that France would not come to Russia's aid in the event of a Russo-Japanese War. Furthermore, Great Britain had recognized Japan's special interests in Korea.

On the international scene, the first concrete result of the new alliance was the promise of Russia to withdraw its troops from Manchuria. These troops had been in occupation since the Boxer Uprising and previous efforts to force their removal had been fruitless. In April, 1902, a Russo-Chinese agreement was signed which specified that evacuation of troops would begin forthwith and would be completed within eighteen months. China also successfully resisted a Russian plea for special privileges in connection with the railways in Manchuria.

From the British point of view, the alliance was accomplishing its purpose. Plans for a Japanese-Russian alliance had been frustrated. Furthermore, Russia had not only been checked in China, it was apparently being forced to withdraw. On the other hand, the alliance produced results of questionable value. Russia's suspicions of England's designs and ambitions were increased to such an extent that Great Britain went to some lengths to explain that the alliance in no way threatened the present position or the legitimate interests of any other power. Russia was not impressed by these explanations. Its ally, France, announced that the Dual Alliance would henceforth be applicable to the Far East as well as to Europe. But this move did little to change the new balance of power in East Asia. The Anglo-Japanese Alliance had established Japan, rather than Russia, as the strongest force in that area.

Such were the apparent, tangible effects of the alliance with England. In retrospect, however, it appears as a symbol of one of the most remarkable national transformations in modern times. It signified not only that Japan had come of age as a modern nation but that its manhood, its vitality, and its potentialities of power and of growth had been recognized and condoned by one of the strongest nations of the world. When viewed in its proper historical perspective, it is nothing less than amazing that Japan had reached a point where Great Britain, at a time when Britannia undisputedly ruled the waves, should have turned to Japan to make an agreement on terms of equality.

In 1852, exactly half a century earlier, Japan was in mortal fear that Great Britain would attack it and wrest from it privileges and concessions, if not actual territory, similar to those obtained in China. In 1852, Katsura Tarō (Japanese Prime Minister in 1902) was five years old. He was raised in a warrior's family in the shadows of the feudal castle in the capital city of the powerful western fief of Chōshū. He grew up in a society in which the warrior class was predominant. Officially Japan was sealed from the outside world. Europeans were treated with reckless arrogance. No one took seriously the reports from the Hollanders that the United States was planning a naval expedition to force Japan to open its ports to the outside world.

In the fifty years from 1852 until Katsura had reached the peak of his career in 1902, his country had changed into a modern, industrialized, military power. While there were distinct limitations to the extent of this modernization and industrialization, in the aggregate this transformation was impressive. Otherwise, how is one to explain Britain's willingness to become Japan's ally? Feudalism had been formally dissolved. A constitution had been promulgated. Universal education had been established. The Civil and Criminal Codes had been revised. A conscript army had overwhelmingly defeated China on the Asiatic mainland. Colonial territories had been added to the traditional homeland. Extraterritoriality had been abolished. All of these things and much more had been accomplished in fifty years. But the most important achievement, in terms of the effect on the Japanese national spirit, was the new Anglo-Japanese Alliance on the basis of equality with a great European, colonial power. Was it little wonder, therefore, that during the next half century a keen sense of invincibility, of uniqueness, of superiority, and of mission to conquer the world should lead Japan blindly to ignominious defeat?

Japan's Diplomatic War With Russia

The first signs of this nascent feeling of invincibility began to emerge in the hardening of the attitude toward Russia. With Great Britain as an ally, the Japanese leaders quickly moved to a solution of other basic outstanding issues. They were not interested in a solution unless it was favorable to Japan. They had previously discovered that the endemic political crises had little effect on the international policies which they formulated. The ineffective struggle of the politicians in the Diet against the oligarchs continued but Katsura met the challenge to his domestic policies in the usual manner. He dissolved Parliament and operated on the budget of the previous year. On matters of foreign policy, he simply ignored the wishes of Parliament.[12]

Foremost among the unanswered questions involving Russia, from Japan's point of view, was whether or not Russia would recognize and respect Japan's special position in Korea. For the past few years, Japanese subjects had slowly acquired increasingly important concessions and property in Korea. Permission had been obtained to build the Pusan-Seoul and Chemulpo-Seoul Railways. Important strategically located real estate had been purchased around the most important harbors. The Bank of Japan had acquired special whaling, fishing, and mining rights. As the Anglo-Japanese Alliance had stated, Japan was "interested in a peculiar degree, politically, industrially and commercially in Korea." It intended to increase these interests and to improve its strategic position in the peninsula. It would brook no interference. It took a dim view of Russia's plans for exploitation of timber in the Yalu River Valley in northwest

Korea. On the other hand, Japan was willing to recognize that Russia had special rights and interests in Manchuria; it also was realistic enough to recognize that it would be far less expensive to win Russian acceptance of its demands by negotiation than by war. Negotiations would also give more time to complete the armament and naval expansion program. If diplomacy failed, the country could easily be mobilized for war to attain by force what could not be wrested by negotiation.

Russian troops had not been withdrawn from Manchuria as provided in the agreement with China in 1902. This fact and a report of new Russian demands on China were used by Japan as the excuse for opening negotiations. Japan considered the permanent occupation of Manchuria by Russian troops to be untenable. Nevertheless, so long as this occupation continued, pressure could be exerted on Russia to recognize Japan's interests in Korea. Consequently, the Japanese Minister at St. Petersburg was ordered to begin negotiations to settle all outstanding differences with Russia.

Political events within Russia made it difficult, if not impossible, however, for such an understanding to be reached. Foreign Minister Lamsdorff agreed that an understanding between the two countries was the best policy; on the other hand, Finance Minister Serge Witte, who had favored a conciliatory attitude toward Japan, was ousted from power by a group of militarists. Moreover, Admiral Alexieff had been appointed special Viceroy of the Far East with headquarters at Port Arthur. He was independent of the control of the Russian Foreign Office and reported only to a special committee selected by the Czar. In fact, on matters relating to Russia's policy in the Far East, he had more power and influence than the Foreign Minister.

Japan proposed that each country recognize the special interests of the other in their respective zones and spheres of interest. Each had the right to take steps to protect these interests. Japanese exploitation of Korea, including construction of a railway in north Korea, was not to be impeded. Finally, Japan was to have the exclusive right to advise the Korean government on administrative reforms and on military assistance.

The Russian counterproposals of October 3, 1903, were only partially satisfactory to Japan. Russia was willing to agree to Japan's request to advise Korea on reforms providing such advice and assistance improved the "civil administration" of the Korean Empire and did not infringe upon its independence. No Korean ports were to be used for strategic purposes and no coastal defenses were to be built along the Korean Straits. Korea north of the thirty-ninth parallel—a line just south of the cities of Wonsan and Py'onyang—should be a neutral zone. Russia also insisted that Manchuria and all of its littoral be completely outside of the Japanese sphere of influence. In other words, Russia intended to keep Manchuria as its exclusive sphere and wanted an unimpeded line of communication by sea from Dairen and Port Arthur to Vladivostok.

The choice left to Japan was clear. It could go to war with the hope that it would drive Russia from Manchuria and emerge as the chief power in northeast Asia. In general, public opinion supported this position. Most people believed that a war with Russia was inevitable and the sooner it was over the better. Premier Katsura and his military colleagues were convinced that they could defeat Russia. The Japanese Navy was equally confident though less vociferous. The other alternative was to settle for a restricted Japanese hegemony over Korea, exclusion from Manchuria, and the continued menace of Russian naval bases on both flanks of Korea at Port Arthur on the west and Vladivostok on the northeast.

To the military-minded leaders in Japan who had easily won a war only a decade earlier, the first alternative seemed both sensible and reasonable. After a Japanese counterproposal was unacceptable to Russia, an Imperial Conference of January 12, 1904, of the Cabinet, the *Genrō,* leading financial and military authorities, and the Emperor, as Chairman, decided on Japan's minimum terms. These included recognition of Manchuria as outside Japan's sphere providing Russia respected the territorial integrity of Manchuria and China and permitted legitimate activities of Japan and other powers in Manchuria. In return, Russia would pledge not to interfere with Japan's activities in Korea. If no satisfactory reply was received to these minimum demands, the issues would be settled by war. The nation as a whole was solidly behind its leaders. As the American Minister in Tokyo reported:

> The Japanese nation is now worked up to a high pitch of excitement, and it is no exaggeration to say that if there is no war it will be a severe disappointment to the Japanese individual of every walk of life. . . . The Japanese nation is in the position of having finally made up its mind to fight, and its costly preparations have been made.[13]

Notes

1. Some of the political developments after 1895 were as follows: The Second Matsukata Cabinet lasted for a little more than a year from September 18, 1896, to January, 1898. Ōkuma was offered the Foreign Minister portfolio. As a further incentive for cooperation from the Progressives, Matsukata promised administrative and financial reforms and the inauguration of the principle of collective responsibility within the Cabinet. As these promises were readily given to win party support rather than from a changed attitude toward the function of the Cabinet and Parliament, they were never implemented. Party support slowly melted away and Ōkuma resigned about a year after his appointment. Shortly thereafter Matsukata's Cabinet fell. The premiership shifted back to Chōshū control under Itō, after the familiar deadlock

between the executive and legislative was resolved in the usual fashion. For the fifth time in eight years the Diet was dissolved in January, 1898. As a result of elections in March, 1898, the parties received an overwhelming majority. Itō had been unsuccessful in his attempt to receive support from the Liberal party. His all-important tax bill was defeated and he was roundly criticized for his weak policy toward China and the concessions obtained by Germany and Russia. He resigned as Prime Minister in less than a year after his appointment. As a bulwark against the rising power of Yamagata's group, Itō recommended a Cabinet supported by the political parties. Hence, in June, 1898, Ōkuma and Itagaki were asked to form the first party Cabinet in Japan's history. After its formation, the parties had as much difficulty in holding together as the oligarchs had had in winning their support. Ōkuma resigned on October 31, 1898, after four months in power. Yamagata then formed his second ministry and silenced the opposition with bribes. He remained in power until October, 1900, during which period a clear Itō-Yamagata rivalry emerged. See Robert A. Scalapino, *Democracy and the Party Movement in Prewar Japan* (Berkeley: University of California Press, 1953), pp. 167-82.

2. Many writers have assumed that inasmuch as Itō and Yamagata were both from Chōshū and were staunch oligarchs, they could not have had basic disagreements. Such is not the case. As Scalapino correctly points out, Yamagata skilfully rallied his forces to embarrass and discredit Itō during his Premiership in 1900-01. The split became even more apparent when it is realized that from 1901 to 1913, the premiership alternated between Katsura and Saionji. As we have noted, the former was from Chōshū and was a protégé of Yamagata. The latter, born in Kyōto in a nobleman's family, was a strong supporter and leader of the Itō faction.

3. Payson J. Treat, *Diplomatic Relations Between the United States and Japan, 1895-1905* (Stanford, Calif.: Stanford University Press, 1938), p. 5.

4. In view of this precedent of suggesting the thirty-eighth parallel as a dividing line for Korea, the Soviet Union accepted it as a logical demarcation in 1945 when it was proposed as the line to separate the Soviet and American zones of occupation.

5. For an account of these rivalries and intrigues see Clarence Weems, *Independence Movement,* Columbia University Ph.D. Thesis, 1954, p. 504 *et seq.* For an account of Kir Alexeviev see *Korean Repository,* vol. 5, (Jan., 1898).

6. China was in no position to retaliate. Furthermore, it was under obligation to repay Russia and the other members of the *triplice* for their action in 1895. The agreement with Germany was signed in March, 1898, which granted a ninety-nine year lease to an area 50 kilometers back from Kiaochow Bay, and mining and railway rights. The Russian convention followed in April on a twenty-five year basis. France's share was to be a lease for a naval station in the south at Kwangchow. Great Britain had stepped into Weihaiwei after the Japanese left in 1896. For details see Hosea Ballou Morse, *The International Relations of the Chinese Empire* (3 vols.; London: Longmans, Green & Co., Inc., 1918), vol. 3, pp. 101 *et seq.*

7. O. Clinard, *Japan's Influence on American Naval Power, 1897-1917* (Berkeley: University of California Press, 1947), p. 10.

8. *Ibid.,* p. 12. See also Treat, *United States and Japan, op. cit.,* p. 30 *et seq.,* for details of the United States–Japanese diplomatic exchanges on the Hawaiian question.

9. This note was dated September 8, 1898. On September 16 President McKinley instructed the Peace Commission not to seek advantages in the Orient which were not common to all. He was ready to accord open door treatment to all. Only the island of Luzon was to be retained. A month later, however, public opinion in the Midwest convinced him to change his instructions to the Commissioners to acquire

all of the islands. When Spain balked, the United States offered to buy them at $20,000,000. The Treaty of Paris, which assigned the islands to the United States, was signed December 10, 1898. Guam was also included. Wake Island was claimed in 1900.

10. Despite Hay's interest in China's territorial integrity, the United States was caught in the general movement to obtain a naval station in China. The U. S. Minister was sent instructions to secure such a base near Fuchow. The project was dropped abruptly, however, when the Japanese objected on the grounds that such a move was contrary to Hay's Open Door Policy and went against the Secretary of State's desires "to preserve the territorial integrity of China." See Treat, *United States and Japan, op. cit.*, p. 110 *et seq.*

11. Prof. Langer has done much to clarify the negotiations with England and Itō's role in the whole affair. Langer concludes his discussion by commenting on the inconsistency of the Japanese government in hoping to obtain both an alliance with England and with Russia. He fails to take into account the fact that the Katsura Government cared nothing about inconsistency. It would have been quite happy to obtain both a British guarantee of help and a Russian recognition of Japan's special interest in Korea. In other words, if Russia had been willing to sign an alliance despite the Anglo-Japanese Alliance, Japan would not have objected. Katsura was not convinced that Itō could have gotten the type of agreement he proposed. When Japan had to decide between an alliance with England or Russia, there was little alternative. See William Langer, *The Diplomacy of Imperialism, 1890-1902* (2 vols.; New York: Alfred A. Knopf, Inc., 1951), vol. 2, p. 725 *et seq.*

12. The following outline of political events will keep the record comparatively complete. As indicated above, Prime Minister Katsura was faced with a political crisis in 1902. In the elections of that year, bribery was widespread but Itō's Seiyūkai party won the largest number of seats (190). Consequently, when Parliament met at the end of that year, the House of Representatives defeated the Cabinet's Budget Bill. The Prime Minister dissolved Parliament. As provided by the Constitution the budget of the previous year automatically went into force. In the election of 1903, subsequent to this dissolution, the Seiyūkai increased its total seats to 193, but later lost control of the Lower House. Itō, who had been defeated in his diplomatic moves for an alliance with Russia rather than with England, had been forced to make several political compromises. From Yamagata's point of view, Itō was a recalcitrant political rival and so was removed from a political position. He was requested by the Emperor to take over the Privy Council. He was able to save some of his political power by appointment of Saionji as President of the Seiyūkai. Katsura survived the next year politically and after hostilities broke out in 1904 with Russia there was no question of replacing him so long as Japan was victorious.

13. Treat, *op. cit.*, p. 194.

13

THE CONSOLIDATION OF THE JAPANESE EMPIRE, 1904-1915

It is no mere coincidence that two significant periods in Japan's recent history encompass approximately a decade. There was a marked change in Japan and its world position in the period from the end of the Sino-Japanese war in 1895 to the breakdown of negotiations with Russia in 1904. In 1895 Japan was largely an unknown quantity. Despite its victory over China, it was still considered by the Western powers as a backward, semifeudal, inferior country. Just prior to the outbreak of the war with Russia, Japan had consolidated its position. It was an ally of Great Britain. It had important and special interests in Korea and had obtained British and Russian recognition of those interests. It was beginning to be recognized as an important world power, and was confident enough in its own strength and ability to be willing to defy Russian threats.

Similarly, the decade from the Russo-Japanese War (1904-5), to the reluctant acceptance by China of the Twenty-One Demands in May, 1915, forms another distinct period in Japan's recent history. In that short time, Japan not only increased but consolidated its empire. In February, 1904, Japan had decided to win control of Korea at all costs and to throw down the gauntlet at Russia's feet. Although it was recognized as a significant force in East Asiatic politics, there was no proof that it was strong enough to challenge successfully a European power. There was even less evidence that it could or would become a successful colonial power, that it would be able to support an efficient modern army and navy, or that it would become a permanent threat to European and American interests in China.

At the end of this second decade, in May, 1915, there was no question as to Japan's capabilities, intentions, or potentialities. It had been transformed into a world power which dominated the entire Far East. It seemed to have been catapulted onto the world stage by an uncontrollable and compelling urge to become strong, to force its will on any who challenged its position, and to be the leader of Asia. Both external and internal developments during this decade must be analyzed, therefore, to determine whether the success in this growth of empire was the result of caprice, of the clever implementation of a master plan, of wise decisions made at times of crises, or of a combination of all of these factors.[1]

The Russo-Japanese War, 1904-5

This analysis logically begins with the outbreak of the war between Russia and Japan. In the early stages, Japan followed the same pattern as against China in 1894 and as against the United States on December 7, 1941. On February 4, 1904, an Imperial Conference decided that the time of waiting had passed. The Japanese negotiators in St. Petersburg were ordered to terminate their discussions. On February 6, Russian troops crossed the Yalu River into Korea, and the Japanese fleet left its naval bases with orders to attack. Port Arthur, the Russian naval base in Liaotung, was bombarded without warning on the night of February 8–9. On February 9, two Russian naval vessels were put out of commission outside of Chemulpo harbor. The next day Japan declared war on Russia. Within three months, the Russian land forces had been driven out of Korea and the naval forces at Port Arthur had been largely crippled. At Mukden, 400,000 Japanese fought tenaciously against 350,000 Russians for two weeks before the city fell in March, 1905.

The defeat of the powerful Russian army was not enough to settle the issue. The Russian Baltic fleet under Admiral Rodjestvensky had been sent around the world to engage the Imperial Japanese Navy. Admiral Tōgō, the Japanese fleet commander, was prepared for the attack, had taken a calculated risk, and had estimated that the Russian fleet would take the most direct route to Vladivostok through the Korean Straits.[2] The main Japanese fleet was at hand when the Russian ships appeared near Tsushima Island on May 27. Within two days, Japanese naval superiority and skill practically annihilated the Russian fleet. Russia's military power in the Far East had been shattered. It was only a matter of time until hostilities ceased and peace negotiations began.

Interrelated Diplomatic Victories and the Treaty of Portsmouth, 1904-5

Both during and immediately following the successes on the battlefields of South Manchuria and in the Tsushima Straits, Japan achieved equally important victories on the diplomatic front. All of these moves were interrelated and directed toward the consolidation of a favored position in Korea and in northeastern Asia. The first of these steps, which took place within a fortnight after the Russo-Japanese War broke out, was the easiest to accomplish. On February 23, 1904, Japan forced the young Korean King to sign a protocol which established a modified Japanese protectorate over Korea. Japan guaranteed to protect the safety of the Korean royal family and the integrity and independence of his country. In return, Korea became a Japanese ally and promised to act on administrative matters only on the advice of Japan. The immediate effect of the protocol was to permit the occupation by Japanese military forces of all important strategic points on the peninsula. In a matter of days all of Korea was secure. In effect, the first irrevocable step had been taken to make Korea an integral part of the Japanese Empire. Japanese merchants and carpetbaggers followed in the wake of their army of occupation and considered themselves above the law. A new and significant sphere of influence had been created on the Asiatic continent.

Economic uncertainty and financial chaos were, however, hampering the exploitation of this newly acquired sphere of influence. Consequently, within six months, Japan moved again. A new protocol was signed in August, 1904, whereby the Korean government agreed to engage Japanese financial and diplomatic advisers. Megata, who became the first financial adviser, immediately inaugurated far-reaching reforms. He established a uniform system of coinage, prepared a budget for the Korean government, and eliminated bureaucratic inefficiency and bribery. Necessary authority was at hand to confiscate land, obtain preferred fishing rights and cabotage privileges for Japanese subjects for inland and coastal waters. The communications system was taken over for purposes of security. Martial law prevented sabotage or other acts inimical to Japan's rapid exploitation of the hard-pressed country. An additional treaty, which solidified and extended the protectorate, awaited the outcome of the War and the Peace Conference.

Even several weeks before the arrival of the Russian fleet in the Tsushima Straits in May, 1905, Japan had seriously considered an armistice. After the defeat of the Russian Army in Manchuria, the Japanese Chief of Staff had reported that 250,000 more men and an expenditure of 1.5 billion yen would be needed for complete victory. This news dampened the ardor of those who pressed for an annihilation of the Russian Army. It made a negotiated peace seem to be the logical solution, especially in view of reports from France to the effect that Russia might be willing to make peace. Consequently, the chief problem which confronted the Japanese Foreign Minister was how to get negotiations started.

Since the United States was in a neutral position toward both the belligerents and President Theodore Roosevelt had shown a personal interest in the matter, he was approached by the Japanese government.[3] His answer was to recommend direct negotiations between the two belligerents and to caution Japan that he expected it to adhere to the Open

Door in Manchuria and to return that territory to Chinese control. Three days after the Battle of Tsushima, Roosevelt was formally requested to mediate. By mid-June, 1905, both belligerents had accepted the President's good offices. On August 9, 1905, the Peace Conference began at Portsmouth, New Hampshire.

Japan's position at the Portsmouth Peace Conference was augmented by two diplomatic developments. In the first place, President Roosevelt had concluded that Korea would inevitably come under the dominance of Japan. In fact, even before the Russian Army was defeated in Manchuria, he had written Korea off. He wrote Hay in January, 1905, "We cannot possibly interfere for the Koreans against Japan. They could not strike one blow in their own defense." Furthermore, he had warned Germany and France that if they made any move against Japan, as they had done in 1895, he would support Japan.

At the same time he feared that Japan's new position of dominance in the Pacific might endanger American interests in the Philippines. He instructed his Secretary of War, William Howard Taft, who was en route to the Philippines, to reach an understanding with the Japanese Prime Minister. Taft informed Katsura that the United States would not interfere if Japanese troops established "suzerainty over Korea to the extent of requiring that Korea enter into no foreign treaties without the consent of Japan." In return, he sought Katsura's assurances that Japan did not have any aggressive designs upon the Philippines.[4] These assurances were incorporated into the Taft-Katsura Agreement of July, 1905. Indirectly, at least, the Agreement showed Japan that it would have America's sympathy at the peace conference.

A second diplomatic victory for Japan was the successful extension and broadening of the Anglo-Japanese Alliance. Because of the increased rivalry between Germany and England in 1904, France and Great Britain had developed a strong community of interest. This shift in the European power alignment made the latter anxious to broaden its alliance with Japan. Only a few days after the Portsmouth Conference began, therefore, a second Anglo-Japanese Alliance was signed. The new Alliance, which was directed both against Russia and Germany, was expanded to include the regions of both East Asia and India. Furthermore, a new proviso required that one of the signatories automatically would come to the assistance of the other when war resulted from an attack on these territories by a third power. In return, Great Britain recognized Japan's right to take measures of guidance and control in Korea.

When the Portsmouth Peace Conference opened in August, 1905, Japan's international position had been rapidly improving. It took a strong position and demanded that Korea be recognized as entirely within its sphere of influence. It was willing to restore Manchuria to China as rapidly as possible but expected that the principle of equal opportunity would be extended to that area. Additional demands included the transfer to Japan of the Russian leases in the Liaotung Peninsula, the lease of the railway in Manchuria from Changchung to Talienwan (Dairen), the cession in full sovereignty of the entire island of Sakhalien, and the payment by Russia of an indemnity to cover the costs of the war.

As the negotiations progressed, the Japanese delegates were in no mood to make concessions. Nevertheless, Japan was not in a position to make unlimited demands. The war had created a financial and economic crisis at home. If negotiations broke down and hostilities were resumed, there was a lack of manpower to assure a quick victory. Russia, on the other hand, found world public opinion swinging to its side as the conference continued. It became increasingly reluctant to accede to demands which it believed to be excessive.

By August 26 the negotiations had reached an impasse. The chief Russian delegate, former Finance Minister Witte, had been instructed to break off negotiations if he was unable to force Japan to drop its demands for an indemnity and for the island of Sakhalien. At this point, President Roosevelt took an active part in the negotiations. He urged the Czar to accept a treaty which required no indemnity and which provided for acquisition by Japan of only the southern half of Sakhalien. Roosevelt also prevailed upon the Japanese delegates to obtain new instructions which would permit them to accept this settlement. Consequently, the Treaty of Portsmouth, which was signed on September 5, 1905, provided for:

1. The recognition of Korean independence and of the paramount political, military, and economic interests of Japan therein.
2. The transfer to Japan of Russia's leases and rights in Liaotung and of the South Manchurian Railway.
3. The withdrawal of foreign troops from Manchuria except Japanese railway guards.
4. The acquisition of the southern half of Sakhalien in full sovereignty by Japan and of special fishing rights in adjacent waters.
5. The noninterference by the signatories in measures which China might take in Manchuria for the commercial and industrial development of that area.

As with the Treaty of Shimonoseki a decade earlier, the Japanese people expected much more from the war. They reacted emotionally and violently against the terms of peace. They demanded Katsura's resignation. They insisted that he should have pressed for an indemnity 50 per cent greater than the cost of the war, for the northern half of Sakhalien, and even for some of the Maritime Provinces in Siberia. Some of the most influential newspapers recommended rejection of the treaty. The comparatively sedate *Asahi* editorialized that the terms of peace had lifted the crown of victory from the nation's head. Other papers suggested the assassination of Cabinet members and the Elder Statesmen. Riots broke out in Tokyo with resultant heavy casualties. Martial law was immediately established. But this time no group of powers forced Japan to give up what it had been granted by the Treaty. Its sphere of influence now encompassed both Korea and Manchuria, and Japan was well along the road toward acquiring a controlling influence over all of Eastern Asia.

A Protectorate Over Korea

When the populace demanded the resignation of Premier Katsura because of his failure to win greater spoils at the Portsmouth Peace Conference, he would have gladly resigned. He was not, however, a free agent. He owed his position and his tenure of office to the Elder Statesmen and the Privy Councilors. They, in turn, realized that there was still important unfinished business to be settled. Japan's new status with Korea had to be regularized. Furthermore, China had not yet recognized the legality of Japan's claim to the former Russian leases in the Liaotung Peninsula. Hence, the Elder Statesmen insisted that Katsura remain at the head of the government until negotiations were completed with both Korea and China.

As for Korea, the two agreements of February and August, 1904, had given Japan a modified protectorate over that country, including the right to appoint financial and diplomatic advisers. These concessions had been obtained during wartime, however, and Japan was insistent on obtaining a more comprehensive and permanent arrangement. Although by the Portsmouth Treaty, Russia recognized the paramount political, economic, and military interests of Japan in Korea, it was another matter to get Korea to verify and to guarantee these interests. Itō Hirobumi, the most venerable statesman, was called upon to negotiate a convention at Seoul with the helpless and hapless peninsular kingdom. By an agreement signed on November 17, 1905, Japan's rights obtained in the earlier conventions were extended. Henceforth, even Korean foreign affairs were under the control of a Japanese Resident General. Itō, who was the first Resident General, explained that propinquity and Japan's own safety had made this action necessary.

Secret requests of the Korean King for help from the United States were of no avail. President Roosevelt declared he saw no practical action open to him in view of the earlier agreements between Japan and Korea. In November, 1905, the United States Minister was ordered to close the American Legation in Seoul. For all practical purposes, Roosevelt considered Korea as a Japanese protectorate and had no objection to such an arrangement.

There was another piece of unfinished diplomatic business before the Katsura Cabinet. China had not yet completed the transfer to Japan of Russia's former rights in the Liaotung Peninsula. By the Portsmouth Treaty, Russia was bound to relinquish its rights in favor of Japan. But Russia had received its rights from China. Since China was not a party to the Portsmouth Treaty, a separate agreement between China and Japan was necessary to make this transfer legal. Consequently, a special mission under Foreign Minister Komura went to Peking to settle the issue. In December, 1905, an agreement was signed which transferred the former Russian leasehold in Liaotung to Japan and gave the latter additional economic concessions. With the successful conclusion of these negotiations there was no real necessity for Katsura to remain in office. He resigned in the first week of January, 1906.

Katsura's resignation, as well as political events in Japan during the next seven years, were largely unconnected with the political realities. In fact, this period witnessed the operation of some of the most blatantly non-democratic aspects of a constitutional monarchy. In the first place, the premiership shifted back and forth between two men, Katsura and Saionji. These shifts were made with complete disregard to their party affiliations and to the strength of the parties in the House of Representatives.

When Katsura resigned, the Elder Statesmen took the responsibility of selecting his successor. Since they were anxious to find someone capable of effectively controlling the domestic scene, they nominated Itō's protégé, Saionji Kimmochi. He had succeeded Itō as head of the Seiyūkai, the strongest political party, but his Cabinet was in no sense a party Cabinet. He selected only two party members to serve with him, one of whom was Hara Kei (1856-1921) as Home Minister.[5] The other portfolios were filled by oligarchs and bureaucrats. Despite the new faces in the Cabinet there was no noticeable shift in policy. A balanced budget, the nationalization of railways, and an expansion program for the Army and Navy were all sponsored and approved.

The most important event during the first Saionji Ministry (1906-8) was the extension of Japanese control over Korea. While the agreement already negotiated with that unfortunate country had theoretically given Japan direction over Korean foreign affairs, the arrangement proved to be far from satisfactory. As Resident General, Prince Itō proposed a comprehensive program of internal "reforms." His plan included the improvement of agriculture and transportation facilities, industrial development, and the reorganization of the courts and the police system.

Since his powers and those of his subordinates appointed to the executive branches of the Korean government were only advisory and since Koreans resented and opposed these infringements on their independence, little progress was made. The King refused to listen to Itō's pleadings that he should approve a protectorate to prevent appointment of a Japanese military governor and outright annexation. When the Japanese Foreign Minister arrived to discuss a new treaty in 1907, the King abdicated rather than be forced to compromise his country's independence.

A new convention was immediately negotiated with his son, the new sovereign. This convention of July 25, 1907, made Korea a protectorate and placed it at the mercy of the Resident General. He could instruct and guide the Korean government on all matters relating to the reform of the Korean administration. His preliminary approval was required for all laws and ordinances and for appointments and removals of high Korean officials. Finally, the Korean government was bound to accept the appointment of any Japanese subject he recommended. To avoid any possible international complication and to protect its flank, Japan also signed a secret convention with Russia. The latter recognized the validity of the protectorate and in return was to receive most-favored-nation treatment for its subjects in Korea.

Even under the protectorate, the reforms advocated by Itō did not progress as rapidly as Japan desired. When one considers the basic attitude of Itō and his colleagues toward the Koreans, it is not surprising that such should be the case. On the one hand, the Japanese had operated under the delusion that the Koreans would willingly accept any "advice" offered them. Such an approach was consistent with Itō's public career. Throughout his long and distinguished service, he had always assumed a paternalistic attitude toward the common man in Japan. He and his contemporaries had displayed a strong self-confidence in the righteousness of their cause and in the wisdom of their decisions.

Naturally, he took this same attitude with him to Korea as Resident General and imbued his subordinates with it. It was strongly tinged with a feeling of superiority over all Koreans. He took immediate steps to implement the new powers granted Japan under the protectorate. Japanese vice-ministers, lesser officials, and clerks and secretaries were attached to the executive departments of the central Korean government. A Japanese secretary and an Inspector of Police with clerical assistants were assigned to each provincial office. Chief justices and procurators were appointed to the principal courts. The Oriental Colonization Company was organized to exploit Korean resources and expand Japanese industry.

On the other hand, Itō found that he had grossly underestimated Korea's love for independence. He had failed to realize that a hard core of Korean nationalism still existed. The more he tried to submerge it, the more buoyant it became. The King and his officials refused to be intimidated. They acted as independently as possible of the Resident General. On all levels of the Korean administration, a conscious policy of obstructionism was followed. Even for Itō, who opposed outright annexation, such a situation was far from satisfactory.[6]

Impotency of the Political Parties and Korea's Annexation, 1910

The growing dissatisfaction within Japan with the Saionji Cabinet also brought Korea's annexation closer. Paradoxically, this dissatisfaction had not been reflected in the regular elections of May, 1908. Despite the unpopularity of Saionji's financial policies, his party (the Seiyūkai) had won eight new seats in the House of Representatives, which gave it a majority for the first time in five years. But Yamagata, the most powerful Elder Statesman, had never let the wishes of the electorate stand in his way. He and his clique had agreed that it was time for a change. Itō was a failure in Korea and Saionji was unpopular at home.

The latter feigned illness and resigned as Prime Minister in July, 1908. His capitulation to the desires of the Elder Statesmen in the face of increased support from the voters was taken as a matter of course. His recommendation that Katsura succeed him was accepted. The Seiyūkai party, despite its majority in the House of Representatives, was content to let the oligarchs call the tune. The actual independence of the Cabinet from the parties was complete.

Katsura was little perturbed over the thought that he would be faced with a hostile Parliament. He had always been disdainful of the parties and their elected representatives. In fact, he was confident that he could force his policies through the Diet despite the opposition. In the final analysis, if he faced a political crisis, he could always turn the premiership back again to Saionji.

Katsura's second Cabinet, composed largely of his own henchmen and representatives from the militarist clique, remained in power for three years (July, 1908—August, 1911). Its domestic policy emphasized austerity and a balanced budget. The naval building program and increases in military expenditures were correlated with a long-term expansion program. To win support for his program, he resorted to bribery and intimidation.[7] The scandals which came to light after the bankruptcy in 1909 of the Japan Sugar Refining Company further weakened the prestige of the politicians. Twenty Diet members were arrested because of bribes which they had received. Furthermore, the legislators evinced a lack of interest in democratic processes. The House of Peers defeated a proposal for universal manhood suffrage. In his speech in opposition to the law, one of the Peers noted: "Nowhere in our Constitution is it stated that the chief object in the creation of the Diet was to give expression to the will of the people."

In the meantime, events were rapidly unfolding toward a climax in Korea. On the international front there were few indications of opposition to its annexation by Japan. A new high point had been reached in American-Japanese friendship. The American battle fleet had been warmly greeted on its official visit to Japan. On November 30, 1908, Secretary of State Elihu Root and Japanese Ambassador Takahira signed an agreement whereby their countries promised to press for territorial integrity and the principle of equal commercial opportunity in China. By inference, Japan could assume that it had a free hand in Korea as it was not mentioned in the joint declaration. In addition, when Japan rejected Root's proposal the next year to internationalize the Japanese-owned South Manchurian Railway, the United States dropped the matter.

On the domestic scene, Katsura pressed for formal annexation but Itō persisted in his opposition to such a move. But pressure from the annexationists continued and the movement gained popular support. It became so strong that in June, 1909, Itō reluctantly resigned as Resident General. He returned to his old post of President of the Privy Council. In October he was sent on an inspection trip to Manchuria where he planned to confer with the Russian Finance Minister on problems of mutual interest to their countries. While in Harbin, Itō was assassinated by a supposedly fanatical Korean. The fact that the assassins' access to him was in no way hampered by his guards led to speculation as to whether or not his political enemies had planned the whole affair. In any case, his death was considered to be more than an adequate pretext for annexation of Korea. Popular opinion at home clamored for such action; those who had previously opposed it remained silent.

The Katsura Cabinet then acted to incorporate Korea into the Japanese Empire. In the process, the Premier followed the usual policy of not disclosing his plans to Parliament. To do so might jeopardize his scheme. After the Diet adjourned in March, 1910, the Cabinet appointed a military man as the new Resident General, as Itō had predicted. General Terauchi Masatake (1852-1919), who had been War Minister continuously from 1902, was assigned to the post. In mid-June, 1910, a detachment of Japanese marines was dispatched to Korea to enforce law and order. A special Cabinet Bureau of Colonial Affairs was established with authority over Korean problems. It was made directly responsible to the Premier.

In July, General Terauchi arrived in Seoul under heavy guard. The entire country had already been under the equivalent of martial law. He suspended or suppressed all organs of public opinion. The Korean King and people were at his mercy. Within a month, after a series of conferences with the King and other officials, Terauchi telegraphed to Tokyo that "the government of Japan and Korea were in complete accord" and sought Imperial sanction for "Korea's request for annexation." On August 22, 1910, Terauchi and the Korean King signed the Treaty of Annexation proposed by Japan.

The Treaty of Annexation was the culmination of a long-standing and a deep-seated desire in Japan to conquer Korea. In 1873, nearly forty years earlier, there had been many who favored an attack on Korea, but the plan was abandoned as impracticable. In the intervening years, Japan had fought successfully in two wars to prevent Korea from falling into the hands of China or Russia. It was now in a position to force its will on the youthful King and proceeded to do so.

By the Treaty, Japan acquired complete sovereignty over Korea and assumed responsibility for its entire government and administration. Korea ceased to exist as a country. Henceforth, Koreans were to be subject to Japanese rulers and to Japanese law. Unfortunately, for both the Koreans and the Japanese, this rule was administered by the military who ruthlessly suppressed any signs of opposition. Every effort was made to eradicate Korean nationalism. This stern attitude toward the people of Korea and disregard for their sensibilities and political aspirations intensified their hatred for their masters. Despite their thirty-five years under Japanese rule, Koreans never lost their thirst for independence.

Having completed the annexation of Korea, Japan moved to consolidate its position by other international agreements. In the same year, a protocol was signed with Russia whereby the contracting parties recognized each other's right to take necessary action to safeguard their interests in Manchuria and Korea. In 1911 Japan pushed for another renewal of the Anglo-Japanese Alliance. The disquietude created over Japan's competition for the China market had created a certain degree of British opposition to the continuance of the Alliance. Nevertheless, fear of German imperialism was more of a formative force in British foreign policy than fear of Japan. As a result, the Alliance was renewed for ten years and some of the provisions were strengthened.

The Domestic Fight for Greater Armaments, 1911-15

Having secured a prominent position on the continent of Asia, the military leaders were convinced that this position could be maintained or improved only through the expansion of the Imperial Army and Navy. Thus, the main attention of the leaders of the government shifted, at least temporarily, from the international to the domestic scene.

The oligarchs, with General Yamagata at the center as the most powerful of the Elder Statesmen, became involved in developing a method whereby they could persuade a hostile House of Representatives to approve a military expansion program without forfeiting any of their executive powers. In other words, how could concessions be made to the party representatives without jeopardizing the basic reactionary concept that the best government was one controlled by the elite group of advisers and ministers of the Emperor?

The details of the Cabinet changes are not necessary to relate in detail. Suffice it to say that Saionji and Katsura continued to alternate as Prime Minister until 1913 and that Parliament was inexorably opposed to greater military expenditures. As a result, the military perfected their procedure whereby they could keep either an obstreperous Cabinet or Parliament in line. For example, in the elections of 1912 during the second Saionji Cabinet, the Seiyūkai party had increased its majority in the Lower House. Retrenchment had been a popular campaign slogan, so the Cabinet refused to approve the budget increases necessary for two new divisions in the Army. The military clique then resorted to a device which was to be "standard operational procedure" throughout the turbulent years after the invasion of Manchuria in 1931. The War Minister, on orders from his superiors, sent in his resignation directly to the Emperor in protest to the Cabinet decision.[8] This action automatically caused the downfall of the Saionji Cabinet because no successor could be found to fill his post.

In 1900, the Privy Council had ruled under pressure from Prime Minister Yamagata, whose leadership was being challenged by Itō, that only Generals and Lieutenant-Generals and Admirals and Vice-Admirals on the active list could serve as Ministers of War and of Navy respectively. This ruling restricted to a mere handful the persons eligible to these two Cabinet portfolios. When the Minister of War resigned in 1912, therefore, all of his colleagues eligible for the post had also been ordered not to accept appointment under Saionji. Saionji knew that he had lost the confidence of the military and had no alternative. He must resign.

Before we proceed further with the discussion of the political history of the prewar years, the death of Emperor Meiji on July 30, 1912, at the age of sixty, must be noted. Since the operations of the constitutional monarchy had become more complicated, the Emperor had participated less and less as an individual in governmental affairs. Imperial Conferences, over which he presided, were called less frequently than in the earlier years of his reign. Now they were held only when the most vital issues, such as those of war and peace, were at stake and their purpose was to secure Imperial consent for decisions already reached by the chief ministers. It was not until the waning days of World War II that they were used to settle differences between contending factions in the government. (See page 387.) On practically all other matters, the Emperor's prerogatives were delegated to his various ministers. On routine matters, his approval was given through the Imperial Household Ministry and the Lord Keeper of the Privy Seal. On formal functions, such as the opening of Parliament, his speech was prepared for him and the whole ceremony was carefully prearranged according to precedent. Meiji as a person had reigned but had not governed. He was protected from public affairs and kept from personal contacts with the people. Divine characteristics were beginning to be attributed to him. The Emperor as a symbol became more important than the Emperor as a person. His death made little difference to the policies of the government.

Meiji's son, who was known as Taishō, reigned until 1926. He was of even less importance in politics than his father. His inexperience, his isolation from the realities of life, and his mental ill-health in the latter part of his life, made him a figurehead rather than a leader. As a new national consciousness emerged as a result of the victories against China and Russia, the institution of the Emperor increased in importance. It became a symbol of patriotism and was to serve as an important and useful instrument of ultranationalism and aggression in the near future.

Shortly after the death of Emperor Meiji, clear signs developed that the oligarchs would have to change their tactics of shifting the premiership from Saionji to Katsura. No progress was being made in Parliament with the armament program. In fact, all political groups were uniting solidly against any program of the Premier. One of the most outstanding and consistent of Japan's liberals, Ozaki Yukio, was brutally frank in his denunciation of the Cabinet. In a speech in Parliament on February 5, 1913, he claimed that the oligarchs:

> always mouth "loyalty" and "patriotism" and advertise themselves as the sole repositories of these qualities but what they are actually doing is to hide themselves behind the throne and shoot at their political enemies from their secure ambush.[9]

Angry mobs in Tokyo battled with the police in protest to the arbitrary rule of the oligarchs. There were simultaneous riots in other cities. Katsura, who was Prime Minister at this point, was forced to resign. The oligarchs realized that if they were to continue to rule, they would have to secure at least partial support from the strongest political parties.

The conciliatory attitude of the next Premier, Admiral Yamamoto Gombei (1852-1933), did little to solve the basic problem. The parties continued to press for real party Cabinets and were hoping to use their power in Parliament to control the bureaucrats. To keep matters from getting out of hand, the *Genrō* selected Ōkuma Shigenobu as the next Premier. As a leader of the former Progressive party, he had shown some interest in party government and still commanded respect within the Diet.

As a Cabinet Minister on several earlier occasions, he had proved to be tractable to policies dictated by the oligarchs. He appeared to be well qualified to control the political scene. He also was amenable to a deal with the military in return for the offer of the office of Prime Minister. The Army apparently secured his approval and support for the two new divisions which they had planned for several years. In any event, after Ōkuma took office on April 16, 1914, his Cabinet members became little more than puppets manipulated by the Elder Statesmen and by the leaders of Yamagata's military clique.

This capitulation of Ōkuma to the desires of the military became clear from his dealings with the Diet. When it rejected his bill which provided for the enlarged Army, he immediately dissolved it. The elections in March, 1915, under the close surveillance of Home Minister Ōura, gave the Cabinet a majority and assured the approval of the Army's plans.[10] It is ironical that Ōkuma, one of the party leaders, should have been the instrument through which the military achieved their aims. It was inevitable, however, from the fact that when he accepted the premiership he had not insisted on Cabinet responsibility to Parliament or other manifestations of representative government. Rather, he capitulated to the wishes of the oligarchs and became their willing tool. Perhaps it was too much to ask of a party leader to press for such reforms in view of the history of the constitutional monarchy up to this point. In any case, it is clearly evident that when he took office, the elements for a truly representative and responsible government simply did not exist.

World War I and the Twenty-One Demands

The outbreak of war in Europe in August, 1914, and its global repercussions swiftly shifted interest from the national to the international stage. Here, too, Ōkuma was to follow an aggressive policy. Despite his interest in earlier life in parliamentary government and the rights of the people, he did not apply his modified concepts of the rights of man to questions of international relations. Indeed, the policies he advocated toward China are a sad commentary on his "liberalism." As Premier in 1915, he sponsored a policy which forced China to become subservient both politically and economically to Japan. To Ōkuma and his colleagues, such liberalism as they advocated could not be allowed to interfere with Japan's destiny to secure a predominant and ruling position in East Asia.

Japan's leading statesmen were constantly on the alert for any opportunity that would permit them to achieve this objective. They had been apprehensive of the effect on Japan of the Chinese Revolution and of the downfall of the Manchu dynasty on February 12, 1912. Although the Japanese public in general supported the revolutionaries, the government announced that it would remain neutral. While the clan bureaucrats were casting covetous eyes on Manchuria and north China and were hopeful that they would be able to extend Japan's influence on the continent, World War I gave them the chance they were seeking.

A new China policy developed rapidly under the leadership of Foreign Minister Katō Kōmei.[11] While Ambassador to London, he had already received assurances from British Foreign Minister Viscount Grey that England would not object to Japan's taking up with China, at an appropriate time, the question of the extension of the leases in Kwantung (Liaotung) and South Manchuria. Upon his return to Tokyo, he continued his efforts to win support for a strong Japanese policy toward China. When the Ōkuma Cabinet was formed in April, 1914, Katō was appointed as Foreign Minister. It was not surprising, therefore, that with the outbreak of World War I in August, 1914, he advocated an aggressive foreign policy. He had concluded that the preoccupation of European countries with the war against Germany and the Entente would leave Japan free to act as it desired in China.

Before we consider Japan's demands on China, however, brief mention should be made of the early effects of World War I on Japan. From the outbreak of hostilities, the Japanese government realized that under the terms of the Anglo-Japanese Alliance it might be called upon to enter the war. On August 7, when Great Britain formally requested Japan's assistance in the destruction of German men-of-war in Chinese waters, Foreign Minister Katō had already decided on his answer. He immediately championed his country's entry into the war on the side of the Allies. He rejected suggestions advanced by Great Britain that the scope of operations of the Imperial Navy be restricted. He clearly saw an opportunity simultaneously to destroy German prestige in Asia and to increase Japanese power. Two days later he had persuaded his colleagues and the *Genrō* to accept the same point of view.

On August 15, 1914, an ultimatum, which set forth Japan's position, was sent to Germany. It demanded that all German men-of-war be withdrawn from Chinese waters or be disarmed. Within a month, the German Leased Territory of Kiaochow in Shantung was to be delivered to Japan with a view to its eventual restoration to China. Finally, an unconditional reply must be received within a week. This decisive action under Katō's leadership had a dual effect. It forestalled any move by Great Britain to limit Japan's zone of operations, and it gave ample cause for entering the war and seizing Germany's possessions in China. No reply having been received within the time specified, Japan declared war. A special session of Parliament was called immediately which gave Prime Minister Ōkuma unanimous support for his war budget. Foreign Minister Katō's address on foreign relations was a mere formality and gave no explanation of the reasons for entering the war.

Actually, Japan's entry into World War I placed far less strain upon the nation than had either of the two previous wars. The naval and military operations were on a much smaller scale than those against China or Russia. Unlike France, Great Britain, or even the United States, Japan had no fear of the power and might of Germany. It was not, in any sense, fighting for its self-preservation or existence. Rather, it was acting in those areas where it was to its direct advantage to do so. Hence, Japanese military and naval operations were confined to the Shantung Peninsula and to the Pacific Ocean. In Shantung immediate action was taken to assure the capitulation of the German forces in Kiaochow Bay. On September 3, 1914, Japanese marines landed at Lungkow on the northern shore of Shantung Peninsula. This move, though it was in violation of Chinese neutrality, permitted a rapid encirclement of the German forces. By November 7, the German contingents and warships had capitulated and the former German-leased territory was in Japanese hands. Furthermore, Japanese troops spread out westward along the Tsinan-Tsingtao Railway in disregard for a new war zone delimited by the Chinese Government.

An interesting sidelight on Japan's attitude toward its partner in the Anglo-Japanese Alliance is revealed by the treatment accorded the British during the Shantung campaign. In view of the Alliance, it was decided for political reasons to permit a British contingent to participate in the campaign against Kiaochow. To avoid any complications in the future, the British forces were kept in complete ignorance of the Japanese plan of attack. The British attachés from the Embassy in Tokyo, who were assigned to the expedition as observers, were not allowed to "observe" any of the actual operations. Upon their return to Tokyo after Kiaochow's fall, they reported that they had been treated to lavish hospitality, had enjoyed a vacation, but had nothing further to report. To Japanese in all walks of life, the war was equally unreal.

The operations in the Pacific Ocean were even more routine. Naval patrols were set up to search for German ships or submarines but few were encountered. The German-owned Marianas, Caroline, and Marshall Islands surrendered without any real resistance. By the beginning of 1915, therefore, Japan considered that its military and naval operations in the war were largely over. It had no military problems comparable in any sense to those created by the entrenchment of the German Army on the Aisne after the Battle of the Marne, by the struggle to win the channel ports, or by the attack being launched on the Eastern Front which was to defeat the Russians in May, 1915. On the contrary, Japan could settle back to profit economically from the manufacture of munitions and other war

Japanese Empire, 1915

goods and from the logistic support its merchant marine gave to the Allies. It also was in the enviable position of being able to carry on a diplomatic offensive of its own when the other Allies were concentrating their every effort on survival.

Consequently, Foreign Minister Katō sought ways and means of capitalizing on the preoccupation of the European powers. Decisions apparently had been made in September, 1914, while the campaign against Kiaochow was under way, that direct negotiations should be started with China after the Germans surrendered. Japan planned to obtain greater concessions in Manchuria and Inner Mongolia and to acquire Germany's rights in Shantung. Katō's thinking on outstanding issues and the maximum desiderata of his country were sharpened and stimulated by the memorandum sent from Peking by Major General Machida Keiu and by ideas proposed by Koike Chōzō, Chief of the Political Affairs Bureau of the Foreign Office. These men, together with Vice-Admiral Moriyama Keisaburō, hammered out proposals for an over-all settlement with China. Their recommendations became the basis for the Twenty-One Demands which Japan presented in May, 1915.[12]

Plans for presenting these demands to China were worked out as carefully as their content. In the first place, inspired articles in the press appeared after Kiaochow's surrender which advocated immediate transfer of the German rights to Japan and the extension of Japanese interests on the continent. Japanese Minister Hioki was recalled from Peking and told to present the Twenty-One Demands to the Chinese Government on a suitable occasion. By the time Parliament had convened at the end of December, 1914, Hioki was back in Peking waiting for a propitious moment to make his *démarche*.

He did not have long to wait. In connection with the capture of Kiaochow, Japanese troops had occupied the Tsinan Railway line well outside of the war zone established by China. China was, quite naturally, apprehensive of the results of the continuance of such a situation. Consequently, in January, 1915, it announced the abolition of the military zone in Shantung and requested that all foreign troops be withdrawn from Chinese territory. Hioki promptly retorted that this act of revocation was improper and arbitrary and betrayed a lack of confidence in his country's good faith. Ten days later, he delivered the Twenty-One Demands directly to the Chinese President, Yüan Shih-kai.

Negotiations concerning these famous Demands began on February 2 and continued through April 17. On Hioki's insistence, no minutes were taken of the discussions. The negotiations were broken off by Japan whenever China showed signs of intransigence. Although Foreign Minister Katō refused to support an expeditionary force against China, he readily agreed to the dispatch on March 22 of Japanese troops to Shantung and Manchuria, "to relieve the garrison." The Chinese government was informed that these additional troops would not be withdrawn "until the negotiations could be brought to a satisfactory conclusion." Through the tried expedient of conscious leaks, the Chinese negotiators circumvented the secrecy of the conference and kept the United States and Great Britain *au courant* with developments. The moral support which China received from these countries helped to offset the military pressure from Japan. In the final analysis, however, China knew that it was powerless to resist Japan unless it had positive help from outside.

In the course of the negotiations, China raised two fundamental questions. The first question concerned the relative importance of the various demands. They had been divided into five groups, the last one being most obnoxious to China. The first four groups, which contained fourteen articles, concerned such questions as the transfer to Japan of the German rights in Shantung, ninety-nine-year leases for the railways in Manchuria, economic concessions in Manchuria and Mongolia, and the operation of the iron deposits near Hankow. The fifth group provided for extensive Japanese rights within China and the appointment of advisers to the government. If this last group had been accepted, the result would have been a practical Japanese protectorate over China. In the early part of the negotiations Japan insisted that all five groups be accepted. Since China continued to refuse to agree to Group V, it was finally withdrawn.

The second basic question concerned the manner in which the demands were presented. As a result of China's firm stand in mid-April, Foreign Minister Katō urged his government to issue an ultimatum requiring immediate acceptance of all of the demands except Group V. His views prevailed in Tokyo, and on May 7 the Chinese government was given two days to make a favorable answer to all of the demands except Group V or accept the consequences. The simultaneous preparations for the mobilization of the Japanese armed forces left no doubt as to what these consequences would be. China capitulated and the main features of Groups I-IV were incorporated in two treaties signed on May 25, 1915. At the Paris Peace Conference China constantly stressed the fact that it had signed the agreements unwillingly and only under duress.

In the decade from the Treaty of Portsmouth of 1905 to the new treaties with China in 1915, the consolidation of the Japanese Empire had been effected. In fact, the main boundaries of that Empire had already been determined. Korea had been made into a colony. Broad concessions had been obtained in Shantung. The Marianas, Caroline, and Marshall Islands were securely under military occupation. There seemed every likelihood that these new acquisitions would be confirmed by the peace conference after World War I. If possession or territorial propinquity had any bearing on the final outcome, Japan's claims would be accepted and confirmed. If such were the case, the unchallenged leadership of Japan in East Asia would be assured. No Japanese official took seriously the note which Secretary of State Robert Lansing sent in protest to the Twenty-One Demands. It said that the United States government could not recognize any agreement which impaired the rights of the United States and its citizens in China, the political and territorial integrity of the Republic of China, or even the Open Door. Surely, they argued, his protest was only for the record and any future conflict of American and Japanese interests in China could be resolved. The world was to wait twenty-six years to discover, however, that Japan had taken another irrevocable step in 1915 on the road to eventual defeat.

Notes

1. It may be argued that Japan's entry into World War I in August, 1914, is a more logical date to use as a terminal one for this period. I would point out, however, that there was never any real doubt as to which side Japan would join either before or after the outbreak of hostilities. The Anglo-Japanese Alliance was only an outward manifestation of a general feeling that it was decidedly to Japan's interest to side with Great Britain in any struggle against Germany. The important decision, therefore, in relation to the consolidation of the Empire, was not to declare war and capture the German possessions in Shantung. Rather, the significant decisions were those made late in 1914 and early in 1915 to force China to accept the Twenty-One Demands which would assure Japanese hegemony over China and over all of East Asia. (See also page 256.)

2. As the fleet was off the Indochina coast during the winter, this conclusion was a natural one to make. Admiral Tōgō Nakagoro (1848-1934) was the commander responsible for this victory. Upon his return home, he was idolized by boisterous crowds in Yokohama and Tokyo. Upon his death, an Imperial rescript declared: "Your sincerity put you in communion with the ancestral gods and your foresight decided victory or defeat." The hero of the capture of Port Arthur, General Nogi, became even more of a deified figure as he followed the Emperor Meiji in death in 1912.

3. The Japanese had made a clever move at the beginning of the War. They had sent Kaneko Kentarō to the United States as a special public relations officer. He was a Harvard classmate of Roosevelt and was received kindly by the President. As the war progressed, Kaneko obtained an increasingly friendly press for Japan. Ironically, he was noticeably inept during the Portsmouth Conference.

4. Tyler Dennett, *Roosevelt and the Russo-Japanese War* (New York: Doubleday & Co., Inc., 1925), pp. 112-13.

5. Home Minister Hara Kei, a commoner, was one of the most talented members of the Seiyūkai party. In a little over a decade, he was to become leader of the party and Premier.

6. There seems little doubt but that Itō honestly wanted to keep the rival military faction at home from getting the upper hand in Korea. He hoped to accomplish this through the continuance of a protectorate. So long as Korea was a protectorate and not a colony, a civilian would be assigned as Resident General. So long as Saionji was Premier, Itō would be able to remain as Resident General.

7. Because of the willingness of party members to support one Premier and then another, regardless of the political complexion of the Cabinet, this period is often referred to by Japanese political scientists as one of "mutual understanding" (*jōi tōgō*) between the party members of the Diet and the Cabinets. Professor Rōyama refers to the "mutual understanding" between the clan bureaucrats and the political parties. When translated into English, however, the term is misleading. It indicates a position of equality for both parties and the oligarchs, a situation which did not exist. While the oligarchs were free to decide the extent to which they would cooperate with the parties, the parties knew that lack of cooperation would make little real difference to the oligarchs. They found it politically expedient therefore, to

cooperate. See Rōyama Masamichi, *Seiji Shi, Gendai Nihon Bummei Shi* (Tokyo: Tōyō Keizai Shimpō Sha, 1940), vol. 2, p. 379.

8. The War Minister was within his legal rights in presenting his resignation to the Emperor. Article XI of the Constitution designates the Emperor as the Supreme Commander of the Army and Navy. Article XII gives him responsibility for its organization. Consequently, the military leaders claimed that they had a constitutional right of "direct access" to the throne on military matters. As we shall see, this concept of "direct access" was the basis for the dual diplomacy which evolved from World War I. (See *infra,* page 329.)

9. Quoted in Robert A. Scalapino, *Democracy and the Party Movement in Prewar Japan* (Berkeley: University of California Press, 1953), p. 194.

10. The Imperial Army had drawn up plans for offensive operations against Russia immediately after the conclusion of the Portsmouth Treaty. It feared Russia would plan a war of revenge. In 1907 the Emperor approved a fifteen-year plan which called for gradual expansion of the armed forces to twenty-five divisions. The refusal of the Saionji Cabinet to approve two new divisions had caused its downfall in 1912. Katsura had been no more successful. After Ōkuma's bill was approved, the total divisions had reached twenty-one. The Navy had likewise obtained approval for a building program but received setbacks from Katsura (an army man) and Saionji (a civilian) while they were Premiers. Even Ōkuma was unable to obtain support for the Navy in 1914. See James Morely, *Japanese Origins of the Siberian Expedition,* Columbia University Ph.D. thesis, 1954, chapter ii.

11. Katō Kōmei (1860-1926) was born in Aiichi Prefecture. He had graduated from law school, studied abroad in England and Europe for two years and married the daughter of Iwasaki Tarō. In 1887, he entered the Foreign Office as personal secretary to Ōkuma who had the unhappy task of trying to persuade the foreign powers to revise their treaties. By 1908 Katō had risen to become Ambassador to London.

12. I am indebted to Prof. James Morely for this information on the origins of the Demands. His conclusions are based on intimate personal knowledge of Foreign Office and War Ministry records. They are far more significant than a secret society memorandum, which one might quote on the question, that has been the chief source used by many historians for some years. See Morely, *op. cit.,* chapter ii.

14

THE ECONOMIC BASIS OF THE NEW EMPIRE, 1890-1915

The economic metamorphosis within Japan during the quarter century before World War I was almost as phenomenal as the outward expansion of the boundaries of the Empire. In 1890, at the inception of the constitutional monarchy, the nation's finances had been placed on a sound basis for the first time.[1] National receipts had actually surpassed expenditures. Agricultural resources had been able to keep pace with the increases in population. In fact, there was a surplus of rice during the quinquennium 1885-89 which permitted the export of an average of over 3,750,000 bushels each year.

Although some progress had been made in the country's industrialization, particularly in the textile and silk industries, there were still many significant gaps. Heavy industries were notably underdeveloped and there was practically no steamship building. Foreign trade, which was carried on almost exclusively in foreign ships, had only just begun to show a favorable balance from 1883 to 1893. Increases in annual expenditures by the central government, which amounted to more than one-third the total, were diverted toward building a modern army and navy.

By May, 1915, when Japan confronted China with an ultimatum demanding compliance with four of the five groups of the Twenty-One Demands, the general economic picture had changed radically. The wars against both China and Russia and the newly created and enlarged military establishments had placed a heavy drain on the nation's finances. There had been an abrupt rise in the annual rate of increase of the population with little new land available for reclamation or few other prospects for increasing rice production. There was also a concomitant shift in the international trade balance from an excess of exports to an excess of imports. These two trends indicated that the future pressure from population might develop into one of the greatest problems facing modern Japan.

Between 1890 and 1915, industrialization, both as a continuation of the traditional policy of strengthening the state and as a result of the stimulus of the two wars, increased at an amazing pace. Just when a depression seemed inevitable, the acute demands of the Allied powers for munitions, shipping, and supplies during World War I enabled Japan to solve, at least temporarily, its major economic and financial problems. So long as the foreign market for Japanese goods and services held, the country's economic future could be left to take care of itself. The present chapter is devoted, therefore, to an analysis of these developments and of their effect on Japan's future.

The displeasure of the Japanese nation with the results of the victory over China in 1895 had been aroused by the intervention of the *triplice* which had forced Japan to retrocede the Liaotung Peninsula to China. This intervention dramatically convinced all classes of society of the validity of the philosophy which had motivated the Meiji leaders in the formulation of political and economic reforms. They had maintained that the country must strengthen itself industrially and militarily if it were to achieve its objectives. This condemnation of the action of the three European powers, this emotional and psychological reaction to foreign meddling had tended to divert men's minds from the actual and potential advantages of the other peace terms.

In the first place, the war had acted as a proving ground for the general operations, tactics, and equipment of the Imperial Army and Navy. This first, full-scale test of the newly created military and naval forces had been a severe one but had not been prolonged enough to place too heavy a drain on resources and on personnel. Nevertheless, the war had been extensive enough to reveal a lack of scientific and up-to-date armaments and a weakness in ability to give logistic support and to coordinate the movements of army and naval units. It had taught the Chiefs of Staff, in a realistic fashion, what improvements were necessary before they could dare to face successfully a powerful, modern nation such as Russia.

Consequently, new orders, which were placed with industry to modernize the Army and the Navy, accelerated the country's building program. These orders from the armed forces stimulated both the government-owned munitions plants and private industry. New plants, such as the Yawata Steel Works, were built at government expense and operated by it. But this compulsion for increased industrial production would have come to nought if Japan had been exhausted economically by the war against China. Actually, the contrary was true. The War had cost an estimated 232.6 million yen, a sum three times the total national expenditures in the fiscal year 1890, but a large portion of these funds had gone back into the Japanese economy and had acted as an incentive to home industries. Furthermore, these expenses were more than covered by the indemnity of 360 million yen which China was required to pay by the terms of the peace treaty. Hence, the Empire's finances were in a stronger position in 1895 than before the outbreak of hostilities. When the indemnity payments began, new, free funds became available for investment in new industries, for expansion of old ones, or for purchases of needed supplies from the domestic market.

But the territorial settlement in 1895 after the Sino-Japanese War was more important for Japan economically than either the increase in armaments or the indemnity payment. Formosa, with its estimated population of 2.6 million in 1898, offered new and tempting markets for the products of Japanese industry. Its area was equal to almost one-tenth of Japan proper; its climate was tropical with abundant rainfall. With a minimum of investment and with the establishment of internal security, the island soon became a valuable source of important raw materials and agricultural products. Camphor and lumber, rice and sugar were soon to be shipped to Japan, and were to become important elements in the Empire's economy.

By the peace treaty of 1895 China had recognized the independence of Korea. From an economic point of view, this meant that so long as political stability could be maintained in Korea, Japanese merchants and investors were free to exploit Korean markets and resources. At home, the country was on the threshold of an era of renewed government spending to expand other state-owned enterprises, such as railways, the telegraph, and telephone. Surplus capital stimulated general industrial activity and created new industries, particularly those of producers' goods. But the future prosperity of the country, its continued industrial activity, was dependent on whether or not a balance could be maintained between the demands of the people for food and the ability of the nation's farmers to meet those demands. If an increasing population tipped the scales, they would have to be counterbalanced by food imports. These imports would then have to be paid for by the sale abroad of manufactured goods if the nation's economy was to be stabilized. Consequently, after the problem of population pressure on agrarian production has been analyzed, an estimate will be made of Japan's financial and industrial strength in 1915.

Population Pressure and Agrarian Production, 1890-1915

In the first quarter century of Japan's modernization, there had been no serious population problem in the sense that the demand for rice, the staple food, could not be met from domestic production. In fact, in these early years rice had been one of the export items and had not been imported until after 1890. During the next quarter century, from 1890 to 1915, there was a complete reversal of this trend and the beginnings of new problems created by continued increases in the population and a higher standard of living. As shown in Table V, rice imports began in the years just before the war with China and rapidly mounted. By 1915 these imports averaged 21 million bushels or about 7 per cent of the total rice consumed. Of even more significance, however, was the fact that these imports were necessary despite the fact that the production of rice increased twice as rapidly as the population. For the five-year period of 1880-84, the average total annual population stood at 37.2 million. During the next thirty years, the population increased by 45 per cent to 52.8 million. (See Table IV.) Through reclamation of waste land, improved methods of cultivation, and the use of better seeds, rice production for the same period had been enlarged by 90 per cent. Thus, in 1880-89, the average yearly production of rice stood at about 150 million bushels, but had risen to 285 million bushels after 1915. Finally, by 1915, imports of rice of nearly 6.3 million bushels from the new colonies of Korea and Formosa decreased by that amount purchases outside the Empire.

TABLE IV

General Trend of Population in Japan Proper, 1872-1935[2]

Year	Population (unit 1000)	Index Number	Average Annual Increase	Rate of Average Annual Increase (per 1000)
"Estimated Actual Population" as of January 1				
1872	34,806	100.0	—	—
1875	35,316	101.5	180.9*	5.1*
1880	36,649	105.3	266.6	7.4
1885	38,313	110.1	332.8	7.9
1890	39,902	114.6	317.8	8.2
1895	41,557	119.4	331.0	8.2
1900	43,847	126.0	458.0	10.8
1905	46,620	133.9	554.6	12.3
1910	49,184	141.3	512.8	10.8
1915	52,752	151.6	713.6	14.1
1920	55,473	159.4	544.2	10.1
Census Returns as of October 1				
1920	55,963	160.8	653.3*	11.8*
1925	59,737	171.6	754.8	13.1
1930	64,450	185.2	942.6	15.3
1935	69,254	199.0	960.8	14.4

* Adjusted to coincide with new date for census.

But the vital facts to be noted in the relationship of these figures on the supply and demand of rice and on the increase in population are that they point to major difficulties ahead. As of the year 1915, the demands for extra rice were met by imports from abroad and these were easily purchased by Japan's exports to the Allies. But for the future, the steady increase in population meant only one thing, namely, a greater demand for rice. There was no assurance, however, that these demands would continue to be met by improved production techniques or by imports paid for from excess exports. In fact, the figures in Table V for later years point to the fact that the peak in the rate of increase of rice production had already been reached. For example, it will be noted that in the five years following the 1910-14 period total production rose only 10 per cent and that there was an actual decrease in production after 1920. To put the matter another way, per capita production steadily decreased despite larger imports from abroad.

The population and food problems could only be solved, therefore, by their close correlation with the over-all industrial program. Contemporary writers and government officials, however, failed to recognize the dangers inherent in the nation's demographic trend. They were fully cognizant of the fact that there was little hope of material increases in the production of staple foods, yet did little to discourage or to prevent rapid population increases.

On the contrary, they considered a large population a boon rather than a hindrance to the growth of the nation. It was argued, for example, that a large population made possible a large army and hence augmented the national strength. The Chief of the Colonial Bureau suggested that the ills from any surplus population could be remedied by industrialization and by the fullest possible use of the new colonial territories such as Korea, Formosa, and Southern Sakhalien (Karafuto). It was not, therefore, until after World War I that Japanese economists and demographers regarded the increases in population as an essentially antagonistic factor in their country's economic welfare.[3] But by that time, their prognostications had little effect on national policy. A militant nationalism had become the accepted policy and foreign nations were told that population pressure made it inevitable and necessary for Japan to expand on the Asiatic mainland.

The amalgamation of the old, feudal, agrarian economy with the new capitalist state had also had other important effects on agriculture and on the nation as a whole. In 1915 the nation was still predominantly rural, so that any impact on the agrarian population was immediately felt throughout the entire empire. The farmer, who traditionally had had difficulty eking out a living, was hard pressed by increases in the size of his family. He supplemented his income from rice by growing silkworms and reeling the silk thread at home. Silk became a profitable cash crop so long as the foreign markets were steady. Furthermore, he found that his daughters formed an abundant, cheap labor supply for industry, particularly for the textile plants.

On the other hand, he was forced to carry a large share of the nation's tax burden. The national policy of encouragement of heavy industries, including public ownership and management of the most important strategic industries, carried with it an obligation to protect these industries

TABLE V

ANNUAL AVERAGE SUPPLY AND DEMAND, PER *Chō* YIELD AND PER CAPITA CONSUMPTION OF RICE, IN *Koku*, 1880-1931[4]

Year	Production (in *koku*)	Per *Chō* Yield	Net Import (—) or Export	Consumption	Population (Unit 1000)	Per Capita Production	Per Capita Consumption	Annual Population Increase (per 1000)
1880-84	29,958,186	11.59	180,139	29,778,047	37,259	0.804	0.779	266.6
1885-89	36,577,309	13.78	735,857	35,841,452	38,703	0.945	0.926	332.8
1890-94	40,355,071	14.64	—366,755	40,721,826	40,508	0.996	1.005	317.8
1895-99	39,265,273	14.00	—1,152,058	40,417,331	42,400	0.926	0.953	331.0
1900-04	44,643,328	15.64	—2,739,903	47,383,231	44,964	0.993	1.054	458.0
1905-09	47,579,742	16.34	—3,175,250	50,754,992	47,416	1.003	1.070	554.6
1910-14	51,166,907	17.06	—2,963,764	54,130,671	50,577	1.012	1.070	512.8
1915-19	56,892,648	18.46	—4,175,061	61,067,709	54,134	1.051	1.128	713.6
1920-24	56,339,472	18.59	—5,907,616	62,247,088	56,798	0.992	1.096	544.2
1925-29	59,452,086	18.71	—10,008,266	69,460,352	60,712	0.979	1.144	
1930-31	61,045,399	18.82	—8,503,000	69,548,399	69,050	0.953	1.086	942
				Indexes				
1880-84	100	100		100	100	100	100	
1925-29	198	161		233	163	122	143	

1 *chō* equals 2.45 acres.
1 *koku* equals 5.11 bushels.

whenever possible. Consequently, the state imposed only light taxes on industry despite the need for greater revenue and the farmer carried a proportionately heavier tax burden than industry. The result was a decrease in the number of farmers who owned their land, an increase in tenancy and rural indebtedness, and a greater concentration of the population in urban areas. The desire of industry to keep wages to a minimum also increased the farmer's difficulties. Such members of the farm family who became wage earners received little recompense for their labors. Insuperable problems, therefore, would appear in the agrarian economy unless drastic reforms in land ownership and in taxation policies were inaugurated. It was far easier for the national government to ignore the growing crisis in agriculture or to hope that it would be solved by Japanese domination of China or by some other diversionary tactics than to sponsor unpopular reforms.

Financial Conditions

After the victory over China, Japan was determined to develop a military machine strong enough to implement its Asiatic policy. Specifically, an expanded army and a modernized and enlarged navy were believed to be requisites for preventing Russian encroachments in Korea. While valuable time was gained through diplomatic agreements (see Chapter 12), unprecedented annual military appropriations could be met only by debit financing. For example, the determination to control Korea and to check Russian imperialistic designs in Eastern Asia necessitated heavy military expenditures which were partially met by floating new bonds. In 1899 an imminent financial panic was avoided by the outbreak of the Boxer Uprising in China. When the Japanese financial world learned of the siege of the foreign legations at Peking, it rallied to this challenge to the nation's prestige abroad. After 1900, however, financial conditions worsened as a result of a noticeable increase in the unfavorable trade balance which caused a 45 per cent decrease in gold specie. Furthermore, the limitless issuance of convertible loans also weakened the financial market. Annual military appropriations had continued to rise by about 10 per cent until they were equivalent to the cost of the war with China (230 million yen). The breaking point had been reached so that a run on the Ōsaka Bank on April 16, 1901, culminated in numerous bank failures and was followed by general economic inactivity for the next two years.

But financial conditions were not desperate enough to cause despair. Despite the increased threat of war with Russia, further financial crises were avoided. Practically the entire nation was convinced that such a war was inevitable and a part of Japan's destiny, so it willingly bore the burden of war preparation. Increases in government expenses were partially met by greater revenue. In 1899 a new tax law was promulgated which increased tax returns. Furthermore, under the terms of the new treaties with the Western powers, which went into effect the same year, Japan had acquired tariff autonomy which increased the income from the new tariffs. Additional expenses were covered by the indemnity payments from China, by foreign loans, by the issuance of notes of the Bank of Japan, and by an increase in the national debt. It will be noted from Table VI, for example, that there was an increase of over 35 per cent in the total number of Bank of Japan notes from 177.8 million yen in 1900 to 233 million yen in 1903 and a jump of nearly 50 per cent to 342 million yen in 1906, the year after the war with Russia. Furthermore, the national debt rose from 207 million yen in 1894 to 435 million yen in 1903.[5]

TABLE VI

NOTE ISSUES,[6] 1881-1913
(In Million Yen)

Year	Government Paper	National Bank Notes	Bank of Japan Notes
1881	118.9	34.0	
1885	93.4	30.2	4.0
1890	40.1	26.4	102.9
1895	15.7	22.3	110.5
1900	5.1	1.6	177.8
1903			233.0
1906			342.0
1910			402.0
1913			426.0

The costs of the Russo-Japanese War of 1904-5, which were estimated at 1.98 billion yen, placed an even heavier strain on the nation's finances. The gap was filled largely by special War Loans, a large proportion of which were bought abroad, especially in London. After Russia was eliminated as a military threat in the Far East, foreign capital became readily available for investment in Japan. The national indebtedness had risen to 2.244 billion yen, over five times that prior to the war. Furthermore, the decline in war orders and the expenditures of huge sums on nonproductive enterprises produced an unsound stock market. Stocks began to decline; new bubble companies went bankrupt; more banks closed in 1907 and 1908. The unfavorable trade balance continued at a yearly average of about 50 million yen. Prime Minister Katsura redeemed the note issue at a lower rate of interest, but general economic inactivity continued until the outbreak of World War I.

In contrast to the financial situation in 1894, therefore, the outlook in the summer of 1914 was not bright. Revenue was well under fixed expenditures; exports continued to run behind imports; the currency in circulation had increased by one-fourth and commodity prices reflected the trend of a steady rise. (See Table VII.)

TABLE VII

NATIONAL FINANCES AND PRICES[7]
Percentage Increases
(Year 1887=100)

Year	Expenditures	Receipts	Currency in Circulation	Commodity Prices	Population
1887	100	100	100.8	100	100
1892				115	
1893	106.5	105.7	120.1	118.1	105.9
1894	98.3	107.6	124.8	126	107
1895	107.4	112.7	142.0	135	108.3
1896	212.5	115.9	151.3	145	109.3
1897				161	
1898	276.6	155.1	143.8	170	112.1
1899				171	
1900	368.5	213.1	160.2	183	114.4
1901				175	
1902	364.0	246.7	164.5	171	117.9
1905	736.8	581.8	306.3	213	131.7
1908				226	
1912				245	

The outbreak of World War I came at a fortuitous time and saved Japan from a financial collapse. The demands of the Allies for munitions, other military supplies, shipping, and services were more than sufficient to increase industrial activity. In 1915, for the third time in twenty years, Japan's exports far exceeded its imports. (See Table XII.)

INDUSTRIAL DEVELOPMENT, 1890-1915

The growth and consolidation of the Empire during the quarter century after the promulgation of the Constitution could not have been achieved without a phenomenal growth in industry. In the period prior to 1890, industrial expansion had resulted from two causes. In the first place, the government had initiated the construction of model factories and the exploitation of resources in the homeland. Many of these plants had then been sold to private capitalists at unusually low prices in order to encourage private capital to form companies. In the second place, private investment had sought new sources of profit. But industrial expansion in old fields and the mushrooming of new enterprises in the twenty-five years from 1890 to 1915 was not so much the result of direct government participation in industry as the effect of outside forces. For example, while subsidies stimulated the creation of an important merchant marine, the logistic demands of both the Sino-Japanese and Russo-Japanese Wars had caused an unprecedented increase in the number of ships sailing under the Japanese flag and constructed in Japanese yards. In nonsubsidized industries, the impact of these two wars was even greater.[8]

To put the matter differently, tremendous strides were taken in the direction of a self-sufficient economy. After the victory over China in 1895, government spending for the expansion of the state-owned railways, for improvements of harbors, and for a large army and navy stimulated general industrial activity. The availability of cash from indemnity payments created a surplus of capital which went into the formation of new industries such as copper, electricity, gas, machinery, shipbuilding, clothing, boots and shoes, and canned goods. During the interbellum years, there was also a marked growth in old industries such as iron manufacturing, mining, weaving and spinning, and lumber manufacturing. To illustrate these general statements, of 8612 companies in existence in 1902, 84 per cent of them had been established since 1894. Of 7800 factories, over 55 per cent of them had grown up in the same period. As can be inferred from Table VIII, most of this development occurred between 1895 and 1898 and was particularly pronounced in the fields of manufacturing, transportation, and banking. Whereas in 1894, paid-up capital in manufacturing companies amounted to 44.5 million yen, by 1896 this amount had more than doubled to reach 89.9 million yen and by 1899 rose to 147.7 million yen. Capital in the transportation companies had also doubled in the four years from 1894 to 1897 from 82.5 million yen to 164 million yen. A similar growth occurred in banking. (See Table VIII.)

TABLE VIII

PAID-UP CAPITAL OF INDUSTRIAL COMPANIES[9]
(In 1000 Yen)

Year	Agricultural Industrial Companies (yen)	Manufacturing Companies (yen)	Commercial Companies (yen)	Sea and Land Transportation (yen)	Banks (yen)	Total (yen)
1894	1,188	44,590	20,015	82,560	101,410	249,763
1895	1,522	58,729	23,835	89,961	127,808	301,855
1896	1,666	89,901	26,535	113,217	166,200	397,519
1897	2,230	105,381	53,512	164,684	206,715	532,522
1898	2,337	122,067	43,446	197,233	256,594	621,677
1899	2,304	147,783	43,904	198,147	291,683	683,821
1900	2,615	158,852	47,129	228,734	341,922	779,252
1901	2,646	166,293	56,085	243,225	361,207	829,456
1902	2,551	173,233	67,353	262,676	372,950	878,763
1903	3,197	170,346	76,994	262,383	374,686	887,606

After Japan defeated Russia in 1905, several factors produced a slightly different type of industrial growth. In the first place, foreign capital was readily available which permitted the growth of new industries. Secondly, some industries had progressed sufficiently so that their products could compete successfully with foreign manufactures. These interests sought to preserve the domestic market for their own goods through tariff protection. Furthermore, the needs of the new colonial territories of Formosa and Southern Sakhalien created new challenges to industry. Finally, the successful elimination of the threat of both Chinese and Russian economic and political control over Korea opened vast opportunities for venture capital in that area. No other power was in a position to challenge Japan economically in the exploitation of this market of some 15 million persons. Little Korean capital was available to profit from the use of the rich resources in that peninsular kingdom, which was over half the size of Japan.

If the new domestic, colonial, and foreign markets were to be supplied, if Japanese industry was to profit from the results of the victories over China and Russia, greater emphasis would have to be placed on a self-sufficient economy. There were clear indications, however, that progress was rapidly being made in this direction. Japanese textiles were beginning to compete in the China market with British, American, and Indian goods. Battleships, steamships, and steam locomotives were no longer purchased abroad but made at home. As one authority expressed it:

> The Russo-Japanese war was a turning point in the history of Japanese industry. After the war, the newly started or developed industries were extended more than ever owing to the post-bellum restoration. The government encouraged the use of domestic products which resulted in the establishment of Japanese industry on an equal footing with their foreign rivals.[10]

But progress toward a self-sufficient economy, particularly in view of expanded military appropriations, was retarded by deficiencies in natural resources such as iron and coking coal. This situation, in turn, had resulted in a late start in iron and steel production. Nevertheless, political necessity, such as the Russian threat in Korea had forced the government to build its own iron and steel plants. For example, in 1901 the Yawata Iron Works was built in northern Kyūshū at a cost of 43 million yen. For many years it was the main steel producing plant in the entire Empire and its completion had a pronounced effect on the total production of iron and finished steel. In 1896, 26,000 tons of pig iron was produced annually. By 1906, after the Yawata works were operating, the figure had risen to 145,000 tons; by 1913 it had increased to 243,000 tons. Since the general demands of industry for iron increased with over-all expansion, however, the domestic smelting plants were able to meet only 48 per cent of requirements.

The steel industry had a similar history. When the war ended with China, this industry had hardly been born. By 1896 only 1000 tons were produced, which equaled only 0.5 per cent of domestic needs. By the end of the war with Russia, however, the Yawata steel mills had been going full blast and total annual steel production was 69,000 tons. By 1913 this figure had risen to 255,000 tons. But this amount was sufficient to take care of only one-third of the nation's demand for steel.

In the important supplementary coal mining industry, the coal mines near Nagasaki had been developed in the 1860's. Thus by 1894, over 2.5 million tons of coal were mined yearly and ten years later the total had climbed to 8 million tons. In another ten years, namely, by 1913, the total production of 22.3 million tons was sufficient to permit the export of 3 million tons.[11] The production of other minerals also increased rapidly, the total in 1913 equaling four and a half times that of 1897. Thus, although the lack of natural resources had prevented a self-sufficiency in iron and steel, by 1915 important advances had been made toward that end.

As for the other heavy industries, it has been indicated previously that attempts were made to encourage the rapid growth of shipbuilding, as well as that of shipping companies, through direct government subsidies. Government yards at Nagasaki and Kōbe were transferred to private ownership and subsidies were paid on all goods shipped in vessels which were over 700 tons and which had been built in Japanese shipyards. Since this policy did little to increase the shipbuilding industry, a double subsidy of 40 yen per ton of cargo was offered to owners of ships built in local yards. The cumulative effect of this direct support from the government was a rapid increase in the tonnage of ships launched and of the percentage of the foreign trade carried in Japanese bottoms. Whereas in 1898 there was an annual average launching of a total of 10,000 tons of ships over 1000 tons displacement, by 1909 the launchings totaled 50,000 tons yearly. Moreover, as will be observed from Table IX below, there was a marked shift in the

TABLE IX

TRENDS TOWARD SELF-SUFFICIENCY IN SHIPPING AND SHIPBUILDING[12]

Year	Average Annual Tonnage Launched Ships Over 100 Tons	Percentage of Exports Carried in Japanese Ships	Percentage of Imports Carried in Japanese Ships	Percentage Japanese Tonnage Entering Ports	Percentage Foreign Masters, Engineers, and Navigators on NYK
1893	10,000	7	9	14	40
1903		40	34	38	
1909	50,000				
1913		52	47	51	25

proportion of the total exports and imports carried in Japanese ships. In 1893, only 7 per cent of exports and 9 per cent of imports were carried in national ships. By 1913, the proportion had risen to over 50 per cent for all foreign trade. In only two decades, therefore, Japan had passed the half-

TABLE X

CAPITAL GROWTH OF SIGNIFICANT INDUSTRIAL COMPANIES[13]
(Paid-Up Capital Above 5,000,000 Yen in 1912)
(Units of 1000 Yen)

	Milling	*Sake* Brewing	Beer	Bean Sauce and Paste	Sugar Refining	Medicine	Paper	Cement	Fertilizer	Cotton Spinning	Wool Spinning
1902											
Number of Companies ..	27	196	8	85	8	54	40	19	21	50	12
Capital	735	4,246	3,262	1,482	2,738	2,710	10,275	3,993	1,683	35,367	7,835
1908											
Number of Companies ..	23	172	4	154	7	80	51	23	53	31	
Capital	3,951	5,707	9,710	7,044	9,213	1,274	17,752	11,061	7,373	52,519	
1912											
Number of Companies ..	31	369	3	225	13	155	70	22	72	32	6
Capital	5,407	9,648	12,464	5,308	15,017	6,566	22,151	11,164	13,760	65,173	6,656

	Thread	Cotton Cloth	Wool Cloth	Machinery	Electrical Equipment	Ship-building	Wood Manufac-turing	Gas	Electricity	Companies Below 5 Million Yen	Grand Total
1902											
Number of Companies ..	301	68	6	23		17	42	4	62	1,263	2,306
Capital	4,788	1,364	2,548	796		10,653	667	4,917	10,347	43,232	153,638
1908											
Number of Companies ..	292	119	8	44	19	17	91	13	114	1,650	3,065
Capital	4,384	3,507	5,582	2,808	2,645	13,062	6,354	18,276	51,717	206,918	440,857
1912											
Number of Companies ..	307	169	17	78	38	25	155	79	270	2,124	4,260
Capital	6,361	11,130	11,369	7,460	5,535	28,033	5,045	54,548	159,808	84,348	546,961

way mark in having met its shipping needs even in the face of an ever larger total in foreign trade.

The whole field of electrical engineering was another industrial activity which grew in this period to have a modicum of self-sufficiency. For example, before the Chinese War in 1894, the manufacture of electrical machinery was restricted to one concern and the total capital of electrical supply companies was 2 million yen. By 1913 capital invested in electrical engineering companies had risen to 61 million yen and electrical supply companies were capitalized at 200 million yen. The importance of electricity in the national economy is even more graphically illustrated by reference to the chart on "Capital Growth of Significant Industrial Companies." (See Table X.) It will be noted that there is no record for electrical equipment companies in 1902. Between 1908 and 1912, however, the number of companies doubled from 19 to 38. The former had paid-up capital at 2.6 million yen, the latter had invested 5.5 million yen. Furthermore, capital investment in electric power companies jumped from 10.3 million yen in 1902 to 51.7 million yen in 1908 and to 159.8 million yen in 1912. In a single decade the generating companies had multiplied fourfold and their investments proliferated sixteen times.

Sugar refining was another comparatively new consumers' industry. Until Formosa was acquired as a colony in 1895, little sugar was produced within the Empire. Prior to 1902 only 2.7 million yen was invested in eight refineries and the nation was compelled to rely heavily on imported sugar. Plans progressed rapidly, however, for the expansion of sugar cane farms in the colony of Formosa and sugar refining investments rose from 9.2 million yen in 1908 to 15 million yen in 1912.

Note should be taken of only three other industries which showed outstanding growth. The first is that of the cement industry whose companies remained practically numerically the same but whose investments nearly tripled in a decade, from 3.9 million yen in 1902 to 11.1 million yen in 1912. Chemical fertilizers, a comparatively new interloper in the national economy, showed phenomenal development. Twenty-one companies with an investment of 1.7 million yen in 1902 had jumped to seventy-two companies with 13.7 million yen investment a decade later in 1912. Finally, the gas industry showed trends similar to that of electricity. Four companies with 4.9 million yen investment in 1902 rose to seventy-nine companies with 54.5 million yen paid-up capital ten years later.

As the Meiji Period progressed, the textile industry became particularly important in the nation's economy and in foreign trade. Both spinning and weaving had been significant industries at an early date, but it was not until after the defeat of China in 1895 that Japanese cloth captured the markets in Korea and China. The large population of otherwise ungainfully employed women was easily absorbed into the industry which retained many characteristics of a feudal society. The mill owners took a proprietary and paternalistic attitude toward their employees. The girls were often under contract for a year or more. They were housed in company dormitories, ate in company restaurants, and had their entire lives regulated by the plant according to a rigid schedule. Bells sounded not only at the close of work but at reveille and at taps.

While this type of labor was cheap and docile, the lack of raw materials increased production costs. For example, raw cotton had to be imported from China, India, or the United States. Nevertheless, the finished product competed with those from Lancashire or southern Europe. There was a steady increase in the growth of the textile industry as a whole. The decrease in the number of spinning companies was in no sense a sign of weakness; it merely indicated a concentration of ownership in the hands of comparatively few companies, each of which increased in size. From 1893 to 1913, the total spindles grew from 382,000 to 2,415,000 and the yearly cotton yarn production rose from 88 million pounds to 607 million pounds. Similar trends appeared in the silk industry, as silk thread exports became one of the largest items in overseas trade.

TABLE XI

JAPANESE TEXTILE DEVELOPMENT[14]
(1893-1913)

Year	Cotton Spindles (in thousands)	Cotton Yarn (in million lbs.)	Spinning Companies	Power Looms	Silk Thread (in thousand *kan*)	Silk Exports (in thousand *kan*)
1893	382	88	40	900	1,110	662
1903	1,381	317	51	5,000	1,924	1,110
1907	1,504	393	42	9,000		
1913	2,415	607	44	24,000	3,375	2,563

Providing constant access could be assured to important sources of raw materials, such as oil, iron, coking coal, commercial salt, and raw cotton, the base was rapidly being laid, therefore, in heavy industries, in utilities, and in consumers' goods industries for a self-sustaining economy. So long as these resources were not within the limits of the Japanese Empire, they could be secured in one of two ways. Profits from exports of raw silk or finished goods could be used to purchase necessary imports of food and of raw materials for processing. Alternatively, territories in which essential natural resources existed in abundance, such as Korea, Manchuria, or North China, could be placed under direct or indirect Japanese control by diplomacy or by force of arms. In reality, both of these alternatives were used. As political unrest threatened accessibility to raw materials in East and Southeast Asia, heavier reliance was placed on territorial expansion than on other methods.

Foreign Trade

While there was a steady increase in exports prior to 1890, they could not keep up with imports essential for the modernization program. Consequently an unfavorable balance in foreign trade soon developed. (See Chapter 9.) This tendency was especially pronounced during the years in which Japan was involved in war against China and later against Russia; it continued down to World War I. (See Table XII.) Even in the period 1909-13, when Japan was not involved in a war, there was an annual average excess of imports over exports of 48 million yen. Only in the first full year of World War I (1915) was this trend dramatically reversed.

TABLE XII

Foreign Trade, 1868-1915[15]

(Annual Average in Million Yen)

Year	Imports	Exports	Balance (—) Unfavorable	Indices of Volume (Year 1913=100)
1868-72	23	16	—7	5.9
1873-77	27	22	—5	9.7
1878-82	33	30	—3	
1883-87	33	42	9	11.0
1888-93	73	77	4	19.7
1894-98	223	139	—84	28.5
1899-03	270	244	—26	40.2
1904-08	441	375	—64	66.0
1909-13	544	496	—48	100.0
1914	596	591	—5	
1915	532	708	176	

An analysis of the structure of this foreign trade reflects the extent of industrialization of the country even more clearly than the over-all trade figures. (See Table XIII, "Structure of Foreign Trade.") For example, prior to 1893 the materials which comprised both exports and imports reflected the undeveloped state of the economy. In the period 1868-72 the value of food, drink, and raw materials totaled nearly as much as the value of all other exports. Similarly, there was a heavy demand for finished goods (44.5 per cent) and semimanufactured products from abroad to meet the needs of the new military machine and of an expanding industrial structure. After the Sino-Japanese War, the value of exports of manufactured goods was equal to the value of food, drink, and raw materials shipped overseas; semimanufactured goods equaled 43 per cent of total exports. Finished goods purchased abroad still led the list of items imported.

From 1908 to 1912, the period before World War I, the value of imports of finished goods had dropped to 24 per cent and raw materials were by far the largest import item (44 per cent). As for exports, one-third of their value was in finished goods and nearly a half was in semifinished products. By 1913, silk thread amounted to 30 per cent of exports.

TABLE XIII

STRUCTURE OF FOREIGN TRADE[16]
(Percentage of Total Value)

Years	Food and Drink		Raw Materials		Semimanufactured Goods		Finished Goods		Other	
	Import	Export	Import	Export	Import	Export	Import	Export	Import	Export
1868-72	29.0	25.4	4.1	23.1	20.2	40.0	44.5	1.9	2.2	8.8
1878-82	14.8	37.1	3.5	11.6	29.9	40.4	48.6	7.2	3.2	3.7
1893-97	20.8	16.8	22.7	10.3	19.1	43.3	35.1	26.2	2.3	3.4
1903-07	23.5	11.9	33.0	9.1	16.7	45.3	25.5	31.1	1.3	2.6
1908-12	12.0	11.1	44.3	9.2	18.9	48.1	24.1	30.5	.7	1.1

In other words, the mills and factories which had already been built were now in need of raw materials such as iron ore, coking coal, and cotton to keep the machinery and mills operating. To a large extent the domestic demands for consumers' goods were met by the products from these mills, and their surplus was shipped abroad. But despite this increase in exports, the national economy had two weaknesses; namely, exports had not been able to keep up with imports, and a large proportion of these exports was in a single item, raw silk. If the bottom should drop out from under the price of raw silk, Japan's economic plight would immediately become precarious.

In 1914, the over-all economic picture was far more gloomy than a quarter of a century earlier. For example, the population was beginning to show an accelerated rate of increase but production of rice in the main islands had almost reached a maximum. The disproportionate share of taxes borne by the farmer either drove him to greater indebtedness or to tenancy. Financially, the country had survived the rigors of the wars against both China and Russia but had suffered some minor financial panics. The cumulative effects of an excess of imports over exports were appearing in the rise in commodity prices, in the increase in public indebtedness, and in a larger amount of currency in circulation. The spate of new companies and factories which had sprouted between the two wars had helped Japan become more self-sufficient. Complete economic independence was impossible, however, in view of scarcities in iron, coking coal, oil, commercial salt, and staple food. Many of the new industries contributed to a more healthy foreign trade structure, but Japan seemed unable by its own efforts to eliminate the annual unfavorable balance of foreign trade. An economic basis of empire had been built, but it rested on a shaky foundation.

But the outbreak of World War I in the summer of 1914 immediately changed Japan's economic status. Japan's limited military operations throughout the war put no special strain on the nation's economy. Furthermore, the immediate purchases by the Allies of Japanese goods and services in the last four months of 1914 were almost sufficient to bring that year's total exports even with imports. The unfavorable trade balance had been cut to a mere 5 million yen. In 1915, the favorable trade balance of 176 million yen was greater than the combined deficit in foreign trade for the past four and a half years. Just as Japan had benefited politically in China in May, 1915, from the preoccupation of the European powers in the war (see Chapter 13), so it gained financially and economically from the continuation of hostilities. Any misgivings which the industrialists or politicians might have had as to Japan's future were dispelled by the profits derived from both military and economic participation in the war on the side of the Allies.

In its own war against China in 1894-95 and against Russia in 1904-5, Japan had acquired new colonial territory and had gained prestige. New profits again appeared from war in 1915. Within two decades Japan had successfully increased and consolidated the Empire as a result of three wars in which it had participated. By 1915, the last one was not yet over but it was fast becoming more profitable and less costly to Japan than any of the others. Consequently, it became increasingly difficult to dissuade even the most "liberal" Japanese that war did not pay.

If in the future, the leading world powers agreed to disarm, history had taught Japan that it should be willing to follow their lead providing it did not weaken itself in relation to the other powers. On the other hand, if international conditions created a changed atmosphere and any important nation resorted to aggression to achieve its objectives, past experience had taught Japan the value of acting in its own self-interest. In any event, the establishment of its hegemony over Eastern Asia had been accepted by practically all groups within the nation as a steadfast principle of foreign policy. If any foreign power, particularly a Western power, failed to recognize Japan's special prerogatives on the Asiatic mainland, it would have to be forced to do so. In the quarter century after 1915, therefore, nothing was to be permitted to interfere with the emergence of Japan as the leader in Greater East Asia.

Notes

1. See Chapter 9, "National Strength in 1890."

2. Ryoichi Ishii, *Population Pressure and Economic Life in Japan* (London: Walter King, Ltd., 1937), p. 59. For the method of estimating the population from 1872-1920 see Japan, Bureau of Statistics, *Population du Japon depuis 1872* (Tokyo: Japanese Government, 1930), pp. 9-10. The census begins with March 8, 1872.

3. Ishii, *op. cit.,* p. 47.

4. Ishii, *op. cit.,* pp. 59 and 165. Quoted from *Kome Tokeihyō* (Statistics Section, Department of Agriculture and Farming, 1931), pp. 10, 15, and 37. A *koku* of rice equals 5.11 bushels and a *chō* equals 2.45 acres.

5. See G. C. Allen, *A Short Economic History of Modern Japan* (London: George Allen & Unwin, Ltd., 1946), p. 42 *et seq.*

6. Adapted from Allen, *ibid.,* pp. 46 and 184.

7. Takahashi Kamikichi, *Meiji Taishō Sangyō Hattatsu Shi* (Tokyo: Kaizosha, 1929), p. 287 and Giichi Ono, *Expenditures of the Sino-Japanese War* (New York: Oxford University Press, 1922), p. 322.

8. Economists have not yet agreed on the extent of government sponsorship of industry or on the influence of this sponsorship on the increase in national wealth. For example, in his penetrating and valuable study, Professor Lockwood emphasizes the importance of private capital in investments in new enterprises, even in the early period. He notes, "After 1882, the state receded into the background as an entrepreneur. Thereafter it confined its own industrial undertakings within Japan to a few strategic industries, notably iron and steel." See William W. Lockwood, *The Economic Development of Japan, Growth and Structural Change 1869-1938* (Princeton: Princeton University Press, 1954), p. 236 ff.

9. Taken from Takahashi, *op. cit.,* p. 301, based on *Statistical Yearbook* and Department of Finance tables.

10. Uchisaburo Kobayashi, *The Basic Industries and Social History of Japan* (New Haven: Yale University Press, 1930), p. 170.

11. Japan has continued to be largely self-sufficient in low-grade bituminous coal. Scarcities have arisen in good coking coal.

12. Allen, *op. cit.,* pp. 76-77 and 86.

13. Based on Takahashi, *op. cit.,* pp. 330-31.

14. Allen, *op. cit.,* p. 65.

15. In 1906, there was a favorable balance of trade of 4.9 million yen and in 1909 of 18.9 million yen. Figures do not include trade with Korea and Formosa. Based on Department of Finance, *Financial and Economic Annual,* Nos. 1 and 36, pp. 45 and 126.

These same tendencies are verified by Lockwood's figures on the balance of international payments of the Japanese Empire from 1873 to 1936 which include merchandise trade, invisibles and gold for the empire. He estimates that there was a net balance of 30 million yen in merchandise trade and of 72 million yen in gold and a deficit of 25 million yen in invisibles for the period 1873 to 1895. These items showed a deficit of 355 million yen, 41 million yen, and 62 million yen respectively from 1896 to 1903. Total net balances for later years were:

1904–13	—1,083 million yen
1914–19	2,431 million yen
1920–29	—2,272 million yen
1930–36	1,302 million yen

See Lockwood, *op. cit.,* p. 257.

16. Allen, *op. cit.,* p. 181.

PART IV

LEADERSHIP IN GREATER EAST ASIA 1915-1941

Our best policy of action is to make skillful use of the War to erect a lasting national policy for the Empire.

From a report of the
Japanese Army Chief of Staff,
October, 1917.

Chronology

1915-1941

1915	Resignation of Foreign Minister Katō
1916, October	General Terauchi becomes Premier
1917	Secret Treaty with Allies, reference Shantung and Pacific Islands
1918	Siberian Expedition
September	First party cabinet under Hara
November	Armistice in Europe
1919	Paris Peace Conference
June	Versailles Treaty
1921	Washington Disarmament Conference
November	Assassination of Premier Hara
1924	Japanese Exclusion Act
1925	Universal Suffrage for men
	Peace Preservation Law
	Shidehara's conciliatory policy toward Russia
1927	General Tanaka is Premier
1928	Murder of Chang Tso-lin in Manchuria
1930	London Naval Treaty
November	Shooting of Hamaguchi
1931, September 18	Manchurian Incident
1932, February	Formation of State of Manchukuo
	Assassinations of Inouye, Dan, and Inukai
1933	Occupation of Inner Mongolia by the Japanese
	Tangku Truce
1934	Rise of Nationalist philosophy under Araki
1936, February 26	Coup by young officers in Army
	Anti-Comintern Pact
1937, June	First Konoye Cabinet
July 7	Incident at Marco Polo Bridge
December	Rape of Nanking
1938	Enactment of National Mobilization Law
	New Order in East Asia
1940	Tripartite Treaty of Alliance
1941, April	United States–Japanese negotiations begin
July	Japan decides to move southward
	United States freezes Japanese assets
October	General Tōjō becomes Premier
December 7	Japanese attack on Pearl Harbor

15

THE FRUITS OF VICTORY IN WORLD WAR I

From the previous discussion of the manner in which the Japanese Empire was extended and consolidated, it is clear that one of the primary concerns of all groups within the nation was to establish their country as the undisputed leader of Eastern Asia. During the first year of World War I, Japan had moved quickly to replace Germany in China and the Pacific Ocean. It had reinforced its new privileged position on the Asiatic mainland by forcing China to sign the Twenty-One Demands. (See page 257 above.) Its chief interest in the war and in the peace settlement continued to be to improve its economic and political position on the Asiatic continent and its strategic advantage in the Pacific. The secret negotiations with Russia and the Allies, the *rapprochement* with the United States, the loans to and new agreements with China, and the Siberian Expedition were all undertaken with these objectives in view. The demands which Japan presented at the Paris Peace Conference were also dictated by this basic policy of expansion.

A brief description of the domestic political scene is necessary, however, before considering the negotiations of the secret treaties. When the Twenty-One Demands were served on China in 1915, Ōkuma Shigenobu was Premier and Katō Kōmei was Foreign Minister. Although they had not let their political philosophy interfere with their ideas on foreign policy, they were both party men and supporters of the concept of party cabinets. While Ōkuma had often identified himself with the oligarchs on many matters, he had never forgiven them for his political ostracism in 1881. Likewise, he had never abandoned the hope that the parties and their leaders might at some time become more powerful than the Elder Statesmen.

His political rivals in the House of Representatives, the members of the Seiyūkai, criticized him harshly. Furthermore, the ultranationalists and the Elder Statesmen were always alert for an opportunity to embarrass and discredit the politicians. Consequently they combined to criticize the Cabinet not for the contents of its policy but for the methods used in implementing it. Specifically, Foreign Minister Katō was blamed for having approved of issuing an ultimatum to China on May 7, 1915. As a result, he was forced to resign in August, 1915, to draw some of the criticism away from his friend and protector, Prime Minister Ōkuma.

But the causes of the struggle between the oligarchs and the leaders of the "political parties" were so deep-seated that the former were not satiated by Katō's resignation. Yamagata had always been inexorably opposed to parliamentary government and still believed that it was against the spirit of the Constitution and the best interests of the country to select the leader of the majority party as Premier. Consequently, when Ōkuma talked of turning the Cabinet over to the leadership of his former Foreign Minister, Katō,[1] the issue was clearly drawn. Yamagata immediately accepted this recommendation as a challenge to the power and prestige of the oligarchs and especially to himself. He seized the initiative and won support for his own candidate, General Terauchi Masatake, the Governor General of Korea. Through his friends, Yamagata had the Governor recalled. In early October, 1916, while Ōkuma's resignation was pending, Terauchi was ordered to form a new Cabinet. This simple maneuver forestalled the appointment of Katō and signaled once more the victory of the conservative oligarchs over the party leaders.

General Terauchi Masatake[2] was Prime Minister until September, 1918. After the public manifested its indignation at the high cost of living by mass riots, which were quieted only when the troops were called out to assist the police, he was forced to resign. He was succeeded by Hara Kei, President of the Seiyūkai, the majority party in Parliament. (See page 299.) But these Cabinet shifts had no practical effect on foreign policy. As in the past, it was considered a special prerogative of the Emperor and was kept above the domestic political struggle.

Consolidation of Gains Through Secret Treaties, 1916-17

From the outbreak of the war to the Versailles Treaty of 1919, the basic theme of Japan's wartime foreign policy remained constant. It was to consolidate the gains already achieved in the war. Having successfully concluded its negotiations with China, Japan now turned to the West to obtain a closer understanding with the leading Allied and Associated Powers and with the United States. Negotiations were first started with Russia, which resulted in a secret treaty being concluded between Russia and Japan on July 3, 1916. The signatories of this treaty agreed to a military alliance, the exact form of which was to be decided jointly, to protect China from political domination by a third power hostile to either Russia or Japan. From Japan's point of view, this treaty was an added guarantee that neither Russia nor a third power would interfere with the exploitation of China as permitted by the Twenty-One Demands.

Even before the Bolshevik Revolution in Russia was to annul the benefits which might have been derived from this treaty, negotiations were begun with Great Britain for support for Japan's war claims. On January 27, 1917, the two governments exchanged views on a secret treaty in which each hoped to gain concessions from the other. The British sought support for their claims to the former German islands in the Pacific, south of the equator. Since Germany announced its resumption of unrestricted submarine warfare a few days after the negotiations began, the Allies were anxious to receive both logistical and naval escort support from Japan for the Atlantic and Mediterranean convoys. Furthermore, the Allies were hopeful that Japan would be able to persuade China to break off diplomatic relations with Germany.

In return for these services, Great Britain was willing to support Japan's demands for the former German rights in Shantung and to the Pacific Islands north of the equator. Despite Japan's refusal to comply with all of the Allies' requests, the British Government agreed on February 16, 1917, to:

> . . . support Japan's claims in regards to the disposal of Germany's rights in Shantung and possessions in islands north of the Equator at the Peace Conference, it being understood that the Japanese Government will treat in the same spirit Great Britain's claims to German islands south of the Equator.[3]

Similar assurances were received in secret by Japan from Russia, France, and Italy in exchange for little more than a promise that efforts would be taken to get China to sever relations with the common enemy. Thus the necessary diplomatic agreements had been made with the Allies to assure transfer to Japan at the peace conference of those territories which had been acquired by military conquest.

But in the early months of 1917, there was still one important flaw in Japan's diplomatic offensive. No understanding had been reached with the United States. So long as this situation obtained, especially after the United States entered the war, Japan could not be certain that its gains would be verified by the peace treaty. On the other hand, if a successful *rapprochement* could be concluded with the United States, and if no new crises arose in the Far East, Japan could sit back and await Germany's defeat by the other Allies.

There were some real difficulties, however, which prevented Japan and the United States from reaching an understanding. Although the two countries were Allies, financial and economic rivalries in China were full of potential dangers. For example, during the war years, Japan had replaced the Allies as the creditors for China and hoped to keep American investors out of the Asiatic mainland. Consequently, Ishii Kikujirō was dispatched to Washington ostensibly on a War Mission but actually to obtain a clear recognition from the United States of Japan's special interests in Asia. After two months of negotiations, Secretary of State Lansing and Ishii agreed on October 31, 1917, that their countries would not take advantage of China's condition in order to obtain special rights or privileges that would abridge those of citizens of other states. Two days later the United States announced that it recognized that "territorial propinquity" created special rights and that hence Japan had special interests in China, especially in the areas contiguous to Japanese possessions.

Secretary Lansing, who apparently was aware of the concessions made to Japan by the other Allies in the Secret Treaties, considered the agreement as a harmless temporization. Nevertheless, to avoid giving the impression that the United States was abandoning its traditional Open Door Policy for China, the United States announced its intention to join the other powers in a financial consortium in China. Before a final understanding was reached on this subject, however, other more significant events arose in the Far East which required American attention if Japanese expansion was to be prevented from getting out of hand.[4]

The Siberian Expedition of 1918-22

From the diplomatic point of view, the Secret Treaties with the Western powers and the Lansing-Ishii Agreement had secured Japan's flank from attack at the Peace Conference. Presumably, there would be no question about the Allies confirming and supporting Japan's demands after victory. On the other hand, there was the constant danger that unpredictable events, which often had unforeseen consequences, such as the constant shifts within the Chinese government and the Bolshevik Revolution in Russia, might jeopardize the chances of reaping the fruits of victory. Thus, whenever it became apparent to the planners within the government that events might be turned to Japan's advantage, direct action followed. Two of the most important results of such actions, both of which were closely interrelated and had an important bearing on the Paris Peace Conference, were the conclusion of a new series of Sino-Japanese agreements and the formation of an Allied Siberian Expedition in which Japan played the decisive role.

As for the former, during the negotiations of the Secret Treaties, Japan had promised to use its good offices to persuade China to enter the war against Germany. As early as February, 1917, Prime Minister Terauchi had dispatched one of his trusted advisers, Nishihara Kamezō, to China to urge it to sever diplomatic relations with Germany. Nishihara, who was to be a key figure in Sino-Japanese diplomatic and financial negotiations for the next year, secretly established close relations with the Chinese

Premier Tuan Chi-jui and the pro-Japanese members of his Cabinet. He offered loans to them in exchange for China's entry into World War I. Consequently China declared war against the Central Powers on August 14, 1917. Subsequently, the Japanese Government publicly declared that its policy was one of nonintervention in the internal affairs of China, but Nishihara quietly followed an opposite policy.[5]

He constantly sought to bind the two countries together through the use of Japanese capital and technicians in the exploitation of China's natural resources. Between the early part of 1917 and September, 1918, he is reported to have negotiated seven separate loans totalling 145 million yen for the development of the telegraph system, mines, lumbering, and railroads. They were often accompanied by agreements giving Japan special concessions.

This personal influence in China of Nishihara, as well as the effects of the large funds at his disposal, must be kept in mind as a specific policy developed toward Siberia and as new political and military agreements were simultaneously made with China. The rapid successes of the Russian Revolution and crumbling of the Eastern Front in Europe had led to British speculation on the advisability of asking Japan to intervene in Siberia.[6] The French had proposed that both Japan and the United States should take possession of the Trans-Siberian Railway at Vladivostok and Harbin, and lead an expedition to Moscow.

In the fall of 1917, the General Staff of the Japanese Imperial Army had already made a careful estimate of the problems involved. It had concluded that logistic difficulties made it unwise to undertake a major effort on the Eastern Front. Consequently, Japan agreed with the United States that force should not be used to intervene in Russia against the Bolsheviks. The Imperial Army urged, just as Nishihara recommended, that efforts be concentrated on securing political and economic supremacy in China through the exploitation of natural resources.

But it was one thing for the Army to decline to participate in a campaign in European Russia and quite another to refrain from taking advantage of the Bolshevik Revolution to improve Japan's position in Eastern Siberia or Northern Manchuria. Furthermore, nearly three-quarters of a million tons of Allied supplies had accumulated at Vladivostok and would be a valuable prize for the Russian revolutionaries or for the Austrian or German prisoners of war in Siberia. In the hands of an army unfriendly to China or to Japan, they might be a decisive factor in the future peace of East Asia. Consequently, Japan acted to protect this property of the Allies in Siberia. It dispatched two warships to Vladivostok to maintain peace and order and to protect the foreign consular corps. One of them arrived on January 12, 1918, to be joined two days later by a British ship sent for the same purpose.

After a robbery early in April of some of the Allied stores, marines were landed to guard the property.

This might have remained only a local incident if events in Siberia had not played into the hands of the chief army policy makers. In February, 1918, an important shift was made in the planning personnel of the Chief of Staff. General Tanaka Giichi, one of the Army's leading specialists on Russian affairs, was appointed chairman of the General Staff's Siberian War Planning Committee.[7] Tanaka and his Committee recommended that the plight of the foreign residents in Siberia be used as the pretext for sending two divisions into the Maritime Provinces of Siberia and three into the Zabaikal to crush the Bolsheviks. They also recommended the use of anti-Bolshevik Russian forces and the conclusion of a military agreement with China.

When the Foreign Minister supported these proposals, the Advisory Council on Foreign Relations insisted that the expedition be undertaken only in self-defense. In the meantime, Tanaka had obtained agreement to the principle of joint Sino-Japanese participation in a Japanese expedition in Siberia. A military agreement of May, 1918, permitted joint planning and tactics, joint use of the transportation system, and the attachment of expert Japanese military advisers to Chinese units. Although the Japanese Army was to operate mainly in North Manchuria, Eastern Mongolia, and Eastern Siberia, this agreement formed a legal basis for its movements within Chinese territory. The first obstacle to a successful Siberian Expedition, mainly, an insecure rear, had been overcome.[8]

Furthermore, a new element had emerged in Siberia which made it possible to overthrow the Bolsheviks with a minimum of effort. Part of the Czecho-Slovak Army, which was fighting for the independence of its country from Austria-Hungary, had been permitted to leave Russia and return home via Siberia and the Pacific. While en route along the Trans-Siberian Railway, this Army had refused to be disarmed, had revolted, and rapidly took over sections of the railway. It soon became the strongest force in Siberia. In June, 1918, it captured Vladivostok and the Czechs immediately received sympathy from the Allies.

The next month Secretary of State Lansing asked Japan to land forces at Vladivostok, to send 7000 troops to defend Irkutsk and the Czechs from the German and Austrian prisoners of war in that area, and to share equally in furnishing arms to the Czech troops. By this proposal, Lansing hoped to win the friendship of the Czechs and also to make unnecessary a Japanese or Allied expedition against Siberia. In effect, his proposal made such an expedition inevitable.

Although the American proposal fell short in most respects of the recommendations of General Tanaka and his Committee, nevertheless, it was too intriguing to the General Staff to be ignored. It was accepted in the belief that such an expedition could be expanded to suit Japan's purposes. On July 31, 1918, the Japanese Government decided that, in harmony with the Allies, it would:

> . . . despatch suitable forces for the proposed mission. . . . Some to Vladivostok and, if called for by the further exigencies of the situation, another detachment will eventually be ordered to operate and to maintain order along the Siberian railway.[9]

The Allies seemed satisfied that Japan was not going to take advantage of the unsettled conditions in Siberia to acquire control over the territory. The United States was informed that a total of only 12,000 troops would be sent to Vladivostok and that the Powers would be notified if they were moved westward. The General Staff was enraged, however, by this concession which the Cabinet had made to the Allies. It considered itself deprived of a chance to carry on "a great war in Siberia to decide the fate of the nation." Once the expedition was launched, therefore, Tanaka's blueprint, not that of the Cabinet, was followed. A total of 3½ divisions were sent immediately to the Amur River Valley and were later reinforced. Japanese troops immediately outnumbered all of the other Allied forces and put Japan in *de facto* control of the whole area.

The Siberian Expedition is a fascinating case study of how the General Staff achieved its objectives in the face of strong national and international opposition. It is equally important as an illustration of power politics at work. While there were small contingents of Allied forces in Vladivostok and the Trans-Siberian Railway was jointly operated, nevertheless, control of the hinterland was in Japanese hands. This situation continued throughout the months of discussion on the peace settlement at Paris. When the issues of racial equality, of Japanese rights in Shantung, and of the Twenty-One Demands were all under discussion, the Japanese Army was well entrenched from Vladivostok to Harbin to Chita to Baikal.[10] The constant realization that the Japanese might remain permanently in that huge area of Siberia acted as a strong incentive to persuade the Allies to accept Japan's demands at Paris. As is so often true in international negotiations, the choice before the Allies was not between a good or bad solution, but rather that of the least objectionable of several unpleasant alternatives. The narrative now shifts away from eastern Siberia to Paris where Japan fought to obtain by negotiations the fruits of victory which it had been promised in the Secret Treaties.

Japan at the Paris Peace Conference

On November 11, 1918, when the Armistice was signed in Europe, Japan viewed the cessation of hostilities with a far more detached attitude than any of the other belligerents. The battlefields of Europe had seemed a long way off and no Japanese soldiers had been involved in the main theater of war. Moreover, in September, 1918, the high cost of living had resulted in rice riots on a national scale which had absorbed the immediate interests of both the people and government. But in the realm of foreign affairs, the course of the Empire was firmly set. Even the appointment of the head of the Seiyūkai party, Hara Kei, as Prime Minister had not caused any deviation in this policy. Internationally, Japan was in a strong position to press at the peace conference for acceptance of its demands. The Army was rapidly spreading westward in Siberia to Lake Baikal and northward into the Amur Valley; the international character of the Siberian Expedition had little retarding effect on this advance. No international agreement had yet been reached on the control of international investments in China, so Japan still operated there with a free hand.

It was taken for granted in Tokyo, therefore, that the Paris Peace Conference would legalize the promises of the Allies set forth in the Secret Treaties. They had promised that the German possessions in Shantung and the Pacific Islands north of the equator would be ceded to Japan. It was also assumed by Japan that it would be free to negotiate bilaterally with China on all outstanding issues and that the latter would play only a minor part in the peace negotiations.

Finally, the Japanese government and people had caught something of the contagious feeling instilled by President Wilson's proposals for a League of Nations which presaged the dawn of a new day for international relations. They accepted the concept of the League and anticipated that the negotiations concerning it would afford an excellent opportunity for the Asiatic countries to seek recognition of both the principle and practice of racial equality. United States Ambassador Roland Morris telegraphed from Tokyo on November 15, 1918:

> It is hoped by the Japanese that the organization of a League of Nations will offer an opportunity to assert the equality of the yellow race, a question which underlies all discussion on the subject.

On January 15, 1919, three days after the Paris Peace Conference was formally opened, Tokyo's leading daily newspaper, the *Asahi,* editorialized that racial inequality was the real obstacle in the way of the brotherhood of nations and that Japan should represent the colored races of the world in seeking equality.

The issue of racial equality was important to the Japanese people and their delegates at Paris because of the discriminatory treatment which Oriental immigrants had received in the United States and Australia. (See page 305.) Since Japan sought world recognition of its status as a leading world power, it could not tolerate the continuance of what the Foreign Minister described as "discriminatory treatment based upon racial prejudice." But the real significance of the debate on racial equality at the Peace Conference was the effect it had on Japan's attitude toward its other demands. Consequently, an account of Japan's role at Paris necessarily begins with its endeavors to obtain a solution to this explosive problem.

All of the leading delegations, including the Japanese, were cognizant of the fact that the whole question of racial equality was an extremely delicate one. After the representatives of the principal powers had been warned that the issue was to arise, President Wilson assigned Colonel Edward M. House to obtain preliminary agreement on a statement which recognized the general principle of racial equality. This statement would then be inserted in the Covenant of the League of Nations. In conversation with Lord Balfour of England, House insisted that the policy of discrimination toward the Japanese could not continue. Balfour was noncommital but Prime Minister Hughes of Australia refused to budge from his position of opposition to any proposal for racial equality.[11]

The issue first came up formally in the middle of February, 1919, at a meeting of the Commission to draft the Covenant of the League of Nations. Makino Shinken, the Japanese member of the Commission, proposed that a clause be added to the draft text of the Covenant which provided for equal treatment for all nationals of all states members of the League, regardless of their race or nationality.[12] In making this proposal, Makino consciously avoided the issue of immigration by referring only to general principles. In defense of his amendment, he argued that the new demands of the League, such as participation by member states in joint actions against aggressors, made it natural that all nationals wanted to be placed on an equal footing with the people they defended with their lives. As was expected from the resistance which Colonel House had encountered, the Japanese proposal was particularly embarrassing to the British. They did not want to offend the Japanese in view of the fact that the Anglo-Japanese Alliance was still in force. They were poignantly aware, however, of the adamant opposition of Hughes of Australia to any proposal which recognized racial equality.

To extricate themselves from this uncomfortable dilemma, the members of the Commission finally decided to delete from the Covenant the entire article which Makino proposed to amend. The delegates from both the United States and Japan had consented to this deletion, however, on condition that they had the right to bring the question of racial equality up again. Thus a final decision was sidetracked for the next two months. But official and nonofficial Japanese statements made it patently clear that they were disappointed with the cool reception which their proposals had received. Doubts were raised in their minds as to Wilson's sincerity when he spoke of the League as a means to obtain justice and equality.

At this point, the Japanese Ambassador in Washington, Ishii, in the hopes of allaying the fears of the critics of racial equality, inadvertently weakened the chances of success of his government's proposals. In March, 1919, he presented a memorandum to President Wilson in which he stressed the importance which his government placed on the nondiscriminatory treatment of races. He concluded his note with the prediction that if this principle were not accepted at the Paris Conference, it would be impossible to eliminate "perpetual friction and discontent among nations and races."[13]

Ten days later, in a public address, he attempted to separate the question of the acceptance of the principle of racial equality, which was before the peace conference, from the question of immigration, which was a domestic issue for each nation to decide. As for the latter, he denied that his government had any thought of forcing a decision on the matter. But he had not calculated on an emotional, rather than a rational, reaction to his speech by a vocal segment of the American people. His speech was used by those opposed to the idea of racial equality as proof that the Japanese government was pressing for acceptance of the concept of racial equality in order to force the United States to revise its immigration laws. (See page 305.) He was also accused by elements in the American press of having issued a veiled threat that Japan would not join the proposed League of Nations unless the concept of racial equality was accepted.

Consequently, the anti-Japanese pressure groups in the United States irrationally concluded that the questions of immigration and racial equality were identical. They began to exert pressure on the American delegation at the Paris Conference. Senator J. D. Phelan of California, who had been one of the most outspoken advocates of Oriental exclusion for the past twenty years, dispatched an alarmist telegram to the American delegation. He misinterpreted Ishii's speech and claimed that Japan had demanded free immigration and other privileges which had aroused the Pacific Coast. He added that Californians were alarmed at the prospects of land being purchased by Japanese in violation of the laws of the state. Despite the inaccuracy of these charges, he concluded with the categorical statement that since the problem was entirely a domestic one, the drafters of the Covenant should "under no circumstances concede to the Japanese demands."

Before the principle of racial equality was officially presented again at the Paris Conference, the Japanese delegation learned that Hughes of Australia would not agree to any reference in the League's Covenant to the principle of racial equality. From the Japanese point of view, however, the matter had now become one of national honor. If they were to participate in the League, they wished to do so on terms of equality with other members. They had not yet received assurances that they would succeed to Germany's former rights in China or in the Pacific Ocean. They saw no reason why they should be intimidated by alarmists in the United States or by Australia's threats.

Consequently, at another meeting of the Commission to draft the Covenant, the Japanese delegation proposed that the text of the preamble to the Covenant include a clause which recognized the principle of the equality of nations and of the just treatment of their nationals. In making this proposal, it was intimated that the failure to accept such a clause might result in Japan's refusal to join the League of Nations. But for Great Britain, since the alternative was between the solidarity of the British Empire or the friendship of Japan, there was no question as to which course should be taken. Hughes remained adamant; Lord Robert Cecil bowed to his wishes rather than those of the Japanese. He refused to approve the proposed clause on the grounds that it would encroach on the sovereignty of member states.

President Wilson, who was Chairman of the meeting on April 11, 1919, hoped that the Japanese would withdraw their proposal. When they insisted on a vote, in which only eleven out of seventeen delegates favored inserting the clause, Wilson ruled that the lack of unanimity had defeated the motion. In an attempt to alleviate any hard feelings which his ruling might engender, he emphasized that the League was obviously based on the principle of the equality of nations and hence such a clause would be superfluous. But it was obvious to everyone, including the Japanese members of the Commission, that the views of the British Dominions had prevailed in London. Even though Makino insisted that he would raise the matter again in the Plenary Session of the Conference, for all practical purposes the question was already settled.

Bitterly disappointed by the fact that the powers would not even recognize racial equality in principle and convinced that discrimination would continue, Japan was determined that it would not be forced to change its position on the Shantung question. Before the Peace Conference had convened, it had assumed that the Secret Treaties of 1917 with the various European Powers, assured support for its claims and made unnecessary negotiations on them. After the Conference got under way, however, Japan realized that some of the powers, notably the United States, questioned Japan's claims and even intended to befriend China and its cause. In the face of this opposition, Japan took the position that the issues outstanding between China and Japan concerned those two countries alone. Consequently China should not be permitted to participate in any of these discussions at the conference. Thus, when the question of the disposition of Germany's rights in Shantung first came up at a meeting of the Council of Ten, on January 27, 1919, Baron Makino insisted that the Chinese representative should not be present. His proposal was overruled and the Chinese attended the meetings.

Makino then presented the views of his government, concentrating on its legal aspects. He argued that his country's contribution to the victory of the Allies rendered it only just and proper that Germany's rights in Shantung should be ceded to Japan. He reminded the delegates that Japan had captured Kiaochow from Germany in the early months of the war and had continued to occupy the province of Shantung. He also maintained that by the Sino-Japanese Agreements of 1915 (the Twenty-One Demands), China had acquiesced in the direct transfer of German rights to Japan. Furthermore, on September 24, 1918, China had signed another set of agreements which were a further recognition of the validity of Japan's position. These later agreements provided for the withdrawal of the Japanese civil administration (military government) from Shantung, for the joint Sino-Japanese management of the railroad from Tsingtao to Tsinan, and for loans from Japan for funds for two new lines.[14]

This position was vehemently and effectively attacked by Dr. Wellington Koo, the chief Chinese delegate. He noted that the Province of Shantung, with its thirty-six million inhabitants, was the cradle of Chinese civilization and the birthplace of the two great sages and philosophers, Confucius and Mencius. Since Shantung was endowed with valuable natural resources, the encroachments of a foreign power in that region could only be for the purpose of exploitation. He maintained that the permanent occupation of Kiaochow by Japan would be for this purpose and would also be a constant threat to the capital of Peking.

He then raised the question of the legal basis of Japan's claims in China, maintaining that the Agreements of 1915 had been agreed to only under duress and had never been considered as permanently binding by his government. Finally, when China had declared war on Germany, it had abrogated "all treaties and conventions theretofore concluded between China and Germany." Consequently, he concluded that there was no legal basis for Japan's claims and that one of the conditions of a just peace required that Shantung should be restored completely and without encumbrances to China.

Dr. Koo immediately won support for his position from practically all the members of the Council of Ten. Popular opinion in the United States and elsewhere recognized China's strong moral position. Consequently, the Japanese delegates became alarmed and emphasized that their country was intent on seeing that it received only what it considered to be its just rewards. Although the Peace Conference concentrated on other matters during the next seven weeks, both China and Japan kept the issue alive by the distribution of memoranda to the other delegations and of pamphlets to the general public in which they set forth the arguments for their respective positions. In this battle of words, the Chinese delegation was the more effective of the two. One of its memoranda, which harped on the moral issue, concluded with the plea:

> The leased territory of Kiaochow with its appurtenant rights is susceptible of only one solution. By restoring it to China, together with the railways and other rights, the Peace Conference will . . . be redressing a wrong . . . and serving the common interests of all nations in the Far East.[15]

By the middle of April, circumstances tended to make both sides begin to show some interest in a compromise solution. On the one hand, Japan had run into strong opposition to its proposal for racial equality. Its position on the Shantung issue was becoming increasingly unpopular. If it were to gain anything at Paris, it might have to make concessions. On the other hand, China realized that its legal position was weak because it had voluntarily acquiesced in the agreements of September, 1918. The promises which the powers had made to Japan in their Secret Treaties might prove to have more force than Chinese eloquence. When the issue was raised at a meeting of the Council of Four on April 15, 1919, four days after the defeat on the issue of racial equality, Makino emphasized that Japan had agreed to the eventual return to China of the leased territory in Shantung. President Wilson vainly sought to solve the problem by suggesting a joint trusteeship for the area. When the Council of Four considered the question a week later, the representatives were confronted with new complications. The Japanese delegation stated that it had received instructions not to sign the peace treaty in the event that the Shantung issue was not settled in its favor. It added that its government would be willing to restore the former German territory in Shantung to China on two conditions. First, Kiaochow should be a free port with a Japanese concession in the city. Second, the railroad in Shantung should be a joint Sino-Japanese enterprise with a Japanese police force to maintain law and order. China continued to press for complete expulsion of Japan from Chinese territory.

President Wilson hoped to find a solution which would be consistent with his policy of the right of nations to determine their own future and with his dream that members of the League would think primarily of their duties toward each other rather than of their self-interests. He was torn between two conflicting claims. He wanted to rectify any injustice which might have been done China; he was determined above all else to win support for the League of Nations from the strongest powers. Lloyd George announced that Britain considered the secret treaties binding and hence would support Japan's demands. This development made it difficult for Wilson to continue to oppose Japan's claims and still keep Britain's support for the League. The whole future of the League had been threatened only the day before by the action of the Italian delegation. It had walked out of the Conference because of dissatisfaction with the proposal to assign Fiume and the Dalmatian Coast to Yugoslavia. Wilson was convinced that if Japan did not receive satisfaction in Shantung, its delegates would follow the example of the Italians. If such an eventuality arose, the League would be lost.

Despite strong opposition from Secretary of State Lansing and from other members of the American delegation, President Wilson agreed to Japan's wishes. On April 30, the Council of Three (Wilson, George, Clemenceau) approved the transfer of Germany's rights in Shantung to Japan. When the Chinese were told of this decision, they raised strenuous objections. As a last resort, they demanded that they be allowed to sign the Treaty of Versailles with reservations on the articles referring to Shantung. When their request was rejected, they refused to sign the Treaty. Thus by the Versailles Treaty the Allied Powers had recognized Japan's new rights in Shantung. China had not done so and Japan's armed forces continued in occupation of the Shantung peninsula. Its diplomats insisted that the decision at Paris implied recognition of the validity of the Agreements of 1915 and of 1918 and began to implement many of their provisions. They ignored China's cries of exploitation and infringement of the Open Door. The problem remained unsolved until the Washington Disarmament Conference of 1922.

In the meantime, there was a tragic sequel to the Paris decision. President Wilson had traded his acquiescence to Japan's demands concerning Shantung for Allied support for his dream of a League of Nations. He had neglected to judge accurately the effect which this compromise would have on the American people and Congress. No matter how he justified his position, it was impossible to make it seem consistent with his earlier advocacy of international guarantees of political independence and territorial integrity of all states. He confidently hoped that the League would right any past wrongs. Colonel House had expressed this thought in a letter sent to the President the day before the decision was made on Shantung:

> My feeling is that while it is all bad, it is no worse than the things we are doing in many of the settlements. . . . Let the League of Nations and the new era do the rest.[16]

Wilson's insistence that nothing that he had agreed to indicated acquiescence in Japanese policy toward China, as set forth in the Twenty-

One Demands, fell on deaf ears. Popular opinion in the United States insisted that a wrong had been done a weak and helpless China to win favor from a militarily powerful Japan. This opinion, combined with a renascent postwar isolationism, resulted in the rejection of the Versailles Treaty by the United States Senate in March, 1920. Japan was securely entrenched in Shantung. The United States was outside the League. Wilson was a broken man physically and spiritually. New means would have to be found to rectify any injustices perpetrated against China.

Another Japanese objective at Paris was to acquire the former German Islands in the Pacific north of the equator. The Secret Treaties of 1917 had specified that the signatories would support Japan's claims to these islands. Makino and other delegates had referred to this fact on several occasions but it was not until near the end of the conference that a final decision was reached. The Council of Four, with President Wilson's consent, agreed to assign the Caroline, Marshall, and Marianas Islands to Japan as a Class C Mandate under the League of Nations. Although it would have preferred to receive them in complete sovereignty, Japan consented to this arrangement.

When the Versailles Treaty was signed on June 28, 1919, therefore, Japan had attained most of its objectives at the Paris Peace Conference. It had been defeated on the issue of racial equality. On the vital issue of new rights in Shantung, however, it had received almost exactly what it had demanded. It had replaced Germany in China. It had bound China to agree to its plans by liberal loans and by promises to transfer, at an indefinite date in the future, any sovereign rights which it held. Although the Pacific Islands were granted Japan under the new system of mandates, as a Class C Mandate the islands could be treated as an integral part of the Empire. The only drawback, from a Japanese point of view, to such an arrangement was that no fortifications were allowed in Class C Mandates. But this limitation was unimportant when the general tendency in the world seemed to be toward less, rather than more, armaments.

In any event, Prime Minister Hara encountered only mild opposition in Parliament to the Versailles Treaty. When asked why the legislature had not been kept informed of the progress of the negotiations, he replied that his government was always ready to supply information consistent with the public interest. He then reminded Parliament that traditionally it had never interfered with the treaty-making prerogatives of the Emperor. He asked for acceptance of the treaty. In view of the general agreement that World War I had strengthened Japan's leadership throughout East Asia and that much had been won at only very limited cost, opposition in Parliament very soon disappeared.

Notes

1. When Katō obtained China's signatures to the May, 1915, notes, his long cherished desire to see Japan control Chinese affairs was largely realized. From his past close relations with Ōkuma, Katō was the natural successor. Ōkuma's complete confidence in him is evidenced by a willingness to support him after he had been forced to resign. On the other hand, elections in 1915 had given Ōkuma a working majority in the House of Representatives and he was confident his man could lead the country.

2. Terauchi Masatake (1851-1919) was basically a soldier. Born in Chōshū in a warrior family, he lost an arm fighting against Saigō in the Satsuma Rebellion of 1877 but remained in the Army. In the Sino-Japanese War he distinguished himself as a brigade commander. He was promoted to Vice-Chief of the Army General Staff and was Minister of War 1902 to 1910 when he became the first Governor-General of Korea. Yamagata's maneuvers had included receiving assurances from Hara, head of the Seiyūkai party, with 111 seats in the Lower House, that he would support Terauchi. On the other hand, Katō was piqued by the fact that he had not been selected as Premier. He formed the Kenseikai (Constitutional party) the day after Terauchi became Premier. Katō publicly denounced the arbitrary action of Yamagata and the Elder Statesmen and promised to fight Terauchi from Parliament. The Kenseikai, an amalgamation of three groups, controlled 197 seats in the House of Representatives. Just when Katō hoped to pass a vote of nonconfidence against Premier Terauchi, Parliament was dissolved. In the elections of April, 1917, the Seiyūkai party, which supported the Cabinet, increased its strength to 160 at the expense of the Kenseikai, which dropped to 119. Hence, Terauchi had vastly improved his political strength. Criticism of foreign policy was kept to a minimum by the Advisory Council on Foreign Relations composed of leaders of the various parties. Katō Kōmei doggedly boycotted the Council.

3. Ray Stannard Baker, *Woodrow Wilson and the World Settlement* (New York: Doubleday, Page & Co., 1922), I, p. 61. For a detailed account of the Secret Treaties see A. Whitney Griswold, *The Far Eastern Policy of the United States* (New York: Harcourt, Brace & Co., 1938), p. 205 *et seq.*

4. As Griswold notes, Wilson was forced to wait until after the Armistice to devote energy to the American diplomatic offensive to check Japan which had been planned in 1917. This offensive sought to prevent independent Japanese capital investments in China, to keep Siberia out of Japanese hands, to restore Shantung to China and to incorporate nonaggressive policies in new treaties on the Far East. *Ibid.,* p. 223.

5. Nishihara Kamezō was well qualified to carry out Terauchi's wishes. He was in Korea in 1908 as head of a group promoting trade between Japan and Korea and Manchuria. When Terauchi became Governor of Korea he was favorably impressed with Nishihara's zeal and interest in expanding Japanese hegemony over the continent. In May, 1915, Nishihara was dispatched to Manchuria to report on the reaction to the Twenty-One Demands. He became a sort of secret private emissary of Terauchi and was a key figure in obtaining further concessions from China.

6. I am greatly indebted to Professor James Morley for the material on the Siberian Expedition which he has set forth in his Ph.D. thesis entitled, *The Origins of Japan's Siberian Expedition, 1919-1922. A Case Study in the Formation of Japan's Foreign Policy,* Columbia University Ph.D. thesis, 1954. He has clarified the whole subject and has made a notable contribution to our knowledge of this aspect of World War I.

7. General Tanaka (1863-1929) was born in Chōshū and graduated from the Military Staff College. He served in the Sino-Japanese War and studied in Russia from 1898-1902. After 1915 he was the chief Russian specialist on the General Staff. As noted below, he was Prime Minister from 1927 to 1929 (see Chapter 16).

8. I have purposely omitted the complications which resulted from the rise and fall of persons such as Semenov and Hovarth and the Japanese and Allied attitude toward them. See Morley, *op. cit.,* chapter viii for these details.

9. See Morley, *op. cit.,* chapter xi. Morley also gives a fascinating account of how the General Staff ignored the Cabinet and its opposition to the basic plan originally proposed by Tanaka and went ahead on its own initiative. One of the most ironical aspects of the whole expedition was the fact that Hara, who became Prime Minister on September 29, 1918, had been unalterably opposed to an expedition except in self-defense. This was particularly true of a move toward the Amur Basin. By the time he was Prime Minister, however, Khabarovosk had fallen to the Japanese and they were on their way to Baikal. He was not strong enough to order the Army home.

10. Japanese forces were withdrawn from Siberia in 1922, over two years after the other Allies had left. They had occupied Northern Sakhalien in 1920 and remained there until 1926.

11. House worked closely with the Japanese in an attempt to obtain a proposal which would be acceptable to Hughes. On February 9, House records that Hughes objected to every solution proposed by the Japanese. Charles Seymour, editor, *The Intimate Papers of Colonel House* (4 vols.; Boston: Houghton Mifflin Co., 1928), IV, pp. 313 ff.

12. Makino Shinken (1862-1949) was a disciple of Ōkubo's. At the age of eleven, he had gone to the United States to study and entered the Foreign Office upon his return in 1879. He served as Minister in Italy and Austria and was Minister of Education in 1906 in the Saionji Cabinet and Foreign Minister in the Yamamoto Cabinet in 1913. He was Minister of the Imperial Household during the Army revolt of February 26, 1936, and narrowly escaped with his life.

Former Premier Saionji was chief delegate at Paris. Despite his familiarity with France during his student days, he was less active in the conference discussions than Makino. For a text of Makino's proposal, which was to be added to Article 21 of the Covenant, see David Hunter Miller, *My Diary at the Conference of Paris* (New York: Appeal Printing Co., 1925), V, Document 355.

13. Baker, *op. cit.,* II, p. 236.

14. For a text of the agreements see Miller, *op. cit.,* VI, pp. 204 ff.

15. *Ibid.,* p. 130. China's legal position was greatly weakened by the agreements of September 24 and 25, 1918. It could not plead duress in this case. Furthermore, since the agreements were made subsequent to the Chinese Declaration of War against Germany, the statement in the Declaration about abrogating former German rights was largely nullified.

16. Seymour, *op. cit.,* IV, p. 454. There has been considerable controversy over the question of whether or not President Wilson was aware of the existence of the Secret Treaties of 1917 when he opposed Japan's claims prior to April 24. Colonel House claims that it was doubtful whether Wilson knew of the understandings between Japan and the Allies in reference to Shantung until he reached Paris. House concludes: "I cannot recall having such knowledge myself." On the other hand, the hearings of the Senate Munitions Investigation Committee indicate that Balfour, on his visit to Washington in May, 1917, had informed Secretary of State Lansing of all of Great Britain's commitments. *Ibid.,* III, pp. 61 ff.; and Griswold, *op. cit.,* pp. 218 ff.

16

THE PRECARIOUS POSITION OF PARLIAMENTARY GOVERNMENT, 1920-1931

The relatively peaceful years between the signing of the Versailles Peace Treaty in 1919 and the outbreak of war in Manchuria in September, 1931, were crowded with contradictions. In reality these events reflected the conflict of diametrically opposed forces which was so typical of modern Japan. They also stand out clearly in retrospect as portents of an unquenchable aggressive nationalism which was to sweep everything before it. For example, the assassination of the two most "progressive" Prime Ministers, Hara and Hamaguchi; the reoccupation of Shantung by Japanese troops; and the independent, overt acts of representatives of the Imperial Army in Manchuria were preliminaries to the military occupation of that entire area following the carefully planned explosion near Mukden on September 18, 1931.

On the other hand, the formation of party cabinets, the singularly powerful position attained by Premiers Hara and Hamaguchi, the active participation in world disarmament, all attest to the existence of a strong group in favor of following parliamentary processes at home and a conciliatory policy abroad. Finally, the inconsistencies of America's policy toward Japan added to the confusion. After taking the lead in checking Japan's international power through naval disarmament and the other Washington agreements of 1922, the United States increased international suspicion and ill will by the passage of an immigration law which excluded Orientals from its shores. The history of the postwar decade is, therefore, that of the interaction of these and many other forces which made the ascendancy of internationally minded civilian leaders prior to September 18, 1931, only an illusion.

Hara's Party Cabinet

In order to understand how such a condition came about, it is necessary to review briefly the postwar political scene. In September, 1918, when Prime Minister General Terauchi had been forced to resign because of the rice riots caused by the high cost of living, conditions were unusually favorable for the emergence of a strong party cabinet. The Elder Statesmen had previously asked their colleague Saionji to form a government but he had refused. Since the Seiyūkai party had more seats in the House of Representatives than any other group and the party's President, Hara Kei,[1] enjoyed a wide popularity, he appeared to be the logical choice under the circumstances. Thus the Elder Statesmen recommended, though reluctantly, that he be appointed. The three most significant facts about his selection were that he was from the north of Japan, was a commoner, and a leader of a political party.

Hara had worked his way to the top as a loyal member of the Seiyūkai party and was an advocate of party cabinets. Hence he immediately appointed Seiyūkai members to all of the posts in his Cabinet, except the Ministers of War and Navy, who were selected as before by their military colleagues. Although his Cabinet came closer than any previous one to being a party cabinet, its operation left much to be desired compared to those in other parliamentary governments.

While Hara led the chorus of those who claimed that militarism was already extinct, he and his Cabinet seemed to lack an understanding of some of the basic elements of democracy. For example, he presented a bill to Parliament which would have permitted universal manhood suffrage. Before it came to a vote, however, he had dissolved the Diet and explained that an extension of the franchise would not contribute to the healthy development of constitutional government. While he favored increases in the number of Imperial universities and modified the rules of colonial administration to permit civilians to be governors of Korea and Formosa, his Home Minister aroused the patriotism of the youth of the country through his eulogization of the Crown Prince and the sponsorship of a militant, nationalistic Young Men's Association. Although Finance Minister Takahashi Korekiyo was opposed to the constantly rising military expenditures, he was powerless to stop them. Despite the election returns of May, 1920, which gave the Seiyūkai a three-fifths majority in the House of Representatives, Hara had qualms about the nation's political stability. He lamented the increased prevalence of radicalism and the beginnings of a vocal labor movement.

Unlike the American Federation of Labor, which refused to champion radicalism and concentrated on improvement in the economic status of the skilled workers, the Japanese labor movement had its origins in socialism. As early as 1912, Suzuki Bunji, a socialist, went to the United States and became inspired by the activities of Samuel Gompers and the American Federation of Labor. Upon his return to Japan, Suzuki formed a society that became the nucleus for organizing the first trade unions. But it was not until after World War I that strikes became important or that the proletarian movement became bellicose.

Following the traditional pattern of the oligarchs toward nonconformity, Hara's government was ruthless in its suppression of strikes and of any other signs of the beginnings of the labor and proletarian movements. Nevertheless, strikes became prevalent after 1919. The workers demanded the right to organize, the abolition of child labor, a minimum wage, restricted working hours, and the amendment of those laws which jeopardized the right to strike. The Kawasaki Dockyard Workers in Kōbe conducted a comparatively peaceful strike which resulted in the workers being granted an eight-hour day. Strikes also broke out in Ōsaka, Yokohama, and other industrial areas.

But the growth of organized labor, which was painfully slow, was retarded by its close connection with the radical movement. The police made numerous arrests, and thugs hired by ultranationalists manhandled and otherwise intimidated persons considered as radicals. But Marxism had become popular among many professors and intellectual leaders who advocated the immediate establishment of a communist state in Japan. Students eagerly responded to their pleas to participate actively in strikes and demonstrations. In 1921, there was a severe clash between the police and the marchers in the May Day parade. A general wave of unrest and a desire for direct action swept over the workers in the cities.

Hara's policy of suppression of these activities only increased the bitterness of labor, not only toward management but also toward the Cabinet and the Seiyūkai. To the worker, there seemed little to recommend a party government as compared to a transcendent cabinet. To some, Premier Hara seemed the personification of all that troubled the nation. On November 4, 1921, he was assassinated by a government railway employee. The reins of government were taken over by Finance Minister Takahashi, but the Seiyūkai had lost its real leader. Despite his genius as a financier, Takahashi was less stern and less capable than his predecessor. He soon lost the confidence of the various factions of the party, some of whom challenged his leadership. Desertions made the Seiyūkai a minority party in the House, so Takahashi resigned in June, 1922. For the next two years the government reverted again to nonparty cabinets.[2]

Even though a party cabinet was in power from 1918 to 1922, Japan had shown no signs of a basic change in foreign policy. There were no indications of relinquishing control in Eastern Asia. Japanese troops continued to be in occupation of Shantung despite the promise at Paris that they would be withdrawn. The Army was solidly entrenched in Manchuria, Eastern Siberia, and in all of Sakhalien. In view of these facts, from the waning months of World War I to the summer of 1921, the

United States entertained deep misgivings concerning the effects of Japan's gains in the war on the future peace and security of Eastern Asia and of the world. Consequently, America had insisted in 1918 on multilateral participation in the Siberian Expedition to prevent Japan's occupation of northeastern Asia. But this action had not restrained the Japanese Imperial Army. (See page 287.)

The United States also attempted to check Japan in the field of international finance. As early as June, 1918, the United States government worked toward the formation of a four-power Consortium to make loans to China on the basis of nondiscriminatory, equal economic opportunity. The Consortium, composed of France, Great Britain, Japan, and the United States, was organized to prevent the continuance of the highly political and exclusive loans negotiated with China by Nishihara and other Japanese agents.[3] After it was conceded that the Consortium would not be applicable to the South Manchurian Railway zone and other areas in which Japan already had special concessions, final agreement for the plan was reached in October, 1920. On paper, at least, a check had been placed on unlimited Japanese investment in China, especially those for political purposes.

The Washington Conference

The most significant postwar American proposal to check Japan's military expansion, however, was the calling of the Washington Conference. By the summer of 1921, several events had contributed to the willingness of the American government to take such a step. In the first place, prior to their victory in the election of November, 1920, the Republicans had advocated general disarmament. Furthermore, many Americans were searching for ways other than the use of the League of Nations whereby future wars could be prevented. The United States placed great hopes on disarmament. It became convinced that a Pacific Disarmament Conference could bring about a significant reduction of both naval and military armaments, could make a renewal of the Anglo-Japanese Alliance unnecessary, and could hamper and obstruct Japanese imperialism in China and Siberia. If these objectives could be achieved, the possibilities of war would be greatly lessened.

Consequently, formal notes were transmitted to Japan, Italy, France, and Great Britain requesting their views on the advisability of holding such a conference. All of the powers accepted, but Japan raised certain questions. It requested a more concise definition of the scope of the problems proposed for discussion; it clearly indicated that questions concerning Sino-Japanese relations, such as the Twenty-One Demands and Shantung, should be scrupulously avoided. But Secretary of State Hughes, like Hay in 1899 when announcing the answers to his Open Door Notes, ignored these objections and declared that all four of the countries approved of such a conference.

In August, 1921, formal invitations were extended to these four powers and to China, the Netherlands, Belgium, and Portugal to convene in Washington. The scope of the conference was expanded to include all of the important outstanding issues in the Pacific area. These were naval disarmament, the Open Door, Japan's position in Shantung, the integrity of China and Russia, the renewal of the Anglo-Japanese Alliance, the status of the German possessions, the Pacific cable, and narcotics. Despite Japan's earlier objections to placing some of these questions on the agenda, it consented to attend. Obviously, it did not want to give the other powers a chance to agree among themselves to limit its freedom of action in China and East Asia. A general curtailment of armaments would be to everyone's advantage, so the question was at least worth discussing. Finally, Hara was Premier when the invitations were issued and took a generally conciliatory attitude toward world disarmament. His murder, a week before the conference opened, had no effect on Japan's attendance.

Representatives of these nine powers with possessions in the Pacific Ocean met in Washington from November, 1921, to February, 1922. Seven treaties and twelve resolutions resulted from the deliberations. These agreements were both interdependent and separate; some of them were signed by only two members, others by all the nations attending the conference.[4] The treaties and agreements generally covered three subjects, namely, nonaggression, naval disarmament, and China. The Four Power Treaty on Insular Possessions laid down certain general principles of nonaggression. In this pact, France, Great Britain, Japan, and the United States pledged to respect each other's rights in the Pacific Ocean. They also agreed to consult jointly whenever a potentially dangerous controversy arose over their rights in the Pacific area.

The two most significant decisions concerning the limitation of naval armaments were the Naval Disarmament Treaty and the agreement between Great Britain and Japan to terminate their alliance. Secretary of State Hughes proposed early in the conference that the most effective method to control naval armaments was by a limitation on the number of capital ships (battleships) to be retained by each of the naval powers. He recommended, therefore, that all capital shipbuilding programs be abandoned, that old capital ships be scrapped, and that the number of battleships owned by each of the five leading naval powers (France, Great Britain, Italy, Japan, and the United States) be reduced in proportion to the existing strength of their respective navies. For Japan, this proposal meant that it would be allowed to retain capital ships at a ratio of three to five in comparison with Great Britain or the United States.

An island empire such as Japan, however, had to rely heavily on its navy for protection and could consider favorably proposals such as a reduction of capital ships or the abandonment of the Anglo-Japanese Alliance providing the potential striking force of the British and American navies was eliminated. In view of the necessity in those days for a task force to have a base from which to operate, Japan would remain safe from attack if American and British naval bases were restricted. Consequently, Admiral Katō Tomosaburō, the chief Japanese delegate and Naval Chief of Staff, proposed that the status quo be maintained with respect to fortifications and naval bases in the Pacific. The United States and Great Britain agreed to this counterproposal so long as it did not apply to their respective naval centers in the Hawaiian Islands and Singapore. Having obtained these specific assurances to protect it from attack, Japan willingly agreed to a reduction of capital ships and did not press further for the renewal of the alliance with England.[5]

As for the treaties dealing with the problems connected with China, they were also closely interrelated. By the Versailles Treaty, Japan had obtained special rights in the Shantung Peninsula, but it had promised to withdraw its troops. Since that time, it had remained in military occupation of the province. Hence, the United States had insisted that both the specific issue of Shantung and the broad question of the over-all relations of the powers toward China should be considered by the Washington Conference. Secretary Hughes proposed that the Open Door Policy be defined in terms of equal economic opportunity for everyone in China. Furthermore, he recommended that a Board of Reference be created to study how this policy could be most effectively carried out and to report and investigate on any infringements of this policy. Since Japan considered that such a Board would be used by the Western powers to keep a constant vigil over its activities on the Asiatic continent, it vigorously opposed the plan. All mention of a Board of Reference was dropped from the Nine Power Treaty, but a new definition was given to the Open Door concept. The treaty required the signatories to respect China's territorial integrity, to refrain from interference in the growth of a stable government, and to take no action which would hamper equal economic opportunities for all.[6]

Progress was also made on the thorny Shantung issue despite the diametrically opposite positions taken by China and Japan. China insisted that there was no real legal basis for any of Japan's claims in Shantung. Japan pointed to the Versailles Treaty and adamantly refused to permit the conference to reopen the question of the legality of the Twenty-One Demands. Nevertheless, under pressure from Great Britain and the

United States, both China and Japan agreed to negotiate the Shantung problem under the eyes of "observers." In January, 1922, Japan's delegate, Foreign Minister Shidehara, made a conciliatory move. He announced that his country had no designs on either Chinese or Russian territory and would begin immediate withdrawal of its troops from Shantung. Under these circumstances, China had little choice but to agree to the Sino-Japanese Treaty of February 4, 1922, in which Japan promised to restore Shantung to China in full sovereignty and to give it a loan to enable it to buy the Tsinan-Tsingtao Railway.

By the various treaties which resulted from the Washington Conference, therefore, many of the most serious problems in the Pacific had been at least temporarily "frozen" and the international atmosphere had been eased. As one authority has expressed it:

> The treaties went as far as pen and ink could go to preserve a peace founded on such antithetical elements as those inherent in the *status quo* in the Far East.[7]

Japan's withdrawal of its military forces from Shantung, shortly after the Conference, and from Siberia in October, 1922, added to a new feeling of amity. The disarmament program also relieved the national expenditures of the five leading naval powers. There was general confidence that the treaty prohibiting new fortifications would be observed and that militarily the status quo would be maintained.

But conditions on the continent continued to be less reassuring. Propinquity, availability of venture capital, and readiness to make the most of China's endemic political instability were too great temptations for Japan's nationalists to withstand. Before they moved to secure extension of their rights in China, however, they received unexpected support for their policies because of America's new exclusion law. Whatever success the Washington Conference may have achieved in easing international tensions in the Pacific was soon to be dissipated by the effects of this exclusion law.

White Man's America

Discrimination against colored races in the United States was as old as the Republic. Slavery, which was an extreme form of discrimination, was abolished only after a civil war had devastated the South. In the far West, where the Oriental immigrants were concentrated, prejudice against them arose at an early date for both economic and emotional reasons. In the 1860's, the Central Pacific Railroad Company imported thousands of Chinese workers to provide cheap labor to construct the transcontinental line across California. By 1880, the economic competition created by the piteously low wages paid to Chinese laborers created the basis for an anti-Oriental movement. Two years later, both skilled and unskilled Chinese laborers were excluded from the United States in order to protect the American labor market.

As for Japanese laborers, they were first brought to the sugar cane and pineapple plantations of Hawaii on a contract basis and later came directly to the continental United States. By 1900, there were about 61,000 Japanese in the Hawaiian Islands, where they comprised the largest element in the population, and 24,000 on the continent. Most of the latter were on the West Coast but equaled only 1 per cent of the California population.[8]

Despite this comparatively small number of Japanese immigrants in California, a strong anti-Japanese movement emerged under the prodding of Mayor James D. Phelan of San Francisco. Mass meetings were held which demanded outright exclusion. The Japanese government moved, however, to check such an eventuality by discontinuing the issuance of passports for laborers to the United States. But the corrupt political situation in San Francisco and California only aggravated the anti-Japanese movement; the politicians used the anti-Oriental movement as a diversionary tactic to squelch criticism of their unscrupulous administration.

The movement reached its peak in October, 1906, when the San Francisco Board of Education passed a resolution excluding Orientals from the city's schools. Since there were only ninety-three persons affected by this order, it had obviously been motivated by racial prejudice against the Japanese. President Roosevelt, who considered the action an unnecessary affront against a sensitive people, was infuriated by this action. He threatened to sue the San Francisco Board of Education. In the meantime, he endeavored to persuade Japan to sign a treaty excluding its subjects from immigrating to the United States. When this move failed, he told the San Francisco Board that he would not go to court against it, providing it rescinded the segregation order in return for his halting immigration of Japanese laborers by executive action. The board finally agreed to this bargain.

To fulfill his promise, Roosevelt had to prevent immigration from two sources, namely, directly from Japan and indirectly from Hawaii and Canada. He achieved the first objective through diplomacy. Early in 1907, Japan agreed not to grant passports to either skilled or unskilled Japanese laborers to the mainland of the United States except to settled agriculturists. This action was formalized the next year by what came to be known as the Gentlemen's Agreement.[9] Henceforth, immigration directly from Japan ceased.

Roosevelt was equally successful in stopping immigrant Japanese from coming into the mainland of the United States from Hawaii and Canada. He persuaded Congress to adopt an amendment to the Immigration Law of 1907 making such entry illegal. But when the Democrats came to power in 1912 under the leadership of Woodrow Wilson, the tension over Japanese exclusion increased between the federal government and California. Phelan was again at the head of the exclusionist vanguard. He sponsored and secured passage of a state law whose purpose and intent was to keep Japanese subjects from owning land. The fact that the law classified them as aliens ineligible for citizenship did not deceive anyone, least of all the Japanese.

The question of exclusion of Oriental immigrants became acute again when the United States Congress began debate on a general immigration law. Mr. Phelan, who was by this time a U. S. Senator, had whipped up extensive support for an exclusion bill. On the other hand, there was a strong group in Congress opposed to any type of discriminatory immigration law. In February, 1924, Secretary of State Hughes wrote to Congressman Albert Johnson in an attempt to restrain Congress from taking precipitous action. Hughes pointed out that the passage of the exclusion bill which was before the House of Representatives was ill-advised and would undo much of the good will created by the Washington Conference.

When the House, ignoring these warnings, was on the point of passing this bill, the Japanese Ambassador protested against its discriminatory character. At this point, Hughes misjudged the mood of Congress. He thought that the antiexclusionist cause would be helped by sending the Ambassador's note to the Congress. The House reacted in exactly the opposite way. On April 12, 1924, it approved the bill with an exclusion clause attached to it. In the debate in the Senate, Henry Cabot Lodge twisted the Ambassador's note so that it appeared that he had maligned the United States. The Ambassador had said that while he did not question the right of any country to regulate immigration, he found it

> difficult to believe that it can be the intention of the people of your great country . . . to resort . . . to a measure which would not only seriously offend the just pride of a friendly nation . . . but would also seem to involve the question of good faith and therefore of the honor of their government. . . . I realize, as I believe you do, the grave consequences which the enactment of the measure retaining that particular clause would bring upon the otherwise happy and mutually advantageous relations between our two countries.[10]

Senator Lodge claimed that the term "grave consequences" implied a threat to the United States. The exclusionist movement spread like wildfire in the Senate which favored retention of the exclusion clause by a vote of 76:2.

The result was the exclusion of Japanese from entry into America. The reaction of the Japanese press was bitter, but on the whole, restrained.

Some Tokyo papers correctly called the bill inequitable and unjust; others described it as a deliberate slap in the face. Officially, the case was closed after the Japanese government sent a formal protest taking exception to the discriminatory aspects of the new law. Although some of them were too polite to say so, the Japanese people understood the action for just what it was—an act of discrimination provoked by an irrational, narrow-minded, militant group with a distorted sense of patriotism and by an emotional reaction in Congress to the explosive problem of race prejudice.

It was all the more difficult for the Japanese to accept this discriminatory treatment with equanimity because only a few months earlier the American people had generously contributed to the relief of those devastated on September 1, 1923, by the earthquake and fire in the Tokyo area. From the Exclusion Law of 1924 until the attack on Pearl Harbor on December 7, 1941, this American law was thrown in the faces of Japanese recruits and subjects alike as proof of the American attitude of disdain and superiority toward Japan. Pronouncements to the contrary by the State Department or by the American Ambassador, notwithstanding, the Japanese people were convinced that Americans wanted to discriminate against them. To the extent that this immigration law was used by the militarists to arouse anti-American hatred in the prewar years, it did contribute to "grave consequences."

National Politics and Expansion, 1924-29

With the passage in 1924 of the law which excluded Japanese from entry into the United States, the center of the stage shifts abruptly from Washington to Tokyo. The crucial issue during the next few years, the outcome of which was to determine the peace of the world, was whether the advocates of military expansionism or of international cooperation were to win control over the government. In terms of domestic politics, it was a question of whether the supporters of party cabinets and constitutional government could control effectively the proponents of Army control and direct action.

In the summer of 1924, conditions were more favorable to the former group than at any previous time. All of the older generation of Elder Statesmen had died and Saionji remained as the only regular member of the *Genrō*. He preferred a party system of government rather than a continuation of oligarchical control. Furthermore, the experiments during the past three years with nonparty cabinets had been most unsatisfactory. For example, during his Premiership of January-June, 1924, Viscount Kiyoura had failed completely to win the confidence of the people. Party members of the House of Representatives had refused flatly to cooperate with the Cabinet. They also united to combat the danger of the continuation of cabinets controlled by the oligarchs. Under the leadership of Katō Kōmei, President of the Kenseikai, the three leading parties in the House of Representatives took an unusually strong stand. They proclaimed:

1. The establishment of a system of party cabinets.
2. The suspension of the arbitrary and monopolistic power and special privilege of the oligarchs.
3. Joint action to achieve these purposes.
4. Repudiation of the Kiyoura government.[11]

This impressive demonstration of unity among the parties and the popular support which they received from the press forced the dissolution of Parliament at the end of 1924.

In the elections which followed, the political parties won 284 seats while the oligarchs mustered only 180. Among the former group, the Kenseikai's total of 153 was by far the largest number of any of the political parties. As President of the party, Katō became the logical choice for Prime Minister. He was, in many other respects, the natural choice. In 1916 he had hoped to succeed Ōkuma as Premier but had been snubbed and passed over by the Elder Statesmen, largely because of the fact that he was a party leader. Since that time, he had often challenged both the *Genrō* and the oligarchs in his fight for parliamentarianism. During World War I, he had refused to participate in the Cabinet's Advisory Council on Foreign Affairs on the grounds that it would compromise his position as a party politician.

On June 11, 1924, he finally achieved his long-sought dream. He was designated Prime Minister and began to put into practice the principle of party cabinets which he had so long advocated. For the next few years, therefore, party leaders supplanted the oligarchs in the key positions in the government, but basic policies differed little from previously.[12] In fact, during the next eight years, which saw the more or less normal operation of the principle of party cabinets, Japan began its invasion of Manchuria.

In view of the fact that the parties failed so miserably to check the growth of ultranationalism, the question arises as to why this was so. Why were the political leaders unable to develop parliamentary procedures and other checks which would have made it difficult, if not impossible, to dislodge them? While momentous social, economic, and political changes were taking place within Japan, why were these insufficient to create a political consciousness which would make the people insist on the creation and continuation of truly representative institutions? Did the party leaders rise to the challenge before them and produce the fearless leadership which the times required? Was the governmental structure such as to choke the growth of democratic processes? For example, did the Constitution, the basic laws, and precedents combine to make it inevitable that an oligarchical form of government should continue under a new type of leadership, the ultranationalists? Were outside forces such as to play into the hands of the nationalists and to discredit the leaders who championed democratic principles?

Some of these questions cannot be answered until the next chapter where the origins of the military occupation of Manchuria by Japan are discussed. On the other hand, a brief analysis of the most significant events of Katō's premiership will give some hint to the answers to these questions. In the first place, the radical movement and labor unrest which had appeared immediately after World War I gained momentum. In 1923, the year before Katō formed his Cabinet, there was a severe clash on May Day between the police and the radicals. Over 200 persons were arrested and the authorities made little effort to determine whether those arrested were real subversives and advocated overthrow of the government or whether they were exercising the privilege of freedom to express their criticism of the government.[13] The leader of the anarchists, Ōsugi Sakae, was killed. These acts increased the bitterness of those who considered themselves unfairly suppressed by the authorities. Such strikes, demonstrations, and overt acts as occurred were manifestations of a new ferment in society and a desire of the people for greater political rights.

Consequently, to meet this dissatisfaction, the Katō ministry sponsored a universal manhood suffrage law. Some party members of the House of Representatives, such as the liberal Ozaki Yukio (1860-1954), had been fighting unsuccessfully for several years to abolish the restrictions on the right to vote. Prime Minister Katō, who had likewise been eager to extend the franchise, capitalized on the majority which his coalition government commanded in the House of Representatives to obtain passage of a new suffrage law. This new law, which was promulgated on May 5, 1925, gave all male citizens above twenty-five years of age the right to vote. This legislation automatically increased the electorate from three to thirteen million, but the effects of the law were not felt until 1928 when the first election under the new law was held.

This step toward broader participation by the people in government was accompanied by an equally important measure which permitted the continuance of autocratic control. Katō and his colleagues had become frightened by the radical movement. They were also firm believers in a central government with strong executive powers supported by a national police. To counteract any ill effects which might result from granting the right of franchise to the adult male population, therefore, they gave the police full powers to cope with the radicals, the advocates of "dangerous thought," and subversives. A new Peace Preservation Law (*Jian Iji Hō*), which extended the authority of the police, was presented to Parliament while the Election Law was under consideration. Since the former acted as a counterbalance against the latter, both laws were passed.

The Peace Preservation Law was promulgated a week after the Election Law and became effective immediately. It provided ten years imprisonment for those convicted of joining societies or parties advocating alteration of the Constitution, of the existing form of government, or of the system of private ownership of property. Thus the Katō Cabinet, despite its emphasis on the principle of party cabinets and cabinet responsibility, followed the same pattern as Itō and the earlier oligarchs. If rights were granted the people, such as universal suffrage, new power was given the executive branch of the government to control the people.[14]

Another important social change which took place during the Katō Ministry was the reorganization of the Imperial Japanese Army. In line with the general trend toward retrenchment in armament expenditures launched by the Washington Naval Conference, general military expenditures decreased from 42 per cent of the national budget in 1922, to 27 per cent during Katō's Cabinet. This curtailment in expenditures for the armed services resulted in the abandonment of four divisions and the reduction of the standing army to seventeen divisions. Officers who were members of the disbanded divisions were not retired from active service. On the contrary, they were assigned to the middle and higher schools and to the universities to be in charge of the new compulsory military training in the schools.

These moves, rather than decreasing the militaristic character of the country, increased it. The reduced number of divisions was adequate for the defensive needs of the country. The money which was saved thereby was invested into new equipment which had been developed during and after World War I. The inauguration of nationwide military training within the schools, and assignment of regular Army officers to the schools exposed a far larger number of persons to militarism than heretofore had been the case. It afforded an excellent opportunity to inculcate into the youths' minds the philosophy of ultranationalism and of the invincibility of the Japanese armed forces.

Finally, these years saw a shift in the social composition of the personnel of the armed services. The predominant influence of leaders of the old warrior class, such as Yamagata, Kuroda, and Terauchi, from Chōshū, was waning. The new cadres of officers were composed increasingly of members from families of the mercantile or small land-owning class. They were not inhibited by personal loyalty to the oligarchs and became more and more dissatisfied with the corruption of the members of Parliament and with the collusion of the Cabinet with big business. They also opposed what they described as an unnecessarily soft policy toward China and toward the Soviet Union.

This criticism by the militarists of Katō's foreign policy was directed against Foreign Minister Shidehara. In general, he supported a conciliatory attitude toward both the Soviet Union and China. As for Japanese-Soviet relations, they had continued to be strained by the lack of a commercial treaty between the two countries, by Japanese demands for restitution for the massacre in 1920 of Japanese residents at Nikolaevsk, and by the presence of Japanese troops in the Soviet portion of Sakhalien. By January, 1925, Foreign Minister Shidehara had reached agreement with the Soviet Union on the most important outstanding issues. He announced that diplomatic relations between the two countries were to be resumed and that earlier fisheries agreements would be revised. In return for a Soviet promise to recognize the provisions of the Treaty of Portsmouth of 1905 (see page 243), Japan promised to withdraw its troops from Northern Sakhalien. By the end of the year, new contracts had been signed for Japanese to exploit petroleum, coal, and timber in the Maritime Provinces in Siberia and in Northern Sakhalien. Relations with the Soviet Union were better than at any time since the Revolution; diplomats appeared to be more successful than militarists in easing Soviet-Japanese tension. Yet the young officers feared that Japan had conceded too much and had revealed its weakness.

But Shidehara was criticized even more severely for his policy toward China. When he had promised at the Washington Conference that Japan would withdraw its troops from Shantung, he had aroused the enmity of his military colleagues who had dreams of the role Japan was destined to play on the continent. In 1925, when he refused to interfere in the civil war in Manchuria, the General Staff considered him an obstructionist. In that year, General Chang Tso-lin, who had exercised independent control over the three Manchurian provinces since 1922, was faced with a civil war. The Japanese commander of the Kwantung Army, who had jurisdiction over the Japanese-owned South Manchurian Railway, declared that the railroad zone was neutral. Since this order had prevented Chang's enemy from moving his troops on the railway, it contributed to Chang's victory.

The Japanese militarists then pressed Shidehara to obtain special concessions from Chang in return for the favor shown him. But Shidehara insisted that Japan should concentrate on the promotion of foreign trade and economic solidarity and should avoid unjust infringement on the interests of any nation. He refused to be a party to deals with Chinese war lords, even though Japan would obtain special privileges in Manchuria. If these views were to prevail, any expansionist dreams of the Kwantung

Army or of any other branch of the Japanese Imperial Army were in jeopardy. Thus Shidehara and his policies were anathema to the militarists.

After Katō's death at the end of January, 1926, it was only a matter of time before his opponents were able to force a change in the Cabinet and the appointment of a military man as Prime Minister. On April 20, 1927, General Tanaka Giichi, President of the Seiyūkai, was selected as Premier.[15] Since he was an army man who had consistently stood for a firm aggressive policy toward both Russia and China, he lost no time in reversing Shidehara's policy. Tanaka was convinced that the threatened unification of China under Chiang Kai-shek and the Kuomintang and recent events in Manchuria were a direct challenge to Japan. He deplored the steady increase in the Chinese population in the Manchurian provinces and a gradual development of a Chinese-owned railway system which could compete with the Japanese-owned South Manchurian Railway. Despite the autonomous control which Chang Tso-lin exerted over Manchuria, these manifestations of Chinese nationalism threatened Japan's special position.

By 1927, when Shanghai fell before the northward advancing troops of the new nationalist leader, Chiang Kai-shek, left-wing elements were in control of the Kuomintang. There had been violent antiforeign outbreaks in Nanking. Tanaka's military and civil advisers, particularly the leaders of the Kwantung Army in Liaotung, urged the necessity of positive action to protect Japanese life and property. The nearer Chiang came to Manchuria, the more concerned the Japanese became.

Prime Minister Tanaka, with the endorsement of his Cabinet, but without divulging his plans to Parliament, decided to dispatch Japanese troops to Shantung to check the advance of the Chinese nationalists. This action intensified an anti-Japanese boycott movement. On May 3, 1928, they clashed at Tsinan with the Kuomintang troops. Four days later, the Japanese commander issued an ultimatum demanding a Chinese apology for the incident, the immediate suspension of hostilities, the suppression of the anti-Japanese boycott, and the withdrawal of Chinese troops along the Tsingtao-Tsinan railroad. Faced with an attack from 25,000 Japanese troops, Chiang Kai-shek was forced to accede to these demands. These Japanese troops continued to straddle the key railroad junction to Peking and thus effectively stopped Chiang's northward advance and simultaneously prevented the union of the Kuomintang forces with those of Chang Tso-lin in Manchuria.

Although Tanaka temporarily avoided criticism of his policy by the adjournment of Parliament, he soon found himself a victim of circumstances. As champion of an expansionist policy, he had anticipated that if Chiang Kai-shek could be checked from advancing northward, then the Manchurian war lord, Chang Tso-lin, could be weaned away from the nationalists and could be won over to a policy of friendship to Japan. In other words, if Chang Tso-lin were willing to become a Japanese puppet, Chiang Kai-shek's new unification drive might come to naught. In any event, Japan would still have a comparatively free hand in Manchuria.

But Tanaka, like many of his predecessors, overestimated his ability to control his hot-headed subordinates and the willingness of a Chinese war lord to become a Japanese puppet. When the Japanese advised Chang to attack a recalcitrant general to the south of him, he refused. Piqued by this independent attitude and believing that his son would be easier to handle, a group of Japanese officers within the Kwantung Army plotted his murder. In early June, 1928, Chang's train was blown up as it crossed the tracks of the South Manchurian Railway.

Since one of the chief duties of the Kwantung Army was the protection of the South Manchurian Railway zone and since Chang was killed within that zone, the implication was clear. He had been murdered by the Japanese military. Prime Minister Tanaka was blamed for this lawless act. To avoid embarrassment, he gave no publicity to the circumstances surrounding Chang's murder. Actually, despite the fact that Tanaka was a general and favored an aggressive policy toward China, he had lost control of the extremists in the Imperial Army. When he insisted that the culprits be punished, his plea was vetoed by the Army Chief of Staff and others. They argued that disciplinary action against those responsible for Chang's murder would weaken the entire discipline of the Army.

What they were actually saying, however, was that there were independent elements in the Japanese Imperial Army, such as the officers of the Kwantung Headquarters, which were out of control and which must be given their own way. But Tanaka's critics would not be silenced and he was forced to resign in early July, 1929. On the basis of information available at the time of his resignation, it appeared as though the antiaggressive and moderate forces had won a victory. But time soon proved that the situation was otherwise.[16]

The Hamaguchi Ministry and the Last of Party Cabinets, 1929-31

The fate which befell Tanaka, a military man, was a mild preview of what was to confront the last of the party cabinets and the entire Japanese nation from 1929 to 1931. The murder of Chang Tso-lin by the Kwantung Army was nothing compared to its carefully executed plans to conquer Manchuria and North China by force of arms. Tanaka's political defeat was insignificant compared to the murder of the next Prime Minister, Hamaguchi Ōsachi, and the disintegration of the political parties, which left the operation of the central government in the hands of the military. Even though a combination of forces were eventually to eliminate the party cabinets and to extinguish the party movement, for a limited period the Hamaguchi Cabinet was able to challenge successfully both the oligarchs and the militarists.

When General Tanaka resigned, the principle was continued of selecting the leader of the main opposition party to become the next Prime Minister. Thus Hamaguchi Ōsachi, President of the Minseitō party, was asked to form a Cabinet.[17] He immediately selected persons for his Cabinet who were leaders in his party. In both domestic problems and foreign relations, the Hamaguchi government, formed on July 2, 1929, adopted policies diametrically opposed to its predecessor. For example, the new Cabinet advocated retrenchment in national expenditures, a balanced budget, a return to the gold standard, and governmental reforms leading toward efficiency and broader powers for the legislative branch of the government. In international affairs, with the appointment of Shidehara as Foreign Minister, there was a return to a conciliatory policy toward China.

On the domestic front, Hamaguchi followed a financial policy which went to the heart of the nation's fiscal instability. He slashed government spending wherever possible. Salaries of government employees were reduced 10 per cent. Savings were advocated in military expenditures. Finance Minister Inouye maintained that Japan should honor its international obligations and should preserve the stability of the yen in the foreign exchange market. Consequently, in January, 1930, he ordered a return to the gold standard.

Unfortunately for the future of party governments and of democratic elements in Japan, this policy could not have come at a worse time. The greatest world depression of modern times had just begun and world prices had dropped. For a country like Japan, which was so dependent on foreign trade, it spelled disaster. All of Inouye's policies, even though they may have been basically sound, aggravated the situation and Japan suffered severely from the effects of depression.[18] Before these ill effects made an appreciable imprint on the nation, however, Hamaguchi had strengthened his political position in a national election. His Minseitō increased its representation in the lower house of Parliament from 217 to 273 and thus obtained an absolute majority.

In reference to the independence of the Prime Minister and the Cabinet from the oligarchs and the military, the high point was reached when Hamaguchi obtained approval of the London Naval Treaty. Consistent with his general interest in a reduction of naval expenses, Hamaguchi agreed in October, 1929, to Japan's attendance at the London Naval Conference under certain specific conditions. He indicated that Japan would be willing to continue to agree to a smaller navy than Great Britain or the United States, providing the accepted ratio did not weaken Japan's power of self-defense. The Japanese delegation to the Conference, therefore, insisted on a 10:7 ratio between the United States and Japan in cruisers and auxiliary craft but with no limitation on submarines. The delegations from the United States and Great Britain refused to agree to this percentage. It was apparent, therefore, that unless Japan agreed to a compromise formula the conference would fail.

Hamaguchi and his Cabinet were interested in international peace and in the reduction of military and naval expenditures to a minimum. Convinced that the actual needs for national defense required only a navy of a ratio of 10:6 with the United States, the Cabinet approved the lower ratio as well as a proposal that no battleships be built for six years. Despite strenuous objections from the Navy, in April, 1930, the Japanese delegates signed the treaty containing these provisions.

But Hamaguchi's troubles over the London Naval Treaty had only just begun. In the first place, he was faced with a hostile press which sympathized with the Navy and argued that 60 per cent was too low a parity to maintain an adequate defense. In Parliament, despite the majority which his party held in the House of Representatives, he was severely criticized for capitulating to American pressure. But the strongest opposition came from the military and from the Privy Council.

From the standpoint of political history, the question was broader than the mere acceptance or rejection of the London Treaty. The central issue was whether or not a Prime Minister and his Cabinet, which apparently had the confidence of a majority of the people as evidenced by the elections, could successfully challenge the militarists and the oligarchs. Since the Constitution provided that the Emperor exercised his treaty-making powers on the advice of the Cabinet alone, Hamaguchi insisted that the Cabinet did not need the approval of the Navy for the treaty. In other words, the military members of the Cabinet did not have a veto on matters of foreign policy. His position was solidified when he forced the resignation of the top members of the Navy General Staff. In July, 1930, the treaty was presented to the Privy Council for ratification. When questioned by the Council concerning his attitude toward the Supreme War Council's latest plans for national defense, Hamaguchi refused to divulge the contents of a memorial on the matter which he had presented to the Emperor. Even though the military had serious objections to the London Naval Treaty, the Premier insisted that it be ratified. On October 1, 1930, the Privy Council reluctantly approved it.

But the victory of Hamaguchi over the military and the oligarchs was of short duration. The Seiyūkai party did its best to embarrass the Cabinet for having neglected to follow the advice of the military experts. The retrenchment in government expenditures, the abolition of the gold embargo, and the world depression were causing widespread unemployment and economic stagnation. The expansionists and ultranationalists in the innumerable secret societies and in key positions in the Imperial Army were convinced that a continuation of Hamaguchi's conciliation toward China and disregard for the opinions of the Chiefs of Staff challenged the foundation of their power. A large proportion of the members of Parliament, the press, and the public at large believed that Japan should continue to have a privileged position in China. They were skeptical of the value of a policy of conciliation.

As was so often the case in Japan's modern century, a single, lawless act dramatized a widespread dissatisfaction with new policies and caused an immediate reaction against them. In mid-November, 1930, while waiting in the Tokyo station, Hamaguchi was shot by a fanatical patriot and member of a nationalist society. Although he survived for nearly a year, this attack shattered his leadership and destroyed at a single blow the principle of supremacy of the civilian branch of the government over the military and over the oligarchs. His immediate successors were unable to hold the Minseitō party together. Of even greater significance was the inability of the party leaders to stop the drive of the Japanese military in China set off by their coup in Mukden on September 18, 1931. A. Morgan Young, one of the most fearless and objective contemporary foreign observers, expressed it:

> Hamaguchi died on August 26th, and a month later all that he had striven for was flung to the winds, and all that he had saved was squandered.[19]

Notes

1. Hara Kei (1856-1921) was born in Morioka. After graduation from college he was a newspaper reporter. From 1881 to 1896 he served in various government posts, including Minister *ad interim* in Paris. He then returned to newspaper work, but in 1900 became Executive Secretary of the Seiyūkai party under Itō. His first Cabinet post was as Communications Minister in the fourth Itō Cabinet in 1900. He was elected to Parliament two years later. He served as Home Minister for both Saionji and Yamamoto and in 1914 became president of the party. He was killed by an assassin November 4, 1921. His diary, *Hara Kei Nikki* (Tokyo: Kangen Sha, 1950-51), contains invaluable material on his activities.

2. There were three nonparty Cabinets from June, 1922, to June, 1924. The first of these (June 12, 1922—September 2, 1923) was that of Admiral Katō Tomosaburō, Naval Minister in the four previous Cabinets and head of the Japanese Delegation to the Washington Conference. With his death from natural causes in August, 1923, his Cabinet resigned. It was followed by that of Admiral Yamamoto Gombei (September 2, 1923—January 7, 1924), which had to struggle with the problems created

by the Tokyo earthquake and fire of September 1, 1923, and which resigned after an attempt was made on the life of the Prince Regent. Viscount Kiyoura, President of the Privy Council, was next appointed Prime Minister and survived until June 11, 1924, when he gave way to Katō Kōmei's party Cabinet, and Japan had another short period of party governments.

3. The conditions laid down by the United States included the pooling of preferences and options of any member banks, the exclusive support of the member governments for the banks in the Consortium, and the maintenance of the administrative integrity and independence of China by all members. See A. Whitney Griswold, *The Far Eastern Policy of the United States* (New York: Harcourt, Brace & Co., Inc., 1938), pp. 223 ff.

4. For example, the five powers (France, Great Britain, Italy, Japan, and the United States) considered the question of limitations of armaments and signed a treaty thereon. Four of these powers (all but Italy) agreed to a Treaty on Insular Possessions in the Pacific. All nine powers negotiated the Nine Power Treaty on Principles and Policies Concerning China. See R. L. Buell, *The Washington Conference* (New York: Appleton, 1922) and Griswold, *Far Eastern Policy* for general surveys. Official documents and texts of the treaties, from which subsequent quotations are taken, are to be found in United States Senate, 67th Congress, 2d Session, No. 126. *Conference on the Limitations of Armaments* (Washington: U. S. Government Printing Office, 1922).

5. The final ratio for capital ships for the five powers was as follows: Great Britain (5), United States (5), Japan (3), France (1.75), and Italy (1.75). The following areas were specifically mentioned as falling under the status quo provisions: the Aleutian Islands, Guam, the Philippines, Hong Kong and British Islands east of 110° meridian, the Kuriles, Bonins, Ryūkyū Islands, Formosa, and Pescadores.

6. Because of the frequency with which parts of this treaty were quoted in the various official exchanges during the next two decades with Japan, some of the clauses of the treaty follow:

Article I.

The Contracting Powers, other than China, agree:

(1) To respect the sovereignty, the independence, and the territorial and administrative integrity of China;

(2) To provide the fullest and most unembarrassed opportunity to China to develop and maintain for herself an effective and stable government;

(3) To use their influence for the purpose of effectually establishing and maintaining the principle of equal opportunity for the commerce and industry of all nations throughout the territory of China;

(4) To refrain from taking advantage of conditions in China in order to seek special rights and privileges which would abridge the rights of subjects or citizens of friendly States, and from countenancing actions inimical to the security of such States.

. . . .

Article III.

With a view to applying more effectually the principles of the Open Door or equality of opportunity in China for the trade and industry of all nations, the Contracting Powers, other than China, agree that they will not seek, nor support their respective nationals in seeking—

(a) any arrangement which might purport to establish in favor of their interests any general superiority of rights with respect to commercial or economic development in any designated region of China;
(b) any such monopoly or preference as would deprive the nationals of any other Power of the right of undertaking any legitimate trade or industry in China, or of participating with the Chinese government . . . in any category of public enterprise, or which . . . is calculated to frustrate the practical application of the principle of equal opportunity.

7. Griswold, *Far Eastern Policy,* p. 331.

8. The problem of the Japanese in America has been more than adequately covered in numerous studies. By far the most inspiring book, which brings the problem down to the relocation of Japanese throughout America after World War II, is Bradford Smith, *Americans From Japan* (Philadelphia: J. B. Lippincott Co., 1949). For tables on the census of Chinese and Japanese in the United States, see R. L. Buell, "Japanese Immigration," World Peace Foundation Pamphlets, VV, and Griswold, *op. cit.,* chapter ix.

9. The Gentlemen's Agreement of 1908 was incorporated into the United States–Japanese Commercial Treaty of 1911. In the latter, the Japanese Government agreed "to maintain with equal effectiveness the limitations and control which they have for the past three years exercised in regulation of the emigration of laborers to the United States." The actual net increase of immigrants for a fifteen-year period had been 8,681, all of whom were women. After 1920, even the admittance of women, so-called "picture brides," was forbidden.

10. House Report No. 350, 68th Congress; or Buell, *op. cit.,* pp. 358-62.

11. Itō, Masanori, *Katō Takaaki* (Tokyo: Katō Hoku Denki Hensan iin-Kai, 1928), II, 460.

12. The Kenseikai, which was formed in 1916, remained in power until April, 1927. Katō's first Cabinet (June 11, 1924—August 2, 1925) had representatives from the other two parties which had joined in the declaration. Takahashi Korekiyo was Minister of Agriculture and Commerce and Inukai Tsuyoshi was Minister of Communications. Katō's second Cabinet was composed exclusively of Kenseikai members except for the service ministers. When he died on January 28, 1926, he was succeeded by his Home Minister, Wakatsuki, who was forced to resign on April 20, 1927, over disagreement with the Privy Council on financial policies. Tanaka Giichi, President of the Seiyūkai, was Premier from April 20, 1927, to July 2, 1929. He was succeeded by the Minseitō Cabinets of Hamaguchi, Wakatsuki, and Inukai until May 26, 1932, when a nationalist Cabinet was formed.

13. Other less extreme examples concerned outstanding professors. In 1920, Professor Morito Tatsuo of Tokyo Imperial University wrote an article on the social ideas of Kropotkin. He emphasized the advisability of achieving individual freedom but the authorities claimed that he had presented communism and anarchism in a favorable light. The court ruled that his writings disturbed the public peace and order. He was dismissed from the university, fined, and imprisoned. The publisher of the article, Ōuchi Hyoe, was accused as an accomplice. Four years later, Professor Yoshino Sakuzō also considered it expedient to resign from the same university because of his writings. Several years earlier, he had criticized the influence of the military in governmental affairs and claimed that neither the House of Peers nor the Privy Council spoke for the people. He was branded as a radical. The argument still continues as to whether that was a fair accusation. For example, in 1952, at the annual meeting of the Political Science Association of Japan, Shinobu

Seisaburō, an outspoken leftist, claimed that Yoshino was nothing more than a liberal. His opponent, Kaji Ryūmei, argued that Yoshino was at least a Socialist.

14. For translations of the first three articles of the law, see Harold S. Quigley, *Japanese Government and Politics, An Introductory Study* (New York: Century, 1932), pp. 57-58.

15. For Tanaka's role in the Siberian Expedition, see above, p. 286. Several months earlier, Tanaka had withdrawn support from Katō. He was an acceptable choice to the military, but was less acceptable to the people because of scandals in which he had been involved while Minister of War (1918-21). He had been charged with having used 3 million yen of the Ministry's funds to bribe parliamentary and party leaders. He attempted to bolster his popularity by the appointment of Takahashi Korekiyo to be Minister of Finance. Since his party controlled only a minority in the House of Representatives, he dissolved Parliament in January, 1928, to avoid the passage of a vote of nonconfidence. The elections which followed were the first under the Universal Manhood Suffrage Law. Although Home Minister Suzuki did his best to assure the success of the Seiyūkai's candidates, Tanaka was able to win only 219 seats, while the Kenseikai elected 217 to the House of Representatives. Thus Tanaka could not command an absolute majority. The most important of the proletariat parties, the Shakai Minshūtō, with a membership of about two-thirds of organized labor, elected eight persons to Parliament. In the next session, Tanaka barely avoided a nonconfidence vote.

16. The Japanese public had no way of knowing at the time of Tanaka's resignation that his downfall was due to insubordination within the Army. Having been a general, he was identified with expansionism and militarism. He made no effort to gain popular favor by accusing his colleagues of disobedience. Perhaps it would have been futile to do so, since his willingness to agree to the Pact of Paris had only increased his woes. Some of his enemies accused him of usurping the Imperial prerogatives. Faced with unpopularity on all sides, he was content to retire from public life and died shortly thereafter in the arms of his mistress, possibly from suicide.

17. Hamaguchi (1870-1931) was Premier from July 2, 1929, to Nov. 15, 1930, and from March 9 to April 14, 1931. In the interim, following the attack on his life on November 14, 1930, Shidehara acted as Premier ad interim. When Hamaguchi resigned on April 14, 1931, because of declining health, the new President of the Minseitō, Wakatsuki, formed another party cabinet which was to survive until December 13, 1931. Technically, therefore, the Wakatsuki Cabinet was the last party cabinet. The Minseitō was the successor to Katō's Kenseikai and received its support largely from the Mitsubishi financial interests, just as the Seiyūkai was supported by the rival Mitsui combine. This intimate connection between parties and the *Zaibatsu* (financial combines) is graphically demonstrated by the family relationship of the Finance Minister with the leading Zaibatsu families. Under Hamaguchi and Wakatsuki, Inouye Junnosuke, son-in-law of the owner of the Mitsubishi, was Minister of Finance.

18. Since the economic position of Japan was one of the important factors which enabled the military to gain control of both domestic and foreign policies in 1931, a general analysis of the nation's economic potentialities is postponed until the next chapter. (See below, p. 322 ff.) Suffice it to note at this point that exports during 1930 dropped 32 per cent and that the value of silk exports, the largest trade item, was only half that of the previous year. Thus the world depression added to the Cabinet's woes, rather than improving its popularity. For a concise and enlighten-

ing account, see Rōyama Masamichi, *Seiji Shi, Gendai Nihon Bummei Shi,* II (Tokyo: Tōyō Keizai Shimpo Sha, 1950), p. 449 *et seq.*

19. Mr. Young, an Englishman, was owner and editor of the *Japan Chronicle.* He continued his attacks on antidemocratic aspects of Japan long after the Manchurian Incident of September, 1931, and after all other foreign or Japanese editorial criticism of militarism within Japan had been silenced. See A. Morgan Young, *Imperial Japan, 1926-1938* (New York: William Morrow & Co., Inc., 1938), p. 61.

17

MILITARISM AND AGGRESSION IN CHINA, 1931-1937

The successful coup d'état of the Japanese military in Manchuria in September, 1931, was caused by events of even more importance than the death of Premier Hamaguchi. While he was indispensable for the continued supremacy of his party, his successors might have been able to control the military if other forces had not been stacked against them. Unfortunately for democratic processes within Japan, for the unification of China, and for the peace of Asia and of the world, the depression only strengthened the hands of the militarists. As economic conditions worsened in Japan, ultranationalists found a receptive audience for their grandiose plans of conquest which promised prestige, wealth, and power for the Empire. Furthermore, this active Japanese expansionism emerged concurrently with a new movement for the unification of China under the leadership of Generalissimo Chiang Kai-shek. When he seriously threatened to incorporate Manchuria into China as an integral part of the Republic, he aroused the Japanese militarists.

The imaginative leaders of the Kwantung Army, which was primarily responsible for protecting Japanese interests in South Manchuria, interpreted these developments as a threat to the special privileges of themselves and of their nation. Inasmuch as they were convinced that their own government leaders were more likely to hinder rather than to help them, they acted on their own initiative. When the Japanese people realized that the military alone had a plan to solve the economic and international crisis which faced the nation, they followed this leadership. As the military successes on the Asiatic continent were ascribed to the divine attributes of the nation and of its sovereign, the Emperor's subjects willingly acquiesced in whatever demands were made of them. The history of the years between the coup in Manchuria in September, 1931, and the outbreak of war in North China in July, 1937, therefore, is that of these demands. It is also an account of how the nation accepted the philosophy of the ambitious and aggressive military and civilian leaders and of how it willingly followed them into war.

Effect of the World Depression

By the summer of 1931 the world depression had placed severe strains on the entire nation. Japan was just completing a long period of capitalist expansion begun under the stimulus of the victory over China in 1895. World War I had enlarged its productive capacity. But the end of hostilities had necessitated the development of new markets for finished goods in order to produce sufficient foreign exchange to purchase imports of staple foods. Since adequate foreign markets could not be maintained and commodity prices at home rose beyond the reach of the domestic purchaser, a postwar liquidation of many small companies ensued.

During the decade of 1920-30, general economic conditions fluctuated but certain features of the economy became accentuated. There was a general concentration of capital into the hands of a few powerful financial concerns or combines (the *zaibatsu*). For example, by 1921, five of the largest coal mining companies, which included the subsidiaries of some of the biggest combines, produced 41 per cent of the total annual coal output. New industries, such as chemical fertilizers and rayon, were encouraged by protective tariffs. From 1913 to 1923, mass production and greater mechanization notably increased output. The production of pig iron, steel, and electric power doubled in quantity and that of machine tools nearly quadrupled in value. By 1927, overexpansion and a rise in national indebtedness to over 5 billion yen caused a financial crisis and several bank failures.

One of the basic policies of the Hamaguchi Cabinet, which took office in July, 1929, was retrenchment and the stabilization of the national economy. Hence, Hamaguchi insisted on a return to the gold standard and a tightening of Japanese money. Unfortunately for him, this move coincided with the spread of the world depression. The prosperity boom collapsed in the United States in October, 1929, and its repercussions spread to Europe. They reached Japan about the same time that it was beginning to feel the effects of the return to the gold standard. Japanese goods, which now sold at prices determined by the gold value of the yen, were at a disadvantage in international markets. The demands in America for raw silk, the largest single export item, fell rapidly. Domestic purchasing power was not sufficiently strong to take up the slack. The unfavorable balance in foreign trade quickly increased. This situation demanded heavy exports of gold specie which rose from 276 million yen in 1930 to 433 million yen in 1931.[1] In other words, the Hamaguchi government could not have chosen a worse time to advocate retrenchment and the return to the gold standard.

Although the depression was late in starting in Japan, it developed rapidly. The government's attempts at rationalization of industry made the industrialists amenable to outside control. The danger of bankruptcy enhanced the tendency toward amalgamation. Society became polarized.

A few exorbitantly rich families controlled a series of subsidiary companies; the farmers, workers, and small businessmen became cogs in the national economy with little voice in its operation. An excess labor population and the general depression kept wages down. A strong, independent, liberal-minded middle class was largely nonexistent. On the whole, the future appeared gloomy to labor and management alike. When the Army, or extreme elements in certain sections of it, predicted that economic exploitation and military expansion on the mainland of Asia would solve Japan's problems, many persons considered them to be prophets.

Furthermore, in addition to the havoc caused by a world depression, a rapidly increasing population had already overtaxed the country's food supply. From a re-examination of the domestic supply and demand of rice (Table V, page 265), it will be observed that after 1920 the steadily increasing population and the limited availability of new lands for cultivation, caused a decline in the per capita production of rice and a drastic increase in rice imports. By 1930, when the world depression and the Hamaguchi policies were paralyzing the Empire's economy, the average annual increase in population amounted to 942,000, and rice imports equaled 42.5 million bushels or 12 per cent of the total amount consumed. Fortunately for Japan, most of the rice imported came from Korea and Formosa, so that a minimum of foreign exchange was needed. But even these areas could not be expected to keep up with the new demands made by an increase in the population of a million persons yearly.

Another economic and social aspect of the population problem was the inability of the national economy to absorb each year approximately 450,000 new workers looking for employment. This increase in the labor force posed an almost insurmountable problem in normal times; it caused a national crisis in years of depression. Finally, although the government had reduced its expenses, it had not lowered the tax burden. The farmer found himself caught, therefore, in a squeeze between the pressure from constant taxes and a reduction in his income. Silk prices had fallen 50 per cent and rice prices had declined almost the same amount.[2] The rural debt rose rapidly, taxes were in arrears, more farmers sold their daughters in prostitution, and tenants sought redress from high rents by resorting to organized tenancy disputes.

In 1931, whether considered from the economic, social, or political point of view, Japan was psychologically ready for momentous events and for an imaginative leadership. For the unemployed, for the debt-ridden farmer, for the low-salaried worker, and for the student who saw little chance of employment after graduation, Marxism and communism had their appeal. For the officers in the lower echelons in the Imperial Army and for the recruits in the ranks, revitalized concepts of a divine mission in Asia and of state control of society appeared to be the salvation for Japan. It was the irony of fate that Premier Hamaguchi could not provide the leadership required to challenge these concepts successfully. His financial policies, which advocated reduced expenditures to balance the budget, were theoretically sound. They gave added importance to the reductions in naval expenditures permitted by the London Naval Treaty. But the effects of the world depression were overriding and turned the people against the government's policies. His death deprived his party of its outstanding leader just when he was needed most.

To add to the tragedy is the fact that while Japan's economic plight seemed gloomy, it was not without hope. Despite a world depression and an ever increasing population in a land with limited resources, raw materials for home industries were at hand in Manchuria and North China.[3] These areas were comparatively rich in strategically important materials such as iron, coking coal, and commercial salt. The Netherlands East Indies had an abundance of oil and rubber. If normal trade relations could have been maintained with these regions, if access to their raw materials could have been assured, there would have been no compelling need for military expansion. The Asiatic market had been important for the purchase of Japanese exports of consumers goods. Exports of cotton goods to China, India, and the Netherlands Indies had increased steadily. In 1929, total exports to China and India had equaled 30 per cent of the total.[4] It was conceivable that these exports could have been increased.

But the advocates of military expansion used the rapidly increasing tensions between China and Japan as an excuse for a bold, positive policy. They argued that conditions in China made it imperative that appropriate steps should be taken to gain political control over the areas on the Asiatic continent in which these important resources were to be found. As a state of emergency developed, their arguments took on added meaning.

Japanese Ultranationalism Confronts Chinese Unification

Thus, though the world depression was increasing Japan's distress, other forces were to contribute to the rapid acceptance by practically all groups in the nation of an aggressive foreign policy and of a form of state socialism. Unfortunately for the peace of the world, the depression coincided with the emergence of two other conflicting forces. These forces were a new nationalism and movement for unification in China and an expansive, irrational, all-inclusive ultranationalism in Japan. It is obvious from previous references to Chinese-Japanese relations that one of the constant aims of Japan's foreign policy had been to obtain and then to solidify special privileges on the Asiatic mainland. This objective had been comparatively easy to achieve, despite foreign intervention, so long as China continued to be politically unstable and disunited.

But conditions were rapidly changing under the leadership of Chiang Kai-shek. By 1928, he had largely pacified northern China and had moved his capital to Nanking. Even the young Manchurian war lord, Chang Hsueh-liang, whom the Japanese military had expected to be able to control after they had killed his father (see page 313), had sworn allegiance to the Nationalist Government and had defied Japan. The political unification of China was closer than it had been for many generations. China had also won some notable diplomatic victories under the impetus of a nationalist resurgence. Great Britain had relinquished its concessions in five Chinese cities; the United States had been only the first of several Western powers to grant China tariff autonomy. By the summer of 1931, plans were afoot for the abolition of extraterritoriality. In a word, China appeared to be on the threshold of a new era in which it would guide its own destinies.

In this task it had the blessing and protection of the Nine Power Treaty signed at the Washington Conference nearly a decade earlier. But this independence from foreign domination could not be complete until Japan's special position in Manchuria had been eliminated. Consequently, a concerted effort was made by the Chinese Nationalist Party (Kuomintang) to integrate Manchuria into the rest of China. Both political and economic means were taken to achieve this objective. In the first place, a Chinese railway system was gradually constructed to compete with the Japanese-owned South Manchurian Railway. A special system of preferential tariff agreements was applied to the various Chinese railways which tended to siphon the freight through these lines to the seaboard exit at Newchang. With the passing of each month, the Japanese-owned South Manchurian Railway increasingly felt the adverse effects of this plan.[5] In the second place, the Kuomintang was sending its organizers to propagandize the schools and to cement the bonds between Nanking and Mukden. As in the case of the competition of the two railway systems, time was on the side of China rather than Japan. The Chinese population had been rapidly increasing and the Japanese had difficulty in buying land. Finally, Chang Hsueh-liang refused to negotiate with the Japanese on any Manchurian issues. He insisted that all matters should be referred to the Nationalist government at Nanking.

Just as the concept of nationalism was taking hold in China, an ultranationalism was firing the imagination of the new civilian and military leaders in Japan. This new ultranationalism, which was redefined as time passed and as new emergencies arose, won acceptability in direct proportion to Chinese unification and to the growth of an anti-Japanese movement. Japanese nationalism also evolved from the reaction against the strengthening of the political parties, against the Cabinet's acceptance of disarmament, and against the increased popularity of the radicals. Since all of these trends were accelerated in the summer of 1931, an explosion at some point seemed more than likely. In fact, in view of the variety and number of the ultranationalist groups, it was surprising that the situation did not get out of hand sooner.

Advocacy of military expansion was not new in Japan. Many of the leaders of the Meiji Restoration such as Kido, Itō, and Yamagata had been influenced in their school years by Yoshida Shōin, who had urged the conquest of Korea and Manchuria. Members of secret societies or their hirelings had gladly intimidated the socialists and other radicals who dared to challenge the wisdom of colonialism. When the founders of the strongest ultranationalist societies were able to convert some of the military leaders to their views, these groups became a determining force in Japanese history.

One of the most important ultranationalists was Kita Ikki (1884-1937). Impetuous and egocentric, Kita advocated a type of state socialism which attempted to harmonize nationalism, liberalism, and individualism. In his *General Outline for the Reconstruction of Japan*,[6] he set forth his program for a social revolution in which the nation was to be reconstructed by the military and by an awakened citizenry. Emphasizing the importance of a tightly knit elite group of leaders for his movement, Kita recommended that the Emperor suspend the Constitution, dissolve the Diet and the Privy Council, and declare martial law. A military junta, to be elected from reserve army officers, would then run the government. Japan's economic ills would be solved by the expropriation by the government of all private property above a fixed amount. Areas such as Manchuria and Siberia would be conquered by force to augment the paucity of natural resources. Through his Society to Preserve the National Essence (Yūzonsha), he exerted a direct influence on many of the hot-headed expansionists, especially the young army officers. Similarly, one of his disciples, Ōkawa Shūmei formed another nationalist group in 1924 whose purpose was to restore "idealism and spiritualism" to Japanese life. Many of the leading political figures and members of the ruling clique of army officers, such as General Araki Sadaō, were admirers of Ōkawa and were members of his group.[7]

Both the effectiveness and strength of this new nationalism is illustrated by a brief description of the plot of March, 1931. Kita and a small group of his most ardent pupils had decided that the time had come to stage a coup d'état to overthrow the government of Hamaguchi and to place it in the firm hands of the generals. The plan called for an attack on the headquarters of the political parties and for a demonstration by 10,000 rightists. The demonstrators were to give mass support to General Ugaki Kazushige and a group of rightist generals who were to appear in the Diet

Building. Ugaki would then announce the formation of a new Cabinet on the grounds that the people had lost confidence in both Parliament and the Cabinet. But Ugaki refused to carry out the role assigned to him by Kita and his group. Consequently some of the other leaders withdrew their support on the grounds that conditions were too immature for such a plot. The whole affair was discovered prior to its execution, but those army officers who were intent on some type of direct action only bided their time.[8]

With such a psychological attitude prevalent among the young army officers, especially those assigned to the Kwantung Army in Manchuria, it was not difficult for them to find what they believed to be a *casus belli* in almost any independent act by the Chinese. Traditional Japanese interests in Manchuria were bound to clash with the Chinese Nationalists' attempts to integrate South Manchuria with the Nanking regime. These basic antagonisms began to explode into incidents which occurred at ever increasing frequency.

In July, 1931, the Chinese residents of southeastern Manchuria revolted against the encroachments of Korean landowners. The Chinese resented the fact that the Koreans, as Japanese subjects, enjoyed extraterritorial rights and protection by Japan and hence were receiving preferential treatment. Unimportant in itself, the incident led to anti-Chinese riots in Korea and to a retaliatory anti-Japanese boycott in China. Negotiations to settle this incident had barely begun when reports trickled in from Inner Mongolia that a Japanese intelligence officer, a Captain Nakamura, had been killed in June by Chinese troops. Nakamura's colleagues, who were imbued with the ultranationalism of Ōkawa, argued that the incident revealed Chinese duplicity and hence the need to settle the Manchurian issue by force. They inflamed Japanese public opinion by insisting that Nakamura was a civilian making a scholarly study and they challenged their own Foreign Office to force a favorable reply out of the Chinese government.

Simultaneously, responsible members of the Army were openly expressing their approval of direct action. For example, in early August, 1931, the Minister of War, Minami Jirō, at a meeting of Army and Divisional Commanders, spoke of the gravity of conditions in Manchuria and of the possibility that Japan might reluctantly have to use force to bring about a favorable settlement. He also attacked "the outsiders in irresponsible positions" who dared to argue in favor of the reduction of armaments and against the Army's plans for expansion. Although he mentioned no names, his audience knew that he referred to the Prime Minister and the civilian members of the Cabinet. A large section of the press supported the Army. While Premier Wakatsuki recognized the seriousness of this attack against him and his Foreign Minister, he did not dare to rebuke General Minami.

The Prime Minister is reported to have stated that he did not wish to criticize the War Minister for fear of the latter resigning and thus jeopardizing the passage of the budget through Parliament. Rumors were also plentiful that the ultranationalists were plotting to have their fellow sympathizers appointed to key positions within the Imperial Palace. Near the end of August, 1931, after reports from Manchuria indicated insubordination by young officers in connection with a "police action," or the suppression by the Japanese of local resistance, Premier Wakatsuki expressed his concern over this matter to the War Minister. He told the War Minister that the Emperor desired to keep on friendly terms with China. He concluded his interview with Minami by saying that Japan wanted to go to war only as a last resort. Apparently, the Premier realized that his entreaties would probably be useless and that the young officers were, in fact, out of control. He feared, worst of all, that Minami and the other Army leaders did not have the inclination to try to stop them.[9]

The Military Occupation of Manchuria, September 18, 1931—January, 1932

If War Minister Minami knew of the plans of his fellow officers in the Kwantung Army in Manchuria to manufacture an incident and thus force the military occupation of that entire area, he refused to divulge these plans to the Prime Minister. It is conceivable that the War Minister might not have known how, when, or where a specific group of officers intended to stage or manufacture an incident which would force the issue. On the other hand, it is inconceivable that he was not aware of the plans which the Chiefs of Staff had developed for the military occupation of Manchuria in case an emergency arose. It also seems likely that he awaited anxiously for some incident, regardless if its nature, which could be used as the pretext for the recourse to force, a possibility about which he had spoken in August. This likelihood is borne out by the report of a visit of the War Minister to the Elder Statesman, Saionji. At that meeting in early September, 1931, Saionji reprimanded Minami for permitting the use of hoodlums and "Fascist gangsters" in Manchuria and Mongolia. The latter readily agreed that it was an unfortunate practice and forthwith did nothing about it. In other words, Minami's position, his past attitude toward the Manchurian problem, and his disdain shown to the civil officials in the government, force one to conclude that he condoned the action of his subordinates.

It is unlikely, however, that all of the events in the first three weeks of September, 1931, will ever be known. But certain facts and their catastrophic effect on world peace are clear. There was mounting support for the insistence by important Army officials that the unsettled questions with China, of which the Nakamura case was the most dramatic, should be settled by force. Colonel Doihara, the Resident Officer of Mukden, who was summoned to Tokyo on September 15, told the press that he favored this policy.

Some of his colleagues took him literally. Sometime between 10:00 and 10:30 P.M. on September 18, 1931, an explosion occurred on or near the South Manchurian Railroad north of Mukden, within the zone protected by the Kwantung Army. Nevertheless, the southbound express from Changchun arrived in Mukden on time at 10:30 P.M. Immediately thereafter and almost simultaneously, over 10,000 Japanese troops in Manchuria from Changchun to Port Arthur were brought into action. When the citizens of Mukden awoke the next morning, they found their city occupied by Japanese soldiers.

By midmorning additional troops had begun to concentrate in northern Korea. In Geneva, the Council of the League of Nations was told by the Japanese delegate that his government had taken all measures possible to prevent a local incident from spreading and would do everything possible to relieve the situation. In Changchun, Chinese troops offered some resistance but were overcome by 3:00 P.M. In Tokyo, at a Cabinet meeting, the War Minister assured his colleagues that the Japanese troops were being used only to protect the South Manchurian Railway zone. Two days later, Japanese troops crossed the border from Korea into Manchuria under orders from Governor General Ugaki but without the Emperor's approval. After the city of Kirin fell on September 21, a semiofficial Army publication announced that all military operations were completed and that no further troop movements were anticipated. On that same date, China officially appealed to the League of Nations to prevent further deterioration of the situation and to demand a re-establishment of the *status quo ante*.

Although it had been suspected in Geneva, London, and Washington, and even in some circles in Tokyo, that the Japanese Army was out of hand, many of the world's leading diplomats believed this to be only a temporary situation. Most foreign observers, blinded partly by wishful thinking and partly by ignorance, held to the opinion that, if the Cabinet and Foreign Minister Shidehara were not embarrassed by precipitate foreign action, then they would be able to regain control. Few persons realized that the only possibility of stopping the irresponsible acts of the military would have been for the Prime Minister, the political parties, the League of Nations, and the United States to have opposed these acts in unequivocal terms.

But the realities of the times made any moves along these lines impossible. In fact, a general timorousness and aptitude for procrastination by opposition groups within Japan and by the powers only stimulated aggressive groups throughout the world. The young officers, who had successfully staged the plot near Mukden, realized that they could do it elsewhere in China with little opposition. They or their colleagues might even be able to overthrow the Cabinet and establish a military dictatorship. A Mussolini or a Hitler could argue that, since Japan's aggression was not checked in Manchuria, it was unlikely that anyone would dare to stop a Fascist or a Nazi drive in Europe or Africa.

But to return to the Manchurian Incident, as it came to be called, two basic questions remain to be answered. They are: (1) What were the effects of the action of the Japanese military in Manchuria? And (2) what were the reasons for these developments? The explosion in Manchuria on September 18, 1931, set off a chain reaction with results, though not immediate, that were to make inevitable a conflict between the Axis Powers and the Allies. Space will not permit a detailed account of all of the phases of this reaction. Suffice it to refer to a few significant aspects of the events which followed. In the first place, the world and the League of Nations were confronted with all of the dangers and irritations emanating from the operation of dual diplomacy in Japan. While the Japanese representative in Geneva was assuring the Council of the League that his government was taking steps to confine the movement of Japanese troops in Manchuria, the military were executing a preconceived plan of the Chiefs of Staff. While the Cabinet reprimanded the Imperial Army for having sent troops from Korea without Imperial consent, the War Minister maneuvered the Emperor into a position of giving *ex post facto* approval of this action.

More specifically, on September 30, 1931, Japan acquiesced in the resolution of the Council of the League. This resolution clearly committed Japan to a speedy withdrawal of its troops to within the South Manchurian Railway zone and to a promise not to aggravate the situation further. At a Cabinet meeting in Tokyo the next day, however, the War Minister inferred that it would be better to withdraw from the League than to give up the military occupation of Manchuria. In defiance of the League, the Japanese bombed Chinchow, the provisional capital of the Manchurian war lord, Chang Hsueh-liang.[10] The Premier reported to the Emperor's closest advisers that the Army should not be permitted to be connected with the formation of an "independent government" in Manchuria. The Kwantung Army leaders ignored this jibe and kept Henry Pu Yi, the heir to the old Manchu dynasty, in protective custody for future use as the head of a new "state."

As the war spread throughout Manchuria, official pronouncements reiterated that military operations had already ceased. But a new offensive action always belied these statements. Officially, Japan insisted that outstanding differences with China should be settled by direct negotiations between the two countries and that they did not concern the League. In reality, the military were determining policy and also deciding on when and how it should be executed. They left to the Foreign Office and its diplomats the task of extricating Japan from any international complications which resulted from these aggressive acts. This involvement of the military in policy and in politics, therefore, was another important result of the Manchurian explosion. While this was not a new phenomenon in Japanese history, the extent and intensity of military dominance over Japan's destiny had been greatly augmented.

Not only were the Foreign Office and the Cabinet forced to follow the Army's lead in Manchuria, but they found themselves forced into subservience to its desires at home. This situation was the result of both overt and covert actions by elements in the Army. After the outbreak of hostilities in Manchuria, Premier Wakatsuki and his colleagues appear to have leaned over backward to avoid any direct criticism of the War Minister. They seemed to sense that any insistence on their part upon a reversal of policy or upon a demand that insubordinate officers be reprimanded would have caused the War Minister to resign. Such a move would have overthrown the Cabinet and might have meant the end of party governments.

Furthermore, in early October rumors emanated from Manchuria, and spread through official circles in Tokyo, to the effect that those who engineered the Manchurian affair were expecting to return to Tokyo, carry out a coup d'état, and establish national socialism. These rumors were suddenly given substance by the premature disclosure of a widespread plot, planned by Colonel Hashimoto Kingorō and other members of the extremist group of officers in Manchuria, to take over the national government by force. Since the plan called for an air attack on the Cabinet during one of its meetings, all of the Ministers realized that they might have been wiped out, and hence they tended to become even more cautious than before.[11]

As the pressure, slight though it may have been, continued to be exerted on Japan by the League's Council and as Prime Minister Wakatsuki became increasingly less able and willing to control the War Minister, the Cabinet became less stable. The Premier wanted to resign but had no appropriate successor to recommend. A policy of opposition to the Army was rapidly losing support. The Privy Council reportedly condoned its activities; the Seiyūkai party, like the War Minister, was recommending Japan's withdrawal from the League of Nations.

After Japan had failed to carry out the League's resolution requiring the withdrawal of troops, the Council met in mid-November, 1931, to consider the next appropriate step it should take. Recommendations for the dispatch of a Commission of Enquiry to investigate conditions on the spot had been consistently opposed by the Japanese delegate. He had also rejected a Chinese offer to settle the issues by arbitration. After the military occupation of the chief cities of Manchuria was completed, however, Japan reversed its position. It agreed to the dispatch of a Commission of Enquiry to Manchuria so long as it had no power to interfere with military matters. Thus, nearly three months after the explosion at Mukden, the Council unanimously approved the dispatch of a Commission to make a study at first hand and to report to the Council any circumstances which threatened to disturb the peace. Long before the Lytton Commission had its first preparatory meeting in Geneva in January, 1932, Japan's military position in Manchuria was secure.[12]

Militant Nationalism at Home

There is a short final chapter in the history of party governments which remains to be told. On December 11, 1931, Wakatsuki resigned as Prime Minister and Elder Statesman Saionji decided to recommend the leader of the Seiyūkai party as his successor. Thus Inukai Ki, became the last party Premier in prewar Japan. In reality, however, a new era was inaugurated with the appointment of this government. General Araki Sadaō, one of the leading exponents of expansion and idol of the aggressive young officers, was the new War Minister. This period, which reached its climax in the attack on Pearl Harbor, was characterized by a steady trend toward facism, direct Army control, and the improvisation of policy to meet constantly recurrent crises following direct action at home or further aggression abroad. It saw the capitulation of the politicians, the intellectuals, the conservative financial interests, labor, and the farmer to the new forces of Nipponism. In fact, it revealed a surprising unanimity among all groups for an aggressive policy toward China, for the eviction of Western imperialism from Eastern Asia, and for its replacement by a Greater East Asia Co-prosperity Sphere with Japan as the guiding force and chief beneficiary.

The unmistakable trend toward military fascism gained momentum rapidly following the appointment in January, 1932, of the Inukai Cabinet. The young officers responsible for starting the occupation of Manchuria had been eulogized rather than disciplined; nothing had happened to Colonel Hashimoto and his colleagues who had planned to seize the national government by force. The people also were far from satisfied with the government's policy toward China or with their economic plight. Unemployment and social unrest, arising from the world depression, provided fertile ground for nationalistic propaganda. The time was ripe for an appeal to people's innate patriotism to make them champion a policy of expansionism rather than the less spectacular task of improving their plight by retrenchment and austerity. The spiritual yearning of the people was easily satisfied by a plea to return to the way of their ancestral gods. Once launched on a program of aggression, there was no turning back; foreign remonstrances and warnings merely served to arouse national feelings.

By February, 1932, Japan was already well along the fascist road.[13] The Army had completed its military campaign in Manchuria and had instigated an "independence movement." In February, 1932, the new "state" of Manchukuo declared its independence. The next month, Mr. Pu Yi, former youthful ruler on the Manchu throne, who had been taken to Dairen under the protective custody of the Kwantung Army, was inaugurated as Provisional President. In the meantime, hostilities had flared up in Shanghai after Japanese troops had landed allegedly to protect their fellow countrymen's lives and property from violent anti-Japanese demonstrations.

At home, the Japanese extremists were taking matters into their own hands. For example, in February, 1932, Inouye Junnosuke, former Finance Minister and campaign manager of the Minseitō party, was shot and killed by a peasant lad. Within less than a month, Dan Takuma, Managing Director of the Mitsui combines, was also murdered. Both of these assassinations were perpetrated in the name of patriotism against men described by their assailants as typical representatives of the politicians and capitalists who were responsible for the ruinous state of the country. Both the civilian and military ultranationalists were also encouraged by the elections for the House of Representatives. Candidates who advocated conservatism at home and an aggressive policy abroad were invariably elected. Prime Minister Inukai's party, the Seiyūkai, which was known for its support of a strong attitude toward China, received an overwhelming majority. There was little likelihood, therefore, that Parliament would place obstacles in the way of the Kwantung Army in its consolidation of Japan's position on the continent.

But many of the old politicians and both of the main parties were anathema to members of some of the ultranationalist groups. The latter argued that if Japan was to be renovated, the first step was to liquidate the political leaders. Hence, on May 15, 1932, a small group of zealous farmers and naval officers tried to overthrow the government. They assassinated Premier Inukai, attacked other officials, and bombed the Bank of Japan and other key spots in Tokyo. Naïve and ill-conceived though this plot may have been, it rang down the curtain on party cabinets and set the stage for the predominance of the Army in the Japanese government.

But resistance from several of the Emperor's key advisers and a struggle for control between two factions within the Army retarded the spread of control by the military. The Imperial Way Faction in the Army supported an avowed fascist, Vice-Chairman of the Privy Council Hiranuma Kiichirō, for the next Premier; another Army group, the Control Faction, was more cautious. Thus Saionji's recommendation of Admiral Saitō Makoto and the formation of a national cabinet were finally accepted.[14] The most significant aspect of this new government, however, was the struggle between War Minister Araki Sadaō and Finance Minister Takahashi Korekiyo. The former, who was the idol of many of the young officers, espoused the expansionist aims of the Imperial Army and justified its action in Manchuria, Inner Mongolia, and North China. Takahashi, although basically a conservative, fearlessly opposed the continuous demands of the military for greater military expenditures.

But Takahashi was faced with insurmountable obstacles. Each new move of the Army on the continent required even greater expenditures. After the pacification of Manchuria and the organization of Manchukuo, Japanese forces advanced on Jehol Province in Inner Mongolia and by March, 1933, occupied its key points. In Geneva, the Japanese delegate, Matsuoka Yōsuke, who was a notorious nationalist and pro-Army man, walked out of the League of Nations in protest over its criticism of the Jehol campaign. In further defiance of world opinion, hostilities were extended to North China. They ceased temporarily, at least, only after the Chinese and Japanese commanders signed a truce at the end of May, 1933, at Tangku. By the Tangku Truce, an area of about 5000 square miles between Peking and the Manchurian border was demilitarized. The Chinese Army was to withdraw from the area. The Kwantung Army had the right to verify this withdrawal and promised to retire northward to the Great Wall. On the other hand, peace and order were to be maintained by a police force friendly to Japan. Consequently, the Kwantung Army was now committed to protect all of Manchuria, the Inner Mongolian provinces of Jehol and Chahar, and China north of Peking.

Faced with these *faits accomplis,* Finance Minister Takahashi was placed in an untenable position. Military expenditures increased from roughly 500 million yen in 1930 to 873 million yen in 1933, and to 941.8 million yen or 43.3 per cent of the entire budget, in 1934.[15] When queried in Parliament as to why the armed services needed this amount, Takahashi could only give evasive answers. War Minister Araki insisted that expenditures would continue to increase in the future and that the reasons were none of Parliament's business. If he could persuade the people to have implicit faith in the Army's leaders and in the invincibility of the Army and Navy, then the dictatorship of the military would be complete. He then set about instilling this attitude among both the Armed Services and the people at large. A man of unselfish motives and simple personal habits, he was at heart a soldier. He was also devoted to strengthening Japan through the dissemination of the Way of the Emperor (*Kōdō*).

Araki's nationalist philosophy, as well as that of many of his colleagues in the Army, was disseminated through a series of Army pamphlets. First published in 1934, these pamphlets emphasized the need of adequate defense to counteract what was described as the menace created by the air forces of the Soviet Union and the United States. The pamphlets argued that the unstable balance of power in the world and the threat of communism dictated a broad economic and social mobilization of the entire nation. The Japanese were destined through the working of the Way of the Emperor to bring peace and order to the Asiatic continent. War, the father of creation, should be encouraged; a new regime of social justice should be promoted.

Another pamphlet, which concentrated on the international crisis created by the Manchurian invasion, maintained that Japan had been insulted. It added:

> Not only in order to work out our protective measures with respect to Manchuria and Mongolia, but also to show the world our brilliant essence, it is necessary . . . that the entire nation be awakened to the convictions and ideals of the Imperial Army. . . .[16]

As the crisis in Asia increased, persons from all classes in society: the political parties, businessmen, laborers, and the farmers, found in the pamphlets philosophical and religious justification for the nation's expansionist program.

Although foreign diplomats at Geneva and elsewhere had often expressed the belief that the Japanese Foreign Office and moderate groups would eventually check the expansionist tendencies of the ultranationalists, their judgment was based as much on wishful thinking as on fact. Those "liberals" who were outspoken in their criticism of the military lived in constant danger of assassination. Political assassins, so long as they pleaded that they had been motivated by patriotism, received ridiculously light sentences from the courts. As time passed, even the Foreign Office, in addition to sponsoring withdrawal from the League, showed clear signs of supporting a strong antiforeign policy and expansionism in China. Following bilateral agreements between the Japanese and North China authorities, it declared in April, 1934 (the Amau Statement), that China should not avail itself of the assistance of any country but Japan. Furthermore, the statement specifically warned that if any other country supplied China with war material or provided funds for political use, Japan would oppose such moves as threats to peace and order in East Asia. In other words, any individual, or concerted action by the Western powers to bolster the faltering resistance of China would not be countenanced by Japan. If China was to be a united nation, it would be so at the sufferance of Japan and under its tutelage.

There were other indications that the Foreign Office largely acquiesced in the general policy of strengthening the Empire's position in Asia. For example, negotiations had begun in 1933 with the Soviet Union for the purchase of the Chinese Eastern Railway, for the settlement of boundary claims, and for the extension of oil and fishing rights. Since the formation of Manchukuo, the Soviet Union realized that the Chinese Eastern Railway had lost much of its strategic and economic importance and hence should be sold. Furthermore, the 2000 miles of contiguous Soviet-Manchukuo frontier had caused innumerable border clashes and disputes. Although both Japan and the Soviet Union had much to gain by successfully negotiating these issues, it took two years before they could agree to mutually acceptable terms. In the spring of 1935, a sale price was agreed upon for the Chinese Eastern Railway, with Japan guaranteeing the payment in money and goods. The year following, both countries agreed in principle to the formation of a commission to adjudicate disputes and to settle the Soviet-Manchukuo boundary.

The Army Gains Control, 1935-37

With the northern flank thus secured by these agreements with the Soviet Union, Japan turned toward a more permanent solution of the China problem. Basically, the points at issue between China and Japan were clear. China claimed in 1935, just as it had maintained at the Paris Peace Conference, that Japan had no legal basis for the special privileges it demanded on the continent. The Nationalist government maintained that the Mukden Incident of September 18, 1931, the Japanese occupation of Manchuria, their "autonomous independence movement" which created Manchukuo, and their penetration into Inner Mongolia and North China all stemmed from the aggressive and inexcusable action of the Japanese militarists. The Kuomintang insisted that the local military agreements between Chinese and Japanese commanders were designed to secure Japan's dominance over the Asiatic continent. The members of the League of Nations, the Soviet Union, and the United States generally supported China's position.

The military situation in Asia was far different in 1935, however, than it had been in 1919. In 1935, the Japanese Army was heavily entrenched in Manchuria, Inner Mongolia, and North China. None of the Western powers were willing to risk a war by challenging Japan's actions. On the other hand, after the world had turned against them for the occupation of Manchuria, the Japanese government and people were rapidly becoming united in a conviction that special conditions in China required special treatment.

They argued that the old standards of international law were not applicable to the unsolved problems between Japan and China. In other words, the Empire's defense requirements, including its economic needs for natural resources and undeveloped land areas, all necessitated the creation of puppet states on the continent. In this manner, Japan could be assured of the friendliness of the puppet governments and simultaneously be able to control and exploit the resources in those areas which would contribute toward a self-sufficient armament industry. The Japanese argument continued that, if the local or national Chinese authorities could not protect Japanese life and property, then the Kwantung Army would take over that responsibility in self-defense. Finally, while Japan recognized that it was natural for China to want to become unified, it should be permitted to do so only if it did not interfere in any way with Japan's plans of expansion on the continent.

If the events, which led to a solid, united front in the Japanese homeland, and to a full-scale war in China, are to be understood, it is not enough to dismiss Japan's position as illegal and groundless or to claim that the arguments are illogical. On the contrary, it must be recognized that many Japanese were firmly convinced of the validity of these claims. Furthermore, they were coming to believe that their country must defend its action in Manchuria and Asia if it were to survive as a nation. Though the military might not have accurately estimated the cost of their China policy, they were not going to be sidetracked. Keeping these general arguments in mind, the main events in Sino-Japanese relations in the last half of 1935 take on added significance. They have a twofold importance: first, because of the increased tension which led toward open hostilities and, second, because the rebuff which Japan received in China stimulated direct action at home.

As relations with the Soviet Union had become at least temporarily stabilized, more attention was given to a solution of some of the basic Sino-Japanese problems. From Japan's point of view, it was necessary to eliminate from the areas which it had conquered those persons and organizations unfriendly to the puppet rulers. Consequently, in June, 1935, the Japanese commander, General Umezu, presented to General Ho Ying-chin, China's War Minister and head of the Peiping Military Council, a series of demands designed to achieve this objective. After a month's delay, General Ho reluctantly accepted the proposals which required withdrawal of Chinese government troops from Hopei. He refused to acquiesce in a subsequent Japanese order, however, which specified that only Chinese friendly to Japan should be appointed to local and provincial positions and that Japan should retain powers of supervision and examination over these local entities.

In other words, Japan's puppet regime in North China was only partially secure. Consequently, in October, 1935, Japan attempted through local negotiations, to form an autonomous government in the north which would sever its financial and political connections with the Chinese Nationalists in Nanking and which would be answerable to Japan's demands. New notes were presented to the Chinese officials in North China on the grounds that they had failed to carry out either the letter or spirit of the Ho-Umezu agreement.[17] This new move to dismember China was met by a new wave of anti-Japanese sentiment. Japan partially met the challenge of assassinations and student strikes by the formation of "Autonomous Councils" in Hopei and Chahar Provinces, but was not yet ready or able to force the issue further.

In fact, internally, Japan was in a turmoil. A struggle was taking place behind the scenes between the radical Imperial Way Faction and the more conservative Control Faction in the Army. General Araki of the former group was replaced as Minister of War by General Hayashi Senjūrō, a leader of the Control Faction. General Mazaki Jinzaburō, another advocate of the Imperial Way and the leader of the young officers, was forced to retire from the all-powerful post of Inspector General of Military Education. One of his followers, Lieutenant-Colonel Aizawa, was convinced that these shifts in the top posts of the Imperial Army were proof that it was rapidly becoming degenerate and must be saved.

Colonel Aizawa then took it upon himself to ask Major General Nagata, Director of the Military Affairs Bureau, a leader of the Control Faction, and the person responsible for Mazaki's dismissal, to resign. The General retaliated by ordering the Colonel transferred to Formosa for his insubordination. But Colonel Aizawa was not to be diverted. In early August, 1935, he made a pilgrimage to the National shrine at Ise where he purified himself. Then he returned to Tokyo, entered General Nagata's office, and murdered him. The Minister of War, who was responsible for the evident lack of discipline within the Army, resigned. Aizawa, who insisted that his motivations were exclusively patriotic, became something of a national hero.

The general turmoil was further aggravated by the political instability of the Cabinet. The Seiyūkai party, which had a majority of the seats in the House of Representatives, had forced a dissolution of Parliament in January, 1936. The elections held the next month were a censure by the people of the extremists. All of the nationalist parties lost, the Seiyūkai dropped sixty-eight seats and the more moderate Minseitō party took the lead.[18]

Military Aggression on the Asiatic Mainland, 1931-37

The Imperial Way Faction and other extremist elements in the Army were confronted with a challenge of either losing ground before an increasingly hostile Parliament and large segments of the public or of forcing their will on the people by a bold coup d'état. Two apparently unrelated events, which occurred on February 25, 1936, clearly show that the Imperial Way Faction had decided on the latter alternative. General Mazaki, whose ouster as Inspector General had been the immediate cause for Aizawa's murderous act was ordered to testify at the latter's trial. Mazaki refused to answer questions at the court martial. In the second place, a notice was placed in the "Personal Column" of the morning edition of the Tokyo *Asahi,* as a signal for a revolt to take place. It read:

> Current Issues Stabilized: There has been a crystallization of the correct judgment of you who are wise and can see into the meaning of things. Let us make every effort —all of us unitedly—to strengthen our national power and to make progress for the Empire by leaps and bounds.
>
> Leader of the Orient,
> Marunouchi Art Club,
> Half-Piercing Solid Star.

Before dawn the next morning, groups of thirty soldiers set out in the snow on their murderous missions to assassinate seven key figures in the government and to take over the War Office, the Premier's residence, the newly erected Diet Building, and the communications centers of the city. When the Tokyo populace went about their usual tasks later that day, those in the heart of the city saw soldiers everywhere and guessed that a coup had taken place. But the radio said nothing. The only cue for those in the suburbs or outside the city that something was amiss was the fact that some morning papers did not appear. Rumors were rampant until official announcements gradually informed the public of the extent of the murders.

The next day, martial law was proclaimed and troops of unimpeachable loyalty were brought from outside the city to quash the rebellion. After a three-day show of strength by these military units and a personal appeal by the Emperor, the insurgents capitulated. Technically, the coup had failed. The Emperor had not been molested and was free to appoint any ministers he chose. In reality, however, only the Imperial Way Faction in the Army had failed to gain control. The Army as a whole and the advocates of a strong policy gained in the end.[19]

While these momentous events were taking place, the people showed an amazing attitude toward the whole affair. During the first day of the attempted coup many white collar workers in Tokyo spent their lunch hour walking between the columns of soldiers facing each other on opposite sides of the busy downtown streets. The strollers tried to find out from the soldiers what group they represented, but had little success. The entire Tokyo populace was completely docile and amenable to any inconvenience caused them by the coup. They carried on their routine activities and left the struggle up to the Army, as they left it up to the ruling cliques to settle their future.

The new power which the Army had acquired from suppressing the coup expressed itself immediately in the selection of a new Cabinet. Hirota

Kōki, though known to be nationalistically minded, was finally chosen as the new Premier. The Army selected a new Minister of War who threatened to refuse to serve whenever the Premier suggested appointments to the Cabinet of persons not acceptable to him and his colleagues. When a colorless national Cabinet was finally selected, the Army rested temporarily on its laurels and endeavored to leave the impression that it alone had saved the country from revolt (even by its own members) and that it had no further intention of centralizing power. A mild reprimand from the Emperor and the execution, in July, 1936, of thirteen young officers involved in the coup caused the War Office to disassociate itself from the ideas advocated by them.

But these moves, as well as the appointment of relatively moderate persons to fill the posts of those who were murdered, were far less significant than the fact that the events of the past few years had prepared the nation to accept the principles and policies of the Imperial Army as basic tenets of Japanese policy. These were described as vindication of the national polity, stabilization of the livelihood of the people, reform of foreign policy, and strengthening of national defense. No group, economic or political, challenged the basic policy of expansion on the continent of Asia. The Army alone had a plan. It advocated the formation of a bloc composed of Japan, Manchukuo, and North China to strengthen the country economically and to protect it from attack from the Soviet Union. In the absence of anything better and lacking a liberal, nonmilitary tradition, the people followed.

By the end of 1936, however, both internal and external conditions had deteriorated and the trend toward totalitarianism was inevitable. The Minister of Finance, Baba Eiichi, had encountered little opposition to a national budget with heavily increased expenditures to develop Manchuria and to strengthen national defenses. For example, total expenditures had increased from 1.5 billion yen in 1932 to 2.3 billion yen in 1936 with an annual average deficit of 638 million yen. During the same period, the amount of the budget devoted to the armed services had increased from 28 to 46 per cent. Baba introduced new taxes on sugar and tobacco and raised postal charges. A sharp rise in wholesale prices developed and retail prices climbed at an average of 2¼ per cent monthly. Increased military demands on heavy industries stimulated their growth at the expense of light industries. The special economic privileges shown some of the new industrialists antagonized the old established families such as Mitsui and Iwasaki.

On the international scene, Japan was less successful in achieving its objectives. In the summer of 1936, these objectives had been set forth in a Cabinet declaration of fundamental principles of national policy. This statement called for the eradication of the Russian menace on the north, the strengthening of Korea, Manchuria, and Japan through close economic cooperation between those areas and China, but the avoidance of antagonizing the Western powers. It also advocated the peaceful penetration of Southeast Asia, and the development of a strong navy in the Western Pacific as a counterbalance to the American navy. All national policies were to be unified, with the military assisting the diplomats and refraining from overt acts whenever possible.[20]

But it was problematical how much longer the military would refrain from some new overt act in China. Incidents of killings of Japanese were occurring with increasing frequency in cities such as Hankow and Shanghai. Kawagoe, who had been advanced to the post of Japanese Ambassador at Nanking, made new demands on the Nationalist government. He insisted that China and Japan jointly attack communism, that the Chinese press be controlled, that Japan have the right to inspect the schools to ferret out anti-Japanese cells, and that the Nanking government assist in the formation of an autonomous government over the five provinces in the north. He was rebuffed by Generalissimo Chiang Kai-shek and negotiations were broken off after the outbreak of a Japanese inspired revolt in western China. When the Hirota government sponsored the signing of the Anti-Comintern Pact with Nazi Germany in November, 1936, it was evident that Japan was rapidly gravitating toward the Rome-Berlin Axis. (See page 348.) In so doing, it was making a full-scale conflict with China that much more likely.

The political crisis from January to June, 1937, had little effect on the Army's control over the government. Only those persons approved by the Army were chosen for Premier and for the various Cabinet posts. Although the Minseitō and Seiyūkai parties, which made common cause against militarism and fascism in government in the elections in April, 1937, won three-fourths of the seats in Parliament, they were not officially represented in the Cabinet of Prime Minister Konoye Fumimarō, which was formed in June.[21] In fact, they no longer were important in the formation of policy or in its execution. That task was assigned to a newly created Cabinet Planning Board which was a coordinating and directing agency which transcended all departments. It had the power to decide the urgency, importance, and priority of proposals presented by the various branches of the government. By July, 1937, when full-scale hostilities broke out in China, the machinery was at hand to mobilize the material and spiritual resources of the nation for war. In the immediate years which followed, totalitarianism slowly and steadily spread throughout the Empire crushing all significant opposition before it.

Notes

1. For an interesting summary of economic conditions in the post-bellum decade see Ōuchi Hyoe, "Keizai," in Yanaihara Tadaō, *Gendai Nihon Shōshi* (Tokyo: Misuzu, 1952), I, pp. 157-88.

2. The export price of silk had fallen even more precipitously. In 1929 it equaled 1420 yen per 100 *kin*. By October, 1930, it dropped to 530 yen and in June, 1932, hit a low of 390 yen. Eventually, this drop affected the amount the farmer received for his silk. G. C. Allen, *A Short Economic History of Modern Japan, 1867-1937* (London: George Allen & Unwin, Ltd., 1946), p. 111.

3. For example, in 1927 Japan imported from overseas (including Manchuria and Korea) 87 per cent of its iron ore requirements, 40 per cent of its pig iron needs, and 35 per cent of the steel ingot and slabs. In comparison to reserves of 40 million tons of iron ore in Japan proper, Manchuria was estimated to have from 300 to 730 million tons. See H. G. Moulton, *Japan, An Economic and Financial Appraisal* (Washington: Brookings Institution, 1931), p. 462 *et seq.;* D. R. Bergsmark, *Economic Geography of Asia* (New York: Prentice-Hall, Inc., 1935), p. 421 ff.; and Allen, *op. cit.,* p. 116.

4. Allen, *Economic History, op. cit.,* p. 105.

5. See C. Walter Young, *Japan's Jurisdiction and International Legal Position in Manchuria* (3 vols.; Baltimore: Johns Hopkins University Press, 1931).

6. Kita's *Nihon Kaizō Hōan Taikō* was first published in 1919. Details of his activities can be found in Robert A. Scalapino, *Democracy and the Party Movement in Prewar Japan* (Berkeley: University of California Press, 1953), p. 334 *et seq.*

7. The interrelationship of leading military and political figures with the various nationalist societies is intriguing yet extremely complicated. Some of the leaders obviously belonged to, or were used by, several of the societies. Both Kita and Ōkawa were accused of implication in some of the same plots. Membership in one society did not exclude membership in another. Thus General Araki Sadaō is purported to have been a strong supporter of Ōkawa's group and at the same time was a member of another group, the *Kokuhonsha.*

Ōkawa Shūmei (b. 1886) studied philosophy at Tokyo Imperial University. He entered the service of the South Manchurian Railway and became director of its Bureau of East Asian Economic Research. He became so active in plots to overthrow the government, particularly that of May 15, 1932, that he was arrested but received an amnesty in 1935 after having served one-third of his sentence.

Araki Sadaō (b. 1877) was a career Army officer who graduated from the War College. In 1931 he entered the Inukai Cabinet as Minister of War, which post he continued to hold until January, 1934. His relationship to the rise of militarism after 1931 is elaborated on pp. 332 *et seq.* In 1948 he was convicted as a War Criminal and given a sentence of life imprisonment.

8. Ugaki Kazushige (b. 1868) was a graduate of the War College and worked his way up through the Army to fill some of its key administrative posts such as Inspector General of Military Education, and War Minister. He served as Minister of War from 1924 to 1927. He served twice as Governor General of Korea after 1927 and was in that post when the plot was conceived.

A word of caution is in order concerning the various plots against the Cabinet. Whenever a plot of this sort was discovered either by the military police (*Kempei tai*) or by the civilian police, great pains were taken not to reveal it to anyone not already aware of its existence. It cannot be concluded, therefore, that the knowledge of the failure of such a coup necessarily had an immediate effect on the Premier and his Cabinet. In some cases, the most that they might learn after several months was that there had been some sort of plot. For example, Harada Kumaō, Secretary to the last Elder Statesman, Saionji, states that August 3 was the first time he heard of the March plot. The details of this particular plot did not come out until 1947 at the War Crimes Trial of the International Military Tribunal for the Far East.

9. According to the *Diary* of Harada Kumaō, Saionji's Secretary, War Minister Minami, was considered to be a real problem by the moderates. When asked about Ugaki's connection with the March, 1931, plot, Minami is reported to have answered that Ugaki had denied any implication in it. The War Minister then accused the Minseitō party of inspiring articles in the press derogatory to the Army. Minami was sentenced to life imprisonment as a War Criminal by the International Military Tribunal on the Far East. See below p. 420; and Harada Kumaō, *Saionji Kō Nikki* (3 vols.; Tokyo: Iwanami, 1952).

10. The Kwantung Headquarters claimed that the bombing, the first of a series of many, was justified by provocative anti-Japanese demonstrations and by the threat to their security from the alleged concentration of Chang's troops for an attack on Japanese forces in Manchuria. These claims fooled no one. See S. R. Smith, *The Manchurian Crisis 1931-1932* (New York: Columbia University Press, 1948), p. 82.

11. Hashimoto was strongly influenced by the nationalist philosophy of Ōkawa Shūmei. He had been active in the Imperial League of Young Officers and after August, 1931, was a leader of the Chosen Men Society. The coup d'état was set for October 24, 1931. After the attack the Emperor was to be asked to appoint a military man as Premier, the parties would be abolished, capital would be confiscated, and state socialism would become a reality. He continued to play an active role in instigating "incidents," including the attack on the U.S. gunboat "Panay" in the Yangtze River, December 12, 1937. At that time he was local commander of the area in which the attack occurred. (See below p. 352.) He was executed as a War Criminal on the basis of the findings of the International Military Tribunal for the Far East.

12. Part of the delay in forming the Commission had been the lack of enthusiasm of the United States and Great Britain for such an inquiry. The United States, after the bombing of Chinchow, had invoked the Kellogg Pact and had agreed to send an observer to the Council meetings. It also agreed to have an observer serve on the League's Commission. In the meantime, the Japanese Army continued its advance. Chang Hsueh-liang extricated his army from Manchuria and on December, 1931, announced his withdrawal behind the Great Wall. On January 3, 1932, Chinchow fell and on the next day the Japanese controlled Shanhaikwan, the gateway to North China.

13. The remainder of this chapter will be devoted to an account of the interrelationship of (1) an outline of only the most significant events of the period, (2) an analysis of how the important groups in society willingly permitted this militarization of their country, and·(3) the relationship of events abroad, particularly on the Asiatic continent, to the growth of a totalitarian state. For a detailed study of the first two of these factors, the reader is referred to the author's *Japan Since 1931, Its Political and Social Development* (New York: American Institute of Pacific Relations, Inc., 1940).

14. The coup d'état of May 15, 1932, and the selection of a Premier illustrates, at once, the vital role of the ultranationalist societies in this period of Japan's history,

and also the complicated nature of the political scene. For example, the *Aikyō Juku,* a rural organization inspired by a priest named Inoue Nisshō, and the Blood Brotherhood League were both behind these and earlier assassinations. Inoue had close contacts with members of the Kwantung Army. They advocated wiping out the political parties, the *zaibatsu,* and traitors with the assistance of the farmers and laborers. When the status quo was destroyed, a new Japan could be built. Hiranuma, who was supported in May, 1932, as Premier, had founded the Society for the Foundation of the State (Kokuhonsha) in 1924. Members in his Society included Generals Ugaki, Araki, Mazaki, and Koiso, President of the Seiyūkai, Suzuki Kisaburō, Managing Director of Mitsui, Ikeda Seihin, and Premier-designate Admiral Saitō. Within the Army, the struggle was between the Imperial Way Faction (Kōdō ha) and the Control Faction (Tōseiha). The former, whose members had engineered the Manchurian Incident, favored direct and immediate action to bring about "reform." The latter, which finally gained the ascendancy after the coup d'état on February 26, 1936 (see page 340), wanted to consolidate its support before acting. On the all-important question of nationalism and the extension of Japanese hegemony over Asia, the two groups agreed in principle but differed only in the time and method of implementing that policy. In fine, all nationalist groups capitalized on the effects of action by any of them. Saitō's Cabinet lasted until July, 1934, when it was succeeded by that of Admiral Okada Keisuke. There was little change in policy and Okada survived until the coup on February 26, 1936. The most comprehensive account of the growth of fascism will be found in Tanaka Sōgorō, *Nihon Fascism no Genryū* (Tokyo, 1949). The fullest account in English is Scalapino, *op. cit.,* pp. 346-92; and Borton, *Japan, op. cit.,* pp. 36-53.

15. See Borton, *op. cit.,* p. 41.

16. Araki was Minister of War, 1931-34. Though out of office for the next four and a half years, he returned to the Cabinet as Minister of Education (May, 1938—August, 1939). He was a close friend of General Mazaki, Inspector General of Military Education until November, 1934. For details on these pamphlets see Borton, *op. cit.,* pp. 44-45.

17. These notes of October 29, 1935, known as the Kawagoe Notes, are significant as an indication of the cooperation developing between the Army and the Foreign Office on problems relating to China. Kawagoe Shigeru was Consul General at Tientsin.

18. The Minseitō increased from 127 to 205. The leftist groups, represented by the Social Mass party, jumped from 3 to 18. See Borton, *op. cit.,* p. 45.

19. Those listed for murder in the coup were the *Genrō,* Saionji, former Lord Keeper of the Privy Seal Makino, Prime Minister Okada, Finance Minister Takahashi, Inspector General of Military Education Watanabe, Lord-Keeper of the Privy Seal and former Premier Saitō, and Grand Chamberlain Suzuki. Of these, the first two were forewarned and took flight. Premier Okada's escape afforded a bit of grim comedy to the melodrama. His brother-in-law, who was in the Premier's official residence when the attack came, was a victim of mistaken identity and was killed while Okada remained hidden. The latter escaped next day in the disguise of a pallbearer for the coffin which presumably contained his own remains. His safe conduct through the lines of insurgent guards around his official residence was then announced to the press and radio, to the amusement of those of us in Tokyo at the time. All other persons on the list were killed except Admiral Suzuki who escaped with wounds. He later was called on by the Emperor to be Premier in the last days of World War II.

20. See International Military Tribunal for the Far East, Defense Exhibit No. 979, Document No. 1634 K, "Fundamental Principle of our National Policy," signed by the Prime Minister and Ministers of War, Navy, Foreign Affairs, and Finance, dated August 11, 1936.

21. The Hirota Cabinet fell on January 23, 1937, after the War Minister resigned in protest to criticisms made against him in Parliament. General Ugaki Kazushige, former Governor of Korea, was unacceptable to the military, so he gave up his efforts to form a Cabinet. Finally, General Hayashi Senjūrō was selected. Without warning Hayashi dissolved Parliament in April and won only fifty seats in the subsequent elections. He finally resigned at the end of May. Prince Konoye's first Cabinet (June 4, 1937—January 5, 1939) was composed largely of pro-Army men and new bureaucrats who were under military influence. Hirota Kōki was Foreign Minister and President of the Planning Board. For a detailed account of these developments see Borton, *op. cit.*, p. 45 *et seq.*

18

PREPARATION FOR TOTAL WAR, 1937-1941

In the early summer of 1937, Japan faced an unprecedented series of crises both at home and abroad. To many persons, the nation's China policy had thus far proved to be only partially successful. The leaders of the Kwantung clique and the advocates of state planning for the puppet regime of Manchukuo had prophesied that their program would bring benefits to all. They had also predicted close cooperation from China in their endeavors. But such had not proved to be the case. Japan's prodigious and unscrupulous efforts to improve Sino-Japanese relations through the promotion of autonomous, indigenous, regional "governments" throughout North China and Inner Mongolia had only strengthened China's movement toward national unification. Since December, 1936, when Generalissimo Chiang Kai-shek was kidnapped at Sian and then released through the intervention of the Chinese Communists, the possibilities of a united China had increased still further.

The Japanese Army, especially the Kwantung clique, looked upon this situation as a threat to their traditional policy of divide and rule. The Foreign Office saw little possibility of Chiang accepting or implementing its minimum requirements for an over-all settlement. It had demanded that China suppress all anti-Japanese activities, recognize the independence of Manchukuo, and cooperate with Japan in the extermination of communism on the Asiatic mainland. Furthermore, China's unification appeared to Japan to be aided and abetted by the Western powers whose special privileges conflicted with its own. In fact, it was claimed that Japan's very existence was being threatened by the encroachments of the United States, Great Britain, and the Soviet Union.

As for the Soviet Union, it had challenged the Kwantung Army's plans for control of all of Mongolia by signing a mutual assistance pact with the Mongolian People's Republic. In fact, General Tōjō Hideki,[1] Chief of Staff of the Kwantung Army, had warned the Army General Staff of the possibility of a coalition of a unified China with the Soviet Union. He advised striking a blow against Chiang at Nanking to prevent such an alliance. To offset this encirclement, Japan had become a partner with Germany in the Anti-Comintern Pact of November 25, 1936. The published clauses of the Pact provided for collaboration in preventing the spread of communism within the borders of the two states and among third powers. The secret clauses were directed against the Soviet Union. They provided that if it launched an unprovoked attack against either of the signatories, the other would not assist the Soviet Union. Furthermore, both parties promised to refrain from making political treaties with the Soviet Union except by mutual consent. Although this single pact was slim protection against a Soviet attack on Manchuria and Korea, it gave Japan moral support in its drive to gain undisputed control of China.

The chief differences of opinion within Japan among the politicians, the financiers, Imperial advisers, and the generals and admirals were on the question of how far Japan should go on the Asiatic mainland. There was no disagreement on who was destined to become the leader of East Asia and possibly of the world. As in previous crises, the differences were over methods rather than over basic aims. The Army extremists were convinced that direct action, regardless of the consequences in Asia, Europe, or America, was the only method. Their opponents, who came from almost all groups including the Imperial Navy and from some cliques within the Imperial Army, are perhaps best described as "moderates." The moderates hoped that Japan's aims in Eastern Asia could be achieved without an open break with the United States, Great Britain, or the Soviet Union. Even after the outbreak of hostilities in China in July, 1937, the moderates naïvely assumed that if the war in China could be terminated successfully in Japan's favor, then the Western Powers would acquiesce in this new "realistic approach" toward Asia.

The various shifts in government, therefore, from the formation of the first Konoye Cabinet on June 4, 1937, to the selection of General Tōjō as Premier on October 18, 1941, were indicative of the struggle for control between the "extremists" and the "moderates." This internal struggle first took the form of an attempt by the latter to prevent the Army from gaining complete political control. As the war in China progressed, however, and as Japan's aims became more closely identified with the Axis powers, the moderates increasingly acquiesced in the plans of the military. They finally capitulated to the admonitions of Tōjō that Japan's national existence could be assured only by waging a successful war against the United States. The present chapter will be devoted, therefore, to an analysis of what steps were taken to centralize political, economic, and social controls, to augment the national strength by alliances with the Axis, and to prevent the moderates from interfering with the war plans.

The Konoye Cabinet Supports War in China in 1937

In view of the domestic and international crisis which faced Japan in the summer of 1937, the selection of the proper person to fill the post of premier was of the utmost importance. Those directly responsible for selecting the Prime Minister and influential persons inside and outside of the government agreed that Konoye Fumimarō was the logical choice. A descendant of one of the oldest families of nobility in Japan, Prince Konoye was enthusiastically proclaimed the man of the hour by the militarists, the bureaucrats, the financiers, and the leaders of the political parties. Because of the close contacts he had had in recent years with key figures in the Army, he was acceptable to both the extremists and the moderates.[2] The extremists were confident that, when necessary, they could persuade him to follow their policies. The moderates recognized that the only hope for the acceptance of their views lay in controlling the extremists in the Army. Konoye was the one person who might be able to throttle them. From the beginning, however, it was evident that Konoye had accepted much of the expansionist philosophy of the militarists and was not willing or able to check them. He readily adopted the broad policies of the Army which were described as clarification of national policy, the strengthening of the defenses, the renovation of the administration of the central government, and the stabilization of the people's livelihood.

The first step toward clarification of a new policy and renovation of the government was the appointment of persons amenable to Army leadership to key posts in the first Konoye Cabinet of June, 1937. In the second place the Cabinet Planning Board, which had been commissioned just prior to the demise of the last Cabinet, became the most important coordinating agency within the government. Charged with making "recommendations . . . both in regard to important national policies and to their coordination and adjustment," it was directly under the Prime Minister and transcended all departments and agencies. Hirota Kōki, former Premier and Foreign Minister, was appointed Chairman of the Board. Through this Board, the new leaders of Japan planned the expansion and mobilization of the nation's strength for any eventuality. As necessity arose, its functions were broadened. For example, after the outbreak of war in China in July, 1937, its Chairman was given rank comparable to that of a Cabinet Minister. The synchronization of its policies with plans for Manchuria was assured by the fact that the Board's Vice-Chairman was also Vice-Chairman of the Cabinet's Manchurian Affairs Board.

But the Cabinet Planning Board and other new organs of control became important in direct proportion to the enlargement of hostilities in China. Since the Ho-Umezu agreement of 1935, Japanese troops had been stationed at strategic points in North China. (See page 337.) At the same time, Chinese Nationalist troops had been in the neighboring regions, so the situation was fraught with danger. During the summer of 1937, the senior Japanese officers in the field were outwardly friendly toward the local Chinese commanders but the lower ranks of each showed increasing enmity toward one another. In fact, the Japanese General Staff had warned its junior officers against taking overt action. During maneuvers of Japanese troops in the strategically important triangle bounded by the Peking-Hankow railway and the Peking-Tientsin line near Marco Polo Bridge (Lukouchiao), firing broke out on the night of July 7, 1937. Although the disposition of both the Chinese and Japanese armies showed that neither side apparently planned an attack, this incident soon flared into a full-fledged conflagration.[3]

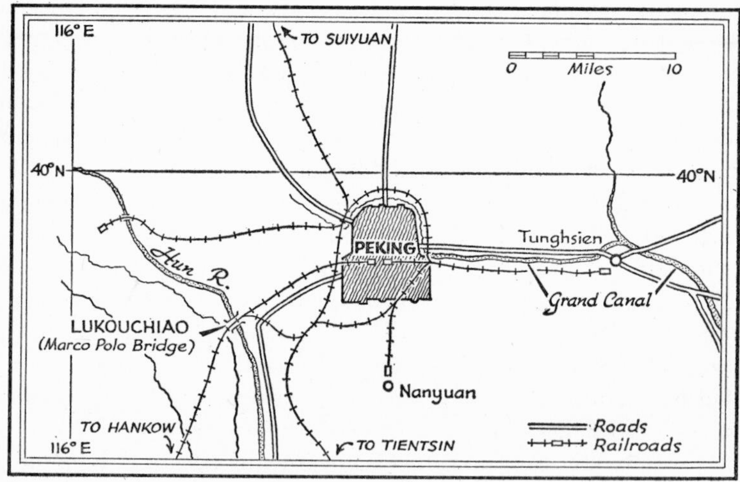

Peking and Marco Polo Bridge, July, 1937

During the next two weeks, attempts to settle the matter locally failed. In Tokyo, Premier Konoye's weakness and vacillation tipped the scales for war. When the Imperial Army insisted on sending reinforcements, he acquiesced. By July 25, 1937, hostilities broke out on a larger scale. In a few days the Japanese became masters of the Peking-Tientsin area. Thus, the second Sino-Japanese War, or perhaps more accurately, the early stages of the East Asia phase of World War II, had begun. By mid-August, hostilities had extended to Shanghai. As in the case of the Mukden Incident in September, 1931, the action of the military officers on the spot had forced the hands of the home government. The Army boasted that their victories would foredoom Chiang Kai-shek to surrender within a matter of months. On the contrary, the Marco Polo Bridge incident proved to be the opening round of a struggle which was resolved only by World War II.

As in previous cases of Japanese aggression on the Asiatic mainland, the Western powers were divided on the best policy to follow. The United States contented itself with an official pronouncement of general principles. In mid-July, 1937, Secretary of State Cordell Hull issued a statement which deprecated the use of force to settle international differences and advocated peaceful negotiation and the faithful observance of international agreements. He wished to avoid any action which could be used by the military in Japan to strengthen their position. Thus he declined an invitation of Great Britain and France for a joint *démarche* and for mediation.

Japan's answer to the American statement revealed, even at this early date, the wide divergence of its policies from those of the United States. The Japanese note maintained that Hull's principles could not be applied to the situation in the Far East unless the Western powers fully recognized the special conditions which existed in that region. In effect, the Japanese government was saying that it would be willing to adhere to these principles only after it had forced the Chinese Nationalist Government of Chiang Kai-shek to recognize its position of superiority in China. Throughout the next four years of war and military occupation of China, any protests to Japan's unilateral, aggressive moves were rejected on the grounds that Chiang's government refused to adopt a friendly policy toward it. Hence, it claimed that it had been forced to take matters into its own hands in self-defense. Despite the conquest of ever larger areas, Japan insisted that it had no territorial designs on China.

During the first few months of the war, the Japanese Army had little difficulty in spreading out along the main railway arteries in North and Central China. By December, 1937, it was ready to attack Nanking, the capital of Chiang Kai-shek. Chiang had not been intimidated by Japanese warnings that they had attacked Shanghai "to chastise the lawless Chinese troops and to impress Nanking with the necessity of a reconstruction of its attitude toward Japan." On the contrary, he had resisted and also appealed to the League of Nations for help. But the Western powers with special interests in China did little to limit the spread of the war. When they met in Brussels in November, 1937, they agreed that, while the conflict was of concern to them, there was no way in which they could bring it to a peaceful conclusion.

But both the people and the governments of Great Britain and the United States were becoming increasingly antagonistic toward Japan. They considered the whole war as the direct result of the aggressive attitude of the Japanese military. They deplored the increasingly frequent bombings of Chinese cities. They were shocked and enraged by a wanton attack on their gunboats which were evacuating their nationals from besieged Nanking. On December 12, 1937, the U.S.S. "Panay" and H.M.S. "Ladybird" were bombed by Japanese planes and strafed by Japanese Army units along the Yangtze. Shortly thereafter, Nanking fell. The triumphant Japanese troops pillaged, looted, and raped at will throughout the city.

Although an apology by the Japanese government and indemnity payments settled the "Panay" and "Ladybird" Incidents,[4] the Rape of Nanking was not so easily forgotten by either China or the Western powers. They were nauseated by Prime Minister Konoye's attributing the fall of Nanking to the "Emperor's august virtue" and to the loyalty and courage of the nation's armed forces. While Japan celebrated the capture of the Chinese capital by lantern parades and anticipated Chiang's early capitulation, the latter moved his capital further inland and made preparations for continued resistance. He rejected the latest peace offerings which required him to recognize the independence of Manchukuo and to permit the stationing of Japanese troops in North and Central China and Inner Mongolia. In return, Japan had promised to cease hostilities and eventually to withdraw its troops from China.[5]

General National Mobilization and a New Order in Asia

Reluctantly, both the military and civilian leaders in Japan realized that the war in China could be won and the nation's defense structure strengthened only by the efforts of the entire nation. Konoye bolstered his country's morale by expressing the hope that the Western powers would eventually become cognizant of Japan's stabilizing influence in the Orient. He insisted that, in the meantime, Japan's mission could be accomplished only by complete mobilization. Militarily, the nation had already been mobilized. The General Staff had begun to execute a previously approved plan for the conquest of key positions on the China mainland. By early November, 1937, an Imperial Headquarters was created to coordinate and to centralize all Japanese military efforts in China. Since the Emperor was Commander in Chief of the Armed Forces, the military leaders could, if necessary, take matters up directly with him. Thus the Cabinet's wishes could be ignored and circumvented.

On the other hand, efforts were made to reconcile differences within the nation by the formation of a Cabinet Advisory Council. This Council was composed of representatives from the most important parties. Although largely advisory, it was organized "to participate in the Cabinet's discussion and planning of important state affairs concerning the China Incident." At its semiweekly meetings, the Council made recommendations on basic national policies. The Cabinet Ministers were thus able to concentrate on administrative matters.

In the meantime, the Cabinet Planning Board speeded up its work on the drafting of a National General Mobilization Bill. This bill was largely an enabling act whose provisions became operative upon the issuance of ordinances. It permitted the government to make full use of the nation's strength for defense purposes in time of war or during "incidents," such as that in China. It permitted the mobilization of the entire personnel and material resources of the nation. It provided for control of prices, goods, services, and finances. It allowed the press and media of information to be placed under strict censorship. The government was given powers to employ or discharge workers, to regulate their wages and working conditions, and to prevent strikes. It could control industrial production and place vital industries under its direct operation. A national registration, wartime taxes, and compulsory savings were all provided for in the law.

When the Konoye Cabinet presented the Mobilization Bill to Parliament, it was opposed by a large number of Representatives. They maintained that its enactment would mean the complete loss of individual liberty and that conditions did not warrant such action. Opposition to the bill dwindled, however, after Konoye promised that its various measures would be implemented only in time of extreme emergency. The Diet passed the new law in March, 1938. Only some provisions of the law were invoked during the first Konoye Cabinet. Nevertheless, the means were at hand to mobilize the nation immediately in the event of a sudden emergency.[6]

Shortly after the passage of the Mobilization Law, Prime Minister Konoye streamlined his government by the formation of a Five Minister Conference composed of the Premier and the Ministers of War, Navy, Foreign Affairs, and Finance. Presumably, all vital and urgent issues were left to this small group to decide. In actuality, however, the military played a dominant role in all vital issues. It directed the war through the Imperial Headquarters. Furthermore, it sponsored administrative shifts in the government which deprived the Foreign Office of much of its powers. For example, War Minister Itagaki Seishirō, who had returned from command of the North China forces after the capture of Hsüchow in May, 1938, insisted that the China Affairs Board be placed under the direct supervision of the Cabinet and hence the Army. When the Foreign Minister insisted that he must retain control of this Board, he was forced to resign. More Army men appeared in the Cabinet. General Araki, former War Minister and advocate of spiritual mobilization through a belief in the Imperial Way, was made Minister of Education. The whole nation was rapidly being cast into a single, submissive unit, subject to the will of the ruling faction.

Premier Konoye also helped to strengthen the position of the military by an expanded interpretation of the policy toward China. The capture of Canton and the occupation of Hankow by Japanese forces by the end of October, 1938, brought the war in China to the end of large-scale territorial conquests. Japan had desperately hoped that Chiang could be forced to capitulate. On the contrary, he and his government had retired to Chungking and gave no signs of surrendering. Consequently, a new policy was essential to fit the new circumstances. Some formula must be found to link the recently conquered territories in Manchukuo, Inner Mongolia, North, Central, and South China with Japan. To meet this need, on November 3, 1938, Premier Konoye issued his famous statement on "A New Order in East Asia." The purpose of the New Order was defined as insuring the permanent stability of East Asia. It was to be achieved by a tripartite relationship of mutual aid and coordination in the political, economic, and cultural fields among Japan, Manchukuo, and China. Konoye asked these three nations, while retaining their respective individuality, to stand united in safeguarding East Asia.

As a first step toward the formation of an effective economic bloc, it was necessary to coordinate the national economy with that of Manchukuo and China. This integration had been accomplished in Manchuria through the government-owned South Manchurian Railway Company and later by the Manchurian Industrial Development Corporation of Aikawa Yoshisuke. (See page 363.) Aikawa, through close connections with leaders of the Kwantung Army, had been given special privileges and his enterprises had made a significant contribution to the industrial growth of Manchuria. After the formation of Manchukuo, control of that "state" by Japan was assured through a General Affairs Board. This Board, whose Chairman was a Japanese appointed by the Kwantung Army, developed plans and programs for the new state. These plans were coordinated with those in Japan through the Cabinet's Manchurian Affairs Board. After the industrial control provisions of the National Mobilization Law went into effect, the authority was at hand to integrate the economies of Japan and Manchukuo.[7]

In China, integration was to be achieved through the Japanese government-owned development corporations which were primarily concerned with the exploitation of the recently conquered areas. The North China Development Corporation made capital and technical assistance available for the mining of coking coal and iron ore in North China in accordance with a plan prepared by the China Affairs Board. (See below, page 363.) Integration and coordination of the activities in all these areas were achieved in Tokyo through the Prime Minister, who was Chairman of the Cabinet Planning Board, the Manchurian Affairs Board and the China Affairs Board. Although experience and new crises required innumerable administrative changes between the passage of the Mobilization Law in

1938 and Japan's decision to attack the United States toward the end of 1941, the basic machinery for complete national mobilization and for co-ordination with the conquered regions of China had been established.

Japan Challenges the Western Powers in Asia, 1938-40

While Prime Minister Konoye had been consolidating the position of the central government and making preparations for national mobilization, his government had also been confronted with some delicate international problems. Although the war in China had strained Japan's relations with the United States, the nearest Western enemy was the Soviet Union. With Vladivostok and other Soviet air bases only a few hours flying time from the industrial and demographic heart of Japan, the fear of Soviet attack always remained in the background. The borders of the Soviet Union were contiguous with those of the Japanese puppet states of Inner Mongolia and Manchukuo, and of Korea. The Japanese General Staff was painfully aware that prolonged hostilities in China weakened their strategic position. They also knew that a deterioration of Soviet-Japanese relations might threaten Japan's whole position on the Asiatic continent.

In the summer of 1938, when Soviet relations came to a crisis, it was problematic whether Japan was militarily prepared to sustain a war in China and, simultaneously, to fight the Soviet Union. While incidents along the ill-defined Manchukuo-Soviet frontier were not unusual, the outbreak of hostilities along the Soviet-Korean border was unusual. In mid-July, 1938, fighting between Soviet and Japanese troops broke out near Changkufeng on the northeastern border. It centered around some strategic heights along the Tumen River. It continued for approximately two weeks. This incident had a sobering effect on the Japanese high command for the incident had threatened to break out into open warfare at any moment. But both sides wanted to avoid war and agreed to negotiate their differences. A border commission was appointed and negotiations were begun to settle contending claims between them. Despite temporary disagreements over terms of a new fishing agreement, friendly relations with the Soviet Union were not threatened again until the summer of 1939. Thus Japan was secure on the northern flank and was free to expand southward to Canton and Hankow. It was also in a position to put pressure on the European powers.

When the Japanese Army began the conquest of China in 1937, one of its objectives was the liquidation of non-Japanese, foreign business and commercial interests on the Asiatic continent. As their forces spread further southward, the Japanese commanders, under the guise of military necessity, constantly placed obstacles in the way of foreign firms. For example, travel on the Yangtze River was restricted to Japanese boats. The Japanese-sponsored currency in North China was the only one recognized officially as legal tender within occupied China. There was constant interference with the shipping facilities of the Western powers.

Despite these challenges and insults, the Western powers, who were in a comparatively weak position, could do little more than endure them. In view of the growing crisis in Europe, one of the basic objectives of British policy was to avoid a frontal attack in either Europe or Asia to gain time for greater military preparedness. Thus it was unwilling to oppose Japan single-handedly. Since isolationist policy was still strong in the United States, it was unlikely to do more than protest each new Japanese move by an official announcement or note. Thus when Konoye announced his policy of a New Order in East Asia, the United States merely protested against the interference with the rights and interests of its nationals by Japan and continued to insist that it would not abrogate any of its rights. On the other hand, it was not yet ready to make a positive move to protect those rights.

By the early part of 1939, therefore, the Japanese Army in China considered its position secure enough to tackle the problem of foreign interference with Japan's plans to control China. It decided to try to cut off foreign aid to Chiang Kai-shek in the belief that he would then have to capitulate. It was also agreed to remove foreign influence by direct action. France and Great Britain were the primary targets of attack. With the northern flank temporarily secured from Soviet attack, Japan defied France, and in February, 1939, occupied Hainan Island off the south coast of China. It also claimed sovereignty over the nearby Spratly Islands. France was too weak to take any countermeasures. Japan had successfully called the bluff of one of the colonial powers. It had, thereby, measurably improved its strategic position.

An even greater moral victory was wrested from Great Britain in Tientsin. In June, 1939, the Japanese charged that the British and French were harboring in their concessions in Tientsin the suspected murderers of a native collaborator. Consequently, the local Japanese commander blockaded these concessions. The real issue was who was to control the silver bullion held by the British as collateral for the Chinese currency. Japan wanted to obtain the bullion and drive the Chinese currency out of circulation. Foreigners entering or leaving the concessions were searched by Japanese soldiers; women were made to strip in public on the pretext of smuggling.[8] This policy of degrading Westerners before Asiatics had a tremendous moral impact both on the perpetrators and on the bystanders. It was a crude but graphic way of deflating the prestige of subjects of the colonial powers. It also tended to elevate the Japanese in the eyes of

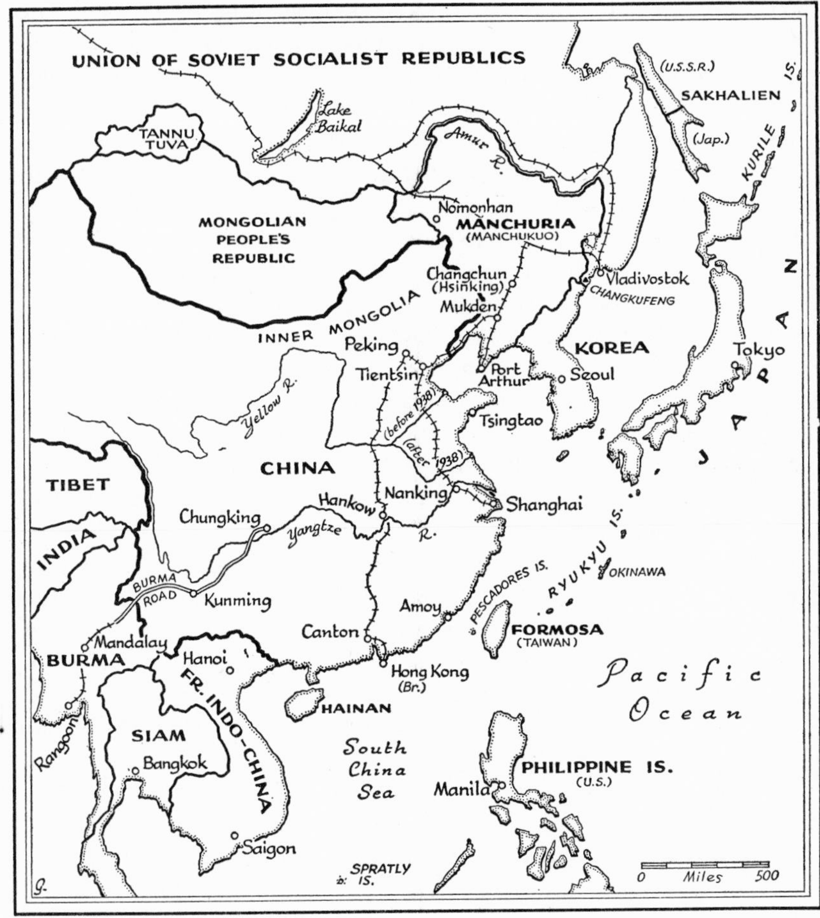

Preparation for Total War, 1937-41

the Chinese as the self-appointed deliverers of Asiatics from European oppression.

But Japan had to pay dearly for its callous attitude and disrespect for the treaty rights of other states in China. Great Britain adamantly refused to surrender the silver bullion. The United States decided that words would have to be replaced by action. Consequently, at the end of July, 1939, it announced its intention to terminate its Treaty of Commerce with Japan after the specified period of six months. This was another way of notifying Japan that unless it ceased its expansionism and other lawless acts, after the expiration date of the treaty, the United States legally could, and might, impose an embargo on the island empire.

At the same time, hostilities on a comparatively large scale had broken out on the Soviet border. This time it was near Nomonhan on the Outer Mongolian-Manchukuo border. By the end of August, 1939, two divisions of Soviet troops with superior mechanized equipment had severely beaten Japanese troops and inflicted 18,000 casualties on the Kwantung Army. These developments threatened to involve Japan in a war with the Soviet Union and to jeopardize its position in China.

As these disquieting reports reached Tokyo, word came from Berlin that Germany and the Soviet Union had signed a nonaggression pact. Japan was in danger of isolation from the Axis. It undertook feverish diplomatic activity directed toward improving its international status. A new Cabinet was formed which promised to follow the "immutable policy of Japan in China," to act independently in dealing with the foreign powers, and to oppose anyone who obstructed Japan's mission.[9] With Hitler's invasion of Poland on September 1, 1939, and the outbreak of World War II in Europe, Japan declared that it would not become involved in the war but would concentrate on the settlement of the war in China. At the same time, negotiations were begun in Moscow which settled the Nomonhan affair. For the second time within a year, therefore, a war with Russia was averted.

But the war in China, the "China Affair," as Japan insisted on calling it, still remained unsettled. In an effort to prevent a closer alliance between the European Axis and Japan, Great Britain had sought to negotiate the Sino-Japanese war. Furthermore, it withdrew its gunboats from the Yangtze River; its troops were recalled from Peking and Tientsin. But these moves were of no avail. During the next few months Japan concentrated on the formation of a strong, pro-Japanese regime for all of China. To this end, the Japanese-sponsored government of Wang Ching-wei was formally inaugurated at Nanking in March, 1940. But even this act had no influence on Chiang and his Nationalist government. He continued to fight Japan as best he could from his temporary capital of Chungking.

The more stubbornly Chiang refused to give up, the more Japan blamed the foreigners for making this resistance possible. Hence, it sought ways and means of preventing the Western powers from continuing to send him aid. Events in Europe soon afforded the opportunity for which Japan was waiting. After the fall of France in the middle of June, 1940, Japan could intimidate Great Britain without fear of reprisals, for the latter was struggling for its very survival. Consequently, Japan demanded that no more military supplies be sent to the Chinese Nationalists over the Burma Road. Great Britain agreed to close the Road for three months. In return, it had avoided war with Japan and gained valuable time during which it won the Battle of Britain.

JAPAN JOINS THE AXIS, 1940

In the meantime, political events within Japan were directed toward the formation of a new political structure which would complete the program for total defense, terminate the war in China, and make Japan an active member of the Axis. Lord keeper of the Privy Seal Kido realized that if elements in the Army were to be placated and kept from engineering a coup d'état, Konoye would have to be reappointed as Premier. The various parties, the Army, Navy, Senior Statesmen, and bureaucrats generally agreed that he was the only acceptable candidate. Before forming his second cabinet, however, Konoye wanted assurances that he would receive support for his policies. Consequently, he consulted his War Minister, General Tōjō Hideki, his Navy Minister, Admiral Yonai Mitsumasa, and his Foreign Minister, Matsuoka Yōsuke, and obtained their agreement for a four-point program. This program called for (1) an alliance with the Axis powers; (2) a planned national economy; (3) a strong economic bloc to be composed of Japan, Manchukuo, and China; and (4) an impenetrable defense based on a new revival of nationalism.

During the summer of 1939, Hitler had unsuccessfully endeavored to persuade Japan to join the Axis. Although it was willing to give a commitment to fight against the Soviet Union, Japan did not want to be committed at that time to fight Great Britain and the United States. Moreover, after Germany had signed a nonaggression pact with the Soviet Union and had invaded Poland, Japan was all the more insistent that it play an independent role.

The military power which the Nazis had demonstrated in Europe from 1939 to 1940, however, had strengthened the position of the advocates of an Axis Alliance. The German victories in Norway, the Netherlands, and France had completely changed the picture. By the autumn of 1940, an Axis victory seemed likely. Thus, unless Japan sided with the Axis, it would not be able to inherit the colonies of Britain, France, and the Netherlands in Asia. Premier Konoye also argued that a tripartite pact would enable his government to arrange for a peace with Chiang and would prevent a war with the Soviet Union. Foreign Minister Matsuoka readily accepted the task of negotiating such a pact. On September 27, 1940, the Tripartite Treaty of Alliance was signed by Japan, Germany, and Italy. The pact recognized the leadership of Germany and Italy in Europe and that of Japan in Greater East Asia. The signatories also promised to come to each other's assistance when attacked by an outside power. Thus the first objective of the Second Konoye Cabinet had been achieved. At the same time, any hopes which the Allies might have had of isolating Japan from the other Axis powers in Europe were shattered.

A New Economic Structure

Despite the passage of the National Mobilization Law in 1938 and the gradual implementation of some of its provisions, the Empire's economy was not operating as a cohesive unit when Konoye formed his second cabinet in July, 1940. The military leaders, such as his new War Minister Tōjō, insisted that government controls be increased and intensified and that they be based on an over-all economic plan. On the other hand, the industrialists, especially the members of the old family combines (the *Zaibatsu*) which comprised the backbone of the nation's economy, insisted that they be permitted to unify and organize industry into cartels which they would control independently of the government. This basic conflict between the militarists and the industrialists, and the bureaucratic jealousies between the old ministries and the new control bodies, had produced a national economy which was partly controlled and partly free. For example, wages were frozen but price controls were more nominal than real. Raw materials presumably were allocated to essential industries but an influential business man could obtain what he needed if he were willing to pay for it. Profit controls had been strengthened and tax reforms had been introduced as a result of Army pressure. Nevertheless, Army dissatisfaction with economic conditions had forced the overthrow of the previous Cabinet.

The appearance of Tōjō as War Minister, Matsuoka as Foreign Minister, and Hoshino Naoki as President of the Planning Board in the Second Konoye Cabinet in July, 1940, was clear proof that the Kwantung clique was going to become active in national economic planning as well as in military strategy and foreign affairs. Since 1932, Hoshino had been a key figure in the formation of the Kwantung Army-controlled, industrial structure in Manchukuo.[10] He was the logical choice, therefore, to carry out the Army's plan of creating a similar structure within Japan proper, which called for a shift from a semiwartime economy to complete control under direction of the military. But Hoshino soon found that it was far more difficult to obtain approval for his plan in Japan, where the industrialists were relatively strong, than in Manchukuo, where his friends in the Kwantung Army called the tune.

Although tremendous advances in industrial production had been made during the decade 1930-40, there were certain obvious weaknesses in the national economy. This production had been directed toward the creation of a strong war machine which had put a heavy strain on the national budget. For example, the value of total industrial output had increased from 6 billion yen at the beginning of the period to 30 billion yen by 1941.

The main emphasis had been on heavy industry, however, which showed a tenfold increase from 1930 to 1942.[11] Military expenditures, which reflected this trend, and the demands of the war in China were largely responsible for a rapid rise in the total national expenditures. Whereas in 1931, military expenses comprised less than half a billion yen and 30 per cent of the budget, in the first year of the China War (1937-38) they totalled about 4 billion yen and over 71 per cent of the budget. By the time Hoshino became President of the Planning Board in 1940 they had increased to 7.3 billion yen. Consequently, the cumulated budget deficit had reached nearly one-fourth of the total national income.

The longer the war in China continued, the more imperative it became for Japan to develop effective planning if the nation was to survive.[12] Despite the efforts of the Cabinet Planning Board, such planning and control as existed prior to 1940 had been haphazard. It had been evolved largely on a basis of trial and error. For instance, effective control over foreign trade was not undertaken until 1937 when high prices at home had caused a slump in exports and a dangerously large adverse balance of trade. In the fall of that year, the first list of prohibited imports was published and strict limitations were enforced. Within a year, by 1938, the former adverse balance had been converted into an export surplus.

But the attempts to control general production and distribution through coordinated plans issued by the Planning Board were far less successful than those for trade. The Planning Board, through a materials mobilization plan, attempted to control such important elements of the economy as oil, iron and steel, power, machine tools, light metals, ships, and minerals. Special policy companies were formed for each of these important industries. But competition for limited raw materials and unwillingness to abide by the regulations resulted in confusion. Even in the strategically important iron and steel industry, there was no fixed pattern of control until November, 1941.

The task of creating an effective economic mobilization was also bedeviled by the plan to create a Greater East Asia Co-prosperity Sphere. As the Japanese Army extended its tentacles over the Asiatic mainland, new raw materials and markets were available for exploitation. The nation was faced, therefore, with a triple task: the exploitation of resources and expansion of industry in the colonies, the industrialization of the newly acquired territories, and the coordination of both of these developments with the new planned economy at home.

During the 1930-40 decade, there was a decided difference in the method of exploitation of the colonies of Korea and Formosa on the one hand, and of Manchukuo and China on the other. As for the two colonies, industrial growth was the result of investment of both private Japanese capitalists and of the Imperial government. In Korea, for example, the sevenfold increase of industrial production in this period was the result of the investment of both the Oriental Development Company and of private companies. The former, which was half-owned by the Japanese government, possessed a large part of the best agricultural land in Korea. It also provided a large share of venture capital. In 1941, it floated 70 per cent of the loans in the colony. On the other hand, the privately owned Japan Nitrogenous Fertilizer Manufacturing Company developed most of the electric power and chemical industry in the Korean peninsula. It reportedly made a profit of 31 per cent. One of its subsidiaries, the Suiho Power Company, built the large hydroelectric plant on the Yalu River, with a yearly output of 3.8 billion kilowatt-hours. With such favorable conditions for high profits and maximum of security, the three leading *Zaibatsu* firms readily invested in new light metal plants, railways, mines, cement, and chemical industries. They also profited from special government subsidies awarded to strategically important plants such as those of synthetic petroleum.

But the economic development of Manchuria had been a different matter. When the Kwantung Army took over that rich, undeveloped, predominantly agricultural area in 1931, it hoped to build its own empire. It dreamt of a self-sufficient continental base of operations free from what it considered the "baneful effects of unbridled capitalism." It proceeded forthwith to make this dream a reality through the creation of the puppet state of Manchukuo. (See page 333.) It soon discovered, however, that the economic exploitation and industrialization of a country was a difficult and complicated matter which required large amounts of capital and a specialized knowledge. During the first few years of the existence of Manchukuo, therefore, its economic expansion was entrusted to the South Manchurian Railway Company. The S.M.R., which was jointly owned by the Japanese and Manchukuo governments, established a number of subsidiary companies to carry on this exploitation.

The Kwantung Army leaders soon recognized, however, that the developmental program of the S.M.R., which concentrated on new railway lines, was not enough. Suspicious of the old-line financial combines, the Kwantung Army sought assistance from one of the most imaginative of the *nouveaux riches,* Aikawa Yoshisuke. In 1936, he became a special economic adviser to the Kwantung Army and soon worked out a plan to transform his financial interests in Japan (*Nissan*) into the Manchurian Industrial Development Corporation (*Mangyō*).

On March 1, 1938, this new corporation began operation under the most favorable conditions for Aikawa, its president. Half of the 400 million yen capital had been supplied by the Manchukuo government which also guaranteed a 6 per cent interest on the investment and underwrote the capital which came from Japan. Manchurian Industrial then began to absorb many of the existing companies. It concentrated its investments in new concerns, such as iron foundries, steel plants, and automobile and aircraft factories. By the end of 1941, its loans had risen to nearly 1.5 billion yen and earnings had equaled 13.6 per cent. While this huge corporation was a profitable enterprise, it was not always looked upon with favor by financial circles in Tokyo. For example, when a new Five Year Plan of expansion for Manchukuo was established in 1937 under its direction, Tokyo bankers were worried over the predominance of Manchurian loans floated on the domestic market. In some cases, they refused to approve new issues of loans for Manchurian enterprises.

Whether by design or by chance, new conquests were started in North China by the Kwantung Army just when it had become difficult to obtain large amounts of new risk capital for investment in Manchuria. These conquests after July, 1937, secured a new supply of resources and opened up new investment possibilities. Exploitation of China was undertaken in various ways. The North China and Central China Development Companies, under Japanese ownership, began an active expansion of transportation, communications, harbor facilities, and natural resources. Private Japanese companies were encouraged to operate industries already developed by Chinese capital. Manchurian companies also participated in the operation of factories and mines. The net result of all this activity was the strengthening of the economic ties among Japan, Manchukuo, and China and the formation of a significant yen-bloc area. For example, in 1940, North China produced 18 million tons of coal and Manchuria mined 21 million tons. By 1941, both areas met all of Japan's salt requirements. In the crucial iron and steel industries, while the continental area manufactured only a small fraction of the ingot and finished steel for the Empire, it produced 30 per cent of Japan's needs for pig iron in 1937 and also in 1941.[13]

Such, in very general terms, was the economic situation within Japan and the occupied areas of China in July, 1940, when Hoshino, as newly appointed President of the Cabinet Planning Board, tried to impose the same sort of controls on Japan proper that he carried out in Manchukuo. He advocated the reorganization and strengthening of the various cartels and the appointment by the Cabinet of their directors. These directors were to be given virtual dictatorial powers to carry out policies formulated by a Supreme Economic Council. But the great family combines were not yet willing to succumb to Army control and refused to relinquish their autonomy. The international crisis was not yet acute enough to convince them that if they did not support the Army they would lose everything. Consequently, the Army had to wait until September, 1941, when a compromise solution was worked out, before it had the power to force industry to comply with state controls. The Second Konoye Cabinet had been less successful, therefore, in the creation of a new economic structure acceptable to the Manchurian clique than it had been in the negotiations for a Tripartite Pact.

In the creation of an impenetrable defense based on a revival of nationalism, the last of the objectives of the Konoye Cabinet, it made notable gains. Although the political parties had not been opposed to Japan's expansion on the Asiatic continent, they had not, on the other hand, been staunch supporters of the program of centralized control at home and indefinite expansion abroad. Even prior to Konoye becoming Prime Minister in July, 1940, he had been active in the formation of a single national party. Under his leadership, several patriotic organizations were merged into a single organization. Later, the old political parties were subjected to "voluntary" dissolution.

The stage was thus prepared for a transcendant ultranationalist body known as the Imperial Rule Assistance Association (IRAA). Its preparatory committee was composed of members of the Cabinet, the Diet, business interests, and the nationalistic societies. It was formally inaugurated in October, 1940, with the Premier as president. It has been claimed that Konoye hoped to use the IRAA to control the Army extremists. Actually, the Army leaders took it over for their own purposes a year later. It then became the vehicle through which outright military party control was exercised. Under its inspiration the nation was prepared to begin its historic march to create a new order in the world, to place, as Konoye had expressed it, the universe under a single roof, namely, the benevolent leadership of the Japanese Emperor.

The Final Steps to War

Underlying all of these ultranationalist developments was a special urge for expansion to the south. The one great weakness in Japan's economic self-sufficiency was a lack of oil, the basic fuel for the Imperial Navy and the Air Force. While large stores of oil had been accumulated, they were not sufficient to sustain a continued, all-out war effort. Domestic production was piteously low and synthetic fuels had not been satisfactorily developed. On the other hand, ample oil supplies, bauxite, tin, and rubber existed just beyond the perimeter of areas directly controlled by the Empire. Thus the expansionists argued that, if the Dutch, for example, would not agree to let the Netherlands Indies become a member of the Co-prosperity Sphere, their rich oil fields might have to be seized.

When considered in this light, the southward military moves of Japan after June, 1940, especially into French Indochina, fall into proper perspective. Beginning that month, Japan steadily increased its pressure. It requested that the Indochina border be closed. Great Britain had likewise acceded to the closing of the Burma Road. By September, 1940, the Vichy Government, and finally the Governor General of Indochina, was forced to concede to demands that Japan be granted the use of three airfields in Indochina with the right to station troops at each. Transit rights were also to be given to Japanese troops for an attack against southwest China.

Despite the strategic advantages which these moves gave to Japan over the Western powers, there was ample evidence available to show that the latter would not, regardless of circumstances, agree to recognize Japan's new rights in Asia. For example, in September, 1940, the Netherlands East Indies had rebuffed a special Japanese economic mission which sought to obtain special concessions for Indonesian oil. While Britain might have been forced to make temporary concessions concerning the closing of the Burma Road, it had no intention of doing so permanently. Secretary of State Cordell Hull told the Senate Foreign Relations Committee in mid-January, 1941, that the United States had repeatedly tried to persuade Japan that its best interests lay in the development of friendly relations with the United States. The United States had not, and would not, sanction the formation of a new order in the western Pacific under Japanese political and economic domination.

But Foreign Minister Matsuoka exemplified the group of nationalists in Japan who held the diametrically opposite view and who ran the government. They were convinced that since the Empire was invincible, it could obtain what it wanted by force. Furthermore, they believed that it was in a strong enough world position to make even the United States concede to its wishes. Consequently, he outlined an impossible program. He proposed the strengthening of the ties with the Axis, protecting his country's northern flank by signing a treaty of nonaggression with the Soviet Union, and working out a general settlement with the United States. Unfortunately for the peace of the world and for his own future, Matsuoka's arrogance and conceit blinded him toward Hitler's motives. Furthermore, despite his early training in America, Matsuoka completely misjudged the seriousness of the basic differences between his own government and those of the United States.

Thus, in March, 1941, he started on his incongruous mission, leaving for Berlin the day after the United States Congress had passed the Lend-Lease Act and thus squarely placed itself by Britain's side against the Axis. In

Germany, he failed to catch the significance of a hint that Hitler was contemplating striking at the Soviet Union. He was more concerned with keeping on the best of terms with both Hitler and Stalin than with their relations toward each other. The Japanese Foreign Minister then went on to Moscow and returned proudly with a Soviet-Japanese Non-Aggression Pact. He believed he had thus protected Japan's northern flank. He then turned his attention toward a *rapprochement* with the United States.[14]

Even before the Foreign Minister had gone to Berlin, a new Japanese Ambassador, Admiral Nomura Kichisaburō had arrived in Washington with the promise from his Foreign Office that he would receive support in negotiations for a basic United States–Japanese understanding. On April 16, 1941, Secretary of State Cordell Hull gave the Japanese Ambassador the first of many notes which were to be exchanged between the two countries during the next eight months of negotiations. During this period, neither country budged from its basic position. Thus Hull's first note contained the four basic principles on which he insisted that agreement must be reached before any final settlement was possible between the two nations. These principles were: (1) the respect for territorial integrity and sovereignty of all nations; (2) the noninterference in the internal affairs of other states; (3) the support of the principle of equality, including equality of commercial opportunity; and (4) the nondisturbance of the status quo except by peaceful means.

The basic Japanese position was expressed in a reply of May 12, 1941. It justified Japan's alliance with Germany and Italy on the grounds that it was defensive in nature with a view to preventing neutral countries from entering the European War. In what was considered as an answer to Hull's first two principles, the note requested the United States to persuade Chiang Kai-shek to agree to negotiate a peace treaty with Japan on the basis of friendship, recognition of the independence of Manchukuo, cooperation against communism, and economic cooperation. In reference to the principle of equal commercial opportunity, Japan proposed normal trade relations between Japan and the United States and that each state should supply the other with needed commodities. The last principle was dismissed by defining Japan's expansion as "peaceful." In fact, it asked the United States to cooperate in the production and procurement for Japan of natural resources such as oil, rubber, tin, and nickel in the southwestern Pacific. Despite the basic divergence of his government's reply from the American position, Premier Konoye hoped that the European War could be confined to Europe and that the United States would agree to force Chiang to sue for peace. If these objectives could be achieved, he was confident that other differences could be resolved.

But international developments, together with the growing strength of

General Tōjō and his group within Japan, quickly obliterated any real chance of a successful conclusion of the American-Japanese negotiations. In the first place, in the early part of June, 1941, the Netherlands had again refused to comply with Japan's demands for oil, rubber, and tin from the Netherlands East Indies. Another note from the United States, received shortly thereafter, indicated that it would not assist Japan in obtaining these strategic materials. Consequently, if these valuable supplies were to be obtained, so Japan's nationalists argued, they would have to be obtained by force.

When Hitler invaded the Soviet Union on June 22, 1941, and failed to advise his Axis partner in the Pacific of his plans, a crisis immediately arose within the Konoye Cabinet. Matsuoka, who had negotiated the Non-Aggression Pact with the Soviet Union, and simultaneously urged closer ties with the Axis, was in an untenable position. To extricate himself, he urged the Emperor to approve entering the war on Hitler's side and advancing southward in the Pacific. While Hitler's armies poured eastward, continuous meetings were held in Tokyo by the Cabinet and the Liaison Conference. After agreement had been reached on July 2, 1941, an Imperial Conference, under the chairmanship of the Emperor, met to give final sanction to a new policy decision.[15]

The importance of this decisive conference cannot be overemphasized. In the first place, Japan's leaders decided to carry out their plan to advance southward on Indochina and Siam *even at the risk of war with Great Britain and the United States.* Secondly, it was agreed to observe the Neutrality Pact with the Soviet Union. Thirdly, if Germany was on the point of defeating Russia, Japan would intervene in the European war. Thus Japan would have a chance to strengthen its position in Eastern Asia at Russia's expense. The decisions of the Conference were kept secret from the people who were told simply that: "A fundamental national policy to be adopted in meeting the prevailing situation has been decided." The decision was that since Japan's very existence depended on moving southward, nothing would stop it from doing so. A general mobilization was ordered. All Japanese merchant ships were called home from the Atlantic Ocean. Time for reaching a settlement was fast running out.

As a first step toward implementing the new policy, Prime Minister Konoye resigned in mid-July, 1941. By so doing, he was able to rid his Cabinet of persons opposed to this basic policy, especially Foreign Minister Matsuoka. The Third Konoye Cabinet, which was formed almost immediately (July 18, 1941 to October 18, 1941), promised to put these policies into practice with speed and fortitude. Pressure was exerted on France and the Vichy Government. They were forced to consent to new Japanese bases in Indochina or suffer invasion. On July 29, 1941, 50,000 Japanese troops poured into the area. As a reprisal, two days later the United States froze all Japanese assets abroad and the negotiations for a general settlement were broken off. In reality, an economic embargo had been imposed on Japan and trade with the United States virtually ceased.

This new development made it all the more advisable, from Japan's point of view, to reach an agreement with the United States, providing such agreement could be achieved on Japan's terms. Premier Konoye proposed, therefore, that he meet with President Roosevelt somewhere in the Pacific to discuss a basic, over-all settlement. In reply, the President told Japanese Ambassador Nomura in August, 1941, that unless Japan stopped its military advances, such as those in Indochina, the United States would have to act to protect its interests and national security. As for the meeting of the heads of state, Japan should furnish a clearer statement of its real attitudes and plans before any such meeting could take place.

On the other hand, the attitudes and plans which were being evolved in Tokyo were making an agreement with the United States impossible. In fact, another Imperial Conference was held early in September. It was decided at that time that the nation should not be deterred in its plans by the possibility of war with the United States. War preparations should proceed at an accelerated rate and be completed by the end of October. Simultaneously, every possible diplomatic means should be used to persuade the United States to agree to Japan's position. If there was no progress by early October, a definite decision should be taken concerning war with the United States.

But the interchange of notes between Japan and the United States which took place during September did little to iron out their differences. On October 2, Hull informed Nomura that Japan's latest proposals formed no real basis for a settlement. He added that the meeting of Konoye and Roosevelt should be put off until there was agreement between the two countries on how the four American principles, originally proposed by him on April 16, should be applied to problems in East Asia.

Thus, early October had arrived without Japanese diplomacy having succeeded in persuading the United States to change its viewpoint. The Japanese High Command demanded that in accordance with the Imperial Conference decision, a definite position should be taken on the question of going to war. The military leaders resented the latest American note which insisted that any basic settlement would entail the withdrawal of Japanese troops from the Chinese mainland. General Tōjō haughtily declared that Japan should fight rather than let the United States interfere with its destiny. He further recommended, and obtained, the resignation of Premier Konoye. On October 18, 1941, Tōjō succeeded to the post of Prime Minister. He and his Manchurian clique were now securely in control.[16]

It was now only a matter of time before his Cabinet approved a war plan which included a simultaneous attack on the naval bases at Pearl Harbor, Manila, and Singapore. Another Imperial Conference, the second in two months, was called. This time a positive decision was taken to make war on both the United States and Great Britain if the pending diplomatic negotiations were unsuccessful. The Conference also approved inviting the European partners of the Axis to join in the struggle. On the other hand, Japan would decline any German overtures to fight the Soviet Union. Consequently, the negotiations in Washington were continued and the Japanese Ambassador was sent a final proposal on which he was ordered to obtain agreement by November 25, 1941. As his instructions noted, procrastination was no longer possible and the United States should seek peace before the last day of negotiations arrived.[17]

On November 17, special Japanese envoy Kurusu arrived in Washington but had no new proposals to offer. Secretary Hull insisted that no settlement was possible until Japan withdrew its troops from China, adopted a liberal commercial policy, and gave up its alliance with the Axis. In the meantime, Premier Tōjō had activated the war plan and Japan's submarines were on their way to rendezvous at Pearl Harbor on December 7, 1941. An alternative plan, a *modus vivendi* which the Japanese government had prepared to keep negotiations continuing until Pearl Harbor Day, was rejected by the United States. Finally, on November 26, 1941, the United States presented its last note which reviewed its position and included the basic points which had been presented at the beginning of the negotiations. It stated that permanent peace could be established only when these principles were adopted. Hull indicated that he was not interested in a *modus vivendi* and that the United States would not modify its position. Unless Japan accepted the American proposals, the economic embargo would continue.

The Liaison Conference in Tokyo agreed unanimously to reject the American note and to fight. Tōjō then secured the Emperor's approval for an Imperial Conference which confirmed this decision. Japan's declaration of war was delayed in reaching the United States. It was still in the process of being deciphered in the Japanese Embassy in Washington when Japan struck at Pearl Harbor on December 7, 1941. The war in the Pacific had begun.

Notes

1. General Tōjō Hideki (1884-1948) was a new figure on the national scene and was to become the most influential person in the government in the critical period from 1941 to 1944. After serving as Chief of the Kwantung Army's military police, he advanced to Chief of Staff. In December, 1938, he returned to Tokyo as Chief

of the newly created Inspectorate General of Military Aviation. In a few months he was raised to be Vice-Minister of War. Under Konoye he held the key post of War Minister from July, 1940, to October, 1941. When he succeeded Konoye as Premier on October 18, 1941, he had already decided on war in the Pacific. He was the first wartime premier but was forced to resign in 1944 after the tide of war had turned against Japan. He was convicted as a major war criminal and condemned to death.

2. Konoye Fumimarō (1891-1945) had remained aloof from politics in the sense that he had never held a Cabinet post. He had long been a member of the House of Peers, however, and was its President from 1933 to 1937, and was also President of the Privy Council from January, 1939, to June, 1940. He appeared to be a weak person, vacillating between a moderate and extremist viewpoint. At the final showdown, however, he did not hesitate. When he learned that he was to be arrested for trial as a war criminal, he committed suicide. There were three Konoye Cabinets as follows: First Konoye Cabinet, June 4, 1937—January 5, 1939; Second Konoye Cabinet July 22, 1940—July 18, 1941; Third Konoye Cabinet, July 18—October 18, 1941. I have adopted the popular spelling of his name.

Konoye's first Cabinet had General Sugiyama Hajime as Minister of War, who had served in that capacity in the previous Cabinet and was one of the strong men in the Army. Admiral Yonai was held over as Navy Minister. Hirota Kōki, former Premier and leader of the bureaucrats but amenable to Army dictates, was Foreign Minister. Kaya Okinori and Yoshino Shinji, both under the influence of the military, were appointed respectively Minister of Finance, and of Commerce and Industry. Baba Eiichi, former Governor of the Hypothec Bank and selected by the Army to be Finance Minister in 1936, was appointed Home Minister. The heads of the two political parties, Nagai and Nakajima, served as individuals on the Cabinet and not as representatives of their parties.

3. Space does not allow nor is this an appropriate place to go into the details of the Lukouchiao or Marco Polo Bridge Incident to establish which side was responsible for the fighting. The real cause of the war was the conflict between Japan's desire to control Manchuria and North China by force, if necessary, and China's drive toward unification. One of the most recent and exhaustive studies of Japan in China will be found in F. C. Jones, *Japan's New Order in Asia: Its Rise and Fall 1937-1945* (London: Oxford University Press, 1954).

4. The Yangtze River attack was another example of independent action by a local unit. Japan was not ready for another war and apologized for the incident the next day. Col. Hashimoto Kingorō, one of the commanders of the units involved in the shooting and an ardent nationalist, was disciplined for his unwarranted act.

5. After Chiang refused to accept the Japanese proposal of December 22, 1937, Konoye announced on January 16, 1938, that his government henceforth would cease to deal with Chiang. See *Tokyo Gazette,* No. 8 (Jan., 1938).

6. For a more detailed analysis of the law, see Borton, *op. cit.,* pp. 60-65 and 129-30; and *Tokyo Gazette,* No. 11 (May, 1938).

7. The Kwantung Army exercised its control over Manchukuo through the General Affairs Board and the Fourth Section of the Army. While all Ministers of State within the Manchukuo government were Chinese, the real power was in the hands of the Vice-Ministers, who were Japanese. All policies, laws, ordinances, and rescripts were first considered by the General Affairs Board under a Japanese Chairman. The Vice-Ministers and Chief of the Fourth Section of the Kwantung Army were the other members of the Board. Thus no action could be taken by

Manchukuo without the approval of the Kwantung Army. Aside from the fact that the latter was nominally responsible to the Chief of Staff in Tokyo, the Japanese government was represented at the Manchukuo capital by the Chief of the Kwantung Army.

8. The smuggling charge had an ironic ring. There is ample evidence to show that agents of the Japanese armed forces had actively engaged in smuggling opium into North China to demoralize the people prior to the formation of puppet regimes. Thus the Japanese came to be feared and despised by the Chinese as much for the fact that they corrupted the country as for the fact that they were conquerors.

9. The shifts in Cabinets which occurred from the resignation of Konoye on January 5, 1939, to the formation of his second Cabinet on July 22, 1940, had little effect on national policy. With various factions and vested interests among the military and civilian leaders seeking to gain power, policies were determined, as always, by a small group of oligarchs who reached an agreed compromise after interminable discussion. Hiranuma Kiichirō, President of the Privy Council after 1936, ardent nationalist, and advocate of the Imperial Way, was Premier from January 5, 1939, to August 30, 1939. General Abe Nobuyuki was then selected as Premier to extricate the nation from a precarious position. Abe was followed by Admiral Yonai Mitsumasa from January 16 to July 22, 1940. The Yonai Cabinet was succeeded by the Second and Third Konoye Cabinets.

10. In 1932, Hoshino became Vice-Minister of Finance in Manchuria. Under the Manchukuo government he rapidly rose to become the most important figure in the government, namely, Chairman of the General Affairs Board, the body which planned and directed all important operations of Manchukuo. He was a close friend of Tōjō and obviously was his choice for his new post. See note 7 above.

11. This change meant that whereas heavy industries accounted for only 38 per cent of the total production in 1930, they had been responsible for 73 per cent in 1942. Other notable changes during approximately the same period were increases of motor vehicle units from 500 annually to 48,000, airplanes from practically none to 5000, aluminum ingots from 19 tons to 72,000 tons, ingot steel from 1.8 million tons to 6.8 million, and naval ships from 15,000 tons in 1931 to 232,000 tons in 1937. In view of the excellent study by Professor Jerome B. Cohen on Japan's wartime economy, a detailed economic analysis of Japan after 1940 has been omitted. Figures will be used only where it is necessary to clarify the general narrative. These figures, as well as those used in the remainder of this section, are taken from Jerome B. Cohen, *Japan's Economy in War and Reconstruction* (Minneapolis: University of Minnesota Press, 1949).

12. In seeking a rationale for expansionism, much was made of the pressure from population. While the argument might have some weight in view of export quotas and the need for foreign markets, it does not seem pertinent in reference to food needs. For example, while the population increased from 64,450,000 in 1930 to 73,114,000 in 1940, rice imports from outside Korea and Formosa declined from 5 per cent of total rice imports in the period 1931-35 to 2 per cent of imports in 1936-38, with total amounts of imports actually less in 1941 than in 1938. Cohen, *op. cit.,* pp. 288 and 369.

13. Cohen, *op. cit.,* pp. 45, 128, and 163.

14. In view of the numerous detailed studies of the intricate foreign relations and negotiations of Japan both with the Axis and with the Allies, it seems unnecessary to do little more than sketch in broadest outline the most significant aspects of these negotiations. For those who wish to consult documentary material, the Proceedings, Records and Exhibits of the International Military Tribunal of

the Far East should be consulted. Also the Report and Hearings of the U.S. Congress Joint Committee in the Investigation of Pearl Harbor, U.S. State Department, *Foreign Relations 1931-41, Japan* (2 vols.), U.S. State Department, *Nazi-Soviet Relations.* Two competent and thorough studies dealing especially with United States—Japanese negotiations, which contain extensive bibliographical material, deserve special mention. They are Herbert Feis, *The Road to Pearl Harbor* (Princeton: Princeton University Press, 1950); and F. C. Jones, *Japan's New Order in East Asia, Its Rise and Fall, 1937-45* (New York: Oxford University Press, 1954).

15. The Liaison Conference thus emerged as the key policy-forming body. Composed of the Premier; Ministers of War, Navy, and Foreign Affairs; and the Chiefs of Staff, it superseded Cabinet decisions. Technically, the Cabinet had to give formal approval to decisions of the Conference. This was the ninth Imperial Conference held to date in Japan's history. It followed the usual pattern of giving formal sanction, without debate and verbal participation by the Emperor, of decisions already agreed to by the Premier and his closest advisers.

16. Tōjō was also concurrently War Minister and Home Minister. Hoshino Naoki, the former author of state control in Manchukuo and President of the Cabinet Planning Board, was the new Chief Secretary of the Cabinet. Kishi Shinsuke, another civilian leader in Manchuria, was Minister of Commerce and Industry.

17. The United States government, throughout all these negotiations, was aware of the instructions sent the Japanese negotiators. It had broken the Japanese codes and was intercepting the messages. Hull gave no inkling, however, of this fact. This information, while helpful, did not reveal all of the decisions in Tokyo of the Imperial Conferences or of the High Command. Hence, no one in Washington knew when, where, or how war might break out.

PART V

JAPAN SURVIVES WAR AND DEFEAT 1941-1955

Unite your total strength to be devoted to the construction for the future. Cultivate the ways of rectitude; foster nobility of spirit; and work with resolution so as ye may enhance the innate glory of the Imperial State and keep pace with the progress of the world.

Imperial Rescript of Emperor Hirohito,
August 14, 1945

Chronology

1941-1955

1941, December 7	Pearl Harbor attacked
December 8	United States declares war on Japan
1942, May	Battle of Coral Sea
June	Battle of Midway
November	Creation of Greater East Asia Ministry
1943, February	Guadalcanal recaptured
November	Munitions Ministry established
1944, July	Fall of Saipan
	Premier Tōjō replaced by Koiso
1945, April 1	Okinawa captured
July 26	Potsdam Declaration
August 6	Atomic bomb dropped on Hiroshima
August 14	Japan agrees to surrender
	General MacArthur appointed Supreme Commander for the Allied Powers
September 2	Japan surrenders
1946, April	First postwar elections in Japan
November	New Constitution adopted
1947, July	United States tries to call peace conference
1948, October	Yoshida forms second Cabinet
1949, May	United States supports Japanese industrial revival
July	Japanese government given greater autonomy
1950, June 25	Invasion of South Korea by Korean communists
	War in Korea
October	United States announces principles for peace treaty
November	Chinese communists enter Korean War
1951, April 10	General MacArthur relieved of his commands
Sept. 8	Treaty of Peace signed at San Francisco
1952, April 28	Peace Treaty in effect, occupation ends
1953, July 27	Armistice in Korea
1954, March	Mutual Defense Assistance Agreement
December	Premier Yoshida resigns
1955, February	Premier Hatoyama's Democratic Party wins elections

19

WORLD WAR II: PEARL HARBOR TO SURRENDER, 1941-1945

At dawn on December 7, 1941, a two-hour Japanese attack hit the naval and air base at Pearl Harbor with devastating suddenness. Eight battleships and ten other ships were either sunk or severely damaged. At one stroke, 90 per cent of the American naval and air strength in the Hawaiian Islands was immobilized. Simultaneously, the Japanese Imperial Navy, Army, and Air Force had collaborated to attack the Philippines, Malaya, Guam, Wake, and Midway Islands, and the British strategic outposts at Hong Kong and Singapore. From the Japanese point of view, these attacks had been eminently successful. The Japanese forces were free to capture their next objectives without hindrance from the American or British Navy or Air Force. The United States declared war on Japan the next day and on the other Axis powers shortly thereafter; England, France, China, and the other Allies soon followed suit.

During the next six months, the Allies were helpless to stop the surge of Japan. Such isolated outposts as Guam and the Gilbert Islands fell almost immediately. Within the first month, there had been landings on the Philippines, Hong Kong had surrendered, and Manila had capitulated. The pressure increased in such widely separated regions as the Netherlands East Indies in southeast Asia and the Bismarck Islands and New Guinea in the south-central Pacific. In mid-February, 1942, after a spectacular jungle campaign by specially trained troops, the Japanese surrounded the great British naval base of Singapore and forced it to surrender. Despite heroic stands such as that of the Filipino and American forces at Bataan in the Philippines, the tide rolled on until it reached its outer perimeter in midsummer. By that time, Japan was in control of a tremendous quadrangle encompassing the entire western Pacific. The four corners of this vast area were the Aleutians in the northeast, the Gilbert Islands in the southeast, Sumatra and Burma in the southwest corner, and Sakhalien in the northwest.[1] (See map, page 380.)

When the Tōjō government went to war, some basic war objectives had already been approved. Others became clarified and refined as the war progressed. These chief objectives might be summarized as follows: (1) the establishment of peace and stability in East Asia through expulsion of the Western colonial powers; (2) the creation of an impenetrable defensive perimeter by the amalgamation of strategic bases such as Manila, Hong Kong, and Singapore with the Empire's defense outposts; (3) the creation of a self-sufficient economy through a Greater East Asia Co-prosperity Sphere; (4) the temporary military administration of former colonial areas to be superseded by "independent governments" friendly to Japan; (5) the successful termination of the war in China; and (6) the enforced acceptance by the United States of peace terms recognizing these accomplishments.

By July, 1942, Premier Tōjō could claim that the first of these objectives had all but been attained. Great Britain, the Netherlands, and the United States had been defeated and humiliated. Actually, these victories had been achieved more rapidly and with fewer losses than anticipated by the Japanese Chiefs of Staff. The nation was proud of its Army and Navy and immensely satisfied. But even the most complacent of Japan's wartime leaders realized that the Allies were preparing for a counterattack as quickly as possible. In fact, the two naval battles of the Coral Sea (May 4-8, 1942) and of Midway (June 3-5, 1942) betokened the difficulties inherent in constructing the planned defense perimeter. The Coral Sea Battle reversed the outward push toward the southeast; the Battle of Midway inflicted heavy losses on a strong Japanese carrier force and protected the western flank of the Hawaiian Islands.

Perfection of Wartime Controls, 1942-44

During the first few months of the war, the entire nation had concentrated its energies on purely military affairs. As the pace of conquest was curbed, then halted, and, finally, reversed, Tōjō and his Cabinet had to cope with two immediate problems. If these conquests were to be solidified and if progress were to be made toward self-sufficiency, he must integrate the various organs of the national government into an effective totalitarian state. In the second place, he must create new administrative machinery to govern the newly conquered overseas territories and to exploit those resources needed by the defense industries and by the armed services. To assist him in building a totalitarian state, the Imperial Rule Assistance Association was transformed into a vehicle to encourage outright military-party control. For example, in April, 1942, it secured the election to the House of Representatives of an overwhelmingly large majority of candidates who had been officially sponsored by Tōjō's government. He was thus assured of political support for whatever he proposed.[2]

But he found the business world less amenable to his leadership. Despite the wide powers which he wielded, the *Zaibatsu* had not yet capitulated to complete governmental control over management, production, and finance. By the summer of 1942, at the height of Japan's military expansion, a compromise system had been evolved whereby industrialists still controlled at least part of their destiny. This cooperation in the government's controls over their affairs was assured by appointment of the cartel heads of the large combines to the highest posts in the Control Associations. The Cabinet Planning Board (see page 342 above), in accordance with a general plan which it originated for Japan and overseas territories, transmitted schedules of production to the Control Associations for execution. Since membership in a Control Association was compulsory for all concerns, presumably a national production quota could be attained. But the heavy demands for increased production soon produced competition among the Control Associations for raw materials and supplies. Furthermore, competition among companies within a single Control Association added to the confusion. As the pace of conquest slackened and was reversed, far more complete and drastic reforms in the governmental structure were necessary.

Furthermore, the swift advances of the Japanese forces in the South Pacific created far-flung and complicated administrative problems. To cope with the situation, an ordinance was drafted for the creation of a Ministry of Greater East Asia. Its purpose was to supervise and administer all matters connected with overseas territories except in Korea, Formosa, and Karafuto. It was to absorb the functions of the powerful Cabinet boards which had been in charge of affairs in Manchuria, China, and the Pacific Mandated Islands. In effect, Premier Tōjō conceived of the new Ministry as a means whereby the newly conquered areas would be integrated into the Empire. Finally, it relegated to the Foreign Office only formal diplomatic functions and thus prevented it from challenging the activities of the Imperial Army in occupied territories. Consequently, when the Foreign Minister resigned in protest, Tōjō was delighted and assumed the post himself.

With the creation of the Greater East Asia Ministry, on November 1, 1942, the protection of Japanese overseas interests and the exploitation of resources in the newly conquered territories were irrevocably placed in the hands of the military. Aoki Kazuo, one of the leading civilian members of the Manchurian clique, was made the first Minister of Greater East Asia.[3] He immediately began to coordinate, as far as it was possible to do so, the political and economic exploitation of the conquered territories.

In general, local independence movements were encouraged for immediate and long-range reasons. For the moment, it made the Japanese appear as liberators and, presumably, reduced resistance to military occupation. Japan hoped that it would also create a situation that would make it difficult for the Western powers, even though they won the war, to retrieve their colonies and their dominant position throughout Asia. This policy was successful in some areas. In Burma, for example, Ba Maw was supported as chief executive. The autonomous movement flourished under his leadership and Japanese tutelage. By August, 1943, the new state was ready to declare its independence and to make a formal alliance with Japan. In the Philippines the reaction was different. Collaborators were at hand who administered the government under Japanese control; when General MacArthur began the reconquest of the islands in October, 1944, however, he was welcomed as the real liberator.

In the British territory of Malaya, and the Dutch colonies in the East Indies, the emphasis was on economic exploitation. In the former, Singapore was developed as a strong Japanese naval outpost and the western anchor of Greater East Asia. Rubber and tin were requisitioned for military purposes but the economy of the Malay States was never successfully integrated into the Co-prosperity Sphere. The Netherlands East Indies were placed under direct military administration with headquarters in Jakarta (old Batavia). Lip service was paid to the aspiration for independence of nationalist leaders such as Soekarno and Hatta, but the Indies were considered important primarily because of their rich resources. Japanese technicians were poured into the islands in a futile attempt to extract oil and other raw materials in sufficient quantity to bolster the Empire's self-sufficiency. But time ran out before this was accomplished.

The other important colonial area in southeast Asia, namely, Indochina, was left under French control because it was to Japan's advantage to do so. The Vichy Government was in no position to oppose any demands which Japan might wish to impose and it administered the territory until shortly before the war's end.

By the end of the first year of the war, Japan had achieved, at least partially, some of the war objectives proclaimed by Premier Tōjō. But the war in the Pacific had been planned by Tōjō and his colleagues independently of their Axis partners. It seemed to be almost detached from the war in Europe, Africa, and the Near East. No meetings of Hitler, Mussolini, and Tōjō were held. They told each other about their plans after they had started to execute them. They viewed each other with awe and with suspicion. For his part, Tōjō thought almost entirely in terms of Japan's future leadership in Asia and of the fundamental need of forcing the colonial powers out of East Asia. His strategists could not think of the war in global terms. They were content to push to their planned perimeter, to stand firm on their conquests, and to await an inevitable counterattack.

In contrast to the relationship of the Axis powers, the Allied leaders worked together. President Franklin D. Roosevelt and Prime Minister Winston Churchill were particularly close. They met on numerous occasions before and during the war; they had conferences with other leaders of the Allies, notably, with Generalissimos Stalin and Chiang Kai-shek. The exigencies of the war in which they were engaged forced them to think in global terms. They synchronized their campaigns; their objectives included the unconditional surrender of all of the Axis powers, not just one of them. After Italy and Germany had been defeated, they intended to concentrate all of their war effort on Japan. Before a campaign could be mounted in the Pacific, the immediate demands of the European and African theaters had to be met. Throughout the entire war, despite occasional disagreements on strategy, the United States and Great Britain cooperated closely on both war plans and postwar policies.

But the relationship of Japan with its Axis partners was of a quite different nature. It had turned a deaf ear to German entreaties to contribute more to the war effort. Despite an agreement among the Axis of January, 1942, which called for a combined naval effort, Japan's operations were away from Europe and the Mediterranean region. They became increasingly confined to the central and western Pacific Ocean. This lack of cooperation was the result of various factors. In the first place, Germany and Japan distrusted each other's motives. Furthermore, the Nordic concept of racial superiority was in direct conflict with the Shintō-inspired Japanese belief in their own racial superiority. Finally, the two countries were in disagreement over policy toward the Soviet Union. Germany was eager to have Japan engage the Soviet Union in the Far East and thus relieve the pressure on the Eastern European front. On the other hand, Japan was determined to avoid war with Russia at all costs. It hoped to be able to persuade Germany to make a compromise peace with the Soviet Union. After Rommel's defeat in North Africa and the decisive German defeat at Stalingrad early in 1943, no Axis arguments could persuade Japan to weaken its own position by going to war against the Soviet Union.[4]

Although it falls within the realm of speculation, one is tempted to ask what might have happened if the Japanese leaders had changed their war plans in the summer of 1942. If the three Axis powers had developed a coordinated, global attack, would they have been able to turn the tide? For example, if Germany had been able to persuade Japan to substitute the conquest of Ceylon for the attack on Midway, would the two ends of the Axis have been joined? Would the Axis powers have been able to consolidate their position in the eastern Mediterranean and would Japan have

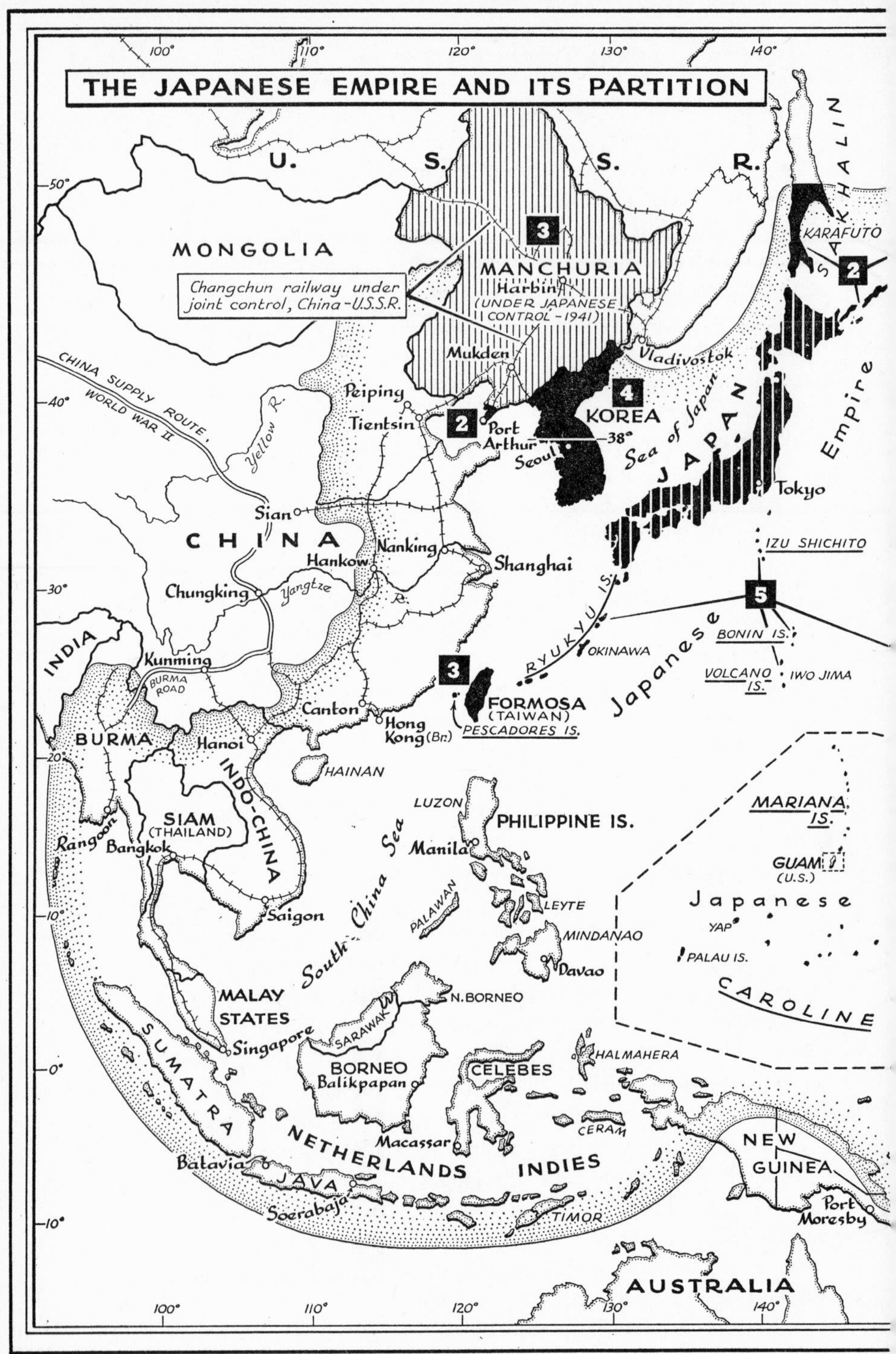

JAPAN IN WORLI

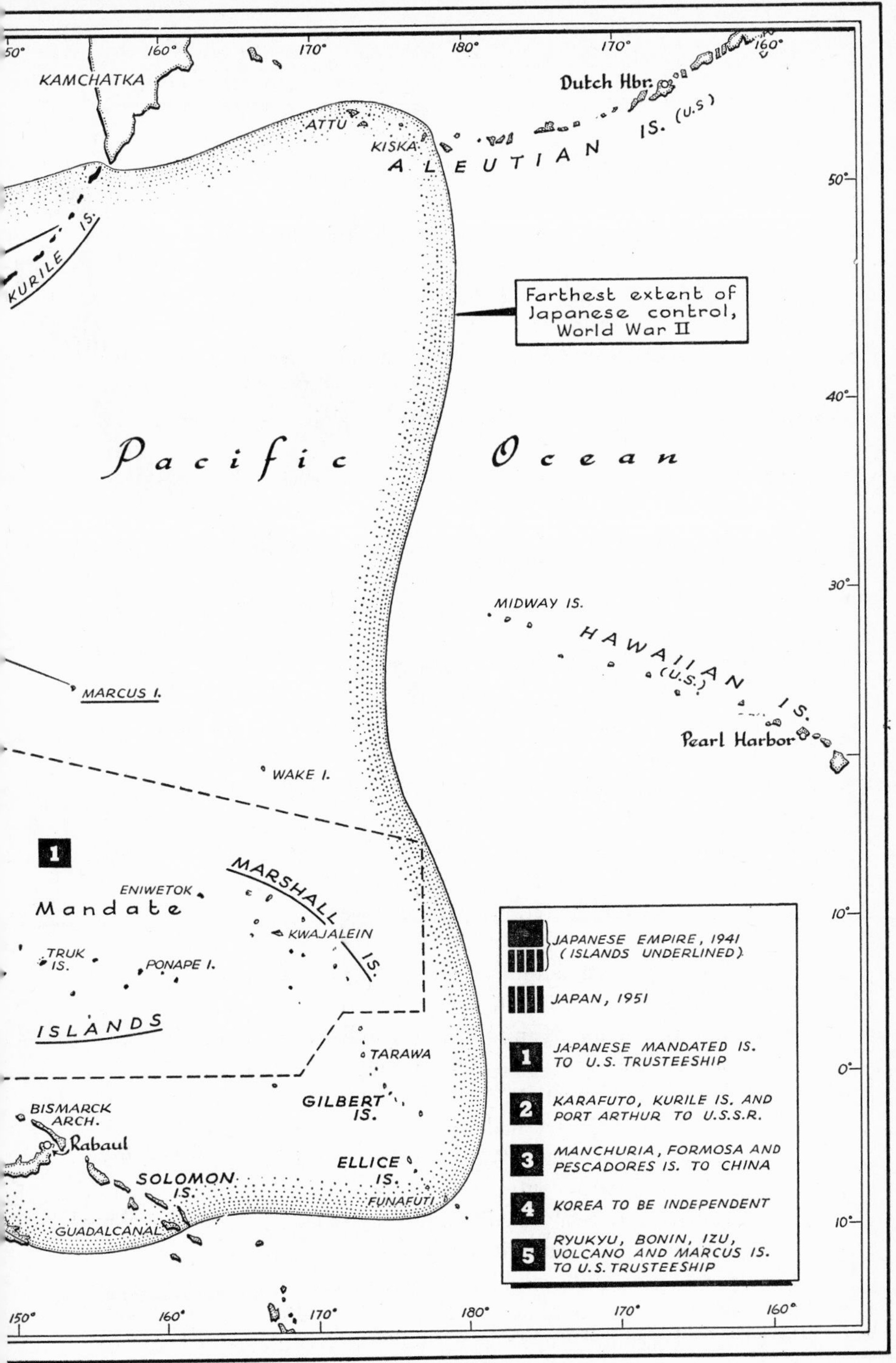

After a map in M.I.T. Series Strategic Area Maps. Copyright by Massachusetts Institute of Technology.

War II and After

had time enough to prepare for a successful attack on Midway to flank the Hawaiian Islands? The answer is probably that even though they had conceived of a coordinated, unified plan, the final results of the war would not have been different.

Since the Axis powers were acting largely independently of each other, their only hope of success was through complete control of the state. For Japan, this meant strengthening control on the home front. Furthermore, significant reverses during the first half of 1943 in the southeast corner of the outer defense perimeter made the situation even more critical. After half a year of some of the most heroic fighting of World War II, the U.S. Marines forced Japan to abandon Guadalcanal in the Solomon Islands. This defeat exposed its flank in that entire quadrant. In the face of this new crisis, Premier Tōjō acted to place complete and direct control of the Empire into his own hands.

In the first place, drastic reforms were inaugurated in local government to increase the production of war materials and to create new, economically self-sufficient, local entities. Thus in July, 1943, Japan proper, including the Ryūkyū Islands in the southwest, and the Kurile Islands and Karafuto in the north, were divided into nine Regional Administrative Districts. These districts were administered by separate councils whose president was the governor of the most important prefecture in each district. Through periodic meetings among the councilors, representatives from the national ministries, and the prefectural governments, conflicts in the enforcement of national policies were eliminated. Furthermore, production quotas were assigned by districts and competitive demands on scarce raw materials were avoided. Finally, in anticipation of damages from air raids, the regions were given discretionary powers over public works to facilitate emergency repairs.

The most significant administrative change within the government, however, was the creation in November, 1943, of the Munitions Ministry. It was set up as the main organ to administer the complete mobilization of Japanese production. The Cabinet Planning Board and the Control Associations proved inadequate to meet the demands for armaments. Thus the new Munitions Ministry had wide powers over any company which engaged in the manufacture of arms, aircraft, warships, and other war materials. As the central control agency for national mobilization, it allotted raw materials, established production schedules, and distributed finished products. It had authority also to regulate capital, labor, and wages. In other words, the family combines, as well as the small companies, were subject to expansion, contraction, or dissolution. After changes were made in the various departments of the government to coordinate their functions with those of the Munitions Ministry, state control over the nation's economy was complete. Prime Minister Tōjō and his Cabinet had dictatorial powers in name and in fact.[5]

But Tōjō, like all other Prime Ministers in modern Japan, was a victim of his environment. Decisions had always been made, even in time of war, by the group rather than by a dictator. Tōjō was unquestionably more responsible than anyone else for taking Japan to war. Furthermore, his authority was also unchallenged during the first two years of the war. When Allied pressure caused a break in Japan's outer perimeter in the central and southwest Pacific, Tōjō was in an untenable position. Allied air and naval attacks had drastically reduced Japanese shipping. Technical deficiency in labor, dwindling stocks of strategic materials, and inefficiency in distribution and production had resulted in a marked decline in war production. In early July, 1944, Saipan, the key base in the Mariana Islands, fell. Japan's cities thus were within easy range of American bombers. The Senior Statesmen (*Jūshin*), former premiers who acted as special advisers to the Emperor, and Lord Keeper of the Privy Seal Kido Kōichi, decided that Tōjō was expendable. On July 18, 1944, he was forced to give way to the will of the group and resigned.

The Beginning of the End: July, 1944—July 10, 1945

The selection of the new Prime Minister, General Koiso Kuniaki, and the members of his Cabinet was the result of a compromise. Some of the Senior Statesmen, though they could not advocate such a policy openly, hoped that the war could be brought to an early conclusion through a compromise peace. They realized that if they even hinted at accepting the territorial settlement proposed by the Allies at Cairo (see page 388), the Army might revolt, liquidate those who opposed it, and dispense with parliamentary government. On the other hand, they were not willing for the Army to retain complete control. They knew that the leaders in the Army advocated an increased national effort to bring victory to Japan. The appointment of General Koiso, a member of the Kwantung clique, as Premier, placated his colleagues. On the other hand, his extremism was balanced by the selection of Admiral Yonai Mitsumasa as Deputy Premier and as Minister of the Navy.[6]

The main objectives of the new Cabinet were twofold: to carry on the war with renewed energy; to be on the alert for a possibility to obtain a compromise peace. Premier Koiso soon discovered that if the war was to progress smoothly closer cooperation between the Cabinet and the High Command must be achieved. A Liaison Conference, which was a group composed of key Cabinet figures and the Chiefs of Staff, had been designed to meet this need. As the war progressed, however, there continued to be a lack of coordination between the government and the armed services.

Consequently, in August, 1944, a Supreme Council for the Direction of War was created. It was composed of the Emperor as Chairman; the Prime Minister; the Ministers of War, Navy, and Foreign Affairs; and the Army and Navy Chiefs of Staff. Its function was "to formulate a fundamental policy for directing the war and to adjust the harmonization of combined strategy for politics and war."[7] It differed from the Liaison Conference in one crucial respect. Since the Emperor was Chairman, he could attend whenever he considered it necessary to break a deadlock in the Council or veto any policy decisions which he did not approve. While in effect the Council usually met without him, he cast the decisive vote for peace in August, 1945.

But in the summer of 1944 Koiso had inherited an impossible assignment. Four months after he assumed office, Japan was subjected to heavy air raids from bombers based on Saipan. These raids, which the Japanese Army had insisted never would occur, were made at will over all parts of the homeland. On March 10, 1945, the first saturation bombing of Tokyo took place. It became apparent to the average Japanese subject, despite the strict control of the press with its reiteration of "victories," that Japan could not hope to win the war. In the meantime, the Philippines were recaptured. On April 1, 1945, even the inner line of defense was pierced by the Allied landings on Okinawa, the largest of the Ryūkyū Islands. Within four days, the Koiso Cabinet fell. It was a victim of the unrelenting pressure from the Allied offensive which no Premier could stop.

The war situation had become so critical that an unprecedented procedure was followed in selecting the next Premier. Lord Keeper of the Privy Seal Kido, who technically overstepped his authority, was the chief organizer of an Imperial Conference to decide on the next Prime Minister. On April 5, 1945, the Senior Statesmen met in the Emperor's audience chamber in an atmosphere of tension.

The die-hards were represented by former Premier Tōjō, who was appearing for the first time as a Senior Statesmen. The news had just been received that the Soviet Union had refused to extend the Neutrality Pact beyond its termination a year hence. In Europe, the Allied Armies had already crossed the Rhine from the west. The Soviet forces were rapidly approaching from the east. The junction of the two forces was expected momentarily. The European end of the Axis was on the point of collapse.

Under these circumstances, the conference with the Emperor immediately turned into a discussion of the question of whether or not to continue the war or to seek peace. General Tōjō insisted on the former alternative and the selection of a Prime Minister who would agree to fight to the finish. He claimed that he spoke for the Army, which would wreck any

Cabinet which followed a contrary policy. He received strong support for his position from ex-Premier Hiranuma.

On the other hand, several of the other Senior Statesmen had been considering for several months ways and means of bringing the war to an end. Together with Kido, they had endeavored to keep themselves informed of the actual military and economic strength of the nation. They had also passed this information on to the Emperor in a series of individual Imperial audiences. They had endeavored to place a representative of the "anti-war group" on the Tōjō Cabinet. They had greatly strengthened their cause when Yonai Mitsumasa was made Deputy Premier and Minister of the Navy under Koiso. Admiral Yonai had learned that one of his colleagues on the Naval Chief of Staff, Admiral Takagi Sōkichi, had completed a study on Japan's war potential. On the basis of his survey, Admiral Takagi had become convinced that Japan could not possibly win the war and hence should work toward a compromise peace. When Yonai was appointed Navy Minister, he instructed Admiral Takagi to make a new, documented study of Japan's actual war potential. The report was to contain recommendations on how Japan could extricate itself from a war which appeared already lost.[8]

Even though this report had not been completed when the Senior Statesmen met with the Emperor in April, 1945, a large group of them favored the selection of a person as Premier who would bring the war to an early close. This same group believed that the Emperor would support such a candidate. Specifically, they had reached a previous understanding that Admiral Suzuki Kentarō was the logical man of the hour. He was held in high esteem by all groups within the country. He had escaped assassination on February 26, 1936, only because of the bravery of his wife. For the past months he had served as President of the Privy Council. The Conference finally agreed to his appointment.

When Kido pressed him to take the position, he doubtless realized that his assignment was to bring the war to a conclusion as rapidly as possible. His new Foreign Minister, Tōgō Shigenori, was also dedicated to the same cause.[9] On the other hand, War Minister Anami and the Chiefs of the Army and Navy General Staff were inexorably opposed to unconditional surrender. In fact, Anami had arrested several hundred persons because of their antiwar views. Officially, therefore, the new Suzuki Cabinet was committed to continue the war to the bitter end. Privately, it was hoped he would bring the war to a speedy conclusion.

In a little over a month after Admiral Suzuki became Premier, therefore, the Supreme Council met in May, 1945, to consider whether or not Japan was capable of continued, effective resistance. The immediate issue before the Council was a proposal by the Foreign Minister concerning

Japan's future relations with the Soviet Union. Japan had been most circumspect in the past in its observance of the Neutrality Pact. It wished, at all costs, to prevent the outbreak of hostilities between the two countries. Germany's capitulation, and Moscow's announced policy that it would not continue the Neutrality Pact, boded no good for the future of these relations. Thus the Foreign Minister was of the opinion that new overtures should be made to Moscow to prevent the situation from deteriorating. Consequently, his plan contained three proposals. These were (1) that the Soviet Union should be prevented from entering the war in the Pacific, (2) that the Soviet Union should be enticed into adopting a friendly policy toward Japan, and (3) that the Soviet Union should be requested to use its good offices to mediate the war in the Pacific on terms favorable to Japan.

The Supreme Council, though divided on the last point, agreed that negotiations should be begun to improve Soviet-Japanese relations. Ex-Premier Hirota was appointed to approach the Soviet Ambassador in Tokyo, Jacob A. Malik. At first, Hirota talked only of an improvement of friendly relations between the two countries; later he proposed a non-aggression pact. In both instances, he received a cool reception. In fact, while these conversations were under way, the Soviet Union was beginning to shift its armies from the European front to Siberia in anticipation of a declaration of war on Japan in accordance with the agreement reached at Yalta. (See page 389.)

During the next few weeks events moved rapidly to a climax. Direct air attacks on Japan proper had begun from Okinawa as a base. The overseas territories were completely isolated from the home islands. The Japanese civilians and occupation forces in these areas had been all but abandoned. A report prepared by the Cabinet indicated clearly that the warmaking power of the nation had been broken. Shipping losses to submarine and air attack were staggering. The total tonnage of vessels had been reduced from 5.5 million to 1.25 million. It was assumed that the loss of Okinawa would preclude surface communication between Japan and the Asiatic continent. Railway transportation had fallen to one-half the previous year. In reference to material resources, the picture was equally grim. Fuel resources had been exhausted; coal production was insufficient to keep industries operating. Steel output had dropped to one-tenth the previous year. Despite priorities given to it, aircraft production was falling rapidly.[10] In fine, the time of decision appeared to be at hand.

This report had made a deep impression on Premier Suzuki who agreed with its gloomy estimate. He forwarded it to the Emperor for his information. In spite of this evidence, War Minister Anami and the Chiefs of Staff continued to insist that more vigorous steps be taken to prosecute the war. At a Supreme Council meeting on June 6, 1945, they stated that the use of suicide squads, a *levée en masse,* and the invincible spirit of Japan would result in a victorious, decisive stand for the homeland. At the very least, the enemy's losses would be so great that he would sue for peace and abandon his demands for unconditional surrender. The Council agreed, with the concurrence of the Emperor, that negotiations for peace would be postponed until after this decisive stand.

During the next two weeks, however, Kido and the Senior Statesmen persuaded the Emperor to reverse this earlier decision of the Council. Consequently, on June 22, 1945, the Emperor called a meeting of the Supreme Council and took the initiative in asking it to approve of peace negotiations to be carried on through the Soviet Union. After a brief discussion, the Council concurred with the Emperor's request. Conversations were again begun between Hirota and Malik. But the Emperor soon became impatient with the lack of progress which was being made. He ordered Premier Suzuki to act immediately and suggested dispatching a special envoy to Moscow with his personal message.

On July 10, 1945, the Supreme Council approved of ex-Premier Konoye as the special peace envoy. In the meantime, the Japanese Ambassador in Moscow was instructed to request the Soviet government to intercede with the Allies on Japan's behalf. The Ambassador was to report that the Emperor expressly wished to end the war promptly. Nevertheless, the Allies should be told that so long as they insisted on unconditional surrender, Japan had no alternative but to continue to fight for its honor and survival. Finally, the Soviet Union was to be asked to act before the Allied leaders met at Potsdam.[11] But the request had come too late. The Allies were in the process of deciding what their next move would be.

Allied Postwar Policy Formation

Although the Supreme Council was not aware of the fact, the question of Japan's surrender was one of the items on the agenda of the Potsdam meeting of Truman, Churchill, and Stalin. The United States government was prepared to seek Allied approval of a joint statement which would give Japan an opportunity to surrender or face destruction. In view of the anticipated successful completion of the first explosion of an atomic bomb, a declaration was called for which clearly defined the objectives of the Allies. By midsummer of 1945, the objectives of the Allies in the Far East had been ill defined. Pronouncements such as the United Nations Declaration of January 1, 1942, reaffirmed in general terms the principles which Roosevelt and Churchill had proclaimed in the Atlantic Charter. The Allies declared, among other things, that they sought no territorial aggrandizement for themselves and that sovereign rights and self-government would be restored to those who had been deprived of them. Each of the United Nations also pledged not to make a separate peace with their common enemies. At the Casablanca Conference held a year later, Roosevelt and Churchill agreed that the war would end only with "the unconditional surrender of the Axis states." But no further attempt had been made to explain what this would mean.

It was not until December, 1943, that any public clarification was made by the Allies concerning the future of the Japanese Empire. In the Cairo Declaration issued by Chiang Kai-shek, Churchill, and Roosevelt, they declared:

> Japan shall be stripped of all the islands in the Pacific which she has seized or occupied since the beginning of the first World War in 1914, and all the territories Japan has stolen from the Chinese, such as Manchuria, Formosa, and the Pescadores, shall be restored to the Republic of China. Japan will also be expelled from all other territories which she has taken by violence and greed. The aforesaid three great powers, mindful of the enslavement of the people of Korea, are determined that in due course Korea shall become free and independent.[12]

They concluded with a promise to persevere with the other United Nations at war with Japan, "to procure the unconditional surrender of Japan."

But even a declaration as specific as the Cairo Declaration left many basic questions unsettled. As early as 1942, a postwar planning section of the Department of State had attempted to anticipate some of these problems. After February, 1944, this work took on added significance. The War and Navy Departments, for purposes of their own future planning for the military occupation of Japan, requested answers to more than twenty fundamental postwar policy questions. These included: What was the meaning, in practical and specific terms, of unconditional surrender? Did it mean, for example, the nonexistence of a Japanese government? What was to be the extent, duration, and type of the military occupation of Japan? Would it be an Allied or entirely American occupation? If the former, would there be one or more zones? What about the future position of the Emperor? What were the basic objectives of the United States in reference to postwar Japan?

In the preparation within the Department of State of definitive policies on these and other post-surrender problems, it soon became apparent that their military and political aspects were closely interrelated. Consequently, a State-War-Navy Coordinating Committee (referred to as SWNCC) was created with responsibility for coordinating and formulating general policies of the United States government. By early January, 1945, when SWNCC appointed a special Subcomittee on the Far East, agreement had already been reached on answers to most of the post-surrender questions. Consequently, when President Roosevelt left for the Yalta Conference later that month, a complete file on studies and recommendations on various Far Eastern problems accompanied him. Although the President did not study these documents in preparation for the conference, they were used later as the basis for Allied policy in Japan.[13]

Although the Yalta Agreement of February, 1945, signed by Churchill, Roosevelt, and Stalin, was concerned primarily with China, it had a direct bearing on Japan. It specified, among other things, that the Soviet Union would enter the war against Japan on the side of the Allies not later than three months after the capitulation of Germany. In return, the Soviet Union was to receive special concessions in China and was to reacquire territories lost to Japan, namely, the southern half of Sakhalien (Karafuto) and the Kurile Islands. For obvious reasons, including the fact that the Soviet Union was at peace with Japan, the Yalta Agreement was kept a closely guarded secret. Even James F. Byrnes, who had been to the conference, did not learn of its existence until after he became Secretary of State in July, 1945.

In the first part of 1945, when military events foreshadowed the defeat of Japan, one of the most important problems confronting the United States government was how to develop a workable definition for "unconditional surrender." This question was tackled by the Subcommittee on the Far East of SWNCC. The Committee reasoned that, while unconditional surrender would mean Japan's military capitulation, it would not necessarily mean the annihilation of the Japanese as a people or the complete destruction of their country. It was further argued that if unconditional surrender were defined in specific terms and if this definition were announced to Japan, it might capitulate before an assault was launched against the home islands. If this came about, the Allies would be spared heavy casualties. The State Department then prepared a document which incorporated these ideas, and which was approved by SWNCC. Thus, by the beginning of July, 1945, a policy statement, which was to be modified later to become the Potsdam Declaration, was ready for Cabinet approval.[14]

The Acceptance of the Potsdam Declaration

On July 10, 1945, when the Supreme Council in Tokyo had decided to ask the Soviet Union to mediate for peace, the United States had already decided to issue a declaration calling on Japan to surrender or to take the consequences. Prior to his departure for a conference with Churchill and Stalin at Potsdam, President Truman and his Cabinet also agreed that if the test of the atomic bomb, scheduled for July 16, proved successful, the bomb would not be used against Japan until after the Allies had issued their declaration.

The news of the success of the atomic bomb reached Potsdam as Truman, Churchill, and Stalin were beginning their deliberations. President Truman then sought and obtained the approval of the United Kingdom and of China for the issuance of the Potsdam Declaration on July 26, 1945. (See Appendix I.)

It was an exposition of Allied postwar aims and objectives, an appeal to Japan to surrender, and a warning that the alternative would be complete and utter destruction. It demanded that the authority and influence of militarists and nationalists must be eliminated for all time and that a new order of peace, security, and justice should be established. It continued that Japan's warmaking power would be destroyed and warned that stern justice would be meted out to war criminals. Furthermore, Japanese sovereignty was to be limited to the four main home islands and their adjacent minor islands.

On the positive side, the Allies promised in their Declaration that the Japanese armed forces abroad would be returned home, fundamental human rights would be established, nonmilitary industries would be permitted, and eventual participation would be allowed in world trade. It required the removal by the Japanese government of all obstacles to the revival and strengthening of democratic tendencies among the people. It warned that the occupation of Japan would continue until the Allied objectives had been achieved and the Japanese people had established by their own free will "a peacefully inclined and responsible government." It concluded by calling upon the Japanese government to proclaim unconditional surrender or face utter destruction.[15]

For the next ten days, the Allies waited in vain for a reply from the Japanese government. The only hint as to how their Declaration had been received was to be found in the Japanese newspapers. On July 28, they quoted the Premier as saying that he considered the Declaration of no great value and that he intended to ignore it.[16] When the Japanese government gave no further signs of accepting the Allied terms, the previous agreement to use the atomic bomb automatically went into effect. On August 6, 1945, the first atomic bomb used in warfare was dropped on Hiroshima.

As reported the next day to the Japanese Army General Staff, "the whole city of Hiroshima was destroyed instantly by a single bomb." Although some of the military chiefs were skeptical of the destructiveness of the new bomb, a special commission sent to investigate the results soon confirmed the terrible news. The threat which the Allies had made at Potsdam that "prompt and utter destruction" awaited Japan if it did not surrender suddenly became a reality. Foreign Minister Tōgō conferred immediately with the Emperor and urged him to accept the Potsdam Declaration.

Before a decision could be reached on this vital question, however, the Soviet Union entered the war against Japan. On August 8, 1945, Soviet Foreign Minister Molotov presented the Japanese Ambassador in Moscow with a declaration of war to be effective the next day. When this news reached Japan, it came as a staggering blow. Premier Suzuki and the military leaders knew that they had no effective plan to stop the Soviet troops in Manchuria and Korea. The pride of the Kwantung Army had long since been withdrawn to protect the homeland. The basic question was no longer whether Japan should continue to fight. It was whether the Potsdam Declaration should be accepted with or without reservations.

Thus, August 9 became one of the most fateful days in Japan's history. Premier Suzuki had an early conference with the Emperor. They decided that the Potsdam Declaration should be accepted immediately. A meeting of the six-man Supreme Council was called by midmorning but it immediately became deadlocked. Half of the members (Premier Suzuki, Foreign Minister Tōgō, and Navy Minister Yonai) favored acceptance of the Potsdam Declaration with the understanding that it did not alter the legal position of the Emperor. The other members of the Council (War Minister Anami, Army Chief of Staff Umezu, and Navy Chief of Staff Toyoda) insisted that the Allies' Declaration should be accepted only on four conditions. These conditions were: (1) no Allied occupation of the homeland, (2) demobilization of the Army and Navy to be under Japanese supervision, (3) war criminals to be prosecuted by the Japanese government, and (4) the status of the Emperor to remain unchanged.

The deadlock in the Supreme Council was not shaken by receipt of the news at midday of the destruction of Nagasaki by the second atomic bomb. On the contrary, the matter was referred to the Cabinet. War Minister Anami and the Chiefs of Staff prevented a decision from being taken. In desperation, Premier Suzuki decided that the Emperor should cast the deciding vote. Late that night, the Emperor presided over another meeting of the Supreme War Council which was held in the Imperial air raid shelter. Privy Council Chairman Hiranuma was also present. The two opposing views were again presented. Those favoring acceptance of the Potsdam Declaration proposed a modification which they believed would assure continuation of the special position of the Emperor. They proposed acceptance with the understanding that the "prerogatives of His Majesty as a sovereign ruler" would not be affected by unconditional surrender. At approximately 3:00 A.M. on August 10, Premier Suzuki emphasized the urgent need for an immediate decision and requested the Emperor to express an opinion. The Emperor then threw his weight on the side of those favoring capitulation. His wish was equivalent to a command which was accepted by the Council. The Cabinet immediately gave its *pro forma* approval. The end of the war was in sight; the Potsdam Declaration had saved both Japan and the Allies from the horrible costs of invasion.

The decision of Japan to accept the Potsdam Declaration with the reservation concerning the Emperor's status was transmitted immediately to the Allied Powers. When this note was received, the United States government, with the consent of the three other Allied powers who sponsored the Potsdam Declaration, decided to ignore this Japanese qualified acceptance which attempted to protect the Emperor's special position. The Allied reply made it patently clear that after surrender both the Emperor and the Japanese government would be subject to an Allied Commander who would be empowered to take whatever steps were necessary to effectuate the surrender terms.

Thus within a period of three days, Japan was again faced with the question of acceptance or rejection of complete capitulation. Acceptance would mean peace; rejection would mean destruction. As during the earlier debates on this issue, the Supreme Council was divided. Premier Suzuki wavered temporarily but finally followed the same procedure as before. The Emperor presided over another meeting of the Supreme Council. He told his military leaders who opposed him that there was no support for their position. He ordered the government to accede to his wishes and to accept immediately the Allied proposal without reservation. On August 14, 1945, President Truman received Japan's reply which he immediately accepted. World War II was over.[17]

The Surrender of Japan, September 2, 1945

After the Japanese government had sent its reply of August 10 to the Allies indicating its willingness to surrender, President Truman proposed to Prime Minister Attlee, Generalissimo Stalin, and Generalissimo Chiang that General Douglas MacArthur be selected as the Allied Commander and that he be designated the Supreme Commander for the Allied Powers. This proposal was approved and General MacArthur's appointment became effective August 14. His immediate task was to make all necessary arrangements for Japan's surrender. His basic assignment was to supervise the occupation of Japan and the execution of Allied postwar policies.

Before the actual surrender ceremonies could take place, however, certain detailed arrangements had to be made. Representatives of the Japanese Chiefs of Staff had to contact MacArthur's headquarters in Manila to receive specific instructions. Advance units of his forces had to land in Japan to prepare for the Allied occupation. The various Allied Theater Commanders had to be notified concerning the units of the

Japanese armed forces which would surrender to them and the areas they would occupy. The Army Corps assigned to the occupation had to be organized, transported, and landed in Japan. Allied prisoners of war in enemy territory had to be contacted and evacuated. Finally, over-all policies for the guidance of the occupation had to be approved by the United States government.

While these preparations were proceeding on schedule, Japan was suffering from the initial shock of defeat. For the people, news of the acceptance of the Potsdam Declaration and of the cessation of hostilities came as a relief. After three and a half years of war, six months of which had been accompanied by intensive bombing, they were too dazed and shocked to understand the true significance of their surrender. Furthermore, no responsible official had given even a hint of what surrender would actually mean. When the Emperor had announced in mid-August that Japan had agreed to capitulate, he had not mentioned specifically the term "unconditional surrender." On the contrary, he had said that the acceptance of the Allied demands would pave the way for a lasting and glorious peace.

It is questionable whether even Premier Suzuki and those who agreed to capitulation, really knew what to expect. Their decision had been forced upon them by their knowledge of their country's desperate straits. But in view of the fact that Japan had never before been defeated, they realized that they had failed and were in national disgrace. Under these circumstances, the least the Cabinet could do was to resign.[18]

In order to preserve as much stability as possible in the interim period between the cessation of hostilities and formal surrender, the Emperor broke precedent and selected the next Premier himself. He chose a blood relative, his uncle, Prince Higashikuni Naruhiko, a general with wide experience. The chief assignment of the new Cabinet, which was formed on August 17, 1945, was to maintain law and order throughout the nation and to surrender formally to the new Supreme Commander. Hence Higashikuni's Cabinet was composed of experienced and respected members of influential segments of society. For example, former Premier Konoye was made Vice-Premier; Shigemitsu Mamoru, a career diplomat, was Foreign Minister; Maeda Tamon, a moderate and an internationalist, was Minister of Education; Higashikuni temporarily assumed the post of Minister of War; and Admiral Yonai continued as Minister of Navy.

Many of the leading militarists seem to have been more aware than anyone else of the consequences, at least for themselves, of unconditional surrender. Together with many important government officials, they used the last two weeks in August, the period between the cessation of hostilities and the formal surrender, to destroy records which would incriminate them and to salvage such profits as they could from the catastrophe. For example, orders were issued by the Army and Navy to dispose of all of their war goods either at a nominal cost or without charge. It was estimated that goods worth 50 billion yen were involved in this gigantic liquidation. Furthermore, payments totalling 10 billion yen, a sum larger than any previous monthly military expenditure, were made for discharge allowances and pensions for senior officers, for canceled contracts, and for the settlement of manufacturers' accounts. When the occupation troops arrived, nothing was said about these questionable transactions.

By the end of August, 1945, the United States government and General MacArthur had completed their preliminary preparations for the surrender and occupation of Japan. General MacArthur and his troops had arrived in the Tokyo area for what he termed the greatest gamble in history. The specific documents for use at the time of surrender had been transmitted to the Supreme Commander for the Allied Powers. A general agreement had been reached on the basic policies under which the occupation was to operate.

On September 2, 1945, the stage was prepared for the final act of World War II. The U.S.S. "Missouri" was anchored in lower Tokyo Bay. The ceremony of signing the Instrument of Surrender took place on its deck. General Douglas MacArthur, Supreme Commander for the Allied Powers, accepted the surrender of Japan on behalf of the four major Allied Powers and "in the interest of the other United Nations at war with Japan." Foreign Minister Shigemitsu Mamoru and Chief of Staff Umezu Yoshijirō signed the document on behalf of Japan. The ceremony was concluded by a short speech from General MacArthur who was to direct the destinies of Japan for the next five and a half years. He set the tone of the occupation he was to command when he said:

> A great tragedy has ended. A great victory has been won. The skies no longer rain death—the seas bear only commerce—men everywhere walk upright in the sunlight.

The Instrument of Surrender (see Appendix II) ordered the immediate cessation of all hostilities and the unconditional surrender of all Japanese armed forces. All officials were commanded to obey all orders issued by the Supreme Commander and to perform their duties until relieved by him. Finally, the Japanese government undertook to carry out the provisions of the Potsdam Declaration and to take whatever action the Supreme Commander might require to implement it.

Another significant and interrelated part of the surrender of Japan was the proclamation issued by the Emperor on the same day. (See Appendix III.) In order to assure the capitulation of all elements in the Japanese armed forces, particularly those in isolated overseas territories, and to guarantee the cooperation of Japanese officials and civilians with the occupation authorities, the United States government considered it advisable to prepare this proclamation for the Emperor. Thus, shortly after the Surrender Instrument was signed, the Emperor proclaimed that he had ordered his government and the Imperial Headquarters to sign the Instrument of Surrender on his behalf. He also commanded his people to lay down their arms and faithfully to carry out all of its provisions and all of the orders of the Imperial Government issued in connection with it. The entire Cabinet pledged its adherence to the surrender and to the proclamation by affixing their signatures to this Imperial Rescript. Thus all military and civil authority in Japan became subject to General MacArthur as Supreme Commander, referred to as SCAP.

But additional steps were necessary to effect the surrender of the Japanese armed forces overseas. Consequently, immediately after the completion of the ceremonies in which he accepted Japan's surrender, the Supreme Commander issued General Order No. 1 which contained detailed arrangements for the surrender of all of the Imperial armed forces. Each of the five Allied Commanders in the Far East was given an area over which he was ordered to continue to have jurisdiction. The Japanese forces were to surrender to the Allied Commander of the area in which they were located. Thus, those in China (excluding Manchuria), Formosa, and French Indochina north of 16° latitude surrendered to Generalissimo Chiang Kai-shek. Those in Manchuria, Korea north of 38° latitude, and Karafuto gave themselves up to the Commander of the Soviet Forces in the Far East. Those in the Pacific Islands capitulated to the Commander of the United States Fleet; those in Southeast Asia to Admiral Mountbatten or the Australian Commander. The Imperial General Headquarters and all Japanese armed forces in Japan proper and Korea south of the thirty-eighth parallel surrendered to General MacArthur.[19]

Finally, the basic policies for postwar Japan had been laid down by the United States in a document entitled, "The United States Initial Post-Surrender Policy for Japan." This over-all policy statement, which was transmitted to General MacArthur at the end of August, 1945, was based on the general principles announced by the Allied leaders at Potsdam. It set forth the two basic objectives of the Allied powers as the prevention of Japan from menacing the future peace of the world and the encouragement of the formation of a responsible government which would respect the rights of others.

This statement then outlined the means whereby these objectives would be achieved. These included:

1. The limitation of Japanese territory to the four main islands and to minor adjacent islands, as provided in the Cairo and Potsdam Declarations.
2. The elimination of militarism in both political and economic life.
3. The trial of war criminals by an Allied Tribunal.
4. The establishment of guarantees for basic human rights.
5. The exaction of reparations and the restitution of stolen goods.
6. The development of democratic organizations in labor.
7. The carrying out of basic reforms in agriculture and industry.

The execution of these policies, as well as the general and specific operation of the occupation, was left to the discretion of General MacArthur as Supreme Commander. He was given wide freedom of action and powers broad enough to meet any exigencies that might develop. If the circumstances warranted it, he could even ignore the Japanese government as the agent for the execution of his orders and act directly. Consequently, the history of the occupation is, in many respects, that of the personal rule of General MacArthur. He conceived his mission to be the transformation of a militaristic state into a peace-loving democratic country. He provided the Japanese with the leadership and the hope they needed so desperately in their darkest hour of history.

Notes

1. No attempt is made to be exhaustive here or elsewhere in this book concerning the campaigns in the Pacific. Detailed information can be found in histories such as Samuel Eliot Morrison, *History of United States Naval Operations* (Boston: Little Brown, 1948). A helpful guide, especially excellent charts, will be found in United States Strategic Bombing Survey, *Summary Report* (*Pacific War*) (Washington: U.S. Government Printing Office, 1946).

2. For a detailed study of the Japanese Government during this period see Hugh Borton, "The Administration and Structure of the Japanese Government," *Department of State Bulletin,* XI (December 24, 1944), pp. 817-33.

3. Aoki Kazuo (b. 1889) spent most of his adult life as a bureaucrat. After 1937 he became Vice-President of the Cabinet's Manchurian Affairs Board and later was Chairman of the Cabinet Planning Board. From 1940 to 1942 he acted as chief financial adviser to Wang Ching-wei's puppet regime in Nanking.

4. For a more detailed analysis of the lack of cooperation in the Axis partnership see F. C. Jones, *Japan's New Order in East Asia, Its Rise and Fall, 1937-1945* (New York: Oxford University Press, 1954).

5. This control was finally clarified and strengthened by the Extraordinary Wartime Administrative Authority to Act which became effective on March 18, 1944. By this law, Tōjō was given the power to decide all questions connected with its enforcement. For the various changes in organization of the government resulting from the creation of the Munitions Ministry, see Borton, "Administration and Structure of the Japanese Government," *op. cit.,* pp. 826-33. It should not be forgotten, however, that rivalries and jealousies continued among the military and

civil branches of the government even under these controls. The dictatorship was weakened by these uncontrollable factors.

6. Koiso Kuniaki (1880-1950) was a career army officer. His various posts put him in close touch with the Imperial Way Faction of the Army. He was Vice-Minister of War under General Araki, Chief of Staff of the Kwantung Army, and was Governor-General of Korea at the time of his appointment as Prime Minister. Tōjō was unable to retain the post of War Minister which he relinquished to General Sugiyama. The most detailed account of the background of events during this period will be found in Robert J. C. Butow, *Japan's Decision to Surrender* (Stanford: Stanford University Press, 1954), pp. 30-58.

7. Foreign Broadcast Intelligence Service, *Radio Report,* November 10, 1944.

8. Konoye, Wakatsuki, Hiranuma, and Okada were the former premiers who had been meeting secretly for several months. For details see Butow, *op. cit.,* p. 14 *et seq.* For a summary of the contents of Admiral Takagi's report and his connection with Admiral Yonai see United States Strategic Bombing Survey, *Japan's Struggle to End the War* (Washington: U.S. Government Printing Office, 1946), p. 3.

9. Considerable confusion has arisen over the question of whether Suzuki took the premiership with the explicit understanding that he was to end the war. Fortunately, Dr. Butow, in his *Decision to Surrender,* p. 70, has correctly emphasized the fact that understandings are often reached in Japan without an explicit commitment (*haragei*). Obviously, Suzuki knew the feelings of the Emperor and most of the Senior Statesmen who wanted to terminate the war. On the other hand, as a retired Admiral, the thought of Japan's unconditional surrender to the Allies was more than he could stomach at this stage. Thus, at several points, he seemed to hesitate. For example, a few days before Germany's capitulation he boasted, "We finally believe that there will surely come in our grasp a golden chance."

10. An exhaustive treatment of Japan's wartime economy will be found in Jerome B. Cohen, *Japan's Economy in War and Reconstruction* (Minneapolis: University of Minnesota Press, 1949). For a summary of the report of Sakomizu Hisamitsu see United States Strategic Bombing Survey, *Japan's Struggle to End the War, op. cit.,* pp. 6 and 16-17.

11. For a survey of these events see *ibid.,* p. 6 *et seq.;* Butow, *op. cit.,* p. 112 *et seq.*

12. Department of State, *Occupation of Japan—Policy and Progress* (Washington: Department of State, Publication 267, Far Eastern Series 17, U.S. Government Printing Office, 1946), p. 51.

13. Dr. Leo Pasvolsky, Special Assistant to Secretary of State Cordell Hull, was primarily responsible for organizing the work of postwar planning within the Department of State. Studies on postwar Japan were begun in the fall of 1942. Tentative conclusions on many of the questions raised by the War and Navy Departments had already been reached prior to February, 1944. Their official request necessitated the revision and formalization of these decisions throughout the next few months. The whole procedure of interdepartmental decisions, especially as far as Japan was concerned, was greatly facilitated by the formation of SWNCC. See Hugh Borton, "United States Occupation Policies in Japan since Surrender," *Political Science Quarterly,* LXII (June, 1947), p. 250 *et seq.;* and U.S. Department of State, *Postwar Foreign Policy Preparation* (Washington: U.S. Government Printing Office, 1949. For verification of the fact that Roosevelt did not use the documents, see James F. Byrnes, *Speaking Frankly* (New York: Harper & Bros., 1947), p. 23.

14. In the narration of events connected with the formation of American postwar policies, the reader may note some divergencies with other accounts. In such places the author has relied on his personal experience. From 1942 to 1948, he was in the Department of State working on postwar policy for Japan. Toward the latter part of this period, he served as Chairman of the Subcommittee of the Far East. Complete documentation of the history of the formulation of American foreign policy during the war and postwar years will have to await the declassification of the documents of the State Department's Inter Divisional Area Committee and the Postwar Planning Committee (PWC) and of the minutes and documents of SWNCC and its subcommittees.

The original drafts of the Potsdam Declaration; the Instrument of Surrender; the Imperial Rescript Announcing Surrender; the United States Initial Post-Surrender Policy for Japan of September 6, 1945; General MacArthur's General Order No. 1; and the Joint Chiefs of Staff Directive to him were considered by the Subcommittee of the Far East and transmitted to SWNCC for formal approval. The Cabinet decision was incorporated into a new document prepared by Secretary of War Stimson which was based on the SWNCC draft. Although Mr. Stimson's document was new, the idea did not originate with him as inferred in his *Memoirs*. See H. L. Stimson and M. Bundy, *On Active Service in Peace and War* (New York: Harper & Bros., 1948), pp. 366 *et seq.* and 620; James F. Byrnes, *Speaking Frankly, op. cit.*, p. 206; F. C. Jones, Hugh Borton, and B. R. Pearn, *The Far East, 1942-1946* (London: Oxford University Press, 1955), p. 311.

15. Department of State, *Occupation of Japan, op. cit.*, pp. 53-55. The term "responsible government" was used in a technical sense. It referred to a government in which the Premier is selected from the party with the most seats in Parliament and in which the Cabinet is collectively responsible for its acts and for its members to Parliament.

16. This refers to the Japanese phrase *mokusatsu* (to ignore by silence), over which there has been much debate. See Butow, *op. cit.*, p. 142 *et seq.*; and Kazuo Kawai, "Mokusatsu, Japan's Response to the Potsdam Declaration," *Pacific Historical Review*, November, 1950.

17. For a detailed chronology of these events and the texts of the exchanges of notes, see Department of State, *Occupation of Japan, op. cit.*, p. 58 *et seq.*

18. True to his promise, War Minister Anami committed suicide. A few dissatisfied officers in the Army made a final, desperate attempt to stop the surrender, but failed. Several loyal subjects, feeling that defeat was too great a disgrace to endure, followed Anami's example and took their own lives in the plaza before the Imperial Palace. On the whole, capitulation was accepted stoically.

19. See Department of State, *Occupation of Japan, op. cit.*, pp. 62-64. The text of General Order No. 1 will be found in SCAP, *Political Reorientation of Japan, September, 1945, to September, 1948* (2 vols.; Washington: U.S. Government Printing Office, 1949), II, p. 442 *et seq.*

20

THE REORIENTATION OF JAPAN UNDER OCCUPATION, 1945-1948

The surrender and occupation of Japan was a gamble because so many variables were involved in the venture. There was no way of predicting with certainty how the nation would react to defeat and particularly to the occupation of its "sacred soil" by foreign troops. Heretofore, all of Japan's wars in modern times had been fought overseas and had been successful. When the Mongols had threatened to invade Japan in the thirteenth century, a divine wind (*Kami kaze*) had saved the Empire. Now that the gods had failed to save them, would the Japanese armed forces obey the Instrument of Surrender? Would the 3½ million Japanese troops overseas, particularly those under fanatical leadership, comply with their Emperor's plea to lay down their arms? Would the thousands of government employees continue to function in their respective positions in the Finance Ministry, in the railroads, in the post and telegraph offices, in the police system, in education and in other government offices? If not, would the personnel of the occupation forces be capable of running Japan?

There were indications, even before the formal surrender on September 2, 1945, that the Japanese would not resist the occupation. The first contingent of Allied troops which landed in Japan had not been molested. The occupation was orderly and devoid of incidents. Initial fear of individual Japanese toward the foreign soldiers quickly disappeared. When the GIs began to befriend the children, their mothers and sisters came out of hiding. Suspicion gave way to trust. SCAP's orders were followed as a matter of course by the armed forces and by civilians alike. Even the overseas contingents of the Army and Navy surrendered in routine fashion.

This docile submission of the military and civilian populace was caused by several factors. In the first place, the Japanese were accustomed to obey their superiors. SCAP had complete and supreme authority. The Emperor told his people to obey this new authority. Of equal importance, perhaps, was the physical and psychological state of shock of most of the people. Nearly 70 per cent of them are reported to have reached a point a month before the end of the war where they felt unable to carry on. Civilian casualties had surpassed three-quarters of a million; over three million homes had been destroyed by raids or had been torn down for firebreaks. The average daily rations afforded about 1680 calories; civilian goods were nonexistent. The will to resist and the physical means to support continued resistance were both nonexistent.[1]

Moreover, the personality, attitude, and reputation of General MacArthur contributed to the success of the occupation. He instilled confidence and acted with benevolence. He exhibited a keen sense of timing in the implementation of the various policies. From the start, he had decided to execute only a restricted number of them at the same time and to give top priority to the most significant ones. In the early days of the occupation, he concentrated on military problems. After the demilitarization program was well under control, he shifted to nonmilitary matters. He then pressed for those reforms that would awaken a new political consciousness among the Japanese, such as the establishment of civil rights, the revision of the Constitution and the elimination of ultranationalists by means of the purge. When progress had been achieved in these fields, he turned to economic problems.

Early Steps Toward Democratization: Human Rights and Constitutional Reforms

Since the foremost mission of the occupation was the elimination of militarism in Japan, SCAP first ordered the demobilization of the Imperial Army, Navy, and Air Force. Allied occupation forces were assigned to specific areas throughout the home islands to supervise this operation. It was completed in six weeks and shortly thereafter the Army and Navy Ministries were abolished. By the end of January, 1946, the demilitarization phase of the occupation had proceeded so smoothly that one of the two American Armies of Occupation was withdrawn.

In the meantime the nonmilitary activities of the occupation increased in importance. General MacArthur perfected his organization and created a General Headquarters, Supreme Commander for the Allied Powers (GHQ, SCAP), with appropriate sections to supervise the various operations of the Japanese government. SCAP directives and orders were then issued to the government, which was held responsible for their execution. On some of the most important issues, however, such as the drafting of the new Constitution, while no formal directives were issued, SCAP played the decisive role.[2] (See page 402.)

On October 4, 1945, SCAP gave the first positive encouragement to new democratic tendencies in Japan. He issued a directive which came to be known as the "Japanese Bill of Rights." Its purpose was to remove the current restrictions on the freedoms of the people. It ordered the abrogation of legislation restricting basic human rights and the release of political prisoners. The Ministry of Home Affairs, center of centralized police control, was deprived of most of its powers. The police were forbidden to interfere with individual liberties.[3]

The immediate effect of this directive was the resignation of Prime Minister Higashikuni. He insisted that he could not maintain peace and order without a Ministry of Home Affairs with strong police powers. Shidehara Kijurō, who as Foreign Minister before the conquest of Manchuria in 1931 had advocated a friendly policy toward China, was selected as his successor. Shidehara's Cabinet was basically conservative and served as a willing tool of SCAP in an interim capacity until after the first postwar elections of April, 1946. During this period, as a result of the political freedom permitted by this directive, the Communists and Social Democrats organized their own parties and began to challenge the old political leaders.

The conservative character of the Shidehara Cabinet and of the House of Representatives was more than counterbalanced, however, by the activities of SCAP in connection with the revision of the Constitution. If representative institutions were to prosper, if individual human freedoms were to be guaranteed, and if a new political reorientation was to be expected, basic revisions of the old Constitution were imperative. (See Chapter 8.) Since no written directives were sent to the Japanese government on the subject of constitutional revision, it is extremely difficult to trace the exact extent of SCAP's participation in this crucial reform. An analysis of the activities of both SCAP and the Japanese government reveals, however, the vital role performed by SCAP officials in this drama.

In the first place, during the first four months of the occupation, General MacArthur made it clear to the Japanese government on several occasions that he believed a drastic change in the Constitution was necessary. He urged the Japanese to undertake this work themselves, under the guidance and general supervision of his headquarters. Vice-Premier Konoye was one of the first to take the initiative in this matter. From a conference with General MacArthur and from a subsequent discussion with his Political Adviser, George Atcheson, Jr., Konoye learned of the minimum reforms which the United States believed necessary to assure a representative form of government for the future. Like Itō two generations earlier, Konoye formed a constitutional drafting commission under his direction and under the immediate protection of the Emperor. But his suicide on December 15, 1945, came before the government had acted on his proposed changes.[4]

In the meantime, General MacArthur had also told Prime Minister Shidehara orally that the reform of the Constitution was one of the most important tasks which his government should undertake. Consequently, the Cabinet formed its own committee under the chairmanship of Matsumoto Joji, a noted professor of law. But all indications pointed to a concerted effort by the Cabinet to avoid making fundamental changes in the old Constitution. Matsumoto publicly talked about the weaknesses of a "government by the people." Proposed drafts of the Progressive and Liberal parties provided for retention by the Emperor of many of his special powers and prerogatives. On February 1, 1946, the Cabinet finally submitted to SCAP its official draft which contained provisions contrary to the aims of the Potsdam Declaration, especially to the concept of "responsible government." The Emperor remained the central figure; the Privy Council continued as his chief advisory body. The Cabinet was not made responsible to the people's elected representatives in Parliament; basic human rights were not guaranteed.

Faced with this apparent disinterest of the Cabinet in basic constitutional reforms, the Government Section of SCAP took the initiative. In conferences on February 2-3, 1946, General Courtney Whitney, Chief of Government Section, and General MacArthur decided on several basic principles to be followed in drafting a new constitution. The Emperor's powers were to be clearly restricted but he was to remain the head of the state. "War as a sovereign right of the nation" was to be abolished and was to be renounced "as an instrumentality for settling disputes." The peerage was not to extend beyond the present generation and the nobility was to be deprived of political power. Finally, the budget was to be modeled on the British system. The Government Section was then assigned the task of drafting a constitution based on these principles.

A new draft was completed in little more than a week. It gave the Cabinet wide powers. Sovereignty, which was to reside in the people, was to be exercised by the executive, legislative, and judicial branches of the government. War was to be outlawed. Civil rights were to be guaranteed and the Cabinet was to be made collectively responsible to Parliament. It provided that if there was a vote of nonconfidence in Parliament, the Cabinet must resign or dissolve the Diet. General MacArthur gave his formal approval to this draft. General Whitney met with representatives from the Japanese Cabinet on February 13, 1946, and showed them the draft his colleagues had prepared.

At this point, the accounts become confused as to what actually took place. The official account is contradictory. It states that there was no compulsion used by SCAP toward the Japanese. On the other hand, it is reported that they were told that if the Cabinet did not act, "General MacArthur was prepared to lay the issue before the people." In any case, they were given a copy of MacArthur's approved draft as a guide in their preparation of a revision. Two days of uninterrupted conference between SCAP officials and Cabinet representatives followed. During these sessions, acceptable English and Japanese texts were adopted. On the next day, March 6, 1946, the text of the new draft Constitution was published in Japan with strong endorsements by both General MacArthur and the Emperor.[5]

Although several months passed before the Japanese expressed their views openly, few doubted that the document was "MacArthur's Constitution." In the light of available evidence, this was clearly the case. An analysis of the official Japanese text indicates that the original text was in English rather than in Japanese. The limited time available for the Cabinet representatives to consider revisions denotes that they had little choice either on the content or on the form of the draft. General MacArthur's endorsement of the final draft on the day after the Cabinet representatives and SCAP officials had agreed on the English and Japanese texts clearly implies that these texts had already incorporated his wishes. The clearest evidence that this was basically a SCAP document, however, is found in its contents. The principles expounded by General MacArthur in early February were incorporated into the final text. But before it could become the basic law of the land, it would require Parliament's approval and the sanction of the Allied powers.

Allied Participation in the Occupation

Up to this point, General MacArthur's actions had elicited only limited criticisms from the Allied powers. They had willingly recognized the fact that the war in the Pacific had been almost exclusively an American campaign and that it was logical for the United States to play the paramount role in the occupation. They were not prepared, however, to relinquish their voice in the determination of basic policies for postwar Japan. When MacArthur published a new Constitution on his own initiative, they protested that he had gone too far.

These protests had some validity in view of the fact that eleven of the Allied nations were members of the Far Eastern Commission which had responsibility for formulating policies for Japan. Before the Instrument of Surrender was signed on September 2, 1945, the United States had taken steps to meet the desires of the Allies to participate in the control of postwar Japan. It had submitted a proposal to China, the Soviet Union, and the United Kingdom for the creation of a Far Eastern Advisory Commission to advise the participating governments on the policies to be adopted to ensure Japanese compliance with the Instrument of Surrender. At the Council of Foreign Ministers in London in September, 1945, Soviet Foreign Minister Molotov offered a counterproposal. He recommended the establishment of a control council for Japan for this purpose. In reply, Secretary Byrnes suggested that this whole problem was an appropriate one for discussion by the proposed Commission.

The United States then invited the ten states which were most concerned with Japan's future to the Commission's first meeting in Washington. The Soviet Union refused to attend on the grounds that it was a purely advisory body. In return, it demanded the formation of a four-power control council. Nevertheless, on October 30, 1945, the Far Eastern Advisory Commission met without a Soviet representative attending. During the next four months, its only important activity was a trip to Japan where its members became familiar at first hand with the problems of the occupation.

When the Council of Foreign Ministers met in Moscow in December, 1945, the problem of the control machinery for Japan was high on its agenda. Most of the Allies were of the opinion that some arrangement should be made whereby they could have more voice in the control of Japan. The United Kingdom tended to favor the Soviet concept of a four-power control council for Japan similar to the Allied Control Council for Germany. It also urged that the Commonwealth countries be given larger representation and that India be included. On the other hand, the United States did not intend to forfeit its favored position in the control of Japan. General MacArthur, even though he was Supreme Commander for the Allied Powers, was an American general and was responsible to his government alone. Any other arrangement could not be seriously entertained. He had already begun to execute his plans for the democratization of Japan. The Foreign Ministers reconciled their differences, however, by the formation of an eleven-nation Far Eastern Commission in Washington with power to formulate policy and of a four-power advisory Allied Council for Japan to sit in Tokyo.[6]

The new Far Eastern Commission was responsible for formulating policies to govern postwar Japan; it could review directives issued by the Supreme Commander or his action on policy matters. On the other hand, it was forbidden to interfere with military matters or to discuss peace treaty problems such as territorial settlements. It recognized the existing control machinery, including the exclusive right of the United States to communicate officially with the Supreme Commander. To meet the Soviet insistence on a veto, and also to protect General MacArthur, the approval of China, the Soviet Union, the United Kingdom, and the United States was required for all policy decisions.

On February 26, 1946, the Commission met for the first time in the Japanese Embassy building under the chairmanship of the United States Representative, General Frank R. McCoy. This was precisely the time that the

Courtesy of East-West

COUNTRYSIDE NEAR THE INLAND SEA

Courtesy of East-West

BURNT-OUT TOKYO FIVE YEARS AFTER SURRENDER

Courtesy of Wide World Photos

Tōjō Hideki, 1885-1948

Yoshida Shigeru, 1878-

Courtesy of East-West

Hatoyama Ichirō, 1883-

Japanese Cabinet was procrastinating on taking a stand on MacArthur's draft of the new Constitution. Unofficial reports from Tokyo indicated extensive activity in Japan in connection with constitutional revision. Just prior to a Commission meeting on March 6, 1946, reports reached Washington that the Tokyo press had published the text of the proposed Constitution and that it had received General MacArthur's personal approval. Several members of the Commission interpreted this action by SCAP as an affront to this international policy-making body and as a challenge to its authority. The next week, approval was sought for a policy decision which would have required General MacArthur to postpone the elections which he had called for April, 1946, and to submit the Constitution to the Commission for approval.

After the American representative threatened to veto any such policy, which would have been completely unacceptable to SCAP, the Commission finally approved a more moderate policy. SCAP was asked to keep the Commission informed on the progress of the draft of the Constitution in the Japanese Parliament. Furthermore, he was requested to apprise the Japanese government of the fact that the Commission must be given an opportunity to approve the final draft. The Commission simultaneously requested SCAP's views on the advisability of postponing the elections to give the new political groups a better chance of victory. MacArthur's reply to this request was an unequivocal, "No." He refused to postpone the elections. He and his Government Section became apprehensive lest the Commission interfere with the acceptance of the Constitution by Parliament.[7]

The other Allied body created by the Council of Foreign Ministers in December, 1945, was the Allied Council for Japan. It was to meet in Tokyo and was limited to four members, the United States, China, the Soviet Union, and a member who represented the United Kingdom, Australia, New Zealand, and India. Unlike the Allied Control Council for Germany, the Allied Council for Japan was not a control body and could not interfere with the execution of policy by SCAP. It could advise SCAP only when he wished to consult with it. In view of General MacArthur's basic desire to avoid interference in the occupation from any quarter, he made the fortnightly meetings of the Council, which first met in April, 1946, as perfunctory as possible. His staff avoided giving the members information which might be used to embarrass him or to hamper his freedom of action. While his representative on the Council, Political Adviser George Atcheson, Jr., made an honest attempt to seek the Council's advice on such questions as land reform, it was an ineffective body and added little to the occupation.[8]

The Political Atmosphere and the Elections, April, 1946

Despite the apprehension of the Far Eastern Commission that an early election would favor the conservatives, SCAP had taken the initiative in pushing for political reforms. At the suggestion of the occupation authorities, the Diet had passed a new election law which gave women the right to vote and which reduced the age of the electorate to twenty years. Furthermore, in order to give the people greater freedom to select persons of their own choice for office, a SCAP directive abolished the terroristic and nationalistic societies and inaugurated a purge of the exponents of militant nationalism and aggression. The old militaristic, ultranationalist leaders were ordered to be removed from public office and forbidden to run for election. Many of the original candidates for the first postwar election were made ineligible by this purge. Places were thus available for new political leaders.[9]

The Bill of Rights Directive of October, 1945, which guaranteed political freedom, had also stimulated political activity. New parties were formed and the old ones were revived. For the first time, the Communists were permitted under the law to organize a party. Their leaders had been released from prison. Others, such as Nozaka Sanzo, returned home from exile, thoroughly indoctrinated with communist doctrine. He became president of the new party, was elected to Parliament in April, 1946, and proved to be one of the shrewdest and most capable postwar politicians. Although the Communist party had only a limited number of members, it won widespread support by advocating popular causes, such as the alleviation of the food shortage, stricter controls on prices, higher wages, the nationalization of basic industries, and the termination of the occupation. The poverty, discontent, and hardship of postwar Japan were fertile ground for the growth of communist dogma. For the time being, the Communist party announced that its program would concentrate on peaceful, evolutionary change rather than on an immediate proletarian revolution.[10]

The Social Democrats refused to join a united front with the Communists and formed a party of their own. Their membership came largely from the growing labor movement and the urban intellectuals. Their platform was far less radical than that of the Communists. Although their goal was the gradual nationalization of the banks and key industries, they concentrated their immediate attack on shortages, stricter controls, and higher wages. They soon became the third strongest party and an important postwar political influence.

The Liberal party and the Progressive party were the largest ones in Japan. They were fundamentally conservative and their members had, for the most part, belonged to the prewar Minseitō and Seiyūkai parties. The Liberal party, which, before the purge, had fifty members in the House of

Representatives, advocated a *laissez-faire* economy, women suffrage, a lower voting age, a reorganization of the House of Peers and the Privy Council, but no major changes in the Constitution. Its chief leaders were Ashida Hitoshi and Yoshida Shigeru, both of whom became premiers later.

Premier Shidehara's Progressive party was the strongest in the Diet but its members were even more conservative than the Liberals. Its candidates supported a minimum of government interference in business and private life. It suffered most from the application of the purge directive which affected even some of the members of the Cabinet.

The results of the election of April, 1946, the first with universal adult suffrage, were not startling. It brought an end, however, to the control of the House of Representatives by members elected during wartime. Three-fourths of these members had been replaced by new persons with a more democratic outlook. The two leading conservative parties, the Progressives and the Liberals, obtained nearly half the seats in the House of Representatives, but their positions were reversed. The Liberals became the leading party with 139 seats. The Social Democrats elected 93 representatives, only one less than the Progressives. The Communists were able to win only five seats. As a result of the poor showing of his party, Premier Shidehara was unable to keep his coalition Cabinet in office and resigned. He was succeeded by the President of the Liberal party, Yoshida Shigeru. The first period of the occupation, when the wartime Parliament and the Cabinets acted in an interim capacity until national elections could be held, had come to an end.

Economic Scarcity

This first period had also been characterized by an economy of acute scarcity. Such essentials as food, shelter, and clothing were in short supply and continued to be rationed. The whole economy was in such a state of collapse that industrial recovery was negligible. But the greatest crisis was in food. The figures clearly indicated an alarming scarcity of the chief staple, rice. Because of the breakdown of the transportation system, the depletion of fertilizer reserves, and poor weather conditions, it was estimated that the average per capita caloric intake for 1946 would be 1530 calories as compared with an average of 1950 calories for the war years. The rice harvest of 1945 had been 27 per cent below that of the previous year; the quantity of rice collected by the government for distribution under rationing had fallen by 50 per cent.[11]

General MacArthur was well aware of the fact, however, that the success of the occupation depended, at least to some extent, on the well-being and tranquility of the people. While his directive specifically prohibited him from taking positive steps to rehabilitate the national economy, it permitted him to request food imports if they were necessary to supplement local resources and "to prevent such widespread disease and civil unrest as would endanger the occupying forces or interfere with military operations." Consequently, simultaneously with ordering the Japanese government to improve its methods of collection and distribution, he forwarded to Washington specific requests for food imports.

Because of the world-wide shortage in grains, particularly in wheat and rice, the food problem in Japan could not be isolated from the world food crisis. Strict rationing was still practiced by many of the United Nations. Widespread starvation and undernourishment were prevalent in China, Southeast Asia, and India. Therefore, MacArthur's request for food for Japan, a former enemy country, was bitterly criticized by several of the members of the Far Eastern Commission. They insisted that the question of food imports was a policy matter which fell within the Commission's competence. This issue, which was one of the most bitterly fought questions in the Commission, was resolved by the Commission deciding that no food imports into Japan would be permitted which would give the Japanese preferential treatment over the peoples of the Allied powers. The first foods imported from the United States were released in April, 1946; their distribution during the next few months amounted to as much as one-fourth of the monthly rationed requirements.

The food shortage was only one aspect of the postwar economic stagnation and retrogression. Inflation, which had been accelerated by the government's financial outlays late in August, 1945, was reaching dangerous proportions. The index figure for the cost of living for the average Tokyo wage earner had increased more than ten times from August, 1945, to January, 1946. Within the same period, the note issue had doubled and prices had risen to nearly three times their previous level. To meet this financial crisis, SCAP ordered the conversion of the currency, the freezing of bank deposits, and the elimination of war profits and indemnities by taxing them out of existence. The results were immediate but not lasting. The money in circulation dropped by 62 billion yen to 15 billion yen. The government announced that note issues would be limited henceforth to 30 billion yen and that the national economy would be stabilized by 1949. But new inflationary trends appeared almost immediately.[12]

Contradictory Forces During Yoshida's First Cabinet

When Premier Yoshida formed his first Cabinet in May, 1946, he faced formidable economic problems. Furthermore, he and his Cabinet were conservatives, yet during his premiership many of the reforms advocated by SCAP were completed. Thus, while he might have been in disagreement with such things as a tightly controlled economy, with the aspects of the Constitution which strengthened the legislative, and with the extension of the purge, he was powerless to stop their execution.

On the other hand, there were indications that certain significant features of representative government were appearing. Premier Yoshida was a man of principle.[13] He had been arrested during the war for his support of the peace movement and had succeeded to the head of the Liberal party because he was beyond the reach of the purges. Furthermore, under his tutelage, the Diet strengthened its position as the sole legislative authority and the House of Representatives showed promise of becoming a genuine agency of popular government. In line with the new policy, which was officially defined as inspiring necessary reforms by suggestion and persuasion, SCAP informally presented proposals to the House of Representatives for improving its function. These proposals advocated the formation of permanent committees, the allotment of sufficient time for deliberations on important items such as the budget, the increase in salaries of the legislators, and the creation of a National Diet Library with a legislative reference service. In August, 1946, the House of Representatives forced its recalcitrant Speaker to resign and cleared the way for the adoption of a Diet Reform Bill, the new Constitution, and temporary laws to implement it.

A New Constitution Is Adopted

In view of the approval which General MacArthur and the Yoshida Cabinet had already given to the draft of the Constitution, it was expected that the Japanese Parliament would approve the new document without many basic changes. In fact, outright opposition to it had dwindled even before the draft was formally presented to Parliament. Only the Communists continued to favor postponement of a vote on its acceptance, but their opposition was not strong enough to cause a delay.

But the opposition in the Far Eastern Commission in Washington to the new draft and to its early adoption was a different matter. Many of the Commission members were convinced that SCAP was pressing for immediate acceptance of the draft of the Constitution to forestall their interference. Consequently, they first concentrated on trying to prevent precipitate action in Japan. In May, 1946, the Commission approved a policy on the criteria to be used in the adoption of the Constitution. The first criterion was that adequate time and opportunity should be allowed for full discussion and consideration of the new document. Secondly, the Commission ruled that it be adopted in such a way as to express the free will of the Japanese people. A month later, after Parliament had opened, General MacArthur dismissed this action of the Commission in an arbitrary fashion. He announced, without referring specifically to the Commission's policy that these criteria had all been scrupulously followed.[14]

Actually, formal consideration of the draft of the new Constitution began in the House of Representatives toward the end of June, 1946. In the meantime, the Far Eastern Commission, which approved a document on basic principles for the new Constitution, insisted that two changes be made in the draft to make it consistent with these principles. The first change was that a majority of the Cabinet should be members of the Diet and that all of the Cabinet members should be civilians. The Commission also insisted that the upper chamber should specifically be made inferior to the House of Representatives. All of these points were incorporated in the draft prior to its approval by the House of Peers in October, 1946.

Shortly thereafter, the Far Eastern Commission cleared the way for final action in Japan. The United States delegation on the Commission avoided a direct vote on the text of the Constitution. The Commission decided instead that a review should be made by the Diet during the second year of the operation of the Constitution. If the operation proved successful, no further action would be necessary. If it proved unsatisfactory, a referendum might be required. After approval by the Privy Council, the new Constitution was promulgated on November 3, 1946, to become effective May 3, 1947.[15]

The new Constitution had diametrically changed the basic political philosophy of Japan's government. (See Appendix IV.) A limited constitutional monarchy had been superseded by a liberal one; the power and right to govern had been taken from the oligarchs and given to the people. A bicameral legislature, not the Emperor, was the highest organ of state. It was the sole legislative branch of the government. Its House of Representatives had superior budgetary and other powers over the new House of Councillors. Initiative for future amendments was vested in the Diet. The Emperor was deprived of all powers of government; he was now the symbol of the unity of the people. Contrary to the old Constitution, the responsibilities of the Cabinet were specifically enumerated. It was invested with all executive authority; it was collectively responsible for its acts to the Diet. The Premier was elected by Parliament; if he lost its confidence, he must resign or order a new general election to be held.

Another important innovation was the requirement that the judiciary be independent of the executive branch of the government. The new judges were not subject to Cabinet regulations. Their tenure in office must be approved by the electorate every ten years. The Supreme Court had full judicial powers. The fundamental human rights of the people were protected, for the first time, by the Constitution. All people were equal under the law, regardless of position, race, creed, or sex. Freedom of thought, religion, assembly, and speech were guaranteed and no longer subject to legal restrictions. Safeguards were provided against unwarranted arrests and against detention without adequate cause. The rights of workers to organize and bargain collectively were emphasized.

As for the elimination of militarism and aggressive tendencies, General MacArthur had taken personal interest in incorporating an article into the Constitution by which Japan renounced war and the use of force. (See page 402.) Article 9, which incorporated his views, stated that the Japanese people renounced war as a right of the nation, and the threat or use of force to settle international disputes. It also specified that land, sea, and air forces would "never be maintained." Ironically, this article on the renunciation of war was to plague the United States in less than five years when it sought to obtain support from Japan for a defense treaty against the Soviet Union.

In view of these and other provisions, this new basic charter of the nation created the legal framework within which "a peacefully inclined and responsible government," as provided by the Potsdam Declaration, could prosper. It remained for the future desires of the Japanese people, the operation of their new laws, and the extent of their adoption of these basic principles to determine whether democratic practices would expand and grow, or whether they would contract and wither.

Temporary Rejection of Conservatism, April, 1947–February, 1948

Even before the new Constitution went into effect in May, 1947, events within Japan reflected a decided reaction against the conservatives. Premier Yoshida lost much of his popularity and was nearly ousted by the Social Democrats who sponsored a vote of nonconfidence in the House of Representatives. To add to the Cabinet's woes, it faced pressure from SCAP to make a drastic extension of the purge. The Government Section of SCAP insisted that the purge should be expanded to include officials in local government, leaders of the largest industrial and financial companies, and influential persons in the various media of information. Yoshida's Cabinet resisted the new purge program but it was finally inaugurated early in January, 1947. A series of ordinances defined the new categories of persons to be included in the purge and set up the necessary national, prefectural, and municipal screening committees to execute it.

These ordinances ordered the removal and exclusion of "undesirable persons" (those who had supported militant nationalism and aggression) from public office in local assemblies and other city, prefectural, town, village and hamlet organizations. Even the heads of the block and neighborhood associations, which had controlled the people on the local level, were included in the purge. Henceforth, these officials were to be elected by the local residents. By subsequent Cabinet action, the neighborhood associations were abolished and their functions were transferred to the new local governments. On paper, at least, extreme nationalists were to be eliminated from local politics.

The economic purge, which was directed at ultranationalists in business, affected a much larger number of persons than any of the other purges. The top executives, directors, and other influential officials of specially designated companies were subject to removal from office. These companies fell into three main categories: government-owned firms such as the Bank of Japan; companies engaged in business in occupied areas; and the family combines, or *zaibatsu* corporations. Elaborate regulations were devised to prevent those persons removed or barred from their positions from operating behind the scenes. Nearly one-fourth of the persons screened under the economic program were adversely affected.

The third category of the revised purge included all those officials who had taken an active part in propaganda which supported expansionism, the war effort, or the exploitation of the occupied territories. Thus writers, leaders in the newspaper and radio world, and publicists were excluded from public office or positions of importance in the media of information.

As originally conceived, the purge was designed to eliminate advocates of ultranationalism and aggression from influential positions to prevent the re-emergence of Japanese militarism. As executed amid the enthusiasm for a "democratic reformation" of Japan, it went far beyond its original purpose. It was designed and enforced by SCAP without the acquiescence of any significant segment of Japanese society. Its arbitrary classifications brought unjust treatment to many. Many business leaders maintained that their removal caused confusion and defeated the purpose of the program. Their criticism was far from wrong. The overzealous SCAP officials who had sponsored such an extensive purge had not stopped to reflect on the transitory character of their efforts. When the occupation ceased, the purge was the first reform to be rescinded.[16]

It was the rank and file of urban workers, particularly those in Tokyo, which gave Yoshida his greatest troubles and which presaged the emergence of a new political force. Since adverse economic conditions continued, labor disputes rose in importance. The Communists were in the forefront of what was described as a "labor offensive." Demands were made for a minimum wage, for larger tax exemptions for persons with low incomes, and for increases in monthly cash payments for wages. In late January, 1947, over 150,000 workers gathered in front of the Imperial Palace in Tokyo and demanded Yoshida's resignation. He stigmatized the leaders as rebellious and irresponsible persons, which only increased their animosity toward him. A general strike was called for February 1, 1947. It was avoided only at the last moment by the personal intervention of General MacArthur. The days of the Cabinet were numbered. Five days later, General MacArthur announced that the momentous changes of the past year required a new election. In other words, he, too, had lost confidence in Yoshida.

While the Communists lost support in the labor movement because of the failure of their plans for a general strike, the Social Democrats gained in strength. The latter had refused to be drawn into the general strike. They had aptly criticized the efforts of the Yoshida Cabinet to check inflation as unrealistic and insincere. They found ready acceptance among the electorate for their program of strict control over the coal, iron, steel, and fertilizer industries as preliminary to their nationalization. They had profited from the extension of the purge which eliminated some of their most formidable conservative rivals.

The most important of the elections scheduled for April, 1947, was that for the House of Representatives. Under the new Constitution, the lower house was recognized as the predominant chamber. It could force the resignation of a Cabinet and precipitate the calling of a new election. It could override the House of Councillors in the designation of the Prime Minister. Consequently, Yoshida's continuance in office was dependent on his party retaining the largest number of seats in the House of Representatives. Although no party won an absolute majority in these elections the Social Democrats obtained 143 seats, the largest number. They had increased their strength by nearly one-half at the expense of the conservative parties; Yoshida's party won only 132. The returns showed a shift away from the conservatives.[17]

Katayama Tetsu, President of the Social Democrats, was finally able to form a coalition Cabinet with the assistance of two of the conservative parties, the Democrats and Cooperatives. But it was an uneasy partnership. The Democrats and Cooperatives, who controlled as many votes as Premier Katayama, were basically opposed to some of his economic policies. As a Christian and an idealist, Katayama enthusiastically supported the democratic institutions created and preserved by the new Constitution. As a politician and Prime Minister, his freedom of action was closely circumscribed because of his shaky political coalition. Practical economic conditions also hampered his program. He had inherited from the Yoshida Cabinet uncontrolled inflation and an economy which had not yet recovered sufficiently to supply essential consumers' goods. His inability to solve these problems, together with a new tendency toward polarization between the Right and the Left, brought his downfall in February, 1948.

SCAP's Interest in Economic Problems in April, 1947

In the meantime, SCAP began to prepare the way for Japan's economic rehabilitation to develop the country as a valuable asset, rather than a liability, in the coming struggle between the Western Democracies and the Soviet Union. As months passed, first the United States, and then the other Western Democracies, began to think of Japan more as an ally than as a former enemy. Controls gave way to assistance; criticism was replaced by encouragement. Responsibilities gradually shifted from SCAP to the Cabinet.

When considered in this perspective, the new interest which General MacArthur took in economic matters in the spring of 1947 is particularly significant. During the first eighteen months of the occupation, he and his headquarters had paid scant attention to economic problems in comparison with military and political ones. In the summer of 1946, he had intervened to alleviate the food crisis and in February, 1947, he had also prevented a general strike. On the other hand, despite an abrupt rise in living costs and the continued scarcity of essential commodities, the occupation authorities had made only desultory efforts to obtain enforcement of controls over finances, wages, prices, and industrial production.

By the spring of 1947, some of General MacArthur's economic advisers had concluded that these adverse economic conditions threatened the success of the entire occupation. Their views were eloquently supported by statistics on the rise in the cost of living. It was estimated, for example, that in early 1946, only one-seventh of the workers earned enough money to meet rising costs. While the wheels of the inflation spiral turned at an increasing speed, those of wages turned more slowly than those of prices. According to a report by the Economic Stabilization Board, by July, 1947, the average income of a Tokyo family equaled 2756 yen per month. Their expenditures totaled 2930 yen, of which three-fourths was spent in the black market. Obviously, drastic action was called for if complete economic chaos was to be avoided.[18]

General economic instability was further aggravated by unfavorable foreign trade balances. This condition was the result of both political and economic factors. As for the former, SCAP was anxious to stimulate foreign trade to lessen the burden of imports of food and other essentials. On the other hand, some of the Allies were reluctant to allow Japan to participate in world trade for fear of the competition from Japanese goods in world markets.

As for the economic factors that had produced this unsatisfactory trade balance, nylon had replaced silk in the world market. Hence, silk, the largest prewar item, was no longer in demand and could not be expected to pay for essential imports. By the end of 1947, despite the creation by

SCAP of a Board of Trade (*Boeki Chō*) to deal with trade matters and the allocation of special funds to stimulate export, the total foreign trade deficit had equaled one-half billion dollars. These difficulties were partially overcome by action of the Far Eastern Commission in Washington. It set up an Inter-Allied Trade Board to facilitate Japanese trade on an inter-governmental basis. Quotas were established for commercial entrants from foreign countries. But by November, 1947, though government trade gave way to private trade, exports were still far below imports.[19]

Until industrial production could be substantially improved, therefore, no basic amelioration could be expected in the nation's economy. The food crisis, the high cost of living, and the trade deficit could not be overcome unless more essential goods were available. Unfortunately, industrial recovery had progressed at an exceedingly low rate. In 1946 it was only 32 per cent of the average for 1930-34; in 1947, it had risen to only 40 per cent of the base average. This sluggishness in industry was explained in various ways. The Japanese business leaders blamed the purge program. SCAP officials hinted that the Far Eastern Commission's lack of decision on the reparations issue and on a postwar level of industry had created distrust in the nation's economic future and had retarded recovery. The labor unions and left-wing politicians accused the Yoshida government of laxness in enforcing controls.

Whatever may have been the causes for the slow rate of recovery, General MacArthur was finally persuaded to take positive action to improve the national economy. He became convinced that Yoshida's Cabinet was not interested in effective controls. Consequently, in March, 1947, he wrote the Prime Minister that controls over wages, prices, and rationing should be enforced and that commodities in short supply should be distributed equitably. He concluded:

> It is essential that the Japanese government, through the Economic Stabilization Board . . . take early and vigorous steps to develop and implement the integrated series of economic and financial controls which the current situation demands.[20]

This warning to Premier Yoshida was also a criticism of the manner in which he had handled the newly created Economic Stabilization Board (ESB) of the Cabinet. Although the ESB had responsibility for economic controls and rehabilitation, Yoshida had done his best to keep it in a subordinate position. When Katayama became Premier in May, 1947, however, he immediately strengthened the Board. It then enforced drastic measures in an attempt to check inflation. In a frank report on current economic conditions, the Board warned of an impending economic crisis. But even these efforts were not enough to check the increases in the national debt or to retard the expansion of currency in circulation. Furthermore, corporations refused to pay their taxes and the tax collectors, in the hope of obtaining higher salaries, refused to collect them. Thus, inflation, higher wages, and a retarded industrial production were the chief evils which hounded the Katayama and successive Cabinets.

Henceforth, both the United States government and SCAP, as well as the Japanese Cabinet, were as much concerned with industrial recovery as with any other single factor. Only as Japan regained its economic strength could it expect to become independent politically; only as it required less direct aid from the United States could it be thought of as an asset rather than a liability in the struggle against world communism. Thus the continuance of the various reforms which SCAP had energetically undertaken depended increasingly on whether they would contribute to Japan's rehabilitation as well as on whether they were acceptable to the Japanese. The agrarian reforms, the growth of organized labor, the new educational movement, and the new status of women would not and could not easily be erased. On the other hand, reforms such as the purge, the dissolution of the *Zaibatsu,* and the decentralization of the police system, which were energetically undertaken, were later either repudiated or left to disappear by desuetude.

Agrarian, Labor, and Zaibatsu Reforms

Of all the economic reforms advocated by SCAP, that in agriculture was the most immediate. Too many people had been trying to eke out an existence for too long a time on too small an amount of land. Furthermore, the population was increasing rapidly and a small minority owned a disproportionately large amount of land.[21] Nearly three-fourths of the farm population was dependent partially or wholly on rented land. They paid rents equal to half or more of their annual crops.

The land reform was designed, therefore, to give those who tilled the soil a chance to own it. A detailed reform program was prepared under SCAP's direction and considered by the Allied Council for Japan. By October, 1946, the Yoshida Cabinet secured the passage in Parliament of two land reform bills. Under the new laws, absentee landowners were to sell their land to the government. Noncultivators who lived on their land could retain 2.5 acres. Cultivators were restricted in most cases to farms of 7.5 acres. Tenant cultivators could buy the land they worked in thirty installments at moderate interest rates. Finally, rentals were not to exceed 25 per cent of the crop and written leases were required to be given by all landowners.

This program, which gained momentum in 1947 and was completed in 1950, enabled 3 million cultivators to acquire possession of 5 million acres of land. Before the program was finally executed, many obstacles had to be overcome. Landowners were reluctant to sell their land for what they considered to be too low a price. Many of the commissions charged with implementing the program were dominated by landowners. Many farmers continued to be ignorant of their rights under the new law. But when completed, and thanks to the profits made by the farmers due to the high price of rice, the heavy rural indebtedness was largely reduced and most tenants had become landowners. Despite the objections of the former landlords, it was unlikely that post-occupation changes could reverse these reforms.

Changes equally as significant as those in agriculture were taking place in labor. The two largest federations, the All-Japan Federation of Labor (JFL) with 900,000 members and the National Congress of Industrial Unions (CIU) with 1,600,000 members were organized during the summer of 1946. The Far Eastern Commission had approved a trade union policy which permitted unions to take part in political activities and to support political parties. While several of the CIU unions had been dominated by left-wing and communist elements, the collapse of the general strike in February, 1947, had spelled defeat for the radicals in an attempt to control the unions and to form a united labor front. The government continued to sponsor legislation for the benefit of labor. New labor standards, which conformed to those set by the International Labor Office, were set. A Labor Ministry was formed and union membership jumped to over six million. Communist control was gradually eliminated from the most powerful executive bodies. A new labor force had emerged in postwar Japanese society which was to become one of the strongest deterrents to a rapid emergence of nationalism and militarism.[22]

One of the most controversial reforms of the occupation was directed at the dissolution of the *Zaibatsu,* the family combines, and at the deconcentration of economic power. Like the unpopular purges, this program, which was designed to break up the family combines, was reversed even before the occupation was completed. The basic American policy for Japan had called for the encouragement of democratic organizations in industry. It favored dissolution of the large banking and industrial combines as part of the demilitarization and democratization of Japan. In fact, the *Zaibatsu* had been described in an official United States government report as, "The greatest war potential of Japan. It was they who made possible all of Japan's conquests and aggressions."[23]

While this castigation of the *Zaibatsu* would be difficult to prove, it is representative of the attitude which motivated the program for the dissolution of the small clique which controlled Japanese economic and financial power. A special holding company was organized to hold and dispose of the securities of the old *Zaibatsu* concerns. Liquidation was then ordered for the five leading firms and later extended to additional combines and their subsidiaries. The personal finances of the ten richest families were strictly controlled; the purge was extended to include prominent officials in those firms listed for dissolution. The industrialists and financiers resisted the reforms as much as possible and hoped that the regulations would be ameliorated in the future.

In effect, they did not have long to wait. In the early part of 1947 the Far Eastern Commission had been considering an American policy paper on the limitations of excessive concentration of economic power. Simultaneously SCAP sponsored a law in the Japanese Diet designed to achieve the same purpose. But this whole policy toward the *Zaibatsu* was sharply criticized by American financial circles. They argued that it would be far better for Japan's future prosperity to permit its economy to develop along traditional lines than to run the risk of stagnation through excessive reforms. This criticism coincided with realization within the United States government that Japan should be strengthened, not weakened, economically. The United States withdrew its paper on excessive concentration of economic power from the Far Eastern Commission. Although the Diet had passed a law to dissolve the huge corporations, the Cabinet, relieved of pressure from SCAP, permitted the new law to lapse. Unlike the agrarian reform and the growth of the labor movement, the *Zaibatsu* reforms had no lasting effect. The Japanese industrial organizations rapidly reverted to their prewar forms and the old financial and industrial concerns and interests again became predominant.

Reforms in the Police Systems and in Education

Another example of the failure of SCAP's reform to become permanent is that of the police system. In prewar Japan, the police had been under the direct control of the Home Minister and thus had been an important element in forming a dictatorial, militaristic government. Since surrender, the new police had not won the confidence of the people nor had their new functions been clearly defined. During the first year of the occupation, a special commission recommended a decentralized police system outside of the control of the Home Ministry. In view of continued resistance to this basic reform, however, a new Police Law was not enacted until December, 1947. The Home Ministry was abolished; the police were divided into local, municipal police and national, rural police. Both groups were free from central government control except during a national emergency; their duties were limited to those normally exercised by a police force.[24] But the new system was never enthusiastically supported by the people. The government constantly sought excuses to revert to the old system of a single, national police force. In 1954, new laws were passed whereby the police system reverted, in many respects, to the prewar pattern.

Since the prewar educational system had been consciously designed to command conformity and absolute obedience and had contributed directly to the growth of ultrapatriotism and militant nationalism, reforms in education were also required. If democratic tendencies were to develop in postwar Japan, a radically different educational philosophy would have to be formed. From the early part of the occupation, schools had been opened but military education and courses in ethics had been stricken from the curriculum. Teachers with records as ultranationalists had been removed from office. Revisions were begun on textbooks in history and geography. On January 1, 1946, the Emperor issued a new rescript in which he denied his divinity and the superiority of the Japanese people. He reiterated, however, the mandate of his grandfather that wisdom and knowledge should be sought throughout the world and thus gave sanction to the new democratic base for education.

A few months later, an education mission reached Japan which worked in close cooperation with SCAP officials and a Japanese advisory committee. Its most important recommendations were incorporated into new laws which were passed by the Diet in the spring of 1947. A new educational philosophy stressed the importance of individual initiative and inquiry, academic freedom, and equal educational opportunities. The twelve years of secondary schools were divided into six years of elementary, three of lower secondary, and three of higher secondary education. Universities were to be four years. Administratively, schools were to be controlled by local elective school boards responsible to the local community.

By the time the new Constitution came into effect in May, 1947, therefore, the educational system had been reformed. But in effect, almost insuperable obstacles prevented a sudden change in the operation of the new educational system. Funds were not available to repair the large number of school buildings made unusable by the war. There was a dearth of adequately trained teachers for the schools and especially for the newly created universities in each of the prefectures. There was no assurance that the teachers would follow the new methods taught them in the normal schools. Finally, the reforms had been initiated by the occupation authorities. With the emergence of a nascent nationalism after the peace treaty, the natural tendency was to revert to a prewar pattern of centralized control over education.[25]

Reparations and War Criminals

Another basic issue which was of paramount importance to the Allies at the time of surrender was the question of reparations. But with the passage of time, most of the Allies lost interest in the reparations question and it was solved largely by default. Before that time arrived, however, the

Allies argued long and hard on the issue. At Potsdam the Allies had decided that postwar Japanese industries should be such as "to permit the exaction of just reparations in kind." Furthermore, reparations payments were considered as a method of reducing Japan's war potential.

In accordance with this policy the Far Eastern Commission endeavored to decide what goods should be made available for reparations. The Commission first agreed that the average industrial production for the years 1930-34 should be used as a base for determining Japan's peacetime needs. Presumably, all industrial equipment above that amount would be available for reparations. But the Commission could not agree on the amount of goods which should be available for reparations, nor the proportion which should be assigned to each country.

In view of this impasse, in April, 1947, the United States government issued an interim directive to the Supreme Commander which authorized him to make available for reparations 30 per cent of the surplus industrial facilities in specified primary and secondary war industries. China was to receive half of these facilities and the Philippine Republic, the United Kingdom, and the Netherlands were each to receive one-sixth. Transfers under this interim program did not begin until the third year of the occupation and were the only reparations paid by Japan on the authority of the Far Eastern Commission.[26]

Another provision of the Potsdam Declaration designed to reduce Japan's future war potential called for the trial of war criminals. The war crimes trials were conceived in the belief that militarism and aggression could be discredited by the punishment of irresponsible militarists. To implement this policy, two types of trials were held. One type, which concerned most of the war criminals, were military tribunals composed of representatives of the states whose nationals had been victimized by Japanese military personnel. The trials were held in the territory where the crimes had been committed.

The second type of trial was international in character and was for the select group of leaders who had planned the war in violation of international law. The International Military Tribunal for the Far East was formed in Tokyo to try those Japanese leaders who had committed "crimes against peace . . . conventional war crimes, [and] crimes against humanity." The Tribunal, which was composed of representatives from the eleven leading Allied powers, began its deliberations on May 3, 1946. The twenty-eight major war criminals included such prominent wartime leaders as former Lord Keeper of the Privy Seal Kido Kōichi; former Prime Ministers Tōjō, Koiso, and Hirota; militarists such as Araki, Itagaki, Matsui, Doihara, and Hashimoto, and the ultranationalist Matsuoka. It took the prosecution nine months to present its case, during which time two of the accused had died and one had become insane. The trial judgment was finally pronounced in November, 1948, at which time all of the accused were found guilty of planning to secure Japan's domination over Asia by waging a war of aggression. Seven were condemned to death, sixteen to life imprisonment, one to twenty-year and one to seven-year imprisonment.[27]

But the trials had failed to accomplish their objective. They were so drawn out that the public lost interest in them. Most Japanese assumed from the start the accused would be found guilty and would be condemned to death. They did not understand or appreciate such technicalities as "due process" and "right of the accused to have counsel and to be heard." Most of the persons tried were old and had already lost the confidence of the people. Those who escaped blamed the leaders not for going to war but for having started a war when they were not certain of victory. Another occupation "reform" had come to naught.

Futile Attempts at a Peace Treaty

But nothing signaled more dramatically a change in Allied policy toward the occupation than the proposal of the United States for a peace conference in the summer of 1947. The failure to obtain agreement among the Allies for such a conference only highlighted the importance of keeping Japan on the side of the Western Democracies in their struggle against world communism. When it was apparent in early 1948 that an immediate peace treaty was impossible, the whole direction of the occupation shifted toward rehabilitation.

In the spring of 1947 a draft of a peace treaty for Japan had been prepared by the Department of State. This draft was then shown to General MacArthur for his comments. Shortly thereafter, on March 19, 1947, he made an impromptu statement on the importance of an early peace treaty. He described the occupation as falling into three phases—military, political, and economic. He believed that necessary precautions had been taken to ensure that Japan would not again menace world peace and that the military phase was over. The framework for political reconstruction had also been established. It was necessary only to watch and control. Finally, the main feature of the economic phase, a blockade, could be ended by signing a peace treaty and by the commencement of normal trade relations. He concluded that the treaty should place Japan under the general supervision of the United Nations for purposes of protective control.[28]

In April, 1947, General MacArthur elaborated further on his desire for an early treaty. He was convinced that an early treaty with Japan would facilitate the settlement of differences in Europe over the German and Austrian treaties. He recommended that a conference be held that summer in Tokyo; six months after the treaty was signed, the occupation forces should begin an orderly withdrawal. The treaty should ensure peace; it should not be punitive in character, like the Versailles Treaty, which only produced another war within twenty-five years. The United States should persuade the other Allies of the advisability of this course of action and, if necessary, should sign a treaty without the Soviet Union.[29]

When General MacArthur's recommendations were conveyed to Secretary of State George Marshall, the latter agreed that a Japanese peace conference should be called in July, 1947. Since international accord on most of the territorial questions had already been reached at the Conferences at Cairo, Yalta, and Potsdam, the United States hoped that the Japanese settlement might prove easier than that for Germany and Austria. To avoid the interminable wranglings on purely procedural problems, which had characterized the meetings of the Council of Foreign Ministers, the United States proposed that a conference of deputies tackle problems of substance in the Japanese treaty. It also recommended that voting in such a conference be by a two-thirds majority; membership should be restricted to the states represented on the Far Eastern Commission.

But the reply from the Soviet Union to the American invitation concentrated on procedural questions. It accused the United States of unilateral action. It insisted that China, Great Britain, Russia, and the United States, should first decide the treaty questions. The issue was further complicated by a Chinese proposal for a compromise voting procedure. During the next six months, the four powers failed to resolve their differences. Although several of the powers, notably Great Britain and Australia, strongly favored an early peace treaty with Japan, the Soviet Union and the Republic of China declined to attend a conference on the basis of the American proposals. In January, 1948, the United States decided that it was inadvisable to press for the conference at that time; the matter was officially dropped for the next two years.[30]

The United States was slowly awakening to the fact that Japan as an ally would be exceedingly useful in the fight against communism in Asia. Since it was assumed that a peace treaty would mean the withdrawal of American occupation troops from Japan, such a move would be advantageous for the Soviet Union. So long as the Soviet Union did not favor a peace conference, it would be more advantageous for the Western Allies to continue the occupation. To counteract the deleterious effects of an indefinite occupation, the Supreme Commander was urged to transfer as much autonomy as possible to the Japanese government. SCAP was to retire from the role of reformer and even permit the reversal by the Japanese, if they so desired, of previous policies. A careful balance was to be struck between the role of a friendly benefactor and of a protector of Japan from Soviet encroachments.

Thus in early 1948, with the demise of the Katayama Cabinet and the decision to postpone holding a peace conference, the general character of the occupation changed rapidly. Encouragement was given to Japanese economic revival; reforms which would hinder this growth were reversed or allowed to lie in abeyance. When war broke out in Korea in June, 1950, Japan was a useful ally. Unless it were given real independence in the foreseeable future, however, it could not be expected to recognize its responsibilities in connection with the United Nations' fight against communism in Korea. A new movement for a peace treaty emerged and with it the idea of a Mutual Security Pact. But the evolution of these new concepts, the emergence of a revitalized Japan squarely on the side of the Western Democracies, and the slow but steady decline of the appeal of communism in Japan, all belong to the next period when the Western Democracies accepted Japan as a trusted ally.

Notes

1. For a more detailed presentation of this subject, as well as other aspects of the first two years of the occupation, see Hugh Borton, "The Allied Occupation of Japan, 1945-47"; in F. C. Jones, Hugh Borton, and B. R. Pearn, *The Far East, 1942-1946* (London: Oxford University Press, 1955), pp. 307-428. Hereafter referred to as Borton, "Occupation."

2. This lack of directives on some of the vital issues is only one of the many problems which baffles the historian of the occupation of Japan. In view of the nature of the occupation and of the assumption of Japanese officials that even the lowest SCAP officer could veto an action taken by the Japanese government, SCAP control was greater than appears on the record. Note that henceforth SCAP came to be used to designate both General MacArthur and his headquarters. See Borton, "Occupation," *op. cit.*, p. 321; and Supreme Commander for the Allied Powers, *Summation of Non-Military Activities in Japan* (Tokyo: GHQ, SCAP, 1945-48), No. 23 (August, 1947). [Hereafter referred to as SCAP, *Summation*.]

3. Automatically, with the surrender of the Armed Forces, the dreaded *Kempeitai* (military police), who were particularly vicious and unscrupulous in the occupied areas, ceased to exist. The text of this directive of October 4, 1945, along with many of the other directives, will be found in Supreme Commander for the Allied Powers, Government Section, *Political Reorientation of Japan, September, 1945, to September, 1948* (2 vols.; Washington: U.S. Government Printing Office, 1949), II.

4. The most extensive material on Constitutional revision will be found in Supreme Commander, *Political Orientation, op. cit.* For a concise account, see Borton, "Occupation" *op. cit.*, p. 326 *et seq.*

5. It was not simply fortuitous that the draft Constitution as approved by General MacArthur contained principles already adopted by the United States government and later presented to the Far Eastern Commission. A SWNCC paper on Constitutional reform had been approved and sent to SCAP before these discus-

sions took place. This same paper later became the basis for the Commission's decision on Constitutional Reform. The principle concerning the renunciation of war, which was not included in the SWNCC document, was MacArthur's own suggestion. See *Political Reorientation, op. cit.,* I, pp. 102 and 105; II, p. 622. See also Borton, "Occupation," *op. cit.,* pp. 330 ff.

6. The initial members on the Commission were Australia, Canada, China, France, India, the Netherlands, New Zealand, the Philippines, the Soviet Union, the United Kingdom, and the United States. Burma and Pakistan joined after 1949. For a history of the Far Eastern Advisory Commission and its successor, the Far Eastern Commission, see George H. Blakeslee, *A History of the Far Eastern Commission* (Washington: U.S. Department of State, Publication 5138, Far Eastern Series 60, 1953).

7. As the United States Representative on the Committee on Constitutional and Legal Reform, the writer well recalls the bitter attacks directed against SCAP's action. The atmosphere was charged with ill will because most of the representatives on that Committee had gone to Tokyo with the Advisory Commission. Prior to their return in January, 1946, they had been told by General Whitney that the problem of constitutional reform was a matter for the Japanese to consider and that no work was being undertaken by SCAP. Their charge that they had purposely been kept ignorant of what was transpiring was made all the more difficult to refute in view of the fact that the United States government had not been kept informed of the activities of the Government Section in February and March, 1946. There were no copies of the new draft Constitution available in Washington when it was published in Tokyo. For the text of the Commission's decisions of March 20, 1946, on the Constitution, see Far Eastern Commission, *Activities of the Far Eastern Commission's Report by the Secretary General, February 26, 1946—July 10, 1947* (Washington: U.S. Government Printing Office, 1947), Appendix 8, p. 63.

8. While on temporary assignment in the spring of 1947 in Tokyo, the writer was consulted on several occasions by Atcheson concerning topics and subject matter to be presented to the Council. The effectiveness of the Council was also reduced because of the following: (1) the Soviet delegate, Lieutenant General Derevyenko used the meetings for propaganda purposes to embarrass SCAP; (2) the Commonwealth member, Mr. Macmahon Ball of Australia, interpreted the Council's functions as being the eyes and ears of the Far Eastern Commission; and (3) General MacArthur was extremely sensitive to adverse criticism which made his subordinates anxious to throttle the Council members to avoid such criticism. For Mr. Ball's views, see his *Japan, Enemy or Ally?* (New York: John Day Co., Inc., 1949).

9. The purge was hardest on the conservatives. The most conservative party, the Progressive party, discovered that only 27 of its 274 members were eligible to continue in office. The Liberals lost 30 of its 50 members.

10. Nozaka had directed Communist activities in Japan from Moscow from 1930 to 1940. During the war he had been with the Communists in China. Other important Communist leaders elected to Parliament in April, 1946, were: Tokuda Kyuichi, Secretary General of the party, and Shiga Yoshio, editor of the Communist daily, *Akahata,* and chief party theorist. For biographical details and an excellent, scholarly account of the communists in Japan, see Rodger Swearinger and Paul Langer, *Red Flag in Japan: International Communism in Action, 1919-1951* (Cambridge: Harvard University Press, 1952).

11. The figures are derived from the following sources. SCAP, *Summation,* Nos. 1-8, Sept./Oct. 1945—May, 1946 and Jerome B. Cohen, *Japan's Economy in War and Reconstruction* (Minneapolis: University of Minnesota Press, 1949), p. 463.

12. See SCAP, *Summation, op. cit.,* No. 6 (March, 1946), p. 201; No. 11 (August, 1946), p. 189; and No. 22 (July, 1947), pp. 18-55.

13. Before the war, Yoshida Shigeru (b. 1878) had been a career diplomat. His highest post was Ambassador to London. He was arrested in 1944 on orders from the War Minister during a roundup of those opposing continuation of the war. His first Cabinet was installed on May 22, 1946, with five Liberals and four Progressives. During the next eight years, he was Premier five times and for a total of nearly seven years. He was nominated Premier in April, 1946, by default. After the elections in April, 1946, the President of the Liberal party, Hatoyama Ichirō, was confident that he could form a Cabinet. His hopes were dashed when the press revealed that he had failed to include some damaging evidence in his purge questionnaire and SCAP found him ineligible for office. It is claimed that Yoshida, when he succeeded to the head of the party, promised Hatoyama the Presidency when his purge charges were cleared. When Yoshida failed to fulfill his promise in 1954, Hatoyama bolted the party and became the next Premier. (See below, p. 451.)

14. For texts of this decision and SCAP's reply, see Far Eastern Commission, *Activities, op. cit.,* p. 20.

15. The rapid decline in importance of the Commission is revealed by the fact that when the review period ended in October, 1948, no member took cognizance of the fact that no review had been made. A more detailed account of the adoption of the Constitution is contained in Borton, "Occupation," *op. cit.,* pp. 348 ff.

16. The total number of persons screened under the various purge programs equaled 717,415. Of these about 115,000 military and 87,000 civilian persons were purged. See Borton, "Occupation," *op. cit.,* p. 360. Texts of the purge directives are contained in SCAP, *Political Reorientation,* II, pp. 501-48.

17. The results of the elections for the House of Representatives of April 25, 1947, were as follows:

Parties	Members Before Election	Elected
Social Democrats	98	143
Conservatives		
Democrats	145	126
Liberals	140	132
Cooperatives	63	31
Communists	6	4
Others	13	30

See SCAP, *Summation,* No. 19 (April, 1947), p. 34; and No. 23 (August, 1947), p. 58.

18. SCAP, *Summation, op. cit.,* No. 22 (July, 1947), p. 30 *et seq.*

19. SCAP, *Two Years of the Occupation: Economics* (Tokyo: SCAP, Public Information Office, 1947); Far Eastern Commission, *Activities, op. cit.,* p. 23; Cohen, *Japan's Economy, op. cit.,* p. 494.

20. Ball, *Japan—Enemy or Ally?, op. cit.,* p. 61.

21. For a concise account of this whole problem by one who was actively engaged in the land reform program, see W. I. Ladejinsky, "Agriculture" in *Japan,* edited by Hugh Borton (Ithaca: Cornell University Press, 1952), pp. 46-64.

22. For the role of the Communists in the labor movement, see Swearinger and Langer, *op. cit.;* and for the labor movement, see Miriam S. Farley, *Aspects of Japan's Labor Problems* (New York: John Day Co., Inc., 1950).

23. Edwin W. Pauley, *Report on Japanese Reparations to the President of the United States, November, 1945 to Apirl, 1946* (Washington: U.S. Government Printing Office, 1946), p. 39.

24. Borton, "Occupation," *op. cit.*, pp. 374.

25. See Robert King Hall, *Education for a New Japan* (New Haven: Yale University Press, 1948); Department of State, *Report of the Education Mission to Japan* (Washington: U.S. Government Printing Office, 1946); SCAP, Civil Information and Education Section, *Education in Japan* (Tokyo: SCAP, 1948).

26. Some of the nations in southeast Asia insisted that Japan pay reparations, so they refused to sign the peace treaty and left the matter for future bilateral settlement. See below p. 460. Borton, "Occupation," *op. cit.*, pp. 403. Far Eastern Commission, *Activities, op. cit.*, pp. 68-80.

27. Those sentenced to death were Doihara Kenju, Chief of the Kwantung Army Secret Service; Hirota Kōki, Premier and Foreign Minister; Itagaki Seishirō, Kwantung Army Chief of Staff and War Minister (1938-39); Kimura Keitarō, Chief of Staff of Kwantung Army and Commander of Burmese Expeditionary Force; Matsui Iwane, Commander of Japanese Forces in China during the rape of Nanking; Muto Akira, Army Commander; and Tōjō Hideki, War Minister and wartime Prime Minister. The records of the trial are valuable not only as a legal record but also as descriptive material of events in Japan from 1931 to the time of surrender. For the Charter of the Tribunal, see Department of State, *Occupation of Japan, op. cit.*, pp. 147-54.

28. The author, who had been chairman of a State Department committee for drafting a treaty, arrived in Japan on March 8, 1947, and the draft was shown to General MacArthur by his political adviser, George Atcheson, Jr. There was no official text of the General's impromptu statement on need for a treaty. The best source is SCAP, *Political Reorientation*, II, 765-66.

29. This concept, which was so much a part of the philosophy of John Foster Dulles when he negotiated the Treaty of San Francisco in September, 1951, was elaborated in an interview which the author had with General MacArthur in Tokyo in mid-April. The idea was counter to most current thinking about the treaty in 1947. A year earlier, Secretary of State Byrnes had proposed a four-power disarmament and demilitarization treaty for Japan, to be enforced for twenty-five years by a Commission of Control. The "Control concept" was universally accepted by the Allies as the most effective method of assuring continued peace. It was included in a modified form in the first draft shown to General MacArthur and modified still further at his suggestion.

30. For details of these abortive negotiations, see Borton, "Occupation," *op. cit.*, pp. 421 ff.

21

AUTONOMY IN A DIVIDED WORLD, 1948-1955

The inability in early 1948 to obtain Soviet agreement for a peace conference for Japan was only one of numerous unsolved international problems which presaged a polarization of the world into two camps. By that date, the Council of Foreign Ministers had made little progress toward a permanent settlement of the German and Austrian questions. In Germany, two zones were rapidly becoming two separate political entities. East Germany was almost as much a part of the Communist World as Poland or Czechoslovakia. West Germany was predominantly oriented toward the Western Democracies.

In the Far East, a similar bifurcation was taking place. Korea continued to be divided at the thirty-eighth parallel; Soviet forces occupied the north and American forces occupied the south. Throughout 1946-47, Soviet-American negotiations had failed to make progress toward unification of the two zones. Consequently, the United States placed the whole matter before the United Nations.[1] The Soviet Union protested vehemently against the decision of the General Assembly that elections be held in 1948 throughout the entire country to select a government.

In China, Generalissimo Chiang Kai-shek and his Nationalist government continued to fight for survival against the Chinese Communists. Throughout 1947 he had held most of his positions but only at the cost of losing his best troops and equipment. His strategy was to try to keep the Communists out of the heart of Manchuria and away from the urban centers in North China. On the other hand, he was rapidly losing control of the hinterland.

The events of the next two years revealed the strength of the Communists on the continent of Asia. Chiang Kai-shek was forced to give up mainland China to them and to retreat to Formosa. The Korean Communists, believing that they could rapidly conquer South Korea, crossed the thirty-eighth parallel. But in the meantime, the United States and the other Western Democracies had come to recognize that they faced a common danger in both Europe and Asia. They began to approach the problem of the treatment of both Germany and Japan from the point of view of how those countries could be strengthened to help to halt the Communist tide. When challenged by the invasion of the Korean Communists, the United Nations, following the leadership of President Truman, decided to fight rather than to capitulate. General MacArthur, who was still the Supreme Commander in Japan, was appointed Commander of the United Nations forces in Korea.

Thus Japan became inextricably enmeshed in the struggles of the Free World against communism. Consequently, its most recent history is more appropriately divided by important events in that struggle rather than by internal developments. Furthermore, the chief characteristics of each of these periods were determined by the growing intensity of this world struggle. Thus, the first period extends from the failure to call a peace conference in 1948 to the outbreak of the Korean War in June, 1950. The chief characteristics of these two years are the growth of Communist power in Asia and the concentration by SCAP on the rehabilitation of the Japanese economy. The second period covers the two years between the Communist invasion of South Korea to the end of the Allied occupation of Japan in April, 1952. The significant feature of this second period is the effort of the United States to obtain Allied sanction for a peace settlement which would recognize Japan's place of equality with the other nations and which would align it on the side against the Communist World.

Finally, the last period embraces the post-treaty years. Since April, 1952, when the treaty went into effect, Japan has been an autonomous country but its actions have been circumscribed by its membership in the general mutual defense community which the Allies have erected against communism. Since many persons in Japan have questioned the advisability of a close alliance with the Western Democracies, strains and stresses have appeared in society. As economic conditions have worsened, the neutralists have found increased support for their position that Japan should befriend both the Western Democracies and the Communist World. Since almost all groups are united on the advantages of closer ties with the Communist regime in China, Japan would like to recognize the Peking Government immediately and begin normal trade relations. But it is bound by treaties to restrict this trade and to resist a Communist attack; it is also dependent on the United States for credits and essential imports. On the other hand, a renascent nationalism strengthens the desire for independence from outside control and influence. Strong opposing forces are working on Japan at the same time. The direction that it finally takes will be determined by the strongest of these forces.

International and Internal Political Developments, February, 1948—June, 1950

In the two and a half years prior to the war in Korea, the spread of communism in Asia, under skilful and unscrupulous leadership, was a direct challenge to the Western Democracies and to Japan. The most dramatic signs of its strength and appeal were the Communist victories in China and the collapse of the resistance of Chiang Kai-shek. By the end of 1949, the Communists had overrun all important areas of China; Chiang had lost general support for his government. He fled to Formosa with the remnants of his Nationalist forces.[2] The new regime of Mao Tse-tung and Chou En-lai rapidly consolidated its position and took on the attributes of a Communist state.

In the meantime, events in Korea divided that country still further into two separate units. The Soviet Union had refused to permit the United Nations Commission on Korea to hold elections in North Korea. In May, 1948, the Korean People's Republic adopted a Constitution which placed North Korea firmly in the Communist camp. The Soviet occupation forces began their withdrawal but Soviet advisers remained to train the North Korean Army. South of the thirty-eighth parallel, the United Nations Commission supervised an election. Dr. Syngman Rhee was elected first President of the Republic of Korea and organized a new governmental structure. He began to form an army under American tutelage in anticipation of the withdrawal of the American forces and the end of the occupation.

All of these events had a direct bearing on Japan. It was still under Allied occupation and continued to be primarily an American responsibility. To allay fears that America might contemplate withdrawal from Japan similar to that from Korea, Secretary of State Dean Acheson clarified his country's position. In January, 1950, he declared that the United States had no intention of weakening the defenses of Japan and that they must and should be maintained. He then referred to an American defense perimeter which ran from the Aleutian Islands in the north to Japan and the Ryūkyū Islands in the south. He added that the strong defense positions in the latter would continue to be held by the United States. At an appropriate time, it would seek a United Nations trusteeship for them.[3] Thus, whether the occupation of Japan were continued as in the past, or whether a peace treaty were concluded, the United States did not intend to abandon it to Communist threats.

The signing in February, 1950, of the Sino-Soviet Treaty of Friendship was another important international development in the growth of communism in East Asia. Its preamble defined its purpose to be "to prevent the rebirth of Japanese imperialism and . . . the repetition of aggression on the part of Japan or any other state which directly or indirectly would unite in any form with Japan in acts of aggression." The signatories bound themselves to give each other military assistance if attacked; they promised to strive for an early peace treaty with Japan. They pledged to develop the economic and cultural ties between them. After a peace was concluded with Japan, or at least by December 31, 1952, the South Manchurian Railway would revert to China and Soviet troops would withdraw from Port Arthur.[4]

The implications of this treaty were clear. The Chinese Communist regime at Peking and the Soviet Union now had a military alliance. Japan was considered by this Peking-Moscow Axis to be as imperialistic and as unregenerate as before the war. The provision in the Sino-Soviet Treaty concerning the signatories' desire for an early peace was an obvious bid for the friendship of the Japanese people. On the other hand, while this treaty ostensibly was directed against Japan, it was obviously aimed at the United States. By linking the United States with Japan and with prewar Japanese imperialism, the Chinese people and the Chinese Communist regime were conditioned to regard both of these countries as their future enemies.

This phenomenal growth of communism in the Far East naturally had its effect on Japan's internal politics. There was a further polarization of political groups to the right and to the left. The general tendency was away from the leftists toward conservatism. When the Social Democratic government of Premier Katayama ended in failure in February, 1948, he was succeeded by a conservative. The Diet, which has the authority to select the Premier, settled on Ashida Hitoshi, President of the conservative Democratic party. After eight months in office, he was ousted by the rival conservative party, the Liberals, under the leadership of Yoshida Shigeru. In October, 1948, Yoshida organized his second Cabinet and remained in power for the next six years. Throughout that entire period the trend was toward greater centralized control and the reversal of many of the liberalizing reforms sponsored by the occupation authorities.

In the elections of January, 1949, the first ones to be held since the electorate had shown a preference for the Social Democrats, Yoshida received overwhelming support for his conservative policies. His Liberal party won a comfortable majority in the House of Representatives. It also maintained its hold over the House of Councillors through amalgamation with the Green Breeze Society. In the elections for one half of the members of the House of Councillors in June, 1950, Yoshida increased his strength still further.

In view of an increased dissatisfaction among the people with the occupation, Yoshida insisted that SCAP put in writing all orders connected with unpopular measures. He thus deflected away from himself adverse criticism of these SCAP-sponsored measures. Criticism of both Yoshida and SCAP was also partially nullified, however, by the markedly reduced scale of intervention by SCAP in internal affairs. In July, 1949, General MacArthur had announced that the necessity no longer existed for the extensive surveillance of Japan by the Occupation. On the contrary, the Japanese government should "be permitted and encouraged to exercise the normal powers of government in matters of domestic administration."

While the Japanese electorate obviously preferred the conservatives, the successes of the Communists in China had strengthened the leftists. Although the Communist party in Japan had an estimated membership of less than 100,000, it exerted an influence out of all proportion to its size. It kept the political and labor fronts in a state of continued agitation. It profited from the discontent created by the struggle between the Communists and the Western Democracies, which made an early withdrawal of the occupation forces unlikely. Thus, in the election in January, 1949, the Communists obtained nearly three million votes or 10 per cent of the total. They apparently had secured votes which previously went to the Socialists. Communist membership in the House of Representatives increased from five to thirty-five.[5]

This election was, however, the high-water mark of the strength of the Japanese Communists. Despite their advocating popular causes in the subsequent elections, their ruthless tactics caused their decline. They resorted to violence and direct action. For example, when the national railways dismissed 30,000 workers to reduce expenditures, the President of the railways was murdered, obviously a victim of the Communist-dominated railway unions. Sabotage and small strikes were frequent. In the National Congress of Industrial Unions, the rank and file of labor refused to follow the Communists' demands that the unions oppose the dismissal of excess government workers. By the summer of 1950, therefore, a strong anticommunist movement had developed in the unions affiliated with the National Congress.

The official attitude of the government toward the Communist leaders was another factor which contributed to the decline of radicalism in Japan prior to the outbreak of the Korean War. In the face of sabotage and lawlessness in the summer of 1949, Premier Yoshida had pleaded for reforms in the police system which would give him the powers he believed necessary to cope with the situation. He even considered the possibility of declaring a state of national emergency which would have made it impossible for the Communist party to operate legally.

But SCAP solved this problem for the Prime Minister. In May, 1950, General MacArthur intimated that because of the lawlessness and stated aims of the Communists, it was open to question whether they should be accorded the protection of the law. He answered his own question in the negative even before the Korean Communists invaded South Korea. He ordered the Japanese government to ban the twenty-four members of the Central Committee of the Communist party, and the seventeen leaders of the Communist daily newspaper, *Red Flag* (*Akahata*), from engaging in political activity, writing, speaking publicly, or working for the government. Rather than run the risk of arrest, the leaders of the party went underground. Although they were thus eliminated from the political scene, Marxist dogma and communist theory continued to have a strong appeal to the intellectuals.

But Premier Yoshida was firmly in control of the domestic political scene. He welcomed the new interest which the United States and SCAP were taking in the economic rehabilitation of Japan as a bulwark in the western Pacific against communism. He was sufficiently shrewd as a politician, and experienced as a diplomat, to appreciate that this new policy was a direct outcome of the rising tide of communism in Asia. While he recognized that this tide posed a real threat to Japan, he was well satisfied that SCAP was meeting the problem in such a way as to be a direct benefit to the national economy.

Economic Rehabilitation, February, 1948—June, 1950

In February, 1948, when the first experiment with a socialist government came to an end, Japan faced basic economic problems that even a peace treaty would not have settled. They were problems which must be solved if political stability and friendliness toward the Western Democracies were to continue. The fundamental question was the old one of how Japan could increase its exports of manufactured goods sufficiently to cover the costs of imports necessary to support a rapidly increasing population. For example, as a result of the return of over six million repatriates after surrender, and a rapid rise in the natural rate of increase, the population had jumped from 72.4 million in 1945 to 80.4 million in 1948. At the same time, the excess of imports over exports in 1948 were valued at $425 million or one and three-fourths times the total amount of exports. Furthermore, grain imports equaled one-tenth of the total amount consumed. Although the United States was sending to Japan foods, fertilizers, and chemicals valued at over $300 million a year, there was no assurance that it would be willing to pay this amount indefinitely. Hence American aid was not a permanent solution.[6]

But an economic stabilization program was needed before an effective foreign trade program could be inaugurated. From the end of World War II to the end of 1948, wholesale prices had increased nearly sixty times, the note issue of the Bank of Japan had grown more than tenfold. Wages were pitiably inadequate to meet ever rising prices and increased living costs.

Consequently, in December, 1948, SCAP ordered the inauguration by the Japanese government of a comprehensive program to achieve fiscal, monetary, price, and wage stability, and to maximize production. Drastic steps were taken to balance the budget, to accelerate the collection of taxes, to limit the extension of credit to useful projects, and to improve the system of rationing and of allocation of supplies. A single rate of exchange for the yen was established at 360 yen to the dollar. Basic changes and reforms were made in the tax structure. Personal income taxes were reduced by about one-third as a remedy to reduce widespread tax evasion. The excess profits tax was eliminated to encourage increased industrial activity.

The economic rehabilitation of Japan was stimulated still further by the new position taken on the reparations issue by the United States representative on the Far Eastern Commission. In May, 1949, he stated that it was the considered view of his government that Japan's capacity to make war should not be permitted to re-emerge. At the same time he insisted that this objective did not require the limitation of its productive capacity of peaceful goods. He added that the problem facing the members of the Commission was one "of reviving these industries to provide the people's barest wants." He concluded by rescinding the directive of April, 1947, ordering the transfer of interim reparations (see page 420), and promising that the United States would not make any future move to secure the transfer of additional reparations from Japan.[7]

This statement placed the United States government squarely behind a program of rehabilitation. This new policy was challenged by some of the members of the Commission who still feared the resurgence of Japanese military forces more than they feared the specter of communism. There were subsequent indications, however, that the Noncommunist World was coming to accept the fact that Japan's participation in world trade was necessary and should be encouraged. For example, in October, 1949, the Economic Commission for Asia and the Far East (ECAFE) approved a resolution to the effect that the expansion of trade between Japan and the countries on the Commission would be beneficial to the region as a whole. It then requested that a special study be made of the potentialities of such trade.

This report recommended that an entirely new emphasis should be placed on export industries. Whereas textiles had comprised a large proportion of Japanese prewar exports to Far Eastern markets, ECAFE urged that Japan concentrate on the manufacture of capital goods. No other Asian country had the machines or skills required for this type of production. The report pointed out, for example, that in 1949 the major capital goods industries had operated at only half capacity. If their full capacity were utilized, they would have an exportable surplus of about $285 million, which would greatly reduce the deficit in the trade balance. It concluded, therefore, that the desired goal was a major expansion of exports of machinery, machine tools, farm implements, and other capital goods from Japan to the ECAFE region. Such expansion would help Japan to stabilize its economy and would strengthen its balance of payments position. Thus aid from the United States could be terminated.[8]

While this ECAFE study predicted that the region would be able to absorb Japan's maximum export possibilities, international developments blocked the effective execution of this plan. The report had noted that if raw materials could be obtained from China on a direct exchange basis, the Japanese iron and steel industry could expand without the use of dollars. If such exchange could not take place, the expansion of heavy industries would be dependent either on technological development or on imports from the dollar bloc. The Communist victories in China closed that area as a large-scale source for these raw materials, however, before the necessary technological advances had been made. Thus, iron ore and coal were shipped from the United States and dollars were needed to purchase them.

Despite these limitations, the program of economic rehabilitation had produced some encouraging results by the outbreak of the war in Korea in June, 1950. The national budget had been kept in balance for two years; the rate of increase of notes issued by the Bank of Japan had diminished. Furthermore, the indices of real wages remained stable. The index of industrial production had risen from 43.7 in 1948 to 73.2 in 1950. Most important of all, during the same period, the unfavorable trade balance had been reduced from $510 million to $220 million.

These levels of industrial production and of export trade had been made possible, however, by direct American aid. From September, 1945, to July, 1950, the United States had poured a total of $1.7 billion worth of goods into Japan. But there was a limit beyond which the United States was not willing to go. Congress had already reduced the aid appropriations for the fiscal year 1950-51 to less than half that of the previous year. Furthermore, the Japanese economy was far from viable. The Economic Stabilization Board had estimated that marked increases in exports would be necessary if a standard of living comparable to prewar days was to be maintained. The basic problem was to find larger foreign markets and new sources of foreign credit. But many of Japan's economic problems were solved, at least temporarily, by the unexpected outbreak of the Korean War.

The Korean War and Japan

On June 25, 1950, the North Korean Army suddenly thrust across the thirty-eighth parallel into South Korea. This action opened the first phase of the Korean War. Except for a military advisory group, there had been no American troops in Korea since June, 1949. The defense of the line which separated the Communist government in the north from the Republic of Korea in the south had been left to the latter's newly organized armed forces. They had been supplied with American equipment but they were no match for the North Korean Communist Army and its Russian-built tanks. President Truman acted immediately to check this invasion which threatened Japan and the chief bastions in the American defense perimeter in the western Pacific. He placed the problem before the Security Council. The Council demanded the immediate withdrawal of the Communist forces to a point north of the thirty-eighth parallel, and the cessation of hostilities. It also asked its members to help carry out its demands. President Truman requested General MacArthur to send aid to the Republic of Korea.[9]

With his appointment shortly thereafter as United Nations Commander, General MacArthur's headquarters immediately became absorbed in the military problems created by the rapid southward advance of the Korean Communists. As the responsibilities of the United Nations headquarters increased, its interest in the business of the occupation of Japan decreased. Prime Minister Yoshida, with his comfortable majority in Parliament, assumed greater responsibility in the operation of his government. Yet his position and that of his country was an anomalous one. Japan was still under the occupation of the Supreme Commander and must obey his orders. At the very least, the Japanese people were expected to accept without protest any demands which the Korean War might make upon them. Presumably, they were expected to approve the action of the United Nations in a war which was not of their doing.

In reality, however, the Japanese public reacted to the Communist attack in Korea in an ominous fashion. They considered it none of their concern. While they refrained from sabotage and willingly worked at any task assigned them by SCAP, they did not realize the significance of the struggle that was going on around them. They appeared prepared to accept without resistance a victory by either side. They failed to accept the thesis that a Communist victory in Korea would be a portentous threat to their own freedom and security.

On the other hand, the shift in American policy toward support of Japan's economic rehabilitation had been predicated on the assumption that such a program would help to keep Japan within the orbit of the Western Democracies. The reaction to the Korean War had indicated, however, that this objective had been only partially achieved. On the other hand, if the occupation were terminated and if Japan were given back its autonomy in a peace treaty, there would be an even greater incentive to side with the Free World. Without such a treaty, promises of equal economic opportunity or freedom to mold one's destiny had little substance.

Renewed Negotiations for a Peace Treaty, October, 1950

During the first year of the Korean War, therefore, the United States devoted much time and effort toward the successful conclusion of a Japanese peace treaty. Before the Allies were ready for a peace conference, however, laborious negotiations were necessary. They still had wide differences of opinion on procedural questions, such as the manner of calling a conference, the voting, and membership. They also disagreed on substantive problems such as the permanent status of Formosa and the Ryūkyū Islands and the extent of future control over Japan's industrial war potential and armaments.

Since the failure in early 1948 to call a peace conference, the United States had not pushed the matter. On the other hand, several of the states directly concerned kept pressing for an early treaty. Members of the British Commonwealth, particularly Australia and New Zealand, were most insistent on this point. At the Commonwealth meeting at Colombo in early 1950, some differences appeared on the question of how severe such a treaty should be; but there was unanimity on the desirability of concluding a peace as soon as possible. As the Canadian Foreign Minister expressed it, there was "need for seizing every opportunity that might lead to a satisfactory early settlement with Japan." General MacArthur also continued to support this view. In February, 1950, even the Soviet Union had pledged to work for the conclusion of a peace in the shortest possible time. But this pledge was made jointly with the Chinese People's Republic. Hence it was a notification to the other powers that the Soviet Union expected Communist China to be one of the signatories.

Despite these differences concerning a peace treaty, the United States was convinced that the Korean War made an early peace with Japan imperative. Consequently, President Truman announced in mid-September, 1950, that the United States intended to begin informal discussions with the Allies on the question. The task of reconciling the differences among the Allies, of negotiating with them, and of obtaining as widespread agreement as possible for a draft treaty was assigned to John Foster Dulles.

Making Silk Thread

Electrical Equipment for a Generating Plant

Courtesy of East-West

Testing Tape Recorders for Export

OLD AND NEW INDUSTRIAL SKILLS

Courtesy of East-West

May Day Riot (1952) in the Imperial Palace Plaza

He approached the problem with wide experience and with imagination. In the development of several general principles which he believed should be incorporated into a Japanese peace treaty, he started from three premises. The first premise was that it was to the military and political advantage of the Western Democracies not to let Japan fall within the Soviet orbit. Secondly, he was convinced that Japan could not be coerced to join the Free World orbit but would doubtless prefer to be an integral part of it rather than part of the Communist World. Finally, there were two types of peace treaties. One type was stern and punitive in character, designed to keep the former enemy in subjection. The other type of treaty was lenient and liberal. Mr. Dulles announced that the United States had rejected the former type. He informed the Allies that it would be unrealistic to impose any military restrictions on Japan and that a liberal attitude was called for. On the matter of procedure, Mr. Dulles adopted a new one. He carried on a series of preliminary bilateral negotiations with representatives of the states that were the members of the Far Eastern Commission. He also made several visits to Japan to conduct such discussions and negotiations as were necessary.[10]

In October, 1950, the United States announced seven principles which it proposed as the basis for the treaty. On the matter of procedure, it was suggested that the signatories should include all the countries at war with Japan and willing to sign the treaty. Thus, despite the war in Korea and the backing the Korean Communists were receiving from Moscow, if the Soviet Union was willing to sign the treaty, it should be permitted to do so. Secondly, the signatories should endeavor to secure Japanese membership in the United Nations. As for the territorial clauses, the American proposal noted that the terms of the Cairo and Potsdam Declarations had largely been carried out but that certain specific settlements must be clarified. In regard to the Ryūkyū Islands, the United States was prepared to assume a trusteeship over them at the appropriate time. In reference to the final disposition of Formosa and Southern Sakhalien (Karafuto), it was recommended that the matter should be settled by the four powers (Great Britain, Republic of China, Soviet Union, and the United States). If they did not reach agreement within a year, the matter should be referred to the General Assembly of the United Nations. On the all-important question of Japan's future security, it was proposed that Japan and the United States should continue a cooperative responsibility until the United Nations could assume it. No provision was suggested for the limitation of rearmament. Japan's commercial interests should be protected by a series of multilateral treaties until such time as new commercial arrangements could be made. Finally, the last American proposals concerned claims and a neutral commission to settle disputes arising from them. The Allies should, in lieu of reparations, confiscate Japanese property within their own territory and their property in Japan should be restored to its rightful owners.[11]

Bilateral negotiations were immediately begun on the basis of these principles. The territorial proposals concerning the Ryūkyū Islands were challenged by the Soviet Union and Communist China, as well as by the Chinese Nationalist government and the Commonwealth nations. Furthermore, Australia and the Philippines led the opposition to the proposal that no restrictions be placed on Japan's future rearmament. The former gave notice that for its own future security, it would resist any attempt to give Japan the right to rearm itself. The Philippines expressed similar views and demanded Japanese payments of $4 billion in reparations before a treaty was negotiated. (See page 460.) Even after the Chinese Communists entered the war in Korea in November, 1950, these states were not yet willing to accede to the proposal that no restrictions be placed on the revival of militarism in Japan. In the south and southwest Pacific, memories of the horrors of the war made the possibility of future Japanese aggression appear to be a danger which must be avoided at all costs. To cope with this problem, the United States proposed that rather than make the treaty restrictive, international guarantees could protect these countries from any danger of aggression. Hence it proposed that special Security Pacts be signed along with the peace treaty to guarantee the future safety of these countries.

As for discussions with the Soviet Union on problems of the peace treaty, on October 29, 1950, Dulles had presented the American principles for a treaty to the Soviet Ambassador at the United Nations. About a month later, the latter requested clarification of some of the American proposals. In an *aide-mémoire,* the Soviet Union insisted that the treaty must first be approved by the four chief Allied Powers, namely, China, the United Kingdom, the Soviet Union, and the United States. Furthermore, China should be represented by the Chinese People's Republic, not by the government of Generalissimo Chiang Kai-shek. The Soviet Union also objected to the suggestion of the United States for a trusteeship for the Ryūkyū Islands. Furthermore, it indicated that continued controls were necessary both to prevent the future rearmament of Japan and to regulate its economy. A few days later, these views were parrotted by the Chinese Communist government which insisted that it participate in the preparation, drafting, and signing of a Japanese peace treaty. The American reply to the Soviet Union refused to concede, however, that "any single nation had the perpetual power to veto the conclusion by others of a peace with Japan." It also rejected the suggestion that the Chinese Communists be included in the negotiations. It then proceeded to continue its negotiations with the other powers in the hope of obtaining agreement by June, 1952.

Dismissal of General MacArthur

The outbreak of the war in Korea in June, 1950, had acted as the catalyst which precipitated renewed discussions among the Allies for a Japanese peace treaty. The military situation in the spring of 1951 also had a direct, if unexpected, effect on Japan. On April 3, 1951, the Chinese and Korean Communist armies had been pushed back by the United Nations forces across the thirty-eighth parallel for the second time since the war began. This development set off a bitter debate on future policy for Korea both within the United States government and between the United States and other members of the United Nations participating in the war in Korea. While there were unlimited variations of opinion, there were two basic, diametrically opposed, alternatives. One alternative, which was vigorously advocated by General MacArthur, proposed an immediate push northward to roll the Communists back across the Yalu River into Manchuria. It also included the destruction by air attack and naval bombardment of their supply bases and airfields in Manchuria. The other alternative, which had widespread support among the United Nations, was to hold the military line around the thirty-eighth parallel, continue to refrain from bombing or attacking any territory outside of Korea, and negotiate for an armistice and peace.[12]

Advocates of the first alternative argued that military necessity required such action. They maintained that it was folly to give the enemy sanctuary in this manner. They believed that such attacks could be carried out without involving the United Nations in a war in China. The supporters of the second alternative, or a modified form of it, including the United States government and several of the governments of the United Nations, argued that such action would mean war in China. Since decisive victory in such a war would be extremely difficult, if not impossible, they considered it of paramount importance to refrain from aggravating the situation by attacking China, despite the military disadvantages of such a policy. In line with this policy and to avoid international complications, General MacArthur had been advised to refrain from making public announcements on questions of policy unless they were first cleared in Washington. Nevertheless, on March 25, 1951, he announced on his own responsibility that "expansion of military operations to (the) coastal areas and interior bases would doom Red China to military collapse." President Truman decided that General MacArthur was no longer able "to give wholehearted support to the policies of the United States government and the United Nations." Consequently, on April 10, 1951, he ordered him relieved of his commands in the Far East. Lieutenant General Matthew B. Ridgway was appointed as his successor.[13]

The Japanese could not believe that the reports were true. They had come to consider General MacArthur as invincible. They had thought of him as the final authority on all things, whether these concerned the occupation of Japan or the war in Korea. They had not even thought of the possibility of another Supreme Commander. Some saw in his dismissal a vivid illustration of the principle that in the United States the civil arm of the government was always stronger than the military. As they recovered from their shock, others feared that his removal might signify a basic change and hardening in American policy. They wondered whether the United States might substitute new and more restricting proposals for the peace treaty than those which Dulles had discussed with the Yoshida Cabinet. Some even feared that the negotiations might be stopped or that Japan would be left in a defenseless position.

But their fears were allayed by a new statement of President Truman regarding post-treaty security arrangements for Japan. He declared that he was sending Dulles to Japan again to discuss further with the Japanese government a security arrangement whereby United States armed forces would remain in and near Japan on a provisional basis. He emphasized the fact that the United States would continue to maintain its bases on Okinawa. It would also carry on further negotiations with Australia and New Zealand concerning a security pact which would bind the three states to act together if any one of them were attacked in the Pacific.[14]

Renewed Bilateral Treaty Negotiations

The bilateral negotiations for both a peace treaty and for security pacts to accompany it continued throughout the first part of 1951. After Dulles returned from Tokyo toward the end of February, the United States believed that it was familiar enough with the views of the fifteen governments which had already been consulted, as well as with those of Japan, to be able to prepare a draft text of the treaty. Such a draft, which took into account the views of the various powers, was prepared and circulated to them for comment. The United States hoped to receive comments on its draft by May 1, 1951. While Malik, the Russian representative at the United Nations, refused to discuss the draft with Dulles, he was sent a copy of it.

But the fact that the Western Democracies were fighting a common enemy in Korea did not necessarily imply that they had yet agreed on all of the principles for a peace treaty for Japan. The British continued to think in terms of economic restrictions and controls; they had drawn up a treaty far more complicated than the American draft. They still regarded Formosa as an integral part of China; they also favored bringing the Chinese Communists into the treaty negotiations. Dulles' task of negotiating a mutually agreeable treaty was not yet completed.

He had also run into difficulty in connection with the security pacts which were proposed to accompany the treaty. The United States had originally planned for a Pacific Mutual Security Pact, similar to the North Atlantic Defense Treaty of 1949. It had hoped that such a pact would give the Pacific powers the assurances which they sought as protection against the possible resurgence of Japanese aggression. But national feelings against Japan among some of the Allies in the Pacific were sufficiently strong to make such a single pact impossible. Consequently, the United States readjusted its approach to the security problem in the Pacific. It proposed that three pacts take the place of one. The first would be a bilateral arrangement between the United States and Japan. The second pact would be a triangular security pact among the United States, Australia, and New Zealand. Finally, the United States and the Philippines should join in a common declaration.

These proposals met the requirements of most of the countries concerned. Furthermore, the other major differences among the Allies had been eliminated, except for those of the Communist nations, so that final arrangements could be made for a formal peace conference. Consequently, in the first half of July, 1951, the United States and the United Kingdom sent a joint invitation to fifty-five of the Allied powers at war with Japan to attend a peace conference to be called at San Francisco on September 4, 1951. The invitation enclosed a draft of a peace treaty with Japan, with accompanying declarations and a protocol. If any state had comments to make on the draft, they were requested to submit them as quickly as possible so that acceptable ones could be included in the final text of the treaty. It was added that August 13, 1951, had been set as the date for the circulation of the final text of the treaty.

It was explained orally to the recipients of the invitations that preparatory negotiations had been carried on for the past ten months among the powers principally concerned. Furthermore, this procedure had been followed to produce a draft which most of the Allied powers would want to sign. Accordingly, the conference at San Francisco was for the purpose of signing the final text of the treaty which would be circulated in August. Changes were not expected to be considered at the San Francisco Conference. Opportunity would be given to the participating governments, however, to make such statements as they considered necessary. Of the fifty-five governments invited to the conference, only three failed to accept the invitation.[15]

The Treaty of Peace With Japan

On September 4, 1951, at the opening ceremony of the Peace Conference at San Francisco, President Truman briefly outlined some of the accomplishments of the occupation of Japan. He then described the treaty as one which would work because it did not contain the seeds of another war but looked to the future. He also noted that as part of the development of regional arrangements for the defense of the Pacific, the United States had recently signed a Treaty of Mutual Defense with the Republic of the Philippines in which the two nations promised to come to each other's defense if attacked. Furthermore, a similar treaty had been signed by Australia, New Zealand, and the United States. He concluded that, in view of Japan's unarmed condition and of a request which it had made to the United States, those two countries would also enter into an agreement concerning Japan's security.

The proceedings of the conference were interrupted by the demand of the Soviet Delegate that the Chinese People's Republic be invited to the conference. The only support for this request came from the delegates from Poland and Czechoslovakia. The Soviet Delegate, A. A. Gromyko, also maintained that the proposed draft treaty "cannot, in any measure, serve the purpose of a peace settlement with Japan or give any guarantees against the recurrence of Japanese aggression in the future." Specifically, he deplored the omission in the draft of restrictions against the re-establishment of militarism and of guarantees for democratic reforms. He claimed that it did not provide for the withdrawal of foreign occupation forces and permitted Japan to join regional security pacts, which he described as a threat to peace in the Far East. He continued his criticism of the treaty by stating that the territorial provisions flagrantly violated the rights of both Communist China and the Soviet Union. Finally, he insisted that the economic clauses were designed to ensure foreign privileges which had been obtained during the occupation. Thus, he used the conference as a public forum to oppose several of the fundamental aspects of the treaty but failed to obtain support for changes in the draft. As was expected, the Soviet bloc refused to sign the treaty.[16]

The Treaty of Peace with Japan was signed on September 8, 1951, by forty-eight Allied nations and Japan. As explained by Dulles, this treaty was nonpunitive and nondiscriminatory and would "restore Japan to dignity, equality, and opportunity in the family of nations." By its Preamble, Japan declared its intention to apply for membership in the United Nations, to conform to the principles of the Charter, and to adhere to the ideals of human rights and freedoms in its new Constitution. The Treaty ended the state of war with Japan and recognized the sovereignty of the Japanese people. Japan formally ratified the territorial clauses of the Potsdam Declaration. It recognized the independence of Korea; it renounced all rights, title, and claims to Formosa and the Pescadores, to the Kurile Islands, to Southern Sakhalien, and to the Mandated Islands in the Pacific. Finally, Japan promised to concur in an American proposal to place the Ryūkyū, Bonin, and Volcano Islands under a United Nations trusteeship.

Another important section of the Treaty concerned problems connected with Japan's future security, including the termination of the occupation (Articles 5 and 6). While Japan accepted the obligations of the Charter of the United Nations to settle international disputes by peaceful means and to refrain from the threat or use of force, the Allied Powers recognized Japan's right of self-defense as a nation. The occupation forces were to be withdrawn within ninety days after the treaty came into force. To avoid the creation of a military vacuum when the treaty became effective, however, it was provided that foreign armed forces might be stationed or retained in Japanese territory under provisions of special international agreements. Since such an agreement was signed between Japan and the United States on the day the Peace Treaty was signed, there was no formal withdrawal of American forces. When the Treaty went into effect on April 28, 1952, the office of Supreme Commander for the Allied Powers was dissolved and the occupation was officially over. The occupation forces were changed into security forces but from outward appearances there seemed to be no difference before and after the Treaty.

In the political and economic clauses (Articles 7-13), Japan was not subjected to permanent disabilities, and no limitations were placed on its economy and trade. Pending the conclusions of treaties between Japan and the Allied Powers on commercial relations, on pelagic fishing, and on international air transport, each Allied Power would be entitled to most-favored-nation treatment on customs duties. The controversial reparation issue (see page 438) was dealt with in two stages. In the first place, the treaty recognized the principle that Japan should pay reparations to the Allied Powers for damage and suffering caused by it during the war. On the other hand, the Powers recognized that, from a realistic point of view, Japan could not possibly pay the billions of dollars in damages.

As for the United States, it had already paid $2 billion since surrender for imports of food and raw materials to make up for current Japanese deficits. It seemed ridiculous, therefore, to think of extracting more from Japan in the form of reparations when it was already unable to pay for its essential imports. But the countries occupied by Japanese during the war still insisted on reparations payments. Consequently, certain Japanese surplus assets, such as excess of skilled workers and of industrial capacity, were made available in lieu of these payments. If these countries desired it, they could negotiate arrangements whereby Japan would process raw materials for them or supply them with expert technical assistance. By these clauses, countries such as the Philippines, Burma, and Indonesia would be able to obtain reparations and at the same time speed their rehabilitation. The remaining clauses of the treaty concerned claims, property, the settlement of disputes, and final clauses.[17]

Post-Treaty Problems

While the Treaty of Peace with Japan ended the occupation and recognized the sovereignty of the Japanese people, it did not solve several essential problems. For example, there were innumerable details which had to be worked out to implement the new United States–Japan Security Pact whereby the former took over temporary responsibility for Japan's defense. Since Japan was expected increasingly to assume responsibility for its own defenses, however, the rearmament question became a burning issue. On the one hand, the increased threat from communism in East Asia and the reluctance of the United States to bear indefinitely the sole burden of the military defense of Japan were strong arguments in favor of the need for a rapid program of rearmament. On the other hand, there was strong resistance within Japan to any move toward the formation of a military establishment.

Politically, Japan continued to favor the conservatives. The successes of communism in Asia and the extensive desire to remain neutral in the East-West struggle in the hope of avoiding involvement in a third World War, however, gave the Socialists and Communists unexpected strength. They fought the efforts of Premier Yoshida to strengthen the authority of the central government. Nevertheless, he sponsored legislation which negated, to a large extent, the reforms of the occupation in the police system, in education, and in the freedom of expression. Economically, dollar expenditures of the United Nations for the Korean War had temporarily relieved Japan's deficit in international trade. No permanent solution had yet been found, however, for the basic problem created by the demands of a rapidly increasing population for large imports of foods and other essentials. When the Korean War stopped, the costs of essential imports far exceeded the value of exports and all indications pointed to a continuation of this situation.

In reference to the important problem of security, the United States and Japan signed a Security Pact on September 8, 1951. It permitted the United States to retain its forces in or near Japan for an indefinite period. Thus Japan was assured of at least temporary protection by American troops. The successful conclusion in February, 1952, of an Administrative Agreement between Japan and the United States provided for the detailed arrangements whereby the American forces continued to remain in Japan without infringing unnecessarily on its sovereignty. Legally, therefore, the American forces were on a different basis and were not an army of occupation.

To comply with this new condition, superficial changes were made in such matters as the name of the armed forces and the location of the headquarters of the American commander. But despite the treaty, anomalies continued which made the return of independence seem illusory to many Japanese and which resulted in increased antiforeign and especially anti-American sentiment. American Air and Naval bases, Army posts, and housing developments for dependents of American military personnel occupied prominent parts of the countryside, the seacoast, or central areas in the cities. G.I.s, from posts in Japan or on leave from the Korean front, crowded the cities and resorts and lavishly spent their accumulated pay. Military personnel and their families were not subject to Japanese police control. Naturally they continued to assume a condescending if not haughty attitude toward their hosts. In fine, so long as foreign troops remained on Japanese soil, the change from occupation to autonomy under the peace treaty seemed to be only a technical matter. The Prime Minister was accused of being more pro-American than pro-Japanese.[18]

The Political Scene

Thus the immediate objectives of the political leaders in the post-treaty period continued to be ambivalent. All of the chief parties, except the left-wing Social Democrats and the Communists, advocated greater autonomy for Japan. At the same time they favored close collaboration with the United States because of the protection such collaboration brought them. Furthermore, all groups theoretically supported the Constitution and human freedoms. On the other hand, the conservative Yoshida government became increasingly intolerant of any opposition to its policies and sought the return of centralized controls over the lives of the people.

When Prime Minister Yoshida was challenged on his policies, he resolved the issue successfully in his favor by resorting to a general election. Since January, 1949, he had been operating with a majority in the House of Representatives. Subsequently, he had increased his following in the House of Councillors. Despite dissident elements within his own party, and the accusation that he was a "One-Man Cabinet," in the general elections in October, 1952, and in April, 1953, his Liberal party won the largest number of seats in the House of Representatives. He continued as Prime Minister. The results of the first of these elections also signified a notable decline in the popularity of the Communists. Whereas they went into the election with thirty-five members in Parliament, they came out without a single representative. On the other hand, even though the Socialist party had split into a right and left wing, their total gains were greater than the number lost by the Communists.[19] This shift away from the extreme left indicated a hardening of the attitude both of the government and of the public toward the Communists.

Nevertheless, by the time the new Treaty of Peace became effective in April, 1952, the Communist party and its sympathizers had obtained appreciable support for their plea that the American troops should be withdrawn from Japan. They had the backing of certain labor groups and of a large segment of the intellectuals and students in the Tokyo area. They controlled the executive body of the Japan Student Federation, the organ which officially represented the students at many of the universities. The Federation had joined with labor in a united front in opposition to the government's proposed Antisubversive Activity Bill. Consequently, when the labor unions planned a big demonstration on May Day, 1952, thousands of students obeyed the posters of the Federation and appeared at the rally.

Tensions had been mounting in Tokyo for several weeks prior to May Day. There had been frequent student strikes at Tokyo University directed by the Federation in opposition to "restrictions on academic freedom." They objected, for example, to police interference in riots on the campus. The organizers of the May Day celebration had been refused permission to hold their rally in the plaza in front of the Imperial Palace. The government clamored for greater police powers; the leftists branded Yoshida as an autocratic ruler and as a tool of America. When some 40,000 persons gathered at the rally in the morning, they were in a mood for excitement. When a small group of leftists began to chant "To the Imperial Palace," they broke up the organized meetings. The crowd picked up the chant. Vanguards broke away, marched across the city, and fought with the police in front of the Imperial Palace Plaza and of the Allied military headquarters. There were several casualties on both sides. As an apparent afterthought, some elements in the crowd vented their anger in a momentary antiforeign demonstration. They destroyed some of the cars parked along the streets and owned by American military personnel.[20]

All respectable elements in society decried the outburst. The *Asahi* newspaper called it regrettable and demanded the trial of the leaders for sedition. It identified them as Communists. It predicted that the incident would be used by the Cabinet as demonstrating that more stringent antisubversive legislation was necessary. Other papers recommended that the Communist party be outlawed. Premier Yoshida quickly pressed for the passage of the Antisubversive Activity Law. Despite the strong opposition of organized labor, which insisted that the loose wording of the law would endanger normal, legitimate union activities, the May Day riots had strengthened support for the Bill. Consequently, it was approved by Parliament in July, 1952. It gave the Cabinet the power to ban activities which would lead to violence. In the hands of a Cabinet which had a high regard for human freedoms, it would not necessarily mean a loss of any of these newly acquired rights. In the hands of unscrupulous persons, it might lead to the serious curtailment of the basic human rights of important groups in society.

Simultaneously with his request for adoption of the Antisubversive Activity Law, Premier Yoshida proposed new legislation to increase the government's control over the police. He requested that the Prime Minister be given power to appoint the key police chiefs. He was also known to favor the abolition of the rural police and the re-establishment of a centralized national police. Since a centralized police force under the direction of the powerful Home Minister had been one of the means whereby the military had formed an ultranationalistic, autocratic state before World War II, his proposals met with vehement protests. In February, 1953, Parliament refused to pass the budget until he withdrew his proposals for police reforms. Shortly thereafter he lost a vote of confidence. In the elections of April, 1953, he was vindicated. His party won far more seats than any other party. But within a year, he was again faced with a recalcitrant Parliament. By the summer of 1954, criticism of his policy toward rearmament and toward the economic crisis created by the falling off of dollar purchases after the Korean Armistice had created a political crisis too great for him to survive.

Rearmament and Mutual Defense

On the matter of rearmament, Prime Minister Yoshida was caught on the horns of a dilemma. He had signed a Treaty of Peace; yet Japan was far from being its own master. In accordance with the provisions of the Treaty, in June, 1952, Japan had applied for membership in the United Nations. The United States had sponsored this application in the meetings of the Security Council, but the Soviet Union had vehemently criticized what it described as the "separate peace" signed at San Francisco and had vetoed the application. A few months later the General Assembly had overwhelmingly resolved that Japan was ready for membership but a Soviet veto still stood in the way of this becoming a reality. Subsequently, Japan sent a permanent observer to the United Nations and joined several of the affiliated bodies such as the International Bank of Reconstruction and Development, the Food and Agricultural Organization, and the World Health Organization.

But the problem of membership in the United Nations was of secondary importance compared to the rearmament issue. On the insistence of General MacArthur, the new Constitution contained Article 9 which outlawed war and forbade the maintenance of land, sea, and air forces. No sooner had the Constitution gone into effect in 1947, however, than American policy began to shift toward the encouragement of Japan's industrial revival. In July, 1950, two weeks after the Korean War broke out, the first formal step was taken toward Japanese rearmament. A Police Reserve of 75,000 was organized to fill part of the gap left by the transfer of American soldiers to the Korean front. After Dulles began active negotiations for a peace treaty in October, 1950, he emphasized that the United States would not place restrictions on future Japanese rearmament. He added that Japan should take immediate steps to develop an internal security force which would be competent to meet any internal threat to its peace and security. He implied that Japan would be expected to expand still further the American trained and equipped Police Reserve.

But the rearmament issue was an explosive one. The occupation had disarmed the Japanese nation completely following its surrender. The Article on the Renunciation of War in the Constitution had psychologically disarmed the Japanese people. The nation was relieved that these things had come about under General MacArthur's benevolent rule. Because of them they believed themselves to be free from the horrors of future wars. As world tensions again mounted and the Western Democracies were lined up against the Communist World, the conviction grew within Japan that if it refrained from rearming then it could avoid involvement in war. People began to realize, however, that so long as the occupation forces remained in Japan their country would become an obvious target in any future American-Soviet war. They reluctantly considered the possibilities of rearmament. The issue was complicated by the debate over the question of whether constitutional revision was essential to permit even a defensive military force. The government argued that constitutional revision was not necessary. The Police Reserve was changed into a National Security Force equipped with modern instruments of war. Premier Yoshida avoided taking a positive stand on the rearmament question by claiming that these forces were purely defensive. At the same time he sought close ties with the United States to assure Japan's protection from attack from the Soviet Union.

He was opposed by a formidable array of political, religious, and social groups. The Communist and Left Wing Socialists vehemently opposed both rearmament and closer alliance with the United States. Many Christians, students, and intellectuals took the same position. The advocates of this neutralist position were motivated by various reasons. Some, but by no means the majority of them, were following the Communist line. Others feared that if new armed forces were permitted, a renewed military leadership and a possible dictatorship would emerge. They pointed to the current economic distress of the country as proof that it could not afford to maintain a military establishment. They resented being used by the United States as a buffer state against Communist China and against the Soviet Union. They maintained that, if Japan were to rearm, the Constitution must first be changed. If rearmament occurred without an amendment, people might lose respect for the Constitution as a whole. All of them believed that Japan and the rest of the world could peacefully coexist with the Communist World. At the other extreme, the conservative Progressive party and the new nationalist leaders were criticizing Prime Minister Yoshida for not openly building up an Army as rapidly as possible.

In the face of these conflicting domestic pressures, Yoshida lost much of his popularity. The complete and final reversal of American policy confused matters further. In December, 1953, when visiting Japan on a world tour, Vice-President Richard Nixon maintained that the United States had made a mistake in 1946 when it advocated disarmament. As far as America was concerned, the more rapidly Japan rearmed, the better. Since the Security Treaty signed with Japan at San Francisco in September, 1951, was not a defensive alliance, the United States had decided that a more extensive and binding agreement was necessary. Throughout the summer of 1953 United States–Japanese negotiations centered on the amount of aid which might be given Japan through the Mutual Security Assistance program.

It was not until March, 1954, however, that the final step was taken which bound Japan militarily to the orbit of the Western Democracies. At that time, Japan and the United States signed a Mutual Defense Assistance Agreement. This Agreement provided for military assistance from the United States in the form of goods, equipment, and services. It specified the means whereby services, property, and information for defense purposes could be exchanged. It compelled both countries to keep a close curb on their trade with Red China. Finally, it required Japan to make a contribution, consistent with its political and economic stability, "to the development and maintenance of its own defensive strength and the defensive strength of the free world."[21] As the newspaper, *Mainichi,* expressed it, the consequences of this treaty were so far-reaching that no one dared to predict the consequences.

Continued Economic Dilemma

If Japan were to embark on a program of active rearmament, which would require heavy outlays for military expenditures, economic problems took on even greater significance. Despite the promise which the United States made in the Mutual Defense Agreement, the type of aid which could be given was restricted by laws governing the Mutual Security Assistance program. Consequently, such help as Japan might receive from the United States would be military rather than general. As expressed by the *Mainichi,* the agreement "turned out to be of little value to the reconstruction of the war-torn Japanese economy." As in the years before the outbreak of the Korean War, the basic problem was that of increasing exports to equal needed imports. (See page 432.) Fortunately, the pace of industrial recovery had quickened prior to the Korean War and increased at an accelerated rate. For example, the index of industrial production rose from 49.7 in 1949 to 85.9 in 1951. Even though production costs were high because of the high shipping costs for raw materials such as cotton, coal, and iron ore, which came from the United States, industrial activity remained well above the levels of those before World War II. In the first half of 1953, the industrial production index stood at 154.[22] It was possible that new orders for the defense establishment would take the place of United Nations orders for the Korean War, and that the industrial production index would remain high.

But there were other less encouraging signs for the future of Japan's economy. In the first place, the rate of population increase was distressingly high. The population in 1955 would probably equal about 88 million. No one could predict when an appreciable decline in the birth rate would appear. There was little new land available for cultivation. Food deficiencies, which amounted to 20 per cent of the total, had to be met by imports. In 1951 the value of these essential imports equaled $558 million. In 1954, the situation had been aggravated by the worst rice crop in twenty years.

The ability to find profitable markets for goods and services to produce foreign exchange for the purchase of imports of foods and other essentials remained the crux of the problem. During the Korean War this problem had been largely solved. For example, in 1951, there had been an unfavorable trade balance of nearly $430 million. On the other hand, an excess of foreign exchange receipts as a result of the war had almost eliminated this deficit. United Nations procurements for the war, the money spent by United Nations troops in Japan, and the costs in dollars of maintenance of United States defense forces totaled $335 million. Thus the unfavorable balance was practically wiped out. In 1952, $800 million payments in Japan more than matched the trade deficit.

With the cessation of the war, the old problem returned. As the war orders ceased after the Armistice in July, 1953, a trade balance deficit of $300 million appeared. Despite new austerity restrictions on the importation of luxuries such as foreign cars, the unfavorable balance continued and no solution was in sight. Premier Yoshida was confronted with a critical economic situation while his political opponents criticized his foreign policy. In the summer of 1954, therefore, it was only a matter of time before his long period of leadership would be over.

Yoshida's Fall, December, 1954

Yoshida's temper and the scandals which involved his close friends and colleagues had not improved his status. He had inadvertently sworn at one of his parliamentary critics. He insisted that the unpopular law to abolish the occupation reforms of the police system and to establish a new national police force should be passed. He also staked his political future on the adoption of laws which would fulfill Japan's obligations under the Mutual Defense Pact. In June, 1954, when these bills were pending, riots broke out in the House of Representatives when the Socialist members tried to force adjournment to prevent their passage. Their tactics failed and the new laws were passed. The question of the need to amend the Constitution was now an academic one; rearmament was a reality. Furthermore, the creation of centralized controls for the police was another sign of rejection of earlier reforms.

Yoshida's final downfall came in December, 1954. While he was on a trip around the world, dissident members of his party refused to obey his orders. When Hatoyama Ichirō, who had been President of the Liberal party, was purged in 1946, he had turned the party over to Mr. Yoshida. By 1953, Hatoyama was again active in politics. He had always been jealous of Yoshida's long tenure of office; he bolted from the Liberals in April, 1953, had returned to the fold, and in July, 1954, was ready to bolt again. When Yoshida returned to Japan from his world trip, Hatoyama rallied his supporters, forced Yoshida out of office in December, 1954, and was elected Prime Minister. The public career of Yoshida Shigeru, the man who had guided his country during most of the past eight years, was over. A new era, that under Hatoyama, who advocated closer ties with both the Soviet Union and Communist China on the one hand and with the United States on the other, had begun. With it new problems faced Japan and its chief ally, the United States.

As Japan entered the year 1955, there were both encouraging and discouraging signs for the future. Though the peace treaty with the Allies had been in force for over two and a half years, international conditions placed heavy restrictions on the freedom of choice of Premier Hatoyama. He had inherited many heavy responsibilities from his predecessor: he was caught inextricably in the struggle between the Free World and the Communist World. Politically, Japan had again selected a conservative government which was basically friendly toward the Western Democracies. On the other hand, there were signs that nationalism was again becoming an important force in Japanese politics. There was increasing evidence that friendly overtures from Communist China and from the Soviet Union were being looked upon with favor by conservatives as well as radicals. If Premier Hatoyama's threat to develop normal relations with these countries became a reality, complications in American-Japanese relations would follow. Economically, the outlook was gloomy and was not likely to be improved by increasingly heavy armament expenditures. In the light of the history of similar problems throughout Japan's modern century, what is the future course likely to be?

Notes

1. For a study of the first two years of the occupation of Korea see Hugh Borton, "Korea Under American and Soviet Occupation, 1945-47," F. C. Jones, Hugh Borton, and B. R. Pearn, *The Far East, 1942-1946* (London: Oxford University Press, 1955), p. 428 *et seq.*

2. In September, 1948, the Communists had formed the North China's People's Republic. Shortly thereafter, Tsinan, the capital of Shantung, was captured, thus cutting off Peking from the south. Mukden fell to the Communists in November, forcing the Kuomintang troops to leave Manchuria. Peking surrendered on January 22, 1949, and Chiang's capital at Nanking fell four months later. In August, 1949, the United States stopped sending aid to Chiang and blamed the collapse of his regime on reactionary elements in his government. He fled to Formosa on December 7, 1949. In January, 1950, Great Britain recognized the Peking regime, but a Soviet resolution in the United Nations to unseat Chiang's representative in the Security Council was later defeated. The Soviet member left the Council in protest.

In the United States, Secretary of State Dean Acheson and his advisers were accused of having played into the hands of the Communists and having foredoomed Chiang to defeat by cutting off aid. The problem was not so simple as it seemed. For example, the Chinese Communist troops, which entered the war in Korea in late 1950, were equipped with American arms. This equipment had been captured from Chiang's troops. If military aid to him had been continued, it would probably likewise have been lost. For the history of Chiang's collapse see U.S. Department of State, *United States Relations with China. With Special Reference to the Period 1944-1949* (Washington: Department of State Publication 3573, U.S. Government Printing Office, 1949).

3. Speech before the National Press Club, January 12, 1950, Department of State, *Bulletin,* January 23, 1950.

4. For a complete text of the treaty see *Sino-Soviet Treaty and Agreements Signed in Moscow on February 14, 1950* (Peking: Foreign Language Press, 1950).

5. Since Ashida had been elected in February, 1948, with the help of the Social Democrats, his Cabinet contained more members from the latter party than from his own. He and some of his colleagues had become involved in bribery scandals, so it was not difficult to cause their downfall. The Yoshida government took office October 19, 1948. In the elections in January, 1949, the Liberals won 264 seats while Ashida's party dropped to 68. The Socialists, who had won 143 seats in 1947, fell to 49. Yoshida survived three more elections and formed five Cabinets before his resignation in November, 1954. For charts on the elections see SCAP,

Political Reorientation of Japan, September, 1945—September, 1948 (2 vols.; Washington: U.S. Government Printing Office, 1949, pp. 321-26 and 345-47.

6. In view of the valuable studies prepared by economists on Japan's postwar economy and the availability of material collected by the Japanese government and by the Economic Commission for Asia and the Far East and other official agencies, only the bare essentials of the problem will be noted here. Figures are taken from Population Problems Research Council, *The Population of Japan* (Tokyo: Population Research Council, 1950); and Jerome B. Cohen, *Economic Problem of Free Japan* (Princeton: Center of International Studies, 1952).

7. Department of State Press Release, No. 436, June 10, 1949.

8. See Economic Commission for Asia and the Far East, Committee on Industry and Trade, *Problems and Prospects of Accelerated Economic Development in the ECAFE Region Through Increased Trade with Japan* (Bangkok: ECAFE, May 9, 1950), E/CN. 11/I & T/21., especially pp. 1, 2, 9, 12, and 14; and Cohen, *op. cit.*, p. 62.

9. President Truman sent this order on June 27, 1950, the same day that the Security Council took action. He also sent the U.S. Seventh Fleet to patrol the Formosa Straits to protect it from attack by Communist China and to prevent the Nationalists from attacking the mainland. Seoul fell before the Communists on June 29, and the next day United States ground forces entered the war. At the request of the Security Council, on July 7, 1950, President Truman appointed General MacArthur as United Nations Commander. The action of the Security Council was not vetoed by the Soviet Union because its representative had not returned to the Council meetings since the walkout at the beginning of the year in protest to the refusal to admit Communist China.

10. This method of approach avoided another stalemate similar to that of 1947. The refusal of one of the major powers to agree to attend a conference could not prevent bilateral discussions with other powers. The new method also left open the question of participation of the Soviet Union in the conference. It enabled the United States to inform the Soviet Union, along with the other Allies, of its proposals for a treaty. If the Soviet Union refused to discuss these proposals, it must bear the onus for not doing so. This procedure also permitted sufficient agreement among the other powers before the peace conference convened to assure their signature at the conference. From a practical, strategic point of view, the Soviet Union could not be completely ignored. In the early months of the Korean War, when the Japanese peace negotiations were begun, Japan was a military vacuum. The United States had practically no tactical troops in that country and there was no Japanese Army, Navy, or Air Force. The United States obviously did not wish to provoke the Soviet Union to the point where it would take direct action against Japan. Dulles was ably assisted in his negotiations and in the preparation of the treaty by John M. Allison, a career Foreign Service Officer. The latter was rewarded for these services by appointment as U.S. Ambassador to Japan in 1953.

11. U.S. Department of State Release, No. 1180, Nov. 24, 1950.

12. The second phase of the Korean War, from the entry of the Chinese Communists on November 26, 1950, to their withdrawal north of the thirty-eighth parallel in April, 1951, had been costly and bitterly fought. After the rapid advance of the United Nations forces in the fall of 1950, following the landings at Inchon in September, General MacArthur had assumed that the Korean Communists would either be driven from Korea or be defeated by the end of the year. He had not realized that as soon as his forces reached the Yalu River in November, 1950, they

would be challenged by the entry of a large Chinese Communist Army into the war and hence be forced to retire southward once more.

13. The Great Debate touched off by General MacArthur's dismissal was one of the bitterest in recent times in the United States. He returned home as a conquering hero and on April 19, 1951, addressed a joint session of Congress. At that time, he modified his views by saying that he felt military necessity required, among other things, "removal of restrictions on air reconnaissance of China's coastal area of Manchuria." The Senate hearings which followed did not result in his being accused of insubordination but all but a loyal few agreed that he had disregarded orders. It was an unfortunate ending to a career which would have remained unblemished if it could have ended before the Korean War began. U.S. Senate, 82d Congress, *Military Situation in the Far East. Hearings Before the Committee on Armed Forces and the Committee on Foreign Relations,* Part V (Washington: U.S. Government Printing Office, 1951), pp. 3179-80.

14. President Truman's statement was made on April 18, 1951. For a text see *New York Times,* April 19, 1951.

15. The problem of whether Nationalist China or Communist China or both should participate in the conference was avoided by not issuing an invitation to either the Nationalist government on Formosa or the People's Republic at Peking. Burma, India, and Yugoslavia were the three states which did not accept the invitation. The Soviet Union accepted even though China was not invited.

16. U.S. Department of State, *Record of Proceedings of the Conference for the Conclusion and Signature of the Treaty of Peace with Japan* (Washington: U.S. Government Printing Office, 1951), pp. 114-17.

17. India was the first nation to make a separate treaty with Japan. Although the Philippines signed the treaty, the Philippine Senate refused to ratify it. As of August 1, 1955, the Soviet Union, the Chinese People's Republic, the Republic of the Philippines, and the Republic of Indonesia were the chief states which had not signed either the San Francisco Treaty or a subsequent peace treaty with Japan.

18. From personal observation, the author can testify to the fact that the changes which occurred in the spring of 1952 in reference to American troops in Japan were almost imperceptible. Some of the steps which were taken to indicate a change were ludicrous. Signs in English with the marking GHQ were painted out or changed but many Japanese didn't know the exact meaning of the signs anyway. U.S. Army cars were painted black but they were easily distinguishable by their licenses or by their occupants. The luxurious living quarters, the special tax exemptions, and the high living standard of the military personnel were obvious indications that "the Welfare State" still existed for the "occupation personnel." Few Japanese excused this situation on the grounds that much of the time and effort of the United Nations military personnel were taken up with the war in Korea.

19. The election results were as follows:

	January, 1949	October, 1952	April, 1953
Liberal Party (Yoshida)	264	240	202
Splinter Liberal Party (Hatoyama)	—	—	35
Progressive Party (Democrats)	68	88	77
Socialists	49		
Right-wing		60	66
Left-wing		56	72
Communists	35	0	1
Others	51	23	13

20. The mob was composed of a large proportion of young people. The campus at Tokyo University was completely deserted that day. There were practically no incidents of attacks on foreigners, not even on those who were in the center of the scuffle. It was basically a fight between the police and the leaders of the vanguard who had come armed with homemade weapons for a fight.

21. For the text of the Mutual Defense Assistance Agreement, signed March 9, 1954, see U.S. Department of State, *Bulletin,* April 5, 1954.

22. These figures are for real production in terms of population increases with the 1935-38 average equal to 100. See Jerome B. Cohen, *Economic Problems, op. cit.,* p. 20; and Mitsubishi Monthly Circular, June, 1954, p. 36.

22

CONCLUSION

The Permanence of a Japanese-American Alliance

If it is reasonable to assume that the cold war has settled down to a period of competitive coexistence, the future of Japan will be largely determined by the part it plays in that competition. In other words, its future international position will be as crucial as any other force in directing its modern destiny. Its domestic economic development will be important in proportion to the influence which economic conditions exert on foreign policy. Likewise, internal political events will have lasting significance only in terms of the contribution which they make to decisions on foreign policy. On the assumption that in this atomic age a state such as Japan still retains a freedom of choice in foreign affairs, there are three alternatives open to it. It might strengthen its alignment with the Free World. It might reverse its present policies and form an alliance with Communist China and the Soviet Union. It might hold tenaciously to a neutralist position and profit as best it can from the East-West conflict.

In view of the history of the postwar years, there is little to warrant the conclusion that in the near future the United States will sever the ties which bind it to Japan. Since the latter's surrender on September 2, 1945, the tendency has been in the opposite direction. The two countries now have a closer alliance than ever before. During the early years of the occupation, the United States evolved a policy of friendliness, rather than of enmity, toward Japan. This led to a lenient peace treaty and to special security arrangements whereby American armed forces have remained in Japan for "the maintenance of international peace and security in the Far East" and for "the security of Japan against armed attack." The Mutual Defense Assistance Agreement of March, 1954, was the culmination of this new policy. By that treaty, both Japan and the United States have pledged to assist each other in their mutual defense against the Communist World. Legally, therefore, there is no question of Japan's aligning with the Free World.

Since the Korean Armistice in 1953 the increased interest of the United States in defending other parts of Asia against communism has tightened this alliance. In January, 1954, President Eisenhower declared that the United States intended to continue to hold indefinitely its bases in the Ryūkyū Islands. It has signed a Mutual Defense Agreement with the Republic of Korea and one with the Chinese Nationalist government on Formosa. It is an active member of the Southeast Asia Treaty Organization. In February, 1955, the United States Congress approved a resolution warning the Chinese Communists that an attack on Formosa would result in immediate retaliation by the American forces. This deep involvement of the United States in the Far East has been predicated on the assumption that its bases in and around Japan would be protected and maintained. So long as the United States continues to resist communism in Asia through a display of force, it will be committed to the defense of Japan.

Such being the case, the United States must be sure that the Pacific defense structure is built on solid ground. If it does not have the wholehearted support of Japan, it must act in such a way as to attract that support. Chester Bowles, former American Ambassador to India, has expressed the problem thus, "An American-inspired, American-managed, American-dominated defense program for Asia is a political dead-end."[1] It cannot be assumed, therefore, that Japan enthusiastically and wholeheartedly accepts the role of a military ally of the United States. Since its defeat, it has not been in a position to choose its foreign policy. It may have followed the lead of the United States reluctantly.

Japan's Relations With the Communist World

There are certain signs which indicate that Japan has not irrevocably and completely accepted this alternative to the exclusion of all others. In the first place, in his election campaign in 1955, Prime Minister Hatoyama pleaded for a "normalization of relations with the Soviet Union and the People's Republic of China." It is impossible to determine to what extent his victory was due to his supporting this policy, but it obviously is not an unpopular position or he would not have been elected. In the election in February, 1955, his Democratic party won the largest number of seats (185) in the House of Representatives.[2]

By 1955 Japan had not yet signed a treaty of peace with either the Soviet Union or Communist China. But both these states, particularly Communist China, have been making friendly overtures to Japan. In effect, both states appear to be doing their best to offer Japan concessions in an effort to isolate it from American influence. In view of the friendly reception these overtures have received in Japan, of the stated policy of Prime

Minister Hatoyama, and of the implications of these facts to future Japanese-American relations, they cannot be ignored.

If any progress is to be made in combating these inroads of the Communist World in Japan, it is necessary to understand certain underlying Japanese attitudes. In the first place, at the time of the elections in February, 1955, the Japanese people had an attitude toward Communist China which was markedly different from that of most Americans. Almost all groups in Japan, not only the Democratic party of Premier Hatoyama, but also the Liberal party of former Premier Yoshida, favor the immediate expansion of trade with the Chinese People's Republic and the early recognition of the Peking regime. Furthermore, both the Left-wing and Right-wing Socialists, who command about one-third of the seats in the House of Representatives, favor a neutralist policy of simultaneous friendship with the Communist World and with the Free World.

The average Japanese is willing to condone the activities of the Chinese People's Republic during its first five years for various reasons. Historically, one of the basic themes of Japanese foreign policy has been a desire to dominate China. This led Japan into four major wars after 1894. Although it gave up all of its special rights in China as a result of defeat in World War II, it did not necessarily abdicate permanently its traditional favored position to the Soviet Union or to anyone else. The hope is doubtless still alive that it will again be able to dominate the continent.

Furthermore, this uncritical attitude toward China, bordering on friendship, stems from certain sentimental feelings. Either before or during World War II, thousands of Japanese have lived in China either as civilians or as members of the Japanese Army. Because of these experiences and of the Chinese origin of many aspects of their civilization, many Japanese believe that they understand the Chinese better than anyone else. As expressed by a contemporary Japanese economist, "What must be . . . stressed is the sense of mutual kinship of Asian nations. Any policy which aims at anything like a complete permanent severing of the ties between the two countries will never be admitted by the national feeling of the majority of the Japanese people."[3]

Another factor which has created a friendly attitude in Japan toward China is the recent reactivation of the repatriation program. Since March, 1953, when repatriation was started again, over 15,000 Japanese have returned home. Some of these repatriates have been thoroughly indoctrinated with communism; others have refused to comment on their experiences for fear of implicating those left behind. While a sizable number of persons still remains to be repatriated, the net effect of these latest moves has been favorable in Japan.[4]

Moreover, the activities of the Chinese People's Republic have invariably been presented in a favorable light in Japan. Japanese editions of official Chinese Communist publications, such as *People's China,* are widely read. Official and private Japanese visitors to Peking and other parts of Communist China have been politely treated. Upon their return home, they write laudatory reports on the accomplishments of the new regime.

Businessmen, manufacturers, politicians, and the press all seem to believe that increased trade with China will alleviate Japan's economic ills. They argue that the Chinese People's Republic is permanently in control of China and that despite the fact that it has a Communist government, Japan cannot afford to lose any possibilities for new foreign markets. It must learn to live with its neighbor and to gain from the potential market of half a billion people. Since European countries such as Great Britain, France, and Germany are already trading with Communist China, no harm should come from Japan's doing so. In any event, they are all firmly convinced that trade and politics are two separate things.

Though some of these arguments may be of questionable validity, they are convincing to many Japanese. They are not concerned over the fact that this further trade will doubtless be limited to a small fraction of prewar trade with the mainland.[5] On the contrary, the enticing statements of Communist officials fall on receptive ears. In April, 1952, Nam Han-chen, chief Chinese delegate to the Moscow Economic Conference, pointed out that Japanese industry requires low-priced Chinese coal, salt, beans, and fats while China needs machines and other products made in Japan. In January, 1954, Vice-Minister of Foreign Trade Lei Jen-min announced that "China is firmly convinced that it can coexist peacefully with countries which have different social and economic institutions, exchange goods with them, and further develop normal trade relations."

While it is unlikely that Japan will give up its alignment with the Free World, it may well decide to recognize the Chinese People's Republic and to seek actively to expand trade with the mainland. If such is the case, it would be unwise for the United States to insist that Japan follow a policy of nonrecognition of Communist China. Such an American policy might alienate Japan from the Free World.

Likewise, it would be unfortunate for the United States to insist that Japanese-Communist trade should not be expanded. Since historical precedent and contemporary forces indicate a trend toward closer ties between Japan and the continent of Asia, the United States might well jeopardize its present favored position in Japan by opposing such a trend. Insistence by the Western Democracies that Japan follow their dictates might have the opposite effect than the one desired. Japan might be wooed away from even a neutralist position toward one of positive friendship with the Communist World. At the very least, it would be in a position to drive a hard bargain for continued cooperation with the United States.

Japan and Southeast Asia

If the Western Democracies are to prevent the alienation to communism of additional areas of Asia, they must demonstrate that they can assist the peoples of underdeveloped areas to raise their standards of living without jeopardizing their political autonomy. Thus, some way has to be found to assist such areas as Burma, Indonesia, Viet-Nam, and the Philippines to rehabilitate their economy, to reduce the possibility of their being absorbed by communism, and to enhance their independence. Japan, with its economic potential, its technical skills, its need for raw materials, and its inadequate foreign markets, appears to be in a position to contribute toward the rehabilitation of these states.

Unfortunately, the problem is far more complex than appears on the surface. During World War II, countries such as Burma, Indonesia, and the Republic of the Philippines, which were occupied by the Japanese Armed Forces, suffered severely under this ordeal. All three of these states retain an understandable enmity toward Japan. Consequently, they have sought heavy reparations payments and rejected the San Francisco Treaty of Peace. Because of the wide discrepancy between their reparations demands and the amount Japan is willing to pay, negotiations on this issue have met an impasse and normal trade relations have not been resumed.

In the summer of 1954, however, the first break appeared in this log jam. Burma and Japan made important concessions in order to profit from the mutual benefits of renewed trade. The two nations agreed on a reparations settlement. Japan promised to pay the equivalent of $200 million in goods, technical services, or cash, and to invest $50 million over a ten-year period in joint enterprises in Burma. In November, 1954, the two countries signed a peace treaty.

If this settlement works out satisfactorily, it should be easier for the Philippines and for Indonesia to come to an agreement with Japan. In the meantime, other interested powers should offer their services to resolve the differences between these countries. If the reparations question can be settled, normal trade relations can be resumed. At that point, Japanese technological skills and production capacity could be integrated into an over-all scheme to raise the living standard of the entire area. Such an international program, with guarantees against encroachment on the political autonomy of any state, would be beneficial both to Japan and to the countries of Southeast Asia. It would also act as an effective counter force against any move by the Communists to win either Japan or Southeast Asia to their camp.

Economic Viability

While the future orientation of Japan may be largely determined by international forces, the importance of economic factors cannot be overlooked. In 1950, the over-all index of industrial production had passed the prewar level and continued to grow at an average rate of 20 per cent yearly. During the same period, gross national production, another important index of total economic activity, had risen annually by at least 10 per cent. The productivity of labor had more than doubled in the four years after 1949. To the casual observer, when the Treaty of Peace went into effect in 1952, the entire country exuded prosperity and seemed to have recovered from the effects of the war. Stores were full of goods, people were well dressed. New streamlined trains carried tremendous crowds on business, vacation, or sightseeing trips. The destruction, scarcities, and poverty of the immediate postwar years were little in evidence. Travelers returning from Europe reported that Japan's standard of living compared favorably with that of West Germany and that of Great Britain under the austerity program.

But these outward signs only belied the underlying state of the nation's economy. They only concealed the need for long-term remedial measures to solve the balance of payments problem. In boldest outline, Japan must import nearly 90 per cent of essential raw materials such as coking coal, iron ore, crude oil, raw cotton, and industrial salt. Population increases have forced necessary food imports up to 20 per cent of the total. In 1954, these imports were estimated to cost 1.3 billion yen. To pay for these essential goods from overseas, exports will have to be increased by 40 per cent.[6]

Several difficulties must be surmounted if these new export totals are to be reached. In the first place, Japan is facing increasingly severe competition in the Asian markets. The high production costs of Japanese manufactures have increased the difficulties of favorable competition. Despite some restrictions placed on imports by Yoshida while he was Premier, no concerted effort was made to enforce a rigid austerity program. Furthermore, Premier Hatoyama will probably not want to run the risk of political suicide by demanding that imports be reduced to a bare minimum. He is more likely to rely on the hope that if conditions become bad enough, the United States will perforce bail Japan out of bankruptcy.

Such a solution of Japan's economic ills is, in effect, no solution. In the near future, the United States Congress will probably not want to appropriate any aid for Japan other than that under the Mutual Security Assistance program. But Japan's economic problems are interrelated with the larger political problem of stopping communism in Asia. The United States should take the initiative, therefore, in working out a plan whereby Japanese technical assistance and manufactured products would be made available for the rehabilitation of those countries in Southeast Asia willing to accept such aid. At the same time, dollar expenditures in Japan for such a program should be dependent on the inauguration of an over-all Japanese austerity program. If unnecessary imports are not stopped by the Japanese government, American aid should then be sent directly to the underdeveloped area.

Such a plan, which integrates a future program for the improvement of conditions in underdeveloped areas with Japanese skills and an austerity program should improve Japan's balance of payments and would seem to have a reasonable chance of success. The noninterference in Japanese-Communist Chinese trade arrangements for nonstrategic items; the encouragement of international trade agreements, such as the General Agreement on Trade and Tariff; and the sponsorship of programs recommended by the Economic Commission on Asia and the Far East should also alleviate the situation. Under these conditions, Japan's economic viability might be achieved.

The Future of Representative Institutions

While economic conditions and international relations will affect the future of representative institutions in Japan the growth or retrogression of democratic practices and forces will also affect the future of the nation. During the greater part of the last century conservatism and absolutism were the guiding political principles that made the growth of democracy practically impossible. One of the basic objectives of the Allied powers for postwar Japan, however, was the creation of conditions which would assist and enhance the growth of democratic institutions. General MacArthur immediately sponsored reforms to achieve this end.

The adoption of a new Constitution based on democratic principles laid the legal foundation for the creation of representative institutions. Under the new Constitution, civil rights had been guaranteed, an independent judiciary was created, the Cabinet was made collectively responsible to Parliament, Parliament was the only legislative body, and full budgetary powers were given to the legislators. The legal foundation was at hand for Japan's democratization.

There were many other reforms inaugurated by the occupation which, so long as they remained in effect, assured the continuance of representative institutions. One of these was the encouragement given to the growth of a strong labor movement through recognizing the right of labor to organize and to bargain collectively. Another was the reform of the old police system through the decentralization of control of the police and the limitation of their powers. A third reform, whose success had a special bearing on the future of democratic institutions, was in the educational system. New educational laws stressed the importance of individual initiative and inquiry and of academic freedom. Local, elective school boards replaced a national Ministry of Education as the supervisory body for the schools.

From the point of view of the permanence of these reforms, they had three weaknesses. In the first place, the innovations were carried out during a military occupation. Though they were formally implemented by the Japanese Diet and Cabinet, the initiative had come from the various staff officers of General MacArthur's headquarters. Many leading Japanese had been consulted in formulating these new policies, yet the Supreme Commander always had the power to exercise a direct or indirect veto on actions which he did not approve. He could also order the Japanese government to carry out any new policy which he considered urgent. In other words, there was no assurance that Japanese acquiescence in these reforms during the occupation meant permanent acceptance of them.

In the second place, throughout Japanese history the men who controlled the government, and the ideas which they held, were far more important than the formal structure through which they operated. The Meiji Constitution of 1889 was made to fit the beliefs and desires of the Meiji leaders. These leaders then made the Cabinet, the Privy Council, and the various government ministries, which they directed, work to implement their political ideas. The leaders were not bound by the will of the people. Under the new Constitution of 1946, the government officials were expected to make the functioning of the national government conform to the democratic principles on which the Constitution was based.

Finally, there were few historical precedents through which the people had become familiar with the operation of representative institutions. In prewar Japan, the Cabinet had not been collectively responsible to Parliament nor had Parliament had full legislative powers. Basic human freedoms had not been guaranteed. It was difficult, therefore, for the Japanese to understand or appreciate the responsibilities and privileges which accompanied postwar democratic institutions.

In view of these facts, and of the predominantly conservative character of the Cabinets after 1948, many of the reforms were modified or rescinded after the end of the occupation. In the first place, the basic civil rights guaranteed by the Constitution were severely threatened by the passage in 1952 of the Antisubversive Activities Law and by the return to a centralized police system. After the riots on May Day, 1952, Premier Yoshida sought the legal power to control the terroristic activities of the extremists, especially the Communists. Under the new law, those who incited or agitated for political action were subject to arrest. Thus, labor unions or political leaders, regardless of their political views, might have their individual liberties and basic human rights threatened by the application of this law whenever they opposed the policies of the party in power.

An even greater threat to the continuance of democratic practices in Japan was the basic alteration of the reforms in the police system. The chief purpose of the reforms during the occupation had been to prevent the police from continuing to be an enforcement agency directly under Cabinet control. Prime Minister Yoshida had insisted, however, that the new system was inefficient and incapable of maintaining internal peace and safety. By the new Police Law of June, 1954, the police in small communities and in the five largest cities were again placed under the supervision of a Central Police Board responsible to the Prime Minister. The Chairman of the Board also had authority to appoint the prefectural police chiefs. The Prime Minister, through his appointive powers, could once more exercise control over the entire police force. If desired, this authority could be used to coerce the people to accept the will of the government.

The movement to amend the Constitution is another important development away from the principle of democracy. It gained momentum after the Treaty of Peace went into effect. Revision has been advocated not only for the chapter on the Renunciation of War (Article 9) to make rearmament legal, but also for other clauses. This revisionist movement is all the more important because it is supported by some of the old nationalists and influential members of the Manchurian clique. For example, Kishi Shinosuke, formerly Director of the General Affairs Bureau of Manchukuo and Minister of Commerce and Industry in Tōjō's wartime Cabinet, has declared, "The time is here for a wholesale scrutiny of the Constitution." As Secretary General of Hatoyama's Democratic party, he is in a key position to press for adoption of his policies.

This philosophy is also supported by the chauvinists who are urging a positive attitude toward rearmament. For example, Colonel Hattori Takushirō, a former aide of General Tōjō, is attempting to win control of the new army. Colonel Tsuji Masanobu, who was wanted by the British for trial as a war criminal because of his activities in Burma, is leader of another group. The emergence of chauvinists of this sort is an indication that new forces may demand and obtain appreciable support for extensive changes in the new Constitution.

Finally, a reversion to prewar educational policies is a further indication of the present trend away from democratization. Prime Minister Yoshida sought ways to control the leftist-dominated Teachers Union. Efforts to restrict their political activity had failed. The new bill places the teachers on the national government payroll. As government employees, they are prohibited from political activity and their unions can now be controlled. Moreover, the power of appointment of teachers reverts to the Ministry of

Education which gives the government the means of preventing Reds from becoming teachers. The teachers and the press severely attacked the Yoshida government for consciously attempting by this law to destroy the liberal basis of the new educational system. As in the case of the Anti-subversive Activities Law and the new Police Law, however, Parliament was in no mood to compromise with the leftists. It passed the new law to control the teachers. The *Asahi,* one of Tokyo's leading papers, editorialized:

> Passage of these laws will have a more far-reaching effect on the freedom of education and perhaps on other freedoms now enjoyed by the people than any other legislation since the war.

A review of these examples of the new legislation adopted since the end of the Allied occupation demonstrates clearly a definite trend away from the Allied policies which were aimed at assisting the process of democratization. It reveals a movement toward authoritarian controls so prevalent before World War II. If the reversal of the program for abolition of the *Zaibatsu,* the cancellation of the purge regulations, and the re-emergence of the military are also considered in this connection, old patterns of action and thought are unmistakably discernible. The reappearance of the large financial combines (*Zaibatsu*) and the rationalization of industry facilitates once more a close alliance between the government and the leading industrialists and financiers. The concentration of police power and educational control within the Cabinet makes possible the regimentation of the thought and action of the people. A rearmament movement and the revitalization of the armed forces give ample opportunity for the old militarists or their protégés to reassert themselves as the guiding force in national policies. With this trend toward the right apparently gaining momentum, and aided and abetted by the continued national and international fear of communism, the pendulum has not yet reached the top of its swing.

But over against this prognosis of a continued swing to the right, new forces are arrayed which should, in the not too distant future, retard and possibly reverse it. In the first place, the labor movement has come of age and the unions have experienced the effect of political power. They and their members will not easily give up their freedom of action. Both wings of the Socialists, which are supported by labor, increased their strength in the election of February, 1955. On the other hand, labor apparently did not support the extreme left as it did in January, 1949, when thirty-five Communists were elected to Parliament. For example, an analysis of the elections of February, 1955, shows that the anticonservative votes went for the Left-wing Socialist candidates rather than for the Communists. On the other hand, the conservative members of the House of Representatives lost less than 6 per cent of their total representation. In other words, the election showed no extreme changes.[7]

The new status of the farmer is another retarding influence in the swing to the extreme right. The agrarian reforms, which affected a large portion of the population, lifted a heavy debt burden from many farm families. As a result, they are reluctant to see a return to prewar conditions for fear that they may lose what they have already gained.

In the third place, the equality of the sexes, guaranteed by the Constitution, has released an entirely new force. Women are coming into their own. They are equal before the law, vote, work, and have greater educational opportunities than ever before. No politician will dare to deprive them of their rights.

Finally, the bitter pill of defeat confronted many Japanese, particularly the youth, with a new political philosophy to guide them; they have found democracy and do not intend to give it up without a struggle . While their understanding of democracy may be distorted, they know that one of its essential elements is individual liberty and freedom. While they may have had only limited experience in the operation of representative institutions, they have appreciated and enjoyed the privileges which democracy brought them.

On balance, therefore, prospects for the continued democratization of Japan are not as bright as they were when the Treaty of Peace was signed in September, 1951. Conversely, it is unlikely that authoritarianism will be able to negate many of the advances already made. The reactions against the occupation-inspired reforms are natural ones. In the end, Japan will probably settle down to a limited form of democracy well to the right of center. Whatever representative institutions remain, they will indicate that a tremendous advance has been made since the beginning of Japan's modern century.

Notes

1. Chester Bowles, "A Fresh Look at Free Asia," *Foreign Affairs,* vol. 33, 1 (October, 1954), p. 58.

2. The election returns for the voting February 27, 1955 were as follows:

	1955	1953
Democrats (former Progressive Party and Hatoyama Splinter)	185	77
Liberals	112	237
Right Socialists	67	66
Left Socialists	89	72
Communists	2	1
Others	12	13

New York Times, March 6, 1955.

3. T. Miyashita, *Observations on Problems of Trade between China and Japan* (Tokyo: Institute of Pacific Affairs, Inc., 1954), p. 31.

4. Although some of these persons may have died, over 46,000 persons are known to have been alive within Communist areas after August, 1945. Three-fourths of them are supposed to be in Communist China.

This figure is exclusive of confirmed deaths of over 252,000 persons within Communist territory. See Japanese Embassy, *Newsletter,* No. 5 (October 5, 1954).

5. Miyashita, *op. cit.,* p. 8.

6. Shigeto Tsuru, "A New Japan?", *Perspective of Japan, An Atlantic Monthly Supplement* (New York: Intercultural Publications, 1955), p. 10.

Final figures on Japan's balance of payments for 1954 were far more encouraging than had been predicted. Thanks to heavy purchases in the sterling area and to invisible credits estimated at $400 million, the deficit was practically eliminated. But economists such as Professor Jerome B. Cohen point out that the market for goods in the sterling area will doubtless decrease and that the basic problems still remain. He believes, however, that if world trade continues to increase and if Japan is able to retain its present position in this trade, its economic difficulties are not insurmountable.

7. It will be observed from the returns given in Note 2, that the total seats for the conservative parties, the Democrats, Liberals, and others changed from 327 in 1953 to 309 in 1955. Likewise, the Right Socialists gained one seat, the Left Socialists seventeen, and the Communists one. Any leftist trend which this might indicate is more than offset by the fact that the Democrats, who replaced the Liberals as the leading party, are more conservative than the latter.

BIBLIOGRAPHICAL NOTE

In view of the availability of both comprehensive and selective bibliographies of material in European and Japanese languages, the following notes are not meant to be exhaustive. They are prepared for the reader who does not have access to these references and who may wish to read further in some of the more important subjects covered in this book. For the sake of convenience, the notes are arranged under the five separate periods covered by each part of the book. More works are listed in European languages than in Japanese on the assumption that those readers who read Japanese will also be familiar with or have access to the extensive Japanese bibliographies.

If the reader is interested in more detailed bibliographical information, the most helpful guide in European languages is *A Selected List of Books and Articles on Japan in English, French, and German* (Cambridge: Harvard-Yenching Institute, revised and enlarged, 1954), compiled by Hugh Borton, Serge Elisséeff, William W. Lockwood, and John C. Pelzel. This annotated bibliography lists over 1700 titles, arranged topically. Both comprehensive and special bibliographies are listed in the first section. For current listings of publications on Japan, the most comprehensive coverage is in *Far Eastern Bibliography,* published annually by the Far Eastern Association.

As for annotated bibliographies in Japanese, the Bibliographical Series of the Center for Japanese Studies of the University of Michigan are the most useful. The following volumes in this series are especially pertinent to the subjects covered by this book: John W. Hall, *Japanese History: A Guide to Japanese References and Research Materials* (Ann Arbor: University of Michigan, Center of Japanese Studies, Bibliographical Series No. 4, 1954); and Robert E. Ward, *A Guide to Japanese Reference and Research Materials in the Field of Political Science* (Ann Arbor: University of Michigan, Center of Japanese Studies, Bibliographical Series No. 1, 1950).

Sir George B. Sansom has written two excellent companion volumes on the cultural background of Japan. They are *Japan, A Short Cultural History* (New York: Appleton-Century-Crofts, Inc., 1943) and *The Western*

World and Japan (New York: Alfred A. Knopf, Inc., 1950). The former covers the period from earliest antiquity through the eighteenth century; the latter describes the impact of European civilization on Japan and its historical development down to about 1894.

For the standard, detailed political history of Japan prior to 1868, see James Murdoch, *History of Japan* (3 vols.; London: Kegan Paul, Trench, Trubner & Co., Ltd., 1926), especially volume II, chapters xiv-xxii and volume III.

A most readable yet condensed history of Japan is *Japan Past and Present* (New York: Alfred A. Knopf, Inc., 1953) by the outstanding scholar Edwin O. Reischauer. His more interpretative study, *The United States and Japan* (Cambridge: Harvard University Press, 1950) is provocative and is especially helpful for understanding contemporary problems.

The only other volume in English which covers a period almost identical with this study is *Japan Since Perry* (New York: McGraw-Hill Book Co., Inc., 1949) by Chitoshi Yanaga. Professor Yanaga has collected within a single volume a vast amount of detailed material based largely on Japanese sources. It also contains a helpful and extensive bibliography of works in both Japanese and European languages.

Bibliographical Notes for Part I: 1850-1868

Several important works have appeared recently on the opening of Japan. The most important is Arthur Walworth, *Black Ships off Japan* (New York: Alfred A. Knopf., Inc., 1941). This study is based on the official *Narrative of the Expedition of an American Squadron under Commodore M. C. Perry,* edited by Francis L. Hawks (3 vols.; Washington: Nicholson, 1856), as well as on other primary sources. Both Hawks and Walworth contain texts of the Kanagawa Treaty. For early American contacts with Japan see "Japan and the United States," by Shunzo Sakamaki, *Transactions of the Asiatic Society of Japan,* 2d series, XVIII (1939). *The Complete Journal of Townsend Harris,* edited by M. E. Cosenza (New York: Doubleday & Co., Inc., 1930), is fascinating and instructive. It also contains texts of the conventions which Harris signed with the Japanese government and of the United States–Japanese Commercial Treaty of 1858. An account of the first Japanese Embassy to the United States in 1860, which is entertaining reading, appeared as *The First Japanese Embassy to the United States of America* (Tokyo: The America-Japan Society, 1920).

There is no single volume in European languages devoted exclusively to the last few years of the Tokugawa dictatorship. Several studies, however, have devoted considerable space to its collapse. One of these is E. Herbert Norman, *Japan's Emergence as a Modern State* (New York: American

Institute of Pacific Relations, Inc., 1940). Much of his economic analysis is, however, open to question. Another valuable book, by one of Japan's outstanding economic historians, which contains background material is Eijirō Honjō, *Economic Theory and the History of Japan in the Tokugawa Period* (Tokyo: Maruzen Co., Ltd., 1943). For a description by a contemporary European observer of internal conditions for a large part of the period see J. H. Gubbins, *The Progress of Japan, 1853-1871* (Oxford: Clarendon Press, 1911).

A few special studies which should be mentioned include E. H. Norman's monograph on the early conscript armies entitled *Soldier and Peasant in Japan* (New York: American Institute of Pacific Relations, Inc., 1943). For details of the early industrialization of the western clans see the author's chapter on "War and the Rise of Industrialization in Japan" in J. D. Clarkson and T. C. Cochran, *War as a Social Institution* (New York: Columbia University Press, 1941); and Henry Smith, "Western Industrialization," *Harvard Journal of Asiatic Studies,* II (1948).

There is a vast amount of source material in Japanese on the opening of the country by the Western powers. The most exhaustive primary sources are *Dai Nihon Komonjo Bakumatsu Gaikoku Kankei* (Japanese Historical Documents, Foreign Relations at End of Tokugawa Period), edited and published by the Shiryō Hensan Jō of Tokyo University. The same office has also published much valuable material in *Ishin Shi* (History of the Restoration), in six volumes, edited by Ishin Shiryō Hensan Kakari (Tokyo; Meiji Shoin, 1939-43). More recently, the Bureau has been publishing *Dai Nihon Ishin Shiryō* (Historical Documents on the Restoration Period), in eight sections. The first two volumes dealing with the period from 1846-53 and 1854-57, are particularly pertinent to this section.

Among the innumerable histories of the Tokugawa Period in Japanese, the most outstanding is Kurita Mototsugu, *Edo Jidai,* I (The Tokugawa Period, Part I), in *Sōgō Nihon Shi Taikei,* IX (Tokyo: Naigai Shoseki Kabushiki Kaisha, 1929). For economic history, see Honjō Eijirō,[1] *Meiji Ishin Keizai Shi Kenkyū* (Studies in Economic History of the Meiji Restoration; Tokyo: Kaizōsha, 1930); and Tsuchiya Takaō, *Zoku Nihon Keizai Shi Gaiyō* (Outline of Japanese Economic History: Continued; Tokyo: Iwanami, 1941).

Two important analytical studies of modern Japan have recently appeared. They are Oka Yoshitake, *Kindai Nihon no Keisei* (The Position of Modern Japan; Tokyo: Kōbun-dō, 1952), and Yanaibara Tadaō (editor), *Gendai Nihon Shōshi* (A Short History of Present-Day Japan; 2 vols.; Tokyo: Misuzu, 1953). Professor Inobe Shigeō was one of the first

[1] To be consistent with common usage, in this "Bibliographic Note" the names of authors of books in Japanese are given with the family name preceding the given name.

scholars to concentrate on the international and political developments of the period in his *Ishin Zenshi no Kenkyū* (Studies of the Early History of the Restoration; Tokyo: Chūbun-kan, 1935). Tsuji Zennosuke's *Kaigai Kōtsū Shiwa* (Historical Essays on Foreign Relations; Tokyo: Naigai Shoseki Kabushiki Kaisha, 1930) is also important. The most representative work by one of the leftist writers is Tōyama Shigeki's *Meiji Ishin* (The Meiji Restoration; Tokyo: Iwanami, 1951).

Bibliographical Notes for Part II: 1868-90

There are numerous works which cover all or part of this period. In political history, one of the most important is W. W. McLaren, *A Political History of Japan During the Meiji Era, 1867-1912* (London: Charles Scribner's Sons, 1916). Significant documents and primary sources for the Restoration and the Constitution have been published in his "Japanese Government Documents," *Transactions of the Asiatic Society of Japan,* vol. 42, part I (1914). It contains the official translations of the Constitution and of the basic laws which accompanied its promulgation. Another important volume on the Constitution is Hirobumi Itō, *Commentaries on the Constitution of the Empire of Japan,* translated by Myoji Itō (Tokyo: Chuo Daigaku, 1931). This concise volume, which has been published in various editions, gives Itō's views on the meanings of the various articles. It came to be considered almost as sacrosanct as the Constitution.

For a study of the Japanese government by a competent political scientist, Harold S. Quigley, *Japanese Government and Politics: An Introductory Study* (New York: Century, 1932), is considered a standard work. For a more recent, interpretative and provocative summary, with emphasis on the role of the oligarchy, see Robert K. Reischauer, *Japan, Government and Politics* (New York: Thomas Nelson & Sons, 1939). Robert A. Scalapino, *Democracy and the Party Movement in Prewar Japan, The Failure of the First Attempt* (Berkeley: University of California Press, 1953) largely supersedes these two studies. It is particularly interesting in its analysis of the social origins of the early parties.

In reference to economic materials, Professor William W. Lockwood has just completed a significant analysis of Japan's industrialization. This work is entitled *The Economic Development of Japan, Growth and Structural Change, 1868-1938* (Princeton: Princeton University Press, 1954). Much of the material in E. H. Norman, *Japan's Emergence as a Modern State, op. cit.,* is devoted to the years 1868-90. A valuable study which connects the problems of population with agricultural production is Ryoichi Ishii, *Population Pressure and Economic Life in Japan* (London: Walter King, Ltd., 1937). A concise and informative article on the nation's finances, written by the man who was Finance Minister after 1882 is Masayoshi Matsukata's "Japan's Finance" in Shigenobu Ōkuma, *Fifty Years of New Japan* (2 vols.; London: Smith Elders, 1910). In fact, this two volume work compiled by Ōkuma, with essays written by the foremost contemporary authorities on the various phases of the development of modern Japan, is an invaluable reference. Its appendices are also helpful.

A thorough study of early Chinese-Japanese relations based on Chinese sources, which throws much light on the Ryūkyū controversy and also on the struggle to control Korea, is T. F. Tsiang's "Sino-Japanese Diplomatic Relations, 1870-94," *Chinese Social and Political Science Review,* 1933. Other important, detailed material on the Korean question is contained in Frederick Nelson, *Korea and the Old Order in Eastern Asia* (Baton Rouge, La.: University of Louisiana, 1946).

The task of selecting representative and significant writings on society in Japan in 1890 is exceedingly difficult. A large number of histories, reminiscences, autobiographies, and interpretative works have been compiled by those who lived in Japan during the Meiji Period. For some of these the reader is referred to Hugh Borton *et al., A Selected List of Books and Articles on Japan, op. cit.* (Cambridge: Harvard-Yenching Institute, revised and enlarged, 1954), especially pp. 48-58 for works on modern history; Chapter IX, "Sociology and Ethnology"; Chapter X, "Education"; Chapter XI, "Mythology, Religion and Philosophy"; and pp. 175-81 for translations of contemporary literature. Some works which should receive special mention are Inazo Nitobe's *Japanese Traits and Foreign Influences* (London: Kegan Paul, Trench, Trubner & Co., Ltd., 1927) and his *Intercourse between the United States and Japan, An Historical Sketch* (Baltimore: Johns Hopkins Press, 1891). While somewhat imaginative and interpretive, the works of Lafcadio Hearn are sensitive and afford valuable insights into the Japanese character. The court physician Dr. Erwin O. von Baelz has written a useful picture in his *Awakening Japan: The Diary of a German Doctor, Erwin Baelz* (New York: Viking Press, Inc., 1932). For an expression of the contemporary, official view of Japanese education, see Dairoku Kikuchi, *Japanese Education* (London: John Murray, 1909).

Studies and sources in Japanese are extensive. As for the previous period, one of the most helpful general surveys is Yanaibara Tadaō, editor, *Gendai Nihon Shōshi, op. cit.* General collections of contemporary material are too numerous to mention. A few of the most valuable include: Itō Hirobumi, editor, *Hisho Ruisan* (Confidential Materials; 27 vols.; Tokyo: Ruisan Kankōkai, 1933-36). This collection contains documents, laws, ordinances, treaties, and other pertinent material on the various phases of history from 1868 to about 1890. Hashimoto Hiroshi, *Ishin Nisshi* (Diaries of the Restoration; Series I, 10 vols.; Series II, 10 vols.); Tokyo: Shizuoka Kyōdō Kenkyūkai, 1932-35) contains a diary of the Council of State and of private diaries. Yoshino Sakuzō, editor, *Meiji Bunka Zenshū* (Collected Works on Meiji Culture; 24 vols.; Tokyo: Nihon Hyōronsha, 1928-30), is an excellent collection of documents and contemporary essays and writings on various aspects of the Meiji Period. The material is arranged topically in separate volumes under subjects such as history, government, foreign relations, finance, literature, etc. Contemporary newspaper material has been reissued by Nakayama Yasumasa in *Shimbun Shūsei Meiji Hennen Shi* (A Chronicle of Meiji History from Newspaper Collections; 15 vols.; Tokyo: Zaisei Keizai Gakkai, 1935-40).

For a general cultural history the reader is referred to *Gendai Nihon Bummei Shi* (A Cultural History of Recent Japan; 18 vols.; Tokyo: Tōyō Keizai Shimpōsha, 1940-44). Foremost among Japanese works on constitutional history is Ōtsu Junichirō, *Dai Nihon Kensei Shi* (A Constitutional History of Japan; 10 vols.; Tokyo: Hōbunkan, 1927-28). Another standard work, though much more condensed, is that of Osatake Takeki, *Nihon Kensei Shi Taikō* (An Outline of Japanese Constitutional History; 2 vols.; Tokyo: Nihon Hyōron Sha, 1938). The studies of Suzuki Yasuzō, especially those written before he emphasized the Marxist interpretation of history, such as *Nihon Kempō Shi Gaisetsu* (A General Outline of the History of the Japanese Constitution; Tokyo: Chūō Koron, 1941) are valuable for the light they throw on the contribution of Prussian political scientists to the framing of the Constitution. For an excellent collection of essays on political problems of the period see Watanabe Ikujirō, *Meiji Shi Kenkyū* (Studies in Meiji History; Tokyo: Rakuno Shōin, 1934).

On economic problems, the material is also abundant. A valuable collection of economic and financial material has been edited by Professors Ōuchi Hyōe and Tsuchiya Takaō and published as *Meiji Zenki Zaisei Keizai Shiryō* (Historical Material on Economics and Finance of the Early Meiji Period; 21 vols.; Tokyo: Kaizō Sha, 1931-36). The *Kōbushō Enkaku Hokoku* (Official History of the Ministry of Industry), frequently referred to in Part II of this book, is in volume 17. Two valuable single volumes are Tsuchiya Takaō, *Zoku Nihon Keizaishi Gaiyō, op. cit.;* and Takahashi Kamekichi, *Meiji Taishō Sangyō Hattatsu Shi* (History of the Expansion of Industry during Meiji and Taishō; Tokyo: Kaizosha, 1927). One of the best analyses of the relationship of landlord-entrepreneur groups with the early parties and with government sponsored industries is Horie Yasuzō, *Nihon Shihon shugi no Seiritsu* (Establishment of Japanese Capitalism; Ōsaka: Daidō Shoin, 1938).

Concerning foreign relations, the two most important collections are those published by the Foreign Office. Its *Dai Nihon Gaikō Bunsho* (Collected Documents on Japanese Diplomacy; Tokyo: Nihon Kokusai Kyōkai, 1936 and later) contains basic documents, arranged chronologically, on foreign relations from 1868. A year is covered by a single volume. By 1952, the latest publication was for the year 1888. The Treaty Division Office has published a collection of treaties in Gaimushō Joyaku Kyoku, editor, *Joyaku Isan* (Collection of Treaties; 9 vols.; Tokyo: Gaimushō Joyaku Kyoku, 1926-29). A relatively objective study by Kiyosawa Kiyoshi, entitled *Nihon Gaikō Shi* (A Diplomatic History of Japan; Tokyo: Tōyō Keizai Shimpōsha, 1941), covers the period from 1868-1931.

An interesting and enlightening publication for social aspects of the Meiji Period is *Gahō Kindai Hyakunen Shi* (An Illustrated History of the Past Century; Tokyo: Kokusai Bunka Johōsha, 1951). This chronological, illustrated history of Japan during the past century is a convenient reference. Arranged in small volumes, each of which covers 5-10 years, it has photographs or drawings of the main events or individuals for each period. For a standard literary history see Homma Hisao, *Meiji Bungaku Shi* (A Literary History of the Meiji Period; 3 vols.; Tokyo: Tokyo Do, 1935-43).

Bibliographical Notes for Part III: 1889-1915

For a general account of political developments during this period, the reader is referred to William W. McLaren, *A Political History of Japan, op. cit.* Political events are also given in some detail in Robert A. Scalapino, *Democracy and the Party Movement, op. cit.* The role of the oligarchs in the early constitutional government is emphasized in Robert K. Reischauer, *Japan, Government and Politics, op. cit.*

In view of the importance to Europe of the Sino-Japanese War of 1894-95 and of the interest of the powers in China, Japan's international relations in this period has received extensive treatment in European languages. William H. Langer devotes a large section of his *The Diplomacy of Imperialism, 1890-1902* (2 vols.; Alfred A. Knopf, Inc., 1935), to events in the Far East, to the problem of concessions in China, and to the Anglo-Japanese Alliance. The same is true of H. B. Morse, *The International Relations of the Chinese Empire* (3 vols.; London: Longmans, Green, 1918). A thorough study based on Chinese sources of the causes of the Sino-Japanese War is T. F. Tsiang, "Sino-Japanese Diplomatic Relations, 1870-1894," *op. cit.* For the role of Korea and its relation with the Western powers see Frederick Nelson, *Korea and the Old Order, op. cit.*

Documentary material on American-Japanese relations, taken from United States archives, is contained in Payson J. Treat, *Diplomatic Relations between the United States and Japan, 1853-1895* (2 vols.; Stanford: Stanford University Press, 1932); and *Diplomatic Relations . . . , 1895-1905* (Stanford: Stanford University Press, 1909). Two significant diaries by Japanese diplomats of this era are A. M. Pooley, editor, *The Secret Memoirs of Count Tadasu Hayashi, 1850-1913* (New York: Nash, 1915); and Kikujiro Ishii, *Diplomatic Commentaries,* translated by William R. Langdon (Baltimore: Johns Hopkins University Press, 1936). For details on how decisions were made by the Japanese government, see S. T. Takeuchi, *War and Diplomacy in the Japanese Empire* (New York: Doubleday, Doran & Co., 1935). A thorough study, which begins with the Open Door Policy, is A. Whitney Griswold, *The Far Eastern Policy of the United States* (New York: Harcourt, Brace & Co., Inc., 1938).

For special books on the Russo-Japanese War, K. Asakawa, *The Russo-Japanese Conflict: Its Causes and Issues* (Boston: Houghton Mifflin Co., 1904), is written in defense of Japan's position. The standard work on President Theodore Roosevelt's role in the Portsmouth Conference is Tyler Dennet, *Roosevelt and the Russo-Japanese War* (New York: Doubleday Doran & Co., Inc., 1925).

Economic sources are also extensive for this period. Various branches of the Japanese government have published statistical material such as Bureau de la Statistique Générale, *Résumé statistique de l'empire du Japon, annuel, 1886-1940* (Tokyo: Imperial Cabinet, Bureau de la Statistique, 1887-1941); Ministry of Finance, *Financial and Economic Annual of Japan, 1901-1940* (Tokyo: Ministry of Finance, 1902-41); and Ministry of Finance, *Annual Return of the Foreign Trade of the Empire of Japan* (Tokyo: Ministry of Finance, 1883-1931).

As for general economic studies, William W. Lockwood covers this period in its entirety in his *The Economic Development of Japan, op. cit.* A concise narrative of Japan's development presented more chronologically than Lockwood is George C. Allen, *A Short Economic History of Modern Japan, 1867-1937* (London: George Allen & Unwin, Ltd., 1946).

Population problems for this period have absorbed the attention of numerous scholars. The results of one group have been published by Ernest F. Penrose in his *Food Supply and Raw Materials in Japan . . . , 1894-1927* (Chicago: University of Chicago Press, 1930). A more recent study is that of Ryoichi Ishii, *Population Pressure and Economic Life in Japan, op. cit.*

In reference to the Japanese material, many of the collections listed under the previous section also cover the period from 1890-1915. For example, see Yoshino, *Meiji Bunka Zenshū, op. cit.;* and Nakayama, *Shimbun Shūsei, op. cit.* Similarly, the collection of treaties published by the Foreign Office in *Joyaku Isan, op. cit.,* include those of this period.

There are various general histories which are largely devoted to the quarter century after the promulgation of the Constitution. Pertinent material on the growth of nationalism will be found in Watanabe Ikujirō, *Meiji Jidai Shi* (History of the Meiji Period; Tokyo: Waseda Daigaku Shuppambu, 1916). While the volumes vary in quality, much factual material can be found in the six-volume collection published by the Asahi Shimbun as *Meiji Taishō Shi* (History of the Meiji and Taishō Periods; 6 vols.; Tokyo: Asahi Shimbunsha, 1930-31).

A word of warning is necessary in reference to many of the political and economic studies on Japan's recent history. Several excellent scholars, such as Rōyama Masamichi, Oka Yoshitake, and Tsuchiya Takaō, who have concentrated on political and economic history of the recent period, have maintained an objective point of view. On the other hand, several of the younger scholars interested in Japan's history after 1890, approach the problem from the Marxist viewpoint. Thus, in using a work such as Shinobu Seisaburō, *Meiji Seiji Shi* (Political History of the Meiji Period; Tokyo: Kenshinsha, 1951), which contains much valuable material, the reader should realize that the author writes from a Marxist viewpoint.

In reference to economic material in Japanese, there are far too many collections to enumerate. As indicated in the section on works in Western languages, the various departments of the government have issued annual statistical reports. Two of the most important collections of economic data are Takimoto Seiichi, editor, *Nihon Sangyō Shiryō Taikei* (Collection of Historical Material on Japanese Industry; 15 vols.; Tokyo: Chūgai Shōgyō, 1926) and Meiji Zaisei Hensankai, *Meiji Zaisei Shi* (Meiji Financial History; 15 vols.; Tokyo: Meiji Zaisei Hensankai, 1905). One of the most useful, single-volume works on Japan's industrial growth after 1868 is Takahashi Kamekichi, *Meiji Taishō Sangyō Hattatsu Shi, op. cit.*

Bibliographical Notes for Part IV: 1915-41

There is no single volume in a European language which covers this period, but two colorful accounts written by a British newspaper editor who resided in Japan overlap most of it. They are A. Morgan Young, *Japan in Recent Times, 1912-1926* (New York: William Morrow & Co., Inc., 1929), and his *Imperial Japan, 1926-1938* (New York: William Morrow & Co., Inc., 1938). Scalapino, in his *Democracy and the Party Movement, op. cit.,* has a concise description of the chief political events. For a survey of the last decade of this period see Hugh Borton, *Japan Since 1931—Its Political and Social Development* (New York: American Institute of Pacific Relations, Inc., 1940). A useful study of the operation of the government during the same period, with emphasis on political institutions, is Charles B. Fahs, *Government in Japan, Recent Trends in Its Scope and Operation* (New York: American Institute of Pacific Relations, Inc., 1940).

For the growth of militarism and nationalism and their relationship to Shintoism, Hillis Lory, *Japan's Military Masters* (New York: Viking Press, Inc., 1943) and John M. Maki, *Japanese Militarism—Its Cause and*

Cure (New York: Alfred A. Knopf, Inc., 1945) will be found especially useful. All of Dr. Daniel C. Holtom's studies on modern Shintō are valuable, but his most outstanding study is *National Faith of Japan: A Study in Modern Shinto* (London: Kegan Paul, Trench, Trubner & Co., Ltd., 1938). For translations of two textbooks on Japanese ethics, which expounded the basis of ultranationalism, see the two volumes edited by Robert K. Hall entitled *Kokutai no Hongi* (Cardinal Principles of the National Entity of Japan), translated by John O. Gauntlett (Cambridge: Harvard University Press, 1949), and *Shūshin: The Ethics of a Defeated Nation* (New York: Teachers College, Columbia University, 1949).

In view of the overwhelming importance of international relations in the years leading to World War II, many of the works on modern Japan were devoted exclusively to these problems. The following titles have been selected, therefore, to give the reader at least one reference to the most important international crises between the two world wars. On the Paris Peace Conference, detailed references to Japan's role are covered by David Hunter Miller, *My Diary at the Conference of Paris* (21 vols.; New York: Appeal Printing Co., 1924). Japan's part in the discussion of the Commission to draft the League's Covenant is treated in his *The Drafting of the Covenant* (2 vols.; New York: G. P. Putnam's Sons, 1928). A standard history of the Conference is H. M. V. Temperley (ed.), *A History of the Peace Conference of Paris* (6 vols.; London: H. Frowde and Hodder & Stoughton, 1920-24).

The basic study on the Washington Disarmament Conference of 1922 is R. L. Buell, *The Washington Conference* (New York: Appleton-Century-Crofts, Inc., 1922). For special reference to events leading to the occupation of Manchuria by Japan in 1931 see Arnold J. Toynbee, *Survey of International Affairs, 1931* (London: Royal Institute of International Affairs, 1933). In S. R. Smith, *The Manchurian Crisis, 1931-1932* (New York: Columbia University Press, 1948), special emphasis is given to the relationship of the Manchurian Incident to the League of Nations. The report of the Lytton Commission has appeared as League of Nations, *Manchuria—Report of the Commission of Enquiry Appointed by the League of Nations* (Washington: U.S. Government Printing Office, 1932).

An excellent study of the background of international events in Asia has been made by F. C. Jones in *Japan's New Order in East Asia: Its Rise and Fall, 1937-45* (London: Oxford University Press, 1954). The outstanding study of events leading to the outbreak of the war in the Pacific is Harold Feis, *The Road to Pearl Harbor; the Coming of the War between the United States and Japan* (Princeton: Princeton University Press, 1950). The basic documents on the negotiations between the two countries have been published by the U.S. Department of State as *Foreign Relations of the*

United States, Japan, 1931-1941 (2 vols.; Washington: U.S. Government Printing Office, 1943).

In reference to economic problems, the American Institute of Pacific Relations, Inc., has published much valuable material in its biennial *Problems of the Pacific* which first appeared in 1928. The most important single volume on economic conditions is Lockwood's *Economic Development of Japan, op. cit.* Other studies for the earlier part of this period include Harold G. Moulton, *Japan, an Economic and Financial Appraisal* (Washington: Brookings Institution, 1931); and John E. Orchard, *Japan's Economic Position, the Progress of Industrialization* (New York: Whittlesey House, 1930). A more recent appraisal, which has some authoritative surveys, but is less valuable on developments after 1936, is E. B. Schumpeter (ed.), *The Industrialization of Japan and Manchukuo, 1930-1940* (New York: Macmillan Co., 1940). One of the best studies on labor problems is that of the International Labor Office entitled *Industrial Labour in Japan* (Geneva: King, 1933). For the background of radicalism and the labor movement, see Roger Swearingen and Paul Langer, *Red Flag in Japan, International Communism in Action 1919-1951* (Cambridge: Harvard University Press, 1952).

Finally, a few monographs which concern special aspects of Japanese society prior to World War II should be mentioned. One of the first field studies to be carried out by a cultural anthropologist was a village study in Kyūshū by Professor John F. Embree. His findings appeared as *Suye Mura, a Japanese Village* (Chicago: University of Chicago Press, 1939). A symposium on Japanese life was edited by Douglas G. Haring and published as *Japan's Prospects* (Cambridge: Harvard University Press, 1946). The outstanding contribution on the question of Japanese in Hawaii and on the American continent has been made by Bradford Smith in his *Americans from Japan* (Philadelphia: J. B. Lippincott Co., 1949).

As for material in Japanese, perhaps the best point of departure is Yanaibara Tadaō, *Gendai Nihon Shōshi, op. cit.* For a general political account, Rōyama Masamichi, *Seiji Shi* (Political History, vol. 2, "Gendai Nihon Bummeishi"; Tokyo: Tōyō Keizai Shimpō Sha, 1940), is also helpful. The standard, detailed political history is Kudō Takeshige, *Taishō Kensei Shi* (A Political History of the Taishō Period; 2 vols.; Tokyo: Okano Shōgakkai, 1930). The most detailed account, though it must be used with caution because of the leftist bias of the author, is Shinobu Seisaburō, *Taishō Seiji Shi* (Political History of the Taishō Period; 4 vols.; Tokyo: Kawade Shobo, 1950-52). For a chronological descriptive reference to political events after 1926 see Ikeda Takeshi, *Shōwa Seiji Keizai Shi* (Political and Economic History of the Shōwa Period; Tokyo: Kokumin Kyoiku Tosho, 1947).

Among the numerous diaries and memoirs written by key officials during the interbellum years, one of the most valuable is that of Premier Hara Kei entitled, *Hara Kei Nikki* (The Diary of Hara Kei; 9 vols.; Tokyo: Kangen Sha, 1949). Another important memoir is the diary of Harada Kumaō, Secretary to the last of the Elder Statesmen, Saionji. This work is entitled *Saionji Kō To Seiryoku* (Diary of Prince Saionji; 8 vols.; Tokyo: Iwanami, 1952). Shigemitsu Mamoru, who was an important diplomat during this period, has written of the turmoil and strains in his *Shōwa no Dōran* (The Upheavals of the Shōwa Period; 2 vols.; Tokyo: Chūō Koron, 1952).

In foreign affairs, two important works are Shinobu Seisaburō, *Kindai Nihon Gaikō Shi* (Recent Japanese Diplomatic History; Tokyo: Chūō Koran Sha, 1946); and Watanabe Ikujirō, *Nihon Kinsei Gaikō Shi* (History of Japanese Diplomacy in Recent Times; Tokyo: Chigura-shabo, 1938). On the negotiations with the United States, the Japanese Ambassador in Washington, Nomura Kichisaburō, has written his memoirs in *Beikoku ni Tsukai-shite* (My Mission to the United States; Tokyo: Iwanami, 1946).

As for economic material, there are innumerable official publications. After 1931, and especially after 1937, statistics on industrial production of strategic and semistrategic industries were withheld for security reasons. For a general economic survey see Ōuchi Hyōe, "Keizai" (Economics) in Yanaibara Tadaō, *Gendai Nihon Shōshi, op. cit.* For a study of the growth of capitalism in Japan the reader is referred to the compilation of Professor Ōuchi and others entitled *Nihon Shihon Shūgi no Kenkyū* (Studies of Japanese Capitalism; 2 vols.; Tokyo: Kōdō Sha, 1948); and to Mori Kiichi's *Nihon Shihon Shūgi Hattatsu Shi Josetsu* (Explanatory History of the Growth of Japanese Capitalism; Tokyo: Hakuyō Sha, 1934). The Research Bureau of the Bank of Japan has written a financial history of Japan since 1931 as follows: Nihon Ginkō Chōsa Kyoku, *Manshū Jihen Igo no Zaisei Kinyū Shi* (Financial and Monetary History from the Manchurian Incident; Tokyo: Nihon Ginkō, 1948). A discussion of public finance during the thirties will also be found in Hijikata Seibi, *Zaisei Shi* (History of Finances, vol. 6, "Gendai Nihon Bummei Shi," Tokyo: Tōyō Keizai Shimpō Sha).

Bibliographical Notes for Part V: 1941-54

The selection of representative studies for the war and postwar years is difficult because events have been so recent that definitive studies on many topics have not yet been completed. Furthermore, after the formation of the General Headquarters of the Supreme Commander for the Allied Powers in Tokyo, a vast amount of material on all phases of postwar life was produced by the various sections of GHQ. Some of this material was printed; a large portion of it was mimeographed. Some of it was carefully edited to prevent adverse criticism of the occupation; some of it was translated from uncritical Japanese reports. We are also much too close to the events to expect that the Japanese would have been able to prepare many thorough, objective studies of their country during and after the war. Finally, material for the most recent years has not yet appeared in book form.

Despite these difficulties some references may be helpful for those wishing to read further on the most modern period. As for works on conditions within Japan during the war and in the immediate postwar years, useful summaries on the various phases and events of the Pacific War will be found in United States Strategic Bombing Survey, *The Campaigns of the Pacific War* (Washington: USSBS, Naval Analysis Division, 1946). The question of the struggle for peace is treated in the Survey's, *Japan's Struggle to End the War* (Washington: U.S. Government Printing Office, 1946). For wartime changes in the Japanese government see Hugh Borton, *The Administration and Structure of the Japanese Government,* U.S. Department of State Publication 2244 (Washington: U.S. Government Printing Office, 1945). A valuable and careful study of the struggle within Japan toward the end of the war over the question of surrender has been made by Robert J. C. Butow in *Japan's Decision to Surrender* (Stanford: Stanford University Press, 1954). The international implications of Japan's foreign policy and military successes during the war are stressed in F. C. Jones, *Japan's New Order in East Asia, op. cit.*

A convenient, official summary of the various international decisions and policies concerning Japan will be found in U.S. Department of State, *Occupation of Japan: Policy and Progress,* Department of State Publication 2671 (Washington: U.S. Government Printing Office, 1946). A first-hand account of the important international conferences and their relation to Japan is James F. Byrnes, *Speaking Frankly* (New York: Harper & Bros., 1947).

For two authoritative reviews of the occupation written by State Department officials, see Edwin M. Martin, *The Allied Occupation of Japan* (Stanford: Stanford University Press, 1948); and Robert A. Fearey, *The Occupation of Japan, Second Phase: 1948-50* (New York: Macmillan Co., 1950). A study of the various phases of the first two years of the occupation has been made by Hugh Borton, entitled "The Allied Occupation of Japan, 1945-7"; in F. C. Jones, Hugh Borton, and B. R. Pearn, *The Far East, 1942-1946* (London: Oxford University Press, 1955), pp. 307-428.

The best single source for data on the occupation are the monthly reports of SCAP which first appeared in October, 1945, and stopped with the issue of September, 1948. They are entitled Supreme Commander for the Allied Powers, *Summation of Non-Military Activities in Japan* (Tokyo: GHQ, Supreme Commander for the Allied Powers, 1945-48). SCAP also published most of the pertinent documents connected with constitutional reform and political movements in Supreme Commander for the Allied Powers, Government Section, *Political Reorientation of Japan, September 1945 to September 1948* (2 vols.; Washington: U.S. Government Printing Office, 1949). The basic study of the role of the Far Eastern Commission is George H. Blakeslee, *A History of the Far Eastern Commission* (Washington: U.S. Government Printing Office, 1953).

For the San Francisco Peace Conference, see U.S. Department of State, *Record of Proceedings of the Conference for the Conclusion and Signature of the Treaty of Peace with Japan* (Washington: U.S. Government Printing Office, 1951). As for Japan's world position in relation to contemporary Far Eastern problems, see the provocative book by Professor Edwin O. Reischauer entitled *Wanted a Far Eastern Policy* (New York: Alfred A. Knopf, Inc., 1955).

It remains to mention a few studies on various aspects of postwar Japanese society and some of the material on economic subjects. As for the former, Roger Swearingen and Paul Langer, *Red Flag in Japan, op. cit.,* have made a careful study of communism in Japan prior to 1951. In the field of educational reform, it is of significance to compare the reports of the U.S. Education Mission to Japan and a survey of postwar education by a SCAP official. For the former see U.S. Education Mission to Japan, *Report of the United States Education Mission to Japan* (Washington: U.S. Government Printing Office, 1946); and *Report of the Second . . . Mission* (Washington: U.S. Government Printing Office, 1950). For the survey by a former SCAP official, which overemphasizes language reform, see Robert K. Hall, *Education for a New Japan* (New Haven: Yale University Press, 1949).

In the field of economics, by far the most important study is that of Jerome B. Cohen, *Japan's Economy in War and Reconstruction* (Minneapolis: University of Minnesota Press, 1949). He has also brought the problems up to date after the Peace Treaty in his *Economic Problems of Free Japan* (Princeton: Center of International Studies, Princeton University Press, 1952). Some of the most significant work on Japan's economic problems has been undertaken by the Cabinet's Economic Stabilization Board. After 1951 it published *Japanese Economic Statistics* (Tokyo: Economic Stabilization Board, December, 1951, and later), a continuation of similar material published by SCAP. Of special interest are the Board's *Economic Survey of Japan 1950-51;* and . . . , *1951-52* (Tokyo: Economic Stabilization Board, 1951 and 1952). Valuable research on Japan's economy has also been carried on by the Economic Commission for Asia and the Far East. One of its most significant reports is United Nations, Economic and Social Council, Economic Commission for Asia and the Far East, Committee on Industry and Trade, *Problems and Prospects of Accelerated Economic Development in the ECAFE Region Through Trade with Japan* (Lake Success: United Nations, Economic and Social Council, 1950). For other postwar economic problems the reader is referred to Borton *et al., Selected List, op. cit.*, pp. 95-101.

As for Japanese works on the postwar years, new material is appearing constantly. On the interpretation of the new Constitution, Minobe Tatsukichi, has written two works. The first, an explanation of each of the articles of the Constitution, is entitled *Shin Kempō Chikujō Kaisetsu* (An explanation of Each Article of the New Constitution; Tokyo: Nippon Hyōron Sha, 1947); the second is a study of the fundamental principles of the new charter and is called *Shin Kempō no Kihon Genri* (Fundamental Principles of the New Constitution; Tokyo: Kokuritsu Shoin, 1947). Two significant works on the last months of the war include Konoye Fumimaro, *Heiwa E no Dōryoku* (Efforts Toward Peace; Tokyo: Nihon Dempō, 1946), an attempt by Konoye to justify his peace efforts; and the invaluable collection of Foreign Office documents on the end of the war edited by Kurihara Takeshi for the Foreign Office as Gaimushō, *Shūsen Shiroku* (Documentary History of the End of the War; Tokyo: Shimbun Gekkan Sha, 1952).

In addition to the various statistical data and official reports published regularly by the Japanese government, general works on postwar economic conditions include the study by Inouye Seimaru and Usami Seijirō, on state monopolistic capitalism, *Kokka Dokusen Shihon Shūgi Ron* (Views on State Monopolistic Capitalism; Tokyo: Chōryū Sha, 1950). Inaba Hidezō has written a two-volume work on the actual state of the nation's economy called *Nihon Keizai no Genjitsu* (Real Conditions of Japan's Economy; 2 vols.; Tokyo: Jiji Tsushinsha, 1949 and 1950). The economic research office of the Mitsubishi interests published a general survey of economic production, namely, Mitsubishi Keizai Kenkyūjo, *Nihon Sangyō Keizai Sōran* (Survey of Japanese Economic Production; Tokyo: Mitsubishi, 1949). Professor Ouchi Hyōe has also written on the probable trend of postwar finances in his *Sengo Nihon Zaisei Ayanda Michi* (The Probable Direction of Postwar Japanese Finances; Tokyo: Jiji Tsushin Sha, 1950).

APPENDIX

APPENDIX I

THE POTSDAM PROCLAMATION

Proclamation Defining Terms for Japanese Surrender

July 26, 1945

(1) WE—THE PRESIDENT of the United States, the President of the National Government of the Republic of China, and the Prime Minister of Great Britain, representing the hundreds of millions of our countrymen, have conferred and agree that Japan shall be given an opportunity to end this war.

(2) The prodigious land, sea and air forces of the United States, the British Empire and of China, many times reinforced by their armies and air fleets from the west, are poised to strike the final blows upon Japan. This military power is sustained and inspired by the determination of all the Allied Nations to prosecute the war against Japan until she ceases to resist.

(3) The result of the futile and senseless German resistance to the might of the aroused free peoples of the world stands forth in awful clarity as an example to the people of Japan. The might that now converges on Japan is immeasurably greater than that which, when applied to the resisting Nazis, necessarily laid waste to the lands, the industry and the method of life of the whole German people. The full application of our military power, backed by our resolve, *will* mean the inevitable and complete destruction of the Japanese armed forces and just as inevitably the utter devastation of the Japanese homeland.

(4) The time has come for Japan to decide whether she will continue to be controlled by those self-willed militaristic advisers whose unintelligent calculations have brought the Empire of Japan to the threshold of annihilation, or whether she will follow the path of reason.

(5) Following are our terms. We will not deviate from them. There are no alternatives. We shall brook no delay.

(6) There must be eliminated for all time the authority and influence of those who have deceived and misled the people of Japan into embarking on world conquest, for we insist that a new order of peace, security and justice will be impossible until irresponsible militarism is driven from the world.

(7) Until such a new order is established *and* until there is convincing proof that Japan's war-making power is destroyed, points in Japanese territory to be designated by the Allies shall be occupied to secure the achievement of the basic objectives we are here setting forth.

(8) The terms of the Cairo Declaration shall be carried out and Japanese sovereignty shall be limited to the islands of Honshu, Hokkaido, Kyushu, Shikoku and such minor islands as we determine.

(9) The Japanese military forces, after being completely disarmed, shall be permitted to return to their homes with the opportunity to lead peaceful and productive lives.

(10) We do not intend that the Japanese shall be enslaved as a race or destroyed as a nation, but stern justice shall be meted out to all war criminals, including those who have visited cruelties upon our prisoners. The Japanese Government shall remove all obstacles to the revival and strengthening of democratic tendencies among the Japanese people. Freedom of speech, of religion, and of thought, as well as respect for the fundamental human rights shall be established.

(11) Japan shall be permitted to maintain such industries as will sustain her economy and permit the exaction of just reparations in kind, but not those which would enable her to re-arm for war. To this end, access to, as distinguished from control of, raw materials shall be permitted. Eventual Japanese participation in world trade relations shall be permitted.

(12) The occupying forces of the Allies shall be withdrawn from Japan as soon as these objectives have been accomplished and there has been established in accordance with the freely expressed will of the Japanese people a peacefully inclined and responsible government.

(13) We call upon the government of Japan to proclaim now the unconditional surrender of all Japanese armed forces, and to provide proper and adequate assurances of their good faith in such action. The alternative for Japan is prompt and utter destruction.

APPENDIX II

INSTRUMENT OF SURRENDER

We, acting by command of and in behalf of the Emperor of Japan, the Japanese Government and the Japanese Imperial General Headquarters, hereby accept the provisions set forth in the declaration issued by the heads of the Governments of the United States, China and Great Britain on 26 July 1945, at Potsdam, and subsequently adhered to by the Union of Soviet Socialist Republics, which four powers are hereafter referred to as the Allied Powers.

We hereby proclaim the unconditional surrender to the Allied Powers of the Japanese Imperial General Headquarters and of all Japanese armed forces and all armed forces under Japanese control wherever situated.

We hereby command all Japanese forces wherever situated and the Japanese people to cease hostilities forthwith, to preserve and save from damage all ships, aircraft, and military and civil property and to comply with all requirements which may be imposed by the Supreme Commander for the Allied Powers or by agencies of the Japanese Government at his direction.

We hereby command the Japanese Imperial General Headquarters to issue at once orders to the Commanders of all Japanese forces and all forces under Japanese control wherever situated to surrender unconditionally themselves and all forces under their control.

We hereby command all civil, military and naval officials to obey and enforce all proclamations, orders and directives deemed by the Supreme Commander for the Allied Powers to be proper to effectuate this surrender and issued by him or under his authority and we direct all such officials to remain at their posts and to continue to perform their non-combatant duties unless specifically relieved by him or under his authority.

We hereby undertake for the Emperor, the Japanese Government and their successors to carry out the provisions of the Potsdam Declaration in good faith, and to issue whatever orders and take whatever action may be required by the Supreme Commander for the Allied Powers or by any other designated representative of the Allied Powers for the purpose of giving effect to that Declaration.

We hereby command the Japanese Imperial Government and the Japanese Imperial General Headquarters at once to liberate all allied prisoners of war and civilian internees now under Japenese control and to provide for their protection, care, maintenance and immediate transportation to places as directed.

The authority of the Emperor and the Japanese Government to rule the state shall be subject to the Supreme Commander for the Allied Powers who will take such steps as he deems proper to effectuate these terms of surrender.

APPENDIX III

IMPERIAL RESCRIPT, SEPTEMBER 2, 1945

Proclamation

Accepting the terms set forth in Declaration issued by the heads of the Governments of the United States, Great Britain and China on July 26th, 1945 at Potsdam and subsequently adhered to by the Union of Soviet Socialist Republics, we have commanded the Japanese Imperial Government and the Japanese Imperial General Headquarters to sign on Our behalf the Instrument of Surrender presented by the Supreme Commander for the Allied Powers and to issue General Order to the Military and Naval Forces in accordance with the direction of the Supreme Commander for the Allied Powers. We command all Our people forthwith to cease hostilities, to lay down their arms and faithfully to carry out all the provisions of Instrument of Surrender and the General Orders issued by the Japanese Imperial Government and the Japanese Imperial General Headquarters hereunder.

This second day of the ninth month of the twentieth year of Syōwa.

Seal of the Emperor

HIROHITO

NARUHIKO-O
Prime Minister
MAMORU SHIGEMITSU
Minister for Foreign Affairs
IWAO YAMAZAKI
Minister for Home Affairs
JUICHI TSUSHIMA
Minister of Finance
SADAMU SHIMOMURA
Minister of War
MITSUMASA YONAI
Minister of Navy
CHUZO IWATA
Minister of Justice
TAMON MAEDA
Minister of Education

KENZO MATSUMURA
Minister of Welfare
KOTARO SENGOKU
Minister of Agriculture and Forestry
CHIKUHEI NAKAJIMA
Minister of Commerce and Industry
NAOTO KOBIYAMA
Minister of Transportation
FUMIMARO KONOE
Minister without Portfolio
TAKETORA OGATA
Minister without Portfolio
BINSHIRO OBATA
Minister without Portfolio

APPENDIX IV

TEXT OF JAPAN'S TWO CONSTITUTIONS*

1889

THE CONSTITUTION OF THE EMPIRE OF JAPAN (MEIJI CONSTITUTION, 1889)

Preamble

Having, by virtue of the glories of Our Ancestors, ascended the Throne of a lineal succession unbroken for ages eternal; desiring to promote the welfare of, and to give development to the moral and intellectual faculties of Our beloved subjects, the very same that have been favoured with the benevolent care and affectionate vigilance of Our Ancestors; and hoping to maintain the prosperity of the State, in concert with Our people and with their support, We hereby promulgate, in pursuance of Our Imperial Rescript of the 12th day of the 10th month of the 14th year of Meiji, a fundamental law of State, to exhibit the principles, by which We are to be guided in Our conduct, and to point out to what Our descendants and Our subjects and their descendants are forever to conform.

The rights of sovereignty of the State, We have inherited from Our Ancestors, and We shall bequeath them to Our descendants. Neither We nor they shall in future fail to wield them, in accordance with the provisions of the Constitution hereby granted.

We now declare to respect and protect the security of the rights and of the property of Our people, and to secure to them the complete enjoyment of the same, within the extent of the provisions of the present Constitution and of the law.

The Imperial Diet shall first be convoked for the 23rd year of Meiji and the time of its opening shall be the date when the present Constitution comes into force.

1946

THE CONSTITUTION OF JAPAN

We, the Japanese people, acting through our duly elected representatives in the National Diet, determined that we shall secure for ourselves and our posterity the fruits of peaceful cooperation with all nations and the blessings of liberty throughout this land, and resolved that never again shall we be visited with the horrors of war through the action of government, do proclaim that sovereign power resides with the people and do firmly establish this Constitution. Government is a sacred trust of the people, the authority for which is derived from the people, the powers of which are exercised by the representatives of the people, and the benefits of which are enjoyed by the people. This is a universal principle of mankind upon which this Constitution is founded. We reject and revoke all constitutions, laws, ordinances, and rescripts in conflict herewith.

We, the Japanese people, desire peace for all time and are deeply conscious of the high ideals controlling human relationship, and we have determined to preserve our security and existence, trusting in the justice and faith of the peace-loving peoples of the world. We desire to occupy an honored place in an international society striving for the preservation of peace, and the banishment of tyranny and slavery, oppression and intolerance for all time from the earth. We recognize that all peoples of the world have the right to live in peace, free from fear and want.

We believe that no nation is responsible to itself alone, but that laws of political morality are universal; and that obedience to such

* For ease in comparing the two documents, the articles of the Meiji Constitution are arranged not in sequence but topically to correspond with the articles of the 1946 Constitution, which are presented *seriatim*. The Meiji Constitution is, nevertheless, complete.

When in the future it may become necessary to amend any of the provisions of the present Constitution, We or Our successors shall assume the initiative right, and submit a project for the same to the Imperial Diet. The Imperial Diet shall pass its vote upon it, according to the conditions imposed by the present Constitution, and in no otherwise shall Our descendants or Our subjects be permitted to attempt any alteration thereof.

Our Ministers of State, on Our behalf, shall be held responsible for the carrying out of the present Constitution, and Our present and future subjects shall forever assume the duty of allegiance to the present Constitution.

laws is incumbent upon all nations who would sustain their own sovereignty and justify their sovereign relationship with other nations.

We, the Japanese people, pledge our national honor to accomplish these high ideals and purposes with all our resources.

Chapter I. The Emperor

Article IV. The Emperor being the Head of the Empire the rights of sovereignty are invested in him, and he exercises them in accordance with the provisions of the present Constitution.

Article I. The Empire of Japan shall be ruled over by Emperors of the dynasty, which has reigned in an unbroken line of descent for ages past.

Article II. The succession to the throne shall devolve upon male descendants of the Imperial House, according to the provisions of the Imperial House Law.

Article III. The person of the Emperor is sacred and inviolable.

Article V. The Emperor exercises the legislative power with the consent of the Imperial Diet.

Article XVII. The institution of a Regency shall take place in conformity with the provisions of the Imperial House Law.

The Regent shall exercise the supreme powers which belong to the Emperor in his name.

Article X. The Emperor determines the organisation of the different branches of the Administration; he fixes the salaries of all

Chapter I. The Emperor

Article 1. The Emperor shall be the symbol of the State and of the unity of the people, deriving his position from the will of the people with whom resides sovereign power.

Article 2. The Imperial Throne shall be dynastic and succeeded to in accordance with the Imperial House Law passed by the Diet.

Article 3. The advice and approval of the Cabinet shall be required for all acts of the Emperor in matters of state, and the Cabinet shall be responsible therefor.

Article 4. The Emperor shall perform only such acts in matters of state as are provided for in this Constitution and he shall not have powers related to government.

The Emperor may delegate the performance of his acts in matters of state as may be provided by law.

Article 5. When, in accordance with the Imperial House Law, a Regency is established, the Regent shall perform his acts in matters of state in the Emperor's name. In this case, paragraph one of the preceding article will be applicable.

Article 6. The Emperor shall appoint the Prime Minister as designated by the Diet.

The Emperor shall appoint the Chief

civil and military officers, and appoints and dismisses the same. Exceptions specially provided for in the present Constitution or in other laws shall be in accordance with the respective provisions bearing thereon.

Article VIII. In case of urgent necessity, when the Imperial Diet is not sitting, the Emperor, in order to maintain the public safety or to avert a public danger, has the power to issue Imperial Ordinances, which shall take the place of laws. Such Imperial Ordinances shall, however, be laid before the Imperial Diet at its next session, and should the Diet disapprove of the said Ordinances, the Government shall declare them to be henceforth invalid.

Article IX. The Emperor issues, or causes to be issued, the ordinances necessary for the carrying out of the laws, or for the maintenance of public peace and order, and for the promotion of the welfare of his subjects. But no Ordinance shall in any way alter any of the existing laws.

Article XI. The Emperor has the supreme command of the army and navy.

Article XII. The Emperor determines the organisation and peace standing of the army and navy.

Article XIII. The Emperor declares war, makes peace, and concludes treaties.

Article VI. The Emperor gives sanction to laws, and orders them to be promulgated and put into force.

Article VII. The Emperor convokes the Imperial Diet, opens, closes, and prorogues it, and dissolves the House of Representatives.

Article XIV. The Emperor proclaims the law of siege. The conditions and operation of the law of siege shall be determined by law.

Article XVI. The Emperor orders amnesty, pardon, commutation of punishments, and rehabilitation.

Article XV. The Emperor confers titles of nobility, rank, orders, and other marks of honour.

Judge of the Supreme Court as designated by the Cabinet.

Article 7. The Emperor, with the advice and approval of the Cabinet, shall perform the following acts in matters of state on behalf of the people:

Promulgation of amendments of the constitution, laws, cabinet orders and treaties.

Convocation of the Diet.

Dissolution of the House of Representatives.

Proclamation of general election of members of the Diet.

Attestation of the appointment and dismissal of Ministers of State and other officials as provided for by law, and of full powers and credentials of Ambassadors and Ministers.

Attestation of general and special amnesty, commutation of punishment, reprieve, and restoration of rights.

Awarding of honors.

Attestation of instruments of ratification and other diplomatic documents as provided for by law.

Receiving foreign ambassadors and ministers.

Performance of ceremonial functions.

Article 8. No property can be given to, or received by, the Imperial House, nor can any gifts be made therefrom, without the authorization of the Diet.

Chapter II. Renunciation of War

Article 9. Aspiring sincerely to an international peace based on justice and order, the Japanese people forever renounce war as a sovereign right of the nation and the threat or use of force as means of settling international disputes.

In order to accomplish the aim of the preceding paragraph, land, sea, and air forces, as well as other war potential, will never be maintained. The right of belligerency of the state will not be recognized.

Chapter II. Rights and Duties of Subjects

Article XVIII. The conditions necessary for being a Japanese subject shall be determined by law.

Chapter III. Rights and Duties of the People

Article 10. The conditions necessary for being a Japanese national shall be determined by law.

Article 11. The people shall not be prevented from enjoying any of the fundamental human rights. These fundamental human rights guaranteed to the people by this Constitution shall be conferred upon the people of this and future generations as eternal and inviolate rights.

Article 12. The freedoms and rights guaranteed to the people by this Constitution shall be maintained by the constant endeavor of the people, who shall refrain from any abuse of these freedoms and rights and shall always be responsible for utilizing them for the public welfare.

Article 13. All of the people shall be respected as individuals. Their right to life, liberty, and the pursuit of happiness shall, to the extent that it does not interfere with the public welfare, be the supreme consideration in legislation and in other governmental affairs.

Article 14. All of the people are equal under the law and there shall be no discrimination in political, economic or social relations, because of race, creed, sex, social status or family origin.

Peers and peerage shall not be recognized.

No privilege shall accompany any award of honor, decoration or any distinction, nor shall any such award be valid beyond the lifetime of the individual who now holds or hereafter may receive it.

Article 15. The people have the inalienable right to choose their public officials and to dismiss them.

All public officials are servants of the whole community and not of any group thereof.

Universal adult suffrage is guaranteed with regard to the election of public officials.

In all elections, secrecy of the ballot shall not be violated. A voter shall not be answerable, publicly or privately, for the choice he has made.

Article XXX. Japanese subjects may present petitions, provided that they observe the proper form of respect, and comply with the rules specially provided for such matters.

Article 16. Every person shall have the right of peaceful petition for the redress of damage, for the removal of public officials, for the enactment, repeal or amendment of laws, ordinances or regulations and for other matters; nor shall any person be in any way discriminated against for sponsoring such a petition.

Article 17. Every person may *sue* for redress as provided by law from the State or a public entity, in case he has suffered damage through illegal act of any public official.

Article 18. No person shall be held in bondage of any kind. Involuntary servitude, except as punishment for crime, is prohibited.

Article XIX. Japanese subjects shall all equally be eligible for civil and military appointments, and any other public offices, subject only to the conditions prescribed and Laws and Ordinances.

Article XX. Japanese subjects are amenable to service in the army or navy, according to the provisions of law.

Article XXVIII. Japanese subjects shall, within limits not prejudicial to peace and order, and not antagonistic to their duties as subjects, enjoy freedom of religious belief.

Article 19. Freedom of thought and conscience shall not be violated.

Article 20. Freedom of religion is guaranteed to all. No religious organization shall receive any privileges from the State, nor exercise any political authority.

No person shall be compelled to take part in any religious act, celebration, rite or practice.

The State and its organs shall refrain from religious education or any other religious activity.

Article XXIX. Japanese subjects shall, within the limits of the law, enjoy liberty in regard to speech, writing, publication, public meetings, and associations.

Article 21. Freedom of assembly and association as well as speech, press and all other forms of expression are guaranteed.

No censorship shall be maintained, nor shall the secrecy of any means of communication be violated.

Article XXII. Subject to the limitations imposed by law, Japanese subjects shall enjoy

Article 22. Every person shall have freedom to choose and change his residence and full liberty in regard to residence and change of abode.

Article XXVII. The rights of property of Japanese subjects shall not be violated. Such measures, however, as may be rendered necessary in the interests of the public welfare shall be taken in accordance with the provisions of the law.

Article XXI. Japanese subjects are amenable to the duty of paying taxes, according to the provisions of law.

Article XXIII. No Japanese subject shall be arrested, detained, tried or punished, except according to law.

Article XXIV. No Japanese subject shall be deprived of his right of being tried by judges determined by law.

to choose his occupation to the extent that it does not interfere with the public welfare.

Freedom of all persons to move to a foreign country and to divest themselves of their nationality shall be inviolate.

Article 23. Academic freedom is guaranteed.

Article 24. Marriage shall be based only on the mutual consent of both sexes and it shall be maintained through mutual cooperation with the equal rights of husband and wife as a basis.

With regard to choice of spouse, property rights, inheritance, choice of domicile, divorce and other matters pertaining to marriage and the family, laws shall be enacted from the standpoint of individual dignity and the essential equality of the sexes.

Article 25. All people have the right to maintain the minimum standards of wholesome and cultured living.

In all spheres of life, the State shall use its endeavors for the promotion and extension of social welfare and security, and of public health.

Article 26. All people shall have the right to receive an equal education correspondent to their ability, as provided by law.

All people shall be obligated to have all boys and girls under their protection receive ordinary education as provided for by law. Such compulsory education shall be free.

Article 27. All people shall have the right and the obligation to work.

Standards for wages, hours, rest and other working conditions shall be fixed by law.

Children shall not be exploited.

Article 28. The right of workers to organize and to bargain and act collectively is guaranteed.

Article 29. The right to own or to hold property is inviolable.

Property rights shall be defined by law, in conformity with the public welfare.

Private property may be taken for public use upon just compensation therefor.

Article 30. The people shall be liable to taxation as provided by law.

Article 31. No person shall be deprived of life or liberty, nor shall any other criminal penalty be imposed, except according to procedure established by law.

Article 32. No person shall be denied the right of access to the courts.

Article 33. No person shall be appre-

Article XXV. Except in the cases provided for in the law, the house of no Japanese subject shall be entered or searched without his permission.

Article XXVI. Except in cases provided for in the law, the secrecy of the letters of Japanese subjects shall not be violated.

hended except upon warrant issued by a competent judicial officer which specifies the offense with which the person is charged, unless he is apprehended, the offense being committed.

Article 34. No person shall be arrested or detained without being at once informed of the charges against him or without the immediate privilege of counsel; nor shall he be detained without adequate cause; and upon demand of any person such cause must be immediately shown in open court in his presence and the presence of his counsel.

Article 35. The right of all persons to be secure in their homes, papers and effects against entries, searches and seizures shall not be impaired except upon warrant issued for adequate cause and particularly describing the place to be searched and things to be seized, or except as provided by Article 33.

Each search or seizure shall be made upon separate warrant issued by a competent judicial officer.

Article 36. The infliction of torture by any public officer and cruel punishments are absolutely forbidden.

Article 37. In all criminal cases the accused shall enjoy the right to a speedy and public trial by an impartial tribunal.

He shall be permitted full opportunity to examine all witnesses, and he shall have the right of compulsory process for obtaining witnesses on his behalf at public expense.

At all times the accused shall have the assistance of competent counsel who shall, if the accused is unable to secure the same by his own efforts, be assigned to his use by the State.

Article 38. No person shall be compelled to testify against himself.

Confession made under compulsion, torture or threat, or after prolonged arrest or detention shall not be admitted in evidence.

No person shall be convicted or punished in cases where the only proof against him is his own confession.

Article 39. No person shall be held criminally liable for an act which was lawful at the time it was committed, or of which he has been acquitted, nor shall he be placed in double jeopardy.

Article 40. Any person, in case he is acquitted after he has been arrested or detained, may *sue* the State for redress as provided by law.

Article XXXI. The provisions contained in the present chapter shall not interfere with the exercise, in times of war or in case of national emergency, of the supreme powers which belong to the Emperor.

Article XXXII. Each and every one of the provisions contained in the preceding articles of the present chapter shall, in so far as they do not conflict with the laws or the rules and discipline of the army and navy, apply to the officers and men of the army and of the navy.

Chapter III. The Imperial Diet

Article XXXIII. The Imperial Diet shall consist of two Houses: the House of Peers and the House of Representatives.

Article XXXIV. The House of Peers shall, in accordance with the Ordinance concerning the House of Peers, be composed of members of the Imperial Family, of Nobles, and of Deputies who have been nominated by the Emperor.

Article XXXV. The House of Representatives shall be composed of members elected by the people, according to the provisions of the Law of Election.

Article XXXVI. No one can at one and the same time be a member of both Houses.

Article LIII. The Members of both Houses shall, during the session, be free from arrest, unless with the consent of the House, except in cases of flagrant delicts, or of offenses connected with a state of internal commotion or with a foreign trouble.

Chapter IV. The Diet

Article 41. The Diet shall be the highest organ of state power, and shall be the sole law-making organ of the State.

Article 42. The Diet shall consist of two Houses, namely the House of Representatives and the House of Councillors.

Article 43. Both Houses shall consist of elected members, representative of all the people.

The number of the members of each House shall be fixed by law.

Article 44. The qualifications of members of both Houses and their electors shall be fixed by law. However, there shall be no discrimination because of race, creed, sex, social status, family origin, education, property or income.

Article 45. The term of office of members of the House of Representatives shall be four years. However, the term shall be terminated before the full term is up in case the House of Representatives is dissolved.

Article 46. The term of office of members of the House of Councillors shall be six years, and the election of half the members shall take place every three years.

Article 47. Electoral districts, method of voting and other matters pertaining to the method of election of members of both Houses shall be fixed by law.

Article 48. No person shall be permitted to be a member of both Houses simultaneously.

Article 49. Members of both Houses shall receive appropriate annual payment from the national treasury in accordance with law.

Article 50. Except in cases provided by law, members of both Houses shall be exempt from apprehension while the Diet is in session, and any members apprehended before the opening of the session shall be freed during the term of the session upon demand of the House.

Article LII. No Member of either House shall be held responsible outside the respective Houses, for any opinion uttered or for any vote given in the House. When, however, a Member himself has given publicity to his opinions by public speech, by documents in print or in writing, or by any other similar means, he shall, in the matter, be amenable to the general law.

Article 51. Members of both Houses shall not be held liable outside the House for speeches, debates or votes cast inside the House.

Article XLI. The Imperial Diet shall be convoked every year.

Article 52. An ordinary session of the Diet shall be convoked once per year.

Article XLII. A session of the Imperial Diet shall last during three months. In case of necessity, the duration of a session may be prolonged by Imperial Order.

Article XLIII. When urgent necessity arises, an extraordinary session may be convoked, in addition to the ordinary one.

The duration of an extraordinary session shall be determined by Imperial Order.

Article 53. The Cabinet may determine to convoke extraordinary sessions of the Diet. When a quarter or more of the total members of either House makes the demand, the Cabinet must determine on such convocation.

Article XLIV. The opening, closing, prolongation of session and prorogation of the Imperial Diet, shall be effected simultaneously for both Houses.

In case the House of Representatives has been ordered to dissolve, the House of Peers shall at the same time be prorogued.

Article XLV. When the House of Representatives has been ordered to dissolve, Members shall be caused by Imperial Order to be newly elected, and the new House shall be convoked within five months from the day of dissolution.

Article 54. When the House of Representatives is dissolved, there must be a general election of members of the House of Representatives within forty (40) days from the date of dissolution, and the Diet must be convoked within thirty (30) days from the date of the election.

When the House of Representatives is dissolved, the House of Councillors is closed at the same time. However, the Cabinet may in time of national emergency convoke the House of Councillors in emergency session.

Measures taken at such session as mentioned in the proviso of the preceding paragraph shall be provisional and shall become null and void unless agreed to by the House of Representatives within a period of ten (10) days after the opening of the next session of the Diet.

Article LI. Both Houses may enact, besides what is provided for in the present Constitution and in the Law of the Houses, rules necessary for the management of their internal affairs.

Article 55. Each House shall judge disputes related to qualifications of its members. However, in order to deny a seat to any member, it is necessary to pass a resolution by a majority of two-thirds or more of the members present.

Article XLVI. No debate can be opened and no vote can be taken in either House of the Imperial Diet, unless not less than one third of the whole number of the Members thereof is present.

Article XLVII. Votes shall be taken in both Houses by absolute majority. In the case of a tie vote, the President shall have the casting vote.

Article 56. Business cannot be transacted in either House unless one-third or more of total membership is present.

All matters shall be decided, in each House, by a majority of those present, except as elsewhere provided in the Constitution, and in case of a tie, the presiding officer shall decide the issue.

Article XLVIII. The deliberations of both Houses shall be held in public. The deliberations may, however, upon demand of the

Article 57. Deliberation in each House shall be public. However, a secret meeting may be held where a majority of two-thirds

Government or by resolution of the House, be held in secret sitting.

[Cf. Article LI.]

Article XXXVII. Every law requires the consent of the Imperial Diet.

Article XXXVIII. Both Houses shall vote upon projects of law submitted to it by the Government, and may respectively initiate projects of law.

Article. XXXIX. A Bill, which has been rejected by either the one or the other of the two Houses, shall not be again brought in during the same session.

Article XL. Both Houses can make representations to the Government, as to laws or upon any other subject. When, however, such representations are not accepted, they cannot be made a second time during the same session.

Article LIV. The Ministers of State and

or more of those members present passes a resolution therefor.

Article 58. Each House shall select its own president and other officials.

Each House shall establish its rules pertaining to meetings, proceedings and internal discipline, and may punish members for disorderly conduct. However, in order to expel a member, a majority of two-thirds or more of those members present must pass a resolution.

Article 59. A bill becomes a law on passage by both Houses, except as otherwise provided by the Constitution.

A bill which is passed by the House of Representatives, and upon which the House of Councillors makes a decision different from that of the House of Representatives, becomes a law when passed a second time by the House of Representatives by a majority of two-thirds or more of the members present.

The provision of the preceding paragraph does not preclude the House of Representatives from calling for the meeting of a joint committee of both Houses, provided for by law.

Failure by the House of Councillors to take final action within sixty (60) days after receipt of a bill passed by the House of Representatives, time in recess excepted, may be determined by the House of Representatives to constitute a rejection of the said bill by the House of Councillors.

Article 60. The budget must first be submitted to the House of Representatives.

Upon consideration of the budget, when the House of Councillors makes a decision different from that of the House of Representatives, and when no agreement can be reached even through a joint committee of both Houses, provided for by law, or in the case of failure by the House of Councillors to take final action within thirty (30) days, the period of recess excluded, after the receipt of the budget passed by the House of Representatives, the decision of the House of Representatives shall be the decision of the Diet.

Article 61. The second paragraph of the preceding article applies also to the Diet approval required for the conclusion of treaties.

Article 62. Each House may conduct investigations in relation to government, and may demand the presence and testimony of witnesses, and the production of records.

Article 63. The Prime Minister and other

the Delegates of the Government may, at any time, take seats and speak in either House.

Article XLIX. Both Houses of the Imperial Diet may respectively present addresses to the Emperor.

Article L. Both Houses may receive petitions presented by subjects.

Chapter IV. The Ministers of State and the Privy Council

Article LV. The respective Ministers of State shall give their advice to the Emperor, and be responsible for it.

All laws, public ordinances, and imperial rescripts, of whatever kind, that relate to the affairs of state require the counter-signature of the Minister of State.

Article LVI. The Privy Council shall, in accordance with the provisions for the organization of the Privy Council, diliberate upon the important matters of State, when they have been consulted by tho Emperor.

Ministers of State may, at any time, appear in either House for the purpose of speaking on bills, regardless of whether they are members of the House or not. They must appear when their presence is required in order to give answers or explanations.

Article 64. The Diet shall set up an impeachment court from among the members of both Houses for the purpose of trying those judges against whom removal proceedings have been instituted.

Matters relating to impeachment shall be provided by law.

Chapter V. The Cabinet

Article 65. Executive power shall be vested in the Cabinet.

Article 66. The Cabinet shall consist of the Prime Minister, who shall be its head, and other Ministers of State, as provided for by law.

The Prime Minister and other Ministers of State must be civilians.

The Cabinet, in the exercise of executive power, shall be collectively responsible to the Diet.

Article 67. The Prime Minister shall be designated from among the members of the Diet by a resolution of the Diet. This designation shall precede all other business.

If the House of Representatives and the House of Councillors disagree and if no agreement can be reached even through a joint committee of both Houses, provided for by law, or the House of Councillors fails to make designation within ten (10) days, exclusive of the period of recess, after the House of Representatives has made designation, the decision of the House of Representatives shall be the decision of the Diet.

Article 68. The Prime Minister shall appoint the Ministers of State. However a majority of their number must be chosen from among the members of the Diet.

The Prime Minister may remove the Ministers of State as he chooses.

Article 69. If the House of Representatives passes a non-confidence resolution, or rejects a confidence resolution, the Cabinet shall resign en masse, unless the House of Representatives is dissolved within ten (10) days.

Article 70. When there is a vacancy in the post of Prime Minister, or upon the first convocation of the Diet after a general election of members of the House of Representatives, the Cabinet shall resign en masse.

Article 71. In the cases mentioned in the two preceding articles, the Cabinet shall continue its functions until the time when a new Prime Minister is appointed.

Article 72. The Prime Minister, representing the Cabinet, submits bills, reports on general national affairs and foreign relations to the Diet and exercises control and supervision over various administrative branches.

Article 73. The Cabinet, in addition to other general administrative functions, shall perform the following functions:

Administer the law faithfully; conduct affairs of state.

Manage foreign affairs.

Conclude treaties. However, it shall obtain prior or, depending on circumstances, subsequent approval of the Diet.

Administer the civil service, in accordance with standards established by law.

Prepare the budget, and present it to the Diet.

Enact cabinet orders in order to execute the provisions of this Constitution and of the law. However, it cannot include penal provisions in such cabinet orders unless authorized by such law.

Decide on general amnesty, special amnesty, commutation of punishment, reprieve, and restoration of rights.

Article 74. All laws and cabinet orders shall be signed by the competent Minister of State and countersigned by the Prime Minister.

Article 75. The Ministers of State, during their tenure of office, shall not be subject to legal action without the consent of the Prime Minister. However, the right to take that action is not impaired hereby.

CHAPTER V. THE JUDICATURE

Article LVII. The Judicature shall be exercised by the Courts of Law according to law, in the name of the Emperor.

CHAPTER VI. JUDICIARY

Article 76. The whole judicial power is vested in a Supreme Court and in such inferior courts as are established by law.

The organization of the Courts of Law shall be determined by law.

Article LX. All matters that fall within the competency of a special Court shall be specially provided for by law.

Article LVIII. The judges shall be appointed from among those who possess proper qualifications according to law.

No judge shall be deprived of his position, unless by way of criminal sentence or disciplinary punishment.

Rules for disciplinary punishment shall be determined by law.

No extraordinary tribunal shall be established, nor shall any organ or agency of the Executive be given final judicial power.

All judges shall be independent in the exercise of their conscience and shall be bound only by this Constitution and the laws.

Article 77. The Supreme Court is vested with the rule-making power under which it determines the rules of procedure and of practice, and of matters relating to attorneys, the internal discipline of the courts and the administration of judicial affairs.

Public procurators shall be subject to the rule-making power of the Supreme Court.

The Supreme Court may delegate the power to make rules for inferior courts to such courts.

Article 78. Judges shall not be removed except by public impeachment unless judicially declared mentally or physically incompetent to perform official duties. No disciplinary action against judges shall be administered by any executive organ or agency.

Article 79. The Supreme Court shall consist of a Chief Judge and such number of judges as may be determined by law; all such judges excepting the Chief Judge shall be appointed by the Cabinet.

The appointment of the judges of the Supreme Court shall be reviewed by the people at the first general election of members of the House of Representatives following their appointment, and shall be reviewed again at the first general election of members of the House of Representatives after a lapse of ten (10) years, and in the same manner thereafter.

In cases mentioned in the foregoing paragraph, when the majority of the voters favors the dismissal of a judge, he shall be dismissed.

Matters pertaining to review shall be prescribed by law.

The judges of the Supreme Court shall be retired upon the attainment of the age as fixed by law.

All such judges shall receive, at regular stated intervals, adequate compensation which shall not be decreased during their terms of office.

Article 80. The judges of the inferior courts shall be appointed by the Cabinet from a list of persons nominated by the Supreme Court. All such judges shall hold office for a term of ten (10) years with privilege of reappointment, provided that they shall be retired upon the attainment of the age as fixed by law.

The judges of the inferior courts shall receive, at regular stated intervals, adequate compensation which shall not be decreased during their terms of office.

Article 81. The Supreme Court is the court of last resort with power to determine the constitutionality of any law, order, regulation or official act.

Article LIX. Trials and judgments of a Court shall be conducted publicly. When, however, there exists any fear that such publicity may be prejudicial to peace and order, or to the maintenance of public morality, the public trial may be suspended by provision of law or by the decision of the Court of Law.

Article 82. Trials shall be conducted and judgment declared publicly.

Where a court unanimously determines publicity to be dangerous to public order or morals, a trial may be conducted privately, but trials of political offenses, offenses involving the press or cases wherein the rights of people as guaranteed in Chap. III of this Constitution are in question shall always be conducted publicly.

Article LXI. No suit at law, which relates to rights alleged to have been infringed by the illegal measures of the administrative authorities, and which shall come within the competency of the Court of Administrative Litigation specially established by law, shall be taken cognizance of by a Court of Law.

Chapter VI. Finance

Article LXII. The imposition of a new tax or the modification of the rates (of an existing one) shall be determined by law.

However, all such administrative fees or other revenue as are in the nature of compensation for services rendered shall not fall within the category of the above clause.

The raising of national loans and the contracting of other liabilities to the charge of the National Treasury, except those that are provided in the Budget, shall require the consent of the Imperial Diet.

Article LXIII. Existing taxes shall, in so far as they are not altered by new laws, continue to be collected as heretofore.

Chapter VII. Finance

Article 83. The power to administer national finances shall be exercised as the Diet shall determine.

Article 84. No new taxes shall be imposed or existing ones modified except by law or under such conditions as law may prescribe.

Article 85. No money shall be expended, nor shall the State obligate itself, except as authorized by the Diet.

Article LXIV. The annual expenditure and revenue of the State shall, in the form of an annual Budget, receive the consent of

Article 86. The Cabinet shall prepare and submit to the Diet for its consideration and decision a budget for each fiscal year.

the Imperial Diet. Any expenditure which exceeds the appropriations set forth under the various heads of the Budget, or those not provided for in the Budget, shall be referred subsequently to the Imperial Diet for its approval.

Article LXV. The Budget shall be first laid before the House of Representatives.

Article LXIX. In order to supply unavoidable deficits in the Budget, and to meet requirements unprovided for in the same, a reserve fund shall be established.

Article LXVI. The expenditure in respect of the Imperial House shall be defrayed every year out of the National Treasury, according to the present fixed amount for the same, and shall not hereafter require the consent thereto of the Imperial Diet, except in case an increase thereof is found necessary.

Article LXVIII. In order to meet special requirements the Government may ask the consent of the Imperial Diet to a certain amount as a continuing expenditure fund, for a previously fixed number of years.

Article LXXII. The final account of the expenditure and revenue of the State shall be verified and confirmed by the Board of Audit, and it shall be submitted by the Government to the Imperial Diet, together with the report of verification of the said Board.

The organisation and competency of the Board of Audit shall be determined by law separately.

Article LXVII. The fixed expenditure based upon the supreme powers of the Emperor and set forth in this Constitution, and such expenditure as may have arisen by the effect of law, or as appertains to the legal obligations of the Government, shall be neither rejected nor reduced by the Imperial

Article 87. In order to provide for unforeseen deficiencies in the budget, a reserve fund may be authorized by the Diet to be expended upon the responsibility of the Cabinet.

The Cabinet must get subsequent approval of the Diet for all payments from the reserve fund.

Article 88. All property of the Imperial Household shall belong to the State. All expenses of the Imperial Household shall be appropriated by the Diet in the budget.

Article 89. No public money or other property shall be expended or appropriated for the use, benefit or maintenance of any religious institution or association, or for any charitable, educational or benevolent enterprises not under the control of public authority.

Article 90. Final accounts of the expenditures and revenues of the State shall be audited annually by a Board of Audit and submitted by the Cabinet to the Diet, together with the statement of audit, during the fiscal year immediately following the period covered.

The organization and competency of the Board of Audit shall be determined by law.

Article 91. At regular intervals and at least annually the Cabinet shall report to the Diet and the people on the state of national finances.

Diet, without the concurrence of the Government.

Article LXX. When there is urgent need for the adoption of measures for the maintenance of the public safety, and when in consequence of the state either of the domestic affairs or of the foreign relations, the Imperial Diet cannot be convoked, the necessary financial measures may be taken by means of an Imperial Ordinance. In such cases as those mentioned in the preceding clause the matter shall be submitted to the Imperial Diet at its next session for its approval.

Article LXXI. When the Imperial Diet has not voted on the Budget, or when the Budget has not been brought into actual existence, the Government shall carry out the Budget of the preceding year.

Article LXXIII. When it has become necessary in future to amend the provisions of the present Constitution, a project to the effect shall be submitted to the Imperial Diet by Imperial Order.

In the above case, neither House can open the debate, unless not less than two-thirds of the whole number of Members are present, and no amendment can be passed, unless a

Chapter VIII. Local Self-Government

Article 92. Regulations concerning organization and operations of local public entities shall be fixed by law in accordance with the principle of local autonomy.

Article 93. The local public entities shall establish assemblies as their deliberative organs, in accordance with law.

The chief executive officers of all local public entities, the members of their assemblies, and such other local officials as may be determined by law shall be elected by direct popular vote within their several communities.

Article 94. Local public entities shall have the right to manage their property, affairs and administration and to enact their own regulations within law.

Article 95. A special law, applicable only to one local public entity, cannot be enacted by the Diet without the consent of the majority of the voters of the local public entity concerned, obtained in accordance with law.

Chapter IX. Amendments

Article 96. Amendments to this Constitution shall be initiated by the Diet, through a concurring vote of two-thirds or more of all the members of each House and shall thereupon be submitted to the people for ratification, which shall require the affirmative vote of a majority of all votes cast thereon, at a special referendum or at such election as the Diet shall specify.

majority of not less than two-thirds of the Members is obtained.

Amendments when so ratified shall immediately be promulgated by the Emperor in the name of the people, as an integral part of this Constitution.

CHAPTER X. SUPREME LAW

Article 97. The fundamental human rights by this Constitution guaranteed to the people of Japan are fruits of the age-old struggle of man to be free; they have survived the many exacting tests for durability and are conferred upon this and future generations in trust, to be held for all time inviolate.

Article LXXIV. No modification of the Imperial House Law shall be required to be submitted to the deliberation of the Imperial Diet.

No provision of the present Constitution can be modified by the Imperial House Law.

Article 98. This Constitution shall be the supreme law of the nation and no law, ordinance, imperial rescript or other act of government, or part thereof, contrary to the provisions hereof, shall have legal force or validity.

The treaties concluded by Japan and established laws of nations shall be faithfully observed.

Article 99. The Emperor or the Regent as well as Ministers of State, members of the Diet, judges, and all other public officials have the obligation to respect and uphold this Constitution.

CHAPTER XI. SUPPLEMENTARY PROVISIONS

Article 100. This Constitution shall be enforced as from the day when the period of six months will have elapsed counting from the day of its promulgation.

The enactment of laws necessary for the enforcement of this Constitution, the election of members of the House of Councillors and the procedure for the convocation of the Diet and other preparatory procedures necessary for the enforcement of this Constitution may be executed before the day prescribed in the preceding paragraph.

Article 101. If the House of Councillors is not constituted before the effective date of this Constitution, the House of Representatives shall function as the Diet until such time as the House of Councillors shall be constituted.

Article 102. The term of office for half the members of the House of Councillors serving in the first term under this Constitution shall be three years. Members falling

Chapter VII. Supplementary Rules

[Article LXXIII.]

[Article LXXIV.]

Article LXXV. No modification can be introduced into the Constitution, or into the Imperial House Law, during the time of a Regency.

Article LXXVI. Existing legal enactments, such as laws, regulations, Ordinances, or by whatever names they may be called, shall, so far as they do not conflict with the present Constitution, continue in force.

All existing contracts or orders, that entail obligations upon the Government, and that are connected with expenditure, shall come within the scope of Article LXVII.

under this category shall be determined in accordance with law.

Article 103. The Ministers of State, members of the House of Representatives and judges in office on the effective date of this Constitution, and all other public officials who occupy positions corresponding to such positions as are recognized by this Constitution shall not forfeit their positions automatically on account of the enforcement of this Constitution unless otherwise specified by law. When, however, successors are elected or appointed under the provisions of this Constitution, they shall forfeit their positions as a matter of course.

INDEX